COMMONWEALTH CARIBBEAN PROPERTY LAW

This 5th edition of *Commonwealth Caribbean Property Law* sets out clearly and concisely the central principles of the law of real property in the region, guiding students through this core but often complex subject area.

Fully revised and updated to include important new case law from the various Caribbean jurisdictions, the book provides comprehensive coverage of the key topics studied by undergraduates, including co-ownership, leaseholds, condominium, restrictive covenants, easements, mortgages and adverse possession. Emphasis is on those areas that are most commonly litigated in the region, and the book contains discussion of, or reference to, many unreported cases. This new edition features expanded coverage of freehold estates, a glossary of key terms, and a new question and answer section at the end of the book.

Commonwealth Caribbean Property Law is essential reading for LLB students in Caribbean universities and students on CAPE Law courses and, with its analysis of the substantive laws across several jurisdictions, it will continue to be an invaluable reference tool for legal practitioners in the region.

Gilbert Kodilinye is Emeritus Professor of Law at the University of the West Indies. He is the author of nine books and numerous scholarly articles. He is a Barrister (England and Wales) and an Attorney at Law (St Lucia).

COMMONWEALTH CARIBBEAN LAW

The Commonwealth Caribbean Law Series is the only series of law books that covers the jurisdiction of the English speaking Caribbean nations. The first titles in the series were published in 1995 to acclaim from academics, practitioners and the judiciary in the region. Several editions followed, and they have now become essential reading for those learning and practising Caribbean law.

This must have series is required holdings for any law library specialising in Caribbean legal information.

Titles in this series include:

Commonwealth Caribbean Contract Law
Gilbert Kodilinye and Maria Kodilinye

Commonwealth Caribbean Employment and Labour Law
Natalie Corthésy and Carla-Anne Harris-Roper

Commonwealth Caribbean Tort Law
Gilbert Kodilinye

Commonwealth Caribbean Business Law
Natalie Persadie and Rajendra Ramlogan

Commonwealth Caribbean Corporate Governance
Edited by Suzanne Ffolkes-Goldson

Commonwealth Caribbean Family Law

Husband, Wife and Cohabitant
Karen Nunez-Tesheira

Commonwealth Caribbean Civil Procedure (Fourth Edition)
Gilbert Kodilinye and Vanessa Kodilinye

Commonwealth Caribbean Company Law
Andrew Burgess

Commonwealth Caribbean Sports Law
Jason Haynes and J. Tyrone Marcus

Commonwealth Caribbean Criminal Practice and Procedure (Fifth Edition)
Dana Seetahal, with updates from Roger Ramgoolam

Commonwealth Caribbean Insurance Law
Lesley Walcott

Commonwealth Caribbean Property Law (Fifth Edition)
Gilbert Kodilinye

For more information about this series please visit: https://www.routledge.com/Commonwealth-Caribbean-Law/book-series/CAV8

COMMONWEALTH CARIBBEAN PROPERTY LAW

Fifth Edition

Gilbert Kodilinye

Routledge
Taylor & Francis Group
LONDON AND NEW YORK

Fifth edition published 2022
by Routledge
2 Park Square, Milton Park, Abingdon, Oxon, OX14 4RN

and by Routledge
605 Third Avenue, New York, NY 10158

Routledge is an imprint of the Taylor & Francis Group, an informa business

First edition published by Cavendish Publishing Ltd 2000

Fourth edition published by Routledge 2014

British Library Cataloguing-in-Publication Data
A catalogue record for this book is available from the British Library

Library of Congress Cataloging-in-Publication Data
Names: Kodilinye, Gilbert, author.
Title: Commonwealth Caribbean property law / Gilbert Kodilinye.
Description: Fifth edition. | Milton Park, Abingdon, Oxon ; New York, NY : Routledge, an imprint of the Taylor & Francis Group, an Informa Business, [2022] | Series: Commonwealth Caribbean law series | Includes bibliographical references and index.
Identifiers: LCCN 2021010065 (print) | LCCN 2021010066 (ebook) | ISBN 9781032019444 (hardback) | ISBN 9781032033662 (paperback) | ISBN 9781003186946 (ebook)
Subjects: LCSH: Real property—West Indies, British. | Leases—West Indies, British.
Classification: LCC KGL5173 .K63 2022 (print) | LCC KGL5173 (ebook) | DDC 346.72904/3—dc23
LC record available at https://lccn.loc.gov/2021010065
LC ebook record available at https://lccn.loc.gov/2021010066

ISBN: 978-1-032-01944-4 (hbk)
ISBN: 978-1-032-03366-2 (pbk)
ISBN: 978-1-003-18694-6 (ebk)

DOI: 10.4324/9781003186946

Typeset in Baskerville
by Apex CoVantage, LLC

CONTENTS

PREFACE

In the preparation of this fifth edition, my main aim has remained that of presenting the subject of Commonwealth Caribbean real property law in a manner accessible to students, which demonstrates the application of legal principles in a modern and practical context. Although designed primarily for students of real property, including conveyancing and landlord and tenant law, it is hoped that practitioners also will continue to derive benefit from the citation and analysis of local statutes and case law. Since the publication of the previous edition, there have been several significant and interesting decisions handed down by the superior courts of the various jurisdictions in the region, and these are discussed in the text.

A new feature of this edition is the appendix of questions and answers, which are intended as a guide for students sitting examinations in Caribbean real property law in institutions of higher learning in the region. The 'suggested answers' are not intended to be definitive, and indeed any answer to a legal problem is bound to be based on the opinions and style of the particular commentator, so the concept of a 'model' or 'definitive' answer hardly exists in this context. Nonetheless, it is hoped that students will derive some real benefit from this section of the book.

TABLE OF CASES

TABLE OF LEGISLATION

CHAPTER 1

STRUCTURE OF REAL PROPERTY LAW

Land law (the 'law of real property') is concerned with the rights and liabilities that arise in respect of immovable property. In its legal sense, 'land' includes not just the soil and things growing naturally on it, but any buildings and fixtures erected thereon. It is a peculiar feature of land that, being immovable and indestructible, it is normally subject to a wide variety of rights, obligations and interests that would not normally affect pure personalty. If X is the owner of a gold watch, it is unlikely that any person other than X will have any right or interest in the watch, nor will X be restricted in his enjoyment of the watch; he may simply use it until it wears out, or until he decides to give it away to someone else. Similarly, if X is the owner of a car, the only other 'person' who is likely to have any right or interest in the car is the finance company (if it has been bought on hire purchase), and X's only obligations in relation to the car will be to insure it, license it, and drive it with due care. On the other hand, if X is the 'owner' of land, there will invariably be several other persons having rights over the land, and he will be burdened with a number of restrictions and obligations (called 'incumbrances') in respect of it. For instance, it is likely that he will have mortgaged it to a bank as security for the loan of the purchase money; that a neighbour, Y, will have a right to run his drains under part of it and to have access over a pathway on it; that the land will be burdened by restrictive covenants prohibiting X and his successors from, for example, sub-dividing the land or using it for a trade or business; and that, if the land is let to a tenant, X will be excluded from possession until expiry of the lease. Furthermore, the 'ownership' of the land may be fragmented. For instance, X may have inherited the land under the will or intestacy of a deceased relative in common with his two brothers, P and Q, so that the land will be 'co-owned' by all three, who will have equal rights to enjoy it. Lastly, X, as 'owner', will be subject to town and country planning legislation, which will require him to seek planning permission to develop the land, and to revenue laws, requiring payment of rates and taxes.

ORIGINS OF LAND LAW

The land laws applicable in Commonwealth Caribbean jurisdictions are derived from English common law and, in Guyana and St Lucia, also partly from Roman–Dutch and civil law respectively. The theory of landholding under the English system was based on the concept of 'tenure'. Under the feudal system, introduced into England by the Normans after the conquest of 1066, all land belonged to the king, who granted possession of areas to certain barons (his 'tenants-in-chief ') in return for services, such as the provision of soldiers for the king's army. These barons in turn granted possession of land to lesser lords, in return for services, and the lords themselves granted subtenancies to others. There was no limit to the number of subtenancies that could be granted and, as a result, 'innumerable petty lords sprang up between the great barons and the immediate tenant of the soil'.[1] This process,

1 Hayes, *Introduction to Conveyancing*, Vol 1, p 9.

DOI: 10.4324/9781003186946-1

known as 'subinfeudation', persisted for 200 years, but was eventually prohibited in 1290 by the statute of *Quia Emptores*, which provided that, thenceforth, no new subtenancies could be granted. If the holder of land wished to grant possession to another, he/she could do so only by outright alienation (called 'substitution'). The effect was that, gradually, the petty ('*mesne*') lords disappeared from the picture, leaving the actual occupant of the land theoretically holding directly from the Crown, but rendering services to no one, and looking to all intents and purposes like the absolute owner.

THE DOCTRINE OF ESTATES

We have seen that, according to the theory of English land law, no one but the Crown actually owns land, and the actual occupant only has 'tenure'. The principle, which still holds good today,[2] is that a person cannot own land; *he/she can own only an interest in land.* The doctrine of estates defines the period for which any such interest will last. In the modern law, there are three principal estates: fee simple estate, leasehold estate and life estate.

Fee simple estate

The fee simple estate (in modern times, often referred to as a 'freehold') is the closest one can come to actual ownership of land. This estate comprises the right to use and enjoy the land for the duration of the life of the grantee and those of his heirs (both lineal and collateral) and successors. A fee simple estate is freely transferable, by *inter vivos* disposition or by will, and although, in theory, it is possible for a person to die without any heirs at all, this is most unlikely to happen, and it is accepted in the modern law that a fee simple is equivalent to permanent ownership of the land.

A fee simple may be 'absolute', amounting to permanent ownership of the land, or it may be 'modified', that is either conditional or determinable.

a) A conditional fee simple is one to which some condition is attached which may have the effect of '*cutting the fee short in mid-flight*'. Such a condition is called a 'condition subsequent' to distinguish it from a condition precedent (a condition which must be satisfied *before* a grant or transaction can take effect). An example of a conditional fee is a disposition by X 'to Y in fee simple *on condition that* Y continues to practise as an attorney-at-law', the effect of which is that if Y does stop practising as an attorney, X can exercise his 'right of entry' and bring Y's fee to an end. Other words which can be used to denote a conditional fee are '*but if*', '*provided that*'. The courts are reluctant to allow estates to be cut short, and so they have developed strict rules as to the conditions they will accept as being valid.

2 In Barbados, however, s 5(1) of the Property Act, Cap 236, expressly provides that 'a fee simple in possession is . . . equivalent, so far as the law permits, to absolute ownership, and all feudal tenure of land is hereby abolished'. For a discussion of the application of the doctrine of tenures in Commonwealth Caribbean territories, see S. Owusu, *Commonwealth Caribbean Land Law*, 2007, London: Routledge-Cavendish, pp 68 *et seq.*

b) A determinable fee, on the other hand, is one in which the *limit or boundary* of the estate is marked by a determining event which may never happen; for example, in a grant by X 'to Y so long as the University of the West Indies shall have an LLM program'. The effect of such a determinable fee is that if the determining event occurs (eg, the UWI ceases to have an LLM program), the fee simple will terminate automatically, without the need for any action on the part of X. Since the determining event merely marks the boundary of the estate and does not cut it short, the courts have adopted a more lenient approach and will uphold the validity of determining events which, if they had been expressed as conditions, might have been declared void. Another reason for the more lenient approach to determining events is that if a determining event is declared void, the whole grant will fail, whereas if a condition is void it will simply be struck out, leaving the grantee with a fee simple absolute. Apart from 'so long as' or 'as long as', other words which denote a determinable fee are 'until', while' and 'during'.

Void conditions

(i) Restraints on alienation

A condition which cuts short the fee simple on the holder alienating the land is void. For example, if X grants land to Y 'on condition that Y never sells the land', or 'on condition that Y does not sell the land to anyone but Z', or 'provided that Y does not mortgage the land', the conditions are void and Y will take a fee simple absolute. However, a *partial* restraint on alienation may be held valid, as in *Re Macleay*,[3] where a condition that the grantee 'never sells out of the family' was held valid. On the other hand, in a determinable fee simple, a restraint on the holder alienating the land is valid. Thus, a grant to Y in fee simple 'until he sells the land' or 'so long as he does not mortgage the land' will be valid, so that if Y sells or mortgages the land, the fee simple will automatically come to an end and the land will revert to the grantor.

(ii) Restraints on bankruptcy

A condition which cuts short the fee on the holder becoming bankrupt is void, as the law prescribes that, if a person becomes bankrupt, the land is to pass to his trustee in bankruptcy (who will sell the land and distribute the proceeds among his creditors). Thus, eg, in a grant 'to Y in fee simple, on condition that he does not commit an act of bankruptcy', the condition is void,[4] so that if Y does become bankrupt, his fee simple absolute will not come to an end but will vest in his trustee in bankruptcy and be available for his creditors. On the other hand, a fee simple which is made determinable on the bankruptcy of the grantee is valid, eg, a grant 'to Y until he commits an act of bankruptcy' is perfectly valid, so that on bankruptcy the fee will automatically terminate and there will be nothing for the trustee in bankruptcy to take.

3 (1875) LR 20 Eq 186.
4 *Re Machu* (1882) 21 Ch D 838.

(iii) Restraints on marriage

In the case of a conditional fee simple, a condition imposing a restraint on marriage is void. Thus, eg, in a grant 'to Y in fee simple, provided that she never marries', the condition is void and will be struck out.[5] However, a condition in *partial* restraint of marriage is valid, eg, conditions against marrying a particular person,[6] or a Roman Catholic,[7] or a Scotsman[8] were all held valid. Moreover, a condition that the grantee will lose his interest on marriage or remarriage will not be void if the purpose of the grant is not to promote celibacy but to provide for the grantee while single, or while a widow or widower.[9] In the case of a determinable fee simple, restraints on marriage, whether partial or total, are valid. Thus, a grant 'to Y in fee simple until she marries' is valid, so that if Y does marry, the fee simple will revert to the grantor.

(iv) Restraints which are contrary to public policy

Conditions which are void as contrary to public policy include: (i) conditions which encourage the separation or divorce of a married couple, eg, a grant of a fee simple to Y (a wife separated from her husband) 'on condition that she never returns to her husband',[10] unless the grant can be construed as a provision of maintenance for a wife while she is unprovided for, rather than as an inducement not to return to her husband;[11] (ii) a condition against undertaking public office[12] or entering the armed forces;[13] (iii) a condition designed to separate a parent from his/her child, even where the parents are divorced (thus, a condition which divested property if the grantees 'should live with or continue under the custody, guardianship or control of their father' was held void[14]).

A determinable fee simple is similarly void if it is contrary to public policy. Thus, a grant 'to Y (a wife separated from her husband) until she returns to her husband' will be void, unless it can be construed as a provision for maintenance during the separation.

(v) Uncertain conditions

The condition in a conditional fee simple is void if the meaning of the words used is not sufficiently certain. For example, a grant that is conditional on the grantee 'residing in' a particular country will be void, as there are many forms and degrees of residence and it would be impossible to determine whether the condition had been satisfied or not;[15] but it has been held that where the words 'permanent residence' are used, there may be sufficient certainty, as permanent residence connotes

5 *Morley v Rennoldson* (1843) 67 ER 235, 239–240.
6 *Re Hanlon* [1933] Ch 254.
7 *Duggan v Kelly* (1848) 10 Ir Eq R 295.
8 *Perrin v Lyon* (1807) 9 East 170.
9 *Jones v Jones* (1876) 1 QBD 279.
10 *Re Johnson's Will Trusts* [1967] 1 All ER 152.
11 *Re Lovell* [1920] 1 Ch 122.
12 *Re Edgar* [1939] 1 All ER 635.
13 *Re Beard* [1908] 1 Ch 383.
14 *Re Sandbrook* [1912] 2 Ch 47.
15 *Sifton v Sifton* [1938] 3 All ER 425.

an intention to live in a place for life,[16] and indeed the concept of permanent residence is defined in many immigration statutes. Other examples of uncertainty can be seen in conditions designed to ensure the observance of a particular religion. It should be noted that the courts have been unwilling to strike down 'religious discrimination' conditions, for it has been held that it is not against public policy for an adherent of a particular religion to discriminate in disposing of his own property, particularly since, to invalidate such conditions 'would bring about a substantial reduction of another freedom, namely that of testamentary disposition'[17]. On the other hand, religious conditions have been held void on the ground of uncertainty, eg, conditions requiring the grantee 'to be a member of' or 'to conform to' the Anglican Church,[18] or not to marry any person 'not of Jewish parentage and of the Jewish faith',[19] because 'faith varies infinitely in degree and, even if it were possible to do so, a donor does not normally specify the exact degree that will satisfy his anxiety . . . Does, for instance, conformity to the Anglican Church necessitate attendance at religious services? If so, how regular must the attendance be?'.[20] However, it has been held that a condition for the forfeiture of an interest if the grantee should 'become a convert to the Roman Catholic religion' was valid, as such conversion requires the performance of certain ceremonies, so that the court could tell with certainty whether or not the condition had been breached. Similarly, the grant of a determinable fee will be void if there is uncertainty as to what terminates the estate.

Fee tail estate

The fee tail estate gives the right to use the land for the life of the grantee and that of his lineal descendants. The fee tail estate theoretically exists in most Caribbean jurisdictions but is almost never encountered in practice and, even in England, no new fee tails could be created after 1 January 1997.

Leasehold estate

A leasehold estate gives a right to possession, use and enjoyment of land for a definite period of time, for example, one month, one year, 21 years, 99 years or any other certain period. A leasehold may be carved out of a fee simple, so that the fee simple owner becomes the lessor (landlord) of the lessee (tenant); a leasehold may also be carved out of a leasehold, in which case the leaseholder becomes the sublessor (landlord) of the sublessee (subtenant). Leaseholds are discussed in Chapters 4–6, below.

Life estate

A life estate is most often found in family settlements where, for example, a deceased leaves his property by will to his widow for life and then to his children or remoter

16 *Re Gape's Will Trusts* [1952] 2 All ER 579.
17 *Blathwayt v Lord Cawley* [1975] 3 All ER 625, 636 where it was held that a condition which divested property if a child became a Roman Catholic was not void either on the ground that it was discriminatory or that it interfered with parental duties regarding religious instruction.
18 *Re Tegg* [1936] 2 All ER 878.
19 *Clayton v Ramsden* [1943] 1All ER 16.
20 Cheshire and Burn, *Modern Law of Real Property*, 16th edn, p 374.

issue. As in the case of leaseholds, a life estate is most often carved out of a fee simple. It gives the holder the right to use and enjoy the rents, profits and income of the property until his or her death, when the estate terminates. A life tenant (as well as a tenant under a lease) is subject to the doctrine of waste. In practice, the doctrine is more likely to be encountered in connection with life estates since, in the vast majority of leases and tenancies, conduct within the definition of waste will be governed by express covenants, such as covenants to repair and user covenants prohibiting actions likely to damage or destroy the property.

Doctrine of waste

(i) *Ameliorating waste* denotes alterations to the property that improve it, such as converting dilapidated warehouses into dwellings.[21] The courts look with disfavour on actions for ameliorating waste, and an action for damages is likely to fail because no damage will have been suffered; unless, perhaps, the building is of historic interest or of a unique quality, and the whole character of the property has been altered.

(ii) *Permissive waste* is the failure to repair property that has fallen into disrepair, such as failure to reinstate dilapidated buildings. A tenant for life is not liable for permissive waste, unless the grant makes him/her 'impeachable for waste', ie, unless an obligation to repair or maintain is expressly imposed. Such an obligation is rare in family settlements.

(iii) *Voluntary waste* consists of actions that diminish the value of the property, such as pulling down or altering houses,[22] or damaging or destroying windows, doors or other fixtures. A tenant for life will not be liable for voluntary waste if the grant makes him/her 'unimpeachable for waste', ie, if the grant expressly absolves him/her from liability for such waste (which is common in grants of life tenancies).

(iv) *Equitable waste* is conduct consisting of acts of wanton destruction committed by a tenant for life who is unimpeachable for voluntary waste. Equity considers it unconscionable for a tenant to ruin the property with impunity. Equitable waste is thus a peculiarly flagrant version of voluntary waste that may be restrained by injunction.

LEGAL AND EQUITABLE ESTATES AND INTERESTS

The distinction between legal and equitable rights is fundamental to English land law. A legal right, estate or interest is one that historically was recognised and enforced by the common law courts, such as the old King's Bench or Common Pleas courts. These courts tended to adopt a very inflexible approach and would deny a remedy to a deserving plaintiff merely because he/she had not observed the proper formalities. The Court of Chancery, on the other hand, where rules of equity were applied, habitually mitigated the harshness of the common law by recognising new rights, such as the beneficiary's interest under a trust, and by granting

21 *Doherty v Allman* (1878) 3 App Cas 709.
22 *Marsden v Edward Heyes Ltd* [1927] 2 KB 1.

new remedies to deserving plaintiffs, such as injunctions and specific performance, despite the absence of the proper formalities. The contribution of equity, therefore, was twofold: (a) it recognised new rights where none existed before – in particular, interests under trusts; and (b) it developed new remedies where the common law remedies would be inadequate. In Commonwealth Caribbean jurisdictions, the superior courts are empowered by statute to apply common law and equitable principles concurrently.[23]

In modern land law, equitable interests fall into three categories, as follows.

(a) Estates and interests taking effect behind trusts – that is, where the legal title to the property is vested in trustees, holding upon trust for the beneficiaries, who have equitable interests in the property. For example, where Blackacre is held by trustees 'upon trust for X for life, remainder to Y and Z', X has an equitable life interest, and Y and Z have concurrent equitable interests in the fee simple. Equitable interests under trusts are usually encountered in family settlements.
(b) Estates and interests created without the necessary legal formalities, which are void at common law, but which may take effect as equitable interests. For example, equitable leases or easements arising under the *Walsh v Lonsdale*[24] principle, and equitable mortgages by deposit of title deeds.[25]
(c) Interests created and recognised by equity, such as restrictive covenants[26] and proprietary estoppel.[27]

It is important to distinguish between legal and equitable interests because, whereas legal estates and interests are rights *in rem*, binding on the whole world, equitable interests suffer from the infirmity that they are not binding on a *bona fide* purchaser of a legal estate in the land who has no notice of the existence of the equitable interest. Such a purchaser will take the land free from the equitable interest, which, in effect, will be extinguished.[28]

In this connection, equity recognises three types of notice: (a) actual notice, where the purchaser in fact knows of the existence of the equitable interest; (b) constructive notice, where the purchaser ought to and would have acquired notice if he/she had made due inquiries and investigated the land and the title; and (c) imputed notice, where the purchaser's legal adviser acquires actual or constructive notice of the interest. A purchaser who is affected by any of these three kinds of notice will be bound by existing equitable interests in the land.

23 See, eg, Supreme Court of Judicature Act, Cap 117, s 31 (Barbados); Supreme Court of Judicature Act, Ch 4:01, s 12 (Trinidad and Tobago); Supreme Court Act, Ch. 53, s 16 (the Bahamas); Judicature (Supreme Court) Act, s 48 (Jamaica).
24 (1882) 21 Ch D 9 (below, p 50).
25 See p 189, below.
26 See Chapter 8, below.
27 See Chapters 3 and 8 below.
28 *Pilcher v Rawlins* (1872) LR 7 Ch App 259; *Robert v Antoine* (2010) High Court, Trinidad and Tobago, No 1950 of 2007, where a purchaser of unregistered land to whom the legal title had been conveyed took free from a prior agreement to sell the land (which was an equitable interest); *cf Anoop v Dhani* (2011) High Court, Trinidad and Tobago, No 964 of 2007 (purchaser of land affected with constructive notice of interest of person in possession of the land at the time of the purchase).

Registration of title

Modern land law systems have been significantly affected by the concept of registration of title, which has been introduced by statutes into most Commonwealth Caribbean jurisdictions.[29] Its main aim is to simplify conveyancing and to ensure that someone dealing with the registered proprietor of title to the land in good faith and for value will obtain an absolute and indefeasible title, whether or not the title of the registered proprietor from whom he/she acquires was liable to be defeated by title paramount or some other cause.[30]

> The object is to save persons dealing with registered proprietors from the trouble and expense of going behind the register, in order to investigate the history of their author's title and to satisfy themselves of its validity.[31]

Put in another way, registration of title is a guarantee by the State that the person registered as proprietor is the true owner of the land, and a purchaser need make no further investigation as to the validity of the title, in the certainty that it would have been thoroughly investigated and approved by the Land Registry officials before it was first registered.[32] By contrast, in unregistered land, the title is to be found in the title deeds, and each prospective purchaser must go to the trouble and expense of investigating the 'root of title'[33] by perusing the title deeds going back for the requisite period (such as 20[34] or 30[35] years), in order to be confident that he/she will obtain a good title to the land. Unfortunately, conversion from the 'old' unregistered system to the 'new' registered system in most jurisdictions takes many years, even where it is provided that registration is 'compulsory' – that is, that on any future sale of unregistered land, the title must be brought on the register, so as to convert the land from unregistered to registered, and to invest the purchaser and all future purchasers with a registered title. It is still, therefore, the case that the majority of titles in Caribbean jurisdictions remain unregistered.[36]

Under the registered system, only the titles themselves can be entered fully on the register. Other interests in the land receive protection in various ways, in accordance with the legislation or the registrar's practice in the particular jurisdiction, such as by the lodging of a caveat to be endorsed on the certificate of title as a warning to persons dealing with the proprietor, or by the entry of a memorandum on the certificate of title, or a caution, inhibition or restriction on the register. Interests requiring protection are mainly equitable ones, such as beneficial interests under

---

29 For example, Registration of Titles Act 1973 (Jamaica); Title by Registration Act, Cap 56:50 (Dominica); Land Registration Act, Cap 229 (Barbados); Registered Land Act, Cap 194 (Belize); Registered Land Act, Cap 374 (Antigua and Barbuda); Real Property Ordinance, Ch 56:02 (Trinidad and Tobago); Land Registry Act, Cap 5:02 (Guyana).

30 *British American Cattle Co v Caribe Farm Industries Ltd* [1998] 4 LRC 547, Privy Council Appeal from the Court of Appeal, Belize, at 552, *per* Lord Browne-Wilkinson.

31 *Gibbs v Messer* [1891] AC 248, at 254.

32 However, the success of a system of registered title depends to a large extent on the efficiency of the administrative machinery in the Registry, including the presence of sufficient and skilled manpower: Wylie, *Land Laws of Trinidad and Tobago*, 1986, Port of Spain: Government of Trinidad and Tobago, p 558.

33 See p 242, below.

34 As in Barbados (s 50(1) of the Property Act, Cap 236).

35 As in Trinidad and Tobago (s 2 of the Law Reform (Property) Act 1976).

36 An exception is Jamaica, where most urban land has been registered and certificates of title issued to the proprietors under the Registration of Titles Act 1973. See Chapter 13, below.

trusts, restrictive covenants, equitable easements, equitable mortgages, and contracts affecting the land, such as agreements to lease or sell, which, if not protected, will be defeated by a transfer of the legal estate in the registered land to a *bona fide* transferee, whether he/she has notice of the interest or not.[37] Accordingly, 'the doctrine of notice, whether actual or constructive, as it may pertain to purchasers of unregistered land, has no application even by analogy to registered land'.[38]

THE MEANING OF LAND

'Land' under the common law means not just the ground and soil, but anything attached to the soil, including all trees, plants, hedges and flowers growing thereon, whether wild or cultivated, and houses and other buildings erected thereon. The principle is expressed in the Latin maxim, *quicquid plantatur solo, solo cedit*,[39] meaning 'whatever is attached to the ground becomes a part of it', a further consequence being that whoever is the owner of the ground area is also the owner of anything attached thereto. Statutory definitions of 'land' in most jurisdictions confirm the common law position regarding buildings. For instance, s 2 of the Property Act, Cap 236 (Barbados) states that '"land" means the surface of the earth, the space above it and the things below it, and includes houses and other structures', and s 3 of the Conveyancing Act 1889 (Jamaica) provides that '"land" . . . includes . . . houses and other buildings'.

Finders

Another consequence of the *quicquid plantatur* rule is that generally anything which is found under or attached to land, and which is not the property of an identified individual, belongs to the person in possession of the land. Thus, for example, it has been held that gold rings found by workmen in mud at the bottom of a pool belonged to the landowner,[40] and a gold brooch excavated by a member of the public using a metal detector in a recreation ground belonged to the local council in possession of the ground.[41] On the other hand, if a chattel is found lying loose and unattached to land, it will *prima facie* belong to the finder, unless before the finding the landowner 'has manifested an intention to exercise control over things which may be upon the land'.[42] In *Parker v British Airways Board*,[43] a passenger who found a gold bracelet lying in the defendant's executive lounge at London Heathrow Airport was held entitled to keep it, as finder, as against the defendant. The court held that the finder of a chattel who was not a trespasser[44] acquired the right to keep it against

37 *Halfmoon Bay Ltd v Crown Eagle Hotels Ltd* (2002) 60 WIR 330, at 336, *per* Lord Millett.
38 *Spiricor v Attorney General of St Lucia* (1997) 5 WIR 123, at 133, *per* Byron CJ; *Forman v Velasquez* (2017) Supreme Court, Belize, No 9 of 2006, *per* Benjamin J.
39 The doctrine has been abolished in Belize (s 13 of the Landlord and Tenant Act, Cap 153).
40 *South Staffordshire Water Co v Sharman* [1896] 2 QB 44.
41 *Waverley Borough Council v Fletcher* [1996] QB 334.
42 Megarry & Wade, The Law of Real Property, 8th edn, para 3–037, p 54.
43 [1982] QB 1004.
44 In *Hibbert v McKiernan* [1948] 2 QB 142, a trespasser had taken golf balls, lost by players, from a golf course. In answering the question whether the golf club, as occupier, or the trespasser had a better right to possession of the balls, Lord Goddard CJ said, at 149–150: 'Every householder or occupier of land means or intends to exclude thieves and wrongdoers from the property

all but the true owner if the chattel had been abandoned or lost, unless the occupier of the building, in which the chattel was found, had shown an intention to exercise exclusive control over the building and the things which were in it. In the circumstances, the defendant had not shown such intention.

The distinction between fixtures and chattels

'Fixtures' are those material things that are physically attached to land so that they become part of the realty and the property of the landowner. An object that becomes a fixture merges, so to speak, with the land and accordingly passes automatically with all subsequent conveyances of the land unless lawfully severed from it. A chattel, on the other hand, is a physical object that never becomes attached to the land, even though placed in some close relation with it, and so does not pass with conveyances of the land. It has been rightly pointed out that the distinction between fixtures and chattels is 'not entirely straightforward',[45] and there is a considerable body of case law on the topic. There are two tests for determining whether an object is a fixture or a chattel: (a) the degree of annexation; and (b) the purpose of annexation.

The degree of annexation

According to this test, an article is a fixture if it is attached to land or a building in some substantial manner, such as by nails or screws, and 'the more firmly or irreversibly the object is affixed to the earth or a building thereon, the more likely is the object to be classified as a fixture'.[46] On the other hand, Lord Blackburn observed that when 'the article in question is no further attached to the land than by its own weight, it is generally considered to be a mere chattel'.[47] Applying this test, it has been held that the following articles were fixtures: looms bolted to the floor of a mill;[48] an automatic car-wash machine bolted to the ground;[49] gasoline pumps on a garage forecourt;[50] gas mains and service pipes embedded in the soil;[51] lockers tacked to a wall; panel doors; three-phase tubing.[52] Items such as air conditioning units and bathroom fittings would also be fixtures under this test.[53] Conversely, the following items have been held to be chattels, principally on the basis that they rested on the ground by their own weight: a cistern;[54] a free-standing greenhouse;[55] a mobile home;[56] printing machinery.[57]

---

occupied by him, and this confers on him a special property in goods found on his land . . . It is unthinkable that this special property would not also allow the occupier to claim a better right to possession'.

45 Gray, *Elements of Land Law*, 2nd edn, 1993, London: Butterworths, p 12.
46 *Ibid.*
47 *Holland v Hodgson* (1872) LR 7 CP 328, at 335.
48 *Ibid.*
49 *Lombard and Ulster Banking Ltd v Kennedy* [1974] NI 20, at 23.
50 *Smith v City Petroleum Co Ltd* [1940] 1 All ER 260.
51 *North Shore Gas Co Ltd v Commissioner of Stamp Duties (NSW)* (1940) 63 CLR 52.
52 *National Business Printing Ltd v Carib Spray Ltd* (1994) 31 JLR 653, Supreme Court, Jamaica.
53 See *Aircool Installations v British Telecommunications* [1995] CLY 821 *Botham v TSB Bank plc* (1996) 73 P & CR DI.
54 *Mather v Fraser* (1856) 69 ER 895.
55 *HE Dibble Ltd v Moore* [1970] 2 QB 181.
56 *Royal Bank of Canada v Beyak* (1981) 119 DLR (3d) 505.
57 *Hulme v Brigham* [1943] KB 152.

Two further considerations are:

(i) 'if an object cannot be removed without serious damage to, or destruction of some part of, the realty, the case for its having become a fixture is a strong one'.[58]

(ii) if the object cannot be removed without serious damage to, or the destruction of the object itself, it will be deemed to be a fixture. In *Elitestone Ltd v Morris*,[59] Lord Lloyd opined that, when one is considering a structure such as a building, the answer to the question whether it has become annexed to the land is 'as much a matter of common sense as precise analysis'. He continued:[60]

> A house which is constructed in such a way so as to be removable, whether as a unit or in sections, may well remain a chattel, even though it is connected temporarily to mains services such as water and electricity. But a house which is constructed in such a way that it cannot be removed at all, save by destruction, cannot have been intended to remain as a chattel. It must have been intended to form part of the realty.

The purpose of annexation

The degree of annexation is not conclusive of the status of an item; it merely provides a *prima facie* categorisation that may be reversed by contrary evidence as to the purpose for which the item was brought onto the land. For instance, objects such as marble statues or other garden ornaments resting by their own weight may be regarded as fixtures, if the circumstances show that they were intended to form part of the landscaping or architectural design of the premises.[61] On the other hand, it has been held that 'white goods', such as an oven, a refrigerator and a dishwasher, are not fixtures, even if they are part of the overall design of a kitchen, because they do not permanently improve it.[62]

It is also an established principle that items substantially fixed to the realty may nevertheless be regarded as chattels if the purpose of fixing them was not to improve the land, but to enjoy them as chattels, and the degree of annexation was no more than was necessary to achieve that purpose: for example, tapestries,[63] display cases of stuffed birds[64] fixed to a wall in a room, or a television cable and equipment.[65] The nature of the premises may also be a relevant factor. Thus, whereas carpets in a private home will usually be regarded as chattels, it has been held that wall-to-wall carpeting affixed to the floors of a hotel was a fixture, since the purpose of its

58 *Berkley v Poulett* [1977] 1 EGLR 86, at 88, *per* Scarman LJ.
59 [1997] 1 All ER 5133; followed in *Makhoul v Foster* (2009) High Court, Antigua and Barbuda, No 2003/0138, *per* Blenman J, upheld (2015) Court of Appeal, Eastern Caribbean, Civ App No 2009/0014, *per* Perreira CJ (chattel building in commercial district of St John's, Antigua 'constructed in such a way that it could not be removed, save by destruction').
60 *Ibid*, at 519.
61 *Ibid*, at 89, 90.
62 *Botham v TSB Bank plc* (1996) 73 P & CR D1.
63 *Leigh v Taylor* [1902] AC 157.
64 *Viscount Hill v Bullock* [1997] 2 Ch 482, at 483.
65 *Credit Valley Cable TV/FM Ltd v Peel Condominium Corp* (1980) 107 DLR (3d) 266, at 275.

attachment was the better use of the building as a hotel rather than the better use of the carpeting.[66]

Chattel houses

In the Caribbean, issues concerning the status of chattel houses as fixtures or chattels have arisen in a number of cases, and there is substantial literature on the topic.[67] The leading case is *Mitchell v Cowie*,[68] in which Wooding CJ, in the Court of Appeal of Trinidad and Tobago, pointed out that there are two distinct types of chattel house in the Caribbean. The first type is a wooden structure resting by its own weight upon a stone or brick base. Applying the degree of annexation test, such a structure would clearly be treated as a chattel, owing to its not being affixed to the land and to the fact that it could easily be removed to another location without causing any damage to the land. The second type of chattel house is affixed to the land in some way and ought therefore to be regarded as a fixture. The house in *Mitchell v Cowie* was of this type, being constructed of hollow blocks standing on concrete pillars that were let into the ground, and it was held to be a fixture. A similar type of house featured in a Bahamian case, *O'Brien Loans Ltd v Missick*.[69] It was described as a wooden house resting on wooden beams, which were bolted at the four corners to four columns. The columns were made of concrete blocks resting on the ground, with cement poured into the hollow spaces to hold them together. The bolts were fixed into the cement. There was also a flush toilet connected to a septic tank in the ground. However, notwithstanding the considerable degree of annexation to the land, Georges JA held, applying the 'purpose of annexation' test, that the house was a chattel. The main ground of the decision was that the owner of the house, being a yearly tenant of the plot of land on which the house stood, had 'no intention to benefit the landlord by adding value to the land'. In a sense, the purpose for which the house was constructed was 'the proper enjoyment of the plot of land', but that did not translate into an intention to benefit the owner of the land.

Wooding CJ, in *Mitchell v Cowie*, had also made the point that, in ascertaining the purpose of annexation, regard must be had to whether the affixation of the house to the land was temporary, and for use as a chattel, or permanent, and intended for the better enjoyment of the land. If a structure that *prima facie* would be a fixture is shown to have been erected for some temporary purpose, then the *prima facie* presumption may be displaced and the structure held to be a chattel. An example given by his Lordship was the English case of *Billing v Pill*,[70] in which an army hut resting on a concrete foundation, to which its floor was secured by bolts let into the concrete, was held to be a chattel because it had been erected for the temporary purpose of providing sleeping accommodation for army personnel in wartime, and could be easily dismantled, removed from the site and re-erected

66 *La Salle Recreations Ltd v Canadian Camdex Investments Ltd* (1969) 4 DLR (3d) 549.
67 See p 103, fn 188, *post*.
68 (1964) 7 WIR 118, Court of Appeal, Trinidad and Tobago.
69 (1977) 1 BLR 49, Court of Appeal, The Bahamas.
70 [1953] 2 All ER 1061.

elsewhere. In a Barbadian case, *Massiah v Hutson*,[71] a similar distinction between buildings intended to be temporary and those intended to be permanent was made, but the chattel house in that case was held to be a fixture on the grounds: (a) that the building was 'of a permanent nature firmly fixed to the soil, the removal or attempted removal of which would be followed by serious loss or material damage to the structure';[72] and (b) that it was erected 'for occupation by the family as their residence permanently'.

71 (1961–63) 3 Barb LR 11.
72 Cf *Elitestone Ltd v Morris* [1997] 2 All ER 513, fn 59, 60 above, where the House of Lords held that a chalet formed part of the land because it was so constructed that it could not be moved, save by demolition. See also *Fields v Modeste* (1966–69) 19 Trin LR 251.

CHAPTER 2

CO-OWNERSHIP

Where two or more persons become entitled to possession of land simultaneously, they are said to hold concurrent interests in the land or to be co-owners: for example, where T by his will leaves a plot of land to his children, X, Y and Z, in fee simple, the children will be co-owners of the land.

There are two types of co-ownership in the modern law:

(a) joint tenancy; and
(b) tenancy in common.

JOINT TENANCY

A joint tenancy occurs where land is conveyed or devised to two or more persons without 'words of severance' – that is, words which indicate that each person is to take a separate share: for example, where Blackacre is devised 'to Bill and Ben in fee simple'.

The essence of a joint tenancy is that there is one title and the joint tenants are collectively regarded as a single owner, although, as between themselves, they have separate rights, such as the right to sever the joint tenancy. The other important characteristic of the joint tenancy is the right of survivorship (*ius accrescendi*) whereby, on the death of one joint tenant, his/her interest automatically accrues to the surviving joint tenants, so that he/she has no interest to transfer under his will or intestacy. He/she may avoid this result, however, by severing his joint tenancy during his lifetime and converting him/herself into a tenant in common with a distinct share, which can pass under his will or intestacy.

As Robinson P explained in the Jamaican Court of Appeal, in *Panton v Roulstone*:[1]

> As against third parties, [joint tenants] are in the position of a single owner, but as against each other, each has equal rights. Each has an equal interest in the land. And the interest of each is severable, should he care to do so in his lifetime. It is only if he dies without having in his lifetime severed that interest, that his interest is extinguished and accrues to the survivor.

Unity between joint tenants

For a joint tenancy to exist, the 'four unities' must be present. They are: unity of possession; unity of interest; unity of title; and unity of time.

---

1 (1976) 24 WIR 462, at 469. The right of survivorship applies equally to joint tenancies in Guyana: *Singh v Mortimer* (1966) 10 WIR 65, at 75, *per* Stoby C.

DOI: 10.4324/9781003186946-2

Unity of possession

This means that each joint tenant is entitled to physical possession of the whole of the land. No tenant can point to any part of the land as his own to the exclusion of the others, and each is entitled to enjoy the fruits of possession, such as rents and profits derived from the land. Unity of possession applies equally to tenancy in common.[2]

Unity of interest

Each joint tenant's interest in the property must be of the same extent, nature and duration, since it would be inconsistent with the nature of a joint tenancy for the tenants to have different interests. Thus, for instance, both must be freeholders or both leaseholders, and both must be entitled in possession or both in remainder.

Unity of title

This means that the joint tenants must have derived their titles from the same document (for instance, from the same will or conveyance), or, where they claim title by adverse possession, they must have taken possession simultaneously.

Unity of time

The interest of each tenant must vest at the same time. Where there is unity of title, there will usually be unity of time also, but not necessarily so. For instance, if land is conveyed 'to X for life, remainder to the heirs of Y and Z', and Y and Z die at different times during X's lifetime, Y's and Z's heirs cannot take as joint tenants, since, although there is unity of title, there is no unity of time,[3] their interests having been acquired at different times.

TENANCY IN COMMON

Tenancy in common differs fundamentally from joint tenancy in that: (a) the only unity is the unity of possession; and (b) there is no right of survivorship. Tenants in common are said to hold 'in undivided shares'. This means that each tenant has a distinct fixed share in the property (for example, one-half, one-third, one-quarter), albeit that the land at present is undivided and treated as a single unit, which can be realised if and when the property is sold; since there is no *ius accrescendi*, a tenant in common may dispose of his share by will or it may pass on his intestacy.

2 *Bull v Bull* [1955] 1 All ER 253; *Forbes v Bonnick* (1968) 11 JLR 67, Court of Appeal, Jamaica; *Dingwall v Wilson* (2013) High Court, Trinidad and Tobago, No 2011–03945.

3 Co Litt 188a.

A tenancy in common arises:

(a) where land is granted to two or more persons with words of severance (such as, 'in equal shares', 'equally', 'to be divided amongst', 'shares respectively');[4]
(b) where equity treats a joint tenancy at law as a tenancy in common;[5] and
(c) where a joint tenant severs his joint tenancy by alienation, acquisition of a greater interest, agreement or course of dealing.[6]

Law and equity

In Commonwealth Caribbean jurisdictions, apart from Belize, the pre-1926 co-ownership rules apply. Under these rules, both joint tenancies and tenancies in common can exist at law and in equity as legal estates and equitable interests respectively. The possibility of creating tenancies in common at law is extremely inconvenient for conveyancers, as the effect of the fragmentation of the legal estate between numerous tenants in common is that each individual title must be investigated before a good title can be transferred to a purchaser of the land. To avoid this problem, the 1925 legislation in England and Wales provided that tenancies in common of the legal estate could no longer exist. The legal title henceforth had to be held by trustees as joint tenants on trust for sale for the benefit of the beneficiaries, who may be either joint tenants or tenants in common of the beneficial (equitable) interest. This scheme of 'statutory trusts' has been adopted in Belize by ss 36–38 of the Law of Property Act, Cap 190.

Equitable presumption of tenancy in common

Whereas the common law favoured joint tenancies, equity has always leaned in favour of tenancies in common, as equity 'preferred the certainty and equality of a tenancy in common to the element of chance which the *ius accrescendi* of a joint tenancy introduced'.[7] Consequently, in the following four instances, equity presumes that a tenancy in common has been created.

Purchase money provided in unequal shares

Where two or more persons together purchase land, providing the purchase money in unequal shares, a tenancy in common of the property is presumed in equity, and the purchasers take shares proportionate to the amounts advanced by each.[8] Thus, for example, if X and Y purchase land for $100,000, with X providing $75,000 of the purchase money and Y $25,000, and take a conveyance to themselves jointly, on X's death, Y will become entitled to the whole of the property at law, but in equity he will be deemed to be a trustee for X's personal representatives of a three-quarters

4 *Christian v Mitchell-Lee* (1969) 13 WIR 302, Court of Appeal, West Indies Associated States.
5 See below.
6 See pp 18–23, below.
7 Hayton, *Megarry's Manual of the Law of Real Property*, 6th edn, 1982, London: Stevens, p 304.
8 *Lake v Gibson* (1729) 21 ER 1052.

share in the property and to take the remaining one-quarter share beneficially.[9] On the other hand, if X and Y had provided $50,000 each, on X's death, Y would have become entitled to the whole property beneficially, both at law and in equity, for where purchase money is advanced equally, equity will presume that the parties intended the *ius accrescendi* to apply.

Loan on mortgage

Where two or more persons advance money, whether in equal or unequal shares, and take a mortgage of the land from the borrower to themselves jointly, they are joint tenants at law, but are treated in equity as tenants in common, and the survivor is a trustee of the deceased mortgagee's share for the latter's personal representatives – for 'though they take a joint security, each means to lend his own and take back his own'.[10]

This rule is unaffected by the practice of inserting a 'joint account clause' in mortgages where two or more persons lend money. The effect of such a clause is that, on the death of one of the mortgagees, the receipt of the survivor shall be a sufficient discharge for the money, so that the mortgagor may safely repay the loan to the survivor, who can re-convey the land without the concurrence of the personal representatives of the deceased mortgagee. The joint account clause is merely a conveyancing device that affects the position as between the mortgagees and the mortgagor; it does not affect the presumption of a tenancy in common as between the mortgagees *inter se*.[11]

Partnership assets

Where business partners purchase land as part of their partnership assets, they are presumed to do so as tenants in common, for *ius accrescendi inter mercatores locum non habet*[12] ('the right of survivorship has no place between merchants'). Although the legal estate may be held on a joint tenancy, in equity, the surviving partners hold a deceased partner's share on trust for his estate. Thus, in *Lake v Craddock*,[13] in which five persons joined in buying some waterlogged land with a view to its improvement by drainage, it was held that they must be presumed to have acquired the land as tenants in common, as the right of survivorship was incompatible with a commercial undertaking.

The presumption extends to any joint undertaking with a view to profit, even where there is no formal partnership agreement between the parties. In *Panton v Roulstone*,[14] two women had purchased six parcels of land, taking conveyances in their joint names. There was no evidence as to the extent of their respective contributions to the purchase price, but a majority of the Jamaican Court of Appeal inferred that the women were business associates and were therefore tenants in common of the

9 See *Gibson v Walton* (1992) 28 Barb LR 113, High Court, Barbados.
10 *Morley v Bird* (1798) 30 ER 1192, at 1193, *per* Arden MR.
11 *Re Jackson* (1887) 34 Ch D 732.
12 Co Litt 182a.
13 (1732) 24 ER 1011.
14 (1976) 24 WIR 462, Court of Appeal, Jamaica.

beneficial interest in the land and, on the death of one, the property did not devolve on the survivor under the *ius accrescendi*. As Watkins JA (Ag) explained:[15]

> Where property is held by A and B in joint tenancy at law, but as tenants in common in equity, upon the prior death of A, B holds the bare legal title by right of survivorship but in trust for himself and the estate of A. Where property is held by A and B in joint tenancy at law and in equity, upon the prior death of A, B takes the property by right of survivorship and the property does not pass under the will or intestacy of A. The right of survivorship operates by law and not by virtue of the intention or pursuant to the will of any deceased co-owner. Any attempt to dispose by will of property in which the legal and beneficial interests subsist in joint tenancy is wholly ineffectual. Contrariwise, where property is held by two persons as joint tenants at law but as tenants in common in equity, the equitable interest of either passes on death either pursuant to his will or on intestacy, and not otherwise.

Robinson P (dissenting) took the view that, on the evidence, the parties were not business partners, pointing out that:[16]

> it is when the joint tenants engage in trade or business such as the buying and selling of lands for profit, or the farming of lands acquired for the purpose, or the building of houses on lands acquired for the purpose and the selling of same for profit, or some trading or business activity other than the mere purchasing and accumulation of land, that equity will presume a tenancy in common of the beneficial interest.

In this case, since the parties had acquired the properties as joint tenants, and in the absence of any evidence that they had used the land in the way of trade or business, Robinson P was unable to agree that they held the beneficial interests as tenants in common.

Individual business purposes

The Privy Council has held, in *Malayan Credit Ltd v Jack Chia-MPH Ltd*,[17] that business tenants who had paid rent and service charges in agreed proportions were tenants in common. In the course of his judgment, Lord Brightman suggested that the cases in which joint tenants at law would be presumed to hold as tenants in common were not necessarily limited to cases of purchases in unequal shares, joint mortgagees and partners, and that there were 'other circumstances in which equity may infer that the beneficial interest is intended to be held by the grantees as tenants in common', such as 'where the grantees hold the premises for their several individual business purposes'.[18]

SEVERANCE OF JOINT TENANCY

It is always open to a joint tenant to avoid the consequences of the *ius accrescendi* by severing his joint tenancy and thereby converting it into a tenancy in common.[19]

---

15 *Ibid*, at 465.
16 *Panton v Roulstone* (1976) 24 WIR 462, at 465.
17 [1986] 1 All ER 711.
18 *Ibid*, at 715.
19 But, see *Mums Inc v Cayman Capital Trust* [1988–89] CILR 485.

In the leading case of *Williams v Hensman*, Page Wood VC identified three types of circumstance that will amount to severance:[20]

(a) act of a joint tenant 'operating upon his own share';
(b) mutual agreement; and
(c) course of dealing (mutual conduct).

Act of joint tenant operating upon his own share

In order to bring about a severance, the act of the joint tenant must be of a final and irrevocable character, which effectively estops him from claiming any interest in the subject matter of the property.[21]

Alienation

Total or partial alienation of his interest by a joint tenant is the clearest type of act within this head. Where a joint tenant alienates his interest *inter vivos*, his joint tenancy is severed and the transferee takes as a tenant in common, since he/she has no unity of title with the other joint tenants. Such severance does not affect the other joint tenants, who remain joint tenants *inter se*. Thus, if X, Y and Z are joint tenants, and X sells his interest to P, P becomes a tenant in common as to one-third and Y and Z joint tenants of two-thirds. If Y then dies, Z will become entitled to two-thirds by the right of survivorship, and P and Z will be left as tenants in common of one-third and two-thirds respectively. Severance by alienation also occurs where a joint tenant mortgages his interest[22] or becomes bankrupt,[23] and, since equity regards that as done which ought to be done, a joint tenancy will be severed by a 'specifically enforceable contract [to alienate] . . . creating an equitable interest in the property, even though the legal act of alienation has not taken place'.[24]

In the Jamaican case of *Gamble v Hankle*,[25] the plaintiff and her husband had been registered as joint proprietors of certain land. After her husband's death, the plaintiff claimed to be solely entitled to the property by virtue of the *ius accrescendi*. The husband had, however, during his lifetime, purported to convey the land to the defendant by a deed of gift. The question in issue was whether the deed of gift had effected a severance of the joint tenancy. Wolfe J held that it had, notwithstanding that the deed of gift was not in the form stipulated in the Registration of Titles Act.

20 (1861) 70 ER 862, at 867. See *Thomas v Davis* [2015] JMCA Civ 22; *Lawrence v Mahfood* [2010] JMCA Civ 38.
21 *Re Wilks* [1891] 3 Ch 59, at 61.
22 *York v Stone* (1709) 91 ER 146. But where the title of the land is registered under a Torrens system, a mortgage of the land does not sever a joint tenancy since a mortgage of registered land operates as a mere security without any transfer or grant of an interest to the mortgagee: Megarry and Wade, *Law of Real Property*, 8th edn, para 13–040; *Lyons v Lyons* [1967] VR 169, at 173, 176–181; see *Vidalis v Piquette* (2011) High Court, Trinidad and Tobago, No 1179 of 2000.
23 *Re Rushton (A Bankrupt)* [1972] Ch 197, at 203.
24 *Seunath v Seunath* (1990) 1 TTLR 437, High Court, Trinidad and Tobago, *per* Gopeesingh J.
25 (1990) 27 JLR 115; followed in *Derby v Townsend* (2006) Supreme Court, Jamaica, No 000974 of 2005, in which it was held that where registered land was owned by spouses as joint tenants, the execution of an instrument of transfer by one spouse had severed the joint tenancy. See also *Francis v Edwards* [2019] JMSC Civ 89 and *Greaves v Chung* [2020] JMSC Civ 118.(instruments of transfer never registered but nonetheless held sufficient to sever).

In Wolfe J's view, the deed of gift was an act that came within the ambit of the first of the three methods of severance mentioned by Page-Wood VC in *Williams v Hensman*.

More recently, in *Francis v Edwards*,[26] Pettigrew-Collins J (Ag) pointed out[27] that section 88 of the Registration of Titles Act of Jamaica requires a transfer of registered land to be in one of the forms A, B, or C in the 4th Schedule to the Act, and further provides that, upon registration of the transfer, the estate and interest of the proprietor as set forth in the instrument of transfer passes to the transferee. In the present case, the transfer document executed by a joint tenant did conform with section 88, but the instrument of transfer was never registered and so could not have operated to pass any interest to the transferee. It was held nevertheless that the execution of the transfer operated to sever the joint tenancy.

Commencement of litigation

There is authority for the proposition that the formal commencement of litigation concerning a joint tenancy is 'an act operating on the share' of the joint tenant commencing the proceedings,[28] notwithstanding that the proceedings could always be abandoned or discontinued.

Mutual agreement

A specifically enforceable contract for the alienation of a joint tenant's interest[29] will certainly have the effect of severing the joint tenancy. However, in order to effect a severance, it is not necessary that an agreement to sever should be specifically enforceable,[30] nor that there should be written evidence of it,[31] nor that any valuable consideration should have passed between the parties;[32] nor will the subsequent repudiation of the agreement prevent a severance.[33]

As for the content of the agreement, it may either expressly provide for severance, or it may simply contemplate a dealing with the property that necessarily involves severance:[34] for example, where joint tenants agree to join in a sale[35] or

26 [2019] JMSC Civ 89.
27 At para 91.
28 *Re Draper's Conveyance* [1967] 3 All ER 853, 857; *Harris v Goddard* [1983] 3 All ER 242, at 246, in which Lawton LJ took the view that the service of a summons with supporting affidavit under the Married Women's Property Act 1882, for an order directing sale of the jointly owned matrimonial home and equal distribution of the proceeds of sale, in *Draper* were acts effectual to sever the joint tenancy within *Williams v Hensman*. This proposition was applied in *Ward v Rawlins* (2017) High Court, St Kitts/Nevis, No 2013/0273 by Ward J, citing this passage in the text.
29 In Antigua and Barbuda, section 101 (1) (a) of the Registered Land Act, Cap 374, prohibits dispositions by one or more co-owners of land held in joint proprietorship without the consent of the other co-owner(s), and an individual joint proprietor cannot compel the other(s) to agree to a disposition. A similar provision is contained in section 100 (1), (2), (3) of the Registered Land Law (2004 Rev) of the Cayman Islands. See *Edwards v Edwards* (2012) High Court, Antigua and Barbuda, No 2002/0204; *Mums Inc v Cayman Capital Trust* [1988–89] CILR 485.
30 Compare with severance under the first head of the *Williams v Hensman* rule (p 000, above) where, in order to constitute 'an act operating upon his own share' sufficient to bring about a severance, the agreement by the joint tenant to alienate his share must be specifically enforceable.
31 *Wilson v Bell* (1843) 5 Ir Eq R 501, at 507.
32 *Burgess v Rawnsley* [1975] 3 All ER 142.
33 *Ibid.*
34 *Ibid.*
35 *Re Hayes' Estate* [1920] 1 Ir 207, at 211.

lease[36] of the property to a third party and to divide the proceeds between them, and where joint tenant spouses enter into a separation agreement that provides for sale and distribution of matrimonial property in specified shares.[37]

The leading case of *Burgess v Rawnsley*[38] may be regarded as an example of severance of a joint tenancy by mutual agreement. Here, an elderly couple, H and R, joined in the purchase of a house, taking a conveyance of the legal title upon trust for sale for themselves as beneficial joint tenants, each providing half the purchase price. When the relationship broke down, H negotiated with R to buy her out, and there was evidence that R had orally agreed to sell her interest to H for a specified price. R later repudiated the agreement and demanded a higher price, but H died before the negotiations could continue. It was held that H had effectively severed the joint tenancy before his death and that his estate was accordingly entitled to a half-share in the proceeds of sale of the property.

Course of dealing

According to Page-Wood VC, severance may be effected 'by any course of dealing sufficient to intimate that the interests of all were mutually treated as constituting a tenancy in common'.[39] This head may be difficult to distinguish from Page-Wood VC's second head (mutual agreement), but it is accepted that the third category is not a mere subheading of the second.

Severance under this head does not require any express act of severance, nor any agreement or declaration of trust. All that is required is 'a consensus between the joint tenants, arising in the course of dealing with the co-owned property, which effectively excludes the future operation of a right of survivorship'.[40] Thus, for example, where spouses who are joint tenants of property negotiate with one another for some arrangement of their interests on divorce, it may be possible to infer from the circumstances a common intention to treat each other as tenants in common, even where the negotiations break down.[41] On the other hand, a unilateral declaration by one party of an intention to sever will not suffice.[42] As Page-Wood VC put it:[43]

> It will not suffice to rely on an intention, with respect to the particular share, declared only behind the backs of the other persons interested.

---

36 *Palmer v Rich* [1987] 1 Ch 134, at 143.
37 *Re McKee* (1975) 56 DLR (3d) 190, at 196; but see *Nielson-Jones v Fedden* [1974] 3 All ER 38.
38 [1975] 3 All ER 142. Cf *Cooper v Coleman* (2007) Supreme Court, Jamaica, No 01803 of 2004; *Miller-Weston v Miller* (2007) Supreme Court, Jamaica, No CLM 094 of 2002; *Mahfood v Lawrence* (2009) Supreme Court, Jamaica, No 1378 of 2006. A joint tenancy in registered land may be severed by mutual agreement, without the need for entry of the agreement on the Register Book of Titles: *Thomas v Davis* [2015] JMCA Civ 22, paras 82–84, *per* Brooks JA.
39 *Williams v Hensman* (1861) 70 ER 862, at 867.
40 Gray, *Elements of Land Law*, 1987, London: Butterworths, p 329. Thus, severance may occur where joint tenants of family land build and occupy individual houses on defined portions of the land, as such conduct shows an intention to hold as tenants in common: *Seunath v Seunath*, fn 43, below.
41 See *op cit*, Hayton, fn 7, p 326.
42 *Nielson-Jones v Fedden* [1974] 3 All ER 38; *Cooper v Coleman* (2007) Supreme Court, Jamaica, No. 01803 of 2004, where McDonald-Bishop J held that communication by the (now deceased) joint tenant of an offer to purchase the other's share in the property, without more, was not sufficient to sever the joint tenancy.
43 *Williams v Hensman* (1861) 70 ER 862, at 867; *Seunath v Seunath* (1990) 1 TTLR 437, at 444, *per* Gopeesingh J.

Other methods of severance

Apart from Page-Wood VC's three methods, there are two other ways of effecting severance of a joint tenancy, one derived from the common law and the other from statute.

Acquisition of an additional estate in the land

Where a joint tenant subsequently acquires an additional estate in the land, the unity of interest between him/herself and the other joint tenants is destroyed and the joint tenancy is severed.[44] For example, if land is granted to X, Y and Z as joint tenants for life, with remainder to R in fee simple, and Y acquires the fee simple from R, Y's life estate will be merged in the fee simple and the joint tenancy will be severed, leaving X and Z as joint tenants *inter se*.

Severance by written notice

Section 36(2) of the Law of Property Act 1925 (UK) provided a new method of severance of a beneficial joint tenancy, viz, by a joint tenant giving notice in writing to the other joint tenants of his desire to sever. This method has been introduced in Barbados and Belize.[45]

This statutory method of severance is convenient, in that it may be unilateral, no consent being required from the other joint tenant,[46] nor is it necessary that the notice should have been actually received by the other tenant; it is sufficient that there is evidence that it was duly posted to him/her.[47] The notice need not be signed, and it is established that it may take the form of a writ or originating summons commencing litigation for the purpose of determining the rights of the parties *inter se*. In *Re Draper's Conveyance*,[48] a wife applied by summons under s 17 of the Married Women's Property Act 1882 (UK) for an order that the jointly owned matrimonial home be sold and the proceeds of sale distributed in accordance with the parties' respective interests. Shortly after the court had made the order requested, the husband died intestate. Plowman J held that the wife's summons, coupled with her affidavit in support, showed an intention inconsistent with a continued joint tenancy, and operated to sever her beneficial joint tenancy during her husband's lifetime, both at common law and under s 36(2).

The principle in *Draper* has been applied by the Barbados High Court. In *Gibson v Walton*,[49] a husband and wife purchased two apartment buildings, which were conveyed to them as beneficial joint tenants. When the relationship became strained, the wife applied under s 191 of the Property Act, Cap 236, for a determination by

44 *Wiscot's Case* (1599) 76 ER 555.
45 Section 43(1) of the Property Act, Cap 236 (Barbados); s 38(2) of the Property Act, Cap 190 (Belize).
46 *Harris v Goddard* [1983] 3 All ER 242, at 246.
47 *Re 88 Berkeley Road, NW9* [1971] 1 All ER 254 (in which notice was sent by recorded delivery, but was never received).
48 [1967] 3 All ER 853. See also *Quigley v Masterson* [2012] 1 All ER 1224 (application to Court of Protection for permission to put jointly owned property on the market with a view to sale, held an effective notice of severance within s 36(2), Law of Property Act 1925).
49 (1992) 28 Barb LR 113. See also *Stuart v Kirton* (1994) 30 Barb LR 405, in which Waterman J held that severance had been brought about by, *inter alia*, a joint tenant's filing a writ and seeking an order of sale of the property and equal distribution of the proceeds of sale.

the court of her interest in the property. The husband died, and the question arose as to whether there had been a severance of the joint tenancy. Belgrave J held that the application by the wife constituted a written notice to the husband of her intention to sever; alternatively, an affidavit sworn by the husband, in which he expressed his desire that the joint tenancy be severed and the property sold and the proceeds of sale distributed in the proper proportions, had the same effect.

PARTITION

Co-owners, whether joint tenants or tenants in common, may agree voluntarily to put an end to the co-ownership by dividing up the property into separate parcels, each former co-owner henceforth becoming a single owner of his parcel. This process is known as 'partition'. At common law, if the co-owners could not agree, there was no right vested in any of them to compel the others to submit to such partition. However, the Partition Acts 1539 and 1540 (UK) conferred a statutory right to bring an action to compel partition, so that one co-owner, whether joint tenant or tenant in common, could insist upon a partition, however inconvenient it might be for the other co-owners;[50] later, the Partition Act 1868 conferred on the court a power to decree a sale of the land instead of partition, which would be desirable where, for instance, the property was too small to be conveniently or sensibly divided up between the co-owners, or 'where partition in the physical sense would be very inconvenient or difficult to operate in a manner fair to all the interested parties'.[51]

The statutory provisions as to compulsory partition and orders of sale in lieu of partition have been reproduced in most Commonwealth Caribbean jurisdictions,[52] so that co-owners can apply to the High Court (or Supreme Court) for an order for partition or, alternatively, for an order of sale,[53] the effect of which will be that each co-owner will obtain a precise share-out of the proceeds of sale.[54]

The statutory provisions regarding sale in lieu of partition in Caribbean jurisdictions are modelled very closely on the English legislation of 1868 and follow a similar

50 In the absence of agreement, partition always requires an application to the court: *Thompson v M'Latamou* (1989) Supreme Court, The Bahamas, No 1187 of 1986, *per* Smith J.

51 *Seunath v Seunath* (1990) 1 TTLR 437, High Court, Trinidad and Tobago, at 448, *per* Gopeesingh J.

52 See ss 3–5 of Partition Act, 1873 (Jamaica); s 2 of Partition Act 1855, Title 26, Item 30, and ss 1, 2 of Partition Act 1914, Title 26, Item 31 (Bermuda); ss 3–5 of Partition Act, Ch 153 (The Bahamas 47); ss 3–5 of Partition Ord, Ch 27, No 14 (Trinidad and Tobago); ss 4, 5, 8 of Partition Act, Cap 225 (Grenada); ss 4, 5, 8 of Partition Act, Cap 54:09 (Dominica); ss 4, 5, 8 of Partition Act, Cap 226 (BVI); ss 3, 15 of Partition Act, Cap 245 (St Vincent); ss 4, 5, 8 of Partition Act, Cap 305 (Antigua); s 2 of Partition Law, Cap 117 (Cayman Islands); cf s 45 of Property Act, Cap 236 (Barbados), which contains a more restricted power to order sale. Compulsory partition has been abolished in England and Wales.

53 See, eg, *Higgs v Leshel Maryas Investment Co Ltd* [2009] UKPC 47. It was held in *Mums Inc v Cayman Capital Trust* [1988–89] CILR 485, Grand Court, Cayman Islands, *per* Harre J, that by virtue of s 100 of the Registered Land Law (Law 21 of 1971, revised 1976) dispositions of land held under joint tenancy are not permitted without the concurrence of all of the joint tenants, so that the court had no power to order a partition or sale of jointly owned property to satisfy a judgment debt.

54 Where one co-owner spends his money for the improvement of the property enjoyed by him/her in common with another co-owner, the *value* of the individual shares of each tenant in common will increase, but the *proportion* in which they hold their respective shares remains constant. The co-owner who has effected improvements cannot recover from the other co-owner(s) a proportionate part of the cost, but if the tenancy in common is brought to an end by *partition*, he may have a lien for the amount by which he increased the value of the share(s) of the other tenant(s) in common: *Patten v Edwards* (1996) 33 JLR 475, Court of Appeal, Jamaica.

pattern. For instance, section 3 of the Partition Ordinance of Trinidad and Tobago, Ch 27, No 14, provides that the court, on the application of any party interested in the property and holding *less than a half-share*, may request a sale of the property and the court may so order if (a) because of the nature of the property, or (b) because of the number of parties interested or presumptively interested, or (c) because of the absence or disability of some of the parties, or (d) because of any other circumstance, a sale of the properties and distribution of the proceeds would be more beneficial for the parties interested than a partition. An illustration of the application of the section can be found in *Mansour v Mansour*.[55] Here, N, the applicant for a sale in lieu of partition, had a one-sixth share in a residential property in Woodbrook, Port of Spain. N's mother, M, who had a one-half share, resided in the property with her 93-year-old mother (N's grandmother). In considering whether to order sale, Rahim J examined the balance of hardship to each party. On the one hand, N was very gainfully employed in Canada, where he had his own accommodation, and he had relatively minimal financial obligations. On the other, M was unemployed and her sole income came from the apartments, which she had constructed at her own expense on the Woodbrook property. She also had the responsibility of looking after her elderly and ailing mother. Rahim J held that, in these circumstances, there was 'no legitimate justification for an order of sale of the property'.

On the other hand, the effect of section 4 is that if a sufficient number of co-owners together holding a half-share or more request a sale, the court must so order unless there is good reason to the contrary, the onus being on the party resisting the sale to show good reason why the sale should not be ordered.[56] In *Suraj v Sookram*,[57] for instance, the claimant sought an order of sale of a house that he owned jointly with his mother, and in which he was entitled to a half share. Boodoosingh J ordered a sale of the property, since it was clear that the family relations had broken down completely and there was such bitterness between the parties that they were not speaking to each other. The learned judge found 'no good reason advanced not to order a sale of the property'. Similarly, in *Pena v Pena*,[58] where the party seeking a sale had a two-thirds share in the co-owned property, Bereaux J held that alleged financial hardship to the party resisting the sale was not 'such as to allow the court to stifle the plaintiff's larger interest in the property and his desire to realise the pecuniary benefits thereof by way of sale'.

Section 5 provides that where a co-owner requests a sale in lieu of partition, the court may direct a sale,

> unless the other parties interested in the property, or some of them, undertake to purchase the share of the party requesting a sale . . . and in case of such undertaking being given, the court may order a valuation of the share of the party requesting a sale.

The proper construction of s 5 was in issue in *Superville v Superville*.[59] Here, the 'other parties interested' (plaintiffs) argued that the effect of s 5 was that, on their

55 (2013) High Court, Trinidad and Tobago, No CV 2012–0256.
56 *Pena v Pena* (2000) High Court, Trinidad and Tobago, No 258 of 1999. See also *Esty v Esty* [2017] JMSC Civ 16, paras 21, 22, *per* Shelly-Williams J; *Patterson v Patterson* [2019] JMSC Civ 10, paras 8–10, *per* D Fraser J.
57 (2011) High Court, Trinidad and Tobago, No 4320 of 2008. See also *Solomon v Solomon* (1988–89) High Court, Trinidad and Tobago, No 2011–04237; *Alexander v Alexander* (2016) High Court, Trinidad and Tobago, No 2014–00250; *Marajh v Marajh* (2018) High Court, Trinidad and Tobago, No 2016–02804.
58 Above, fn 56.
59 (1999) High Court, Trinidad and Tobago, No 57607 of 1999.

undertaking to purchase the share of the party requesting a sale (defendant), the court could order the defendant to sell to them at a valuation. The defendant, on the other hand, argued that he could not be compelled to sell his share to the plaintiffs. Mendonca J held, following English authorities, that it was 'clear from the cases that under section 5 the court cannot compel a part owner to sell his share to the other part owner(s)'. The true position was that 'if he is prepared to accept a sale of his share at a valuation, the court may so order on the undertaking of the other part owner(s) to purchase the share'. His Lordship regarded *dicta* of Lords Watson and Blackburn in *Pitt v Jones*[60] as most apposite. Lord Watson had said that:[61]

> the provisions of section 5 cannot be enforced, except at the instance of the party requesting a sale and *voluntarily* offering, as an alternative, to sell his own share to the other parties interested, at a price to be fixed by the court, and also that he may retract that alternative at any time before a judicial contract has been completed by these parties, or any of them, giving the requisite statutory undertaking to purchase. The result of retraction will be to deprive him of the right to insist on a sale under section 5, leaving him to seek his remedy under section 3 or 4, if he can bring his case within them, or by a decree of partition. [Emphasis added]

Similarly, Lord Blackburn had explained the position thus:[62]

> Section 5 says that, in every case of a suit for partition (whether the sale would or would not be more beneficial for the parties than a partition), if any party . . . requests a sale, the court shall have a discretion to order such a sale, unless the parties opposing the sale are willing to take his share at a valuation. But it does not say, nor do I think it is intended to say, that a party who requests a sale of the whole *must* take that valuation. I think it means that if a party presses for a sale, and the court thinks that the opposing parties in fairness ought either to buy him out or consent to a sale, it may order a sale unless they will agree to take his share at a valuation, in which case the party requesting a sale either accepts that valuation or not.

Accordingly, in *Superville*, Mendonca J refused to order the defendant to sell his share to the plaintiffs.

Equitable accounting and occupation rent

In a partition suit and/or order for sale, adjustments as to the respective shares of the co-owners may be made by the court, 'the guiding principle being that neither party could take the benefit of an increase in value of the property without making an allowance for what has been expended by the other in order to obtain it'.[63] This applies particularly where the co-owners are husband and wife and one of the parties has effected repairs or renovations to the matrimonial home. Further, where one of the parties has remained in sole occupation of the home, he/she may be required to pay to the other an 'occupation rent', whether that other party was ousted from the home or left voluntarily.[64]

60 (1879–80) 5 App Cas 651.
61 *Ibid*, at 663.
62 *Ibid*.
63 *Re Pavlou* [1993] 1 WLR 1046, at 1048–1049, *per* Millett J, followed in *Marajh v Marajh* (2018) High Court, Trinidad and Tobago, No 2016–02804, *per* Kokaram J.
64 *Re Pavlou*, *ibid*, at 1050.

CHAPTER 3

LICENCES AND PROPRIETARY ESTOPPEL

A licence is essentially a permission given by the owner or occupier of land (the 'licensor') to another person (the 'licensee') to enter upon the land for some purpose, for example to lodge in a room, to view a film, or to swim in a pool: acts that might otherwise amount to a trespass.

Until fairly recently, a licence was considered to be, at most, a mere contractual arrangement between two persons, subject to the usual privity rule, but in the last 50 or so years, some licences have come to be regarded almost as proprietary interests in land, which are binding not only on the licensor, but also on third parties. This is particularly the case with licences arising by estoppel, where a party has no recognised legal or equitable interest in the land, but it would be inequitable in the particular circumstances for him/her to be denied a right to occupy. This is an area of the law that is still in the process of development, and it may be that a new right *in alieno solo* is emerging.

TYPES OF LICENCE

There are four generally accepted categories of licence:

(a) bare licence;
(b) licence coupled with an interest;
(c) contractual licence; and
(d) estoppel licence.

Bare licence

A bare licence is one granted otherwise than for valuable consideration. It amounts to a mere permission to enter upon the licensor's land: for example, an invitation to dinner, or to play a game of tennis. Such licences may also be implied: for instance, a postman has an implied licence to enter premises in order to deliver mail, and it has been suggested that, in the absence of a locked gate, the occupier of a dwelling house gives an implied licence to any member of the public to pass through his garden or yard and up to his front door in order to communicate with him/her;[1] also, a commercial organisation may be taken to give implied licences to persons who enter in good faith in order to do business or acquire information.[2] A bare licence can be withdrawn at any time by the licensor without notice, but the licensee must be given a reasonable time to leave. What is a reasonable time will depend on the circumstances.[3]

---

1 *Robson v Hallett* [1967] 2 QB 939.
2 See *Davis v Lisle* [1936] 2 KB 434; *Great Central Rly Co v Bates* [1921] 3 KB 578.
3 *Robson v Hallett* [1967] 2 QB 939.

DOI: 10.4324/9781003186946-3

Licence coupled with an interest

The prime example of this type of licence is where a person who has been granted a *profit à prendre*, such as a right to take growing timber or game from the land, acquires a licence to enter the land in order to enjoy the right. Such a licence is not effective at law unless the profit has been formally granted by deed.[4] Being incidental to the enjoyment of an interest in land, a licence coupled with an interest is irrevocable[5] and binding on third parties.

Contractual licence

A contractual licence is one granted for valuable consideration. It may be 'short-term', for example, where a person buys a ticket in a cinema, or for a football or cricket match,[6] or for temporary car parking;[7] it may be 'medium-term', an example of which would be annual membership of a golf or tennis club; or 'long-term', as in the case of the lodger who is given the right to occupy a dwelling house for a period, such right not amounting to a lease or tenancy.

Revocability of contractual licence

At common law, a licence other than one coupled with a grant or interest is revocable at any time by the licensor, whether the licence is gratuitous or contractual.[8] Thus, in *Wood v Leadbitter*,[9] in which Wood had bought a ticket to view horse racing and was forcibly ejected from the racecourse in breach of the contract, it was held that Leadbitter, the licensor, was entitled to revoke Wood's licence at any time and that, once he did so, Wood became a trespasser who could be lawfully ejected with reasonable force. Wood's argument that he had an irrevocable licence to enter and remain in the racecourse enclosure during the whole period of the race meeting was rejected. Accordingly, Wood could not sue Leadbitter for assault and his only remedy was for damages for breach of contract, which would be nominal.

However, equity may come to the aid of the licensee in that, where a contractual licence purports to confer a right to enter and remain on land for a particular purpose or for a specified period, the court may imply a negative contractual term to the effect that the licensor will not revoke the licence before the purpose or period has been completed. Accordingly, a court of equity may grant an injunction to restrain the licensor from revoking the licence in breach of the contractual term[10] and, where appropriate, may compel the licensor to carry out the bargain by means of a decree of specific performance.[11] Of course, in the case of very short-term licences, such as that in *Wood v Leadbitter*, the award of an injunction or specific performance would

4 *Wood v Leadbitter* [1843–60] All ER Rep 190.
5 *Ibid.*
6 See, eg, *Winter Garden Theatre (London) Ltd v Millennium Productions Ltd* [1947] 2 All ER 331; *Hurst v Picture Theatres Ltd* [1915] 1 KB 1, in which the court somewhat misleadingly categorised the licence as one coupled with an interest; *Mayfield Holdings Ltd v Moana Reef Ltd* [1973] 1 NZLR 309.
7 *Ashby v Tolhurst* [1937] 2 KB 242, at 249.
8 See *Hardware v Levy* (1971) 12 JLR 330, Court of Appeal, Jamaica.
9 [1843–60] All ER Rep 190.
10 *Winter Garden Theatre (London) Ltd v Millennium Productions Ltd* [1947] 2 All ER 331.
11 *Verrall v Great Yarmouth BC* [1980] 1 All ER 839.

be impracticable, and so the licensee's only remedy would be damages. But, where there is a long- or medium-term contractual licence, which, on a proper construction of the contract, is irrevocable, then its revocation may be prevented by injunction and/or specific performance. As Lord Denning MR explained:[12]

> Since *Winter Garden Theatre (London) Ltd v Millennium Productions Ltd*,[13] it is clear that once a man has entered under his contract of licence, he cannot be turned out. An injunction can be obtained against the licensor to prevent his being turned out. On principle, it is the same if it happens before he enters. If he has a contractual right to enter, and the licensor refuses to let him come in, then he can come to court and in a proper case get an order for specific performance to allow him to come in.

The concept of the contractual licence has been applied with a degree of flexibility in the family home context where, in order to do justice to 'deserted' cohabitees, the courts have been willing to imply contractual licences in situations in which there was little evidence of any contractual arrangement between the parties. In Lord Denning's words, the court may 'imply a contract by [the licensor] . . . or, if need be, impose the equivalent of a contract by him'.[14] An example is *Chandler v Kerly*.[15] Here, Chandler and Mrs Kerly, who was separated from her husband, formed a relationship. Chandler later purchased the matrimonial home of Mrs Kerly and her husband, and moved in with Mrs Kerly and her two children. However, Chandler later ended the relationship and sought possession of the house. It was held that Mrs Kerly had a contractual licence terminable by reasonable notice, which, in the circumstances, was taken to be 12 months. Another example is *Tanner v Tanner*,[16] which concerned an unmarried couple with children. The father had purchased a house for the mother and children to live in, and the mother had given up Rent Act protected accommodation to move into the house. The mother was held to have no proprietary interest in the house, but she was entitled to a contractual licence to live in the property, which the father could not revoke until the children were no longer of school age.

In this context, the contractual licence is used as a flexible device in order to achieve an equitable result. Accordingly, there are no rigid rules or principles as to when a court will, and when it will not, find a contractual licence in the family home situation. It appears rather that the courts first decide what would be a desirable result and then work backwards, utilising whatever legal concept seems best to bring about the result, whether contractual licence, estoppel licence, or resulting or constructive trust. For this reason, it will be found that some cases decided on the basis of a contractual licence may seem to fit more neatly into the category of estoppel licences, or vice versa; in others, it may be extremely difficult to determine, from legal reasoning, into which category the case falls.

Contractual licences and third parties

Notwithstanding the enhanced status of the contractual licence as against the licensor brought about by the use of equitable remedies, it seems that a contractual

12 *Ibid*, at 844.
13 [1947] 2 All ER 331.
14 *Tanner v Tanner* [1975] 3 All ER 776, at 780.
15 [1978] 2 All ER 942.
16 [1975] 3 All ER 776.

licence remains incapable of binding third parties, even with notice. The traditional view is that a contractual licence binds only the parties to it, and does not confer any proprietary interest in land capable of running with the land. One of the leading cases is *King v David Allen and Sons (Billposting) Ltd.*[17] There, the licensor gave to the licensee the exclusive permission to affix advertisements to the walls of a cinema. Subsequently, the licensor granted a lease of the cinema to a third party, without any express mention of the licence. The lessee refused to allow the licensee to continue affixing the advertisements, and the licensee sued the licensor for breach of contract. The licensor would be liable for damages for breach if the lease had the effect of depriving the licensee of his right to affix the advertisements – in other words, if the licence were not binding on the lessee. The House of Lords held that the licence was not binding and therefore the action for damages succeeded.

Cases such as *King v David Allen and Sons (Billposting)* Ltd[18] had clearly established that a contractual licence would not be binding on third parties, with or without notice, but two cases, in both of which Lord Denning MR gave the leading judgment, suggested that it could be so binding. The first of these was *Errington v Errington.*[19] Here, a father purchased a house in his own name, subject to a mortgage. Wishing to provide a home for his son, who had recently married, he agreed that his son and daughter-in-law could occupy the house and that, provided they paid all monthly mortgage instalments, he would convey the legal estate to them. They paid the instalments as they became due, but the payments were not completed when, nine years later, the father died, having devised the house to his widow. Shortly after the father's death, the couple separated; the son went to live elsewhere, and the daughter-in-law remained in occupation and continued to pay the mortgage instalments. The widow brought an action for possession, but her action was dismissed by the Court of Appeal on the ground that the son and daughter-in-law were contractual licensees. The promise of the house in return for paying the mortgage instalments could not be revoked, and this 'licence coupled with an equity' was binding on the widow.

The reasoning in *Errington* does not necessarily lead to the conclusion that a contractual licence can bind third parties, as the decision in that case would seem to be better explained on the ground of estoppel. Moreover, in *National Provincial Bank Ltd v Ainsworth,*[20] the House of Lords was reluctant to regard a contractual licensee as having more than a personal right, holding that such a right could not be converted into an equitable interest binding on third parties merely because the licensor could be restrained from revoking the licence.

The other case in which a contractual licence was held to bind a third party is *Binions v Evans.*[21] Mrs Evans had been allowed by the trustees of the estate, for which her late husband had worked, to reside rent-free in a cottage on the estate for the rest of her life. This licence was part of a written agreement that imposed on Mrs Evans an obligation to keep the interior of the cottage in repair and to maintain the garden. Subsequently, the trustees sold and conveyed the cottage to Binions expressly subject to the agreement, and Binions paid a reduced price because of this. In an action by

17 [1916] 2 AC 54.
18 See also *Clore v Theatrical Properties Ltd* [1936] 3 All ER 483.
19 [1952] 1 All ER 149.
20 [1965] 2 All ER 472.
21 [1972] 2 All ER 70.

Binions for possession of the cottage, the Court of Appeal held that Mrs Evans was protected. Megaw and Stephenson LJJ found for Mrs Evans on the ground that she was a tenant for life under the Settled Land Act 1925. Lord Denning MR, on the other hand, held that Binions was bound by Mrs Evans' contractual licence because, in the first place, Binions had purchased the cottage expressly subject to Mrs Evans' rights and could not ignore them, and, secondly, because the licence gave rise to a constructive trust, which bound Binions to allow Mrs Evans to live in the cottage for the rest of her life.

It is clear that neither *Errington* nor *Binions* is authority for any general principle that contractual licences are binding on third parties, for both decisions can be supported only on their special facts. Furthermore, in the later case of *Ashburn Anstalt v Arnold*,[22] the Court of Appeal held, *obiter*, that where land was conveyed to a purchaser expressly 'subject to' a contractual licence, the licence was not a proprietary interest capable of binding such purchaser. Fox LJ said:[23]

> The far-reaching statement of principle in *Errington* was not supported by authority, not necessary for the decision of the case, and *per incuriam* in the sense that it was made without reference to authorities which, if they would not have compelled, would surely have persuaded the court to adopt a different *ratio*. Of course, the law must be free to develop. But as a response to problems which had arisen, the *Errington* rule (without more) was neither practically necessary nor theoretically convincing. By contrast, the finding on appropriate facts of a constructive trust may well be regarded as a beneficial adaptation of old rules to new situations . . . The court will not impose a constructive trust *unless it is satisfied that the conscience of the estate owner is affected* [emphasis added] . . . The words 'subject to' will, of course, impose notice. But notice is not enough to impose on somebody an obligation to give effect to a contract into which he did not enter.

Licence protected by estoppel

The doctrine of proprietary estoppel prevents the revocation of a right affecting land that one party has been led by the other to believe to be permanent. The doctrine is founded on the wider equitable principle against unconscionability, and its effect is to prevent a person from enforcing his strict legal rights when it would be inequitable for him/her to do so in the light of the parties' conduct and the dealings that have taken place between them. Thus, where X, the owner of land, allows Y to expend money on that land or otherwise act to his detriment under an expectation, created or encouraged by X, that Y will be able to remain on the land or acquire an interest in it, equity will step in and ensure that Y's expectations will not be defeated.

The estoppel doctrine is inextricably bound up with the law of licences in two respects. Firstly, in many of the cases, the owner of the land has given a person a licence to do something on the land, such as a licence to build a house on the land, or to exercise a right of way across it. Such licence may be protected by estoppel if the requirements of the doctrine, such as an assurance by the licensor and detrimental

---

22 [1988] 2 All ER 147; followed in *Arthurs v Berry* (1994) 31 JLR 100, Court of Appeal, Jamaica, *per* Patterson JA (Ag).
23 [1988] 2 All ER 147, at 164.

reliance by the licensee, are present.[24] Secondly, in order to 'satisfy the equity' that may have arisen in favour of the person who has relied on the owner's assurance, the court may grant that person an irrevocable licence to occupy the land.

The three classes of cases to which the doctrine of proprietary estoppel may apply are as follows:

(a) cases of incomplete gifts;
(b) cases in which a reasonable expectation of acquisition of a right to remain in occupation of land was created; and
(c) cases of unilateral mistake.

Incomplete gifts

An estoppel may arise where X intends to make a gift of land to Y, but the gift is incomplete because the appropriate formalities have not been complied with. A well-known example is *Dillwyn v Llewelyn*,[25] in which a father allowed his son to have possession of his (the father's) land and signed an informal memorandum purporting to transfer the fee simple to the son. The latter spent a large sum on building a house for himself on the land. After the father's death, the son claimed to be entitled to the fee simple. It was held that the father's representations, together with the son's expenditure, entitled the son to call for the imperfect gift to be perfected (as an exception to the maxim that 'equity will not perfect an imperfect gift') by conveyance of the fee simple to him.[26]

An analogous situation is where the owner of land expressly promises that he will make a gift of the land at some time in the future and the promisee incurs expenditure in reliance on the promise. Two Commonwealth Caribbean cases neatly illustrate the application of proprietary estoppel in this context. In the Barbadian case of *Sealy v Sealy*,[27] a father had invited and encouraged his son to erect a dwelling house on half an acre of the father's land, promising that, when the building reached a certain stage, he would convey the land to the son by way of gift. The father failed to carry out his promise. King J (Ag) held that an equity had arisen in the son's favour, which would be satisfied by ordering the father to convey the plot to the son:

> Lord Westbury in *Dillwyn v Llewelyn* [said]:[28]
>
> > If A puts B in possession of a piece of land, and tells him, 'I give it to you that you may build a house on it', and B, on the strength of that promise, with the knowledge of A, expends a large sum of money in building a house accordingly, I cannot doubt that the donee acquires a right from the subsequent transaction to

---

24 This passage in the text was cited with approval by Seepersad J in *Davidson v Joseph* (2016) High Court, Trinidad and Tobago, No 201–0263, paras 48, 51.

25 [1861–73] All ER Rep 384. A Jamaican example of an estoppel arising from an incomplete gift is *Raffington v McIntosh* (2009) Court of Appeal, Jamaica, Civ App No 5 of 2007.

26 The equity arising in such a case is a 'requirement and liability' within s 88 of the Registration of Titles Act: *Lungrin v Monelal* (2004) Court of Appeal, Jamaica, Civ App No 8 of 2003, *per* Downer JA.

27 (1990) High Court, Barbados, No 1492 of 1987. See also *Hassanali v Mohammed* (2011) High Court, Trinidad and Tobago, No 58 of 2007.

28 [1861–73] All ER Rep 384, at 387.

> call on the donor to perform the contract and complete the imperfect donation which was made.
>
> It is clear from the above that, once an equitable right has arisen, the donee may call on the donor to complete his promise. In other words, the plaintiff in this instant case may sue for the promise to be made good and this court has jurisdiction to hear and determine the matter.

After stating that ss 47 and 60 of the Property Act, Cap 236, had no application to the case, King J (Ag) continued:

> The defendant not only invited and encouraged the plaintiff, but worked on building the house . . . The defendant failed to carry out his promise after falling out with the plaintiff. What relief is the plaintiff entitled to? The defendant had offered to execute a declaration at the plaintiff's expense that he holds 809.70 square metres of land on trust for the plaintiff. The plaintiff had made his final plea for a conveyance of the fee simple in half an acre of land.

In *Chalmers v Pardoe*, Sir Terence Donovan said:[29]

> There can be no doubt on the authorities that where an owner of land has invited or expressly encouraged another to expend money on part of his land on the faith of an assurance or promise that part of the land will be made over to the person so expending his money, a court of equity will *prima facie* require the owner by appropriate conveyance to fulfil his obligation; and when, for example for reasons of title, no such conveyance can effectively be made, a court of equity may declare that the person who has expended the money is entitled to an equitable charge or lien for the amount expended.
>
> I have given careful consideration to all of the cited authorities and have chosen to be guided by the above, together with *Pascoe v Turner*,[30] in which a considerable number of cases were commented on, and approaches to be adopted in these matters recommended. All those authorities point to the conclusion that this plaintiff is entitled to a conveyance of the fee simple by the defendant.

Another example is the Trinidadian case of *Khan v Khan*.[31] Here, the plaintiffs were the son and daughter-in-law of the defendant. The plaintiffs purchased a parcel of land on which they had intended to build their matrimonial home, but the defendant persuaded them instead to come and live with him in his house, which they did, having been assured by the defendant that he would leave his share of the house to them by his will. The plaintiffs subsequently spent their money on repairing and renovating the defendant's house and building a garage, with the encouragement of the defendant. Later, a dispute arose between the parties and the defendant ordered the plaintiffs to leave the house. Shah J held that the plaintiffs had acquired an equity in the defendant's house by estoppel, which would be satisfied by the court's ordering

29 [1963] 3 All ER 552, 555. This statement of principle was applied by Barnett CJ in *Gonzales Bros Furniture Ltd v Godet* (2011) Supreme Court, The Bahamas, No 563 of 2001, where a purchaser was allowed by the vendor to take possession of the property before completion and before payment of the deposit, and incurred expenditure in improving the property in the expectation of receiving the fee simple.

30 [1979] 2 All ER 945.

31 (1994) High Court, Trinidad and Tobago, No S-1022 of 1993. See also *Bhopa v Bhopa* (1998) High Court, Trinidad and Tobago, No 1101 of 1997; *Sooknanan v Sooknanan* (1995) High Court, Trinidad and Tobago, No S 622 of 1994; *Mohammed v Damarsingh* (2009) High Court, Trinidad and Tobago, No 984 of 1983. Cf *Baldeo v Baldeo* (2011) High Court, Trinidad and Tobago, No 4311 of 2007.

the defendant to convey his share in the house to himself for life, with remainder to the plaintiffs in fee simple.

Reasonable expectation of acquisition of a right

Proprietary estoppel may arise in cases in which there is no clear express promise of a gift by X, but where X and Y have nevertheless consistently dealt with one another in such a way as to cause Y to believe that he would acquire a right to remain in possession of X's land. In a dissenting judgment in *Ramsden v Dyson*,[3231] Lord Kingsdown said:

> If a man, under a verbal agreement with a landlord for a certain interest in land, or, what amounts to the same thing, *under an expectation, created or encouraged by the landlord* [emphasis added], that he shall have a certain interest, takes possession of such land with the consent of the landlord, and upon the faith of such promise or expectation, with the knowledge of the landlord and without objection by him, lays out money upon the land, a court of equity will compel the landlord to give effect to such promise or expectation.

This type of case thus resembles the cases of incomplete gifts, but the main difference is that, in this class of case, there is no attempted gift or express promise to give in the future, only conduct that causes an expectation in the mind of the person expending his money that the expenditure will be justified. In order to satisfy the equity in this type of case, the court may grant an irrevocable licence to occupy the land. The leading example is *Inwards v Baker*,[33] in which a father allowed his son to build a house on his (the father's) land. The son was under the impression that he would be permitted to live there as long as he wished. When the father died, the trustees of the father's will allowed the son to remain in occupation for 12 years, after which they sought possession. Possession was refused by the Court of Appeal on the ground that the son had acquired, as against his father, an irrevocable licence arising by proprietary estoppel. The licence gave the son the right to remain in occupation for the rest of his life, and the trustees were bound by the licence because they had acquiesced in the son's continued occupation after they had notice of it. Lord Denning MR said:[34]

> If the owner of land requests another, or indeed allows another, to expend money on the land under an expectation created or encouraged by the (owner of the land) that he will be able to remain there, that raises an equity in the licensee such as to entitle him to stay.

Two Commonwealth Caribbean cases that illustrate the application of the rule are *Clarke v Kellarie* and *Denson v Bush*. In *Clarke*,[35] C acquired a tenancy of leasehold premises occupied by K, her brother-in-law, and his family. C assured K that he and his family could continue to occupy the premises until K's death. K thereafter decided to erect a building on the land and, although C did not give K any express permission to build, she regularly visited the site and raised no objection to the

32 (1866) LR 1 HL 129, at 170.
33 [1965] 1 All ER 446. A recent example is *Peters v Lewis* (2010) High Court, Trinidad and Tobago, No 36 of 2001.
34 *Ibid*, at 448.
35 (1970) 16 WIR 401, High Court, Trinidad and Tobago.

construction work. After the building had been completed, C acquired a long lease of the property and shortly afterwards sought to dispossess K. According to the evidence, K was illiterate and 'of very limited intelligence', whereas C was 'intelligent, alert and keenly alive to her interests'. Rees J held that K was a licensee. An equity by estoppel had been created by C's conduct, which would be satisfied by an order that K be entitled to occupy the land as licensee for so long as C was a lessee thereof, and that K should pay to C an amount equivalent to the rent reserved under the lease for the specified period.

In *Denson v Bush*,[36] R, the owner of a house, lived abroad. The defendants, who were close relatives of R, were encouraged by other members of the family to occupy the property, and were led to believe that they could remain in occupation for the rest of their lives. The property was dilapidated, and the defendants spent their money in carrying out repairs, with the acquiescence of R. No rent was paid by the defendants, nor did R spend any money on repairs to the property. R subsequently transferred the property to his son, the plaintiff, who had full knowledge of the position of the defendants. The plaintiff later gave the defendants notice to quit. Summerfield CJ held that since the defendants had been encouraged to believe that they would be allowed to remain in occupation indefinitely and had spent money on repairs to the property in reliance on that belief, an equity had arisen in their favour, which would be satisfied by giving them a licence to occupy the house for the rest of their lives. The learned Chief Justice said:[37]

> The case of *Inwards v Baker* has much in common with this one. The only difference here is that the expectation was induced or encouraged by the apparent agent of the owner, but that does not affect the principle. Where the circumstances point to the fact that a person giving permission to occupy premises, and giving assurances in relation to the occupancy, is acting as the agent of the owner and the person receiving those assurances has no reason to doubt that he is the agent, and the owner, with the knowledge that occupation has been permitted on his behalf, does nothing to disabuse the resultant possessor of any assurances given on his behalf before the possessor acts on them to his detriment then, in my view, the principles in *Inwards v Baker* apply as if those assurances had been given by the owner himself. Certainly, in this case, the owner's acquiescence in the state of affairs which existed over 16 years, with full knowledge that the house would have to be repaired and maintained by the defendants, encouraged the expectation which his apparent agents had given to the defendants.
>
> One must remember that this was a family affair, with one member of the family dealing with another and none would question the authority of the other to do what he or she purported to do. It was also at a time when the owner, Robert Chesley Bush, had been away from the island continuously for about 14 years with no apparent prospect of an early return if, indeed, there was any prospect at all. Although the money was raised by the second defendant, the defendants are husband and wife and there

36 [1980–83] CILR 41, Grand Court, Cayman Islands.

37 *Ibid*, at 46. See also *Flores v Wright* [1985] Bz LR 385, Supreme Court, Belize; *White v Ramroop* (2010) High Court, Trinidad and Tobago, No 7245 of 1986. As far as chattel houses are concerned, it was pointed out by Husbands J in a Barbadian case, *Skinner v Daniel* (1981) 16 Barb LR 21 (High Court, Barbados), that: 'to say that no equity arises . . . merely because the money expended is in respect of a chattel house rather than of a wall structure is . . . to take too narrow a view. In many cases, so to hold would be inequitable. Today, many chattel houses are substantial buildings with characteristics and facilities similar to those of wall structures. Others, more modest, are no less firmly rooted to the land they occupy by the special relationship of their owners to the family plot on which they stand, and the settled intention and expectation of the owners to occupy the houses on the land for the rest of their days'.

> can be no doubt that the repairs and maintenance were a joint enterprise, the first defendant doing a lot of the work himself.
>
> I am of the opinion that the principle in *Inwards v Baker* applies to this case and that the defendants have a licence coupled with an equity in the property and it is accordingly so declared.
>
> The plaintiff was not a *bona fide* purchaser for value without notice of that licence coupled with an equity so as to destroy the defendant's equitable rights in the property.
>
> There remains the question of the manner in which the equity should be satisfied. The nature of the equity was that it gave each defendant the right to remain in occupation of the property for the remainder of his or her life. There is no reason why the protection afforded by this court should not reflect the nature of the equity – as was done in the case of *Inwards v Baker*. The equity should therefore be satisfied by allowing either or both defendants to remain in occupation of the property for as long as either desires.

Unilateral mistake

The application of estoppel principles to cases of unilateral mistake was explained by Lord Cranworth in *Ramsden v Dyson*:[38]

> If a stranger begins to build on my land supposing it to be his own, and I, perceiving his mistake, abstain from setting him right, and leave him to persevere in his error, a court of equity will not allow me afterwards to assert my title to the land in which he had expended money on the supposition that the land was his own. It considers that, when I saw the mistake into which he had fallen, it was my duty to be active and to state my adverse title, and that it would be dishonest in me to remain wilfully passive on such an occasion in order afterwards to profit by the mistake which I might have prevented.

The requirements for a successful plea of estoppel under the *Ramsden v Dyson* rule were outlined by Fry J in *Willmott v Barber* (often referred to as 'the five *probanda*').[39] These may be summarised as follows, A being the true owner and B the person who has expended money.

(a) B must have been mistaken as to his legal rights;[40] if he was aware that he was infringing the rights of another, he cannot resist the claims of that other.

(b) B must have expended some money or must have done some act on the faith of his mistaken belief; otherwise, he will not suffer by A's subsequent assertion of his rights.

(c) A must have known of the existence of his own right, which is inconsistent with the right claimed by B, since acquiescence is founded on conduct with knowledge of one's legal rights.

(d) A must have known of B's mistaken belief as to his rights;[41] with such knowledge, it is inequitable for him to remain silent and allow B to proceed on his mistake.

---

38 (1866) LR 1 HL 129, at 140.

39 (1880) 15 Ch D 96, at 105.

40 In *Lettsome v Flanders* (1999) High Court, British Virgin Islands, Benjamin J preferred to invoke this requirement rather than the broader principle advocated in *Taylors Fashions*.

41 Such knowledge was lacking in the Cayman case of *Solomon v Solomon* [1989–89] CILR 144, at 154, *per* Collet CJ. In *Arawak Homes Ltd v Dean* (2010) Supreme Court, The Bahamas, No 1883

(e) A must have encouraged B in his expenditure of money or other act, either directly or by abstaining from asserting his legal rights.

The modern approach

Social and economic changes in the second half of the 20th century have given increased significance to the doctrine of proprietary estoppel, and some courts have moved away from applying restrictive criteria such as those in *Willmott v Barber*. According to Oliver J, in *Taylors Fashions Ltd v Liverpool Victoria Trustees Co Ltd*,[42] the courts should adopt a 'much broader approach' to the doctrine 'which is directed . . . at ascertaining whether, in particular individual circumstances, it would be unconscionable for a party to be permitted to deny that which, knowingly or unknowingly, he has allowed or encouraged another to assume to his detriment'. Further, as Allen Sr J pointed out in a recent Bahamian case,[43] Oliver J had drawn a clear distinction between the 'reasonable expectation of a right' cases and the 'unilateral mistake' cases, suggesting that while all five of the *Willmott v Barber* probanda might be relevant to the latter class of case, they would not all be appropriate to the former.

In the modern law, therefore, it has become accepted that a claimant will be able to establish an estoppel if he can prove: (a) an assurance; (b) reliance; and (c) a detriment, in circumstances in which it would be unconscionable to deny a remedy to the claimant.[44]

Assurance

In order that an equity may arise by proprietary estoppel, it is essential that the claimant can show some assurance on the part of the person to be estopped, amounting to 'a representation or expectation created by the landowner'.[45] Mere 'expenditure with consent' does not give rise to an estoppel, and 'one who voluntarily improves another's land without encouragement or promise of reward does so "entirely at his own risk" '.[46] In the well-known dictum of Bowen LJ,[47] 'liabilities are not to be forced upon people behind their backs, any more than you can confer a benefit upon a man against his will'.

There must be an express or implied assurance made by the landowner or his employee or agent that led the claimant reasonably to believe that he had or would acquire some rights over the land in question. Such assurance was lacking in the Jamaican case of *Lewis v McLean*,[48] in which a tenant, with the permission of the

---

of 2002, Allen Sr J found on the evidence that the defendant was well aware that he had no title to the land on which he erected two buildings; accordingly, there was no equity to satisfy, and there was 'no principle of equity which would prevent [the owner of the land] from claiming the land with the benefit of all the expenditure made on it'.

42 [1982] 1 All ER 897, at 915. See also *Blue Haven Enterprises Ltd v Tully* (2006) Privy Council Appeal No 57 of 2004.

43 *Arawak Homes Ltd v Dean* (2010) Supreme Court, The Bahamas, No 1883 of 2002.

44 See, eg, *Peters v Lewis* (2010) High Court, Trinidad and Tobago, No 36 of 2001; *Sookraj v Sookraj* (2010) High Court, Trinidad and Tobago, No 550 of 2000; *Mills v Roberts* (2012) High Court, Trinidad and Tobago, No CV 2011–04300.

45 *Savva v Costa* (1981) 131 NLJ 1114.

46 Gray, *Elements of Land Law*, 1987, London: Butterworths, p 397; *Miller v Isaac* (2016) High Court, Trinidad and Tobago, No CV 2013–0159, para 49, *per* Rahim J.

47 *Falcke v Scottish Imperial Insurance Co* (1886) 34 Ch D 234, at 248.

48 (1982) 19 JLR 56, Court of Appeal, Jamaica.

landlord, erected on the rented land a two-bedroom dwelling house, a licensed bar, and a hardware and lumber store. When the landlord gave the tenant notice to quit, the tenant claimed for reimbursement of his expenditure, basing his claim on proprietary estoppel. The Jamaican Court of Appeal held that the tenant's claim failed, since 'there never was any promise or assurance of the land to the [tenant] on the faith of which he erected the building'. Campbell JA (Ag) distinguished the Barbadian case of *McCollin v Carter*,[49] in which Carter entered into possession of McCollin's land as a licensee. McCollin had promised to make a gift of the land to Carter's daughter. McCollin, knowing that there was no enforceable agreement to transfer the land to Carter, acquiesced in Carter's carrying out substantial improvements on the land, and Douglas CJ accordingly held that Carter was entitled to compensation for his expenditure. In *Lewis v McLean*, there was no such assurance and acquiescence.

In a Trinidadian case, *Flanders v Teesdale*,[50] F and T had enjoyed a romantic relationship, as a consequence of which T had moved into F's house. When the relationship came to an end after nine years, F sought to evict T through an action for possession. According to the evidence, T had gone to the USA, where for about five years she had worked as a domestic and remitted funds to F for the refurbishment of the house, under the assurance that F would marry her and that the house would be their matrimonial home. Describing the case as containing 'all the classic elements of a proprietary estoppel', Dean-Armorer J held that T had acted to her detriment in reliance on F's promise, and F would be entitled to possession of the house only on payment to T of the sum of $23,000 (US), the minimum amount required to satisfy her equity.

Reliance

For an estoppel to arise, it is essential that the claimant should have relied on the assurance, in the sense that he was induced to act in a certain way because of the assurance given to him. Since a claimant may in practice have difficulty in proving reliance on his part, the court may infer reliance in cases in which such reliance may plausibly explain the claimant's conduct, as, for example, in *Greasely v Cooke*,[51] in which it was held that if clear assurances have been made and a detriment has been suffered, the court may presume that there has been reliance. The effect of cases such as *Greasely v Cooke* is to shift the burden of proof on to the defendant to show that there has been no reliance. He may discharge this burden by showing that the claimant would have done the detrimental acts irrespective of any assurance given to him.

Detriment

The requirement that a claimant in proprietary estoppel must show that he has suffered some detriment in relying on the defendant's assurance is a manifestation of the principle that equity does not assist volunteers – that is, persons who have given no consideration in the form of a benefit or a detriment in return for a promise. A detriment in this context may take any form, so long as it is not minimal or

49 (1974) 26 WIR 1, High Court, Barbados.
50 (2009) High Court, Trinidad and Tobago, No 127 of 2006.
51 [1980] 3 All ER 710 (see below).

trivial.[52] The most common example of a sufficient detriment is expenditure of money in building on the land, but it is not necessary that the detriment be related to the land at all. For instance, it has been held to be sufficient that the claimant has given up employment or property in another place in order to come and live with the defendant.[53] Another example is *Greasely v Cooke*.[54] There, C, in 1938, then aged 16, came to live as a maid in a house occupied by a widower, his three sons K, H and O, and his mentally handicapped daughter. In 1946, C and K started to cohabit as man and wife and, from 1948 onwards, C received no wages, but continued to manage the house and nursed the daughter until the latter's death in 1975. She had been given vague assurances by H and K that she would be able to live in the house for as long as she wished but, after K's death, H and O's daughters, in whom the house had vested, sought possession. It was held that: (a) the statements of K and H were sufficient to amount to assurances for the purposes of proprietary estoppel; (b) it could be assumed that C had acted on the faith of those assurances, and it was for the plaintiffs to prove otherwise; and (c) the expenditure of money is not a necessary element of detriment – it is sufficient that the party to whom the assurance was made has acted on the faith of the assurance in circumstances in which it would be inequitable for the parties making the assurance to go back on it.

A somewhat similar case that came before the Jamaican Court of Appeal is *Trenchfield v Leslie*.[55] Here, L lived in her uncle's house for three years, physically taking care of him without payment, and spending her money on repairs to the house. There was some evidence that the uncle had promised to leave her the house by his will, but no concluded agreement to that effect.[56] After the uncle's death, T, an executrix of his will and devisee of the house, sought possession of the house. The magistrate refused to grant possession to T and the Court of Appeal dismissed T's appeal. In the words of Patterson JA (Ag):[57]

> A person may obtain an interest in land if he is led by the owner thereof to believe that he will be granted such an interest and, as a result, he acts to his detriment . . . The respondent's occupation was that of licensee . . . the respondent's licence may aptly be described as a 'licence coupled with an equity'.

In a later case decided by the House of Lords, *Thorner v Major*,[58] M had, for about 30 years, worked without pay on T's farm, having been encouraged by T to believe that he would inherit the farm on T's death. It was held that proprietary estoppel was established, even though the evidence was that T never made any express representations concerning the farm, but rather that it was a matter of implication and inference from indirect statements, oblique remarks and conduct. Lord Neuberger said that although any representations or assurances had normally to be 'clear and

52 M Dixon, *Principles of Land Law*, 3rd edn, 1999, London: Cavendish Publishing, p 305.
53 *Dodsworth v Dodsworth* (1973) 228 EG 1115. In *Taylor v Vincent N Taylor Construction Ltd* (2011) High Court, Trinidad and Tobago, No CV 2009–01825, the detriment consisted of 'the personal sacrifices and social dislocation involving the whole family to [leave Trinidad and] make a new life in Tobago'.
54 [1980] 3 All ER 710.
55 (1994) 31 JLR 497, Court of Appeal, Jamaica.
56 Patterson JA (Ag) pointed out that it was common in Jamaica for persons to enter into valid contracts whereby someone would care for a person in his sickness or old age in return for a devise of land in the will of that person, but there was no such valid contract in this case.
57 (1994) 31 JLR 497, at 500, 501.
58 [2009] 1 WLR 776.

unequivocal' in order to give rise to a proprietary estoppel, it might be 'sufficient for the person invoking the estoppel to establish that he reasonably understood the representor's statements . . . to be an assurance on which he could rely', and ambiguity in the representor's statements 'should not deprive a person who reasonably relied on the assurance, of all relief'. Accordingly, in an appropriate case, a testator's freedom of testamentary disposition may be interfered with,[59] subject to the court's jurisdiction to decide how to satisfy the claimant's equity.

In *Henry v Henry*,[60] a St Lucian case, one of the issues was whether the claimant, who had lived with and cared for G, an elderly relative, on the faith of a firm assurance that she would leave her share in a plot of land to him in her will, had in fact suffered a detriment. The trial judge held that the claimant had not acted to his detriment since he had lived on the plot rent-free for decades, the plot had been his source of livelihood, and he had reaped the produce of the plot and sold and kept the proceeds of any surplus. The Eastern Caribbean Court of Appeal, on the other hand, held that the claimant had acted to his detriment and awarded him G's promised share of the land – his 'expectation interest'. The Privy Council, revisiting the issue of detriment, stated that in order to determine the matter it was necessary to weigh the advantages against the disadvantages suffered by the claimant[61] in relying on G's assurance. The Privy Council's finding was that the claimant had established detriment because, by working on the land (which the other family members had declined to do), caring for G, and providing food for her, he had 'effectively deprived himself of the opportunity of a better life elsewhere', and that detriment was not outweighed by the advantages referred to by the trial judge. In Sir Jonathan Parker's words:

> Overall, the strong impression which the evidence conveys to the Board is that, in reliance on Geraldine Pierre's promises, Callistus Henry has opted for a hard life in which he has had to struggle to make ends meet and to provide for his family, in circumstances where more attractive prospects beckoned elsewhere.

On the other hand, it has been emphasised by the Privy Council that

> while recourse to the doctrine of estoppel provides a welcome means of effecting justice when the facts demand it, it is equally important that the courts do not penalise those who, through acts of kindness, simply allow other members of their family to inhabit their property rent-free.[62]

This observation has particular resonance in those Caribbean societies where extended family relationships are particularly strong. In *Knowles v Knowles*,[63] V and G, the co-owners of an estate in Antigua, in 1984 gave a licence to J (V's son and

59 'The broad inquiry in a case such as this is whether, in all the circumstances, it is unconscionable for a testator to make a will giving specific property to one person if, by his conduct, he has previously created the expectation in a different person that he will inherit it': *Uglow v Uglow* [2004] EWCA 987, at para [8], *per* Mummery LJ.

60 [2010] UKPC 3.

61 See also *Baldeo v Baldeo* (2011) High Court, Trinidad and Tobago, No 4311 of 2007.

62 *Knowles v Knowles* [2008] UKPC 30 (Privy Council Appeal from the ECS Court of Appeal, Antigua and Barbuda), *per* Sir Henry Brooke, para 27.

63 *Ibid.* See also *Mahabir v Mangatoo* (2008) High Court, Trinidad and Tobago, No 1621 of 2002. But in *Barrow v Sheppard* (2014) High Court, Trinidad and Tobago, No 2008–4220, Dean-Armorer J, distinguishing *Knowles* and *Mahabir* on the facts, held that the defendant's proprietary estoppel claim succeeded.

G's brother) and J's wife, E, to occupy a house on the estate. After V's death in 1992, G allowed J and E to continue their occupation of the house. In 2003, J and E separated and J went to live elsewhere, whereupon G gave E three months' notice to quit. E contended that she had acquired an interest in the house by proprietary estoppel, on the basis of her having carried out various repairs and improvements to the property with G's acquiescence and encouragement. The Privy Council held that there was no evidence that G had encouraged J and E to believe that they were being given an interest in the house, as opposed to merely being allowed to occupy the property as family members, and so no estoppel had arisen in favour of E.

Satisfying the claimant's equity

We have seen that, in Lord Denning's words, where a claimant has acquired a right by estoppel, 'it is for the court in each case to decide in what way the equity can be satisfied'.[64] Thus, it is open to the court to award the claimant any remedy it considers appropriate. He may be awarded: the fee simple in the land;[65] an easement over the land;[66] a right under a testamentary disposition;[67] a charge or lien over the land;[68] a long lease;[69] or a licence to occupy for life[70] or for a shorter period.[71]

A Caribbean case that is illustrative of the issue of satisfying a claimant's equity is *Seymour v Ebanks*.[72] In this case, S, in 1958, went into possession of E's land on which, with E's consent, he built a cinema at a cost of £4,500. In 1977, after operating the cinema for almost 20 years, S was dispossessed of the land by an order of the court, and the land was later sold to a third party. S claimed that he had a licence coupled with an equity, and the question arose as to how that equity should be satisfied. The lower court awarded S compensation of £3,000, being the value of the building at the time of dispossession. It was held, on appeal, that S had occupied the land by licence, and the fact that E had acquiesced in S's expenditure of money in reclaiming the land and building a cinema thereon raised an equity in S's favour.

64 *Ives (ER) Investments Ltd v High* [1967] 1 All ER 504, at 507.

65 *Pascoe v Turner* [1979] 2 All ER 945; *Sealy v Sealy* (1990) High Court, Barbados, No 1492 of 1987; *Khan v Khan* (1994) High Court, Trinidad and Tobago, No 1022 of 1993; *Sookraj v Sookraj* (2010) High Court, Trinidad and Tobago, No 550 of 2000. In *Mills v Roberts* (2016) Court of Appeal, Trinidad and Tobago, Civ App No T243 of 2012, the Court replaced the trial judge's award of a life interest with an award of the fee simple, on the grounds that (a) the statement of Lord Westbury in *Dillwyn v Llewelyn*, *supra*, that 'no one builds a house for his own life only' was 'no less true in Trinidad and Tobago', and (b) that, with a life interest only, the appellant 'would not be able to obtain a mortgage by using the property as security, or charge the property to obtain a loan for any purpose' (*per* Jamadar, JA), a point that had been made in *Pascoe v Turner*, *supra*.

66 *Crabb v Arun DC* [1975] 3 All ER 865; *Ives (ER) Investments Ltd v High* [1967] 1 All ER 504; *Sawyer v Butler* (1991) Supreme Court, The Bahamas, No 356 of 1990; *Colley-Clarke v Colley* (2001) High Court, Trinidad and Tobago, No 1216 of 1999.

67 *Re Basham* [1987] 1 All ER 405.

68 *Unity Joint Stock Mutual Banking Association v King* (1858) 53 ER 563; *Chalmers v Pardoe* [1963] 3 All ER 552; *Seymour v Ebanks* [1980–83] CILR 252, Court of Appeal, Cayman Islands.

69 *Griffiths v Williams* (1977) 248 EG 947.

70 *Inwards v Baker* [1965] 1 All ER 446; *Williams v Staite* [1978] 2 All ER 928; *Matharu v Matharu* (1994) 68 P & CR 93; *Skinner v Daniel* (1981) 16 Barb LR 21, High Court, Barbados; *Greaves v Barnett* (1978) 13 Barb LR 129, High Court, Barbados; *Taylor v Vincent N Taylor Construction Ltd* (2011) High Court, Trinidad and Tobago, No CV 2009–01825.

71 *Dodsworth v Dodsworth* (1973) 228 EG 1115.

72 [1980–83] CILR 252, Court of Appeal, Cayman Islands. See also *Cranston v Samuels* [2019] JMCA Civ 42.

It was this licence coupled with an equity that was lost when S was dispossessed of the land. Accordingly, S was entitled to be compensated by means of an equitable charge or lien on the property for the amount of his expenditure, which was £4,500, and not merely for the value of the building.

Rowe JA explained the decision, thus:[73]

> The learned Chief Justice in the lower court asked the question as to how the equity should be satisfied and the answer he gave was that, as the appellant had had the use of the premises for 20 years before he was dispossessed, in all the circumstances the proper way to satisfy the equity was by compensation, which should be the value of the building at the time of the dispossession . . .
>
> In my opinion, the equity which the appellant lost was the equity to continue to operate his cinema for his own benefit. It can be inferred from the facts found by the learned Chief Justice that the appellant had in contemplation a tenure for an indefinite period at his option. The appellant clearly did not wish to give up his cinema operations, nor did he wish to confer a benefit upon the respondent to the extent of his original expenditure on the respondent's land. My first inclination, therefore, is that the most favourable way to arrive at the value and extent of the appellant's equity is to take evidence to show what would be an appropriate period for an indefinite personal licence to operate a cinema. Problems might, however, arise as to whether any period between 20 and 40 years, having regard to the age of the appellant at the time when the equity arose, could be regarded as the optimum period and consequently speculation might therefore replace sound reasoning.
>
> I have therefore considered the alternative course proposed by White JA, which is that in the circumstances of the case, where the property has been sold to a third party, a court of equity can declare that a person who has expended his money on another's land is entitled to an equitable charge or lien for the amount so expended. What the appellant expended on the respondent's land is the known and accepted sum of £4,500. The appellant had reclaimed the respondent's land and had rendered it suitable for building purposes. He had built a cinema thereon, which structure was still in existence at the time of his dispossession. The appellant should surely have an equity equivalent to his complete outlay.

The proper approach to satisfying an equity in circumstances where D made an assurance to C that, in return for C rendering services to D or physically taking care of D without pay, D would leave property to C in his (D's) will, was exhaustively examined by the English Court of Appeal in *Jennings v Rice*.[74] Here, R, a childless widow, died in 1997 at the age of 93, leaving an estate worth £1.3 million (sterling), which included her house and furniture valued at £435,000. J, a self-employed mason, had worked for R, initially as a part-time gardener for a small hourly payment but later as a general carer, assuming more and more onerous and time-consuming duties. After 1980, R stopped paying J, but told him that he need not worry because he 'would be alright', she would 'see to it', and 'this will all be yours one day'. Subsequently, R became almost completely dependent on J, and, after a burglary at the house, J would sleep almost every night on a sofa in the sitting room. In these circumstances, J claimed that under the doctrine of proprietary estoppel he should receive the whole of R's estate or, alternatively, the value of the house and furniture, as that was his expectation. The trial judge, whose decision was affirmed

73 *Ibid*, at 259.
74 [2002] EWCA Civ 159.

by the Court of Appeal, considered that to award R's entire estate or the full value of the house to J would be excessive, and he held that J's equity would be satisfied by awarding him the cost of employing a full-time carer for the period, which was assessed at £200,000. Aldous LJ stressed that 'the most essential requirement is that there must be proportionality between the expectation and the detriment', and the overall objective is to avoid unconscionable conduct and to 'do justice' to the promisee. In Walker LJ's view, a distinction had to be drawn between cases of firm promises of specific amounts or property, and cases of more vague assurances, as in the present case. In the first type of case, it is easier for the court to award the expected benefit whereas, in the second, the 'expected benefit' may not be the appropriate test.

Estoppel licences and third parties

It is well established that a licence protected by estoppel is binding on third parties with notice of its existence.[75] Thus, for example, in *Inwards v Baker*,[76] in which, as we have seen, a father encouraged his son to build a house on the father's land in the expectation that he would be allowed to live there indefinitely, the court refused to permit the trustees of the father's will to evict the son, who was held to be entitled to a licence to occupy the land for as long as he wished; in *Ives (ER) Investments Ltd v High*,[77] in which X had informally granted his neighbour, Y, a right of way across his land, and Y had incurred expenditure in building a garage so sited that it could only be approached over X's land, and X acquiesced in the building, it was held that purchasers of X's land with notice of Y's right were not entitled to revoke it. It seems, however, that such a right will be defeated by a *bona fide* purchaser of the legal estate without notice of the right.

75 *Ives (ER) Investments Ltd v High* [1967] 2 QB 379, at 400,405. See *Lyons v Lindsay* [2020] JMSC Civ 92, para [107], *per* Thomas J: though in *Haynes v Minors* (1972) 2 OECSLR 235, at 238, 239, Cecil Lewis JA, in the OECS Court of Appeal, took the view that an estoppel licence, as a mere equity, was incapable of binding successors in title, even with notice.
76 [1965] 1 All ER 446.
77 [1967] 1 All ER 504.

CHAPTER 4

CREATION OF LEASES

The law of landlord and tenant governs the relationship between lessor and lessee (otherwise called 'landlord' and 'tenant' respectively), defines the rights and obligations of the parties to leases and tenancies, and lays down the formalities for the creation and the termination of the lessor/lessee relationship. Leaseholds, also known as 'demises' or 'terms of years', have a long history. In early medieval times, leaseholds were regarded merely as contractual rights to occupy land. A lessee could be evicted at any time. He had no estate in the land, and his/her only remedy for wrongful dispossession was an action for damages against the dispossessor. Later, with the development of the action of ejectment, by the end of the 15th century, it became possible for a dispossessed tenant to recover possession of the land, and at that point the leasehold may be said to have acquired the status of a proprietary interest and an estate in land. Leaseholds, in fact, always remained outside the feudal system of landholding, to which the freehold estates belonged, but when leaseholds 'became a new type of estate, it was impossible to deny that they were also a new type of tenure; for every tenant must hold by tenure of some sort if he is to hold an estate at all'.[1] Ironically, the leasehold, originally conceived outside the doctrine of tenures, is today the only form of 'tenure' that has any practical significance. The nature of this tenure, signified by the words 'landlord' and 'tenant', is that the tenant pays 'rent service' (now known simply as 'rent') to the landlord in return for his/her right to occupy the land, and the landlord retains a right to levy distress against the tenant's goods in the event of non-payment of rent and, more importantly, in some circumstances a right to forfeit the lease if the tenant is in breach of his/her obligations.

ESSENTIAL CHARACTERISTICS OF LEASES

There are two requirements for a right to occupy land to be capable of taking effect as a lease:

(a) the right to exclusive possession must be given; and
(b) the duration of the lease must be certain.

These requirements must now be considered in turn.

Exclusive possession

It is a necessary characteristic of a lease or tenancy that the tenant must have exclusive possession of the premises. This means that the tenant must be given the right to exclude all other persons from the land, including the landlord. However, the mere fact that a person has exclusive possession of land does not necessarily make him/her a tenant; he may be only a licensee, having merely a personal privilege to

---

1 Megarry and Wade, *The Law of Real Property*, 8th edn, para 3–015.

DOI: 10.4324/9781003186946-4

occupy and no interest in the land. The most important distinctions between a lease and a licence are:

(a) a lessee, holding a legal lease, has an interest in land that is binding on the whole world; a licensee has a mere personal right that, at most, binds only licensor and licensee;
(b) a lessee, but not a licensee, may maintain an action in trespass against any person who interferes with his/her right to possession;
(c) a lessee may assign his/her lease, whereas a licensee has no proprietary interest capable of assignment; and
(d) In Trinidad and Tobago, a lessee, but not a licensee, is entitled to claim a statutory, 30-year lease in respect of land on which a house is erected, under the Land Tenants (Security of Tenure) Act 1981.[2]

Distinguishing between leases and licences

In determining whether a lease or a licence has been created, it was once the rule that, where exclusive possession was granted, there was a lease.[3] Later, a more flexible test was used, viz, that the answer to the question depended on the intention of the parties to be inferred from the surrounding circumstances, and the fact that exclusive possession was granted was not decisive in favour of a lease.[4] Then, in 1985, the decision of the House of Lords in *Street v Mountford*[5] appeared to abandon the flexible test in favour of the more rigid proposition that:[6]

> where the only circumstances are that residential accommodation is offered and accepted with exclusive possession for a term at a rent, the result is a tenancy . . .

In other words, if the three requirements, viz, exclusive possession, a fixed or periodic term, and rent are present, there will be a tenancy, unless there are exceptional circumstances that point to a licence. Under this test, it appears that the intentions of the parties as to whether a lease or a licence was to be created are irrelevant, and the only intention that is to be regarded as relevant is the intention to give exclusive possession of the premises.[7]

Lord Millett, in the Privy Council, in *Ramnarace v Lutchman*,[8] assumed, without discussion, that *Street* was applicable in Trinidad and Tobago, though this has not

2 Ch 59: 54. See *Mahadeo v Dass* (1988) High Court, Trinidad and Tobago, No 1570 of 1980; *Thomas v Barath* (1986) High Court, Trinidad and Tobago, No 1686 of 1980; *Cyrus v Gopaul* (1989) Court of Appeal, Trinidad and Tobago, Mag App No 69 of 1987. See pp 56–60, below.
3 *Lynes v Snaith* [1989] 1 QB 486; *Glenwood Lumber Co Ltd v Phillips* [1904] AC 405.
4 See, eg, *Cobb v Lane* [1952] 1 All ER 1199; *Isaac v Hotel de Paris* [1960] 1 All ER 348, PC; *Quan v Gonzales* (1966–69) 19 Trin LR (Pt V) 331.
5 [1985] 2 All ER 289. The decision in *Street v Mountford* was designed to prevent landlords from avoiding the consequences of the Rent Restriction Acts by framing what were essentially tenancy agreements as 'licences'. The courts are now astute in detecting such 'sham' licences, described by Lord Templeman in *Antoniades v Villiers* [1988] 3 All ER 1058, at 1064, as 'a pretence intended only to get round the Rent Acts'.
6 [1985] 2 All ER 289, at 300.
7 *Ibid.*
8 [2001] 1 WLR 1651.

been borne out by some Trinidadian decisions.[9] On the other hand, the Jamaican courts appear to have accepted the principle as good law.[10]

In any event, it is likely that, in the following circumstances, a licence and not a lease will be created:

(a) where a person is given exclusive possession of premises as an 'act of friendship or generosity'[11] or by way of family arrangement;[12]
(b) where services, such as regular cleaning and meals, are provided by the owner of the property, which require the owner to have unrestricted access to the premises;[13]
(c) where an employee occupies premises belonging to his/her employer in order that he can carry out his/her duties more effectively (called a 'service occupancy');[14]
(d) where the physical situation of the premises indicates that only a licence was intended – for example, a stall in a market[15] or a kiosk in a theatre foyer.[16]

Examples of the lease/licence dichotomy in the Caribbean

In *Sylvester v Cyrus*,[17] S was in urgent need of accommodation, as the house in which she was living was to be demolished. As a result of a conversation between S and C, in September 1957, C let S into occupation of a house of which C was herself a monthly tenant. It was agreed that S would pay a premium of $150, and $12 a month as rent. C moved out of the house, taking her telephone with her, and had the electricity meter removed. When, in February 1958, C re-entered the house, S brought an action for trespass. The trial judge held that the relationship between the parties was one of licensor and licensee; that the licence had been effectively revoked by C's re-entry; and that C was not liable in trespass.

---

9 In *Ramdeen v Hansraj* (2000) High Court, Trinidad and Tobago, No 1041 of 1998, for instance, Mendonca J applied the 'intention of the parties' test without mentioning *Street*; and in *Algoo v Tom* (1999) High Court, Trinidad and Tobago, although *Street* was cited, it formed no part of Barnes J's judgment, whilst the 'intention of the parties' test did.

10 See *Urban Development Corp v Hamilton* [2013] JMSC Civ 56, para 28, *per* Morrison J; *Mattar v Salmon* [2020] JMSC Civ 48, paras 39–45, *per* D Fraser J.

11 *Marcroft Wagons Ltd v Smith* [1951] 2 All ER 271; *Facchini v Bryson* [1952] 1 TLR 1386.

12 *Cobb v Lane* [1952] 1 All ER 1199; *Edwards v Brathwaite* (1978) 32 WIR 85; *Romany v Romany* (1972) 21 WIR 491.

13 *Abbeyfield (Harpenden) Society Ltd v Woods* [1968] 1 WLR 374; *Marchant v Charters* [1977] 3 All ER 918; *Street v Mountford* [1985] 2 All ER 289 ('a lodger is entitled to live in the premises, but he cannot call the place his own', *per* Lord Templeman, at 293).

14 *Smith v Seghill Overseers* (1875) LR 10 QB 422, at 428. A Caribbean example is *Hekmati v Scherer* (1998) Supreme Court, The Bahamas, No 859 of 1998, in which it was held that a person appointed as a personal secretary to W and granted the right to live in a house owned by W was a licensee and not a tenant. It was also held by Brooks J in *Farquharson v Everglades Farms Ltd* (2011) Supreme Court, Jamaica, No 820 of 2010, following *Ivory v Palmer* [1975] ICR 340, that where a contract of employment has been terminated, whether or not in breach of contract, the right to occupy the accommodation provided by the employer is also terminated.

15 *Kassim v Georgetown Clerk* (1961) 4 WIR 135, Supreme Court, British Guiana.

16 *Clore v Theatrical Properties Ltd* [1963] 3 All ER 483.

17 (1959) 1 WIR 407. In *Simonette v Ahoy* (2009) Court of Appeal, Trinidad and Tobago, Civ App No 156 of 2005, Warner JA noted that 'difficulties sometimes arise in distinguishing a licence from a tenancy at will, since both may share the characteristic of a grant of exclusive possession. A person cannot, however, be a tenant at will where it appears from the surrounding circumstances that there was no intention to create legal relations'.

On appeal, the Federal Supreme Court held that, from the fact that S was given exclusive possession of the house, an intention to create a monthly subtenancy was to be inferred, and there were no special circumstances to negative the inference. C was, accordingly, liable for trespass. Lewis J said:[18]

> I am unable to find in the evidence any special circumstances or conduct of the parties which negative the inference normally to be drawn where a person having a possessory interest in land puts another person into exclusive possession of that land, namely an intention to create a tenancy. The facts as found by the trial judge all point to that inference as being the proper one. It is true that in July to September 1956, when [S] was negotiating with [C], she was in urgent need of a house, but that is not an unusual situation, and the fact that [C] demanded and received a premium of $150 suggests that this was a business transaction rather than a personal privilege motivated by charitable or humane considerations. It is also clear that [C] wished to be in a position to recover possession of the apartment should she at any time need to do so, but this she could have done by giving the proper notice to [S], who would not, in the circumstances, have been able to avail herself of the protection of the Rent Restriction Ordinance. I have come to the conclusion, therefore, that the trial judge erred in holding that the relationship between the parties was that of licensor and licensee. In my judgment, this was a simple case of subtenancy at a monthly rental.

In *Isaac v Hotel de Paris*,[19] the respondent company was the lessee of part of a building in Port of Spain, which was used as a hotel. In December 1955, the company let the appellant into possession of the first floor of the building under an arrangement that the appellant would operate a night bar for the company.

In February 1956, after a dispute between the parties, it was agreed that the appellant would pay $250 a month as 'rent' (the amount payable by the company as head rent) and all expenses incurred in the running of the bar, and in return that the appellant could retain all of the profits for himself. In May 1956, the company gave the appellant seven days' notice to quit the premises.

It was held by the Privy Council that the circumstances in which the appellant was allowed to occupy the premises showed that the company never intended to accept him as a tenant and that he was fully aware of that fact. A licence had been created, and the notice was sufficient to terminate it. Lord Denning said:[20]

> It was submitted by counsel for the appellant that there were all the *indicia* of a monthly tenancy. There was not only exclusive possession but there was also the payment and acceptance of rent. (Furthermore, the appellant paid the disbursements, and so forth.) Counsel admitted that these would not be decisive to establish a tenancy in the case of premises within the Rent Restriction Acts such as *Marcroft Wagons Ltd v Smith*[21] and *Murray, Bull and Co Ltd v Murray*,[22] but it was altogether different, he said, in the present case where

18 *Ibid*, at 412.
19 [1960] 1 All ER 348, PC, on appeal from the Federal Supreme Court. See also *Spencer v Esso Standard Oil (SA) Ltd* (1969) 13 WIR 108, Court of Appeal, West Indies Associated States, in which it was held that an agreement, whereby the appellant had been permitted to occupy land for the specific purpose of operating a motor service station erected thereon by the respondent company, was a licence and not a lease, as his possession was of a restricted nature, amounting to a personal privilege, with no interest in the land. On the other hand, in *Hadad v Elias* (1993) High Court, Trinidad and Tobago, No 97 of 1992, it was held that, where H had entered into an agreement with the owner of the premises whereby H was to operate a patisserie therein, a tenancy had been created.
20 [1960] 1 All ER 348, at 351.
21 [1951] 2 All ER 271.
22 [1952] 2 All ER 1079.

the premises were not subject to rent restriction legislation. The only proper inference here was a monthly tenancy. Their Lordships cannot accept this view. There are many cases in the books where exclusive possession has been given of premises outside the Rent Restriction Acts and yet there has been held to be no tenancy. Instances are *Errington v Errington*[23] and *Cobb v Lane*,[24] which were referred to during the argument. It is true that in those two cases there was no payment or acceptance of rent, but even payment and acceptance of rent – though of great weight – is not decisive of a tenancy where it can be otherwise explained: see *Clarke v Grant*.[25] As Lord Greene MR said in *Booker v Palmer*:[26]

> There is one golden rule which is of very general application, namely, that the law does not impute an intention to enter into legal relationships where the circumstances and the conduct of the parties negative any intention of the kind.

It appears to their Lordships that the law on this matter was correctly interpreted and applied by Archer J in the Federal Supreme Court when he said:

> It is clear from the authorities that the intention of the parties is the paramount consideration and, while the fact of exclusive possession together with the payment of rent is of the first importance, the circumstances in which exclusive possession has been given and the character in which money paid as rent has been received are also matters to be considered. The circumstances in which the [appellant] was allowed to occupy the Parisian Hotel show that Joseph never intended to accept him as a tenant and that he was fully aware of it. The payments he made were only part of the disbursements for which he made himself responsible, and the so-called rent was in the nature of a reimbursement of the rent payable by the [respondent company].

Their Lordships are, therefore, of opinion that the relationship between the parties after 17 February 1956 was not that of landlord and tenant, but that of licensor and licensee. The circumstances and conduct of the parties show that all that was intended was that the appellant should have a personal privilege of running a night bar on the premises, with no interest in the land at all.

In *Quan v Gonzales*,[27] the plaintiff and the defendant executed a deed whereby the defendant, the owner in fee simple of business premises, granted to the plaintiff an option exercisable during a five-year period to purchase the premises for $75,000, payable by monthly instalments. It was also provided that 'in order the better to enable the [plaintiff] to determine whether or not he shall exercise the said option, the [defendant] has agreed to allow him to occupy and carry on the business of a drug store' in the premises on certain terms, among them the payment of $25 per month during the currency of what was described as the 'licence'.

The main issue for determination was whether the plaintiff was in occupation of the premises as a tenant protected by the Rent Restriction Ordinance, or whether he was merely a licensee. It was held that:

(a) there is a strong presumption in favour of a tenancy where a person is given exclusive possession of premises;
(b) in the present case, the parties had entered into a formal agreement that purported to define their relationship and rights. There were clauses in the

23 [1952] 1 All ER 149.
24 [1952] 1 All ER 1199.
25 [1949] 1 All ER 768.
26 [1942] 2 All ER 674, at 677.
27 (1966–69) 19 Trin LR (Pt V) 331.

deed that were consistent with a tenancy agreement but, equally, they were not inconsistent with a licence coupled with an option to be exercised over an extended period;

(c) it was impossible in the circumstances of the case to impute any intention on the part of the parties to enter into the relationship of landlord and tenant – their relationship was as set out plainly in the deed, that of licensor and licensee; and

(d) the option not having been exercised during the period, the licence that was concurrent with it terminated by effluxion of time.

In *Edwards v Brathwaite*,[28] B's mother, the owner of a parcel of land, had, before her death in 1939, put B in possession of a house spot and curtilage. B placed his chattel house on the land and lived there up to the time of the action. After the mother's death, B's father had continued to live on the land. At no time did he require B to pay any rent. During the period of his occupation, B erected a fence around his house and cultivated a kitchen garden and fruit trees. The main question that arose was whether B was a tenant at will or a licensee, for only if he were a tenant at will would he be able to acquire a possessory title under s 8 of the Limitation and Prescription Act, Cap 232, Laws of Barbados.

Worrell J held that B was a licensee. He said:[29]

> The first question which must be determined here is whether the claimant's occupation of the land was under a tenancy at will or under a licence . . . On the evidence before me, I find that, when the claimant went into occupation of the land, it was nothing more than a family arrangement. I also find that, on the death of the claimant's mother, he continued in occupation by family arrangement during the lifetime of his father.

In *Ramnarace v Lutchman*,[30] the appellant, R, had, in 1974, been let into possession of a piece of land in central Trinidad, owned by her uncle, on the understanding that she would buy the land when she had sufficient funds. R and her family remained in exclusive and rent-free possession of the property until the time of the present action. During the period of her occupation, R built a three-bedroomed wooden house on part of the land and later replaced it with a concrete one. The uncle died in 1977, and the respondent, who was a beneficiary of the uncle's estate, sought possession as against R. R claimed she had acquired a title by adverse possession, and one of the issues in the case was whether R was a licensee or a tenant at will.[31] The Court of Appeal of Trinidad and Tobago, reversing the trial judge, held that R was a licensee, but in the Privy Council, Lord Millett, delivering the judgment of the Board, held that she was a tenant at will, despite the family arrangement and the 'act of generosity' on the uncle's part. The Court of Appeal had given

> insufficient weight to the facts that the appellant was throughout in exclusive possession and that her occupation was attributable not merely to her uncle's generosity, but to the parties' intention that she should purchase the land in due course . . . She

28 (1978) 32 WIR 85. See, also, *Lucas v Jordan* (2001) High Court, Trinidad and Tobago, No 1917 of 1994.
29 *Ibid*, at 90.
30 [2001] 1 WLR 1651.
31 See also *Simonette v Ahoy* (2009) Court of Appeal, Trinidad and Tobago, Civ App No 156 of 2005.

must be taken to have entered into possession of the disputed land in July 1974 as an intending purchaser and as a tenant at will.

Certainty of duration

The general rule is that a lease must have a certain beginning[32] and a certain ending. This requirement will be satisfied where, for example, L grants to T a lease of Greenacre 'for a term of five years commencing on 1 March 2014'. The requirement of certainty of duration is also satisfied where a periodic tenancy (such as a weekly, monthly or yearly tenancy) is granted, since although, in the absence of notice to quit by either party, the tenancy may continue indefinitely, each period of the tenancy is of certain duration. Where, however, L granted T a lease of premises 'for the duration of the war', the lease was held void, since there was no certainty as to when the war would end;[33] and where a local authority granted a lease of a strip of land fronting a public road on terms that 'the tenancy shall continue until the land is required by the [local authority] for the purpose of widening the road', the lease was held void for uncertainty.[34]

Certain other principles have been established, viz:

(a) the requirement that the commencement date must be certain is satisfied where the parties agree that it shall begin upon the occurrence of an uncertain event, as, for example, upon possession of the premises becoming vacant;[35]
(b) a lease for the life of a person or persons is not void for uncertainty – for example, a term granted to T for life, or to T during the lives of X and Y, is valid at common law, as also is a lease for a period determinable with a life or lives, for example, 'to T for five years if X shall so long live';
(c) a lease may be validly granted for a discontinuous period, as in the case of some timeshare agreements relating to holiday homes – for example, it has been held that the lease of a house for one week in each year for 80 consecutive years was a valid lease for a discontinuous period of 80 years.[36]

FORMALITIES FOR CREATION OF LEASES

Statutory provisions in the various jurisdictions require certain formalities for the creation of legal leases. In England, the effect of ss 52 and 54 of the Law of Property Act 1925 (re-enacting, in substance, s 1 of the Statute of Frauds 1677 and s 3 of the Real Property Act 1845) is that a lease for a period of more than three years must be made by deed in order to be valid at law, whilst leases for three years or less may be made by simple writing or orally, provided that they are to 'take effect in

32 *Harvey v Pratt* [1965] 1 WLR 1025; *BR&S Marketing Ltd v National Agricultural Marketing and Development Corporation* (2013) High Court, Trinidad and Tobago, No 2007–02154.
33 *Lace v Chantler* [1944] KB 368.
34 *Prudential Assurance Co Ltd v London Residuary Body* [1992] 3 All ER 504.
35 *Brilliant v Michaels* [1945] 1 All ER 121.
36 *Cottage Holiday Associates Ltd v Customs and Excise Commissioners* [1983] QB 735.

possession . . . at the best rent reasonably obtainable without taking a fine'. Periodic tenancies may be validly created orally or by simple writing.

In Commonwealth Caribbean jurisdictions, the statutory requirements are varied. Examples are:

(a) Guyana: Landlord and Tenant Act, Cap 61:01, section 6 – leases for more than three years must be made by deed; leases for three years or less must be in writing;
(b) Barbados: Property Act, Cap 236, section 149 – leases for more than one year must be made in writing; leases for one year or less than one year may be oral; periodic tenancies may be oral;
(c) Trinidad and Tobago: Landlord and Tenant Act, Ch 27, No 16, section 3 – leases for more than three years must be made by deed;[37] leases for three years[38] or less may be made by deed or in writing; periodic tenancies and tenancies at will may be oral.

Effect of non-compliance with formalities

A lease that does not comply with the necessary statutory formalities is void at law, but it has long been the rule that if the intended tenant goes into possession with the landlord's consent, a tenancy at will arises, and if the tenant then pays rent, which is accepted, he becomes a yearly or other periodic tenant depending on the period with reference to which rent is paid.[39] Thus, for example, if T goes into possession under a lease that is void for lack of formality and pays rent monthly, he becomes a monthly tenant at law.[40]

In equity, on the other hand, a lease that fails to conform with the statutory formalities nevertheless takes effect as *an agreement for a lease*, which, if specifically enforceable, will be effective as between the parties.[41] Such an informal lease is known as an 'equitable lease'. The relationship between an agreement for a lease in equity and a yearly tenancy at law is illustrated by the leading case of *Walsh v Lonsdale*.[42] In this case, L agreed in writing to grant to T the lease of a mill for seven years. It was agreed that a deed should be executed containing, *inter alia*, a term that, on demand, T would pay one year's rent in advance. No deed was executed, but T was let into possession and paid rent, in arrears, for a year and a half, thereby becoming a yearly tenant at law. L then demanded a year's rent in advance and, upon refusal by T, distrained for the amount. T brought an action for, *inter alia*, damages for illegal distress and an injunction to restrain the distress.

37 The deed must be duly registered. Section 3 of Ch 27, No 16, goes on to provide that any agreement in writing to let land for a period of more than three years shall take effect as an agreement to lease; the person in possession pursuant to the agreement may, from payment of rent or other circumstances, be construed to be a tenant from year to year. See also *John v McNeil* (2019) High Court, Trinidad and Tobago, No CV 2018–01115, para 13, *per* Donaldson-Honeywell J.
38 See *Walker v Marcano* (1990) High Court, Trinidad and Tobago, No 2085 of 1988.
39 *Martin v Smith* (1874) LR 9 Ex 50.
40 See *Metcalfe and Eddy Ltd v Edghill* (1963) 5 WIR 417, Court of Appeal, Trinidad and Tobago (see below).
41 *Broadway Import and Export Ltd v Levy* (1996) 33 JLR 26, Supreme Court, Jamaica, *per* Langrin J.
42 (1882) 21 Ch D 9.

T argued that he was under no obligation to pay rent in advance since he was, at law, only a yearly tenant and the payment of rent in advance was inconsistent with a yearly tenancy, which could be determined by half a year's notice; L's distress was, therefore, illegal. It was held, however, that a tenant who holds under an agreement for a lease of which specific performance will be decreed is in the same position vis-à-vis the landlord (as regards rights and liabilities) as if a formal lease had been executed ('equity regards that as done which ought to be done') and, since L would have been entitled to distrain for rent had the lease agreed upon been granted by deed, the distress was lawful in equity. In so far as there was a conflict between the position at law (in which there was a yearly tenancy) and the position in equity (where there was an equitable lease for seven years), the equitable rule prevailed.

The principle in *Walsh v Lonsdale* was applied in *Metcalfe and Eddy Ltd v Edghill*.[43] In this case, there was an oral agreement for a lease for a period of 3 years and 15 days. The tenant went into possession of the landlord's premises, paying $350 a month as rent in accordance with the agreement. The oral agreement was subsequently reduced into writing and signed by both parties, but no deed, as required by s 3 of Ch 27, No 16, was executed. Shortly afterwards, the tenant gave one month's notice to quit and, on expiry of the period of notice, vacated the premises. The landlord disputed the validity of the notice and claimed specific performance of the agreement. The tenant argued that he had entered into possession under a monthly tenancy that had been validly determined, and this argument was accepted by the trial judge.

The Court of Appeal of Trinidad and Tobago held, on appeal, that, under the rule in *Walsh v Lonsdale*, there was a binding contract to execute a lease for the fixed term stated therein, and it was specifically enforceable as such.

LEASE AND AGREEMENT FOR LEASE COMPARED

We have seen[44] that, as between the landlord and the tenant, 'an agreement for a lease may be as good as a lease', particularly having regard to the rule that the stipulations in the agreement are as binding on the parties as if they had been contained in a formal lease binding in law. However, in two respects,[45] an agreement for a lease is not as effective as a lease. These are as follows.

Dependency on specific performance

An agreement for a lease depends for its effectiveness on the willingness of the court to grant specific performance of the agreement. As Stamp J explained:[46]

> The equitable interests which the intended lessee has under an agreement for a lease do not exist *in vacuo*, but arise because the intended lessee has an equitable right to specific performance of the agreement. In such a situation, that which is agreed to be

43 (1963) 5 WIR 417, Court of Appeal, Trinidad and Tobago. Another example of the application of the *Walsh v Lonsdale* principle is the Jamaican case of *Brown v Silvera* [1898] Stephens' R 1257.

44 See p 50, above.

45 See pp 52, 53, below.

46 *Warmington v Miller* [1973] 2 All ER 372, at 377.

and ought to be done is treated as having been done and carrying with it in equity the attendant rights.

Specific performance, like other equitable remedies, is discretionary, and if, for any reason, the court will not grant the remedy, an agreement for a lease will be ineffective. Instances in which the court may refuse the remedy are where the tenant is unable to perform the covenants to be contained in the lease because he is insolvent,[47] or where he has already been in breach of a covenant that would have formed part of the lease.[48]

In any event, in order to be enforceable, an agreement for a lease must conform with the provisions of the Statute of Frauds and its equivalents, which require such an agreement to be evidenced by a sufficient note or memorandum containing all of the material terms, and it must also be clear that the parties have indeed reached a concluded agreement. The essential terms of a lease agreement were stated by Rattray P and Patterson JA, in the Jamaican Court of Appeal, in *Singer Sewing Machine Co v Montego Bay Co-operative Credit Union Ltd*,[49] to be: (a) the identities of lessor and lessee; (b) the identity of the property; (c) the rental to be paid; (d) the commencement date; and (e) the duration of the lease.[50]

The memorandum need not be in any special form. Any written evidence, such as a letter (or series of letters) or a receipt for rent will be sufficient, provided that it is signed by the party against whom the agreement is being enforced, or his/her agent.[51]

If there is no written memorandum, the agreement will be unenforceable, but if there is a sufficient act of part performance by one party,[52] such as in the *Singer* case where the tenant went into possession and spent money on adapting the premises for its business purposes, then the agreement will be enforceable in equity by that party.

Third parties

An agreement for a lease is less effective than a lease where third parties are involved. This is so in two respects.

(a) Since an agreement for a lease creates a mere equitable interest, it may be defeated by a *bona fide* purchaser for value of a legal estate in the land.[53] Thus, for example, if L agrees to grant a five-year lease of Blackacre to T, and one week later sells and conveys the fee simple to P, who has no notice of the agreement, P will take free of the agreement, which will be extinguished.

47 Cheshire and Burn, *Modern Law of Real Property*, 14th edn, 1988, London: Butterworths, p 363.
48 *Coatsworth v Johnson* (1886) 55 LJQB 220.
49 (1997) 34 JLR 251, at 257, 275.
50 See also *Exotic Fruits and Flowers Ltd v Agricultural Development Corp* (1999) Court of Appeal, Jamaica Civ App No 110 of 1998, in which it was held that the memorandum was not sufficient as it did not state the duration of the lease, nor was the deficiency cured by reference in a newspaper advertisement to the proposed duration of the lease, as an advertisement inviting applications could not be used to determine what was contained in any subsequent agreement between the parties.
51 See also Chapter 12, below.
52 See also pp 237, 238, below.
53 *Broadway Import and Export Ltd v Levy* (1996) 33 JLR 26, Supreme Court, Jamaica.

If, on the other hand, it is possible in the particular jurisdiction to protect equitable interests by an entry on the land register, and the agreement is entered on the register before conveyance of the fee simple, the purchaser will take subject to it.

(b) In a lease, there is privity of estate between landlord and tenant, and those covenants that 'touch and concern' the land are enforceable by and against assignees of the lease,[54] but in an agreement to lease the normal principle of contract law applies, which is that only benefits, and not burdens, are assignable.[55] Thus, for example, where T1 assigns his equitable lease to T2, T2 may enforce the landlord's covenants since they are benefits to him, but he is not liable on the tenant's covenants – for example, the covenant to pay rent.[56]

TYPES OF TENANCY

Lease for a fixed period

A lease may be granted for any fixed period, however short or long, provided that there is a certain beginning and a certain ending within the principles previously described. Leases for one year, two years or five years, on the one hand, and leases for 21, 99 or 999 years, on the other, are common.

A lease for a fixed period terminates automatically when the period expires; there is no need for any notice to quit by the landlord or the tenant. Another basic characteristic of a fixed-term lease is that the landlord cannot terminate the lease before the end of the period unless the tenant has been in breach of a condition in the lease, or the lease contains a forfeiture clause and the tenant has committed a breach of covenant that entitles the landlord to forfeit the lease. Nor can the tenant terminate the lease before it has run its course; he may only ask the landlord to accept a surrender of the lease, which offer the landlord may accept or reject as he pleases.[57]

A lease for a fixed term is a proprietary interest that, on the death of the tenant, passes under his/her will or intestacy; similarly, the landlord's reversion is capable of passing under his/her will or intestacy.

Periodic tenancy

Weekly, monthly, quarterly and yearly tenancies are the commonest examples of periodic tenancies. Such tenancies continue indefinitely until terminated by a proper notice to quit by the landlord or the tenant. Subject to agreement to the contrary,

---

54 See p 79 *et seq*, below.
55 See Gray, *Elements of Land Law*, 2nd edn, 1993, London: Butterworths, pp 870–873.
56 *Purchase v Lichfield Brewery Co* [1915] 1 KB 184. But, in *Boyer v Warbey* [1953] 1 QB 234, at 246, Lord Denning expressed the view that an assignee of an equitable lease should be bound in the same way as an assignee of a legal lease.
57 This paragraph in the text was cited as 'a correct statement of the law' by Smith JA in the Jamaican Court of Appeal in *Brady and Chen Ltd v Devon House Development Ltd* (2010) Court of Appeal, Jamaica, Civ App No 62 of 2009, para 30. See also *Tewani Ltd v Tikal Ltd* [2016] JMCC Comm 8, paras 28, 29, *per* Batts J.

the length of notice required to terminate a periodic tenancy depends on the form that the tenancy takes, viz, a weekly tenancy can be terminated by a week's notice; a monthly tenancy by one month's notice; and a quarterly tenancy by three months' notice. An exception to this rule is the yearly tenancy, which is terminable by half a year's notice.

A periodic tenancy may be created expressly or by implication. It is created expressly where some words such as 'yearly tenant' or 'monthly tenant' or 'tenant from year to year' (or from month to month) are used. More often, such a tenancy will arise by implication of law. In such a case, the periodic tenancy will be measured according to the frequency of payment of rent. Thus, if L lets land to T at '$12,000 a year', a yearly tenancy arises; if it is at '$1,000 per month', there is a monthly tenancy,[58] and so on. Where a tenant under a lease for a fixed term 'holds over' – that is, remains in possession after expiry of the term – and rent is paid and accepted on a periodic basis, for example, monthly, a periodic tenancy arises,[59] but no such tenancy will be implied where the tenant remains in possession as a statutory tenant under the rent restriction legislation, or where there is evidence that the landlord wished to evict the tenant, or where he did not know the relevant facts, such as where the tenant had died, unknown to the landlord, and the landlord had accepted rent from the tenant's widow.[60–61]

Tenancy at will

If L permits T to occupy L's land as tenant on the terms that the tenancy may be terminated by L or T at any time, a tenancy at will arises.

This type of tenancy was described by de la Bastide JA in *Romany v Romany* thus:[62]

> A tenancy at will exists when a person occupies the land of another on the understanding that he may go when he likes and that the owner may terminate his interest at any time the owner wishes so to do. A tenancy at will has been properly described as a personal relationship between the landlord and his tenant and it is important, in this case, to note that it is determined by the death of either of them or by one of a variety of acts, even by an involuntary alienation, which would not affect the subsistence of any other tenancy.[63]

In *Cyrus v Gopaul*,[64] Edoo JA further emphasised: 'The rule is clear. A tenancy at will can only exist as a result of an agreement between the parties and an intention on the part of the landlord to create such a tenancy.' Thus, where, in this case, the owner of land permitted the plaintiff, who was a friend of a deceased statutory tenant, to remain in occupation of the land for four years after the tenant's death, it was held that she occupied the land as a mere licensee and

58 *Brooks v Ammon* (1987) High Court, Trinidad and Tobago, No 57 of 1979.
59 See *Kanhai v Gosine* (1988) Court of Appeal, Trinidad and Tobago, Mag App No 125 of 1988; *Pantin v Williams* (1995) High Court, Trinidad and Tobago, No 1379 of 1991.
60–61 *Tickner v Buzzacott* [1965] Ch 426.
62 (1972) 21 WIR 491, at 496.
63 *Wheeler v Mercer* [1956] 3 All ER 631, at 634.
64 (1989) Court of Appeal, Trinidad and Tobago, Mag App No 69 of 1987. See also *Moonan v Moonan* (1988) Court of Appeal, Trinidad and Tobago, Mag App No 12 of 1987.

not as a tenant at will, since there was no intention on the part of the owner to accept her as a tenant.

A tenancy at will may be created either expressly or by implication. Examples of a tenancy at will arising by implication include: where T takes possession under a void lease or under an agreement for a lease and has not yet paid rent; where T 'holds over' after expiry of his lease, without having yet paid rent;[65] and where T is allowed to occupy a house rent-free for an indefinite period. Unless it is agreed that the occupation is to be rent-free, T must pay L compensation for the 'use and occupation' of the land.[66]

An example of a rent-free tenancy at will is to be found in the Trinidadian case of *Deen v Mahabir*.[67] Here, M verbally agreed to allow D, with whom he was on friendly terms, to occupy his house, rent-free, for three to four months whilst D's house was under construction. After some considerable time had elapsed, M repeatedly requested D to leave the house, but D remained in occupation. An ejectment order was made by the magistrate, against which D appealed on the ground that the magistrate had no jurisdiction to determine the complaint because the relationship of landlord and tenant had not existed between the parties, within s 3 of the Summary Ejectment Ordinance, Ch 27, No 17. The Court of Appeal held that, where exclusive possession was given to a new occupant, it was to be inferred that a tenancy had been created, unless special circumstances existed to show that only a licence had been intended. In the present case, the fact that D did not pay rent or that his occupation of the premises had been the result of 'generosity or indulgence' on the part of M, was as consistent with the grant of a rent-free tenancy at will as it was with the grant of a gratuitous licence, and there were no special circumstances or conduct to negative a tenancy.

A tenancy at will terminates when either party does an act that is incompatible with its continuance, for example, where T commits voluntary waste, or where L enters the land and cuts trees or carries away stone, or where either party gives notice of termination to the other.

Tenancy at sufferance

Where T remains in possession of the land after the expiry of his lease without L's assent or dissent,[68] a tenancy at sufferance arises. A tenant at sufferance differs from a trespasser in that his original entry was lawful, and differs from a tenant at will in that his tenancy exists without L's consent. L may claim possession at any time, and he is entitled to claim compensation for T's 'use and occupation'. The relationship may be converted into a periodic tenancy by the payment and acceptance of rent.

---

65 See, eg, *Antoine v Almandoz Tobago Ltd* (2010) High Court, Trinidad and Tobago, No 838 of 2007.

66 *Howard v Shaw* (1841) 151 ER 973. See Megarry and Wade, *Law of Real Property*, 6th edn, para 14–075.

67 (1970) 17 WIR 21.

68 The commencement of ejectment proceedings constitutes dissent by the landlord, and precludes the implication of a tenancy at sufferance: *De Hayney v Ali* (1986) Court of Appeal, Trinidad and Tobago, No 169 of 1984, *per* McMillan JA. Similarly, where the landlord protests at a holding over by the tenant: *Alexander v Rampersad* (1989) High Court, Trinidad and Tobago, No 1780 of 1988, *per* Blackman J.

The following definition of tenancy at sufferance from *Woodfall*[69] was quoted with approval by Deyalsingh J in *Seetahal v Batchasingh*:[70]

> A tenant at sufferance is one who has entered by a lawful demise or title, and, after that has ceased, wrongfully continues in possession without the assent or dissent of the person next entitled; as where a tenant for years holds over after expiry of his term; or where anyone continues in possession without agreement after a particular estate is ended . . . An undertenant who is in possession at the determination of the original lease, and is suffered by the reversioner to hold over, is only a tenant at sufferance. Where a tenancy at will is determined by the landlord exercising acts of ownership, and the tenant remains in possession, he becomes a tenant on sufferance only: but slight evidence would be sufficient to show a new creation of a tenancy at will, or he may by payment of rent, or other acknowledgment of tenancy, become tenant from year to year.

In the *Seetahal* case, S's claim that he had become a tenant at sufferance was rejected since he could not show that he had ever owned an estate in the land; at most, his occupation had been as a licensee. He was not, therefore, protected by the Land Tenants (Security of Tenure) Act 1981.[71]

Tenancy by estoppel

If L purports to grant a lease of land to T, but L has no title to the land, L is estopped from repudiating the tenancy and T is also estopped from denying L's title and the tenancy's existence.[72] In such a case, there arises a 'tenancy by estoppel', which, although invalid vis-à-vis third parties, is binding on L and T and, as between them, has the attributes of a true tenancy. As Farwell LJ described it:[73]

> It is true that a title by estoppel is only good against the person estopped and imports from its very existence the idea of no real title at all, yet as against the person estopped it has all the elements of a real title.

Thus, covenants contained in the lease are enforceable by and against L and T and their successors.

THE LAND TENANTS (SECURITY OF TENURE) ACT 1981 (TRINIDAD AND TOBAGO)

The object of this legislation,[74] which has spawned voluminous litigation in the courts of Trinidad and Tobago, is to provide security of tenure for any residential tenant who, on the date on which the Act came into force ('the appointed date'),

69 *Landlord and Tenant*, 28th edn, 1978, London: Sweet & Maxwell, p 8.
70 (1987) High Court, Trinidad and Tobago, No 89 of 1983.
71 See below. Cf *Ramoutar v Abdool* (1993) High Court, Trinidad and Tobago, No 957 of 1983, in which Permanand J held that the plaintiffs, as tenants at sufferance of building land, were entitled to rely on s 4 of the Act.
72 *Meredith v Gray* (1968) 11 JLR 100, Court of Appeal, Jamaica; *Harrysingh v Ramgoolam* (1984) High Court, Trinidad and Tobago, No 744 of 1978; *White v Cotterell* (1971) 12 JLR 386, Court of Appeal, Jamaica.
73 *Bank of England v Cutler* [1908] 2 KB 208, at 234.
74 See also Land Tenants (Security of Tenure) (Amendment) Act 1983.

was entitled to possession of building land on which he had erected or was in the process of erecting a chattel house. In *Ghany Investments Ltd v Ward*,[75] Hamel-Smith JA explained the purpose of the Act thus:

> The Act was established at a time when certain tenants of land (known as 'building land') found themselves in the invidious position of having to vacate the land, the tenancy having come to an end, but being unable to remove the dwellings which they had erected thereon. These dwellings, unlike the common law chattel house, were 'attached' to the ground and were incapable of being removed without destruction. The Act sought to regularise such tenancies of land by giving a measure of security of tenure to such tenants by converting the tenancies into 30-year 'statutory' leases. It also contained another provision giving the tenants an option to purchase the reversionary interest of the landlord at 50% of the open market value.

'Chattel house' is accordingly given an extremely wide definition by section 2, to include any 'building erected[76] by a tenant upon land comprised in his tenancy with the consent or acquiescence of the landlord and affixed to the land in such a way as to be incapable of being removed from its site without destruction'. In *Angel v Scott Land and Investment Co Ltd*,[77] for instance, Crane J held that two buildings comprising nine separate apartments were within the definition of chattel houses, as they were buildings that could not be removed without their demolition, rather than chattel houses in the generally accepted sense of houses complete in themselves that could easily be removed as chattels and which a tenant had a right to remove at common law.[78]

On the other hand, in *Joseph v Edwards*,[79] in which there was an old tapia house on the land, described by the valuer as 'obsolete', and practically destroyed, Lucky J held that the tenant was not entitled to claim a statutory lease since, under the Act, 'there must be a structure of some permanency . . . which is being used as a dwelling house . . . The Act protects tenants from being evicted from their dwelling houses by unscrupulous landlords of the lands on which the house has been erected. Therefore, if there is no chattel house on the lands, the provisions of the Act are not applicable'.

Somewhat surprisingly, Lord Walker in the Privy Council in *Gopaul v Baksh*[80] took the view that a building will come within the definition of 'chattel house', 'whether or not it is capable of being removed without destruction', on the ground that section 2 states that 'chattel house' *includes* a house that cannot be removed without its

---

75 (1995) Court of Appeal, Trinidad and Tobago, Civ App No 5 of 1989 1995.

76 'Erected' includes cases where a tenant 'does substantial work to what may be an existing structure on the land so as to convert it into a chattel house intended to be used as a dwelling . . . The house need not be built by the tenant "from the ground up"': *Blackman v Cooper* (2013) Court of Appeal, Trinidad and Tobago, Civ App No 107 of 2010, *per* Mendonca JA.

77 (1987) High Court, Trinidad and Tobago, No 187 of 1987. It was also held in this case that the buildings were 'used as a dwelling' within s 3(1) of the Act. The Act does not preclude two or more dwelling houses from falling within its purview, if they exist on premises let by a landlord under the same tenancy. According to the general rule of statutory interpretation in s 16(2)(a) of the Interpretation Act, Ch 3:01, the singular ('dwelling') includes the plural ('dwellings'). See also *Ghany Investments Ltd v Ward* (1995) Court of Appeal, Trinidad and Tobago, Civ App No 5 of 1989. See also the observations of Archie J in *Kumar v Ramcharitar* (2000) High Court, Trinidad and Tobago, No 3924 of 1989.

78 See p 103, below.

79 (1994) High Court, Trinidad and Tobago, No 508 of 1991.

80 [2012] UKPC 1.

destruction, so that the definition is not restricted to such buildings. This view was confirmed, *obiter*, in *Blackman v Cooper*[81] by Mendonca JA who said that

> the question whether the house was affixed to the land in such a way as to be incapable of being removed without its destruction is irrelevant to determining whether it is a chattel house within the meaning of the Act.

It is respectfully submitted, however, that this interpretation of the Act is contrary to the perceived purpose of the legislation which, as Lord Walker seemed to recognise elsewhere in his judgment, was to give security of tenure to tenants who had erected substantial buildings on rented land, rather than to benefit those who had merely placed on the land temporary and easily removable structures. If, indeed, Lord Walker's view were correct, there would have been no need for the section to have contained any reference at all to the destructibility of the building.

The Act applies only to contractual tenancies (including tenancies at will and at sufferance);[82] it does not apply to statutory tenancies arising under the (now lapsed) Rent Restriction Act.[83] Thus, it was held by McMillan JA, in *De Hayney v Ali*,[84] that, where a contractual tenancy had been determined by a valid notice to quit, but the tenant remained in possession as a statutory tenant, he could not claim the benefit of the Land Tenants Act. This conclusion resulted from the definition of 'tenant' in section 2, which included 'any person entitled in possession to land *under a contract of tenancy*, whether express or implied'. Nor, as has been held in several cases,[85] is a mere licensee within the purview of the Act; nor, *a fortiori*, is a squatter who erects a house on the land;[86] and, in *Seetahal v Batchasingh*,[87] Deyalsingh J held that the child of a deceased tenant never had an estate in the land, and so was not protected by the Act.

---

81 Fn 76, above.

82 In *Ramoutar v Abdool* (1993) High Court, Trinidad and Tobago, No 957 of 1983, Permanand J held that the plaintiffs, as tenants at sufferance of building land, were entitled to rely on section 4 of the Act. A tenancy at sufferance exists where a tenant is in possession without the assent or dissent of the landlord. The commencement of ejectment proceedings constitutes dissent by the landlord and precludes the implication of a tenancy at sufferance: *De Hayney v Ali* (1986) Court of Appeal, Trinidad and Tobago, Mag App No 169 of 1984, *per* McMillan JA. Similarly, where the landlord protests at a holding over by the tenant: *Alexander v Rampersad* (1989) High Court, Trinidad and Tobago, No 1780 of 1988, *per* Blackman J. In *Ramdeen v Hansraj* (2000) High Court, Trinidad and Tobago, No 1041 of 1998, Mendonca J held that there was nothing in the Act that restricted its application to tenants paying rent. Accordingly, the Act applied to rent-free tenancies.

83 Since persons occupying premises by virtue of a statutory right conferred by the Rent Restriction Act are treated as licensees with no interest in the land: *Kumar v Ramcharitar* (2000) High Court, Trinidad and Tobago, No 3924 of 1989, *per* Archie J. See also *Bahaw-Nanan v Ramdass* (2007) High Court, Trinidad and Tobago, No 393 of 1996; *Arman v HV Holdings Ltd* (2007) High Court, Trinidad and Tobago No CV 03746 of 2006; *H V Holdings Ltd v Hamid* (2013) High Court, Trinidad and Tobago, No 2009–03221.

84 (1986) Court of Appeal, Trinidad and Tobago, Mag App No 169 of 1984. A similar view was taken by Blackman J in *Alexander v Rampersad* (1989) High Court, Trinidad and Tobago, No 1780 of 1988, and on appeal by Hamel-Smith JA in *Rampersad v Alexander* (1998) Court of Appeal, Trinidad and Tobago, Civ App No 11 of 1989. See also *Dickson v Singh* (2003) High Court, Trinidad and Tobago, No 211 of 1991.

85 *Mahadeo v Dass* (1988) High Court, Trinidad and Tobago, No 1570 of 1980, *per* Hamel-Smith J; *Thomas v Barath* (1986) High Court, Trinidad and Tobago, No 1686 of 1980, *per* Edoo J; *Cyrus v Gopaul* (1989) Court of Appeal, Trinidad and Tobago, Mag App No 69 of 1987; *Singh v Sakai* (2004) High Court, Trinidad and Tobago, No 115 of 1999; *Moses v George* (2011) High Court, Trinidad and Tobago, No 4869 of 2008.

86 *Superville v Eversley* (1986) High Court, Trinidad and Tobago, No 2651 of 1985.

87 (1987) High Court, Trinidad and Tobago, No 89 of 1983.

It was established in *Ghany Investments Ltd v Ward*[88] that it is not necessary that a tenant who wishes to enjoy the benefits of the Act should have been in actual occupation of the chattel house on the appointed date. It is sufficient that the chattel house was being used as a dwelling[89] on that date, so that, for instance, it is 'possible for a person acquiring an interest by operation of law (for example, under a will or on intestacy[90]) to inherit the tenancy with a chattel house thereon "used as a dwelling" and so claim the protection of the Act without assuming occupation thereof'.[91]

By section 4, all tenancies to which the Act applies, and which were subsisting immediately before the Act came into force, are converted into 30-year leases, with an option to renew for a further 30-year term.[92] Section 5 contains detailed rent control provisions, and further gives sitting tenants the option of purchasing the land

> at any time during the term of the statutory lease at a price not exceeding 50% of the open market value of the land without the chattel house, ascertained at the date of the service on the landlord of notice of purchase under s 9(1).

A tenant who exercises the option to purchase is precluded from reselling the land at a higher price to any purchaser other than the State for a period of five years.

Section 5(4) provides that if the rent payable or any part thereof is in arrears for six months, the landlord may apply to the Land Commission for redress, which redress includes the power to terminate the statutory lease. It was held in *Gocool v Rambachan*[93] that, in the absence of a Land Commission, the court has jurisdiction to make such orders. Section 7(3) provides, however, that any order made under s 5(4) shall be conditional on the failure of the tenant to pay all arrears of rent within 30 days of the order. The Act further provides that until an application for a review of the rent is made, the rent under a statutory lease shall be the rent payable immediately before 1 June 1981.

By section 5(8), a statutory tenant has the right to assign the lease or sublet the property with the consent of the landlord, which is not to be unreasonably withheld. Under section 10, a tenant who wishes to assign or sublet must serve on the landlord an application in writing for consent. Within one month of receipt of the application, the landlord must serve the tenant with a notice in writing, either consenting

---

88 (1995) Court of Appeal, Trinidad and Tobago, Civ App No 5 of 1989.

89 A building used partly as a dwelling and partly for commercial purposes is within the purview of the Act: *Gopaul v Baksh* [2012] UKPC 1; *Mackay v Jesse Henderson & Co Ltd* (2011) High Court, Trinidad and Tobago, No CV 2009–01602.

90 See, eg, *Hector v Keith* (2013) Court of Appeal, Trinidad and Tobago, Civ App No 6 of 2010; *Jordan v Lucas* (2012) Court of Appeal, Trinidad and Tobago, Civ App No 189 of 2009; *Gooding v George* (2009) High Court, Trinidad and Tobago, No 2425 of 2007; *Cooper v Blackman* (2010) High Court, Trinidad and Tobago, No 6 of 2005. *In Guyadeen v Guyadeen* (2009) High Court, Trinidad and Tobago, No 2264 of 2008, Delzin J held that the unexpired residue of a statutory lease under the Act formed part of the deceased's estate and fell to be distributed in accordance with the provisions of the will.

91 *Per* Hamel-Smith JA, adopted by Archie J in *Kumar v Ramcharitar* (2000) High Court, Trinidad and Tobago, No 3924 of 1989. See also *Campbell v HV Holdings Ltd* (1998) High Court, Trinidad and Tobago, No S 951 of 1995 1998.

92 Section 4(3) required the tenant to give at least six months' written notice in order to exercise his/her right of renewal, but under the Land Tenants (Security of Tenure) Act, 2010 (No 10 of 2010) it is sufficient to give notice on or before the expiration of the original term of the statutory lease; see *Jordan v Lucas* (2012) Court of Appeal, Trinidad and Tobago, Civ App No 189 of 2009, *per* Jamadar JA; *Greene v Greene* (2020) High Court, Trinidad and Tobago, No CV 2014–04369, *per* Harris J.

93 (2005) High Court, Trinidad and Tobago, No S-1533 of 1996.

or refusing and, in the case of a refusal, the landlord must give his reasons for such refusal. In the absence of any notice by the landlord, he is deemed to have consented.

In *Khan v CGAS Development Co Ltd*,[94] the statutory tenant was in breach of section 5(8) by subletting without seeking the landlord's consent. Jones JA, in the Court of Appeal, pointed out that the Act does not give the landlord a right of re-entry to determine the statutory lease on account of breach of any covenant other than the covenant to pay rent; however, section 5(1) and (2) provided for the incorporation of the terms and conditions of the original contractual tenancy into the statutory lease, so long as they were not inconsistent with the provisions of the Act, and the original tenancy in this case did include a right of re-entry; accordingly, the landlord had the right to re-enter, but since he had failed to take steps to do so, the statutory tenant had retained (i) his right to renew the lease for another 30 year term under section 4 (3), and (ii) his option to purchase the property under section 5.

94 (2019) Court of Appeal, Trinidad and Tobago, Civ App No P-183 of 2014.

CHAPTER 5

LEASEHOLD COVENANTS

The liabilities of lessor and lessee are normally to be found in the express covenants (that is, obligations) contained in the deed of lease, or in the covenants implied by statute or by the common law. They may be considered under the following heads.

LANDLORD'S IMPLIED OBLIGATIONS

Covenant for quiet enjoyment

At common law, there is implied in every lease a covenant on the part of the landlord that the tenant shall be put into possession[1] of the demised premises and that he/she shall have 'quiet enjoyment' of the premises during the continuance of the lease.[2] The word 'quiet' in the covenant does not refer simply to absence of noise, but rather to enjoyment without interference.[3] Accordingly, a tenant is entitled to recover damages from the landlord if the landlord, or any other person claiming through him/her, substantially disturbs or physically interferes with the tenant's enjoyment of the land.[4]

Examples of breaches of this covenant are where L, having reserved the right to work minerals under the demised land, conducts mining operations in such a way as to cause the land to subside;[5] or where L, in order to 'get rid of' T, removes the doors, windows or roof of the building,[6] causes the electricity or water supply to be

---

1 *Miller v Emcer Products Ltd* [1956] 1 All ER 237. In *Singh v Szala* (1975) Full Court, Guyana, L granted to T a monthly tenancy of a cottage and a storeroom below. L kept the storeroom locked and never gave T possession of it up to the time of the present action. Bollers CJ and Mitchell J held that 'there was a direct physical interference with the room . . . by keeping it locked', and 'impliedly [L] was under an obligation at the commencement of the tenancy to put [T] into possession of that tenancy . . . and to see that he remained quietly in possession of it. It is our view that if he did not put him in possession of the tenancy to which he was entitled, [T] has a cause of action in Guyana for breach of the implied covenant for quiet enjoyment'. Similarly, in *Massai Aviation Services v Attorney General* (2007) Privy Council Appeal No 58 of 2005, in which the Bahamas government granted to the appellants a 21-year lease of a site at the Nassau International Airport but allowed Bahamasair to remain in occupation of some buildings on the site, it was held that the government, as lessor, was in breach of the covenant for quiet enjoyment in failing to give the lessee possession of the whole premises let.

2 *Markham v Paget* [1908] 1 Ch 697.

3 *Southwark London Borough Council v Mills* [2001] 1 AC 1, at 22, *per* Lord Millett.

4 *Jones v Lavington* [1903] 1 KB 253; *Ferreira v Mansfield* [1947] LRBG 73; *Saul v Saul* [1963] LRBG 299, High Court, British Guiana; *Wells v Bayparl Ltd* (1991) Supreme Court, The Bahamas, No 1058 of 1983; *Green v Thomas* (1977) High Court, Trinidad and Tobago, No 301 of 1972; *Narine v Narine* (1973) High Court, Guyana, No 437 of 1972. In *Branchett v Beaney* [1992] 3 All ER 910, the English Court of Appeal held that damages for mental distress caused by a breach of the implied covenant for quiet enjoyment were not recoverable, but in *Mackenzie v Ward* (2000) High Court, Trinidad and Tobago, No 1272 of 1996, Tiwari J, following earlier authority, did award such damages. It is submitted that such damages should be recoverable.

5 *Markham v Paget* [1908] 1 Ch 697.

6 *Lavender v Betts* [1942] 2 All ER 72; *Ram v Ramkissoon* (1968) 13 WIR 332; *Lyons v Quamina* (1989) High Court, Trinidad and Tobago, No 97 of 1986.

DOI: 10.4324/9781003186946-5

cut off,[7] or subjects T to persistent harassment[8] or intimidation;[9] and the acts of L and a hired bailiff in removing the tenant's goods from the premises without a valid termination of the lease.[10]

There are many examples of breaches of the covenant for quiet enjoyment in the Commonwealth Caribbean. In the Guyanese case of *Ali v Enmore Estates Ltd*,[11] for instance, the plaintiff was a yearly tenant of agricultural land owned by the defendants. The defendants wished to extend their sugar cane agriculture and attempted to persuade the plaintiff to surrender his tenancy in return for a tenancy of other land. On the plaintiff's refusal to vacate his plot, the defendants moved in with a bulldozer, dismantled the plaintiff's palings and threatened to remove his house. Gonsalves-Sabola J held that there had been a flagrant breach of the implied covenant for quiet enjoyment for which the defendants were liable. He said:

> The defendants' self-help, whether inspired by ignorance, *bona fides* or pressing need, was executed with a high hand and the court, in stepping forth to the rescue and protection of the humble tenant of at least 25 years' standing, can perceive the landlord's conduct in no other light than as attracting aggravated damages.

In *Ram v Ramkissoon*,[12] the appellant was a statutory tenant of two rooms in a central portion of a building in which he carried on business as a jeweller. The building was old and in a bad state of repair, and its two end portions had been unoccupied for several years. The respondent landlord, who owned the whole building, wished to obtain vacant possession of the central portion also. While ejectment proceedings were pending, the respondent removed the galvanised iron sheets from the roof of both end portions of the building. The appellant complained that, as a direct consequence of the removal of the roof, rainwater seeped through the rooms he occupied, causing annoyance, discomfort and physical damage to his property. He claimed damages for, *inter alia*, breach of the landlord's implied covenant for quiet enjoyment. The Court of Appeal of Trinidad and Tobago held, reversing the trial judge's decision, that the damage suffered by the appellant was sufficiently substantial to constitute a breach of the covenant for quiet enjoyment. Wooding CJ said:[13]

> It was agreed that a covenant for quiet enjoyment must be implied from the respondent's contract of letting. It was also agreed that, to constitute an actionable breach, the interference with the tenant's enjoyment of the tenancy must be substantial: see *Browne v Flower*.[14] But I am not at all sure that the parties are at one as to what is meant by sub-

7 *Tapper v Myrie* (1968) 11 JLR 102, Court of Appeal, Jamaica; *Perera v Vandiyar* [1953] 1 All ER 1109. In *McKenzie v Ward* (2000) High Court, Trinidad and Tobago, No 1272 of 1996, Tiwari J held that, in a lease of commercial premises, the landlord was in breach of the covenant for quiet enjoyment by (a) preventing deliveries from being made to the premises, and (b) falsely reporting to the electricity company that the tenant and/or his employees had engaged in current stealing, such report resulting in disconnection of the electricity supply.

8 *Valentine v Rampersad* (1970) 17 WIR 12, Court of Appeal, Trinidad and Tobago.

9 *Kenny v Preen* [1962] 3 All ER 814.

10 *John v McNeil* (2019) High Court, Trinidad and Tobago, No CV 2018–01115, *per* Donaldson-Honeywell J.

11 (1971) High Court, Guyana, No 3619 of 1969. See also *Jagroop v Khan* (1990) High Court, Trinidad and Tobago, No 1041 of 1985, in which L unlawfully entered land in the possession of T and destroyed T's boundary fences.

12 (1968) 13 WIR 332, Court of Appeal, Trinidad and Tobago. See also *Bartholomew v Young* (1990) High Court, Trinidad and Tobago, No 2363 of 1981.

13 (1968) 13 WIR 332, at 334.

14 [1911] 1 Ch 219, at 228.

stantial. Be that as it may, what was alleged here? The appellant's tenancy related to the central portion of a building which was to a large extent protected by the two end portions against wind and weather. The rented premises were deprived of that protection by the deliberate act of the respondent who was under no pressure or notice to do what he did. The end portions had been unoccupied and in a state of dilapidation for some five or six years at least, so it seems odd that he should suddenly have decided to remove their roofs. He had terminated the appellant's contractual tenancy and was currently pursuing ejectment proceedings to put an end to his statutory tenancy. Three months after instituting these proceedings, he effected the first removal. And three months later he began some more. The appellant points to all this as evidencing a resolve on the part of the respondent, and a carrying out of the resolve, to nudge him out of his possession of the rented premises. It may well be so. But, even then, the facts here would fall very far short of those in *Kenny v Preen*,[15] upon which his counsel relied.

In that case, it was found that:

> There was a deliberate and persistent attempt by the landlord to drive the tenant out of her possession of the premises by persecution and intimidation, and intimidation included threats of physical eviction of the tenant and removal of her belongings.

And, in the view of the court:

> That course of conduct by the landlord seriously interfered with the tenant's proper freedom of action in exercising her right of possession, tended to deprive her of the full benefit of it, and was an invasion of her rights as tenant to remain in possession undisturbed, and so would in itself constitute a breach of covenant, even if there were no direct physical interference with the tenant's possession and enjoyment.

Here, it may be, as I said, that the respondent had begun to embark upon a campaign deliberately planned to drive the appellant out of his possession of the rented premises. But there was no finding to that effect. Nor was it any part of the appellant's case at the trial . . . although he admitted taking off the galvanised roofing while the ejectment proceedings were pending, he denied that he did so in order to 'smoke out' the appellant.

Nevertheless, I think there was some physical interference with the enjoyment of the tenancy. By depriving the central portion of the building of such protection against wind and weather as the two end portions afforded, there was, whenever rain fell, enough irruption of water upon the rented premises to cause Dr Singh to regard the seepage as at least not minimal. So there was an invasion of the appellant's right as tenant to remain in possession undisturbed by such irruptions. In my judgment, that was damage sufficiently substantial, if only because of its frequency, to constitute a breach of the covenant. And I so hold.

In *Tapper v Myrie*,[16] a tenant of residential accommodation paid an agreed rent of £2 15s a month and a further sum of 5s for electricity. When the landlord demanded an additional payment of 5s a month for rent, the tenant refused to pay, whereupon the landlord gave him notice to quit.[17] The tenant did not leave, and one night, when he returned home, he found there was no electricity in his room. He spoke to the landlord

15 [1962] 3 All ER 814.
16 (1968) 11 JLR 102.
17 There was no discussion in Fox JA's judgment as to whether or not the notice to quit had validly terminated the tenancy or, if it had, whether the tenant remained in possession as a statutory tenant.

about it, and the latter retorted: 'I cut off your light because I want you to come out, and you won't come out'. The Jamaican Court of Appeal, affirming the decision of the trial magistrate, held that the action of the landlord in disconnecting the electricity supply was a breach of the implied covenant for quiet enjoyment, notwithstanding that the act complained of was done off the premises, since it was 'a physical interference with the demised premises'. Nor was there any merit in the landlord's argument that there were two separate contracts – one for renting the premises, and one for the supply of electricity – and even if there had been a breach of the latter contract, this did not amount to a breach of the covenant for quiet enjoyment. Fox JA said:[18]

> It is clear that the parties had bargained on the footing that electric current should come into the premises. This became a benefit which was in no way dissimilar from other benefits incidental upon the rental of the premises. Viewed in this manner, it is idle to inquire whether the arrangement in respect of electricity is regarded as having been embodied in the contract of rental, or independent thereof. To deprive the plaintiff of his supply of electricity would be in breach of the defendant's implied undertaking not to do so, and would render him liable, as the learned resident magistrate has found.

On the other hand, since there must be some physical interference with the enjoyment of the premises let, mere noise or disorderly conduct emanating from the landlord's adjoining premises may not amount to breach of the covenant for quiet enjoyment,[19] although it may be actionable as a nuisance or constitute a derogation from the lessor's grant if the latter has participated in it. Where no participation by the lessor is proved, he will not be liable merely for having failed to take steps to prevent it.[20] Furthermore, a disturbance of enjoyment, even where caused by the lessor, which is merely temporary and which does not interfere with the lessee's possession, is not a breach of the covenant.[21]

Covenant not to derogate from the grant

There is an implied covenant that the landlord will not derogate from his grant. As Bowen LJ said, 'a grantor, having given a thing with one hand, is not to take away the means of enjoying it with the other'.[22] In the context of leaseholds, this means that the landlord 'must not frustrate the use of the land for the purposes for which it was let'.[23] For instance, there was a breach of the covenant where L, having let land to T for the purpose of carrying on a business as a timber merchant, erected buildings on adjoining land that interrupted the free flow of air to the sheds that T used

---

18 *Tapper v Myrie* (1968) 11 JLR 102, at 105.

19 *Jenkins v Jackson* (1888) 40 Ch D 71; *Jaeger v Mansions Consolidated Ltd* (1902) 87 LT 690, at 694. But in *Alexander v Maritime Leasing Co Ltd* (2009) High Court, Trinidad and Tobago, No 2235 of 2006, a case where the claimant had rented a shop in the defendant's shopping mall, Stollmeyer J held that the defendant had been in breach of the covenant for quiet enjoyment by subjecting the claimant to substantial vibration, noise and dust from building works in the mall for a period of two months. In the absence of evidence of loss of trade, nominal damages were awarded.

20 *Belbridge Property Trust Ltd v Milton* (1934) 78 SJ 489, in which the lessor was held not liable for an invasion by rats, where he had done nothing to attract them to the demised premises, nor let them loose there.

21 *Manchester, Sheffield and Lincolnshire Rly Co v Anderson* [1898] 2 Ch 394, at 401.

22 *Birmingham, Dudley and District Banking Co v Rose* (1888) 38 Ch D 295, at 313.

23 *Browne v Flower* [1911] 1 Ch 219, 225–27; Cheshire and Burn, *Modern Law of Real Property*, 14th edn, 1988, London: Butterworths, p 378.

for drying timber.[24] Similarly, where L lets to T an apartment in a building intended for purely residential use, he commits a breach of covenant if he subsequently lets most of the other apartments in the building for business purposes.[25]

To constitute a breach of the covenant, L must do some act that renders the demised premises 'substantially less fit for the purposes for which they were let'.[26] Thus, there will be no breach where L, having let premises to T for use in a particular trade, later lets adjoining premises to a rival trader, because the premises let to T will still be fit for the purpose for which they were let, albeit that T's profits may be reduced.[27] Nor will an act by L that constitutes a mere invasion of T's privacy amount to a breach of the covenant, as where, for example, having let a ground-floor apartment to T, L erects an outside staircase to an upper apartment that passes directly in front of T's bedroom window.[28]

Many acts that constitute a breach of this covenant may also constitute a breach of the covenant for quiet enjoyment: for instance, where L operates machinery on adjoining land that causes structural damage to the house let to T; or where excessive dust and fumes emitted from neighbouring land seriously interfere with T's enjoyment of his premises.

Covenant as to fitness for habitation

At common law, there is no implied covenant by a landlord that the premises let are or will be fit for human habitation, nor is there any implied covenant that the landlord will do any repairs whatever.[29] However, there are the following exceptions.

Furnished lettings

Where residential premises are let furnished, there is an implied condition that they are fit for habitation at the commencement of the tenancy:[30] for example, the drains must not be defective,[31] nor must the premises be infested with bugs.[32] However, the landlord has no obligation to *keep* the premises habitable, so, if they subsequently become unfit, the landlord is not liable.[33]

High-rise apartment buildings

It was held in *Liverpool CC v Irwin*[34] that a landlord of residential apartments in a high-rise building is under an implied duty to keep in a reasonable state of repair the lifts, staircases and other common facilities, such as lighting and garbage chutes, for the benefit of all of the tenants in the building.

---

24 *Aldin v Latimer, Clark, Muirhead and Co* [1894] 2 Ch 437.
25 *Newman v Real Estate Debenture Corp Ltd* [1940] 1 All ER 131.
26 Megarry and Wade, *Law of Real Property*, 6th edn, 2000, London: Stevens, p 696.
27 *Port v Griffith* [1938] 1 All ER 295.
28 See *Browne v Flower* [1911] 1 Ch 219.
29 *Op cit*, Cheshire and Burn, fn 22, p 373.
30 *Collins v Hopkins* [1923] 2 KB 617.
31 *Wilson v Finch-Hatton* (1877) 2 Ex D 336.
32 *Smith v Marrable* (1843) 152 ER 693; (1843) 174 ER 598.
33 *Sarson v Roberts* [1895] 2 QB 395.
34 [1976] 2 All ER 39.

Statutory provisions

The common law position has been modified or altered by statute in some Commonwealth Caribbean jurisdictions. For instance, s 157(d) of the Property Act, Cap 236 (Barbados), provides that, 'in the case of a lease of a dwelling house, or part thereof', there is an implied covenant 'that the house or part thereof is fit for human habitation at the commencement of the tenancy'; and s 6 of the Landlord and Tenant Act, Cap 189 (Belize), s 44(1) of the Landlord and Tenant Act, Cap 61:01 (Guyana), and s 3 of the Letting of Houses (Implied Terms) Act, Ch 27, No 8 (Trinidad and Tobago), provide that

> in any contract for letting any house for human habitation there shall, notwithstanding any stipulation to the contrary, be implied a condition that the house is, at the commencement of the tenancy, and an undertaking that the house will be kept by the landlord during the tenancy, in repair and in all respects reasonably fit for human habitation.

It will be seen that s 157(d) of Cap 236 modifies the common law position in that it imposes an obligation on a landlord of any dwelling house – not merely furnished dwellings – to ensure that it is fit for human habitation at the commencement of the tenancy. Caps 189, 61:01 and 27, No 8, on the other hand, extend the obligation still further by providing that a landlord of any dwelling house must not only make the house fit for habitation at the commencement of the tenancy, but also keep it in such a state throughout the tenancy.

The meaning of 'fit for human habitation' within cl 2 of the Rent Restriction Exclusion of Premises Order 1954 was in issue in a Trinidadian case, *Hamblin v Samuel*.[35] In this case, the owner of a house decided to convert the basement area into two self-contained apartments. Officials of the Rent Assessment Board visited the premises and found that the ventilation in the apartments was inadequate, that the single bedroom window in each apartment could not be opened at all, and that the sitting-room windows in each had generally to be kept closed because of the prevailing dust. According to Wooding CJ, 'the Board would appear to have regarded the conditions to which the apartments were subject as almost, if not wholly, subhuman'. In ascertaining the meaning of 'fit for human habitation', the learned Chief Justice gave it 'its natural meaning', which may tersely be said to be 'fit for human beings to live in'.

Wooding CJ regarded s 4(1) of the Housing Act 1957 (UK) as a reasonable guide as to whether premises are fit for human habitation. The subsection provided:

> In determining for any of the purposes of this Act whether a house is unfit for human habitation, regard shall be had to its condition in respect of the following matters, that is to say:
>
> (a) repair;
> (b) stability;
> (c) freedom from damp;
> (d) natural lighting;
> (e) ventilation;

35 (1966) 11 WIR 48.

(f) water supply;
(g) drainage and sanitary conveniences;
(h) facilities for storage, preparation and cooking of food and for the disposal of waste water,

and the house shall be deemed to be unfit for human habitation if and only if it is so far defective in one or more of the said matters that it is not reasonably suitable for occupation in that condition.

Covenant to repair

Repairing covenants, other than covenants as to fitness for habitation, are normally expressly inserted in leases. At common law, there is no implied obligation on a landlord to do repairs, but statutory obligations are imposed on landlords in some jurisdictions. For instance, s 157(c) of Cap 236 (Barbados) implies a covenant 'to keep in repair the roof, main walls and main drains and, where part only of a building is leased, the common passage and common installations', and s 157(e) imposes an obligation 'to repair the leased premises in the case of destruction by fire, earthquake, hurricane, flood or riot'.

Where a landlord has covenanted or is subject to a statutory obligation to repair[36] and, having been notified by the tenant of the need for certain repairs,[37] fails to carry them out, the tenant is entitled to arrange to have the repair work done and to deduct the cost from future payments of rent.[38] A Bahamian example is *Milo Butler and Sons Investment Co Ltd v Monarch Investments Ltd*,[39] in which the landlord had covenanted 'to keep and maintain the main structure and all exterior parts . . . including the roof . . . in good and tenantable repair'. The tenant informed the landlord in writing that the roof was in urgent need of repair and, after the landlord's failure to respond, the tenant gave notice of his intention to effect the repairs and to deduct the cost from future rent payments. Allen J, in the Supreme Court of The Bahamas, held that the tenant was not liable for failure to pay rent equivalent to the cost of carrying out the necessary repairs.

TENANT'S IMPLIED OBLIGATION

Obligation not to commit waste

A tenant for a fixed term is liable for both voluntary waste (that is, positive acts of injury to the property, such as altering or destroying it) and permissive waste (that is, allowing the property to become dilapidated through omission to repair) and,

---

36 The court has a discretionary power, which should be cautiously exercised, to order a landlord to do some specific work under a covenant to repair. Where there has been a clear breach of a repairing covenant, and there is no doubt as to what is required to be done to remedy the breach, an order of specific performance ought to be made: *Jeune v Queen's Cross Properties Ltd* [1973] 3 All ER 97.

37 A landlord's liability to repair does not arise until he has been notified of the need for repair, or otherwise acquires knowledge of such need: *O'Brien v Robinson* [1973] 1 All ER 583; *Uniproducts (Manchester) Ltd v Rose Furnishers Ltd* [1956] 1 All ER 146.

38 *Lee-Parker v Izzett* [1971] 3 All ER 1099. See PHL Rank (1976) 40 Conv (NS) 190; A Waite [1981] Conv 199; PF Smith (1980) 130 NLJ 330.

39 (1998) Supreme Court, The Bahamas, No 10 of 1989.

therefore, in the absence of an express stipulation to the contrary, he/she must keep the premises in proper repair.[40]

A yearly tenant is certainly liable for voluntary waste,[41] but there is uncertainty as to the extent of his/her liability for permissive waste. According to one view, a yearly tenant's liability is the same as that of a tenant for a fixed term.[42] Another view is that he/she is merely liable to keep the premises wind- and water-tight, fair wear and tear excepted.[43] A third view is that his/her liability is no greater than that of a weekly, monthly or quarterly tenant, viz, his/her only obligation is to use the premises 'in a tenant-like manner'.[44] The meaning of this latter phrase was explained by Lord Denning thus:[45]

> The tenant must take care of the place . . . He must clean the chimneys, when necessary, and also the windows. He must mend the electric light when it fuses. He must unstop the sink when it is blocked by his waste. In short, he must do the little jobs about the place which a reasonable tenant would do. In addition, he must, of course, not damage the house, wilfully or negligently; and he must see that his family and guests do not damage it: and if they do, he must repair it. But, apart from such things, if the house falls into disrepair through fair wear and tear or lapse of time, or for any reason not caused by him, then the tenant is not liable to repair it.

Section 11 of Cap 189 (Belize) and s 8 of Cap 61:01 (Guyana) impose liability on all tenants for voluntary waste, but are silent as to liability for permissive waste. The sections provide that 'a lessee shall not make voluntary waste of the land held under the tenancy without the permission of the lessor and, if he does so, the lessee shall be liable to pay damages to the lessor', but 'no action shall be brought by any landlord against any tenant on or in whose land or buildings any fire shall accidentally begin in respect of any damage suffered by him in consequence thereof'.

Registered land

Section 95(b) of the Registration of Titles Act of Jamaica provides that, in every lease made under the provisions of the Act, there is to be implied a covenant that the lessee 'will keep and yield up the leased property in good and tenantable repair, accidents and damages from storm and tempest, or other acts of God and the Queen's enemies, and reasonable wear and tear excepted'.[46]

EXPRESS COVENANTS

To a large extent, the rights and liabilities of landlord and tenant are regulated by express covenants inserted in the lease or tenancy agreement. There is an infinite variety of such covenants, but those that are most significant and

40 *Yellowly v Gower* (1855) 156 ER 833.
41 See *Warren v Keen* [1954] 1 QB 15, at 21.
42 Yates and Hawkins, *Landlord and Tenant Law*, 2nd edn, 1986, London: Sweet & Maxwell, p 205.
43 *Op cit*, Megarry and Wade, fn 25, p 882.
44 *Op cit*, Cheshire and Burn, fn 22, p 379; *Milo Butler and Sons Investment Co Ltd v Monarch Investments Ltd* (1998) Supreme Court, The Bahamas, No 10 of 1989, *per* Allen J.
45 *Warren v Keen* [1954] 1 QB 15, at 20.
46 See *Frater v Wedderburn* (2010) Court of Appeal, Jamaica, Civ App No 23 of 2009.

commonly encountered concern payment of rent, obligation to repair, and obligation not to assign, underlet or part with the possession of the premises without the landlord's consent.

Covenant to pay rent

The rent payable by a tenant under a lease is more properly called 'rent service', which signifies that, historically, T held the land in return for services, which were later commuted into fixed money payments. Although, today, rent almost invariably consists of money payments, there is nothing to prevent rent taking the form of delivery of chattels or produce,[47] or the performance of personal services.[48]

The amount to be paid as rent must be sufficiently certain. It need not be certain at the date of the lease, but it must be 'calculated with certainty at the time when payment comes to be made'.[49] It has been held that an option to renew a lease is void for uncertainty if the rent is 'to be agreed',[50] or 'subject to renegotiation',[51] but a term in a council tenant's rent book to the effect that rent was 'liable to be increased or decreased on notice being given' was held valid,[52] as also was an option to renew a lease 'at a rent to be fixed at a price to be determined, having regard to the market valuation of the premises at the time of exercising the option'.[53] It is also sufficient if the parties provide that the rent shall be fixed by a third party.[54] Further, once a lease has been granted, the court will do what it can to interpret provisions as to rent in such a way as to achieve sufficient certainty. Thus, for example, where, in a ten-year lease, rent was fixed for the first five years and was thereafter to be 'as agreed', it was held that a reasonable rent, to be assessed at the end of the first period, was payable for the second period.[55]

A lease may contain a 'rent review clause', enabling rent to be raised at regular intervals to reflect the fair market value of the demised premises. The clause may provide for reviews, for example, every seven, five or three years, and will specify the administrative procedure for ascertaining the fair market rent.[56]

At common law, rent is payable in arrears, but this may be, and usually is, displaced by agreement between the parties or by a custom that the rent should be paid in advance.[57]

47 Co Litt 142a.
48 *Duke of Marlborough v Oxborn* (1864) 122 ER 758.
49 *Op cit*, Cheshire and Burn, fn 22, p 381.
50 *King's Motors (Oxford) Ltd v Lax* [1970] 1 WLR 426; but in *Adam v Besseling* (1987) High Court, Trinidad and Tobago, No 2504 of 1987, Mustapha Ibrahim J pointed out that, where there was an option to renew a lease at a rent to be agreed, the uncertainty could be cured and the agreement rendered valid if the parties agreed on a rent before the time for the exercise of the option had arrived; in *Fiore v Paradise International Corp Ltd* (2000) Supreme Court, Belize, No 518 of 1998, Shanks J held that if the option does not state the terms of the renewal, the lease will be for the same period and in the same terms as the original lease, so far as those terms arise out of the landlord/tenant relationship. See also *Brown v Gould* [1971] 2 All ER 1505.
51 *Hemmings v Attorney General* (2004) Supreme Court, Jamaica, No E 315 of 1998.
52 *Greater London Council v Connolly* [1970] 1 All ER 870.
53 *Brown v Gould* [1971] 2 All ER 1505.
54 *Lloyds Bank v Marcan* [1973] 3 All ER 754.
55 *Beer v Bowden* [1981] 1 WLR 522.
56 See Hill and Redman, *Law of Landlord and Tenant*, Issue 46, Vol 1, London: Butterworths, [3581]–[3588]; *op cit*, Cheshire and Burn, fn 22, p 382.
57 See *Francis v Daley* (1964) 6 WIR 256.

Covenant to repair

The obligation to repair the demised premises may rest on the landlord, or on the tenant, or partly on the landlord and partly on the tenant. The matter is entirely one for negotiation between the parties, and the extent of the obligation depends on the wording of the covenant.[58] Expressions often used are 'good tenantable repair',[59] 'sufficient repair', 'good and substantial repair', although it has been suggested that these phrases do not increase the burden imposed by the single word 'repair'.[60] If there is no express provision for repairs in the lease, the tenant may be held liable for them under the doctrine of waste.[61] Further, statutory provisions may impose obligations to repair. For instance, as we have seen, s 157(c) of Cap 236 (Barbados) implies a covenant by the landlord 'to keep in repair the roof, main walls and main drains and, where part only of a building is leased, the common passage and common installations'; s 158(c) of the same Act imposes an obligation upon the tenant 'to keep the interior of the leased premises in good repair, reasonable wear and tear excepted'. Both of these implied covenants are, however, subject to any express provision to the contrary in the lease.

At common law, the standard of repair required is that in which, after making due allowance for the locality, character and age of the premises at the date of the lease, a reasonably minded owner would keep them.[62] This standard is also required by s 159(1) of Cap 236, which provides that 'repair' means 'the state of repair in which a prudent owner might reasonably be expected to keep his property, due allowance being made for the age, character and location of the premises at the commencement of the lease'.

As regards locality, it is clear that a house situated in an exclusive residential suburb would demand a higher standard of repair than one situated in a run-down urban or inner city area.[63] As regards character, it is equally clear that the standard of repair applicable to a mansion house would be much higher than that applicable to an agricultural worker's cottage.[64] An important principle is that it is the character of the premises and the locality at the beginning of the tenancy that must be considered. Thus, if, at the commencement of a long lease, the house is a desirable one situated in an expensive and fashionable locality, but after several years the neighbourhood and the property become run-down, the covenantor must put the property back into its original state: he cannot argue that his obligation is to be measured by the current low standards of the locality.[65]

With regard to the age of the property, the covenantor is under an obligation to keep it in a reasonably good condition for a building of that age.[66] If, in order to keep

58 See Hill and Redman, *op cit*, fn 55, [6330] *et seq; Milo Butler and Sons Investment Co Ltd v Monarch Investments Ltd* (1998) Supreme Court, The Bahamas, No 10 of 1989.

59 'Good tenantable repair' has been held to mean 'such repair as, having regard to the age, character and locality of the house, would make it reasonably fit for the occupation of a reasonably minded tenant of the class who would be likely to take it': *Proudfoot v Hart* (1890) 25 QBD 42, 52, *per* Lord Esher MR; *Milo Butler and Sons Investment Co Ltd v Monarch Investments Ltd* (1998) Supreme Court, The Bahamas, No 10 of 1989.

60 *Anstruther-Gough-Calthorpe v McOscar* [1924] 1 KB 716, 722, at 723.

61 See p 6, above.

62 *Lurcott v Wakely* [1911] 1 KB 905; *Anstruther-Gough-Calthorpe v McOscar* [1924] 1 KB 716.

63 *Op cit*, Cheshire and Burn, fn 22, p 385.

64 *Ibid.*

65 *Anstruther-Gough-Calthorpe v McOscar* [1924] 1 KB 716.

66 *Op cit*, Cheshire and Burn, fn 22, p 385.

the property in such a condition, it becomes necessary to renew or replace parts of the building, such as a defective wall or roof, the covenantor must do the renewal or replacement. However, the covenantor is not bound to *reconstruct* the building; so, for example, 'the tenant of an old house is not bound to replace defective foundations with foundations of an entirely different character',[67] because that would, in effect, amount to reconstruction. The obligation to repair does not normally require the rebuilding of premises that 'through inherent defects, have passed beyond repair, or doing work which cannot fairly be called repairing the premises as they stood when demised',[68] and

> it is always a question of degree whether that which the tenant is being asked to do can properly be described as repair, or whether, on the contrary, it would involve giving back to the landlord a wholly different thing from that which he demised.[69]

In the Jamaican case *International Hotels Ltd v Cornwall Holdings Ltd*,[70] in which a lease of a hotel required the tenant to keep and maintain the premises, with its fixtures and fittings, 'in good and substantial repair and condition', Harris J held that it was 'obligatory on the part of a tenant, who is under liability to substantially repair demised premises and to keep them in a state of good repair, to do so, even if they were not in a state of tenantable repair at the inception of the tenancy', so long as it will not 'involve giving back to the landlord a wholly different thing from that which he demised'. In this case, the replacement of dilapidated equipment with upgraded equipment, currently available on the market, could 'not be regarded as the [tenant] giving back to the landlord a wholly different thing from that for which it had covenanted at the commencement of the lease'.

These principles were first established in *Ravenseft Properties Ltd v Davstone (Holdings) Ltd*,[71] in which it was held that where an inherent defect has caused damage, the tenant may be under an obligation to rectify not only the damage but also the cause of the damage, even though it is an inherent defect, if it is the proper practice to do so, or it is necessary to do so in order to do 'the job properly once and for all'. Thus, in the *Ravenseft* case, in which the stone cladding on a building became cracked owing to the absence of expansion joints, which were not included in the original design, the tenant was obliged not only to replace the stone cladding, but also to insert expansion joints in order to prevent recurrence of the problem.

Fair wear and tear

Tenants frequently covenant to keep the premises in repair, 'fair wear and tear excepted'. The effect of the phrase is to absolve the tenant from liability for:

(a) damage due to the ordinary operation of natural causes, such as wind and rain; and
(b) disrepair resulting from the reasonable use of the premises.

---

67 *Ibid; Sotheby v Grundy* [1947] 2 All ER 761.
68 *Op cit*, Megarry and Wade, fn 25, p 27.
69 *Ravenseft Properties Ltd v Davstone (Holdings) Ltd* [1979] 1 All ER 929, 937, *per* Foster J.
70 (1996) 33 JLR 314, Supreme Court, Jamaica.
71 [1979] 1 All ER 929.

However, although the tenant is not liable for the original damage or deterioration constituting wear and tear, he/she is liable for any consequential damage resulting from his/her failure to rectify the original damage, where it should be obvious to a reasonable person that, if not rectified, further and lasting damage would ensue. As Talbot J put it in *Haskell v Marlow*:[72]

> The tenant is bound to do such repairs as may be required to prevent the consequences flowing originally from wear and tear from producing others which wear and tear would not directly produce. For example, if a tile falls off the roof, the tenant is not liable for the immediate consequences; but if he does nothing and in the result more and more water gets in, the roof and walls decay and ultimately the top floor, or the whole house, becomes uninhabitable, he cannot say that it is due to reasonable wear and tear . . . On the other hand, take the gradual wearing away of a stone floor or staircase by ordinary use. This may in time produce a considerable wear and tear, and the tenant is not liable in respect of it.

Covenant not to assign, sublet or part with possession of the demised premises

In the absence of any express stipulation to the contrary, a tenant is free to assign, sublet or part with the possession of the demised premises to a third party. However, in order to ensure that the premises do not fall into the hands of an irresponsible person, it is usual for a lease to contain an express covenant either that the tenant will not assign or sublet the premises (an 'absolute covenant') or, more commonly, that the tenant will not assign or sublet *without the consent of the landlord* (a 'qualified covenant'). The qualified covenant may be subject to an express proviso that the landlord will not unreasonably refuse his/her consent to an assignment or subletting. Such a proviso is implied in England under s 19 of the Landlord and Tenant Act 1927, but there is no such statutory implication in Commonwealth Caribbean jurisdictions, apart from that contained in the registered land legislation in some jurisdictions.[73] In Barbados, s 158(f) of Cap 236 provides that there is an implied covenant that the tenant shall not 'transfer, charge, sublet or otherwise part with the possession of the leased premises or any part thereof without the written consent of the lessor'.

The courts construe covenants against assigning, subletting or parting with possession strictly against the landlord. Thus, for instance, a covenant against parting with possession is not broken where the tenant allows another person to have the use of the premises without giving him/her legal possession,[74] nor is a covenant against assignment broken by a subletting of the premises, and a covenant 'not to sublet' the premises is not broken by a subletting of *part* of the premises.[75]

72 [1928] 2 KB 45, at 58, 59.
73 See, eg, s 53(h) of the Registered Land Act (Cap 374, Laws of Antigua and Barbuda, 1992 Rev); s 53(i) of the Registered Land Ordinance (Cap 229, Laws of the Virgin Islands, 1991 Rev). Cf Land Tenants (Security of Tenure) Act 1981, s 5(8) (Trinidad and Tobago).
74 *Chaplin v Smith* [1926] 1 KB 198.
75 *Cook v Shoesmith* [1951] 1 KB 752, at 753; *Esdaile v Lewis* [1952] 2 All ER 357, at 359; *Montrichard Enterprises Ltd v Attorney General* (1998) High Court, Trinidad and Tobago, No CV 350 of 1989. Accordingly, a well-drawn lease should include a covenant against assigning, underletting or parting with possession *of all or any part* of the premises.

Effect of breach

The effect of breach of a covenant against assigning or underletting may be summarised thus:

(a) an assignment or subletting made in breach of an absolute or qualified covenant is nevertheless valid,[76] but the breach may give rise to forfeiture of the lease and/or a claim for damages;

(b) in the case of a qualified covenant, if the tenant omits to apply for consent to an assignment or underletting, he/she is liable for damages in any event and to forfeiture of the lease,[77] although the court may grant relief against forfeiture;[78]

(c) in the case of a qualified covenant containing a proviso that the landlord will not unreasonably refuse consent, a tenant to whom consent has been refused may nevertheless go ahead with the assignment or subletting and, if it is later found that the landlord's refusal was unreasonable, the tenant will not be in breach of covenant; if, on the other hand, the landlord's refusal is found to be reasonable, there will be a breach of covenant and the tenant will be liable for damages and to forfeiture, as in (b).[79]

Reasonableness of refusal of consent

The question of reasonableness of a refusal of consent is essentially a question of fact depending on all of the circumstances of the case,[80] but there is strong authority for the view that, in order to be reasonable, the reason for refusal must be connected with the personality of the assignee, or with the user or occupation of the premises.[81] For example, it may be reasonable to refuse consent where the proposed assignee intends to use the demised premises for a purpose that will be injurious to the property or to other property owned by the landlord,[82] or where the assignee's financial position is precarious, or where the assignment will enable the assignee to acquire a statutory tenancy protected by the rent restriction legislation, such protection not being available to the assignor.[83]

Option to purchase the reversion

An option to purchase the reversion will often take the form of a covenant in the lease to the effect that if the lessee within a specified period gives to the lessor notice in writing (of a specified length) of his/her desire to purchase the freehold reversion

76 *Samad v Jordan* (1972) High Court, Guyana, No 1289 of 1970.
77 *Barrow v Isaacs* [1891] 1 QB 417.
78 *Home Property and Investment Co Ltd v Walker* [1947] 1 All ER 789.
79 *Lewis and Allenby Ltd v Pegge* [1914] 1 Ch 782, at 785.
80 *Bickel v Duke of Westminster* [1976] 3 All ER 801, at 804.
81 *Houlder Bros and Co Ltd v Gibbs* [1925] 1 Ch 575, at 585, *per* Warrington LJ; although, in *Bickel v Duke of Westminster* [1976] 3 All ER 801, at 804, 805, Lord Denning MR advocated a broader approach to the question of reasonableness. See G Kodilinye [1988] Conv 45.
82 *Bridwell Hospital Governors v Fawkner* (1892) 8 TLR 637.
83 *Lee v K Carter Ltd* [1948] 2 All ER 690.

of the premises, the lessor will, on payment of a specified purchase price and all arrears of rent, convey the freehold of the demised premises to the lessee.[84]

The nature of such an option was described by Langrin J, in the Jamaican Supreme Court, in *Broadway Import and Export Ltd v Levy*:[85]

> An option to purchase is the right to purchase a particular estate in land for a particular sum within a particular period. The holder of the option can call for the sale of the land to him for the agreed price at any time within the agreed period. Thus, with an option to purchase, the option holder is the prime mover. The option agreement constitutes an irrevocable offer to sell and, once the plaintiff has accepted that offer by exercising the option, a contract has come into being.

In *Caribbean Asbestos Products Ltd v Lopez*, Luckhoo P had this to say:[86]

> An option, when granted for value, confers a right or privilege in the optionee to call for the sale to him of the land in accordance with the conditions specified for the exercise of the option, and the lessor undertakes that he will not within the time, if any, specified in the option clause, which is indeed a separate contract, deal with the land in any way inconsistent with the right of the optionee to purchase the land, together with a binding agreement not to revoke the offer during the time, if any, specified in the option. If the offer is accepted within the time specified, a contract of sale is made . . . If the lessor, in breach of his agreement, purports to revoke his offer, his revocation is ineffectual to prevent the formation of a contract by the acceptance of the offer within the specified time.

It is an established principle that an option to purchase affects the parties *qua* vendor and purchaser, not *qua* landlord and tenant.[87] It does not 'touch and concern' the land, and, therefore, does not run automatically with the lease or the reversion.[88] However, an option to purchase the reversion is a proprietary interest, which forms part of the lease, and the benefit will pass on an assignment of the lease,[89] even, it seems, where the assignment makes no mention of the option.[90] It has been held that an option that is expressed to be binding on the lessor's successors in title will be binding on an assignee of the reversion if it has been registered as an estate contract,[91] which, in Commonwealth Caribbean jurisdictions, would mean that it will be binding on a purchaser of the reversion having notice of the option[92] or, where title to the land is registered, where it is protected by entry of a caution or caveat on the register or certificate of title.[93] On the death of the lessee, the benefit of the option devolves with the lease on his personal representatives.[94]

---

84 *Op cit*, Hill and Redman, fn 55, [735].
85 (1996) 33 JLR 26, 28, Supreme Court, Jamaica.
86 (1974) 21 WIR 462, at 466.
87 *Woodall v Clifton* [1905] 2 Ch 257, at 279, *per* Romer LJ. In *Arima Agricultural Co-operative Society Ltd v Armstrong* (1987) High Court, Trinidad and Tobago, No 217 of 1980, it was held that an option to purchase fixtures and fittings did not touch and concern the land, being a merely personal agreement.
88 See p 78, below.
89 *London and South Western Rly Co v Gomm* (1882) 20 Ch D 562; *Griffith v Pelton* [1957] 3 All ER 75, at 84.
90 *Griffith v Pelton* [1957] 3 All ER 75.
91 *Ibid.*
92 *Broadway Import and Export Ltd v Levy* (1996) 33 JLR 26, Supreme Court, Jamaica.
93 Such an option may qualify as an 'overriding interest' in some registered land systems, eg, Registered Land Act, Cap 194, section 31 (1) (g) (Belize): *Rodriguez v Aldana* (2018) Supreme Court, Belize, No 661 of 2016, paras 11–16, *per* Griffith J, following *Webb v Pollmount Ltd* [1966] 1 All ER 481.
94 *Re Adams and Kensington Vestry* (1884) 27 Ch D 394.

It has also been established that:

(a) an option to purchase the reversion will usually terminate on expiry of the lease and will not be exercisable by a tenant who holds over after such expiry;[95]

(b) where certain matters are made conditions precedent to the exercise of the option, the conditions must be observed strictly –[96] for example, notice of a desire to exercise the option must be given within the specified period, as time will normally be of the essence of the contract,[97] and, if payment of the purchase money at the expiration of the notice is made a condition precedent, the payment must be duly made, otherwise the option will be unenforceable.[98] Again, if the lease expressly states that performance of all of the covenants therein is to be a condition precedent for the exercise of the option, the lessee must show such performance,[99] although strict performance may be waived by the lessor;[100]

(c) the lease will normally require notice of interest to exercise an option to be in writing,[101] and where writing is not expressly required, such a requirement will be implied;[102] and

(d) the purchase price of the freehold will normally be specified; in the absence of an agreed price, it will be the open market value of the freehold subject to the existing lease.[103]

Option to renew a lease

A lease may contain a term granting the lessee an option to renew the lease for a further period.[104] Such an option will devolve upon the lessee's, and will be binding on the lessor's, personal representatives.[105] Unlike an option to purchase the reversion, it touches and concerns the land, and, therefore, runs automatically with the lease and the reversion.[106] It is an interest in the land, is capable of assignment, and is binding on a purchaser of the freehold with notice or, where the land is registered, is binding on purchasers if protected by an entry on the register or certificate of title.[107]

A lessee who seeks to exercise the option must abide by any terms or conditions as to its exercise expressed in the lease. Further, if the option is made conditional on

95 *Bradbury v Grimble and Co* [1920] 2 Ch 548. See also *Barrett v Dale* [2020] JMCA Civ 13.
96 *West Country Cleaners (Falmouth) Ltd v Saly* [1966] 3 All ER 210. In *Jamaica Omnibus Services Ltd v Wharfing Services Ltd* (1991) 28 JLR 403, one of the conditions was that written notice of a desire to exercise the option should be accompanied by payment of a deposit of 10 per cent of the purchase money. The plaintiff's cheque for the amount was dishonoured. Cooke J held that the option had not been properly exercised.
97 *Lord Ranelagh v Melton* (1864) 62 ER 627. See *Robertson v Surbiton Property Developments Ltd* (1982) 19 JLR 90.
98 *Ibid.*
99 See *Bassett v Whiteley* (1982) 45 P & CR 87.
100 *Friary Holroyd and Healey's Breweries Ltd v Singleton* [1899] 2 Ch 261.
101 See, eg, *Cherkiss Enterprises Ltd v Depass* (1989) 26 JLR 196, Supreme Court, Jamaica.
102 *Buckingham Canal Co v Cartwright* (1879) 11 Ch D 421, at 434.
103 *Grimes (AP) Ltd v Grayshott Motor Co Ltd* (1967) 201 EG 586.
104 *Moss v Barton* (1866) LR 1 Eq 474.
105 *Op cit*, Hill and Redman, fn 55, [764].
106 *Weg Motors Ltd v Hales* [1961] 3 All ER 181.
107 *Beesley v Hallwood Estates Ltd* [1960] 2 All ER 314.

the lessee having complied with all of the terms of the lease,[108] any breach of covenant existing at the relevant date will disentitle the lessee from exercising the option, even though the breach may be trivial and the lessor has not complained of it.[109] On the other hand, past breaches, which have become 'spent', will not prevent exercise of the option, whether the covenants concerned were positive or negative.[110] Usually, an option to renew must be exercised by a written notice[111] given at or before a stated time before the termination of the lease;[112] if no time is stipulated for exercise of the option, it may be exercised so long as the relationship of landlord and tenant exists, even though the original lease has terminated.[113]

108 As in *Broadway Import and Export Ltd v Levy* (1996) 33 JLR 26, Supreme Court, Jamaica.
109 *West Country Cleaners (Falmouth) Ltd v Saly* [1966] 3 All ER 210; *Janwani v Goolat* (1993) High Court, Trinidad and Tobago, No S 1728 of 1992.
110 *Bass Holdings Ltd v Morton Music Ltd* [1987] 2 All ER 1001.
111 But where there is no stipulation for the option to be exercised in writing, an oral exercise will be valid: *Hadad v Elias* (1993) High Court, Trinidad and Tobago, No 97 of 1992.
112 *Biondi v Kirklington and Piccadilly Estates Ltd* [1947] 2 All ER 59.
113 *Moss v Barton* (1866) LR 1 Eq 474; *Coe v Bush* (1983) 20 JLR 99, Court of Appeal, Cayman Islands, in which Carey JA also held that where the lease is silent as to the mode of exercising an option to renew, it may be exercised either expressly or by conduct.

CHAPTER 6

ASSIGNMENT, TERMINATION OF LEASES AND DISTRESS

ASSIGNMENT OF LEASE AND REVERSION

Since a lease is a proprietary interest, it may be assigned by the lessee to another person. Similarly, the reversion is property in the hands of the lessor, and he may assign it. Where a lessee assigns the lease or the lessor assigns the reversion, the question arises as to whether the assignee:

(a) is entitled to the benefits of the covenants made in favour of the assignor; and
(b) is subject to the burdens of the covenants entered into by the assignor.

In other words, where T1 assigns his lease to T2, is T2 entitled to enforce the landlord's covenants (for example, where the landlord has covenanted to repair), and is T2 bound by the tenant's covenants (for example, where T1 has covenanted to pay rent)?

Similarly, where L1 assigns the reversion to L2, is L2 entitled to enforce the tenant's covenants, and is L2 bound by the landlord's covenants?

The principles may be summarised as follows: where there is *privity of contract* between the parties, both are bound. There is privity of contract between the original lessor and the original lessee. This relationship, created by the contract of lease itself, continues to subsist between lessor and lessee despite any assignments of their respective interests. Thus, if L1 and T1 are parties to a lease, and T1 later assigns the lease to T2, L1 remains liable to T1 and T1 remains liable to L1 on the covenants in the lease because there is privity of contract between them. Similarly, if L1 assigns the reversion to L2, L1 and T1 remain liable to one another on the covenants, because there is privity of contract between them.

Where there is merely *privity of estate* between the parties, only covenants that touch and concern the land are enforceable. Privity of estate 'describes the relationship between two parties who respectively hold the same estates as those created by the lease'. It arises 'when the relationship of landlord and tenant exists between them under the lease which contains the covenant in question'.[1] Thus, there will be privity of estate between the parties where:

(a) T1 (the original lessee) holds the lease and L1 (the original lessor) holds the reversion – that is, where there has been no assignment of the lease or the reversion, in which case, there is also privity of contract between T1 and L1;
(b) T2 (an assignee) holds the lease and L1 (the original lessor) holds the reversion;

---

1 Cheshire and Burn, *Modern Law of Real Property*, 14th edn, 1988, London: Butterworths, p 431.

DOI: 10.4324/9781003186946-6

(c) T1 (the original lessee) holds the lease and L2 (an assignee) holds the reversion; and
(d) T2 (an assignee) holds the lease and L2 (an assignee) holds the reversion.

Touching and concerning the land

A covenant 'touching and concerning' the land has been defined as one that 'affects the landlord in his normal capacity as landlord, or the tenant in his normal capacity as tenant'.[2] Examples of such covenants are:

(a) to pay rent;[3]
(b) to repair;[4]
(c) to insure the premises against fire;[5]
(d) not to assign or sublet without consent;[6]
(e) to renew the lease;[7]
(f) not to serve notice to quit for three years, unless the premises are required for the landlord's own occupation;[8]
(g) not to allow a third party, X, to participate in the running of a business on the premises;[9] and
(h) not to build on adjoining land so as to interfere with the enjoyment of the demised property.[10]

On the other hand, personal or collateral covenants do not touch and concern the land, since they are not directly relevant to the relationship of landlord and tenant. Examples are:

(a) a covenant by either party to pay a sum of money to the other[11] (unless inextricably bound up with some other covenant that touches and concerns the land);[12]
(b) a covenant entitling the tenant to purchase the reversion at any time during the lease[13] (because it affects the parties *qua* vendor and purchaser, not *qua* landlord and tenant); and
(c) a covenant by the landlord that he would not open another public house within half a mile of the demised premises (because it did not oblige the landlord to do or refrain from doing anything on the demised premises).[14]

---

2 *Op cit*, p 425.
3 *Hill v Booth* [1930] 1 KB 381.
4 *Williams v Earle* (1868) LR 3 QB 739.
5 *Vernon v Smith* (1821) 106 ER 1094.
6 *Goldstein v Sanders* [1915] 1 Ch 549.
7 *Weg Motors Ltd v Hales* [1960] 3 All ER 758.
8 *Breams Property Investment Co Ltd v Stroulgar* [1948] 1 All ER 460.
9 *Lewin v American and Colonial Distributors Ltd* [1945] 2 All ER 271.
10 *Ricketts v Enfield Churchwardens* [1909] 1 Ch 544.
11 *Re Hunter's Lease* [1942] 1 All ER 27.
12 *Moss Empires Ltd v Olympia Ltd* [1939] 3 All ER 460.
13 Cheshire and Burn, *Modern Law of Real Property*, 15th edn, 1994, London: Butterworths, p 448.
14 *Thomas v Hayward* (1869) LR 4 Ex 311.

Running of the benefits and burdens of covenants

At common law or under statutory provisions, the position now is that, in a legal lease, the benefits and burdens of covenants touching and concerning the land are enforceable not only by and against L1 and T1, but also by and against L2 and T2 and further assignees of the lease and the reversion, viz:

(a) under the rule in *Spencer's Case*,[15] the benefits of the landlord's covenants and the burdens of the tenant's covenants run with the lease;

(b) by ss 10 and 11 of the Conveyancing Act 1881 (UK), the benefits of the tenant's covenants and the burdens of the landlord's covenants 'go with' the reversion. These provisions were reproduced in ss 141 and 142 of the Law of Property Act 1925 (UK) and in most Commonwealth Caribbean jurisdictions.[16] Section 18 of Cap 61:01 (Guyana) contains a much shorter provision, which would appear to have the same effect. Sections 160 and 161 of Cap 236 (Barbados) are also of similar effect.

It has been held[17] that the effect of s 141 of the 1925 Act is that the assignee of the reversion is the only person entitled to sue the tenant for rent or for any breach of covenant, whether such rent accrued or such breach occurred before or after the assignment. Thus, for example, on 1 February 2000, L1 grants a ten-year lease to T1. On 1 April 2001, T1 assigns the lease to T2. On that date, T1 owes L1 arrears of rent amounting to $6,000. On 1 May 2001, L1 assigns the reversion to L2. T2 owes no arrears of rent. In this case, only L2 can sue T1 for the $6,000 rent, even though the obligation arose before L2 acquired the reversion, and there never was any privity of estate between L2 and T1.[18]

TERMINATION OF LEASES AND TENANCIES

A lease or tenancy may be terminated by:

(a) forfeiture;
(b) surrender;
(c) merger;
(d) effluxion of time;
(e) notice to quit; or
(f) frustration.

---

15 (1853) 77 ER 72. It should be noted, however, that assignees are liable and able to sue only if they hold the estate with which the covenant runs, so that such persons must he assignees and not sublessees or squatters Maudsley and Burn, *Land Law Cases and Materials*, 9th edn (2009), p 475.

16 See, for example, ss 10, 11 of Ch 138 (The Bahamas); ss 66, 67 of Cap 271 (St Kitts/Nevis); ss 12, 13 of Conveyancing Act 1973 (Jamaica); ss 66, 67 of Ch 56:01 (Trinidad and Tobago); ss 66, 67 of Cap 54:01 (Dominica); ss 10, 11 of Conveyancing Act 1983 (Bermuda); ss 65, 66 of Cap 220 (BVI); ss 19, 21 of Cap 189 (Belize).

17 *Re King* [1963] 1 All ER 781 (covenant to repair); *London and County Ltd v Wilfred Sportsman Ltd* [1970] 2 All ER 600 (covenant to pay rent).

18 See *Arlesford Trading Co Ltd v Servansingh* [1971] 3 All ER 1130.

Forfeiture

At common law, a distinction is drawn between breach of a condition[19] and breach of a covenant.[20] Where a condition in a lease is broken, the landlord is entitled to resume possession by re-entry upon the premises and the lease will be terminated, as the continuance of the lease has been made conditional on the tenant's carrying out his/her obligations. Where on the other hand, a covenant is broken, the landlord is entitled to re-enter only if the lease contains an express forfeiture clause. Whether a stipulation in a lease amounts to a condition or a covenant depends on the intention of the parties.[21] In practice, covenants are far more common than conditions.

It is, in any event, the usual practice for a lease to contain a forfeiture clause[22] reserving to the landlord the right of re-entry if the tenant is in breach of one or more of the covenants in the lease, and providing that, upon re-entry, the lease shall be forfeited. If there is a breach of covenant, the lease becomes voidable, in the sense that the landlord has the option whether to terminate it or not. It is only when the landlord does some unequivocal act that shows that he intends to terminate it that the lease will be avoided. Such an act may be:

(a) actual re-entry by the landlord; or
(b) the granting of a new lease to a third party; or
(c) the commencement of ejectment proceedings, in which the landlord seeks a possession order from the court.

An action for ejectment is the most usual method of forfeiting a lease in modern times; this is because, if force is used in re-entry, the landlord may be criminally liable for forcible entry.[23] Where ejectment proceedings are commenced, the forfeiture does not become final until the court grants a possession order. Before then, the tenant has a right to seek relief against forfeiture, which, if granted, will re-establish the lease. In the meantime, the court may order the tenant to pay to the landlord an amount as '*mesne* profits' (where the landlord's action is successful) or rent (where the tenant succeeds in obtaining relief).[24]

---

19 That is, where the lease is granted, for instance, 'on condition that' or 'provided always that' certain things are done or are not done. In such a case, the continuance of the lease is made conditional on the tenant performing his obligations.

20 For example, where 'the tenant hereby covenants with the landlord as follows'.

21 *Doe d Henniker v Watt* (1828) 8 B & C 308.

22 For example, 'If any part of the said rent shall be in arrears for 21 days, whether lawfully demanded or not, the lessor or his assigns may re-enter upon the said premises, and immediately thereupon the said term shall absolutely determine'. See *Davidson v Ward* (2009) High Court, Trinidad and Tobago, No 1397 of 2000, *per* Rampersad J.

23 Forcible Entry Acts 1381–1623; Forcible and Clandestine Entries Act, Cap 132 (Barbados). See *Duplessis v Moore* (1993) High Court, Barbados, No 1082 of 1988; *Patrick v Beverley Gardens Development Co Ltd* (1974) Court of Appeal, Jamaica, Civ Apps Nos 36 of 1972 and 21 of 1974. Further, such entry may be perilous for the landlord. In *R v Hussey* (1924) 18 Cr App R 160, a tenant who shot his landlady while she was trying to evict him forcibly, pursuant to an invalid notice to quit, was held not guilty of unlawful wounding.

24 See Megarry and Wade, *Law of Real Property*, 5th edn, 1984, London: Stevens, pp 672, 673.

Waiver of forfeiture

Where a landlord (a) knows of a breach of covenant that makes the lease liable to forfeiture, and (b) does some unequivocal act recognising the continued existence of the lease,[25] he/she is said to waive the forfeiture and he loses the right to terminate the lease. A merely passive attitude on the landlord's part does not amount to waiver,[26] nor is there waiver where the landlord refrains from taking action because he believes he will not be able to prove a suspected breach of covenant.[27] On the other hand, it is well established that there is waiver if the landlord, with knowledge of the breach, demands,[28] sues for[29] or accepts[30] rent falling due after the breach, notwithstanding that his/her acceptance is stated to be 'without prejudice',[31] or that an agent of the landlord accepted it by mistake.[32] There is also waiver where the landlord distrains for rent, whether due before or after the breach.[33]

A waiver of a breach of covenant extends only to the particular breach in question; it does not extend to future breaches. Where there is a continuing breach – for example, where there is breach of a repairing covenant – a demand for or acceptance of rent waives the forfeiture only up to the date of the demand or acceptance; it does not preclude the landlord from forfeiting the lease if the breach continues.[34]

Another established rule is that, once the landlord has shown his final decision to treat the lease as forfeited by commencing an ejectment action, a subsequent demand or acceptance of rent will not amount to waiver.[35] This principle was applied in a Trinidadian case, *Ramjattansingh v Khan*.[36] Here, R let a building to K for a five-year term from 1 December 1975, at a monthly rent of $400. K covenanted in the lease 'not to use or permit the demised premises or any part thereof to be used otherwise than for business purposes, such business to include only grocery, bar, poultry depot, and for residential purposes'. K later erected an extension to the building in the form of a shed, which he used as a pool room. This constituted a breach of the covenant. R knew of the breach in August 1976 and, in December 1976, he issued and served a writ claiming possession. There was evidence that, in December 1977, K paid and R accepted one month's rent. K argued that the acceptance of rent with knowledge of the breach operated as a waiver of R's right to forfeiture. Cross

---

25 *Matthews v Smallwood* [1910] 1 Ch 777, at 786.
26 *Perry v Davis* (1858) 140 ER 945.
27 *Chrisdell Ltd v Tickner* [1987] 2 EGLR 123.
28 *Segal Securities Ltd v Thoseby* [1963] 1 All ER 500; *Cayman Arms (1982) Ltd v English Shoppe Ltd* [1990–91] CILR 299, Grand Court, Cayman Islands.
29 *Dendy v Nicholl* (1858) 140 ER 1130.
30 *Central Estates (Belgravia) Ltd v Woolgar (No 2)* [1972] 3 All ER 610; *Bates v Sylvester* (1960) 3 WIR 136, Supreme Court, Appellate Jurisdiction, Trinidad and Tobago.
31 *Segal Securities Ltd v Thoseby* [1963] 1 All ER 500.
32 *Central Estates (Belgravia) Ltd v Woolgar (No 2)* [1972] 3 All ER 610.
33 *David v Williams* (1835) 57 ER 485.
34 See *op cit*, Megarry and Wade, fn 24, pp 674, 675. See also *Higgins v Texaco Bahamas Ltd* (1987) Supreme Court, The Bahamas, No 233 of 1986, *per* Georges CJ. Where there has been a waiver of a breach by demand or acceptance of rent after a 's 146 notice' has been served, and the breach is a continuing one, no further notice need be served where the landlord wishes to forfeit the lease at some time in the future: *Cayman Arms (1982) Ltd v English Shoppe Ltd* [1990–91] CILR 299, *per* Harre J, following *Greenwich LBC v Discreet Selling Estates Ltd* (1991) 81 P & CR 405.
35 *Civil Service Co-operative Society Ltd v McGrigor's Trustee* [1923] 2 Ch 347; *Grimwood v Moss* (1872) LR 7 CP 360.
36 (1977) High Court, Trinidad and Tobago, No 3210 of 1976.

J held that the issue and service of the writ for possession demonstrated clearly and unequivocally R's decision to treat the lease as forfeited, and the subsequent acceptance of rent did not affect it. He said:

> The question is, does the acceptance of rent after knowledge of breaches of the covenants constitute an unequivocal affirmation of the tenancy and therefore operate as a waiver, as the defendants maintain by the amended defence?
>
> In *Halsbury's Laws of England*,[37] it is stated that:
>
> > Probably also an absolute and unqualified demand of rent due after the cause of forfeiture, made by the landlord or his duly authorised agent, operates as a waiver. But if the landlord has already shown a final determination to take advantage of the forfeiture, for instance by commencing an action to recover possession, no subsequent act, whether receipt of rent, or distress, or otherwise will operate as a waiver.
>
> If further authority for this view were needed, it is to be found in the judgment of Lord Coleridge in *Evans v Enever*,[38] where the learned judge says:
>
> > But there is a series of cases which establish that if an action is brought for recovery of possession for breaches of covenants in the lease, that is an irrevocable election to determine the lease, and that no subsequent acts of the plaintiff can be relied on as qualifying that position.
>
> In his closing address, counsel for the defendants urged that even if the plaintiffs were entitled to re-enter, this was a proper case for the court to grant relief against the forfeiture. This relief has not been sought in the pleadings nor is there any evidence to warrant such an exercise of the court's power. For the reasons stated, there will be judgment for the plaintiffs for possession.

Forfeiture for non-payment of rent

The procedure for forfeiture for non-payment of rent differs from the procedure for forfeiture for breaches of other covenants. At common law, unless exempted by the terms of the lease, a landlord who intends to assert his right of re-entry is required before doing so to make a 'formal demand' for the rent due. A formal demand is made by the landlord, or his agent, demanding on the demised premises the exact sum due between sunrise and sunset on the day when it is payable.[39] Section 10 of the Common Law Procedure Act 1852 (UK) modified the position by providing that if (a) half a year's rent is in arrears, and (b) there are not sufficient chattels to be found on the premises to enable the landlord to recover the arrears due by levying distress, then the landlord is exempted from making a formal demand. In practice, a well-drawn lease will expressly exempt the landlord from the requirement of making a formal demand.[40]

---

37 3rd edn, Vol 23, [1397].
38 [1920] 2 KB 315, at 320.
39 Notes to *Duppa v Mayo* (1668) 1 Wms Sound 282, 287.
40 See, above, fn 22, and *Lewis v Bailey* (2009) High Court, St Vincent and the Grenadines, No 248 of 2007; *Amberly Ltd v National Parks Authority* (1996) High Court, Antigua and Barbuda, No 282 of 1996. This passage in the text was cited with approval by Rampersad J in *Davidson v Ward* (2009) High Court, Trinidad and Tobago, No 1397 of 2000, at paras 9, 10.

Relief against forfeiture

A tenant whose lease is being forfeited for non-payment of rent may apply for relief. The court's jurisdiction to grant relief has been explained thus:[41]

> The function of the court in exercising this equitable jurisdiction is to grant relief when all that is due for rent and costs has been paid up, and (in general) to disregard any other causes of complaint that the landlord may have against the tenant. The question is whether, provided all is paid up, the landlord will not have been fully compensated; and the view taken by the court is that if he gets the whole of his rent and costs, then he has got all that he is entitled to so far as rent is concerned, and extraneous matters of breach of covenant, and so forth, are, generally speaking, irrelevant.

In most cases, relief will be granted as a matter of course where the tenant pays the arrears of rent and costs, but the court must also be satisfied that it is just and equitable to grant it, and there may be circumstances in which, in the exercise of its discretion, the court will refuse relief: for example, where the tenant has been guilty of inordinate conduct, or where, in the meantime, the landlord has altered his position in the belief that the forfeiture was effective.[42] Moreover, relief may be granted on terms, for example, that the tenant should carry out outstanding repairs. The effect of a grant of relief is that the tenant holds under the terms of the original lease.

Where a lease is forfeited, any sublease is automatically destroyed,[43] but the sublessee has the same right to apply for relief against forfeiture as the tenant under the headlease. Similarly, a mortgagee of a leasehold interest holding under a subdemise or under a charge by way of legal mortgage may apply for relief. However, relief is not available to a squatter who has dispossessed the lessee.[44]

Forfeiture for breaches of other covenants

Before a lessor can proceed to forfeit a lease for breach of any covenant other than the covenant to pay rent, he must first serve on the tenant[45] a statutory notice:

(a) specifying the particular breach complained of; and
(b) if the breach is capable of remedy, requiring the lessee to remedy the breach; and
(c) requiring the lessee to make compensation in money for the breach.[46]

---

41 *Gill v Lewis* [1956] 1 All ER 844, at 853, *per* Jenkins LJ.
42 *Stanhope v Haworth* (1886) 3 TLR 34.
43 *Great Western Rly v Smith* (1876) 2 Ch D 235, at 253.
44 *Tickner v Buzzacott* [1965] 1 All ER 131.
45 *Pantin v Williams* (1995) High Court, Trinidad and Tobago, No 1379 of 1991, *per* Warner J. Where a lease has been assigned in breach of a covenant against assigning without consent, the notice must be served on the assignee and not on the original lessee; *Old Grovebury Manor Farm Ltd v W Seymour Plant Sales and Hire Ltd (No 2)* [1979] 3 All ER 504; *Caribbean Commercial Bank Ltd v Turney* (1990) High Court, Barbados, No 236 of 1987; *International Real Estate Consultants Ltd v Taurus Services Ltd* (2004) High Court, Trinidad and Tobago, No 1113 of 2003.
46 See, eg, s 15(1) of Cap 189 (Belize); s 16 of Ch 138 (The Bahamas); s 70 of Cap 271 (St Kitts/Nevis); s 17 of Conveyancing Act 1973 (Jamaica); s 70 of Cap 54:01 (Dominica); s 69 of Cap 220 (BVI); s 10(1) of Cap 61:01 (Guyana); s 167 of Cap 236 (Barbados); s 70 of Ch 56:01 (Trinidad and Tobago). See also s 56 of the Registered Land Law 1971 (Revised), (Cayman Islands); *Cayman Hotel and Golf Inc v Resort Gems Ltd* [1992–93] CILR 327. The corresponding passage in

If, within a reasonable time, the lessee fails to remedy the breach (if it is capable of remedy), and to pay reasonable compensation to the satisfaction of the lessor, the lessor may proceed with the forfeiture. The notice must be sufficiently precise to direct the tenant's attention to the particular matters of which the landlord complains, so that he may understand with reasonable certainty what he must do to remedy the situation.[47]

Manning J pointed out in the Antigua High Court in *Colonial Minerals Ltd v Joseph Dew & Son Ltd (No 1)*[48] that the object of these statutory provisions (which first appeared in s 14 of the Conveyancing Act 1881 (UK) and were reproduced in s 146 of the Law of Property Act 1925 (UK) and in equivalent legislation in Commonwealth Caribbean jurisdictions) was:

> clearly to curb landlords in insisting on their rights of re-entry and forfeiture accruing from breaches of covenants by tenants. In what seemed reasonably clear terms, it provided that, in all cases, the tenant should be given the opportunity of paying compensation for the breach, and that if such compensation was paid to the satisfaction of the lessor, there should be no re-entry and no forfeiture.

However, as Manning J pointed out, in subsequent cases the provision was interpreted unfavourably to tenants, in that the words 'requiring the lessee to make compensation in money for the breach' were interpreted as applying only where the landlord wanted compensation: thus, where the breach is incapable of remedy, the landlord can decide not to seek compensation, but to insist on forfeiture. In Manning J's words:[49]

> One learned judge asked, 'Why should the landlord ask for compensation if he doesn't want it?' The answer was that statute law said he must ask for compensation before insisting on his right of re-entry. The construction placed on the words dates back to *Lock v Pearce*,[50] and it is too late now for a court in the Colonies to construe them in any other way.

Reasonable time

Where a breach is capable of remedy (for example, where there is breach of a repairing covenant), three months is usually regarded as a 'reasonable time' for the tenant to comply with the notice;[51] but where the breach is incapable of remedy (for example, where there has been breach of a covenant against immoral user and a 'stigma' has attached to the premises), it has been held that the lessor may proceed to forfeit the lease after 14 days.[52]

In *Colonial Minerals Ltd v Joseph Dew & Son Ltd (No 2)*,[53] D Ltd granted a ten-year mining lease of a plantation to G, who later assigned the lease to C Ltd. The lease contained a term to the effect that, if the tenant at any time during the period of the

---

the text was cited with approval by Donaldson-Honeywell J in *John v McNeil* (2019) High Court, Trinidad and Tobago, No CV 2018–01115, paras 47, 48.

47 *Fletcher v Nokes* [1897] 1 Ch 271, at 274.
48 (1959) 2 OECSLR 243, at 246.
49 *Ibid.*
50 [1893] 2 Ch 271.
51 Hayton, *Megarry's Manual of the Law of Real Property*, 6th edn, 1982, London: Stevens, p 354.
52 *Scala House and District Property Co Ltd v Forbes* [1973] 3 All ER 308.
53 (1959) 2 OECSLR 248.

lease ceased to work the mine for 12 successive calendar months, the landlord should have the right to re-enter and forfeit the lease.

Manning J, in the lower court, held that there had been a breach of the covenant since the tenant had ceased to work the mine for 12 successive months, and the only issue remaining was whether a proper notice had been served within s 9(1) of the Law of Property Amendment Act, Ch 93 (Leeward Islands), which was an almost exact replica of s 14 of the Conveyancing Act 1881 and s 146 of the Law of Property Act 1925. In this case, a notice revoking C Ltd's 'licence, liberty and authority . . . to work [the] mine' was served on C Ltd on 9 September 1949, the same day as D Ltd re-entered. There was no request for compensation in the notice and no request to remedy the breach. Manning J held that, in accordance with earlier authorities, there was no need for a landlord to ask for compensation if he did not want it, and so there could be no objection to the lack of such a request in the instant case. Nor could there be any objection to the lack of any request to remedy the breach of covenant, as the breach in this case was incapable of remedy in so far as 'it was impossible for [C Ltd] to put the clock back and work the mine properly for the 12 months preceding 9 September 1949'.

On appeal by C Ltd, D Ltd put forward a different argument. D Ltd conceded that the notice of 9 September, standing alone, did not comply with s 9(1) and that it was only an intimation that D Ltd had already re-entered. However, D Ltd contended that a letter addressed to C Ltd, dated 26 April 1948, had given notice of D Ltd's intention to re-enter on 31 July 1948 if C Ltd did not commence working the mine before that date. The Court of Appeal held that the letter of 26 April did not constitute a proper notice within s 9(1) because the breach alleged in that letter was not the same as the breach alleged in the notice of 9 September. Perez CJ, delivering the judgment of the court, said:[54]

> The respondent . . . now seeks refuge in this expressed intention to re-enter if certain conditions were not fulfilled. In support of his argument counsel cited the case of *New River Co v Crumpton*.[55] There the defendant, a tenant to plaintiff under a lease containing a covenant to repair, was on 11 December 1914 served with a notice under the Conveyancing Act 1881 specifying the breach of the covenant to repair and the repairs required to be done. On 22 March 1916 the notice to repair was substantially uncomplied with and the plaintiff on that date brought an action for possession. It was held that as the only object of the notice under the Act was to inform the tenant what she was required to do, no new notice was necessary to support the action even though so long an interval as 12 months had elapsed between the expiry of the notice and the commencement of the action. In that case the breach was a continuing one, was clearly specified and was not subject to change, whereas in the present case the period of the breach envisaged by the covenant is peculiarly related to the date of the notice; the breach must in our view on the date of the notice have existed for 12 months last past; that is for the 12 months immediately preceding the notice. The breach alleged in the letter of 26 April 1948 is not the same as that alleged in the notice of 9 September 1949 and is not the same as that pleaded. The respondent's submission must therefore fail. To sustain the view submitted on behalf of the respondent would be to permit after a lapse of years the revival of a conditional notice to re-enter for a limited and specified breach of a non-continuing nature. This would be concordant neither with the spirit nor language of the statute, and, moreover, would be a violation of its plain meaning.

54 *Ibid*, at 252.
55 [1917] 1 KB 762.

Remediability of the breach

The question of whether a breach of covenant is capable of remedy is important since, if it is so capable, the statutory notice must require it to be remedied, otherwise the notice will be ineffective. There is no doubt that where a *positive* covenant, for example, a covenant to repair, has been broken, the breach is capable of remedy and so the notice must require the tenant to remedy the breach,[56] but where the covenant is *negative*, it may be difficult to decide whether the breach can be remedied. One view is that all breaches of negative covenants are incapable of remedy,[57] so that recovery of possession by the landlord would then depend solely on whether the court was willing to grant relief against forfeiture.[58] It has been held, for instance, that breach of a covenant against subletting without consent is a 'once-and-for-all' breach, which cannot be remedied, even by obtaining a surrender of the sublease from the subtenant,[59] and it has been held that breach of a covenant against immoral user cannot be remedied where the immoral user causes a 'stigma' to be attached to the premises (and, therefore, to the landlord's reputation), which cannot be erased.[60] On the other hand, where the immoral user is not by the tenant but by his subtenant, and the tenant takes immediate steps to forfeit the sublease, then the breach may apparently be regarded as capable of remedy.[61] It has been suggested that, in order to avoid such difficulties, the landlord in his statutory notice should require the tenant to remedy the breach 'if capable of remedy', so that the landlord may claim in his action either that the breach is incapable of remedy or, if it is capable of remedy, that it has not been remedied.[62]

Relief against forfeiture

As soon as the landlord has served his statutory notice, the tenant may apply to the court for relief against forfeiture. Statutory provisions in Belize[63] and Guyana,[64] which are modelled on s 146(2) of the Law of Property Act 1925, and in Barbados,[65] which are differently worded, but of similar effect, provide that the court may grant or refuse relief as, having regard to the conduct of the parties and all other circumstances, it thinks fit. The discretion given to the court is wide, and there are no firm rules upon which relief may be granted or refused,[66] although it has been held that, where the breach involves immoral user, relief will be granted only in rare cases.[67] If the court decides to grant relief, it may do so on such terms as it deems proper.

56 *Expert Clothing Service and Sales Ltd v Hillgate House Ltd* [1985] 2 All ER 998, at 1008, in which it was held that, where a tenant had committed a once-and-for-all breach of covenant by failing to carry out repairs by a certain date, the breach was capable of remedy, even after that date.
57 Although this view was strongly disapproved by Neuberger LJ in *Akici v LR Butlin Ltd* [2006] 1 WLR 201.
58 *Hoffmann v Fineberg* [1949] Ch 245, at 254, *per* Harman J.
59 *Scala House and District Property Co Ltd v Forbes* [1973] 3 All ER 308.
60 *Rugby School Governors v Tannahill* [1935] 1 KB 87.
61 *Glass v Kencakes Ltd* [1964] 3 All ER 807.
62 *Op cit*, Cheshire and Burn, fn 13, p 438.
63 Section 15(2) and (4) of Cap 189.
64 Section 10(2) and (4) of Cap 61:01.
65 Section 168(1) and (2) of Cap 236.
66 *Hyman v Rose* [1912] AC 623, at 631, *per* Lord Eldon LC.
67 *Central Estates (Belgravia) Ltd v Woolgar* [1971] 3 All ER 647, at 649.

Where relief is granted, the effect is as if the lease had never been forfeited.[68] If the court grants relief on terms, for example, where the tenant is ordered to carry out repairs within a certain period of time, and those terms are not observed, the order for relief is nullified, unless the court gives the tenant extra time to satisfy the terms.[69]

Under the statutes, a sublessee (including a mortgagee) may apply for relief against the forfeiture of the headlease for breach of any covenant, whether or not the tenant under the headlease can claim relief. If the court decides to grant relief, it may make an order vesting the whole or any part of the demised premises in the sublessee 'for the whole term of the lease or any less term' on such terms and conditions as it thinks fit, but the sublessee is not 'entitled to require a lease to be granted to him for any longer term than he had under his original sublease'. It has been held that the second of these two conflicting provisions prevails, and the court will not grant the sublessee a term longer than his sublease.[70] The court may impose conditions, such as one that the sublessee is to pay to the head landlord a higher rent than that required under the original sublease,[71] or that the sublessee is to make good the breaches of covenant in the headlease that caused the forfeiture, and to perform for the future the covenants in the forfeited lease.[72]

Surrender

Where a tenant surrenders his lease to his immediate landlord, the lease is extinguished, although the landlord will be bound by any sublease previously granted by the tenant.[73]

Surrender releases both landlord and tenant from all future obligations under the lease, but they remain liable for obligations already incurred.[74]

Surrender may be express or implied by law. Express surrender requires writing,[75] even where the lease or tenancy was created orally.

Surrender by operation of law occurs where the conduct of the parties shows an intention that the lease shall be yielded up, in circumstances in which it would be inequitable for either party to rely on the lack of an express surrender by deed or writing. Estoppel is thus the basis of this type of surrender. Examples are:

(a) where the tenant gives up possession of the premises by delivery of the key, and the landlord accepts it;[76]

---

68 *Scala House and District Property Co Ltd v Forbes* [1973] 3 All ER 308.
69 *Op cit*, Cheshire and Burn, fn 13, p 440.
70 *Ewart v Fryer* [1901] 1 Ch 499, at 515, *per* Romer LJ.
71 *Chatman Empire Theatre Ltd v Ultrans Ltd* [1961] 2 All ER 381.
72 *Ewart v Fryer* [1901] 1 Ch 499; *Gray v Bonsall* [1904] 1 KB 601, at 608.
73 *Schwab v McCarthy* (1976) 31 P & CR 196.
74 *Torminster Properties Ltd v Green* [1983] 2 All ER 457.
75 For example, under s 165(1)(a) of Cap 236 (Barbados); s 3 of the Statute of Frauds 1677 (applicable in Jamaica by virtue of s 41 of the Interpretation Act: see *Brady and Chen Ltd v Devon House Development Ltd* (2010) Court of Appeal, Jamaica, Civ App No 62 of 2009, *per* Smith JA). Under s 3 of the Landlord and Tenant Ordinance, Ch 27, No 16 (Trinidad and Tobago), surrender of a lease must be made 'by deed duly registered': see *Humphrey v Trinidad and Tobago National Petroleum Marketing Ltd* (2005) High Court, Trinidad and Tobago, No 601 of 1991.
76 *White v Brown* (1969) 13 WIR 523, Court of Appeal, Jamaica; *Banks v Arch* [2004–05] CILR 441, at 447 (Grand Court, Cayman Islands), *per* Sanderson J (Ag). In *Diego Martin Consumers Co-operative Society Ltd v Liverpool* (1997) High Court, Trinidad and Tobago, No 2752 of 1996,

(b) where it is agreed that the tenant will remain in possession rent-free, not as tenant, but as a licensee;[77]
(c) where the tenant has been absent from the premises for a long time and owes substantial arrears of rent – although mere abandonment will not in itself constitute surrender, for the landlord may wish the lease to continue;[78] and
(d) where the tenant accepts a fresh lease from the landlord, even though the new lease is for a shorter term than the original one.[79]

Merger

A lease and a reversion cannot be held by the same person at the same time. Accordingly, if they both become vested in the same person – for example, where the landlord conveys his fee simple to the tenant – the lease is said to be 'merged' into the fee simple and is destroyed.[80]

Effluxion of time

On expiry of the agreed period in a lease for a fixed term, the lease terminates automatically 'by effluxion of time'.[81] There is thus no need for notice to quit to be given by either party. The position has, however, been drastically affected by the rent restriction legislation, which gives a tenant a statutory right (amounting to a 'statutory tenancy' or a 'status of irremovability') to remain in possession of the premises after expiry of the contractual lease and subject to the same terms.[82]

Notice to quit

As has been seen,[83] a periodic tenancy is determinable by a proper notice to quit by either the landlord[84] or the tenant, subject, as in the case of a lease for a fixed term, to the application of the rent restriction legislation. In the absence of a valid notice to quit, a periodic tenancy will continue indefinitely, and will not expire at the end of a period.[85]

Warner J held that surrender could be implied from the fact that the tenant had given up possession of the premises, notwithstanding that he never handed over the keys to the landlord.

77 *Foster v Robinson* [1950] 2 All ER 342.

78 See *Preston Borough Council v Fairclough* (1982) The Times, 15 December, in which Griffiths LJ stated that the mere fact that the tenants of a house had vacated it while owing rent did not constitute a surrender by them of the tenancy; see also *Kumar v Ramcharitar* (2000) High Court, Trinidad and Tobago, No 3924 of 1989, *per* Archie J; *Madho v Jagroo* (2009) High Court, Trinidad and Tobago, No 2555 of 2003, *per* Boodoosingh J (Ag).

79 *Metcalfe v Boyce* [1927] 1 KB 758.

80 *Blackstone's Commentaries*, Vol 2, p 177.

81 It was held by the Jamaican Court of Appeal in *Scott v Lerner Shop Ltd* (1988) 25 JLR 219 that, in making a possession order on expiry of a lease by effluxion of time, the resident magistrate had a discretion to postpone the order for possession for a period (*eg*, 12 months) to give the tenant time to find alternative accommodation.

82 See, eg, Rent Restriction Act (Jamaica).

83 See pp 53, 54, above.

84 Notice to quit given by one co-owner of the property is sufficient to determine a tenancy: *Harrysingh v Ramgoolam* (1984) High Court, Trinidad and Tobago, No 744 of 1978.

85 *Richards v Walker* (1982) 19 JLR 236, Court of Appeal, Jamaica.

The rules relating to notice to quit may be summarised thus.

(a) A notice to quit must be unconditional, in the sense that there must be 'plain, unambiguous words claiming to determine the existing tenancy at a certain time'.[86] Thus, for example, a notice by a tenant would be void if it stated his intention to quit the premises on a certain date 'unless I am unable to obtain accommodation elsewhere' by that date.[87]

(b) In the absence of agreement to the contrary,[88] a yearly tenancy is determinable by a half-year's notice expiring either on the last day of a year of the tenancy (that is, the day before the anniversary of the beginning of the year) or on the following day. This may be achieved by the following formula: 'at the expiration of the year of your tenancy which will expire next after the end of one half-year from the service of this notice'.[89]

(c) In the absence of agreement to the contrary, a weekly, monthly or quarterly tenancy is determinable by a full period's notice – that is, a weekly tenancy by one week's notice, a monthly tenancy by one month's notice, and a quarterly tenancy by a quarter's notice.[90]

(d) A notice to quit 'on or before' or 'by' a certain date is valid if given by the landlord,[91] but void if given by the tenant for, in the former case, the tenant can be in no doubt as to when he is required to leave, whereas, in the latter, the landlord is left in doubt as to when the tenant will leave.[92]

(e) In the case of a weekly tenancy, the notice need not be seven clear days. Thus, for example, a weekly tenancy commencing on a Wednesday can be terminated by a notice to quit given on or before one Wednesday to expire at midnight on the following Tuesday.[93]

(f) In the case of a monthly tenancy, the notice must expire at the end of a month of the tenancy. 'Month' means a calendar month; the notice must therefore expire on the corresponding day of the following month or, it seems, on the previous day[94] (for example, notice to quit given on 15 March must expire on 15 or 14 April). Where there is no corresponding day in the following month (for example, where notice to quit is given on 31 August), the notice will expire on the last day of that month (that is, 30 September).

The validity of a notice to quit in the case of a monthly tenancy was an issue in the Trinidadian case of *Pollonais v Gittens*.[95] Here, a monthly tenancy commenced on 3 April 1969. On 10 February 1973, the landlord (respondent) served a notice on the tenant to quit 'at the end of one full month which will expire on 9 March'. The

---

86 *Gardner v Ingram* (1889) 61 LT 729, at 730, *per* Lord Coleridge.
87 *Op cit*, Cheshire and Burn, fn 13, p 461.
88 See *Shirley Apartments Ltd v Rogers* (1987) Supreme Court, The Bahamas, No 198 of 1985, *per* Georges CJ.
89 See *op cit*, Megarry and Wade, fn 24, p 651.
90 *Ibid.*
91 *Dagger v Shepherd* [1946] KB 215; *Harrysingh v Ramgoolam* (1984) High Court, Trinidad and Tobago, No 744 of 1978; *Chang v Empire Flats Ltd* (2006) High Court, Trinidad and Tobago, No CV00364 of 2005, in which a notice that stated, 'If you are not prepared to pay this increased rent, you are required to vacate the apartment on or before 1st October 2005', was held valid (*per* Jones J).
92 Megarry and Wade, *Law of Real Property*, 6th edn, 2000, London: Sweet & Maxwell [14–073].
93 *Crate v Miller* [1947] KB 946.
94 *Ibid.*
95 (1975) Court of Appeal, Trinidad and Tobago, Mag App No 224 of 1974.

Court of Appeal held that the notice was invalid, because the date of expiry of the notice was not the end of a current period of the tenancy, which ran from the third of each month to the third of the following month. Rees JA explained:

> There has been a conflict of judicial opinion whether, in the case of a monthly or weekly tenancy, notice to quit must expire at the end of the current period, but the question is now well settled that, to determine a monthly tenancy, a month's notice expiring with a month of the tenancy is required. In *Simmonds v Crossley*,[96] a Divisional Court consisting of Swift and Acton JJ decided that in the case of a monthly tenancy it was not necessary for a notice to quit to expire at the end of a current period of the tenancy, but in the later case of *Queen's Club Garden Estates Ltd v Bignell*,[97] to which we were referred, Lush J, in a very careful judgment, analysed and examined the question in detail and rejected as incorrect the view expressed in the *Crossley* case. He said:[98]
>
>> I think the true view is that in any periodic tenancy, whether it be yearly, quarterly, monthly or weekly, the notice to quit must expire at the end of the current period.
>
> In *Precious v Reedie*,[99] Bailhache J supported the view of Lush J in giving the decision of the court. After referring to the *Crossley* case and the *Bignell* case, he said that they came to the conclusion that, to determine a monthly tenancy, a notice to quit must correspond in length with the period of the tenancy and must terminate on the date of the month on which the tenancy began, unless there was some agreement to the contrary.

On the other hand (for instance, in the case of a monthly tenancy), provided that the date of expiry of the notice to quit corresponds with the end of a current period of the tenancy, a notice served more than a month before the end of the period will be valid. In *Mohammed v Radoo*,[100] the tenancy commenced on the 11th of the month. On 22 July 2003, the landlord served the following notice on the tenant:

> Take notice that you are hereby required to quit and deliver up vacant possession of the premises situate at 6 Sagram Street, El Dorado, which you hold and occupy of me as a monthly tenant on 11 September 2003, or at the end of the next complete period of your tenancy which shall expire one month next after service of this notice upon you.

The tenant argued, citing *Pollonais v Gittens*, that the notice was bad, as it should have been served exactly one month prior to the date on which it took effect. The Court of Appeal of Trinidad and Tobago rejected that contention. As Mendonca JA explained:

> It is not in dispute that the tenancy . . . commenced on the 11th of the month, and it is also not disputed that the landlord, in order to determine the tenancy in this case, may give one month's notice either expiring on the 10th of the month or on the 11th of the month . . . Nowhere [in *Pollonais v Gittens*] is it stated that the notice to quit must be served exactly one month before it took effect . . . What the law requires is that the tenant must be given *at least* one month's notice to determine the tenancy, and not exactly one month.

---

96 [1922] 2 KB 95.
97 [1924] 1 KB 117.
98 *Ibid*, at 124.
99 [1924] All ER 573.
100 (2007) High Court, Trinidad and Tobago, Civ App No 73 of 2005. See also *Chang v Empire Flats Ltd* (2006) High Court, Trinidad and Tobago, No CV 00364 of 2005, in which a notice served on 30 August 2005, to expire on 1 October 2005, was held valid.

Another Trinidadian case in which the validity of a notice to quit was in issue is *Hernandez v Rewan*,[101] in which there was a monthly tenancy that ran from the first day of the month to the last, the rent being payable on the first day of each month. On 27 August 1998, the landlord served on the tenant a notice to quit dated 26 August 1998, in the following terms:

> Take notice that you are required to quit and deliver up to me or to whom I may appoint possession of the property situate at Adventist Street, Sangre Grande . . . which you hold of me as a monthly tenant on the 1st day of September 1998 or the next complete month of your tenancy which will expire next after the end of one month from the date of the service upon you of this notice.

Jamadar J held that the notice in effect contained two options: the first (with notice expiring on 1 September) was void, as less than a clear one month's notice had been given; but the second (with notice expiring after the end of one month from the date of service of the notice) was valid, as it followed a precedent established in *Precious v* Reedy[102] and described as a 'saving option', which was 'a standard alternative that saves a notice in the event that a first and specific option is for some reason invalid'.

In *Ramlal v Chong*,[103] McMillan JA emphasised that 'a notice to quit need not be served on a tenant personally. It may be served on a person constituted the agent of the tenant for the purpose of receiving the notice'. Thus, service made at the house of the tenant upon a person whose duty it would be to deliver the notice to the tenant was sufficient to sustain ejectment proceedings. Accordingly, service on a servant of the tenant at the latter's residence or on someone left in control of the premises would be sufficient. Similarly, in *HV Holdings Ltd v Jumadeen*,[104] Blackman J held that service of notice to quit on a member of the tenant's household – in this case, the tenant's common-law wife[105] – was sufficient, and the Court of Appeal upheld that decision.[106]

In *Williams v Colonial Life Insurance Company (Trinidad) Ltd*,[107] however, Alexander J explained that notice may be served on a person expressly appointed as agent to receive the notice (for example, where notice was received by the solicitor who was authorised to pay the rent for the tenant[108]), in which case, service on the agent is deemed to be service on the tenant, or the notice may be handed to a member of the tenant's household, such as his wife or servant, in which case, there is only a rebuttable presumption of service on the tenant. He explained:

> Apart from any question of agency, the fact that the notice has been delivered to the wife or servant of the tenant raises a strong presumption that it has reached him, especially if an explanation of the notice was given when it was delivered. The presumption can only be rebutted by proof that the notice did not come to the knowledge of the tenant at all.

101 (2007) High Court, Trinidad and Tobago, No CV 0084 of 2005.
102 [1924] 2 KB 149.
103 (1990) Court of Appeal, Trinidad and Tobago, Mag App No 107 of 1989.
104 (1988) High Court, Trinidad and Tobago, No S 2483 of 1986.
105 See also *H V Holdings Ltd v Hamid* (2013) High Court, Trinidad and Tobago, No 2009–03221, *per* Seepersad J.
106 Civ App No 93 of 1988.
107 (2008) High Court, Trinidad and Tobago, No S 359 of 1998.
108 *Doe d Prior v Ongley* (1850) 138 ER 11.

This approach had been taken in the earlier case of *McQuilkin v Duprey*.[109] In that case, the appellant carried on a dressmaking business in premises rented from the respondent. One P, on the respondent's directions, went to the premises to serve the appellant with a notice to quit. The appellant was absent, so he handed the notice to 'the lady in charge' of the premises. It was held by the Trinidad and Tobago Court of Appeal that there was a presumption of fact that the notice had come to the knowledge of the appellant, and since the presumption had not been rebutted, the notice would be deemed to have been duly served. In the words of McShine JA:[110]

> I am of the view that this notice was passed on. I think so because the *prima facie* inference in such a case as the instant one is that, being handed the notice, this lady in charge constituted the agent of the appellant, and that a responsible agent does what duty to his principal would seem to require. I do not put this as a rule of law but as a presumption of fact. Such a presumption can no doubt be rebutted by evidence of failure so to act on the part of the agent, but in this case this lady in charge was not called in rebuttal and the presumption remained.

The effect where one notice to quit is followed by another was in issue in *Lee Kin v Cumana Consumers Co-operative Society Ltd*.[111] In this case, the landlords served a valid notice to quit on the tenant on 30 March 1979. The tenant remained in possession, asking for two extensions of time, which were granted. Finally, on 20 March 1981, the landlords served a second notice to quit, requiring possession on or before 30 April 1981. When the tenant failed to vacate the premises, the landlords brought proceedings for possession. Collymore J, in the Trinidad and Tobago High Court, held that *Lowenthal v Vanhoute*[112] was authority for the proposition that, where a valid notice to quit has been given, a subsequent notice is of no effect unless it can be inferred from other circumstances that a new tenancy has been created after expiry of the first notice. An agreement to grant a new tenancy cannot be inferred from the fact that a second notice to quit was given; nor is the first notice waived by the second. In the instant case, no new tenancy had come into being; the tenant had merely been granted the indulgence of more time to find alternative accommodation. The clear inference from the parties' conduct was that the tenancy had been terminated by the first notice in 1979, and the second notice in March 1981 was therefore superfluous, as far as the termination of the tenancy was concerned; its only effect was to bring to the notice of the tenant that the landlords intended to pursue their right to possession by legal action, and the granting of the indulgence could not defeat that right.

Similarly, in a case from the British Virgin Islands, *Lettsome v Flanders*,[113] in which a valid notice to quit had been served, but the tenant remained in possession paying rent that was accepted by the landlord, Benjamin J held that the effect of the principle in *Lowenthal*[114] was that the acceptance of rent by the landlord subsequently to the notice did not detract from the effectiveness of the notice. He pointed out that, in *Clarke v Grant*,[115] Goddard LCJ had reasoned that 'if proper notice to quit

109 (1963) 6 WIR 122.
110 *Ibid*, at 127.
111 (1984) High Court, Trinidad and Tobago, No 2109 of 1981.
112 [1947] 1 All ER 16.
113 (1999) High Court, British Virgin Islands, No 46 of 1993.
114 [1947] 1 All ER 16.
115 [1949] 1 All ER 768, at 769.

has been given in respect of a periodic tenancy . . . the effect of the notice is to bring the tenancy to an end just as effectively as if there has been a term which has expired'. Therefore, the tenancy having been brought to an end by a notice to quit, a payment of rent after the termination of the tenancy would operate in favour of the tenant only if it could be shown that the parties intended that there should be a new tenancy.

Frustration

The question of the application of the doctrine of frustration to leaseholds is a problematic one. The orthodox view was that the doctrine could never apply to a lease because a lease is not merely a contract, but creates an interest in land that, once vested in the lessee, cannot be divested except by one of the methods described above. However, in *National Carriers Ltd v Panalpina Northern Ltd*,[116] the House of Lords accepted that the doctrine could apply to a lease on the same basis as frustration of a contract, although the occasions on which it would be applicable must be extremely rare. A majority of their Lordships in the *National Carriers* case took the view that a lease might be frustrated not only by physical catastrophe, such as where 'some vast convulsion of nature swallowed up the property altogether, or buried it in the depths of the sea',[117] but also by a supervening event so far beyond the contemplation of the parties that it would be unjust to enforce the lease. On the facts of the case itself, in which there was a ten-year lease of a warehouse, it was held that there was no frustration and rent remained payable by the tenant when the local authority closed the only access road to the warehouse, rendering it unusable for a 20-month period in the middle of the ten-year term, although a larger interruption might have frustrated the lease, the matter being treated as one of degree. Earlier cases are examples of leases not being frustrated. In *Cricklewood Property and Investment Trust Ltd v Leighton's Investment Trust Ltd*,[118] for instance, it was held that a building lease for 99 years from May 1936 was not frustrated and rent remained payable when wartime legislation prohibited building. Similarly, it has been held that the tenant remains liable for rent notwithstanding that a building on the demised land is destroyed by fire,[119] or by an enemy bomb,[120] or requisitioned by the government,[121] and it has been held that a covenant to repair imposes an absolute obligation on the covenantor, and he remains liable in damages for failure to carry out repairs, notwithstanding that he has been prevented from doing so by some extraneous cause, such as the requisitioning of the premises[122] or the refusal of the authorities to grant him a building licence.[123] It may be assumed, however, that, since the *National Carriers* case, the court may exceptionally treat any such circumstances as being so far beyond the contemplation of the parties as to give rise to frustration.

116 [1981] 1 All ER 161.
117 *Cricklewood Property and Investment Trust Ltd v Leighton's Investment Trust Ltd* [1945] AC 221, at 229, *per* Lord Simon.
118 *Ibid.*
119 *Matthey v Curling* [1922] 2 AC 180.
120 *Redmond v Dainton*[1920] 2 KB 256.
121 *Eyre v Johnson* [1946] 1 All ER 719.
122 *Smiley v Townshend* [1950] 1 All ER 530.
123 *Eyre v Johnson* [1946] 1 All ER 719.

DISTRESS

Distress is an ancient common law remedy, a survival of the feudal concept of tenure, which entitles a landlord, where rent is in arrears, to seize the tenant's goods and chattels found on the premises and to sell them in order to recover the amount of rent owed. Its great advantage is that it is a remedy of 'self-help', and enables the landlord to recover his rent speedily and without the necessity for court proceedings. The remedy is rarely exercised in England nowadays, but it is still sometimes invoked in Commonwealth Caribbean jurisdictions.[124] Distress for rent has been abolished in Jamaica.[125]

Time and place

The right to 'levy distress' (or to 'distrain') does not arise until rent is 'in arrears', which does not occur until the day after it falls due.[126] At common law, distress cannot be levied between sunset and sunrise, nor on a Sunday.[127]

The right to distrain is *prima facie* limited to goods found on the premises out of which the rent issues, but statutory provisions in some jurisdictions provide that, where the tenant has fraudulently or clandestinely removed his goods from the demised premises in order to prevent the landlord from distraining on them, they may be seized by the landlord wherever they are found.[128] Such a provision was in issue in *White v Brown*, a Jamaican case decided before distress for rent was abolished in that country.[129] Here, W rented a room from B on a monthly tenancy. B served W with a notice to quit, but W continued to occupy the room after expiry of the notice. B filed ejectment proceedings against W. W moved to new premises on 24 September 1965, handing B the key to the room on the same day. On 26 October 1965, B employed a bailiff to levy distress on W's furniture at her new residence, for arrears up to 28 September 1965. W brought an action against B for trespass consequent on illegal distress. B pleaded s 3 of the Landlord and Tenants Law, 1838 (Laws of Jamaica), which permitted a landlord to levy distress on chattels found on premises other than those out of which the rent issued, where the tenant had fraudulently

124 Particularly in Trinidad and Tobago, where ss 8 and 9 of the Landlord and Tenant Ordinance, Ch 27, No 16, give to landlords and tenants the same rights to levy distress and to replevy respectively as are given by the law of England in like cases: *Cornwall v Trincity Commercial Centre Ltd* (1996) High Court, Trinidad and Tobago, No 1437 of 1995, *per* Warner J; *Diego Martin Consumers Co-operative Society Ltd v Liverpool* (1997) High Court, Trinidad and Tobago, No 2752 of 1996, *per* Warner J; *Sealandaire Ltd v Paul* (1994) High Court, Trinidad and Tobago, No 169 of 1994, *per* Bharath J.

In St Vincent and The Grenadines, the recovery of rent by common law distress was abolished by s 3 of the Rent Recovery Ordinance, Ch 19, unless reserved by deed, although ss 4–8 provided a procedure for the attachment and sale of goods for arrears of rent. See *Re Hutchinson* (1992) High Court, St Vincent and The Grenadines, No 504 of 1991. See now ss 3–19 of the Rent Recovery Act, Cap 94.

125 By s 3 of the Law Reform (Landlords and Tenants) Act 1979.

126 *Dibble v Bowater* (1853) 118 ER 879.

127 *Werth v London and Westminster Loan Co* (1889) 5 TLR 521; *JJ Pharmacy Ltd v Parillon Investments Ltd* (1988) High Court, Trinidad and Tobago, No 1495 of 1988.

128 For example, s 19 of the Landlord and Tenant Ordinance, Ch 27, No 16 (Trinidad and Tobago); s 22(3) of the Landlord and Tenant Act, Cap 61:01 (Guyana). See also ss 16, 19 of the Landlord and Tenant Act, Cap 230 (Barbados).

129 (1969) 13 WIR 523.

or clandestinely removed his chattels in order to prevent the landlord from levying distress on them. The Jamaican Court of Appeal held that:

(a) the tenancy had been brought to an end when B accepted the key to the room on 24 September, and B's right to levy distress ceased at that moment;[130]
(b) there was no evidence that W's removal of her furniture to the new premises was fraudulent or clandestine or designed to elude distress, so B had no right to seize W's goods there.

B was therefore liable in damages for illegal distress.

The distrainor may enter the premises through an unlocked door,[131] and he may enter by unlocking a door or padlock with a key in the normal way,[132] but he may not break open an *outer* door,[133] nor may he enter through a closed window.[134] In another Jamaican case, *Thompson v Facey*,[135] F was the headlessee of a house of which T was landlord. The house consisted of four apartments, three of which were occupied by F, the fourth being sublet to E. When F fell into arrears with his rent, T decided to distrain upon F's goods. Being unable to enter through F's front door, T gained access to F's part of the building by first entering E's room through an unlocked door, then breaking the lock of the door connecting E's room with F's part of the building.

One of the issues in the case was whether T's entry into F's part of the premises was lawful. T contended that his entry was lawful, since the connecting door broken by him was an inner, not an outer door; the magistrate held that, although the door was inside the building, it was to be treated as an outer door because it in fact separated F's holding from E's. The Jamaican Court of Appeal held that the real test for determining whether a door is an outer door is whether it 'served the purpose of a protection against the outer world'. The door broken in this case did not serve that purpose: it 'served only to provide privacy as between the respective occupants of the rooms on either side thereof'. T's entry was, therefore, not unlawful. Watkins JA explained the position thus:[136]

> Was the levy illegal? This was of course the paramount question. 'An illegal distress is one which is wrongful at the very outset, that is to say, either where there was no right to distrain or where a wrongful act was committed at the beginning of the levy, invalidating all subsequent proceedings so as to render the distrainor a trespasser *ab initio*': *Halsbury's Laws of England*, 2nd edn, Vol 10, para 738. That learned author proceeded to give examples of illegal distress, among which the following are relevant:
>
> (a) when no rent is in arrear;
> (b) a distress made in an unlawful manner, as by breaking open an outer door.
>
> In the instant case, it was not challenged that rent was in arrear and, indeed, the single question was as to whether that door intervening between Miss Edwards' and Facey's respective abodes which was admittedly forcibly opened was indeed an *outer* door. The

130 See also *Reyes v Ali* (1998) High Court, Trinidad and Tobago, No 4278 of 1995, *per* Gobin J.
131 *Southam v Smout* [1963] 3 All ER 104.
132 *Atkin's Court Forms*, 2nd edn, Vol 15, London: Butterworths, p 207; *Romany v Guelmo* (1994) High Court, Trinidad and Tobago, No 1688 of 1991.
133 *American Concentrated Must Corp v Hendry* (1893) 62 LJQB 388.
134 *Nash v Lucas* (1867) LR 2 QB 590.
135 (1976) 14 JLR 158.
136 *Ibid*, at 160.

answer is to be determined not only by a consideration of the structure of the house but also by reference to a consideration of the policy and purpose behind the ancient and long-settled rule of law that a distrainor for rent may break an inner door but may not break open an outer door. In *American Concentrated Must Corporation v Hendry*,[137] the matter was the subject of extensive and learned analysis by Bowen LJ, who said:

> The doctrine of the inviolability of the outer doors of a house and its precinct has long been established by English law. The principle is one which carries us back in imagination to wilder times, when the outer door of a house, or the outer gates and enclosures of land, were an essential protection, not merely against fraud, but violence . . .
>
> All creditors and all aggrieved persons who respected the King's peace, the sheriff in a civil suit, and the landlord in pursuit of his private remedy for rent and services, were both of them held at bay by a bolted door or barred gate. To break open either was to deprive the owner of the protection against the outer world for his family, his goods and furniture and his cattle.

See, also, *Lee v Gransel*.[138] Applying this purpose of the ancient law to the facts of the instant case, could it be really asserted with any conviction that this intervening door served the purpose of a protection against the outer world for the respondent? The outer door to the area in his occupation was by way of a veranda which the landlord bailiff had tried but, having found barred and bolted, had left untouched. It was contended, however, that whilst that intervening door constituted an inner door looking at the house as a whole, it in fact constituted an outer door in relation to the area occupied by the respondent and this indeed was the ground on which the decision of the learned resident magistrate in his favour rested. 'For all practical purposes', he said, 'this was the plaintiff's outside door, for it separated his holding from that of the subtenant Vera Edwards.' With respect to the learned resident magistrate and to counsel at the Bar, this, it seems on the authorities, is not the test at all. First of all, the right of distress extends over all the demise out of which the rent issues. The entire house in the instant case formed a part of the relevant demise and not merely the portion in actual occupation by the respondent. Next, the real test is as to whether the door or other apparatus, whatever it may be, which has been broken or forcibly unbarred, served as a protection against the outer world. This intervening door served only to provide privacy as between the respective occupants of the rooms on either side thereof.

Distrainable goods

At common law, the basic rule is that all goods and chattels found on the premises out of which the rent issues are distrainable, whether they belong to the defaulting tenant or to a third party,[139] such as a lodger, but this power has been severely curtailed by:

(a) the concept of privileged goods; and
(b) statutory provisions designed to protect third parties from seizure of their chattels.

---

137 (1893) 62 LJQB 388, at 390.
138 [1558–1774] All ER Rep 468.
139 *Lyons v Elliott* (1876) 1 QBD 210; *Plantel Ltd v Manick* (1987) High Court, Trinidad and Tobago, No 2315 of 1987; *Cornwall v Trincity Commercial Centre Ltd* (1996) High Court, Trinidad and Tobago, No 1437 of 1995.

It has also been held in Trinidad and Tobago that a chattel house is not distrainable, on the basis that chattel houses are so fixed to the land as to form part of the land during the period of tenancy. The position was explained by Wooding CJ in *Doolan v Ramlakan*,[140] following his earlier decision in *Baptiste v Supersad*,[141] as follows:

> It is a long established practice in this country that, if a house is let to a tenant who gets into arrear with his rent, the landlord distrains the tenant's furniture if the tenancy is of a house, but if building land is let to a tenant who is likewise in arrear, he distrains or purports to distrain the building of the tenant standing thereon. How this practice began it is difficult to say, but it certainly has become established. However, as the landlord discovered in the case to which I referred, the practice is wrong and indefensible in law. The mistaken notion that it is the right thing to do should therefore be removed from the minds of landlords and bailiffs as speedily as possible. So although it does not arise in this case . . . we have gone out of our way to call attention to the law on the point so that not only tenants, landlords and bailiffs may be guided by what is really no more than a restatement of the law of distress, but also the attention of those who administer the courts will be directed accordingly.

Privileged goods

The list of privileged goods is derived partly from the common law and partly from statute. Examples are:

(a) things in actual use;
(b) things delivered to a person by way of his trade or business, such as cloth handed to a tailor to be made into a dress;[142]
(c) wearing apparel and bedding of the tenant or his family up to a certain value;[143]
(d) tools and implements of the tenant's trade up to a certain value; and
(e) machinery belonging to a third party that is on an agricultural holding under a contract of hire.[144]

Third parties' goods

Statutory provisions in some jurisdictions have given to third parties, whose goods are found on the demised premises, a means of avoiding their seizure. These statutes[145] provide that a subtenant or lodger, or any other person not being a tenant

140 (1967) 12 WIR 146, at 148.
141 (1967) 12 WIR 140.
142 *Simpson v Hartopp* [1558–1774] All ER Rep 453. In *Cornwall v Trincity Commercial Centre Ltd* (1996) High Court, Trinidad and Tobago, No 1437 of 1995, Warner J held that musical equipment hired from the plaintiff by the tenant who operated a discotheque on the premises was privileged under this head, since the equipment had been delivered to the tenant for use in his business of providing music for dancing.
143 Section 35(a) of Cap 189 (Belize); s 14(a) of Cap 61:01 (Guyana); s 78 of Ch 54 (The Bahamas).
144 Section 14(b) of Cap 61:01 (Guyana); s 35(b) of Cap 189 (Belize).
145 See, eg, s 44 of Cap 189 (Belize); s 36 of Cap 61:01 (Guyana); cf s 27 of Ch 27, No 16 (Trinidad and Tobago).

of the premises and not having a beneficial interest in the tenancy, may serve a notice on the landlord declaring that:

(a) the tenant has no property in the goods;
(b) the goods are not goods excepted by the statute;
(c) so much rent (if any) is due from him to the tenant;
(d) future instalments of rent will become due on stated days; and
(e) he will pay such rent to the landlord.

With this notice, the third party must send an inventory of his goods. If the landlord levies distress on the third party's goods after receipt of the notice and inventory, he will be guilty of illegal distress, and the third party may apply to the court for replevin (that is, the restoration of his goods).

Procedure for levying distress

Statutory provisions govern the procedure for levying distress. For instance, s 29 of Cap 153 (Belize)[146] provides that, when any rent not exceeding $3,600 becomes due and the tenant remains in default of payment for seven days thereafter, the landlord may apply to a magistrate for a distress warrant. The magistrate may then issue a warrant authorising a police officer or bailiff to enter the premises, if necessary by force, between 8 am and 4 pm, and to distrain the goods found therein, subject to any privilege from distress at common law or under the statute. The landlord must then make out and leave with the tenant an inventory of the goods distrained.[147] The goods may be set up for sale by public auction five days after the distress, unless the tenant, before the sale, serves the bailiff with a notice that he desires to replevy the goods and deposits the amount of the rent due and $25 as security for costs.

Impounding

Impounding is the act of keeping custody of goods in a secure place or enclosure, which may be on the demised premises or elsewhere, after they have been seized.[148] The distrainor must not use the goods impounded, since he holds them merely as a pledge, and he is answerable for the condition of the pound, so that if the goods are stolen or damaged, he will be liable.[149] The effect of impounding is that the goods are placed in the custody of the law. Any person who removes them from the pound without the distrainor's consent, and with knowledge of the impounding, commits the tort of pound breach, and is liable for 'treble damages' – that is, for three times

146 Cf ss 22–24 of Cap 61:01 (Guyana).
147 It has also been pointed out that, at common law, the distrainor, on completion of the seizure, is required to make an inventory of the goods intended to be included in the distress, and to give notice of the distress to the tenant. See *JJ Pharmacy Ltd v Parillon Investments Ltd* (1988) High Court, Trinidad and Tobago, No 1495 of 1988. In Trinidad and Tobago, a bailiff who levies distress must deliver to the tenant a notice of the distress, including an inventory and a statement of authorised charges; the goods cannot be sold until this has been done: *Diego Martin Consumers Co-operative Society Ltd v Liverpool* (1997) High Court, Trinidad and Tobago, No 2752 of 1996, *per* Warner J.
148 *Op cit, Atkin's*, fn 132, p 208; Daniel, *Law of Distress for Rent*, 7th edn, 1960, London: Estates Gazette, p 65.
149 *Ibid*, Daniel, p 65.

the value of the goods removed – even where the distress itself was unlawful.[150] However, if the distrainor himself takes the goods out of the pound for the purpose of using them unlawfully, the owner is entitled to retake possession from the distrainor without being liable for pound breach.[151]

Pound breach must be distinguished from 'rescue', which is the removal of distrained goods without the distrainor's consent *after seizure but before impounding.* If the distress was illegal, and impounding has not yet taken place, the owner may lawfully rescue the goods;[152] otherwise, rescue is a tort giving rise to a claim for treble damages, as in the case of pound breach.[153]

Replevin

Replevin is the remedy whereby a tenant may recover possession of goods that have been illegally distrained. The process was explained by Bharath J, in the Trinidad and Tobago High Court, in *Sealandaire Ltd v Paul,* thus:[154]

> This type of action, where an illegal distress is alleged and a claim is made for restoration of the goods, is known as an action in replevin, the procedure for which is set out in s 10 of the Landlord and Tenant Ordinance, Ch 27, No 16. That section provides, on complaint to the magistrate for the district, for security to be provided for the goods by means of a bond in double the value of the goods distrained before deliverance, and for returning the goods and chattels and prosecuting a suit for illegal distress without delay in the Supreme Court.

The remedy thus consists of two parts:

(1) the replevy, by which the tenant obtains redelivery of the goods; and
(2) the action of replevin, in which the validity or otherwise of the distress is determined.[155]

Replevin is available only where the distress was illegal: not where it was merely excessive or irregular. Examples of illegality giving rise to replevin are: (a) where no rent was due; (b) where there was no demise at a fixed rent; and (c) as in *Sealandaire,*[156] in which the relationship of landlord and tenant had terminated before the distress was levied.

The tenant may exercise his remedy at any time, so long as the goods have not been sold;[157] although, as Warner J pointed out in *Cornwall v Trincity Commercial Centre Ltd,*[158] under s 11 of the Landlord and Tenant Ordinance of Trinidad and Tobago, the distrainor is empowered to sell the distrained goods if replevy is not made within five days, so the claimant must act promptly, otherwise he will be without remedy. Proceedings may be brought by the person whose goods have been seized, whether

150 *Cotsworth v Betison* (1696) 91 ER 965.
151 *Smith v Wright* (1861) 158 ER 338.
152 *Cotsworth v Betison* (1696) 91 ER 965.
153 See *Smith v Wright* (1861) 158 ER 338.
154 (1994) High Court, Trinidad and Tobago, No 169 of 1994.
155 *Op cit,* Daniel, fn 148, p 86.
156 *Ibid.*
157 See s 34 of Cap 189 (Belize); ss 23, 24 of Cap 230 (Barbados).
158 (1996) High Court, Trinidad and Tobago, No 1437 of 1995.

the tenant or a third party,[159] against either the bailiff who levied or the landlord, if he authorised the distress, or both.[160]

The action of replevin is commenced, in High Court actions, by issue of an ordinary claim form. If the claimant is successful, he will not be entitled to damages for the value of the goods if they were returned to him when the replevy was made (as would normally be the case), but he may recover general damages for annoyance and for injury to trade, credit and reputation.[161]

Illegal, excessive and irregular distress

A wrongful distress may be: (a) illegal; or (b) excessive; or (c) irregular.

Illegal distress occurs where there was no right of distress at all, for example, where the relationship of landlord and tenant had ceased to exist at the time of the distress,[162] or where goods were seized in order to recover a debt other than arrears of rent.[163] Distress will equally be illegal where, although there was a right of distress, a wrongful act was committed *in the course of the levy itself* (for example, where privileged goods are seized).[164]

Excessive distress occurs where more goods are seized than are reasonably necessary to satisfy the arrears of rent and proper charges of the distress.[165]

Irregular distress occurs where, although there was a right of distress, a wrongful act was committed at some stage of the proceedings *subsequent to the seizure*[166] (for example, where the proper procedure for selling the distrained goods was not followed[167]).

The difference between the three types of wrongful distress is significant with respect to: (a) the persons against whom action can be brought; and (b) the damages available. Where distress is illegal, action should be brought against the bailiff

159 *Fenton v Logan* (1833) 131 ER 767.
160 *Jones v Johnson* (1850) 155 ER 377.
161 *Smith v Enright* (1893) 63 LJQB 220.
162 As in *White v Brown* (1969) 13 WIR 523 (p 56, above); *Sealandaire Ltd v Paul* (1994) High Court, Trinidad and Tobago, No 169 of 1994; *McKenzie v Ward* (2000) High Court, Trinidad and Tobago, No 1272 of 1996; *Bristol v Ramoutar* (1996) High Court, Trinidad and Tobago, No 231 of 1993, in which Sealey J also held (following *Bridges v Smith* (1829) 130 ER 1119) that, where a landlord brings ejectment proceedings, he thereby treats the tenant as a trespasser, and the landlord no longer has any right to distrain, although he may have a right to claim for *mesne* profits in an action in trespass; nor is the effect of the commencement of ejectment proceedings nullified by the subsequent withdrawal of the proceedings. However, s 16 of the Landlord and Tenant Act, Ch 27, No 16 provides an exception to the rule that a landlord may not levy distress after the determination of a lease or tenancy; the section provides a right to distrain after the determination of (i) a lease for life or lives, (ii) a tenancy for years, and (iii) a tenancy at will: see *Antoine v Almandoz Tobago Ltd* (2010) High Court, Trinidad and Tobago, No 838 of 2007 (tenant holding over after expiry of lease with landlord's consent held a tenant at will, so landlord entitled to distrain).
163 *Alexander v Maritime Leasing Co Ltd* (2009) High Court, Trinidad and Tobago, No 2235 of 2006.
164 *Op cit*, Daniel, fn 148, p 80; *op cit, Atkin's*, fn 132, Vol 15, p 213.
165 *Carter v Carter* (1829) 130 ER 1118. However, it has been held that an excessive levy will give rise to a cause of action only where the value of the goods seized was out of all proportion to the amount of rent actually due: *Thompson v Facey* (1976) 14 JLR 158; *Hernandez v Rewan* (2007) High Court, Trinidad and Tobago, No CV 00084 of 2005. The above passage in the text together with this footnote were cited with approval by Boodoosingh J in *Garner & Garner Ltd v Chootoo* (2013) High Court, Trinidad and Tobago, No CV 2010–03244.
166 *Op cit, Atkin's*, fn 132.
167 See, eg, *Banks v Arch* [2004–05] CILR 441 (Grand Court, Cayman Islands) (distrainor failed to take inventory, contrary to Landlord and Tenant Law (1998 Rev), s 21).

who actually committed the illegal act, not against the landlord, unless the latter expressly authorised or ratified it.[168] Damages obtainable for illegal distress extend to the full value of the goods removed and sold, with no deduction for the rent owed,[169] although the landlord can counterclaim for arrears of rent.[170] Where distress is excessive, action may be brought against the landlord or the bailiff.[171] The measure of damages for excessive distress is the value of the goods wrongfully seized, less the arrears of rent and the costs of the distress.[172] Where the excess goods seized have not been sold, so that the tenant has suffered no actual damage, he will recover only nominal damages,[173] though he will be entitled to recover for any consequential losses suffered, such as for the loss of use of the goods taken in excess of the permitted distress.[174] In the case of irregular distress, action may be brought against either the landlord, or the bailiff, or both.[175] The tenant may recover only for any special damage sustained.[176]

Action for double value

Where (a) no rent was owed at the time of the distress, and (b) the distrainor has sold the goods, the owner may recover against the distrainor double the value of the goods distrained and the full costs of the action.[177]

Injunction

Where a tenant alleges wrongful distress, or where he anticipates that a wrongful distress will take place, he may obtain an interlocutory injunction to restrain the distress until the matter can be brought to trial,[178] but the court will usually grant an injunction only on the terms that the tenant pay into court the full arrears of rent.

TENANT'S RIGHT TO FIXTURES

At common law, the maxim *quicquid plantatur solo, solo cedit* ('whatever is attached to the soil becomes part of the soil') applies, so that any fixture attached by a tenant during his tenancy *prima facie* belongs to the landlord.[179] However, it has long been established that, as an exception to this rule, a tenant is entitled to remove any

168 *Lewis v Read* (1845) 153 ER 350. There was ratification by the landlord in *Hernandez v Rewan* (2007) High Court, Trinidad and Tobago, No CV00084 of 2005 (unreported).
169 *Attack v Bramwell* (1863) 122 ER 196.
170 *Op cit*, Daniel, fn 148, p 81.
171 *Megson v Mapleton* (1884) 49 LT 744.
172 See *Poggott v Birtles* (1836) 150 ER 507.
173 *Chandler v Doulton* (1865) 34 LJ Ex 89.
174 *Antoine v Almandoz Tobago Ltd*, above, fn 162.
175 *Haseler v Lemoynes* (1858) 141 ER 214.
176 *Plasycoed Collieries Co v Partridge* [1912] 2 KB 345. See also Landlord and Tenant Ordinance (Trinidad and Tobago), s 25; *Hernandez v Rewan*, above.
177 *Op cit*, Daniel, fn 148, p 82; s 5 of Ch 164 (The Bahamas); s 36 of Cap 189 (Belize); s 32 of Cap 230 (Barbados).
178 *Op cit*, Daniel, fn 148.
179 *Holland v Hodgson* (1872) LR 7 CP 328; *Moonan v Moonan* (1988) Court of Appeal, Trinidad and Tobago, Mag App No 12 of 1987. See pp 10–13, above.

trade,[180] ornamental or domestic fixtures attached by him; these are classified as 'tenant's fixtures'.[181] Trade fixtures are those items that have been affixed for the purpose of carrying on a particular trade: examples are fixed engines and boilers; a shed for making varnish; the fittings of a public house or bar; shrubs planted by a market gardener; and gasoline pumps installed at a petrol station.[182] Ornamental and domestic fixtures are those items that have been attached to a house 'for the sake either of ornament or convenience': for example, air conditioning units, mirrors, kitchen stoves and window blinds; fixtures that are in the nature of a permanent improvement to the house and which cannot be removed without causing substantial damage – such as a conservatory connected by a door to one of the living rooms – are not removable as ornamental or domestic fixtures.[183]

At common law, the tenant's right to remove trade, ornamental and domestic fixtures must be exercised during the tenancy (including a statutory tenancy), otherwise they become a gift to the landlord.[184] However, there are at least three exceptions to this rule, viz:

(a) a further period of grace is permitted for removal where the tenant continues in possession of the demised property after expiry of a fixed term 'under a reasonable supposition of consent on the part of the landlord';[185]
(b) where a periodic tenancy (for example, a weekly tenancy) or a tenancy at will is terminated by the landlord, the tenant is allowed a reasonable time after the expiration of the notice to quit to remove his fixtures;[186]
(c) the right of removal will continue where the landlord exercises a right of forfeiture and the tenant remains in possession for such a reasonable time as would enable him to remove his fixtures.[187]

In some jurisdictions, the common law principles regarding removal of fixtures by a tenant have been superseded by statutory rules; for instance, s 13 of Cap 189 (Belize) and s 15 of Cap 61:01 (Guyana) provide, in summary, as follows:

(a) the doctrine *quicquid plantatur solo, solo cedit* does not apply to tenant's fixtures, which are the property of and are removable by the tenant before or after the termination of the tenancy;
(b) in removing any fixture, the tenant must not do any avoidable damage to any part of the demised premises; and the tenant must immediately make good any unavoidable damage;
(c) before removing any fixture, the tenant must give one month's notice in writing to the landlord of his intention to remove it, and the landlord may, before expiry of the notice, elect by notice in writing to purchase such fixture

180 *Poole's Case* (1703) 91 ER 320.
181 In *Pro-Jam Ltd v Gibraltar Trust Ltd* (1997) 34 JLR 65, Supreme Court, Jamaica, Chester Orr J held that the following items were tenant's fixtures: air conditioning units; carpeting; burglar alarm system; mirrors; and company directory sign.
182 See *op cit*, Hayton, fn 51, p 21; *Smith v City Petroleum Co Ltd* [1940] 1 All ER 260.
183 See Woodfall, *Landlord and Tenant*, Vol 1, 28th edn, 1978, London: Sweet & Maxwell, [1557], [1558]; *op cit*, Hayton, fn 51, p 21.
184 *Lyde v Russel* (1830) 109 ER 834. See generally G Kodilinye [1987] Conv 253.
185 *Re Roberts, ex p Brook* (1878) 10 Ch D 100, at 109, *per* Thesiger LJ.
186 *Smith v City Petroleum Co Ltd* [1940] 1 All ER 260, at 262, followed in *Pro-Jam Ltd v Gibraltar Trust Ltd* (1997) 34 JLR 75, Supreme Court, Jamaica.
187 *Re Roberts, ex p Brook* (1878) 10 Ch D 100, at 109.

at the fair value thereof to an incoming tenant; any dispute about the valuation is to be adjudicated upon by the court.

Chattel houses

There has been much discussion in the Caribbean as to the legal consequences of a tenant's placing a chattel house on land (sometimes called a 'house spot') of which he is tenant.[188] In particular, the question may arise as to whether the chattel house, when placed on the land, remains a chattel, or whether it is to be regarded as a fixture.[189] As far as the law of landlord and tenant is concerned, the question would seem to be a sterile one, as, in any case, the tenant will be entitled to remove his chattel house at the end of the tenancy, either because it is deemed to be a chattel, or because it comes within the category of domestic fixtures which are removable before or at the expiration of the tenancy, so long as no damage is caused to the land.

188 See, eg, F Alexis, PK Menon and D White (eds), *Commonwealth Caribbean Legal Essays*, NJO Liverpool, pp 197–203; SCR McIntosh (1995) 5 Carib LR 32; M Gibson (1984) 10(3) Bulletin of Eastern Caribbean Affairs 56–87, pp 70–75; JM Glenn and C Toppin-Allahar (1997) 7 Carib LR 368–70; S Owusu, *Commonwealth Caribbean Land Law*, 2007, London: Routledge-Cavendish, Chapter 2.

189 See *Mitchell v Cowie* (1964) 7 WIR 118, Court of Appeal, Trinidad and Tobago, *per* Wooding CJ; *O'Brien Loans Ltd v Missick* [1977] 1 LRB 49, at 55–57, Court of Appeal, The Bahamas, *per* Georges JA, pp 7, 8, above. In *Ramkelawan v Alexander* (2005) Court of Appeal, Trinidad and Tobago, Civ App No 1 of 2002, Mendonca JA pointed out that it was not uncommon in Trinidad for a tenant of land to sell the chattel house standing on the land, without assigning the tenancy. It was held that the purchase of such a chattel house did not give the purchaser any interest in the land.

CHAPTER 7

CONDOMINIUM

Unlike in North America and elsewhere, condominium development in the Caribbean has not been brought about by the pressures of land shortages in the metropolitan areas or the desire for city living, but rather by the needs of the tourism industry. Thus, condominium structures in the Caribbean tend not to be high-rise, multistorey edifices used by local residents as their only or principal home, but relatively small two- or three-storey buildings sited near the sea and used by vacationing foreign residents. The condominium concept is intended to incorporate the economic advantages of co-operative apartment living with the economic and psychological advantages of home ownership, but, in the Caribbean, these aims are perhaps less important than the desire to enjoy or benefit from holiday accommodation in an idyllic location. In addition, condominium development in the Caribbean is often commercial – utilised by small businesses, such as beauty salons, boutiques and souvenir shops in resort areas.

CONDOMINIUM LEGISLATION

Although several Commonwealth Caribbean jurisdictions have introduced condominium legislation,[1] only the Bahamian Act has attracted significant case law. The account in this chapter will, therefore, focus primarily on the Law of Property and Conveyancing (Condominium) Act, Ch 139,[2] of The Bahamas, and the similarly drafted Condominium Act, Cap 224A, of Barbados. Both Acts are based substantially on the Model Act prepared in 1961 by the American Federal Housing Administration (FHA), which has been the model for much of the condominium legislation in the USA and Canada.

NATURE OF THE INTEREST OF THE UNIT OWNER

In *Bank of Nova Scotia v GLT Corporation Ltd*,[3] Smith J explained the genesis of the condominium concept in The Bahamas:

> Up until the coming into operation of the Law of Property and Conveyancing (Condominium) Act 1965, there was no provision in our law for the horizontal division-up of the fee simple estate in land. In other words, the fee simple estate in a part of a second or other storey of a building could not be in a totally different ownership than that of the ground floor of the same building. The Act was passed to make provision for the ownership in fee simple of units in multi-unit buildings, thus providing for horizontal division of a fee simple.

---

1 See, eg, Cap 60 (Grenada); Condominium Act 1986 (Bermuda); Registration (Strata Titles) Act 1973 Rev (Jamaica); Cap 227 (St Vincent).
2 Statute Law of the Bahamas, 2000.
3 (1986) Supreme Court, The Bahamas, No 112 of 1982.

DOI: 10.4324/9781003186946-7

And, in the words of Gonsalves-Sabola J in *Triple Ecstasy Ltd v Bay View Village Management Ltd*:[4]

> The Condominium Act, enacted in 1965, introduced in The Bahamas the condominium concept of ownership, whereby a building could be subdivided among several owners, each owner owning absolutely his compartmentalised unit, but yet having defined rights over other parts of the property, subject to his liability to make financial contributions towards the general maintenance of the condominium.

Under the Act, therefore, the purchaser of a condominium acquires a fee simple interest in the individual unit purchased, together with an individual share in the 'common property'. As with most condominium legislation (an exception being the Condominium Act 1981 of Trinidad and Tobago), Ch 139 and Cap 224A preclude the creation of a condominium on a leasehold, because of the disadvantage that, in a leasehold, the financial independence of individual unit owners from the other unit owners may be compromised. The legislation also contemplates the use of individual mortgages for each unit, and the separate alienability of each. The provision, in s 6(3) of Ch 139, to the effect that each unit together with the individual share in the common property 'shall for all purposes constitute an estate in real property' ('estate in land' in Cap 224A) seems to have been intended to allay any fears on the part of mortgagees as to the nature of the security. Finally, in *Southair (Bahamas) Ltd v Signet Bank (Bahamas) Ltd*,[5] Strachan J stated that a unit owner's fee simple estate has the maximum lifespan that the law permits, and survives the destruction of the building. This seems to settle, for The Bahamas at least, the vexed question as to whether a unit owner's interest is confined to the tangible parts of the property (the earth, bricks and plaster) inside its boundary, or whether it includes the air space within the boundary. In the case of the former, where a building containing units is destroyed by fire, earthquake, etc, the units will vanish; in the case of the latter, they will not be affected.

DEFINITION OF 'UNIT' AND 'COMMON PROPERTY'

'Unit' is defined in s 3 of Ch 139 as:

> a part of the property to which a declaration relates, intended for any type of independent use, and which includes one or more floors or parts thereof in a building, and which has direct access to a street or to common property leading to a street, and may include any appurtenance such as a balcony, terrace or patio or any other structure such as a garage, store or parking place which may be situated in some other part of the property.

The requirement in the section that each unit must have a direct exit to a public street or common area leading to a public street[6] is clearly intended to preclude the further subdividing of apartments into smaller units.

The Act defines 'common property' somewhat unhelpfully as 'so much of the property as is not contained within the boundaries of any unit'. The FHA Model

4 (1988–89) 1 Carib Comm LR 334, at 347.
5 (1993) Supreme Court, The Bahamas, No 112 of 1992.
6 See *Wineberg v Pro-De Ltd* (2007) Supreme Court, The Bahamas, No 264 of 2006.

Act is much more specific, and states that the common property is to include, *inter alia*: (a) the land on which the building is located; (b) all structural members, bearing walls, lobbies, roofs, halls, corridors, stairways, etc; (c) basements, yards, gardens, parking and storage space; (d) caretakers' lodgings; (e) central utilities such as power, water, air conditioning; and (f) all other parts of the property normally in common use.

It is possible that, should the need arise, reference will be made to the Model Act for the purpose of defining common property in The Bahamas. Preferably, however, each declaration should contain a comprehensive definition of 'common property'.

METHOD OF ESTABLISHING A CONDOMINIUM

The Act requires the following documents: (a) declaration; (b) bylaws; and (c) individual unit deeds.

The declaration

Section 4(1) of Ch 139 and Cap 224A specify what a declaration must contain. This includes:

(a) a description of the property sufficient to identify it and its location precisely;
(b) a description of the building (with number of storeys, basements, cellars and units), and the principal materials of which it is constructed;
(c) a description of every unit by reference to its floor area, limits, boundaries, etc;
(d) drawings and plans of the building;
(e) a statement of covenants, conditions and restrictions affecting the use of the units;
(f) the bylaws applicable to the property; and
(g) the method of amendment of the declaration by the unit owners.

In addition, a declaration may contain any other matters (not inconsistent with the Acts) that the person executing the instrument considers desirable.

In *Goodyear v Maynard*,[7] Henry J emphasised that the 'declaration is the foundation stone on which the entire legal edifice in the Act was built', and 'if the declaration is defective, the edifice must fall'.

In this case, the defendant refused to complete the purchase of a condominium apartment in Freeport, on the ground that the declaration failed to comply with s 4(1) of the Act. By that section, a declaration must provide for 'the methods . . . to be observed and the conditions to be fulfilled for the amendment of the declaration by the unit owners'. The plaintiff vendor argued that cl 10 of the declaration, which provided, *inter alia*, that the unit entitlement of each owner could be varied by the consents by deed of all of the unit owners affected, satisfied s 4(1)(1). Henry J did not accept this argument. He pointed out that a variation within cl 10 of unit

7 (1983) Supreme Court, The Bahamas, No 981 of 1982.

entitlements prescribed in the schedule to the declaration would certainly result in an amendment of the declaration *pro tanto*, but it did not provide for the amendment of any other portion of the declaration – but, were the provisions of s 4(1)(1) mandatory, so that failure to comply with them would render the declaration void? There was a conflict of authority on this question. In *Roberts Realty of The Bahamas Ltd v Innscinz*,[8] Brice CJ had held that although some of the particulars required by s 4(1) obviously had to 'be included in order to carry out the purpose and intention of the Act', others, like s 4(1)(1), were 'more in the nature of ancillary matters', so that a declaration need contain provisions for the amendment only of those particulars that were contemplated as being capable of amendment. Henry J disagreed with this view, and preferred the contrary view of da Costa J, in *GLT Corp Ltd v Bank of Nova Scotia*,[9] that the provisions of s 4(1)(1) were mandatory. Henry J pointed out that, under s 6(4), the provisions of the Act, and the declaration when recorded,[10] were binding on the owners of all units in the building. The Act clearly recognised the necessity to empower the unit owners in appropriate cases to amend the declaration, and, to this end, it was necessary for the declaration to contain a provision for such amendment. In the absence of any such provision, the declaration was void, the vendor was unable to show a good title, and the defendant was, therefore, entitled to refuse to complete.

Who must execute the declaration

Section 4(1) of Ch 139 provides that a declaration must be executed by 'the person or persons having the legal and equitable title in fee simple absolute to the property to which the declaration relates'. In other words, the developer of the condominium will be responsible for executing the declaration.

This requirement has been discussed in a number of cases, in which the courts have consistently held that the provisions relating to execution of the declaration are mandatory, and failure to abide by them will render the declaration and, therefore, the whole condominium scheme invalid. In *Johnson v Wallace*,[11] for instance, a declaration was held void on the ground that a prior mortgagee had not joined in its execution. Georges CJ accordingly set aside the conveyances of units to several purchasers on the ground that they had been based on a false assumption, common to vendor and purchaser, that the property being conveyed was, in fact, a condominium under the Act. These were instances of 'common mistake', in which 'equity would regard the contract as a nullity and set it aside notwithstanding that it has been executed; imposing terms if necessary to ensure justice between the parties'. It was also held that, on the assumption that the developer executed and registered a new declaration, it would be sufficient, in order to cure the defects in the purchasers' titles, to execute confirmatory conveyances reciting the facts that made such conveyances necessary.

8 No E 419 of 1972, cited in *Goodyear v Maynard* (1983) Supreme Court, The Bahamas, No 981 of 1982.
9 No E 56 of 1980, cited in *Goodyear v Maynard* (1983), above.
10 Also, when a declaration is recorded (ie, when it is filed in the Registry of Records), it constitutes constructive notice to subsequent purchasers and all other persons of the conditions and restrictions governing the condominium unit owners: *Hampton Ridge Condominium Association Ltd v Bannister* (2017) Supreme Court, The Bahamas, No 2016/CLE/gen/00406, *per* Charles J.
11 (1988–89) 1 Carib Comm LR 49. In *Grant v Francis* (1997) Supreme Court, The Bahamas, No 957 of 1996, Allen J held that a wife who was entitled to dower rights in her husband's property, to which a declaration related, was not 'a person having the legal and equitable title in fee simple absolute', and so a declaration executed without her concurrence was not void.

In *Glinton v Albacore Developments Ltd*,[12] the question arose as to whether it was permissible to include, in a new declaration, terms that were different from those contained in the original defective one. One argument was that, since the original declaration was void, it was to be treated as if it had never existed in law, so there was no reason why the new declaration should adhere to its terms. On the other hand, it could be argued that, although the original declaration was invalid, it in fact constituted representations made by the developer to prospective purchasers of the condominiums, and such purchasers agreed to buy units on the faith of those representations. Now that it had been discovered that the declaration was invalid, the developer was under a duty to convey in keeping with the representations then made. If the terms of the declaration were altered, this would amount to an alteration of the contractual terms, so that there was a danger of actions being brought against the developer by aggrieved purchasers. Georges CJ held that the original declaration constituted a contractual warranty that could not be varied, and the terms of the new declaration should, therefore, not differ from those in the old one, except where necessary to cure any defects.

Registration of the declaration

In Barbados, a declaration must be registered in the Condominium Land Register, which the Registrar of Titles is required to compile under s 12 of the Land Registration Act, Cap 229 (s 6 of Cap 224A). In The Bahamas, where there is no system of registration of title, the declaration must be lodged for recording at the Registry of Records (s 6(1) of Ch 139).

Unit entitlement

The declaration must contain a schedule stating the 'unit entitlement' of each unit in the scheme, expressed as a fraction or percentage of the aggregate estimated value of all of the units taken together, or of the aggregate floor area. This is a crucial factor in any condominium scheme because it determines: (a) the voting rights of each unit owner in the body corporate; and (b) the amount of contribution to the common expenses required of the unit owner (s 4(5) of Cap 224A; s 4(4) of Ch 139).

Drawings and plans

Section 4(1) and (6) of Cap 224A and s 5(1)–(3) of Ch 139 provide for a complete set of drawings and plans of the building to be annexed to the declaration. Such plans must be accompanied by a certificate of a qualified architect (and, under Cap 224A, must also be approved by the Chief Town Planner), certifying that the drawings are accurate. In *Sawyer v Family Guardian Insurance Co*,[13] the question arose as to whether an architect's certificate submitted subsequently to an original void declaration could be incorporated into a second valid declaration without express words of incorporation. Strachan J was able to answer this question in the affirmative, following *Roberts*

12 (1988) Supreme Court, The Bahamas, No 488 of 1988.
13 (1992) Supreme Court, The Bahamas, No 503B of 1992.

v Albacore Developments Ltd[14] and *Johnson v Wallace*.[15] Section 5(2) of Ch 139 also provides that where, at the date of recording of the declaration, the building is not complete, the architect's statement is to be lodged for record in the Registry upon completion[16] of the building and before any unit is conveyed. It was emphasised in *Sawyer* that the provisions of s 5(1) and (2) are mandatory. On the other hand, it is arguable that the provisions of s 4(1) and (6) of Cap 224A are not mandatory, as the Act speaks of the annexation of such plans 'as are deemed necessary or convenient'.

Existing mortgages

Section 6(2) of Ch 139 provides that where, before the first conveyance of any unit, there is in being any mortgage or charge affecting such unit, every such mortgage or charge must be satisfied, or the unit must be released from the incumbrance, or the mortgagee or chargee must join in the conveyance. In *Bank of Nova Scotia v GLT Ltd*,[17] an argument to the effect that the execution of a declaration of condominium had the effect of extinguishing an existing mortgage over the building was rejected by the court.

No partition of common property

The Acts provide that no share in the common property shall be disposed of, except as appurtenant to the unit to which it relates, and no unit owner may bring an action for partition of any interest in the common property. An exception to the latter is where the court orders the removal of the property from the provisions of the Act.[18]

Bylaws

In addition to the declaration, every condominium scheme must have bylaws providing for such matters as the composition of the board of management, procedure for election to and removal from the board, duties and powers of the board, method of calling meetings of unit owners, voting procedures and the duties of unit owners. Some of these rules may be duplicated in the declaration. In the absence of expressly drafted bylaws, those set out in the schedules to the Acts are deemed to apply.

THE BODY CORPORATE

Under s 13(1) of Cap 224A and s 13(1) and (2) of Ch 139, as from the date of the recording of the declaration, all of the owners from time to time of the units constitute a 'body corporate' in whom the operation of the property is vested. It is to be a non-profit-making body, having perpetual succession and a common seal, and capable of suing and being sued in its corporate name.[18a] Further, s 19 of both

14 (1988) Supreme Court, The Bahamas, No 267 of 1988.
15 (1988–89) 1 Carib Comm LR 49.
16 It is debatable whether 'completion' in s 5(2) includes substantial completion.
17 (1986) Supreme Court, The Bahamas, No 795 of 1982.
18 Section 7(2) of Ch 139; s 7(2) of Cap 224A.
18a See *The Landings Proprietors Unit Plan No 2/2007* v *Two Seas Holdings Ltd* (2019) High Court, St Lucia, No 2018/0263.

Acts removes personal liability of a unit owner for the acts or omissions of the body corporate, and limits the unit owner's liability for common expenses to the amount of contributions levied upon him from time to time. In many US jurisdictions, the equivalent body is not a company but an unincorporated association (for example, in the US Virgin Islands).

In *Cannes Resort (Freeport) Ltd v Gaudet*,[19] there was a conflict between the declaration, the bylaws and the provisions of the Act. Clause 22 of the declaration stated that 'the company reserves the right to appoint the majority of the directors of the body corporate until such time as all the units in the condominium have been sold', whereas the bylaws (as set out in the Schedule to the Act) gave the unit owners the sole power to elect the members of the board of directors. Before all of the condominium units had been sold, the unit owners held a meeting at which the defendants were duly elected to the board of the body corporate. Representatives of the company then sought the determination of the court as to whether the defendants were entitled to exercise the powers of the board to the exclusion of the company, notwithstanding cl 22 of the declaration. Isaac J held that there had been 'a thinly veiled attempt by the plaintiffs, in drafting clause 22 into the declaration, to control the property by controlling the board of management'. Clause 22 of the declaration could not be reconciled with the provisions of s 15(1)(a) of the Act (setting out the content and scope of the bylaws) without every unit owner being a member of Cannes Resort (Freeport) Ltd, and none of the unit owners were in fact members of the company. Since cl 22 was in contravention of s 15(1) of the Act, it was void, and it followed that the defendants had been validly elected to the board.

Duties of body corporate

The main duties of the body corporate under s 14 of Ch 139 and s 14 of Cap 224A are:

(a) to operate the property for the benefit of all unit owners and to be responsible for the enforcement of the bylaws;
(b) to keep the common property in good repair; and
(c) to insure the building to its replacement value against fire, hurricane and seawave.

Questions may arise as to the extent of the duty of a body corporate to enforce the bylaws against defaulting unit owners, in the light of the provisions of s 14(1) and s 23(3) of Ch 139 and Cap 224A. As stated above, s 14(1)(a) provides that the duties of the body corporate include responsibility for the enforcement of the bylaws, and s 23(3) provides that an action to enforce compliance with the bylaws 'shall be maintainable by the body corporate acting on behalf of the unit owners, or by an aggrieved unit owner'. The issue has not yet arisen in the courts of The Bahamas or Barbados, but there is a British Columbia case in which the question arose. In *Strachan v The Owners, Strata Corporation VR574*,[20] a unit owner applied under s 40 of the Condominium Act (BC) for an order requiring the strata corporation to enforce bylaws prohibiting the

19 (2004) Supreme Court, The Bahamas, No FP/CLS/206 of 2003. 'The company' in this case was the developer of the condominium scheme.
20 (1992) 28 RPR (3d) 279.

owners from making alterations to the exterior of the condominium structure without the written permission of the condominium council, and prohibiting use of strata lots for commercial purposes. Section 14 of the Condominium Act was similar in its terms to s 14 of the Bahamian and Barbadian Acts: 'The strata corporation is responsible for the enforcement of the bylaws, and the control, management and administration of the common property, etc.'. On the other hand, the British Columbia statute contained a provision, in s 40, which does not appear in the two Caribbean statutes:

> Where a strata corporation fails to fulfil an obligation under this Act or bylaws, the owner of a strata lot, or a registered mortgagee, may apply to the court for a mandatory injunction requiring the strata corporation to perform the obligation.

Blair J held that the strata corporation had an obligation to enforce its own bylaws (and, indeed, the defendant corporation admitted that it was under such a duty), and that failure to do so gave the petitioning lot owner the right to seek a mandatory injunction. It seems that, should the issue arise in The Bahamas or Barbados, the court should come to the same conclusion on the wording of s 14 of Ch 139 and Cap 224A for, despite the absence of any provision equivalent to s 40 of the British Columbia statute, s 23(3) of the Caribbean statutes, giving the aggrieved unit owner the right to enforce compliance with the bylaws, should ultimately have the same effect.

Section 17 of Ch 139 (and the similarly, but not identically, worded s 17 of Cap 224A) provides that 'the body corporate shall keep detailed and accurate records . . . of the receipts and expenditures arising from the operation of the property', and 'such records and any vouchers authorising any payments shall be available for inspection by any unit owner at all reasonable times'. Further, 'annual accounts duly audited by a qualified auditor shall be rendered by the body corporate to all unit owners at least once in every year'.

Appointment of administrator

In *Marcoplos v Silver Sands Sea Lodge Condominium Management Co*,[21] Isaacs J (Ag) held that the accounting provisions were mandatory, and any unit owner who claimed to have been denied access to the audited financial records concerning the management of the condominium had *locus standi* as 'a person having any interest in any unit' to apply to the court under s 27 of Ch 139 for an order appointing an administrator to take over the operation of the property from the body corporate.

In an Antiguan case, *Unit 301 South Point Ltd v The Proprietors, Condominium Plan C200800028 Rols Ltd*,[22] an application was made by unit owners seeking the appointment of an administrator under section 13 of the Registration of Condominium Titles Act, Cap. 376, which provides that the body corporate ('corporation', under the Act) or any person having an interest in a condominium lot may apply to the court for the appointment of an administrator, and the court may in its discretion make such appointment for a fixed or indefinite period on such terms and conditions as it thinks fit. The main complaint of the unit owners in this case was that the

21 (2004) Supreme Court, The Bahamas, No 2002/CLS/FP/231. See also *Cannes Resort (Freeport) Ltd v Gaudet*, above.

22 (2014) High Court, Antigua and Barbuda, No 2014/0070.

defendants could not fairly conduct the affairs of the body corporate because they owned the majority of the condominium units, and they were also operating, for their own benefit, a hotel on adjacent land. This allegedly amounted to a conflict of interest. In coming to his decision, Cottle J referred to *Lum v Strata Plan VR 519*[23], a Canadian case applying legislation similar to the Antiguan Act, where Harvey J set out some factors to be considered when the court is exercising its jurisdiction to appoint a condominium administrator. These included:

(a) whether there was a demonstrable inability to manage the body corporate ('strata corporation', under the Canadian legislation);
(b) whether substantial misconduct or mismanagement of the body corporate's affairs had been demonstrated;
(c) whether the appointment of an administrator was necessary to bring order to the body corporate's affairs;
(d) whether there was a struggle within the body corporate among competing groups such as to impede or prevent proper governance;
(e) where only the appointment of an administrator would produce a reasonable prospect of bringing to order the body corporate's affairs.

Cottle J took the view that 'the court should only interfere in the management of a condominium corporation where the majority uses its might to unfairly oppress the minority unit owners'. In the present case, the claimants had not alleged mismanagement on the part of the defendants, and 'the democratic government of the condominium corporation should not be overridden by the court except where absolutely necessary'; lastly, in declining to appoint an administrator, the learned judge was mindful of the inevitable expense involved in such appointment.

Duty to insure

The duty of the body corporate to insure the property was in issue in *Maychem v Lucayan Towers South Condominium Association*,[24] in which Strachan J rejected an argument to the effect that there was no mandatory duty to insure because the body corporate was empowered to decide by unanimous resolution not to do so. In Strachan J's view, the association had a duty, under s 14(1)(c), to insure against the specified risks for the full replacement value of the building, unless the unit owners by resolution decided otherwise.

A body corporate is invested by the statutes with certain powers of management, among which are the power to raise money to cover administrative expenses, employment of staff,[25] insurance premiums, capital improvements and renewals of common property; such amounts may be raised by levying contributions on the unit owners in proportion to their respective unit entitlements.

23 [2001] BC.J NO 641.
24 (1993) Supreme Court, The Bahamas, No 1581 of 1991.
25 In *Maillis v Town Court Ltd* [1989–90] 1 LRB 184, in which a unit owner had been robbed and shot by a masked bandit in the condominium car park, Gonsalves-Sabola J emphasised that the scope of the duty of care in the management of the condominium, including the provision of illumination and the employment of security personnel, was restricted by the financial resources made available to management through the contributions of the unit owners.

Default in payment of contributions

As Gonsalves-Sabola J pointed out in *Triple Ecstasy Ltd v Bay View Village Management Ltd*,[26] the success of the condominium idea depends on the punctual discharge by the unit owners of their financial obligations. To ensure this, the legislature has provided 'machinery for effectively protecting the rights of the unit holders against breach by any of them of these financial obligations'. Thus, where a unit owner is in default in payment of contributions levied by the body corporate for common expenses, the body corporate has two methods of recovery, which exist concurrently: (a) to bring an action for debt in respect of the amount owed (s 18(2) of Ch 139; s 18(2) of Cap 224A); and (b) to enforce a charge (s 21 of 139) or a lien (s 21 of Cap 224A) against the unit of the offender. In the *Triple Ecstasy* case, Gonsalves-Sabola J rejected an argument to the effect that the charge created by s 21 was equitable only, holding that the Act must be interpreted as providing for a legal charge, otherwise the body corporate would only be able to put up for sale an inferior interest, and this would defeat the purpose of the Act. Further, it is noteworthy that s 21(4) gives the body corporate the same powers of sale for the purpose of enforcing the charge as a mortgagee under the provisions of ss 21–23 of the Conveyancing and Law of Property Act, Ch 138.[27]

An issue that arose on similar legislation in the US Virgin Islands was whether the obligation to pay contributions (called 'common assessments') was independent of the condominium association's duty to repair and maintain the units and common areas; a further question was whether the condominium association had the authority to disconnect the water supply to recalcitrant unit owners who had failed to pay their assessments. In *Towers Condominium Association v Lawrence*,[28] the Territorial Court of the Virgin Islands held that the alleged breaches of duty by the association in failing to maintain the buildings, facilities and common areas of the condominium did not justify the unit owners' withholding of the common charges payable by them. Meyers J emphasised that:[29]

> Nowhere in the declaration, the bylaws or the Condominium Act is a unit owner authorised or permitted to withhold the payment of common assessments for any reason. This payment is mandatory, without any exceptions.

A unit owner's duty to pay assessment fees was conditional solely on his acquisition of title. Thus, a unit owner who was involved in a dispute with the association concerning its services and operations was not entitled to 'exert leverage in that controversy by withholding payment, but must seek other remedy'.[30] The obligation to pay assessments was independent of the association's obligation to carry out repairs, and it was further held, in this case, that the association had acted within the scope of its authority and was justified in disconnecting the water supply of delinquent unit owners, as the policy had been approved by the board of directors as a means of

26 (1988–89) 1 Carib Comm LR 344, at 347.
27 See p 000, below; *Edelweiss Chalets Condominium Association v Davis* (1998) Supreme Court, The Bahamas, No FP160 of 1997.
28 [1995] VIR 185; applied in *The Proprietors, Condominium Plan No 2/1989 v Trinity Investment Co Ltd* (2016) Court of Appeal, OECS (Antigua and Barbuda), Civ App No 2008/0009.
29 *Ibid*, at 188.
30 *Ibid*, at 189, citing *Forest Villas Condominium Association v Caneiro* (1992) 422 SE 2d 884 (Ga App 1992), at 886.

abating violations of the bylaws, and in order to prevent the disconnection of the entire complex by the water authority because of the refusal of a few unit owners to pay their assessments.

TERMINATION OF CONDOMINIUM SCHEME

Property may be removed from the Acts by an Order of the Supreme Court (under s 31(1) of Ch 139) or the High Court (under s 31(1) of Cap 224A), where the court is satisfied that either at least 90 per cent of the unit owners have resolved to terminate the scheme and all mortgagees have consented, or the building has been destroyed or damaged and is not to be reconstructed, or it is just and equitable to remove the property from the Act.

Upon dissolution, the building is deemed to be owned in common by all unit owners in undivided shares in the same proportions as they had originally been entitled to the common property.

CHAPTER 8

RESTRICTIVE COVENANTS

Freehold covenants – that is, covenants entered into by one freeholder in favour of another freeholder – are an important means of controlling the use of land. The majority of such covenants are restrictive in substance – for example, a covenant not to carry on any trade or business on the land, or a covenant not to build more than one dwelling house thereon; consequently, this topic is usually referred to as the law of 'restrictive covenants'.

Covenants, being promises made by deed, are contractual obligations that remain enforceable as between the original parties. The main difficulty is in determining whether: (a) the benefit of such a covenant has run to a successor-in-title of the covenantee; and (b) the burden has run to a successor-in-title of the covenantor. The basic problem may be illustrated as follows: V (covenantee) sells part of his land to P (covenantor), who covenants not to use the land other than for residential purposes. Later, V sells his retained land to X and P sells his land to Y. In what circumstances can X (the assignee of the covenantee) enforce the covenant against Y (the assignee of the covenantor)?

In this example, the covenantee was the vendor of land, and the covenantor the purchaser. This would be the usual position; however, the positions may be the reverse, viz, the vendor may be covenantor and the purchaser covenantee. Further, the parties may not be vendor and purchaser at all, but may have acquired their respective plots (Blackacre and Whiteacre) from a third person, or from two different persons; later, in order to preserve the value of Blackacre, the owner may agree to pay the owner of Whiteacre $50,000 in return for a covenant that Whiteacre should be used for residential purposes only. When the owner of Whiteacre enters into the covenant, the value of Whiteacre will depreciate, whilst the value of Blackacre will appreciate.

The position may thus be summarised by saying that:

(a) covenants usually involve a sale between covenantee and covenantor, but do not necessarily do so; and
(b) if a sale is involved, the vendor may be covenantee or covenantor, and the purchaser may be covenantor or covenantee.

In dealing with the running of the benefits and the burdens of covenants between freeholders, it is essential to bear in mind that common law and equity have different rules, and that there are always two main questions, as follows.

(a) Has the benefit of the covenant passed to the assignee of the covenantee?
(b) Has the burden of the covenant passed to the assignee of the covenantor?

For purposes of exposition, it is more convenient to deal with the passing of the burden before considering the passing of the benefit.

DOI: 10.4324/9781003186946-8

RUNNING OF THE BURDEN

The position at common law

It is well established that the burden of a covenant between freeholders does not run at common law. The position is different where leaseholds are concerned, as the burden of a covenant in a legal lease runs under the rule in *Spencer's Case*.[1]

The leading case that illustrates the proposition that the burden of a freehold covenant does not run at common law is *Austerberry v Oldham Corp*.[2] In this case, X conveyed the freehold of part of his land to trustees, who covenanted for themselves, their heirs and assigns, that they would form the piece of land into a road, and would forever afterwards keep it in repair. The road was duly made, and, later, X sold to the plaintiff the part of his land that ran along both sides of the road. The defendant corporation then took over the road from the trustees under statutory powers, and sought to make the plaintiff bear a share of the cost of maintaining the road for which frontagers were liable by statute. The plaintiff contended that the burden of the covenant to maintain the road had passed from the trustees to the defendant corporation, and that the latter was accordingly liable to bear the cost of maintaining the road. It was held that the plaintiff's argument failed, since the burden of a freehold covenant can never run with the land of the covenantor at common law.

It will be noticed that, in *Austerberry*, the covenant was *positive* – that is, it required the covenantor to do some positive act on the burdened land that would involve expenditure on the part of the covenantor. If the covenant had been *restrictive* (that is, negative in substance), then, as we shall see, the burden would have run in equity under the rule in *Tulk v Moxhay*.[3] Since the covenant was positive, however, the burden could not run either at common law or in equity.

The position in equity

In the leading case of *Tulk v Moxhay*, equity introduced what was then a revolutionary principle, to the effect that the burden of a *restrictive* covenant entered into by the owner of Whiteacre with the owner of neighbouring Blackacre imposes an equitable burden on Whiteacre that is enforceable against all successors-in-title, except for a *bona fide* purchaser for value of the legal estate in Whiteacre having no notice of the covenant. In other words, where the covenant is restrictive, the common law rule that the burden of a freehold covenant does not run with the burdened land is outflanked, and equity will enforce the covenant against successors in title by granting an injunction to restrain any breach. The rule in *Tulk v Moxhay* introduced a new right of property, since its effect was that a restrictive covenant was not only enforceable against the original covenantor as a contract, but also became an incumbrance on the land binding on successors-in-title of the covenantor.

---

1 See pp 78, 79, above.
2 (1885) 29 Ch D 750. The principle in *Austerberry* was followed in *E and GC Ltd v Bate* (1935) 79 LJ News 203, in which it was held that the burden of a covenant to construct a road did not pass to the devisee of the covenantor. See also *Half Moon Bay Ltd v Crown Eagle Hotels Ltd* (2002) 60 WIR 330.
3 (1848) 41 ER 1143.

The facts of *Tulk v Moxhay* were simple. In 1808, the plaintiff, who was owner in fee simple of a plot of vacant land in the centre of Leicester Square, London, as well as other land in the Square, sold the plot to one Elms, who covenanted for himself and his assigns that he and they would forever keep the plot in an open state, uncovered by any buildings. The plot passed by various conveyances into the hands of the defendant, who admitted that he had taken the land with notice of the covenant. He then proposed to erect buildings on the land. The plaintiff, who was still the owner of several adjacent houses, sought an injunction to restrain the threatened breach of covenant, and he succeeded. The basis of the decision was simply that the defendant had purchased the land with notice of the covenant, and a court of equity would not permit him to disregard it. It was contrary to conscience that a person should come to the land with notice of a covenant affecting it, and to act in a manner inconsistent with such covenant.

This principle was applied in several later cases,[4] but, at the end of the 19th century, there was a change of emphasis. By then, it had become clear that to rest the doctrine solely on the question whether the defendant had notice of the covenant or not would mean that a burden would be imposed on land without any corresponding interest in the plaintiff that required protection. It was at this point that, by analogy with the law of easements, the concept of dominancy and serviency emerged in the law of restrictive covenants; thus, in *Formby v Barker*,[5] it was established that equity would enforce a restrictive covenant against an assignee of the burdened land only if the covenant had been made for the protection of other land retained by the covenantee. In other words, there must be a dominant as well as a servient tenement; the covenant must touch and concern the dominant tenement of the covenantee; and the covenant must be intended to protect that land against certain uses of the servient tenement that would be detrimental to the enjoyment or value of the dominant tenement.

Requirements for the running of the burden in equity

The covenant must be negative in nature

The burden of a positive covenant – that is, one that involves expenditure of money by the owner of the burdened land, for example, a covenant to maintain a road or drains – does not run in equity: the covenant must be negative – for example, a covenant not to use a building for any trade or business. It should be noted that what is required is that the covenant must be negative in substance, not necessarily in form. For instance, the covenant in *Tulk v Moxhay* – to keep the land as an open space – was positive in form, but negative in substance (that is, it required the covenantor *not to build* on the land). Conversely, a covenant not to let premises fall into disrepair is negative in form, but positive in substance, as it requires expenditure on the part of the servient owner, and is therefore outside the rule.

The reason why equity will enforce only negative covenants against successors-in-title of the covenantor is that, where the covenant is negative, all the court needs to do is to issue an injunction restraining breach of the covenant; whereas, in the case of a

4 See, eg, *Luker v Dennis* (1877) 7 Ch D 227.
5 [1903] 2 Ch 539.

positive covenant, the court may be called upon to supervise the performance of the covenant – for example, to ensure that repairs are satisfactorily carried out under a covenant – something that courts of equity have always been reluctant to do.

The covenant must be made for the protection of other land retained by the covenantee

As we have seen, there must be a dominant land capable of deriving a benefit from the restriction on the use of the servient land. If, at the time the covenant was made, the covenantee retained no adjacent land capable of being protected by the covenant, the burden will not run to assignees of the covenantor, but will be enforceable only against the covenantor; in other words, it will be treated as a merely personal contract between covenantor and covenantee, and will not be an incumbrance on the covenantor's land. In *London CC v Allen*,[6] A, a builder, in return for permission to lay out a new street on his land, entered into a covenant with the council not to build on a plot that was located across the end of the proposed street. The plot was eventually conveyed to X, who built three houses on it, and mortgaged it to Y. The question was whether the covenant was binding on X and Y. It was held that it was not, since the council never had any land capable of being protected by the covenant, and the fact that X and Y had notice of the covenant was irrelevant. On the other hand, in *Re Gadd's Land Transfer*,[7] it was held that, in the circumstances of the particular case, the retention by the covenantee of a road leading to the servient tenement was sufficient to enable him to enforce a restrictive covenant against successors-in-title of the original covenantor.

There is an apparent exception to the rule that the covenantee must retain some land adjacent to the servient tenement. This exception concerns leaseholds. Where a restrictive covenant is contained in a lease, there will be no need to depend on the *Tulk v Moxhay* principle, as the lessor will be able to enforce it against assignees of the original lessee under the rule in *Spencer's Case* and the doctrine of privity of estate.[8] However, if the lessee grants a sublease, there will be no privity of estate between lessor and sublessee, so that any negative covenants in the lease will be enforceable against the sublessee only if the post-*Tulk v Moxhay* requirements are satisfied. With respect to the requirement of retention of adjacent land by the covenantee (the lessor), it seems that the lessor's reversion in the demised premises is sufficient to satisfy the requirement. There is no need for him to have retained any other land that could be called a dominant tenement.[9]

It must have been the common intention of the parties that the burden of the covenant should run with the covenantor's land

It is provided by statute in some jurisdictions that, unless a contrary intention appears, covenants relating to the covenantor's land are deemed to have been made by the covenantor on behalf of himself, his successors-in-title, and the persons deriving title

6 [1914] 3 KB 642.
7 [1966] Ch 56.
8 See pp 78, 79, above.
9 *Hall v Ewin* (1887) 37 Ch D 74. See also *Regent Oil Co v JA Gregory (Hatch End) Ltd* [1966] Ch 402, at 433, *per* Harman LJ, in which it was held that a mortgagee's interest in the mortgaged property is a sufficient interest to enable him to enforce a restrictive covenant affecting the land.

under him or them.[10] In other words, in the absence of any express words indicating that the covenant is to be binding on the covenantor alone and not his successors in title, it will be inferred that the intention was to bind successors.

In other Caribbean jurisdictions, it would seem that affirmative evidence will be required to establish an intention that the burden of a restrictive covenant should run to successors-in-title of the covenantor, such as by express words to that effect in the covenant.

Persons bound by restrictive covenants

Under *Tulk v Moxhay*, the burden of a covenant is a burden not on the estate of the defendant, but on the servient tenement itself. Thus, it is not necessary to show that the defendant holds the same estate that the covenantor held. The defendant is bound merely by the fact that he occupies the servient land, whether as fee simple owner, or lessee, or sublessee, or as a mere licensee having no interest in the land. The occupier is bound irrespective of the nature of his occupation. Thus, for example, in *Mander v Falcke*,[11] a lessee had covenanted not to use the demised premises for any purpose that would cause annoyance or inconvenience to adjoining property owned by the lessor. The lessee sublet the premises, and the sublease eventually became vested in X, who did not occupy the premises himself, but gave an occupational licence to his father. While in occupation, X's father used the premises ostensibly as an oyster bar and refreshment room, but in reality as a notorious brothel, 'to the great annoyance of the neighbourhood'.[12] The plaintiff, who had acquired the reversion, sought an injunction to restrain breach of the covenant, and the injunction was granted. The mere occupation by the father was sufficient to enable the covenant to be enforced against him by injunction.

Registration

Being an equitable interest only, a restrictive covenant will not be binding on a *bona fide* purchaser of a legal estate in the servient land without notice of the covenant. However, in those jurisdictions in which the system of registration of title operates, a restrictive covenant can be protected by entry of a memorandum on the certificate of title or a caution on the register of the servient tenement.[13]

Positive covenants

We have seen that the burden of a positive freehold covenant – that is, one that requires expenditure on the part of the servient owner – does not run with the land of the covenantor, either at common law or in equity, so that only the original

---

10 See, eg, s 84(1) of the Property Act, Cap 236 (Barbados); s 62(1) of the Law of Property Act, Cap 190 (Belize); s 22(1) of the Conveyancing Act 1983 (Bermuda).
11 [1891] 2 Ch 554.
12 *Ibid*, at 555.
13 See, eg, s 33 of the Land Registration Act, Cap 229 (Barbados); s 33 of the Registered Land Act, Cap 194 (Belize); s 30 of the Registered Land Act, Cap 374 (Antigua and Barbuda); s 30 of the Registered Land Ordinance, Cap 229 (BVI); s 30 of the Land Registration Act 1984 (St Lucia); s 70 of the Registration of Titles Act 1973 (Jamaica).

covenantor will be liable on it.[14] This is recognised as a serious defect in the law, particularly where there are housing estates in which purchasers have covenanted to contribute towards the cost of maintenance of facilities, such as access roads, drainage, or fences and hedges. Such liability for maintenance costs will be essential for the convenience of the various owners and for the preservation of the value of the properties. In some jurisdictions, 'condominium' legislation[15] has solved the problem, as far as multi-storey apartment buildings are concerned, by creating enforceable obligations as between freehold purchasers and their successors-in-title, but such condominium legislation does not usually apply to freehold properties on residential housing estates.

In order to avoid the consequence of the non-enforceability of positive covenants against successors, a number of methods or devices may be used.

(a) Leasing the land to be burdened instead of selling the freehold, so that the burden of the covenants will run by privity of estate, under the rule in *Spencer's Case.*[16]

(b) Chains of indemnity covenants. Since an original covenantor remains liable even after he has parted with the land, he may protect himself by taking a covenant of indemnity from his purchaser. Each successive purchaser may enter into a similar covenant with his vendor, so that a 'chain' of indemnity covenants will be created. In theory, the original covenantee should be able to secure the observance of the positive covenant by the current owner of the servient land by suing the original covenantor. However, as has been pointed out,[17] in practice, this device will sooner or later become ineffective, as a result of the death or disappearance of the original covenantor, or because of a break in the chain of indemnity covenants.

(c) A right of re-entry may be reserved in the conveyance, exercisable on events amounting to a breach of the positive covenant. The right of re-entry will run with the burdened land, but will be subject to the rule against perpetuities.[18]

(d) The rule in *Halsall v Brizzell.*[19] Under this principle, a person who wishes to take advantage of a shared service or facility, such as drains, a park, or an access road on a residential estate, must comply with any corresponding obligation to contribute to the cost of providing or maintaining it. The principle is expressed by the maxim, 'he who accepts the benefit must accept the burden', and is illustrated by the facts of the case itself. There, a building estate had been developed in 1851 and the various plots sold freehold. Each purchaser covenanted that he and his successors would contribute to the cost of maintaining the roads and sewers on the estate, and a promenade and sea wall. The question was whether the defendant, who was a successor-in-title of one of the purchasers, was bound to make the agreed

14 See pp 116, 117, above.
15 See, eg, Law of Property and Conveyancing (Condominium) Act, Ch 139 (The Bahamas); Condominium Act, Cap 224A (Barbados). See Chapter 7, above.
16 See pp 78, 79, above.
17 *Report of the Committee on Positive Covenants Affecting Land*, Cmnd 2719, 1965, [8].
18 See Maudsley and Burn, *Land Law: Cases and Materials*, 5th edn, 1986, London: Butterworths, pp 756–58.
19 [1957] 1 All ER 371.

> contributions. It was held that, since the covenant was positive, it did not run with the burdened land at law or in equity, but because the defendant, along with the other plot owners, needed to use the roads and other amenities, he had to accept the burden of contributing to their upkeep.

The scope of the principle in *Halsall v Brizzell* was considered in *Rhone v Stevens*,[20] where Lord Templeman emphasised that the 'enforcement of a positive covenant lies in contract', and

> equity cannot compel an owner to comply with a positive covenant entered into by his predecessors-in-title without flatly contradicting the common law rule that a person cannot be made liable upon a contract unless he was a party to it.

Accordingly, he took the view that the *Halsall v Brizzell* principle should apply only in circumstances where the enjoyment of the benefits (such as the right to use certain facilities) was made *expressly or impliedly conditional* on the acceptance of the burden of contributing to their maintenance. This meant that, for the rule to apply, it had to relate to reciprocal benefits and burdens. In *Rhone*, such reciprocity was lacking. The case involved the division of a house into two units, with a party wall and a common roof. It was accepted that each unit was entitled to and subjected to mutual easements of support. The original owners sold one unit (Unit A), retaining the other (Unit B), and covenanted in the conveyance of Unit A to keep the entire roof in good repair. The successor-in-title to Unit A later brought an action against the successor-in-title to Unit B to enforce the repairing covenant, relying on the rule in *Halsall v Brizzell*. The House of Lords held that the rule did not apply because the reciprocal benefits and burdens in the conveyance related only to the easements of support: the repairing covenant relating to the roof was an independent provision and, since it was a positive covenant, the burden had not run to the successor to Unit B.

The principles in *Halsall* and *Rhone* have been discussed and applied in the Eastern Caribbean Court of Appeal in two recent cases.

In the first of these, *Westerhall Point Residents' Association Ltd v Batihk*,[21] an action was brought by the Association against B, a lot owner in a residential development in Grenada, to recover maintenance contributions allegedly due in relation to the upkeep of an estate road giving access to the various lots in the development. B's lot had originally been conveyed by the developer to B's predecessor-in-title, P, subject to the following covenant:

> The company hereby covenants with the purchaser that the company will at its own expense maintain for a period of three years from the date of completion all roads laid down in the present development and shown on the layout plan, and the purchaser covenants with the company that thereafter the purchaser will share proportionately in the maintenance and upkeep of the said roads.

The Association contended that, although admittedly the covenant to pay contributions was positive and its burden did not run automatically to B at law or in equity, B was liable to pay the contributions under the rule in *Halsall v Brizzell* because B had enjoyed the benefit of using the estate road, which was in fact the

20 [1994] 2 AC 310.
21 (2016) Court of Appeal, Eastern Caribbean, Civ App No 2015/0004.

only means of access to the properties in the development, and he was therefore bound to accept the burden. Following the reasoning of Lord Templeman in *Rhone v Stephens*, to the effect that accepting the burden of the positive covenant must be a condition of enjoying the benefit of the facility, Webster JA noted that, in the deed of conveyance between the developer and P, it was not expressly stated that the use of the estate road was conditional on the payment of a maintenance fee, but it was clear that, by placing 'the obligation to pay for the maintenance and upkeep of the road squarely on the shoulders of the residents of the development after the first three years', the use of the road 'was conditional . . . on the payment of a proportionate share of the maintenance costs'. The Association's claim therefore succeeded.

The second case is *Half Moon Bay Home Owners Co Ltd v Platinum Properties Ltd*,[22] where the original purchaser of a villa (No 14) in a development in St Kitts obtained a certificate of title endorsed with the following clause:

> The registered proprietor shall have full right and liberty, conditional upon the payment by the registered proprietor to the management company of maintenance fees in accordance with the standard management of the said development, (i) to use the roads, paths and walkways to gain access to the land transferred, and (ii) to use the sewage system to which the development was from time to time connected.

The defendant, P Co, ultimately became the proprietor of Villa No 14. The management company, HMB, requested payment of maintenance fees but PCo failed to comply. HMB brought an action to recover the fees. It was held that the principles in *Halsall* and *Rhone* applied. In the present case, the benefit of using the sewage system and the burden of paying for its maintenance were reciprocal. The endorsement on the certificate of title expressly stated that the exercise of the right was conditional on the payment of maintenance fees to HMB (unlike in *Westerhall*, where conditionality was implied by the court). P Co had a choice whether to exercise the rights specified in the certificate of title and pay the maintenance fees, or to opt to use an alternative method such as a private sewage system. Since P Co had opted to exercise the right to use the development's sewage system, it was obliged to pay the fees.

Two further points in this case are worthy of note. First, in addition to the requirement of reciprocity of benefits and burdens, *Halsall* and *Rhone* established that a successor-in-title of the original covenantor will be bound by a positive covenant only if he had the opportunity to choose whether to take the reciprocal benefit or decline it. In *Westerhall*, the lot owner's option to decline use of the access road was purely theoretical, because it was the only means of access to his property, but in the *Half Moon Bay* case P Co did have the genuine, if inconvenient, option of using a private sewage system rather than that belonging to the development. Secondly, the maintenance fees claimed by HMB were for a wide range of services not limited to the maintenance of the sewage system, and P Co contended that since it did not utilise all of those benefits but only the sewage system, it should only be required to pay a proportion of the maintenance fees. Thom JA rejected that contention, on the authority of *Wilkinson v Kardene*,[23] where it was held that provided a maintenance fee relates to at least some of the benefits taken and the owners had, at least in theory,

22 (2018) Court of Appeal, Eastern Caribbean, Civ App No 201/0003.
23 [2013] EWCA Civ 44.

the option to decide not to take some benefits, then the entire maintenance fee will be payable.

RUNNING OF THE BENEFIT

The position at common law

The benefit of a covenant between freeholders, unlike the burden, is capable of running at common law, provided that two conditions are fulfilled:

(a) the covenant touches and concerns the covenantee's land; and
(b) the covenantee has a legal estate in the land benefited.

Covenant must touch and concern the land

This requirement will be satisfied if the covenant is made for the benefit of the covenantee's land and not merely for the covenantee's personal advantage. It must affect the value of the dominant land. Whether a covenant touches and concerns the land is a question of fact to be determined on expert evidence presented to the court. The onus is on the covenantor to show that a covenant does not touch and concern either originally (that is, when it was entered into) or at the date of the action.

Covenantee must have a legal estate

Any legal estate suffices here. Thus, not only an assignee of the fee simple of the dominant land, but also a tenant under a legal lease of the land, will be entitled to enforce the covenant.

POSITIVE AND NEGATIVE COVENANTS

As far as the running of the benefit of a covenant at common law is concerned, it is immaterial whether the covenant is positive or negative: in either case, the benefit may run. Thus, for example, in *Sharp v Waterhouse*,[24] it was held that the benefit of a covenant to supply the covenantee's land with pure water was enforceable by successors of the covenantee; and in *Smith and Snipes Hall Ltd v River Douglas Catchment Board*,[25] it was held that the benefit of a covenant by the Catchment Board to maintain the banks of a river had passed to a tenant of the assignee.

NO NEED FOR SERVIENT TENEMENT

For the running of the benefit of a covenant, there must be a dominant tenement, but there need not be a servient tenement; in other words, there is no requirement that the covenant should impose a burden on any land belonging to the covenantor, and the latter will be bound even though he owns no land. Thus, in *Smith and Snipes*

24 (1857) 119 ER 1449.
25 [1949] 2 All ER 179.

Hall,[26] the benefit of the covenant passed, despite the fact that the Catchment Board did not own any servient land; and in *The Prior's Case*, in which a prior covenanted with the lord of a manor to sing divine service regularly in the manor chapel, it was held that the lord's successor could sue the prior for failure to perform the covenant.[27]

The position in equity

If it is possible for the assignee of the covenantee to enforce the covenant under common law principles, there is no difficulty. However, there are a number of severe limitations to the running of the benefit at common law, the effect of which is that it is rarely possible to rely on the common law rules. Accordingly, in the vast majority of cases, the assignee will be obliged to depend on the equitable rules for the running of the benefit.

The circumstances in which the equitable rules must be relied on are as follows:

(a) where the covenantee or the assignee are merely equitable owners of the land benefited;[28]
(b) where the covenantor is no longer the owner of the servient tenement, but has assigned it, so that enforcement against the assignee of the servient tenement depends upon the rule in *Tulk v Moxhay*;[29]
(c) where only part of the benefited land is assigned to the plaintiff, since at common law the benefit cannot be assigned in pieces;[30] and
(d) where the plaintiff relies upon his land being part of a scheme of development.[31]

In order to establish that the benefit of a covenant has run in equity, the plaintiff must show that there has been:

(a) annexation of the benefit to the dominant land; or
(b) express assignment of the covenant; or
(c) a scheme of development.

Annexation

If the assignee of the covenantee can show that the covenant is annexed to the land benefited, then he and his successors-in-title can enforce the covenant – that is, the benefit will pass to them. Annexation is an abstract concept, whereby the covenant is deemed to be attached to the title of the land so that all future owners will automatically be entitled to the benefit. Whether a particular covenant is annexed to the land benefited depends upon 'the intention of the parties to be inferred from the language which they used in the deed creating the covenant'.[32]

---

26 *Ibid.*
27 (1368) YB 42 Ed III, Pl 14, fol 3A.
28 *Fairclough v Marshall* (1878) 4 Ex D 37.
29 *Marten v Flight Refuelling Ltd* [1961] 2 All ER 696.
30 *Re Union of London and Smith's Bank Ltd's Conveyance, Miles v Easter* [1933] Ch 611, at 630, *per* Romer LJ.
31 See pp 130–135, below.
32 Cheshire and Burn, *Modern Law of Real Property*, 15th edn, 1994, London: Butterworths, p 623.

The requirement is that the land benefited must be clearly identified in the conveyance of the servient land that contains the covenant.

The classic formula for annexation is that used in the leading case of *Rogers v Hosegood*, as follows:[33]

> with intent that the covenants might so far as possible bind the premises thereby conveyed and every part thereof and might enure to the benefit of the vendors . . . their heirs and successors and others claiming under them to all or any of their lands adjoining or near to the said premises.

In *Drake v Gray*,[34] Greene LJ suggested that it was sufficient for annexation that a covenant is made 'with X, owner or owners for the time being of Blackacre (the dominant tenement)', or simply 'for the benefit of Blackacre'. In other words, the benefit will be annexed to the dominant land so as to run with it if in the conveyance of the servient land the covenant is either stated to be made with the covenantee in his capacity as owner of the dominant land, or stated to be made for the benefit of the land, for in either case it would be obvious that future owners of that land are intended to benefit.

On the other hand, it was held in *Renals v* Cowlishaw[35] that there was no annexation where the covenantor covenanted with 'the vendors, their heirs, executors, administrators and assigns', because there was no reference to any land, and the reference to executors, etc, left it uncertain as to whether the covenant was intended to benefit the successors to the covenantee's land or the successors to his personalty; in *Pass v Ramsahoye*,[36] Williams J in the Barbados High Court held that, where the covenantor covenanted in the conveyance 'to the intent that the burden of the covenant shall run with the land hereby granted', there was no annexation, in the absence of any 'indication of an intention to annex the *benefit* of the covenant to any particular land'.

Again, in *Halfmoon Bay Ltd v Crown Eagle Hotels Ltd*,[37] in which the purchaser for itself and its successors covenanted 'with the vendor, its successors and assigns', Langrin J in the Jamaican Supreme Court held there was no annexation of the benefit of the covenants. He said:[38]

> There is no expression of the covenants being for the benefit of any land or made with the vendor as owner of any particular parcel of land . . . to be benefited. Even if it is clear that the parties intended to annex the benefit of the covenant to some land, by express words or necessary implication, three further questions arise. The court

33 [1900] 2 Ch 388.
34 [1936] 1 All ER 363, at 377, *per* Greene LJ.
35 (1878) 9 Ch D 125.
36 (1986) High Court, Barbados, No 231 of 1986. See also *Lamb v Midac Equipment Ltd* (1996) 52 WIR 290, Court of Appeal, Jamaica, *per* Carey JA.
37 (1996) 33 JLR 103, Supreme Court, Jamaica. On appeal to the Privy Council ((2002) 60 WIR 330, 335), it was observed by Lord Millett that the appellants in this case were the original covenantees and, as such, were certainly entitled to the benefit of the covenants. Annexation was 'relevant only where the party who is seeking to enforce the covenant is a successor-in-title of the original covenantee'.
38 *Ibid*, at 110. Similarly, in *Lamb v Midac Equipment Ltd* (1999) Privy Council Appeal No 576 of 1997, it was noted that a covenant made with 'Frank Watson, his heirs, executors, administrators, transferees and assigns' had not been expressed to be made for the benefit of land identified by the covenant itself. The reference to 'heirs, executors' etc., was consistent with the covenant being intended for the benefit of Frank Watson himself, as distinct from specific property. There was therefore no annexation.

> must ascertain the identity of the land to which the covenant is annexed; determine, upon the construction of the words by which the annexation is effected, whether the covenant is annexed to the whole of the land referred to as a whole, or to such land as a whole and also to each and every part of it; and decide whether the land to which the parties have purported to annex the benefit of the covenant is 'touched and concerned' by the covenant: if not, the annexation fails.

The insistence upon a strict form of words, such as those used in *Rogers v Hosegood*, has been much criticised and, as Professor Wade has pointed out,[39] it seems that a struggle has been taking place between, on the one hand, conveyancers who insist on strictness of form in the interest of conveyancing convenience and certainty, and, on the other, certain judges who seek to liberalise the law by looking for the intention of the parties rather than a mechanical formula.

Implied annexation

One theory that has been canvassed and relied upon by the Jamaican Court of Appeal is that of 'implied annexation'. According to Megarry and Wade, annexation can be implied where the facts make the connection with the benefited land so obvious that to ignore it would be not only an injustice, but a departure from common sense.[40] Thus, if annexation can be implied, the benefit of the covenant will run even though the accepted form of words is not used. Arguments against insistence on formal annexation, and therefore in favour of implied annexation, include the following:

(a) no formal annexation is required in order that the benefit of a covenant may run at common law – the only requirements are that the covenant should touch and concern the covenantee's land and that the assignee should have a legal estate, and it is out of character for equity to be more formalistic than the common law;
(b) express annexation is not required in order that the burden of a covenant may run, nor for the running of benefits or burdens in leases under *Spencer's Case*, nor for the running of the benefit or burden of easements; and
(c) the benefit of a covenant can be assigned in equity without the need for any particular form of words.

In *Jamaica Mutual Life Assurance Society v Hillsborough Ltd*,[41] there were no express words in the conveyance to the covenantor stating that the restrictive covenants contained therein were intended for the benefit of any land retained by the covenantee. Nevertheless, the Jamaican Court of Appeal held that annexation could be implied from the surrounding circumstances. In Carey JA's words:

> The real question is . . . one of intention, which it is permissible to ascertain from an examination of the surrounding facts at the time of sale.

On appeal to the Privy Council, however, the Board appeared to rule out the possibility of implied annexation, and held that, since there were no express words

39 (1972) 31 CLJ 163, 164.
40 Megarry and Wade, *Law of Real Property*, 5th edn, 1984, London: Stevens, p 784.
41 [1989] 1 WLR 1101.

'stating that the restrictions . . . were intended for the benefit of any land retained by (the covenantee)', there was no annexation of the covenants.

Statutory annexation

According to *Federated Homes Ltd v Mill Lodge Properties Ltd*,[42] s 78 of the Law of Property Act 1925 has the effect of annexing the benefit of a covenant to the dominant land, without the need for express words of annexation. Section 78, the wording of which has been substantially reproduced in some Commonwealth Caribbean statutes,[43] provides that:

> a covenant relating to any land of the covenantee shall be deemed to be made with the covenantee and his successors-in-title and the persons deriving title under him or them, and shall have effect as if such successors and other persons were expressed. For the purposes of this subsection, in connection with covenants restrictive of the user of land, 'successors-in-title' shall be deemed to include the owners and occupiers for the time being of the land of the covenantee intended to be benefited.

In *Federated Homes*, M Ltd owned a site that included three areas of land, coloured red, green and blue on the plan. M Ltd obtained planning permission to develop the site by erecting up to 1,250 houses. In February 1971, M Ltd sold and conveyed the blue land to the defendants. In the conveyance, the defendants covenanted with the vendor that, in carrying out the development of the blue land, they would not build 'at a greater density than a total of 300 dwellings so as not to reduce the number of units which the vendor might eventually erect on the retained land under the planning consent'. The retained land was described as 'any adjoining or adjacent property retained by' M Ltd (that is, the red and green land). By a series of transfers, the plaintiffs became the owners of the red and green land. In 1977, the plaintiffs obtained planning permission to develop the red and green land. They then discovered that the defendants had obtained planning permission to develop the blue land at a higher density than permitted by the covenant, and that the density was likely to prejudice the development of the red and green land. The plaintiffs sought an injunction to restrain the defendants from building on the blue land at a density that would be in breach of the covenant. The main question for decision was whether the benefit of the covenant had passed to the plaintiffs, either by annexation or assignment. As regards annexation, the trial judge held that the benefit of the covenant had not been annexed to the retained land because the conveyance to the defendants had not expressly or impliedly annexed it, and s 78 did not have the effect of annexing the benefit to the retained land. However, the Court of Appeal overruled the trial judge on this point, holding that, since the covenant touched and concerned the covenantee's land, s 78 had the effect of annexing the benefit to the land.

One important feature of *Federated Homes* is that the defendants were the original covenantors, not assignees. Thus, there was no need to rely on the *Tulk v Moxhay* principle, and it was possible to decide the case on common law principles, but it can be presumed that, in view of the interpretation put on s 78, the Court of Appeal

42 [1980] 1 All ER 371.
43 See, eg, s 83(1) of the Property Act, Cap 236 (Barbados); s 21 of the Conveyancing Act 1983 (Bermuda); s 61 of the Law of Property Act, Cap 190 (Belize).

would have reached the same decision if the defendants had been assignees of the burdened land, provided, of course, that the requirements for the running of the burden were satisfied.

It seems, however, that in those Caribbean jurisdictions where the Property legislation is based not on s 78 of the Law of Property Act 1925 but on the earlier Conveyancing Act of 1881 (such as s 61 of the Conveyancing Act of Jamaica), the statutory annexation principle in *Federated Homes* may not apply, as it has been held that the wording of the earlier statute is significantly different, and insufficiently precise to annex the benefit of a covenant to the dominant land.[44]

Further, it was held in *Roake v Chadha*,[45] that where the original covenanting parties had expressly stipulated that the benefit of their covenant should not pass to subsequent purchasers of the dominant tenement, unless the benefit were expressly assigned, s 78 could not apply so as to pass the benefit.

Area to be benefited

It was established in *Re Ballard's* Conveyance[46] that there will be no effective annexation if the area of the dominant land is greater than can reasonably be benefited; put in another way, there can be no annexation unless substantially the whole of the dominant land is capable of benefiting from the covenant. In that case, a covenant was stated to be made for the benefit of 'the owners for the time being of the Childwickbury Estate'. The area of the estate was about 1,700 acres, and the restriction was imposed on a plot of only 18 acres. It was found as a fact that most of the estate could not possibly be directly affected by a breach of the covenant. It was accordingly held that the covenant was not enforceable by assignees of the *whole* of the dominant tenement. Clauson J refused to sever the covenant so as to regard it as annexed to the part of the estate that was in fact benefited. On the other hand, if the covenant had been stated to be for the benefit of the whole *or any part* of the estate, it could have been enforced by the successor-in-title to any part of the land that the covenant in fact benefited.[47]

An additional reason for annexing the benefit expressly to the whole or any part of the dominant tenement is that, if the benefit is annexed only to the whole, and the covenantee or a successor sells part of the land, the purchaser of the part will be unable to enforce the covenant. Thus, in *Re Jeff's Transfer (No 2)*,[48] following the earlier case of *Russell v Archdale*,[49] it was held that a covenant expressed to be 'for the benefit of the remainder of the Chorleywood Estate belonging to the vendor' was annexed only to the whole and not to each and every part of the estate, so that a purchaser of part only could not enforce the covenant. On the other hand, in *Re Selwyn's Conveyance*,[50] it was held that a covenant 'for the benefit of the adjoining or

44 *Sainsbury (J) plc v Enfield LBC* [1989] 1 WLR 590. *Contra*, Wade, HWR [1972B] CLJ 157, who argued that the earlier section should be interpreted as effecting annexation.
45 [1983] 3 All ER 503.
46 [1937] 2 All ER 691.
47 See *Marquess of Zetland v Driver* [1938] 2 All ER 158.
48 [1966] 1 All ER 937.
49 [1962] 2 All ER 305.
50 [1967] 1 All ER 339.

neighbouring land part or lately part of the Selwyn Estate' did annex the benefit to separate parts of the land.

The rule that the benefit of a covenant that is annexed to the whole of the dominant land cannot be enforced by a purchaser of part of the land has been criticised as 'arbitrary and inconvenient', and, in *Federated Homes Ltd v Mill Lodge Properties Ltd*,[51] in which the plaintiffs, who were seeking to enforce the covenant, were purchasers of two separate parts of the dominant land, Brightman LJ said:[52]

> It was suggested by counsel for the defendants that if this covenant ought to be read as inuring for the benefit of the retained land, it should be read as inuring only for the benefit of the retained land as a whole and not for the benefit of every part of it . . . I find the idea of the annexation of a covenant to the whole of the land but not to a part of it a difficult conception fully to grasp . . . I would have thought that if the benefit of a covenant is, on a proper construction of a document, annexed to the land, *prima facie* it is annexed to every part thereof, unless a contrary intention appears.

It was accordingly held that the plaintiffs could enforce the covenant.

Express assignment

Express assignment of the benefit of a covenant will occur where the dominant land, to which no covenant has been annexed, is sold and conveyed 'together with the benefit of covenants entered into by X (the covenantor)'. There are five requirements, which were laid down by Romer LJ in *Re Union of London and Smith's Bank Ltd's Conveyance, Miles v Easter*:[53]

(a) the covenant must have been taken for the benefit of the land of the covenantee;
(b) the dominant tenement must be indicated with reasonable certainty, which indication need not appear in the conveyance creating the covenant – it is sufficient if, in the light of the surrounding circumstances, the identity of the dominant land is in some other way ascertainable with reasonable certainty;
(c) the dominant tenement must be retained in whole or in part by the plaintiff;
(d) the dominant tenement must be capable of benefiting from the covenant; and
(e) the assignment of the covenant and the conveyance of the land to which it relates (that is, the dominant land) must be contemporaneous.

Unlike in the case of annexation, there is no doubt that an express assignment of the benefit of a covenant to a purchaser of part only of the dominant tenement is effective.[54] The benefit of a covenant can also be assigned by operation of law: for instance, on the death of a covenantee, the benefit automatically passes to his personal representatives upon trust for the devisee of the dominant tenement, and may be assigned to the devisee.[55] A final question is whether the effect of expressly

51 [1980] 1 All ER 371.
52 *Ibid*, at 380.
53 [1933] Ch 611.
54 *Op cit*, Cheshire and Burn, fn 28, p 629.
55 *Newton Abbot Co-operative Society Ltd v Williamson and Treadgold Ltd* [1952] 1 All ER 279.

assigning the benefit of a covenant on the sale of the dominant land is to annex it to the land, so that it will automatically pass to future owners without the need for express assignment, or whether, each time the dominant land is sold, there must be a fresh assignment of the benefit, viz, a continuous chain of assignments. In *Re Pinewood Estate*,[56] it was assumed without argument that a chain of assignments is necessary, but *dicta* in other cases[57] suggest the contrary – that is, that assignment of the benefit does have the effect of annexing it to the land so that no further assignments are necessary.

Schemes of development

Where a scheme of development (or 'building scheme', as it is often called) exists, restrictive covenants are enforceable in equity by and against successors of the original contracting parties. Cheshire and Burn explain the nature of the concept thus:[58]

> A scheme of development comes into existence where land is laid out in plots and sold to different purchasers or leased to different lessees, each of whom enters into a restrictive covenant with the common vendor or lessor agreeing that his particular plot shall not be used for certain purposes. In such a case these restrictive covenants are taken because the whole estate is being developed on a definite plan, and it is vital, if the value of each plot is not to be depreciated, that the purchasers or lessees should be prevented from dealing with their land so as to lower the tone of the neighbourhood. When the existence of a scheme of development has been established, the rule is that each purchaser and his assignees can sue or be sued by every other purchaser and his assignees for a breach of the restrictive covenants. In such an action for breach, it is immaterial whether the defendant acquired his title before or after the date on which the plaintiff purchased his plot. In other words, the restrictive covenants constitute a special local law for the area over which the scheme extends, and not only the plot-owners, but even the vendor himself, become subject to that law, provided that the area and the obligations to be imposed therein are defined. They all have a common interest in maintaining the restriction. This community of interest necessarily requires and imports reciprocity of obligation.[59] There thus arises what Simonds J has called 'an equity which is created by circumstances and is independent of contractual obligation'.[60]

A scheme of development has the following advantages:

(a) no special formula for annexation is required, since the annexation of the benefit of the covenants to every plot still unsold proves itself from the surrounding facts;

(b) the owners of plots sold previously are shown by the facts to be within the benefit of the covenants, even though they are not expressly mentioned as covenantees;

(c) no unsold plot can later be disposed of by the vendor without his requiring the purchaser to enter into the covenants of the scheme; and

---

56 [1957] 2 All ER 517.
57 *Reid v Bickerstaff* [1909] 2 Ch 305, at 320; *Rogers v Hosegood* [1900] 2 Ch 388, at 408.
58 *Op cit*, Cheshire and Burn, fn 28, p 630.
59 *Spicer v Martin* (1888) 14 App Cas 12, at 25, *per* Lord Macnaghten.
60 *Lawrence v South County Freeholds* [1939] 2 All ER 503, at 524.

(d) a restrictive covenant normally is discharged where the titles to the dominant and servient tenements become vested in the same person, but where there is a scheme of development, such 'unity of seisin' does not automatically discharge a covenant within the area of unity, and it will revive on severance, unless the parties intended otherwise.[61]

As soon as the first sale under the scheme has been made, the scheme crystallises, and all of the land within the scheme is bound. There is no need for the vendor to have bound himself by the covenants, since he is in the position of a trustee and cannot authorise breaches of the covenants.

The subject matter of a scheme of development is usually freehold land that is to be sold off in lots to persons who wish to build houses, but it may also apply to apartment blocks or to houses already built, and to leaseholds as well as freeholds. It is also possible to create a sub-scheme within an area subject to an existing scheme of development.

The requirements for the existence of a scheme of development were formulated by Parker J in *Elliston v Reacher*:[62]

(a) both the plaintiff and the defendant in the action for breach of the restrictive covenant must have derived their titles to the land from a common vendor;
(b) before the sale of the plots to the plaintiff and the defendant, the common vendor must have laid out his estate for sale in lots subject to restrictions that it was intended to impose on all the lots, and which were consistent only with some general scheme of development;
(c) the restrictions were intended by the common vendor to be for, and were for, the benefit of all of the lots sold, which intention is gathered from all of the circumstances of the case, but if the restrictions are obviously calculated to enhance the value of each lot, the intention is readily inferred;[63]
(d) the original purchasers must have bought their lots on the understanding that the restrictions were to enure for the benefit of the other lots; and
(e) the geographical area to which the scheme extends must be ascertained with reasonable certainty.

Although the requirements in *Elliston v Reacher* are still considered to be a valuable guide as to the existence or otherwise of a building scheme, there are cases in which schemes of development have been held to exist despite the absence of one or more of the requirements. In *Baxter v Four Oaks Properties*,[64] for instance, the second requirement was lacking, as there was no evidence that the common vendor had laid out the estate in lots before beginning to sell it off. He merely sold plots, of the size that each purchaser wished to take, to purchasers as they came along. Nevertheless, Cross J held that there was sufficient evidence of an intention to create mutually binding covenants. Also, in *Re Dolphin's Conveyance*,[65] Stamp J found the existence of a scheme of development despite the absence of both a common vendor and prior lotting.

61 *Texaco Antilles Ltd v Kernochan* [1973] 2 All ER 118, PC, appeal from the Court of Appeal of The Bahamas.
62 [1908] 2 Ch 374, at 385.
63 See *British Hoffman Ltd v Bella Vista Beach Apartments Ltd (No 2)* (1979–80) 1 LRB 519, Supreme Court, The Bahamas.
64 [1965] 1 All ER 906.
65 [1970] 2 All ER 664.

The modern position

It now seems to be generally accepted that, under the modern law, the two requirements that are needed in order to establish a scheme of development are that:

(a) the land to which the scheme relates must be identified; and
(b) there must be a common intention on the part of the purchasers that there should be 'reciprocity of obligation'.[66]

These requirements were confirmed by the Privy Council in two cases, originating from Jamaica and Trinidad and Tobago respectively.

In the first case, *Jamaica Mutual Life Assurance Society v Hillsborough Ltd*,[67] the predecessors-in-title of the applicant and of the first and second objectors had purchased their respective parcels of land from common vendors, subject to covenants not to subdivide the land into lots of less than one acre each, and not to carry on any trade or business thereon. The instruments of transfer did not annex the benefit of the covenants to any land retained by the vendors, nor was there any subsequent assignment of the benefit of the covenants to any of the objectors' predecessors-in-title. The third and fourth objectors were purchasers of neighbouring land subject to the same restrictions. The applicant proposed to develop its land as a multi-unit residential complex, and sought a declaration in the Jamaican Supreme Court under s 5 of the Restrictive Covenants (Discharge and Modification) Act 1960 as to whether its land was affected by the restrictions and as to whether and by whom the restrictions were enforceable.

On the question as to whether there was a scheme of development, so that the covenants in the applicant's title would run with the land and enure to the benefit of the objectors and their successors, the Privy Council held that there was nothing in the instruments of transfer to suggest that the vendors were selling off a number of lots as part of a scheme, nor was there any indication that the purchasers had assumed obligations to any persons other than the vendors[68] or had acquired the benefit of obligations incurred by other persons. Further, there was no evidence as to whether the sales of the lots were advertised or as to what, if any, representations were made by the vendors to the purchasers:[69]

> In the absence of any such extraneous evidence, the terms of the instruments of transfer alone [fell] far short of what is required to establish community of interest or reciprocity of obligation between purchasers . . . To imply a building scheme from no more than a common vendor and the existence of common covenants would be going much too far.

In the Trinidadian case of *Emile Elias and Co Ltd v Pine Groves Ltd*,[70] the Privy Council again found that there was no scheme of development. In this case, a company, in 1938, divided an area of its land into five lots, which were sold to four purchasers.

66 See Gray, *Elements of Land Law*, 1987, London: Butterworths, pp 718, 719; *Laurenciago Ltd v Anthony*, High Court, Antigua and Barbuda (2017), para 21.
67 [1989] 1 WLR 1101.
68 See also *Lamb v Midac Equipment Ltd* (1996) 52 WIR 290, Court of Appeal, Jamaica, *per* Carey and Patterson JJA.
69 [1989] 1 WLR 1101, at 1108.
70 [1993] 1 WLR 305.

Lot 5 was shown on a plan annexed to the conveyance to the purchaser of lots 4 and 5, but not on the general plan annexed to the other conveyances. The purchasers of lots 1, 4 and 5 covenanted with the company and its assigns, *inter alia*, not to erect any building other than one dwelling house on each lot, and the purchasers of lots 2 and 3 entered into a similar covenant, but they also entered into other covenants that were substantially different from those applicable to lots 1, 4 and 5. The plaintiff and defendant subsequently became the owners of lots 3 and 1 respectively. When the defendant started to build more than one house on his lot, the plaintiff brought proceedings to enforce the restriction, contending that a building scheme had been established in 1938. Lord Browne-Wilkinson, delivering the judgment of the Board, held that, apart from the requirement of derivation of title from a common vendor and the laying out of the land in lots, none of the *Elliston v Reacher*[71] requirements were satisfied. He continued:[72]

> *Was the area of the scheme defined?*
>
> The rationale for the requirement that the area of a scheme should be defined is explained in *Reid v Bickerstaff*[73] by Cozens-Hardy MR:
>
> > In my opinion, there must be a defined area within which the scheme is operative. Reciprocity is the foundation of the idea of a scheme. A purchaser of one parcel cannot be subject to an implied obligation to purchasers of an undefined and unknown area. He must know both the extent of his burden and the extent of his benefit.
>
> This shows that it is not sufficient that the common vendor has himself defined the area. In order to create a valid building scheme, the purchasers of all the land within the area of the scheme must also know what that area is.
>
> In this case, there was one plan, the general plan, which was attached to all four 1938 conveyances, but this plan did not show lot 5. If, therefore, lot 5 falls to be treated as part of the designated scheme area, it has not been proved that in 1938 the purchasers of lots 1, 2 and 3 were aware of that fact. Mr Fitzpatrick suggested that it could be inferred from the fact that all the purchasers were associated with the golf club and, by the time of the 1948 deed, were aware of lot 5, that they were so aware in 1938. Their Lordships feel unable to attach to any such inference sufficient probative force to reach an affirmative conclusion that all the purchasers of the lots in 1938 knew that lot 5 was included. If lot 5 was to be part of a scheme area giving rise to mutually enforceable obligations between all the lots, it would surely have been shown on the plan annexed to each of the conveyances.
>
> In the view of the Board, if there was any intention to create mutually enforceable rights in a scheme area, lot 5 must have been part of that area. It was sold at the same time as lots 1–4 and was subjected to the same covenants as affected lot 4 and lot 1. It is entirely incredible that there was any intention to create rights which would be mutually enforceable between the owners of lots 1, 2, 3 and 4 but not enforceable by and against the owner of lot 5.
>
> Accordingly, lot 5 being part of any scheme that could be established and it not having been shown that the purchasers of lots 1–3 were aware of that fact, the requirements of a defined scheme area known to the original purchasers cannot be satisfied.

71 [1908] 2 Ch 374.
72 [1993] 1 WLR 305, at 310.
73 [1909] 2 Ch 305, at 319.

> *Lack of uniformity in the covenants*
>
> It is one of the badges of an enforceable building scheme, creating a local law to which all owners are subject and of which all owners take the benefit, that they accept a common code of covenants. It is most improbable that a purchaser will have any intention to accept the burden of covenants affecting the land which he acquires being enforceable by other owners of the land in the scheme area unless he himself is to enjoy reciprocal rights over the lands of such other owners: the crucial element of reciprocity would be missing. That does not mean that all lots within the scheme must be subject to identical covenants. For example, in a scheme of mixed residential and commercial development, the covenants will obviously vary according to the use intended to be made of each category of lot. But if, as in the present case, the lots are all of a similar nature and all intended for high-class development consisting of one dwelling on a substantial plot, a disparity in the covenants imposed is a powerful indication that there was no intention to create reciprocally enforceable rights.
>
> The covenants imposed on lots 1, 4 and 5 differ in matters of substance from those imposed on lots 2 and 3. Lots 2 and 3 (in addition to the restriction against erecting more than one dwelling house) contain a covenant restricting the use of the building when erected to use as a private dwelling house only. Lots 4, 5 and 1 contain no such restriction on the user. It cannot be realistically supposed that, for example, the purchaser of lot 2 ever intended to enter into an obligation whereunder the owner of lot 1 could restrain him from taking lodgers whereas, if lot 1 were to take lodgers, lot 2 could not object.
>
> Again, the owners of lots 2 and 3 entered into a covenant not to cause a nuisance to those occupying lands in the neighbourhood, whereas lots 4, 5 and 1 were not subjected to such covenants. This disparity again militates against the finding of any intention to create a mutually enforceable local law based on reciprocity. Therefore, the second of the requirements laid down by Parker J in *Elliston v Reacher*[74] is not satisfied in the present case.
>
> *Generally*
>
> If one steps back and looks at the matter generally, there is no convincing proof that the parties' intention was to produce mutually enforceable covenants. The covenants in the 1938 conveyances were made with the company alone and were not expressed to be made for the benefit of any land not owned (because previously sold) by the company. The company itself as owner of the rest of the golf course had an interest in obtaining the covenants so as to preserve the character of the land retained. The purchasers of lots 1–3 did not know of lot 5.
>
> There is no consistent set of covenants affecting each of the lots. Therefore, all the contemporaneous evidence of what the parties intended in 1938 is far from being consistent only with an intention to create a building scheme giving rise to mutually enforceable rights.

The necessity for reciprocity of obligation and benefit was highlighted by the Privy Council in another Jamaican case, *Lamb v Midac Equipment Ltd*.[75] Here, the appellant lived in an apartment in a residential block. On the other side of the road, diagonally opposite, the respondent company carried on a garage and repair shop business. The appellant claimed not only that noxious fumes and gases coming from the garage had adversely affected his and his wife's health and were therefore an actionable nuisance, but also that the respondent's use of its premises was in breach

74 [1908] 2 Ch 374, at 384.
75 (1999) Privy Council Appeal, No 57 of 1997.

of a covenant restricting user to residential purposes. Since the appellant was not the original covenantee, it was necessary for him to show either that the benefit of the covenant had been annexed to his land or that the covenant had been entered into as part of a scheme of development. On the latter point, the facts were that there had been a division of the land of the common vendor into a number of lots, and that the lots had been sold by him subject to similar covenants. Was this sufficient to give rise to a scheme of development? Lord Nicholls answered the question in the negative. He said that it was well established that the essence of a scheme of development was reciprocity of obligation, where each purchaser from the common vendor is intended to be subject to similar obligations and each is intended to have the benefit of the obligations entered into by his fellow purchasers, and continued:

> The existence of this intended reciprocity is a matter of proof by evidence,[76] having regard to the circumstances of each case. Proof, as here, of the division of land by a common vendor into several lots, and the taking of similar covenants from each purchaser, goes some way towards the desired goal. By itself, however, this evidence is insufficient. It leaves open the possibility that the common vendor took the covenants, not for the benefit of the purchasers of the several plots but for his own benefit. He might, for instance, be the owner of neighbouring land. In the present case this possibility cannot be dismissed as a fanciful imagining. The plan attached to Frank Watson's[77] certificate of title relating to the five acres suggests that the remaining part of no. 17 Waterloo Road, abutting onto the five acres, also belonged to Frank Watson . . . It is . . . clear that Mary Christie,[78] and presumably each of the purchasers, knew she was buying a plot of land in a defined area laid out in lots. But there is no evidence, such as might be provided by a contract of sale, from which a court could properly infer that each purchaser knew that purchasers of the other lots had entered into, or would enter into, similar covenants. The absence of this evidence is fatal to Mr Lamb . . . In the absence of such evidence there is a lack of material from which intended reciprocity of obligation and benefit between all the purchasers can be inferred.

DISCHARGE AND MODIFICATION

The court has an inherent power to discharge or modify a restrictive covenant if there is sufficient evidence: (a) that a covenantee (or any of his assignees) has acquiesced in a course of conduct that is inconsistent with its continuance, as where he has disregarded past breaches of the covenant; or (b) that the character of the neighbourhood has changed to such an extent that it would be inequitable or senseless to continue to insist on observance of a covenant that, in effect, has become redundant.[79]

76 It is not necessary for each conveyance to contain 'an expressed declaration that the covenants are intended to enure and to be for the benefit of all, whether prior or subsequent purchasers or their successors-in-title, and to be enforceable by them', nor 'to find any express contract by the vendor or the several purchasers to that effect. It may be collected or inferred from the nature of the transaction'. All of the circumstances of the case must be taken into account in determining whether the restrictions were imposed 'merely to protect the vendor himself . . . or for the mutual benefit and advantage of the purchasers': *Reid v Bickerstaff* [1909] 2 Ch 309, at 311, *per* Joyce J; *Donald v Igmant Development* (1999) OECS Court of Appeal (Grenada), Civ App No 15 of 1999.

77 The original common vendor.

78 The predecessor in title of the respondent company and one of the original covenantors.

79 *Chatsworth Estates Co v Fewell* [1931] 1 Ch 224; *Paradise Island Ltd v Condor Enterprises Ltd* (1993) Supreme Court, The Bahamas, No 873 of 1992.

In addition to the inherent power, statutory provisions in Barbados and Jamaica, which are modelled on the original s 84 of the Law of Property Act 1925 (UK), provide for the discharge or modification of restrictive covenants; in those jurisdictions, it is invariably the statutory provisions that are relied upon. Section 3(1) of the Restrictive Covenants (Discharge and Modification) Act of Jamaica[80] provides that an application for discharge or modification may be made to a judge of the Supreme Court[81] on all or any of the following grounds:[82]

(a) that, by reason of changes in the character of the property or the neighbourhood or other circumstances of the case which the judge may think material, the restriction ought to be deemed obsolete; or
(b) that the continued existence of such restriction, or the continued existence thereof without modification, would impede the reasonable user of the land for public or private purposes, without securing to any person practical benefits sufficient in nature or extent to justify the continued existence of such restriction or, as the case may be, the continued existence thereof without modification; or
(c) that the persons of full age and capacity for the time being or from time to time entitled to the benefit of the restriction, whether in respect of estates in fee simple or lesser estates or interests in the property to which the benefit of the restriction is annexed, have agreed either expressly or by implication by their acts or omissions to the same being discharged or modified; or
(d) that the proposed discharge or modification will not injure the persons entitled to the benefit of the restriction.

Obsolescence (ground (a))

This provision essentially reproduces the ground (b) of inherent jurisdiction (above). The requirements of this ground have proved to be extremely difficult to satisfy since, as Smith JA pointed out in the Jamaican Court of Appeal in *Stephenson v Liverant*,[83]

> a change in the character of the neighbourhood[84] does not necessarily result in the covenant being deemed obsolete. The court is obliged to consider the further question whether the changes are such that the covenant ought to be deemed obsolete.

80 Section 196(1) of the Property Act, Cap 236 (Barbados) is similarly worded; cf s 96 of the Registered Land Law (Cayman Islands), which provides for the discharge or modification of easements, 'restrictive agreements' and profits on similar grounds, but omitting the ground of agreement to discharge. See *Murmarson Ltd v Eldemire* [1988–89] CILR 61.

81 Under s 196(1) of the Property Act, Cap 236 (Barbados), application is made to a 'judge in chambers'.

82 The burden of proof lies on the applicant to satisfy the court that one or more of the grounds has been made out; even if he succeeds in doing so, the court still has a discretion as to whether or not to order discharge or modification: *Re 13 Gainsborough Avenue* (1990) 27 JLR 491, Supreme Court, Jamaica, *per* Bingham J; *Re 39 Wellington Drive* (1991) Supreme Court, Jamaica, No ERC 139 of 1990, *per* Courtenay Orr J. There is no burden of proof on the objectors as, in objecting, they are merely exercising their right to preserve their entitlement to the benefit of the covenants which they enjoy.

83 (1972) 18 WIR 323, at 336.

84 The test to be applied in determining whether the character of a neighbourhood has changed is the 'estate agent's test' – that is, 'What does the purchaser of a house in that road or part of the road expect to get?: *Regardless Ltd v Hadeed* (1996) 33 JLR 417; *Re 39 Wellington Drive* (1991) Supreme Court, Jamaica, No ERC 139 of 1990, *per* Courtenay Orr J; *Re 48 Norbrook Avenue*

The test for determining whether a covenant ought to be deemed obsolete was laid down by Romer LJ in *Re Truman, Hanbury, Buxton and Co Ltd's Application*,[85] viz, whether the original purpose for which the covenant was imposed can or cannot still be achieved: if it can, the covenant is not obsolete; if it cannot, it is. An example given by Romer LJ of a sufficient change that might render covenants obsolete is where an area once intended to be residential has, through express or tacit waiver of the covenants, become substantially commercial.[86]

In *Stephenson v Liverant*,[87] purchasers of lots in a private residential development entered into covenants prohibiting the erection of any building other than a private dwelling, and prohibiting the use of any building for any trade or business. The applicants, who owned two of the lots in the development, sought the modification of the covenants, so as to enable them to erect a number of apartment blocks for letting to tourists. The main ground of the application was that, by reason of changes in the character of the neighbourhood and breaches of the covenants by the owners of other lots in the development (of the 15 lots built upon, nine had been developed in breach of covenant, in that they contained more than one dwelling house), the covenants should be deemed obsolete. One of the questions before the court was whether, by letting their houses to tourists, the owners were in breach of the covenants prohibiting use of the land for any trade or business and, if the answer were in the affirmative, whether, in the light of such breaches, there could be said to have been a change in the character of the neighbourhood sufficient to enable the court to hold that the covenants ought to be deemed obsolete.

The Jamaican Court of Appeal, affirming the decision of Parnell J, held that, notwithstanding any proved or admitted breaches of the covenants, the changes in the character of the neighbourhood were not so far-reaching as to render the covenants obsolete.

Fox JA explained the decision thus:[88]

> The contention that, by renting to tourists, business is being carried on upon the land, requires a closer examination. It is clear that the owners of nearly all the houses derive a steady annual income from such rent. Looked at in this light, it is true to say that the

(1994) Supreme Court, Jamaica, No ERC 80 of 1990, *per* Harris J (Ag); *Re 15 Kensington Crescent* (1996) 33 JLR 57, Supreme Court, Jamaica, *per* Harrison J.

85 [1955] 3 WLR 704.

86 Applications for discharge or modification under this subsection failed in *Re Bay Distributors Ltd* (1988–89) 1 Carib Comm LR 358 and *Re Landfall* (1970) 17 WIR 178, High Court, Barbados, on the ground that the areas in which the covenants existed had retained their residential and secluded character. See also *Re Haloute's Application* (1986) High Court, Barbados, No 156 of 1986; *Re 39 Wellington Drive* (1991) Supreme Court, Jamaica, No ERC 139 of 1990; *Central Mining and Excavating Ltd v Creswell* (1993) 30 JLR 503, Court of Appeal, Jamaica; *Re Covenant Community Church* (1990) 27 JLR 368, Supreme Court, Jamaica; *Re Mona and Papine Estates* (1994) Supreme Court, Jamaica, No ERC 147 of 1991. An application for modification was granted on grounds (a), (b) and (d) in *Re 15 Kensington Crescent* (1996) 33 JLR 57, Supreme Court, Jamaica.

87 (1972) 18 WIR 323.

88 *Ibid*, at 331. See also the observations of Parnell J in the lower court, *sub nom Re Lots 12 and 13 Fortlands* (1969) 15 WIR 312, at 321, who pointed out that a balance had to be struck between the public interest in satisfying the demand for residential accommodation and the need to protect the private benefits that flowed from the enjoyment of enforceable restrictions. In *Re 39 Wellington Drive* (1991) Supreme Court, Jamaica, No ERC 139 of 1990, Courtenay Orr J emphasised that the general economic state of the country and the housing shortage factor were irrelevant considerations in determining whether a covenant was obsolete. The Court of Appeal, by a majority, dismissed an appeal against the decision of the trial judge refusing discharge of the covenant.

> houses are being used for the purposes of business. But it should be noticed that within the houses themselves no business is being carried on. The houses are not being used as a shop, a school, a chapel, or a nursing home or a racing stable. They are being used as private dwellings. Such user does not really jeopardise to any significant extent those incidents which the first part of covenant 5 was intended to secure. Neither would the transactions, which may be necessary to conclude a contract of tenancy, impeach the spirit of the latter part of that covenant. If, in fact, those transactions took place upon the land, and as to this the evidence is vague (they could have been effected elsewhere), in their nature the transactions do not go beyond the business which the owner of any dwelling house may be obliged to complete in his home from time to time. In addition, the business is done with delicacy, discretion, and an absence of physical exhibition. There is no evidence that any lot is used for advertising, or contains an office set apart for the discharge of formalities, or is possessed of any means of entertainment beyond those that may be expected in any private dwelling house. Having regard to these considerations, I take the view that even if it is admitted that most houses are being used for the purpose of a business, such user has not caused such a change in the residential character of the neighbourhood as to justify a conclusion that the covenants are obsolete.

More recently, in *Re 48 Norbrook Avenue*,[89] Harris J (Ag) found on the evidence that there had been a general tendency towards subdivision of lots in the neighbourhood, resulting in differences in the style, appearance and arrangement of the houses. Whereas there had been single family dwellings on some lots, there were now multiple dwellings, such that it could be said that there had been changes in the character of the neighbourhood. However, applying the test in *Re Truman, Hanbury*, Harris J (Ag) held that the covenants ought not to be deemed obsolete.

A more liberal approach to discharging covenants on the ground of obsolescence was taken by Greenidge J in a Barbadian case, *Re Boyce*,[90] in which an application was made under s 196 of the Property Act to discharge a covenant not to erect more than one single dwelling house on a lot in Rowans Park, an old-established residential development. The applicant had been granted planning permission to subdivide the lot into four separate lots and to build thereon four townhouses. In considering whether to order a discharge, Greenidge J found that there had indeed been a change in the character of Rowans Park, in that what was originally a development of single dwelling houses had seen a growth in multi-unit dwellings and 'construed literally, this covenant is obsolete against the background of the increasing demand for housing as evidenced by the erection within the past ten years or so of multi-dwelling units', which were 'now a prominent feature of the Rowans Park neighbourhood'. The conclusion was that 'the particular sort of residential user required by the covenant' had become obsolete.

A similar approach was taken in Jamaica by Wright JA in his dissenting judgment in *Re 39 Wellington Drive* (sub nom *Central Mining and Excavating Ltd v Croswell*). He said:

> It cannot be assumed that a neighbourhood which has been transformed from being a quiet single-family neighbourhood to one which is now interspersed with high-density dwellings would retain its character unchanged. In some instances, several families now occupy the land space which the covenant reserved to a single family. With the

89 (1994) Supreme Court, Jamaica, No ERC 80 of 1990.
90 (2005) High Court, Barbados, No 2163 of 2003.

> infusion of town houses, the style, arrangement and appearance of the houses have changed. This is evident from the planametric map; and it is unlikely that the social customs of multiple family dwellings would be the same as those of the single family envisaged by the covenant.

Wright JA's approach was applied by Anderson (P) J in *Burke v Whitters*,[91] where the applicant sought the modification of covenants prohibiting, *inter alia*, the building of more than one residence on each lot. Expert evidence of an experienced realtor referred to the rapid urbanisation of Jamaica, and the necessity to utilise scarce land resources in Kingston and St Andrew in the most effective manner, by increasing densities of occupation in the Corporate Area. It was pointed out that, to satisfy this demand, restrictive covenants in the area under consideration had been gradually relaxed, giving way to a host of town house and apartment complexes, as the need for 'large manorial residences' no longer existed on a large scale. Anderson J found on the evidence that there had in fact been 'substantial and substantive' changes in the character of the neighbourhood, and the question for the court was whether, by virtue of those changes, 'or other circumstances of the case which the court might think material', the restriction ought to be deemed obsolete. After referring to a number of Australian cases in which the meaning of 'obsolete' in this context had been considered, Anderson J found additional support in the dissenting judgment of Wright JA (referred to above), and concluded that the covenants in the instant case were indeed obsolete.

Again, in *Re 30 Dillsbury Avenue, St Andrew*,[92] where the applicant sought an order of modification of restrictive covenants so that she could lawfully erect four town-houses and a bungalow on her lot, Lawrence-Beswick J, in considering whether there had been a change in the character[93] of the neighbourhood, accepted the unchallenged evidence of an experienced surveyor to the effect that whereas, initially, practically all the lots in the Avenue had 'single family dwellings' erected on them, at the time of the present action the majority of the lots contained 'multi-family dwellings' and, applying the 'estate agent's test', 'today's purchasers would therefore expect to find on Dillsbury Avenue multiple dwellings on lots as small as 2000 square feet'. In the view of the learned judge, 'the face of the neighbourhood has permanently changed and . . . the covenants concerning such dwellings and land space ought to be deemed obsolete'.

Thus, on the basis of recent cases in Jamaica and Barbados, it appears that the courts may be more willing in the future to countenance the discharge or modification of restrictive covenants on the ground of obsolescence. Increasing urbanisation and the profound changes in modes of living in the 21st century make it inevitable that many restrictive covenants imposed on land in the 1920s or earlier will be deemed obsolete by the courts.[94]

91 (1993) 30 JLR 6.

92 (2011) Supreme Court, Jamaica, No 961 of 2003. But see *Re 23–25 Seymour Avenue* (2011) Supreme Court, Jamaica, No 360 of 2008, where Brooks J refused to order a discharge or modification of similar covenants since, although the trend in the neighbourhood was towards multi-family developments, 'if single family units still exist in numbers, and the residential character of the neighbourhood remains', it could not be said that the original object of the covenants could not still be achieved. Brooks J also adverted to the constitutional right of property owners to have their property rights supported by the restrictions.

93 (2011) Supreme Court, Jamaica, No 856 of 2006.

94 'Character' derives from the 'style, arrangement and appearance of the houses on the estate and from the social customs of the inhabitants': *Re Davis' Application* (1950) 7 P&CR 1.

Impeding the reasonable user of the land (ground (b))

In order to satisfy this ground, it must be shown:

(i) that the restriction impedes the reasonable use of the land; and
(ii) that the restriction does not secure practical benefits to any person sufficient to justify its continued existence.

The courts have taken a very restrictive approach to this provision, and successful applications under (b) are rare. One difficulty, of course, is that the requirement of (b) is a double one. Another difficulty is that in *Stannard v* Issa[95] the Privy Council emphasised that, in order to succeed under this ground, an applicant for the discharge or modification of a restrictive covenant on the ground that it 'impedes the reasonable user of the land . . . has to go a great deal further than merely to show that, to an impartial planner, his proposal appeared a good and reasonable proposal'. Where, for instance, a developer who purchases land subject to a covenant restricting building to a single dwelling house proposes to erect an apartment block for rental to tourists or residents, it is not sufficient for him to argue that this proposal is one that would make a reasonable user of the land, 'having regard to current pressures of population and current notions of optimum density', nor will the fact that he has obtained planning permission for his proposal necessarily assist his case. The majority of the Jamaican Court of Appeal in *Stannard v Issa* seemed to have been of the view that all the applicant needed to show was that the proposed use was: (a) reasonable; and (b) impeded to a sensible degree by the restrictions sought to be modified. They adverted to the fact that the neighbourhood in this case was a tourist resort area, and the proposed development was in harmony with it. The Privy Council, however, preferred and, indeed, wholeheartedly endorsed the 'powerful' dissenting judgment of Carey JA,[96] who had stated that the applicant must show that the restrictions '*have sterilised the reasonable use of the land*'.[97] Put in another way, the court must be satisfied: (a) that the permitted use is no longer a reasonable one; and (b) that the applicant's proposed use is the only reasonable one. These tests are very difficult to satisfy.

Even if the applicant succeeds in showing that the restrictions have sterilised the reasonable user of the land, he has another hurdle to surmount, which is to show that the restrictions do not secure practical benefits to any person.

The statutes do not define 'practical benefits', but it is accepted that they would include such benefits as privacy and view, low density of occupation, peace and quiet, security, and maintenance of property values.[98] Most of these benefits were enjoyed by the residents in *Stannard v Issa*.[99] In this case, an area of land on the coast

95 [1987] AC 175, at 187; (1986) 34 WIR 189, at 196; *Re Ghey and Galton's Application* [1957] 3 All ER 164, at 171, *per* Lord Evershed MR.
96 Cf *Re Boyce* (2005) High Court, Barbados, No 2163 of 2003, in which Greenidge J, in discharging a covenant, emphasised that the proposed development was a 'viable economic response to the need for accommodation in the tourism sector' and fitted within the Barbados National Development Plan. However, the decision in this case seems to have been based primarily on grounds (a) (changes in the character of the neighbourhood and obsolescence) and (d) (no injury likely to persons entitled to the benefit of the covenants).
97 [1987] AC 175, at 195.
98 See HW Wilkinson (1979) 129 NLJ 523, 524.
99 See also *Re Constant Spring and Norbrook Estates* (1961) 3 WIR 270, Supreme Court, Jamaica; *Re Bengal* (1994) Supreme Court, Jamaica, No ERC 71 of 1992; *Hsia v Lyn* [2020] JMSC Civ 5.

between Ocho Rios and Tower Isle in Jamaica was, in 1952, subdivided into 11 lots, 10 of which were sold subject to common covenants not to subdivide the lots, not to erect any building of less than £2,000 prime cost, and not to carry on any trade or business or use the land for any commercial purposes, save that of a medical practice. Up to the end of 1952, the development was entirely residential, constituting, in the trial judge's words, a 'peaceful seaside enclave of a family nature'. The applicant, an original covenantor, who was the owner of two lots, obtained planning permission to erect 6 blocks of three-storey buildings, comprising 40 residential apartments together with amenities, including two swimming pools. She applied to a judge in chambers for modification of the covenants so as to permit this development. The owners of other lots subject to the same restrictions objected to the application. Theobald J rejected the application, holding that the continued existence of the covenants in their present form did not impede the reasonable user of the applicant's land, and that the proposed modification would adversely affect the practical benefits secured to the objectors by the covenants. The Jamaican Court of Appeal, by a majority, reversed that decision and granted the modification. The Privy Council advised that Theobald J's decision be restored. There was no evidence of any difficulty in developing the applicant's land or in disposing of it for development within the framework of the existing restrictions, nor was there any suggestion that the restrictions had the effect of sterilising the land.[100]

It was also emphasised by the Privy Council in this case[101] that it was incorrect to interpret s 3(1)(b) of the Jamaican Act as if it were identical to the equivalent English provision (s 84(1) of the Law of Property Act 1925 (UK)), as the latter section had been amended in 1969 by s 28 of the Law of Property Act 1969 by substitution of the phrase 'some reasonable user' for 'the reasonable user'. The purpose of this amendment had been to widen the scope of the section and thereby make it easier for applicants to secure discharge or modification where money would be adequate compensation for the objectors. The Jamaican section had thus to be interpreted in the light of cases decided before 1969, and based on the narrower wording.

Agreement to discharge or modification (ground (c))

A covenant may be discharged or modified where the dominant owners[102] have agreed, either expressly or by implication, by their acts or omissions, to such discharge or modification. This ground is rarely relied upon, and it must be regarded as virtually redundant since, if all of the dominant owners come to such an agreement, they will normally execute a deed to that effect. Applying to the court in such a case would be a waste of time and money. It seems that the only situation in which an application on ground (c) might be needed is where the dominant owners indicated that they would agree to a discharge or modification, but then refused to execute the formal deed.

A more useful application of this ground would be in cases of implied consent, viz, where the persons entitled to the benefit of covenants have acquiesced in past breaches to such an extent that they must be presumed to have consented to the

100 See also *Re 13 Gainsborough Avenue* (1990) 27 JLR 491, Supreme Court, Jamaica, *per* Bingham J.
101 [1987] AC 175, at 186, 187.
102 It is essential that all of the dominant owners are in agreement; the agreement of some only is not sufficient: *Re 13 Gainsborough Avenue* (1990) 27 JLR 491, Supreme Court, Jamaica, *per* Bingham J.

discharge of the covenants. This argument was rejected, however, in *Re Federal Motors Ltd's Application*,[103] in which the applicant company sought the discharge of a restrictive covenant in order to enable it to service vehicles on its land. Graham-Perkins J (Ag), in the Jamaican Supreme Court, held that the fact that the surrounding owners had not objected to the applicant's breaches of covenant for more than two years did not indicate agreement by implication to the discharge of the covenant.

No injury to objectors (ground (d))

Under ground (d), a covenant may be discharged or modified on the ground that the proposed discharge or modification will not injure the persons entitled to the benefit of the restriction. This paragraph has much in common with the second limb of ground (b): 'without securing to any person practical benefits sufficient in nature or extent to justify the continued existence of such restriction'; in many cases, where an applicant fails to satisfy the second limb of ground (b), he will inevitably fail to satisfy ground (d) also. For instance, in *Stannard v Issa*,[104] once it had been decided that the continued existence of the covenants did secure substantial practical benefits to the objectors in the preservation of 'the privacy and quietude of an enclave of single dwellings in large gardens', it was a short step to holding that the objectors would be injured by the proposed modification of the covenant, in the sense that it would have seriously interfered with those benefits by permitting the construction of 40 residential apartments. Similarly, in *Re Bay Distributors*,[105] an application under ground (d) failed since the applicant was unable to produce sufficient evidence to show that the practical benefits of peace, privacy and seclusion hitherto enjoyed by the objectors would not be adversely affected by the proposed modification.

The scope of ground (d) has been severely limited by the restrictive interpretation put on it in *Ridley v Taylor*[106] by Russell LJ, who stated that the ground was 'designed to cover the case of the, proprietorially speaking, frivolous objection', and that it was 'so to speak, a long-stop against vexatious objections to extended user'.

This narrow interpretation of the scope of ground (d) was applied in *Re System Sales Ltd's Application*,[107] in which lots within a residential scheme of development, described as 'a quiet and peaceful enclave', were subject to covenants not to erect more than one freehold dwelling house on each lot, not to subdivide any lot, and

103 (1966) 9 WIR 375, at 381.
104 [1987] AC 175, at 187; (1986) 34 WIR 189, at 196.
105 (1988–89) 1 Carib Comm LR 358; affirmed in *Bay Distributors Ltd v Goddard* (1989) Court of Appeal, Barbados, No 19 of 1988.
106 [1965] 2 All ER 51, at 58. In *Ministry of Housing v Raynor* [2016] JMCA Civ 31, para 34, Brooks JA listed the requirements, as gleaned from decided cases, to be satisfied for the discharge of a covenant within ground (d), as follows: (i) the onus of proof lies on the applicant to satisfy the requirements of s 3(1) (d); (ii) the objector is not obliged to adduce evidence of the injury that he complains about; (iii) the injury to the objector must be related to his own proprietary interest; (iv) the onus is on the applicant to show that the objection is frivolous; (v) the applicant must show that granting the application would not amount to a relaxation of that covenant which would constitute a real risk, as a precedent, of disturbing the pattern that the covenant was designed to protect. In other words, the applicant must show that the mere existence of an order modifying the covenant would not undermine the intact system of restrictions; (vi) even if no injury to the objector is proved, the court still has a discretion to refuse the application to modify or discharge the covenant; (vii) each case turns on its own facts.
107 (1992) 43 WIR 19.

not to use the land for any trade or business. The Barbados Telephone Company wished to erect a substation on part of one lot, and, with the consent of the owner of the lot, S Ltd, had obtained planning permission to do so. S Ltd sought a discharge or modification of the covenants. Objections were raised that the volume of vehicular traffic would grow, the value of the properties would fall, and the removal of the restrictions attaching to the applicant's lot would encourage other lot owners to make similar applications for subdivision or for setting up other types of business. After citing Russell LJ's dictum, Williams CJ, in the Barbados High Court, stated that

> the issue is whether [S Ltd] has established that the objections raised are trifling and insubstantial and can be dismissed as no more than frivolous . . . Under [para (d)] I am not authorised to weigh the practical benefits of one course against the other. I am only concerned with whether [S Ltd] has established that the objectors, as persons who have bought into the development, have raised only insubstantial matters.[108]

Concluding that the objections were not insubstantial, Williams CJ refused the application for modification.

In *Re Lot 10, McAuley Heights*,[109] on the other hand, in which a lot of land situated in an isolated area was burdened with covenants restricting subdivision of the land and prohibiting the erection of more than one private dwelling house thereon, modification so as to permit a subdivision into two lots and the erection of a dwelling house on each lot was granted under ground (d), on the basis that the objections to modification were insubstantial, and the proposed modification would 'not injure in any way the persons entitled to the benefit of the restriction'.[110] The circumstances in this case were a far cry from those in *Stannard v Issa* and *Stephenson v Liverant*.[111] Here, there was:

> a dwelling house designed to give the appearance of a single unit, the architecture of which [was] consistent with the design and external appearance of the houses already built in the subdivision, but capable of accommodating two families because of its internal dividing wall. Each unit would provide security for the other in an isolated area of a crime-prone parish, and, by their very presence, would provide additional security for the neighbourhood, including the houses of the objectors.[112]

The 'thin end of the wedge' argument

Mention should be made of an argument accepted in some of the cases, notably *Stephenson v Liverant*,[113] *Re System Sales Ltd's Application*[114] and numerous English cases,[115] to the effect that a discharge or modification should not be approved within ground (d) where this might set a precedent for the granting of future applications for

---

108 *Ibid*, at 27.
109 (1989) Supreme Court, Jamaica, No ER R/C 70 of 1983. See also *Re Lot 49, Ebony Glades* (1996) 33 JLR 4, Supreme Court, Jamaica, *per* Chester Orr J.
110 *Per* Edwards J.
111 (1972) 18 WIR 323.
112 *Re Lot 10, McAuley Heights* (1989) Supreme Court, Jamaica, No ER R/C 70 of 1983, *per* Edwards J.
113 (1972) 18 WIR 323, at 330. See also *Earl v Spence* (1992) Court of Appeal, Jamaica, Civ App No 69 of 1989.
114 (1992) 43 WIR 19, at 28.
115 See *op cit*, Wilkinson, fn 94, p 524; *Re Ghey and Galton's Application* [1957] 3 All ER 164.

discharge or modification – the 'thin end of the wedge', which might ultimately lead to the dismantling of the entire residential scheme. In *McMorris v Brown*,[116] a Privy Council appeal from Jamaica, Lord Cooke expressly approved of this approach. He said:[117]

> Cases may arise in which it is very difficult to say that the particular thing which the applicant wishes to do will of itself cause anyone any harm; but that harm may still come to the persons entitled to the benefit of the restriction if it were to become generally allowable to do similar things. Or such harm may flow from the very existence of the order making the modification, through the implication that the restriction is vulnerable to the action of the Lands Tribunal in England or the Supreme Court of Jamaica . . . The prevailing approach is as indicated in *Re Snaith and Dolding's Application*,[118] where it was observed that:
>
> > . . . it is . . . legitimate, in considering a particular application, to have regard to the scheme of covenants as a whole and to assess the importance to the beneficiaries of maintaining the integrity of the scheme. In so far as the application would have the effect, if granted, of opening a breach in a carefully maintained and outstandingly successful scheme of development, to grant the application would . . . deprive the objectors of a substantial practical benefit, namely the assurance of the integrity of the building scheme.

Lord Cooke continued[119] by stating that the onus was on the applicant to show that a first relaxation of the covenant against subdivision in the *McMorris* case would not 'constitute a real risk as a precedent, so disturbing the pattern of a block of family homes in exceptionally extensive grounds'; '. . . bearing in mind the subdivisional tendencies and pressures for housing sites in Forest Hills generally', the applicant had not discharged that onus. Accordingly, the application for modification under ground (d) failed in this case.

The 'thin end of the wedge' argument has not been universally accepted, however, and a contrary view is that if a modification will in itself cause no injury to the objectors, it should not be refused on the ground that subsequent successful applications for modification might do so, since each application must be decided on its merits.[120] This view has particular validity in the Caribbean, where applications are heard by a High Court or Supreme Court judge, for, as Edwards J observed in *Re Lot 10, McAuley Heights*,[121] 'the "thin end of the wedge" argument assumes that the judiciary is incapable of exercising the discretion which Parliament saw fit to entrust to it'.

In the Barbadian case of *Re Packer*,[122] in which there was an application to modify restrictive covenants so as to permit the erection of a condominium apartment building on one lot in a residential development of seven lots, Blackman J (Ag) took the view that it would be absurd in this case to give any weight to the 'thin end of the wedge' argument, as it was highly unlikely that the current lot owners would

116 [1998] 3 WLR 971.
117 *Ibid*, at 978.
118 (1995) 71 P & CR 104, at 118.
119 [1998] 3 WLR 971, at 979.
120 *Re Farmiloe's Application* (1983) 48 P & CR 317. See, also, *Re Forgac's Application* (1976) 32 P & CR 464.
121 (1989) Supreme Court, Jamaica, No ER R/C 70 of 1983.
122 (2000) High Court, Barbados, No 1152 of 1998.

demolish their dwelling houses so as to exploit the precedent created by a discharge or modification. Having visited the *locus in quo* and found that the area was by no means a 'quiet and peaceful enclave', and having accepted evidence that the proposed building was in harmony with the architectural character of the neighbourhood, he held that modification of the covenants would not injure the objectors and should therefore be allowed. The Court of Appeal, however, reversed that decision,[123] Williams CJ observing that 'Barbados is a small island, but that does not mean that every bit of it must be subjected to the hustle and bustle of modern day traffic and congestion; or that those who legitimately contracted to live in a low density development must have their choice overridden by or in favour of others who want to make money'. There was no absurdity in giving weight to the 'thin end of the wedge' argument, as other owners in the development might indeed be encouraged to seek modifications as well. Admittedly, this would entail their demolishing existing buildings before they could construct apartment/condominium blocks, but the financial gains could well make such demolition worthwhile. In coming to the conclusion that modification should not be allowed, Williams CJ relied on the restrictive approach of Russell LJ in *Ridley v Taylor*.[124]

123 (2001) Court of Appeal, Barbados, Civ App No 7 of 2000.
124 [1965] 2 All ER 51, at 58 (p 000, above).

CHAPTER 9

EASEMENTS

DEFINITION

An easement is a right *in alieno solo* (over the land of another). Circumstances can arise in which a landowner may wish to grant certain rights over his/her land to another person that fall short of a grant of possession. For example, he/she may wish to grant to an adjoining landowner a right to pass and repass over his land on foot or with vehicles (an easement of way), or a right to lay pipes under his land to convey water or sewage; or he/she may agree to curtail his own rights in favour of another, for example, to agree not to build on a defined portion of his land so as to ensure that light continues to reach his neighbour's windows (an easement of light), or he/she may agree not to pull down his own portion of a duplex house so as to withdraw support from his neighbour's portion (an easement of support).[1] Interference with an easement may give rise to an action for damages in nuisance, and for an injunction[2] to restrain further interference.

Some of these rights may be granted not only by way of easement, but also by means of restrictive covenant[3] or licence.[4] Restrictive covenants are particularly appropriate where the right granted is a 'negative' one – that is, one under which the grantor agrees not to use his land in a particular way (for example, not to erect a building on his land). Licences are more appropriate where the right granted is 'positive' – that is, one that allows the grantee to use the grantor's land in a particular way (for example, to use a footpath on the grantor's land). Both types of right, positive and negative, can be created by easement. It should be noted, however, that there is another sense in which the words 'positive' and 'negative' are used. The other meaning is that a right is positive if it requires expenditure of money by the grantor; it is negative if it does not require expenditure. The general rule is that the law does not recognise positive easements in this sense – in other words, a right will not be held to be an easement if it requires expenditure of money by the grantor. The one exception to this is the easement of fencing, which requires the grantor to maintain a fence for the benefit of the grantee; this easement is well accepted, but it is anomalous, and has been called a 'spurious easement'.[5]

Of these three rights – easements, restrictive covenants and licences – the fullest in law is the easement, since a legal easement is a right *in rem*, binding on the whole world, whereas a restrictive covenant is binding only in equity and may be defeated by a *bona fide* purchaser for value of the legal estate without notice of the covenant or, where title to the burdened land is registered, it may be void against a subsequent purchaser unless protected by an entry on the register.

A licence is a much less valuable right than an easement, since it is a right *in personam*, and, if contractual, is generally binding only on the original parties to the

---

1 See, generally, Jackson, *Law of Easements and Profits*, 1978, London: Butterworths.
2 *Lush v Duprey* (1966) 10 WIR 389, Court of Appeal, Trinidad and Tobago.
3 See Chapter 8, above.
4 See Chapter 3, above.
5 See p 155, below.

DOI: 10.4324/9781003186946-9

agreement and is not binding on successors-in-title to the original parties;[6] an estoppel licence, on the other hand, is binding only on successors-in-title having *notice* of its existence.[7] If the licence is neither contractual nor arising by estoppel – for example, an oral permission unsupported by consideration to use a footpath on the licensor's land – then the rights of the grantee can be revoked at any time by the licensor and cannot be legally enforced at all, even against the licensor.

An easement must also be distinguished from a customary or public right. As will be seen, the essence of an easement is that it is a right 'appurtenant' to a particular parcel of land – that is, a right that is exercisable by the owner for the time being of the land for the benefit of which the easement exists. A right that is exercisable by the general public may take effect as a local customary right or a public right, but it is not an easement, because it is not appurtenant to any land. For example, at common law, the right of the inhabitants of a village to walk across another's land to reach the local church, or the right of fishermen to dry their nets on another's land, may be valid customary rights, but they are not easements; the rights of the general public to pass along a highway, to fish in the sea, or to bathe on a beach, are not easements, but public rights.[8]

REQUIREMENTS FOR A VALID EASEMENT

Easement are based on the concept of 'dominant' and 'servient' tenements. An easement may be defined broadly as a right attached to land (the dominant tenement) that gives the owner of that land a right to use the land of another (the servient tenement) in a particular way (for example, to walk or drive across it), or to prevent the servient owner from using the servient tenement in a particular way (for example, to prevent the servient owner from building so as to obstruct the light coming to the windows of the dominant tenement). Such a right is enforceable by all successors-in-title to the dominant tenement against all successors-in-title to the servient tenement, irrespective of whether the successors to the servient tenement had notice of the existence of the easement.

For such rights to exist as easements, certain requirements must be satisfied, as follows.[9]

There must be a dominant and a servient tenement

It is essential that the right must be *appurtenant* to land – that is, that there must be a dominant tenement to which the right is attached. If X, the owner of Whiteacre,

6 *Ashburn Anstalt v Arnold* [1988] 2 All ER 147, at 164, *per* Fox LJ, disapproving earlier authorities, such as *Errington v Errington* [1952] 1 All ER 149 and *Binions v Evans* [1972] 2 All ER 70. See pp 29, 30, above.

7 See *Ives (ER) Investments Ltd v High* [1967] 1 All ER 504; *Denson v Bush* [1980–83] CILR 141, Grand Court, Cayman Islands.

8 See Megarry and Wade, *Law of Real Property*, 6th edn, 2000, London: Stevens, pp 1086, 1087, 1096. Under s 3A(1) of the Prescription Act (Jamaica), a right to use a beach for fishing, bathing or recreation may be acquired by prescription in the same way as an easement of light. See *Beach Control Authority v Price* (1961) 3 WIR 115, pp 178, 179, below.

9 See *Re Ellenborough Park* [1953] 3 All ER 667; *Majid v Beepath* (1981) High Court, Trinidad and Tobago, No 882 of 1976.

grants to Y, who does not own any neighbouring land, the right to use a pathway running across Whiteacre, Y's right cannot be an easement. It is a privilege that is personal to Y, as there is no dominant land to which the right can be said to be attached. Y's right will be, at most, a mere licence. But if Y is the owner[10] of adjoining land, Blackacre, then the right will be an easement (assuming that the other requirements of an easement are satisfied), since X has granted the right not to Y personally, but to Y in his capacity as owner of Blackacre, and the right may be said to have been granted for the benefit of Blackacre. Thus, not only Y, but also all Y's successors-in-title will be entitled to exercise the right of way.

A technical expression that is often used to describe the rule is that 'there cannot be an easement in gross' – that is, an easement that is independent of the ownership of land by the claimant. It should be noted that 'ownership' here includes not only the fee simple owners of the dominant tenement, but also those who own lesser estates in the land: for example, a lessee of the dominant tenement is entitled to enjoy all easements that exist for the benefit of that tenement.

As well as a dominant tenement, there must be a servient tenement over which the easement is to be exercised. The servient tenement must be defined sufficiently clearly in the grant. That is normally done by means of a plan of the servient tenement, as in *Keefe v Amor*,[11] in which land was conveyed 'together also with a right of way on foot or with vehicles over the land shown and coloured brown on the plan hereto annexed'. It should be noted that, where an easement is acquired by prescription – that is, by virtue of long usage and without any express grant – there will be no documents to define the dominant and servient tenements. Oral evidence will thus be required to establish what those tenements are.

An easement must accommodate the dominant tenement

This requirement means that the right claimed must be sufficiently connected with the enjoyment of the dominant tenement and must be for its benefit.[12] The easement must not merely confer some personal benefit on the grantee, but must serve to make the dominant tenement 'a better and more convenient property'.[13] In deciding whether an alleged easement benefits the dominant tenement, regard must be had to the purposes for which the dominant tenement is used. For example, if the dominant tenement is a dwelling house, a right to use a garden on adjoining property[14] or to cross adjoining land to reach a beach[15] will accommodate the tenement, since it enhances its use and enjoyment. If the dominant tenement is an apartment used for business purposes, the right to use a washroom in the apartment immediately above will accommodate

10 In *Boodhoo v Jammuna* (1989) High Court, Trinidad and Tobago, No 438 of 1987, Hamel-Smith J emphasised that one who claims to be entitled to an easement must show that he owns the fee simple or is lessee of the dominant tenement. In this case, the El Socorro Sanatan Dharma Sudhar Sabha, being an unincorporated association, was incapable of owning land, unless trustees were appointed in whom the land could be vested. In the absence of appointment of trustees, there could be no claim to an easement. See also *Kuarsingh v Stephens* (1996) High Court, Trinidad and Tobago, No 1497 of 1991.

11 [1964] 2 All ER 517.

12 Gale, *Easements*, 15th edn, 1986, London: Sweet & Maxwell, pp 17–20.

13 *Op cit*, Megarry and Wade, fn 8, p 1080.

14 *Re Ellenborough Park* [1955] 3 All ER 667.

15 *Hart v Pierce* (1967) 11 WIR 179, High Court, Barbados.

the dominant tenement since it enhances its use.[16] Where the dominant tenement is a public house, an easement to fix a signboard to an adjacent building will accommodate the dominant tenement, even though it benefits the business carried on in the pub rather than the dominant tenement itself.[17] The fact that the existence of the easement increases the value of the dominant tenement is not conclusive as to whether it accommodates the tenement, but it is a relevant factor to be considered.

Propinquity

Normally, the dominant and servient lands will be adjacent to one another, but it is not essential that this should be so, provided that they are sufficiently close so that the dominant land receives a practical benefit from the right. On the other hand, if the two tenements are many miles apart, clearly there can be no easement in favour of one against the other. As Byles J once said:[18] 'You cannot have a right of way over land in Kent appurtenant to an estate in Northumberland [about 300 miles from Kent]'. An unusual example of a servient tenement being held to be sufficiently close to the dominant tenement to accommodate it was where a pew in a church was held to be sufficiently close to a house in the parish, so that the owners of the house acquired an easement to use the pew.[19]

Personal advantages

A right will not accommodate the dominant tenement if it is granted solely for the personal benefit of the grantee, and not for the benefit of the land occupied by him/her. The leading case is *Hill v Tupper*.[20] A canal company leased land adjoining the canal to Hill, granting him the sole and exclusive right to put pleasure boats on the canal. Tupper disregarded this privilege by putting his own rival boats on the canal. Hill sought to restrain Tupper, claiming that Tupper was interfering with his easement to put pleasure boats on the canal. It was held that the right granted to Hill was not an easement, but only a licence, since it was not acquired in order to benefit Hill's land as such, but merely so that he could further an independent business enterprise. The result might have been different if, for example, the right granted had been to cross the canal in order to have access to and from Hill's land, and if Tupper's boats had been so numerous that they interfered with that right.[21] In such a situation, Hill would have had an easement of way and he could have obtained an injunction to restrain Tupper from interfering with the easement.

Dominant and servient tenements must not be both owned and occupied by the same person

Since the essence of an easement is that it is a right *in alieno solo* (over the land of another), it is a basic rule that a person cannot have an easement over his own land. For example, if X is the fee simple owner of two adjacent plots, Blackacre and

16 *Miller v Emcer Products Ltd* [1956] 1 All ER 237.
17 *Moody v Steggles* (1879) 12 Ch D 261.
18 *Bailey v Stephens* (1862) 142 ER 1077.
19 *Phillips v Halliday* [1891] AC 228.
20 [1861–73] All ER Rep 696.
21 *Op cit*, Megarry and Wade, fn 8, p 1081.

Whiteacre, and he/she is in the habit of driving across Whiteacre in order to reach the main road, he/she is not exercising an easement of way over Whiteacre; he/she is simply exercising his rights of ownership of Whiteacre itself. X's right in this case is called a 'quasi-easement' for some purposes, and, as will be seen later, if X later sells the quasi-dominant tenement (Blackacre) and retains the quasi-servient tenement (Whiteacre), the purchaser of Blackacre may acquire a permanent easement over Whiteacre.

It is only where the dominant and servient tenements are both owned and occupied by the same person that an easement is incapable of arising. In the example given, X is both owner and occupier of both tenements – but suppose that X, whilst remaining the fee simple owner of both plots, lets Blackacre to T, a tenant. The two plots are now occupied by different persons. The question is, can T, the tenant occupying Blackacre, acquire an easement over Whiteacre occupied by his landlord, X? The answer is that T can acquire such an easement over Whiteacre by express or implied grant,[22] but he/she cannot acquire an easement by prescription.[23] Similarly, if X lets Blackacre to T and Whiteacre to S, there will be diversity of occupation, and T can acquire an easement over Whiteacre by implied or express grant,[24] although not by prescription.[25]

The right must be capable of forming the subject matter of a grant

The basic principle is that all easements 'lie in grant' – that is, in theory, every easement is created by grant, whether express, implied or presumed. Thus, no right can be an easement unless it is capable of being granted. This proposition is somewhat unhelpful since it does not define what characteristics a right must possess in order that it may be granted. However, it appears from the case law that there are at least three requirements.

(i) The right must be sufficiently defined – that is, it must not be too vague

If the right claimed as an easement cannot be reasonably defined, then it cannot exist as an easement: for example, a right to light shining into a particular window on the dominant tenement is sufficiently certain, but a general right to the air flowing indiscriminately over the servient tenement is too vague to be an easement. Thus, in *Webb v Bird*,[26] in which the plaintiff claimed an easement of the free access of air to the sails of his windmill, which he had enjoyed for 30 years (that is, the claim was by prescription) and which had been obstructed by a building erected by the defendant, it was held that he could not acquire a right to wind and air coming in an undefined channel, for this was not a right known to the law; it was too vague and uncertain.

22 As in *Miller v Emcer Products Ltd* [1956] 1 All ER 237 and *Wright v Macadam* [1949] 2 All ER 565.
23 *Kilgour v Gaddes* [1904] 1 KB 457.
24 In *Majid v Beepath* (1981) High Court, Trinidad and Tobago, No 882 of 1976, Edoo J pointed out that 'a tenant may acquire an easement against another tenant of the same landlord by grant, but for a period not exceeding that of the latter tenant's lease'.
25 *Kilgour v Gaddes* [1904] 1 KB 457.
26 (1861) 143 ER 332.

Another example of a right held to be too uncertain to rank as an easement is a right to privacy. In *Browne v Flower*,[27] an apartment consisting of 12 rooms on the ground, first and second floors of a building was let to T. Later, another apartment on the ground floor was let to the plaintiff. Both apartments had windows overlooking a garden used by the landlord. Sometime afterwards, T subdivided her apartment and, with the landlord's consent, built an iron staircase leading from the garden to an entrance to her apartment on the first floor. The staircase was erected in such a way that persons going up and down could see directly into the plaintiff's bedroom. It was held that there was no easement that had been interfered with by the building of the staircase. The law does not recognise any easement of privacy.

Another type of right that is generally considered to be too vague to be an easement is the *jus spatiandi* – a right to wander at large over the servient tenement, for example, where the servient tenement is a park or field. The right to use a defined pathway across the servient tenement to pass from the dominant tenement to a place beyond the servient tenement is, of course, recognised as an easement of way, but the right to wander at large for recreation has always been considered to be too vague and uncertain to be an easement.

However, in the leading case of *Re Ellenborough Park*,[28] there appeared to be a change of judicial attitude. The facts were that the 'White Cross Estate', which included Ellenborough Park, was being developed as a housing estate. The land surrounding the park had been divided into lots and sold to different purchasers. The conveyances of each lot granted to the purchaser 'full enjoyment at all times hereafter, in common with the other persons to whom such easements may be granted, of the pleasure ground'. The vendors covenanted to keep Ellenborough Park as an ornamental pleasure ground, the expense to be shared by all of the purchasers. It was held that the rights were valid easements, notwithstanding that they might involve a *jus spatiandi* or some analogous right, since:

(a) there were clearly dominant and servient tenements;
(b) the servient tenement accommodated the dominant tenements (the adjacent dwelling houses) since the right to use the park was connected with the enjoyment of the residences; the park was to be a communal garden for the benefit of the owners of the adjoining houses and clearly enhanced the enjoyment of those houses; and
(c) the right was not too vague or uncertain, since it was for the benefit of a limited number of houses, all bordering the park.

A recent case, *Regency Villas Title Projects Ltd v Jordan*[29] was, as the English Court of Appeal noted, the first time since *Ellenborough Park* that the Court had the opportunity to consider the validity of easements relating to various kinds of recreational facilities. Sir Geoffrey Vos, Chancellor, delivering the judgment of the Court, pointed out that, in the more than 60 years since *Ellenborough Park* was decided, the culture and expectations of the population of England and Wales had radically changed, and

27 [1911] Ch 219. See also *Phipps v Pears* [1964] 2 All ER 35, in which it was held that an easement of protection from the weather was too uncertain to be the subject matter of a grant.
28 [1955] 3 All ER 667.
29 [2017] EWCA Civ 238.

the present case had to be considered in the light of those changes. The question to be decided (which, incidentally, seems to be particularly relevant to villa owners in Caribbean resort developments), was whether rights benefiting timeshare owners in a holiday park to use, *inter alia*, a swimming pool, golf course and tennis courts were capable of existing as easements. In response to the principle expressed in earlier cases that an easement should be 'a right of utility and benefit and not one of mere recreation and amusement', the Court stated:[30]

> Easements in the modern world must, of course, retain their essential legal qualities. But the views of society as to what is mere recreation or amusement may change, even if the exclusion of such rights were authoritative, which we rather doubt. Physical exercise is now regarded by my most people in the United Kingdom as either an essential or at least a desirable part of their daily routines. It is not a mere recreation or amusement. Physical exercise can, moreover, in our modern lives, take many forms, whether it be walking, swimming or playing active games and sports. We cannot see how an easement could either in 1981 or in 2017 be ruled out solely on the grounds that the form of physical exercise it envisaged was a game or a sport rather than purely a walk in a garden.
>
> In our view, the requirement that an easement must be a 'right of utility and benefit' is the crucial requirement. The essence of an easement is to give the dominant tenement a benefit or a utility as such. Thus, an easement properly so called will improve the general utility of the dominant tenement. It may benefit the trade carried on upon the dominant tenement or the utility of living there . . . an easement should not in the modern world be held to be invalid on the ground that it was 'mere recreation or amusement' because the form of physical exercise it envisaged was a game or a sport.
>
> There are also other important aspects of the tests adumbrated in *Ellenborough Park* that are particularly relevant to the correct determination of the validity of the grant in this case.
>
> First, the rights must not be too wide or vague.
>
> Secondly, an easement cannot impose a positive obligation on the owner of the servient tenement. In *Rance v. Elvin*[30a] the Court of Appeal held that an easement could not impose a positive requirement for the servient tenement to pay to maintain a water supply, but only imposed on the servient tenement the negative obligation not to impede the flow of water that did enter the relevant pipes . . . *Rance v. Elvin* did not, however, decide . . . that an easement is invalid if it requires positive action by the servient owner in order to allow its continued enjoyment; only that the easement granted did not impose a positive obligation on the servient owner to pay for the water . . . If the servient owner wants to maintain a right of way in good repair, he may do so, but there is no obligation on the servient owner to do so. If the servient owner fails to maintain it, the dominant owner may do so.
>
> Thirdly, an easement is unlikely to be valid if it requires the dominant owner to exercise a right to joint occupation or deprives the servient owner of proprietorship or legal possession. . . This factor is . . . of some importance in the context of sporting facilities that may require much maintenance to remain useable as such, for example a golf course that requires daily mowing to be properly playable. It is here that the right to cease the business that maintains the facilities becomes relevant. If, in such a situation, the owner of the dominant tenement had to take actual occupation or possession of part of the servient tenement in order to give continued effect to the easement, for example, to play golf, that fact might, in our view, at least point against the existence of such an easement in the first place.

30 At para 54.
30a Fn 42, below.

Ultimately, the Court held that the right to enjoy the swimming pool,[31] golf course and tennis courts[32] did take effect as easements, notwithstanding that they may have been granted for 'mere recreation or amusement'. It did not matter that the servient owner might cease to maintain them, since the dominant owners had the right under the general law of easements to enter the servient land in order to carry out necessary repairs or maintenance. The Supreme Court later substantially affirmed the Court of Appeal's reasoning.[33]

(ii) The right must not substantially deprive the servient owner of possession of the servient tenement

Since an easement is essentially a right to do an act on land in the occupation of someone else, a right will not be recognised as an easement if it substantially deprives the owner of the servient tenement of his possession of the land, or if it amounts to a claim to joint possession of the servient tenement. The leading case is *Copeland v Greenhalf*.[34] There, the plaintiff was the owner of an orchard and an adjoining house. Access to the orchard was by way of a strip of land (also owned by the plaintiff) about 150 ft long and averaging 25 ft in width. The defendant was a wheelwright whose premises were directly opposite the strip of land. The defendant proved that, for 50 years, he and his father before him had, to the knowledge of the plaintiff, used one side of the plaintiff's strip of land to store and repair vehicles in connection with his business. He always left room for the plaintiff to have access to the orchard. The defendant claimed that he had acquired an easement by prescription to park and repair his vehicles on the strip. The plaintiff sought to restrain him from doing so. It was held that the right claimed by the defendant was not an easement, since it 'was virtually a claim to possession of the servient tenement', in that the defendant claimed to leave as many vehicles as he liked there, for as long as he liked, and he claimed to enter whenever he liked and do repair work there. Upjohn J said:

> In my judgment, that is not a claim which can be established as an easement. It is virtually a claim to possession of the servient tenement; if necessary, to the exclusion of the owner; or at any rate to a joint user.[35]

In so ruling, his Lordship appeared to be of the view that the right claimed was both too uncertain and too extensive to be an easement. He was careful to point out, however, that this was a claim to an easement by prescription, and he expressly left open the question whether such a right could be acquired as an easement by express grant or reservation.

---

31 The Court accepted that modern swimming pools will often have sophisticated filtration, heating, chlorination, and water circulation systems. But such systems are not essential to the benefit and utility of using the pool. Water was obviously essential, but that could be provided by the owner of the dominant tenement if the servient owner closed its business or allowed the pool to fall into disrepair.

32 The Court suggested that 'the utility and benefit to a dominant dwelling or timeshare property of the ability to use a next-door tennis court was obvious to any modern owner'.

33 [2018] UKSC 57.

34 [1952] 1 All ER 809.

35 Another consequence of this proposition is that 'no right to which attaches the characteristics of an easement of way, and which would seek to prevent the servient owner . . . from making ordinary use of his land, can ever be acquired by prescription': *Ross v Cable and Wireless (WI) Ltd* [1952–79] CILR 240, Grand Court, Cayman Islands, *per* Graham-Perkins J (Ag).

The principle in *Copeland* was followed in *Grigsby v Melville*,[36] in which Brightman J held that the right to occupy a cellar in the plaintiff's house could not be an easement since, to all intents and purposes, it would give an exclusive right to use the whole of the servient tenement (the cellar) and would substantially deprive the owner of the servient tenement of possession of it.

Brightman J expressly followed *Copeland*, although, for the following reasons, it seems he need not have done so:

(a) In *Grigsby*, the easement of storage was claimed by way of express reservation in the conveyance, which read: 'there is reserved to the vendor such rights and easements as may be enjoyed in connexion with the said adjoining property'. As was noted earlier, *Copeland* was a case of prescription; Upjohn J, in that case, pointed out that his decision was concerned only with cases of prescription, and he expressly left open the question whether an easement such as the one claimed could have been acquired by express grant or reservation. Thus, it was not necessary for Brightman J to have followed *Copeland*.

(b) *Grigsby* is difficult to reconcile with the earlier decision of *Wright v Macadam*,[37] in which it was held that the right of a tenant to store her coal in a shed was capable of being an easement and could pass on a conveyance under s 62 of the Law of Property Act 1925. Brightman J, in *Grigsby*, disposed of *Wright* on the ground that the facts were not wholly clear from the report, so that it was difficult to know whether the tenant had exclusive use of the coal shed or of any defined part of it. There is also the case of *Miller v Emcer Products Ltd*,[38] in which an easement to use a washroom was upheld, even though it could be argued that the servient owner would be dispossessed from the washroom when it was in use. It thus seems that it is still uncertain whether rights of storage can rank as easements.

Parking

It is also doubtful whether a right to park a vehicle in a particular place can be an easement. It has been suggested that a right to park a car anywhere in a large area does not amount to a claim to possession of any space and so can rank as an easement (this was confirmed in *Newman v Jones*),[39] but that a right to park a car in a particular reserved space amounts to a claim to possession of the whole servient space, and so cannot be an easement. This would be particularly inconvenient where there are apartment blocks with ground floor or basement car parks, and where car spaces are allotted to the residents. It has been suggested[40] that if this interpretation of

36 [1973] 1 All ER 385.
37 [1949] 2 All ER 565.
38 [1956] 1 All ER 237.
39 22 March 1982, unreported, Chancery Division, England and Wales. In *London and Blenheim Estates Ltd v Ladbroke Retail Parks Ltd* [1993] 1 All ER 307, at 317 (affirmed [1993] 4 All ER 157), Judge Paul Baker QC said: '. . . the essential question is one of degree. If the right granted in relation to the area over which it is to be exercisable is such that it would leave the servient owner without any reasonable use of his land, whether for parking or anything else, it could not be an easement, though it might be some larger or different grant'. See also *Handel v St Stephens Close Ltd* [1994] 1 EGLR 70; *Hair v Gillman* (2000) 80 P & CR 108; *Moncrieff v Jamieson* [2007] UKHL42.
40 See DJ Hayton (1973) 37 Conv (NS) 60.

Copeland and *Grigsby* is correct, the most practical solution would be either to grant leases or licences of each parking space to each resident, or to grant a general easement of parking to all of the residents, ensuring that some sort of practical arrangement is worked out as between all of the residents involved.

(iii) There must be a capable grantor and grantee

As a corollary to the rule that the right must be capable of being the subject matter of a grant, there must be a capable grantor and a capable grantee. In the case of the grantor, it is obvious that if the grantor has no power to grant easements (for example, where the grantor is a company or a statutory corporation and the grant would be *ultra vires*), then any purported grant would not create an easement. As regards the grantee, the example usually given of an incapable grantee is a wide and fluctuating body of persons, such as the inhabitants of a village. Such a body cannot acquire an easement, although, as we have seen,[41] it can acquire a customary right to do something: for example, to use a footpath across private land in order to reach the local church, or to play cricket on an area of land.

An easement must be negative from the point of view of the servient owner – that is, it must not involve the servient owner in any expenditure

A right cannot be an easement if it involves expenditure by the alleged servient owner. By the same token, a servient owner is under no obligation to carry out any maintenance or construction work that may be needed for the enjoyment of an easement.[42] For example, a dominant owner who has an easement of way across a bridge cannot require the servient owner to carry out repairs to the bridge.[43]

To this general rule, there are at least two recognised exceptions:

(a) where there is an easement of fencing, the servient owner is bound to maintain the fence for the benefit of the dominant tenement, notwithstanding that the maintenance will involve expenditure of money;[44] and

(b) where the parties have expressly or impliedly agreed that the servient owner is to be responsible for maintenance – for example, a local authority, which had let apartments in a high-rise building to tenants, was held liable, as under an implied contract, to maintain easements of access over the common parts of the building.[45]

41 See p 147, above.

42 See, eg, *Rance v Elvin* (1983) 49 P & CR 65; *Regis Property Co Ltd v Redman* [1956] 2 All ER 335; *Stokes v Mixconcrete (Holdings) Ltd* (1978) P & CR 448.

43 *Jones v Pritchard* [1908] 1 Ch 630, at 637. But the dominant owner has a right to enter the servient tenement in order to carry out the necessary repairs himself: *ibid; Bulle v Gallagher* (1987) High Court, British Virgin Islands, No 38 of 1984; *Nanton v Rooks* (1969) High Court, St Vincent and the Grenadines, No 191 of 1966.

44 *Crow v Wood* [1970] 3 All ER 425; *Jones v Price* [1965] 2 QB 618.

45 *Liverpool CC v Irwin* [1976] 2 All ER 39.

Legal and equitable easements

Easements have been recognised at common law from medieval times, and they usually take effect as legal interests binding all successors-in-title to the servient tenement. However, in order to be valid at law, an easement must be created by deed[46] or writing. Legal easements may also be acquired by prescription, in which case long use in effect takes the place of a deed.[47]

An easement that is granted without the proper formalities may take effect as an equitable easement under the *Walsh v Lonsdale*[48] principle (for instance, where a right of way is granted by a written agreement not under seal[49]) and, in Barbados and Belize, as in England, an easement other than one for an interest in fee simple or for a term of years (for example, an easement for life) will take effect as an equitable easement only.[50]

ACQUISITION OF EASEMENTS

Express grant

No special form of words is required for the express grant of an easement, provided that the extent of the easement and the description of the dominant and servient tenements are reasonably clear. Usually, the dominant tenement will be described in the deed, but, if it is not, the court may consider all of the surrounding circumstances in ascertaining whether there is a dominant tenement.[51]

Express reservation

The question of reservation arises where the owner of land sells part and retains the rest, and wishes to reserve an easement over the land sold in favour of the land retained by him/her. At common law, a vendor cannot directly reserve for him/herself any easements over the land sold. He/she can only do so indirectly by getting the purchaser to regrant the easement back to him/her. Statutory provisions[52] in some jurisdictions have now made such a regrant unnecessary, by providing that the reservation of a legal estate or interest shall 'operate at law without any execution of the conveyance by the grantee or any regrant by him'. In other words, it is possible on the sale of land for the vendor to reserve for him/herself an easement in favour of the land retained by him/him and against the land sold. An example where this was done is *Johnstone v Holdway*,[53] in which the vendor conveyed land to the purchaser, and in the conveyance inserted the following words: '. . . except and

46 This is the position at common law, although statutory provisions in some jurisdictions require only writing. See, eg, s 43 of Cap 190 (Belize); s 60 of Cap 236 (Barbados).

47 See p 168 *et seq*, below.

48 (1882) 21 Ch D 9. See pp 50, 51, above; *Ramkissoon v Sookwah* (1990) High Court, Trinidad and Tobago, No 169 of 1971.

49 *Jamaica Public Service Co Ltd v Campbell* [2013] JMSC Civ 22.

50 See s 3 of the Property Act, Cap 236 (Barbados); s 3 of the Law of Property Act, Cap 190 (Belize).

51 *Johnstone v Holdway* [1963] 1 All ER 432; *Shannon Ltd v Venner Ltd* [1965] 1 All ER 590.

52 Section 65(1) of the Law of Property Act 1925 (UK); s 69 of Cap 236 (Barbados).

53 [1963] 1 All ER 432.

reserving unto the company and its successors-in-title . . . a right of way at all times and for all purposes (including quarrying)'. It was held that an easement of way had been validly reserved by the vendor.

Implied grant

We have seen that a person cannot have an easement over his own land.[54] If D owns two adjacent plots, Blackacre and Whiteacre, and D habitually crosses Whiteacre in order to reach a minimart on the other side of Whiteacre, D is not exercising any easement, but simply making use of his rights as owner of Whiteacre. The position we have to consider now, however, is what happens when D sells Blackacre and retains Whiteacre, or when D sells both Blackacre and Whiteacre, but to different persons; for, although a person cannot have an easement over his own land, there is nothing to prevent a purchaser of land from acquiring an easement over other land retained by the vendor. In this case, Blackacre is called the quasi-dominant tenement and Whiteacre the quasi-servient tenement. Such an easement may be granted expressly, as we have already seen, but if, owing to incompetent drafting of the conveyance or for any other reason, no express grant of easements is made, the purchaser may still be able to rely on the rules of law whereby easements are implied in his favour. There are three categories of easement that may be implied in favour of the purchaser:

(a) easements of necessity;
(b) intended easements; and
(c) easements within the rule in *Wheeldon v Burrows*.[55]

Easements of necessity

An easement of necessity most often arises where the land sold is completely surrounded by the land retained by the vendor, or by the retained land and land in the possession of a third party, and unless a right of way is implied over the surrounding land, the purchaser of the landlocked plot will have no access to and from his land. In such cases, an easement of way may be implied over the quasi-servient tenement.[56]

In *Nickerson v Barraclough*,[57] Megarry J, at first instance, took the view that the doctrine of easements of necessity is based on public policy, in that it is against public policy that land should be made inaccessible; the English Court of Appeal,[58]

---

54 See p 148, above.
55 (1879) 12 Ch D 31.
56 *Lush v Duprey* (1966) 10 WIR 389, Court of Appeal, Trinidad and Tobago; *Antigua v Boxwill* (1971) 16 WIR 136, PC appeal from the Court of Appeal, Guyana; *Henderson v Griffith* (1970) High Court, Guyana, No 2488 of 1967; *Crooks v Browne* (1986) 23 JLR 475, Court of Appeal, Jamaica; *Sookoo v Edgecombe* (1997) High Court, Trinidad and Tobago, No 412 of 1990; *Colley-Clarke v Colley* (2001) High Court, Trinidad and Tobago, No 1316 of 1999. In registered land, the omission to indicate the landlocked parcel and the proposed right of way on the certificate of title of the servient land does not prevent an easement of necessity from arising: *Crooks v Browne* (1986) 23 JLR 475, Court of Appeal, Jamaica.
57 [1979] 3 All ER 312.
58 [1981] 2 All ER 369, at 379, *per* Brightman LJ.

however, denied that view, starting that the doctrine was based on the presumed intention of the parties. In so doing, the Court of Appeal appears to have blurred the distinction between easements of necessity and intended easements.

Another case in which the distinction between easements of necessity and intended easements became blurred is *Wong v Beaumont Property Trust*,[59] which is also unusual in that it was not a case of a landlocked plot. The facts were that, by a lease made in 1957, three cellars were let to the predecessor-in-title of the present tenant by the predecessors of the present landlord, for a period of 21 years. In the lease, the tenant covenanted to use the premises as a 'popular restaurant' and to control all odours according to health regulations, so as not to create a nuisance. Although the parties did not realise it at the time the lease was made, it was necessary, in order to prevent smells, to construct a ventilation duct to the outside wall of the premises, the wall being in the possession of the landlord. Because the parties did not realise the necessity for this, no duct was built. In 1961, the plaintiff bought the remainder of the lease and developed the premises into a successful Chinese restaurant. The odours coming from the restaurant caused the occupant of the floor above to complain, and the public health inspector required the duct to be built. The landlord refused to allow the duct to be built, and the plaintiff sought a declaration that he was entitled to do so. Lord Denning MR said:[60]

> The question is: has the tenant a right to put up this duct without the landlord's consent? If he has any right at all, it must be by way of easement . . . in particular, an easement of necessity.

All three judges in the Court of Appeal agreed that the plaintiff was entitled to an easement of necessity, since the covenants in the lease relating to the carrying on of the restaurant business, viz, not to cause a nuisance by odours, and to comply with the Public Health Regulations, could not be performed without the ventilation duct. The result was that the plaintiff was entitled to construct the duct and to enter the landlord's part of the premises in order to maintain and repair it.

Meaning of 'necessity'

It is well established that an easement of necessity will be implied in a conveyance only where, without such an easement, the property could not be used at all. It will not be implied merely on the ground that it would be necessary for the reasonable enjoyment of the property. Thus, in *MRA Engineering Ltd v Trimster Co*,[61] the court refused to read into the conveyance of the quasi-dominant tenement an easement of necessity in the form of a driveway for cars. Certainly, there was no existing access to the property by car, but there was access by foot over a public footpath. The lack of access by car made the use of the quasi-dominant tenement more difficult and inconvenient, but it was not inaccessible.

Similarly, in *Manjang v Drammeh*,[62] in which access was available by water across the River Gambia, 'albeit less convenient than access across *terra firma*', the Privy

59 [1964] 2 All ER 119.
60 *Ibid*, at 122.
61 (1987) 56 P & CR 1.
62 (1990) 61 P & CR 194; applied in *Ramkissoon v Pooransingh* (2017) High Court, Trinidad and Tobago, No 2012–0052.

Council held that no easement of necessity would be implied; and in the Trinidadian case of *Boisson v Letrean*,[63] Hamel-Smith J refused to imply an easement of necessity where there was a means of access, albeit over mountainous and difficult terrain. He said:

> The law is clear. The right only arises by way of necessity, not convenience. I fully appreciate that this is mountainous terrain and access . . . to the dominant land is going to be difficult. But there is access, and a way of necessity can only exist where the alleged implied grantee of the easement has no other means of reaching his land. If other means of access exist, no matter how inconvenient, an easement of necessity cannot arise, for the mere inconvenience of an alternative way will not itself give rise to a way of necessity.

The scope of the doctrine of easements of necessity was further examined by Hamel-Smith J in *Rampersad v Jattan*[64] and *Ramdass v Ramdass*.[65] He emphasised the following points.

(a) The doctrine applies not only where the common owner of two parcels of land sells one for value (retaining the other), but also where one parcel is devised by will or conveyed voluntarily *inter vivos*.[66]
(b) Once the plaintiff has established that his parcel is landlocked, the onus shifts to the defendant to show the existence of an alternative route.[67]
(c) The defendant must show that there is a legally enforceable means of access. Any access over private land, where use is by permission of the owner, will be disregarded.[68]
(d) Where the court does imply an easement of necessity, it must be a convenient one.[69]
(e) A way of necessity, once created, may not be varied by the servient owner, even where the altered way is equally convenient.[70]

Intended easements

In *Pwllbach Colliery Co Ltd v Woodman*,[71] Lord Parker stated:

> The law will readily imply the grant or reservation of easements as may be necessary to give effect to the common intention of the parties to a grant of real property, with

---

63 (1989) High Court, Trinidad and Tobago, No 4435 of 1985. See also *Rivers v Darceuil* (1997) High Court, Trinidad and Tobago, No 2024 of 1984; *Mohammed v Ali* (1998) High Court, Trinidad and Tobago, No 1737 of 1980; *Emmanuel v Ace Engineering Ltd* (2013) High Court, Dominica, No 281 of 2009; *Brand v Creasy* (2013) Supreme Court, Belize, No 156 of 2012; *Maduro v Penn* (2017)High Court, BVI, No 2015/111.
64 (1989) High Court, Trinidad and Tobago, No 4556 of 1988.
65 (1989) High Court, Trinidad and Tobago, No 1171 of 1988.
66 *Rampersad v Jattan* (1989) High Court, Trinidad and Tobago, No 4556 of 1988.
67 *Ibid.*
68 *Ibid.*
69 *Ramdass v Ramdass* (1989) High Court, Trinidad and Tobago, No 1171 of 1988. It was held in *Lush v Duprey* (1966) 10 WIR 388, Court of Appeal, Trinidad and Tobago, *per* Wooding CJ, at 395, that the convenience to be afforded by a way of necessity 'falls to be determined as at the date of the acquisition of the right, and the claimant cannot claim any enlargement of that right simply because he subsequently executed work which improved the convenience and facilities of the way'.
70 *Ramdass v Ramdass* (1989) High Court, Trinidad and Tobago, No 1171 of 1988.
71 [1915] AC 634, at 646.

> reference to the manner or purposes in and for which the land granted . . . is to be used. But it is essential for this purpose that the parties should intend that the subject of the grant . . . should be used in some definite and particular manner.

It has been pointed out[72] that intended easements in this sense are not essentially different from easements of necessity, in that a common intention to grant a particular easement will normally exist only in cases of necessity. *Wong v Beaumont Property Trust*[73] is an example of a case that can be categorised under either heading; similarly, the mutual easements of support implied in favour of adjoining duplex houses would appear to fall under both heads. In a Jamaican case, *J & O Operators Ltd v Kingston and St Andrew Corp*,[74] Anderson J held that, in the particular circumstances of the case, a developer, in seeking approval to subdivide the area of the proposed development and secure registered titles, must have intended that the plaintiffs' lots should have access over the defendants' adjacent parking lot, as 'in all other directions they would cross onto lands of other registered proprietors . . . In this context, the plaintiffs may claim that they are entitled to an easement of common intention (see *Wong v Beaumont Property Trust*)'. The Court of Appeal, however, overruled the decision of the lower court on the ground that there was

> no evidence that, at the time of the disposition of the lots now owned by the plaintiffs, the parties had a common intention that the lots would be used in a definite and particular manner, and that the easement claimed was necessary to give effect to that intention.[75]

Ultimately, on further appeal to the Privy Council, it was held that no easement should be implied as there was a public right of way between the various lots and the principal streets of the development, and this right of passage was available to the appellants in the same way as to any member of the public.[76]

Easements implied under the rule in Wheeldon v Burrows

Where X owns two adjoining tenements, Greenacre and Blueacre, and he is in the habit of walking or driving across Blueacre as an alternative means of access from Greenacre to the outside world, one cannot speak of X enjoying an easement over Blueacre, as X is merely exercising his right as owner of Blueacre itself; but if X sells Greenacre to Y, the doctrine of non-derogation from grant requires that Y should not be in a less favourable position than X was, and Y may become entitled to an easement of way over Blueacre. In this context, X's enjoyment of the access across Blueacre may conveniently be called a quasi-easement, which, on the sale of Greenacre, ripens into a full legal easement. This principle was established in *Wheeldon v Burrows*,[77] in which it was held that upon the grant of part of the grantor's land, there would pass to the grantee, as easements, all quasi-easements over the land retained that:

(a) were continuous and apparent; and
(b) were necessary to the reasonable enjoyment of the land granted; and

---

72 Gray, *Elements of Land Law*, 1987, London: Butterworths, p 671.
73 [1964] 2 All ER 119.
74 (2005) Supreme Court, Jamaica, No CLJ-116 of 1999.
75 (2009) Court of Appeal, Jamaica, Civ App No 80 of 2005.
76 [2012] UKPC 7.
77 (1879) 12 Ch D 31, at 49.

(c) had been, and were at the time of the grant, used by the grantor for the benefit of the part granted.

'CONTINUOUS AND APPARENT' QUASI-EASEMENTS

These are quasi-easements that are 'accompanied by some obvious and permanent mark on the land itself, or at least by some mark which will be disclosed by a careful inspection of the premises',[78] such as a made road,[79] or a worn track,[80] drains discoverable with ordinary care,[81] and windows enjoying light.[82]

'NECESSARY TO THE REASONABLE ENJOYMENT OF THE LAND'

This does not mean that the easement must be one of necessity, and the requirement may be satisfied despite the presence of some alternative means of access.[83] It seems that if the easement simply enhances the enjoyment of the land – for example, where it affords a 'short cut' to some place outside – the requirement will be satisfied.

'USED PRIOR TO AND AT THE TIME OF THE GRANT'

An easement cannot be acquired under *Wheeldon v Burrows* unless there is evidence of actual use by the common owner prior to and at the time of the grant. In *Sovmots Investments Ltd v Secretary of State for the Environment*,[84] a large, high-rise office complex, 'Centre Point', was owned by Sovmots. At the time of the action, the building had never been occupied, although it had been completed several months previously. Thirty-six maisonettes on the top six floors of the building were compulsorily acquired by Camden Borough Council, which claimed that it had acquired easements of support for the maisonettes from the building below. The council argued, *inter alia*, that the easements had passed under the *Wheeldon v Burrows* doctrine. The House of Lords held that the doctrine did not apply since: (a) it was based on the principle that a grantor must not derogate from his grant, and it had no application where the quasi-dominant tenement was acquired by compulsory purchase order; and (b) the third requirement of the *Wheeldon v Burrows* rule was not satisfied, viz, that there must be actual use and enjoyment of the quasi-easement by the grantor at the time of the grant. This was not satisfied, since Centre Point had never been occupied.

An example of the application of the rule in *Wheeldon v Burrows* in the Caribbean is *Meyer v Charles*.[85] In this case, M agreed to sell a parcel of land in Antigua to C. The only means of access to the parcel was by an access road over land retained by M. Although it seems that, in any event, C was entitled to an easement of necessity over the road, the Court of Appeal of the Eastern Caribbean States in fact held that C had acquired an easement under the rule in *Wheeldon v Burrows*. Floissac CJ said:[86]

---

78 Cheshire and Burn, *Modern Law of Real Property*, 16th edn, 2000, London: Butterworths, p 592.
79 *Brown v Alabaster* (1887) 37 Ch D 490.
80 *Hansford v Jago* [1921] 1 Ch 322.
81 *Pyer v Carter* (1857) 156 ER 1472.
82 *Allen v Taylor* (1880) 16 Ch D 355.
83 *Horn v Hiscock* (1972) 223 EG 1437, at 1441.
84 [1977] 2 All ER 385. See C Harpum (1977) 41 Conv (NS) 415.
85 (1992) 43 WIR 169.
86 *Ibid*, at 173. Another ground for the decision was that, because M had represented to C, during negotiations leading up to the sale, that a right of way over the access road would be available for the benefit of the parcel to be sold, M was estopped by this assurance from denying C's right of way (at 174).

> All the prerequisites to the implication of a grant of an easement in the form of a right of way over the access road have been satisfied. Firstly, the appellants were the common owners of parcel 55 and the access road. Secondly, during the common ownership, the appellants used the access road as the sole means of access to parcel 55 from the public road, and vice versa. Thirdly, the user of the access road was continuous and apparent (in the sense that it was exercised over a visible access road) and was evidently necessary for the reasonable enjoyment of parcel 55. Fourthly, had parcel 55 and the access road belonged to different owners, the user of the access road would have been indicative of an easement or right whereby parcel 55 would have been classified as the dominant tenement and the access road would have been classified as the servient tenement.

In these circumstances, when the appellants severed their ownership by selling parcel 55 (the quasi-dominant tenement) to the respondents and retained the access road (the quasi-servient tenement), the grant of an easement or right of way over the access road for the benefit of parcel 55 had to be implied.

Implied reservation

Implied reservation may arise where the common owner of two tenements sells the quasi-servient tenement and retains the quasi-dominant tenement. Because of the principles (a) that a grant is construed in favour of the grantee, and (b) that a grantor must not derogate from his grant, the law is reluctant to imply easements in favour of the vendor of land. If the vendor wishes to retain rights over the quasi-servient tenement, he/she should expressly reserve them in the conveyance. The only easements that will be implied in favour of the vendor are:

(a) easements of necessity; and
(b) intended easements.

Easements of necessity

The same rules apply here as apply to implied grant. Thus, if the quasi-dominant tenement (Blackacre) is completely surrounded by other land and the only means of access to and from it is by way over the quasi-servient tenement (Whiteacre), on a sale of Whiteacre by the common owner, an easement of way over Whiteacre will be impliedly reserved for the benefit of Blackacre retained by the vendor.

Intended easements

As in the case of implied grant, any easements that are required in order to carry out the common intention of the parties will be impliedly reserved for the grantor. For example, where the owner of a duplex house sells one part and retains the other, an easement of support will be impliedly reserved for the vendor's part,[87] since this would be necessary to carry out the parties' common intention.

87 *Shubrook v Tufnell* [1916] 2 Ch 120.

Non-applicability of Wheeldon v Burrows

The rule in *Wheeldon v Burrows* does not apply where the quasi-servient tenement is sold and the quasi-dominant tenement retained. Therefore, if the vendor wishes to reserve easements in his favour, he should do so expressly in the deed of conveyance.[88]

Sales of both quasi-dominant and quasi-servient tenements

Where the common owner does not retain any land, but sells both tenements to different purchasers, the result depends on whether the sales are contemporaneous or not.

(a) Where the sales are contemporaneous, the rule in *Wheeldon v Burrows* applies.[89] Thus, all of those continuous and apparent quasi-easements that were in use at the time of the sales pass by implication with the quasi-dominant tenement. In other words, where V sells the quasi-dominant tenement to X and the quasi-servient tenement to Y, and the sales are contemporaneous, the result is the same as if V had sold the quasi-dominant tenement and retained the quasi-servient tenement; X will be entitled to easements of necessity, intended easements and continuous and apparent easements under *Wheeldon v Burrows*.

(b) Where the sales take place at different times, the rule is that the later purchaser is in the same position as his vendor. Thus, if the vendor first sells the quasi-servient tenement, he will not, in the absence of an express reservation, be entitled to easements over the land sold, except for easements of necessity and intended easements, nor will a subsequent purchaser of the quasi-servient tenement be in any better position; but if he first sells the quasi-dominant tenement, the purchaser may also enforce continuous and apparent easements under *Wheeldon v Burrows* against a subsequent purchaser of the quasi-servient tenement to the same extent as he could have done against the vendor.[90]

ACQUISITION UNDER STATUTORY PROVISIONS

Section 62(1) of the Law of Property Act 1925, re-enacting s 6(1) of the Conveyancing Act 1881, provides that, unless a contrary intention is expressed in the conveyance:

> A conveyance of land shall be deemed to include, and shall by virtue of this Act operate to convey with the land, all buildings, erections, fixtures, commons, hedges, ditches, fences, ways, water-courses, liberties, privileges, easements, rights, and advantages whatsoever, appertaining or reputed to appertain to the land or any part thereof, or reputed or known as part or parcel of or appurtenant to the land or any part thereof.

Similar provisions have been enacted in most Commonwealth Caribbean jurisdictions.[91]

---

88 *Majid v Beepath* (1981) High Court, Trinidad and Tobago, No 882 of 1976, *per* Edoo J; *Badall v Du Four* (1980) High Court, Trinidad and Tobago, No 919 of 1977, *per* Bernard J.
89 *Schwann v Cotton* [1916] 2 Ch 120.
90 *Op cit*, Cheshire and Burn, fn 73, p 513.
91 Section 66 of Cap 236 (Barbados); s 6 of Ch 138 (The Bahamas); s 7 of Conveyancing Act 1983 (Bermuda); s 16 of Cap 220 (BVI); s 16 of Cap 54:01 (Dominica); s 3 of Cap 64 (Grenada); s 9 of Conveyancing Act 1973 Rev (Jamaica); s 16 of Ch 56:01 (Trinidad and Tobago); s 16 of Cap 271 (St Kitts/Nevis).

Purpose of the provisions

The object of the provisions is to ensure that a purchaser of land will automatically acquire the benefit not only of easements appurtenant to the land, but also of other rights and privileges that have previously been enjoyed by the owners and occupiers of that land. Thus, the purchaser will acquire all such rights without the need for express words in the conveyance. The significance of the provisions is that their wording is so wide that the purchaser will acquire even those privileges that were previously enjoyed only by way of permission of the vendor – that is, the provisions have the effect of converting mere licences into easements. Thus, for example, in *International Tea Stores Ltd v Hobbs*,[92] the defendant, who owned two houses, let one of them to a tenant for business purposes, and frequently gave permission to the managers of the business to pass and repass across a yard in the defendant's possession. The tenant later purchased the reversion of the property let, nothing being expressed in the conveyance about any right of way across the yard. It was held that he had acquired an easement of way by virtue of s 6 of the Conveyancing Act 1881, since the statute was wide enough to convert mere licences into easements.

The provisions apply whenever there is a conveyance of land. It has been held that 'conveyance' includes not only a conveyance on sale of the fee simple, but also the renewal of a lease, provided that it is made by deed or writing and not merely by word of mouth. The leading case is *Wright v Macadam*.[93] In 1940, M let a top-floor flat in his house to W for one week. After the end of the week, W continued in occupation as a statutory tenant under the Rent Acts. In 1941, M gave W permission to use a shed in the garden (in the occupation of M) to store her coal.[94] In 1943, M granted a new tenancy of the flat to W by an unsealed written document that made no reference to the use of the shed. W enjoyed the use of the shed until 1947, when M demanded that she pay an extra rental for the privilege. When W refused, M denied her further use of the shed. It was held that W had acquired an easement to use the shed under s 62, and was entitled to an injunction to restrain interference with her use of it. Several points emerge from the judgment, as follows.

(a) The word 'conveyance' in s 62(1) included a tenancy made in writing, since the agreement passed a legal estate and therefore amounted to a conveyance.
(b) A right enjoyed by mere permission can pass as an easement under s 62 (as in *Hobbs*).[95]
(c) To pass as an easement, the right must be one known to the law – that is, one that is capable of being recognised as an easement. A right to use a coal shed for the purpose of storing coal for domestic use could clearly be recognised as an easement. It was a right of a kind that could have been included in a lease or conveyance by the use of appropriate express words.

---

92 [1903] 2 Ch 165. See also *Hair v Gillman* (2000) 80 P & CR 108.
93 [1949] 2 All ER 565.
94 Cf *Chinfatt v Solomon* (2007) High Court, Trinidad and Tobago, No 1101 of 1998.
95 [1903] 2 Ch 165.

(d) In the circumstances of the case, it could not be said that the parties intended a merely temporary right to use the shed, since no time limit was set for the use.

Limitations on the application of the provisions

We have seen that, for a licence to be converted into an easement under s 62 and its equivalents, it is irrelevant whether the purchaser had an enforceable right over the vendor's land before the conveyance. The question is solely whether a licence or privilege was in fact enjoyed by the purchaser. If it was enjoyed, then it will ripen into an easement by virtue of the section. Thus, the vendor of land (as in *Hobbs*), or the lessor about to renew a lease, should take care expressly to exclude the operation of the provisions from the conveyance, lest any licences or privileges should be converted into fully fledged easements.

The right claimed under the provisions must be capable of being an easement –that is, it must be recognised by the law as an easement

If the right claimed under the provisions is not capable of being an easement, such as a right to protection from the weather,[96] or a right to privacy, the claim will fail. Another case in which a claim to an easement under s 62 failed on this principle is *Green v Ashco Horticulturalist Ltd.*[97] There, the landlord, B, in 1939, granted a lease of premises to Green for use as a shop. When this lease expired, in 1945, B renewed the lease; in 1959, the lease was further renewed. B, who also owned adjoining property, had allowed Green to use a passageway that ran from the back of the demised premises to the main street, for the purpose of loading and unloading his fruit. Green made considerable use of this passageway, but B had told him he could not use it at certain times when B required it for his own purposes. Green acquiesced to that restriction. Green claimed that this privilege had been converted into an easement of way by virtue of s 62 when the lease was renewed in 1945. It was held that the right claimed was incapable of being an easement, since Green's alleged right of way was restricted, in that he could exercise it only when B permitted him to do so. Cross J said that 'a purported right of way for such period as the servient owner may permit one to use it would not confer any legal right at all'. Such a restriction is inconsistent with an easement of way, the essence of which is that it can be exercised at any time, without regard to the wishes of the owner of the servient tenement. Green could not, therefore, claim that he had acquired an easement under s 62.

On the other hand, we have seen that, in *Wright v Macadam*,[98] the right to store coal in a shed on the servient land was held to be capable of being an easement and passed as such under s 62. Similarly, in *Newman v Jones*,[99] Megarry VC said:

> In view of *Wright v Macadam* . . . I feel no hesitation in holding that a right for a landowner to park a car anywhere in a defined area nearby is capable of existing as an easement.

96 *Phipps v Pears* [1964] 2 All ER 35.
97 [1966] 2 All ER 232.
98 See p 164, above.
99 22 March 1982 (unreported), Chancery Division, England and Wales.

He therefore went on to hold that a right to park on the forecourt of an apartment block passed as an easement under s 62.

Section 62 will not operate unless there has been some diversity of ownership or occupation of the dominant and servient tenements prior to the conveyance

This principle, which was established in *Long v Gowlett*,[100] has been criticised by academic writers,[101] and there was some authority to the contrary,[102] but it was confirmed by the House of Lords in *Sovmots Investments Ltd v Secretary of State for the Environment*,[103] the facts of which have been mentioned earlier.[104] One of the claims of Camden Borough Council was that the effect of the compulsory purchase order relating to the maisonettes in the Centre Point complex was to bring s 62 into play, so that the council acquired all ancillary rights of support, drainage, etc, automatically as easements. It was held, however, that s 62 did not apply, since there had been no diversity of ownership or occupation prior to the conveyance, in that Sovmots Ltd had at all times owned the entire complex and no part of it had been occupied by anyone else. Lord Wilberforce explained the reason for the rule thus:[105]

> The reason is that when land is under one ownership, one cannot speak in any intelligible sense of rights or privileges or easements being exercised over one part for the benefit of another. Whatever the owner does, he does as owner, and until a separation occurs, of ownership or at least of occupation, the condition for the existence of rights, etc, does not exist.

More recently, in *P&S Platt Ltd v Crouch*,[106] the English Court of Appeal has retreated from the requirement of prior diversity of occupation by holding that where V, the common owner of Blackacre and Whiteacre, conveys Blackacre to P and retains Whiteacre, there will pass to P, under section 62, all those continuous and apparent quasi-easements that were enjoyed by V at the time of the conveyance, whether or not they were necessary for the reasonable enjoyment of Blackacre, and in such cases it will be unnecessary to rely on the rule in *Wheeldon v Burrows*.[107] In *P&S Platt*, V were fee simple owners of a hotel and an adjoining plot of land adjacent to a river, on which there were moorings used for the benefit of the hotel guests. When P purchased the hotel from V (who retained the adjoining land), P claimed that it had acquired the right to use the moorings as an easement under section 62. P's claim was upheld by the court. Peter Gibson LJ said:[108]

> English law has long recognized that a conveyance by a grantor of part of his property carries with it certain rights over the retained land which are not expressly conveyed by the conveyance. Because of the common ownership of the property, such rights cannot have been easements prior to the conveyance . . . Somewhat similar [to the rule in *Wheeldon v Burrows*] but more extensive in effect is section 62 of the Law of Property

100 [1923] 2 Ch 177.
101 See P Jackson (1966) 30 Conv (NS) 340; P Smith [1978] Conv 449.
102 *Broomfield v Williams* [1897] 1 Ch 602.
103 [1977] 2 All ER 385, at 391, 397; see C Harpum (1977) 41 Conv (NS) 415.
104 See p 161, above.
105 [1977] 2 All ER 385, at 391.
106 [2003] EWCA Civ 1110.
107 See pp 160–162, above.
108 *Ibid*, at paras 1, 2 *et seq*.

> Act 1925, replacing section 6 of the Conveyancing Act 1881, and designed to make it unnecessary to set out the full effect of every conveyance . . . This appeal gives rise to the question whether, on a transfer by vendors of part of their property, certain quasi-easements over the retained property became legal easements by the operation of section 62 . . . To my mind, the evidence is clear that the rights in question did appertain to and were reputed to appertain to and were enjoyed with the hotel, being part of the hotel business and advertised as such and enjoyed by the hotel guests. The rights were continuous and apparent, and so it matters not that prior to the sale of the hotel there was no diversity of occupation of the dominant and servient tenements. Accordingly, I reach the conclusion that section 62 operated to convert the rights into full easements.

It remains to be seen whether the blurring of the distinction between the effects of section 62 and the rule in *Wheeldon v Burrows*,[109] and the avoidance of the rule clearly confirmed by the House of Lords in *Sovmots*, will find favour with the courts in the UK and the Caribbean. The authors of the UK Law Commission Consultation Paper of 2008 noted that the precise relationship between section 62 and the *Wheeldon* rule is 'doubtful and uncertain' and, more significantly, were critical of the 'transformative effect' of section 62, pointing out that it often operated 'in circumstances where the parties would not necessarily expect an easement to be granted'. It was accordingly recommended that the section should be amended so as to remove its transformative effect, while retaining its 'useful word-saving function'.

There must be a 'conveyance' of land

We have seen that, in *Wright v Macadam*,[110] the word 'conveyance' was interpreted widely to include not only deeds of conveyance and leases by deed, but also tenancies made by writing. Not included, however, are purely oral tenancies,[111] nor agreements to lease.[112] This is another respect in which an agreement to lease within the *Walsh v Lonsdale*[113] principle is less effective than a legal lease.[114]

Section 62 may be excluded by express exception in conveyance

It is always open to the vendor or lessor expressly to exclude the operation of s 62 or its equivalents in the conveyance or lease. The best way to do this is to insert a clause in the conveyance or lease expressly excepting from it any advantages, privileges or licences hitherto enjoyed in respect of the land sold. Indeed, the prudent vendor or lessor should always ensure that such a clause is inserted.

An example of the application of the above principles in the Caribbean is *David v Stollmeyer Ltd*,[115] a case decided under s 16(2) of the Conveyancing and Law of Property Ordinance, Ch 56:01 (Laws of Trinidad and Tobago). In this case, in April 1946, CS granted a 99-year lease of a parcel of land with a dwelling house

109 (1879) LR 12 Ch D 31.
110 [1949] 2 All ER 565.
111 *Rye v Rye* [1962] 1 All ER 146.
112 *Re Ray* [1896] 1 Ch 468.
113 (1882) 21 Ch D 9.
114 See pp 51–53, above.
115 (1959) 1 WIR 153.

thereon to the defendant/appellant. The lease contained the usual covenants, but there was no reference in the lease to the supply of water. At the time of the execution of the lease, water was supplied to the premises by a pipe through which it was conveyed by natural gravitation from a reservoir situated on premises that were retained by CS. The source of the water that flowed into the reservoir was a natural spring. These waterworks had been operated by CS for many years prior to the lease, and, after execution of the lease, the appellant continued to receive water from the reservoir. In February 1951, the reversion in the parcel of land demised to the appellant, together with the other part of the estate retained by CS, was sold and conveyed to the plaintiff/respondent company. The company brought an action claiming the sum of $74 for water supplied to the appellant. The appellant argued that he had a right to the supply of water by way of easement that had arisen on the execution of the lease, by virtue of s 16(2) of the Conveyancing and Law of Property Ordinance, which provided that 'a conveyance of land, having houses or other buildings thereon, shall be deemed to include and shall . . . operate to convey with the land . . . all watercourses, liberties, privileges, easements, rights and advantages . . . appertaining . . . to the land . . . or at the time of the conveyance . . . enjoyed with . . . the land'.

Gomes CJ held that, at the time of the execution of the lease, the appellant acquired a right to the normal supply of water that flowed from the reservoir to the demised premises, such right being capable of passing to a lessee as an easement under s 16(2) of the Ordinance.

ACQUISITION BY PRESUMED GRANT (PRESCRIPTION)

Under this method of acquisition, the law presumes that a person who has, in fact, enjoyed a right for a considerable period of time was, at some time in the past, granted an easement by deed. This concept of acquisition by long enjoyment is called prescription. The doctrine of presumed grant is, of course, a legal fiction, designed, on the one hand, to uphold a right that has been continuously enjoyed and, on the other, to pay lip service to the principle that every easement must originate in a grant.

Basis of prescription

The doctrine of prescription is based on acquiescence by the servient owner in allowing somebody to exercise what amounts to an easement over his land for a long time without doing anything to stop him/her. Fry J, in *Dalton v Angus*, explained the nature of prescriptive acquisition thus:[116]

> In my opinion, the whole law of prescription and the whole law which governs the presumption or inference of a grant or covenant rests upon acquiescence. The courts and the judges have had recourse to various expedients for quieting the possession of persons in the exercise of rights which have not been resisted by the persons against whom they are exercised, but in all cases it appears to me that acquiescence and nothing else is the principle upon which the expedients rest. It becomes, then, of the highest importance to consider of what ingredients acquiescence consists. In many

116 (1881) 6 App Cas 740, at 773.

cases, as, for instance, in the case of that acquiescence which creates a right of way, it will be found to involve, first, the doing of some act by one man on the land of another; secondly, the absence of a right to do that act in the person doing it; thirdly, the knowledge of the person affected by it that the act is done; fourthly, the power of the person affected by the act to prevent such act either by act on his part or by action in the courts; and lastly, the abstinence by him from any such interference for such a length of time as renders it reasonable for the courts to say that he shall not afterwards interfere to stop the acts being done. In some other cases, as, for example, in the case of lights, some of these ingredients are wanting; but I cannot imagine any case of acquiescence in which there is not shown to be in the servient owner:

(i) knowledge of the acts done;
(ii) a power in him to stop the acts or to sue in respect of them; and
(iii) an abstinence on his part from the exercise of such power.

Requirements for prescription

The long enjoyment must be:

(a) as of right;
(b) continuous; and
(c) in fee simple.

User as of right

This requirement means that the enjoyment must not have been by force, in secret or by permission (*nec vi, nec clam, nec precario*).

Nec vi: User by force includes not only physical violence (for example, where the claimant breaks open a locked gate or pulls down a fence), but also where the claimant continues his user despite the servient owner's continual protests,[117] for in neither case can the enjoyment be said to have been acquiesced in by the servient owner.

Nec clam: Where the user was secret – that is, without the knowledge of the servient owner – there can be no prescription: for example, where the plaintiffs claimed an easement to discharge waste fluid from a factory into sewers belonging to a local authority, it was held that the plaintiffs had not acquired an easement by prescription, since the discharge had been nocturnal and intermittent, and without the knowledge of the local authority.[118] Similarly, where D claimed an easement of support for his/her wharf, the claim failed because D had fixed his/her wharf to P's land by means of underwater rods that were invisible, apart from two nuts protruding above the surface of the water.[119] It should be noted, however, that if the servient owner deliberately shuts his eyes to the conduct of the claimant, the defence of *nec clam* will not avail him, since he/she will be held to have had constructive knowledge of the user.[120] In *Diment v Foot (NH) Ltd*,[121] D and F owned adjacent farms. F claimed that, between

117 (1881) 6 App Cas 740, at 786.
118 *Liverpool Corp v Coghill* [1918] 1 Ch 307.
119 *Union Lighterage Co v London Graving Dock Co* [1902] 2 Ch 557.
120 *Ibid*, 571. See *Baboolal v Ali* (2004) High Court, Trinidad and Tobago, No S 1303 of 2003.
121 [1974] 2 All ER 785.

1936 and 1976, he and his predecessors-in-title had used a way across an outlying part of D's farm. The only visible evidence of access from F's farm to D's farm was a gate fixed at the point where F claimed the access. During the period of user, D had been absent from her farm, visiting it only once a year. The farm had been let on four separate agricultural tenancies, and a firm of surveyors had been appointed as agents to manage the land during D's absence. D argued that F could not have acquired an easement by prescription since she (D) was unaware that F or his predecessors were crossing her land. Her argument succeeded. It was held that:

(a) D did not have constructive knowledge of F's user – the mere sight of a gate leading to F's land would not have put D on any further inquiry as to why the gate was there;
(b) although there is a presumption that the servient owner knows of a user of way, the presumption could be rebutted by evidence that he did not have such knowledge, as was the case here; and
(c) no knowledge was proved to have been acquired by D's agent, so no knowledge could be imputed to D.

Nec precario: User that has been enjoyed with the permission of the servient owner cannot become an easement by prescription, for the fact that the permission was granted shows that the servient owner cannot have acquiesced in the claimant's exercising the easement *as a matter of right*, since a permission can be withdrawn at any time. User by permission can only be, at most, a licence. The leading case is *Gardner v Hodgson's Kingston Brewery*,[122] in which it was held that a woman who had used a cartway from her stables through the yard of an adjoining inn for 60 years did not acquire an easement, because she paid 15 shillings a year for the privilege. The user was by permission and not as of right. This case shows that a landowner can easily prevent a neighbour from acquiring a prescriptive easement of way over his land by requiring that the neighbour make a nominal periodic payment for the use of the way.[123] It is equally clear that a licence or permission granted as an act of good neighbourliness cannot be converted into an easement by prescription.[124]
Finally, it may be noted that, although a licence to do something on the servient owner's land, whether gratuitous or contractual, cannot develop into an easement by prescription, since the user will be by permission, it may be converted into an easement under s 62 of the Law of Property Act 1925 (UK) or its equivalents, if the conditions of the sections are met.[125]

Continuous user[126]

This requirement does not necessarily demand that the user be non-stop or on a 24-hour basis; rather, the degree of continuity needed depends on the type of easement claimed.[127]

122 [1903] AC 229.
123 *Ibid*, at 231.
124 *Ironside v Cook* (1978) 41 P & CR 326.
125 See p 163 *et seq*, above.
126 The following passage in the text was cited with approval by Blenman J in *Mapp v Matthews* (2007) High Court, St Vincent, No 560 of 2002, para 39.
127 *Hollins v Verney* (1884) 13 QBD 304.

For instance, an easement to receive support from a building must necessarily be enjoyed 'round the clock', whereas an easement to receive an uninterrupted flow of light must be enjoyed during the daylight hours. An easement of way, on the other hand, will be regarded as sufficiently continuous even where it is used only intermittently, for, by its very nature, it will be used from time to time.[128] If, however, the user is very occasional, as, for example, in one case in which a way was used only three times in 36 years, clearly there can be no claim to an easement by prescription.[129] Whether the user of the way is sufficiently continuous is thus a matter of degree. Megarry and Wade suggest that user 'whenever the circumstances require it'[130] will normally be sufficient to satisfy the requirement of continuity, provided that the intervals are not excessive. It may also be noted that the user need not have been by the same person throughout the whole period. It is sufficient that the user is by successive owners or occupiers of the dominant tenement – which would be the most usual case[131] – nor need the user be by the owner or occupier personally. It is sufficient if members of his family or regular employees enjoy the user.[132]

User in fee simple

The user cannot ripen into an easement unless it is by or on behalf of a fee simple owner against another fee simple owner. This rule has the following practical effects.

(a) An easement for a term of years cannot be acquired by prescription[133] (although it can be acquired by express or implied grant or reservation).[134] An easement acquired by prescription must be for an estate equivalent to a fee simple estate.

(b) In order to acquire an easement by prescription, it must be shown that the user began at a time when the servient tenement was in the hands of a fee simple owner, since only then could a grant by a fee simple owner be presumed. Thus, if, at the time when the user began, the servient tenement was occupied by a tenant under a lease, no easement can be acquired by prescription.[135] However, provided that the servient tenement was occupied by a fee simple owner at the beginning of the period of user, an easement may be claimed despite the fact that, subsequently, the servient tenement was let to a tenant.[136]

(c) A tenant can claim an easement by prescription only on behalf of his/her landlord – that is, he/her cannot claim an easement for the remainder of his/her tenancy only.

---

128 *Ibid.*
129 *Ibid.*
130 *Op cit*, Megarry and Wade, fn 8, p 874.
131 *Op cit*, Cheshire and Burn, fn 73, p 516.
132 *Ansaldi v Lee Lum* [1920] Trin LR 80, at 82, West Indian Court of Appeal, but it was held in this case that use of a way by occasional day labourers going to and from their work did not confer an easement on the employer.
133 *Ansaldi v Lee Lum* [1920] Trin LR 80.
134 See eg, *Wright v Macadam* [1949] 2 All ER 565, p 164, above.
135 *Daniel v North* (1809) 103 ER 1047.
136 *Pugh v Savage* [1970] 2 All ER 353.

The rule that the tenant's claim must be on behalf of his landlord has the following further consequences:

- A tenant cannot claim an easement by prescription over other land occupied by his/her landlord, since a person cannot have an easement against him/herself. Thus, for example, if L, the owner of a two-storey building, lets the upper apartment to T, and occupies the lower apartment him/herself, T cannot acquire by prescription an easement to use a washroom on the ground floor – although he/she could acquire such an easement by express grant or under s 62 of the Law of Property Act 1925 and its equivalents.[137]
- If the landlord leases two separate plots to two tenants, one tenant cannot acquire an easement by prescription against the other tenant, since the landlord cannot have an easement against him/herself.[138]

METHODS OF PRESCRIPTION

There are three separate methods whereby an easement may be acquired by prescription. These methods are cumulative and it is common for claimants to rely upon all three simultaneously.

Prescription at common law

In order to acquire an easement by prescription at common law, the claimant must show that he/she has enjoyed the user since time immemorial – that is, from the time at which legal memory is taken to have begun. The date from which legal memory begins was fixed at 1189 by the Statute of Westminster 1275. The claimant must, therefore, show enjoyment since 1189. In order to relieve the claimant from discharging this impossible burden of proof, the courts are willing to presume that enjoyment has lasted from 1189, if proof is given of an actual enjoyment for 20 years.[139] This concession, however, is subject to one major difficulty: it is that the presumption that user has been since time immemorial can be rebutted by proof that the easement could not possibly have existed since 1189. For example, if an easement of light to a building is claimed, the servient owner can rebut the presumption of user from 1189 by proving that the building was constructed in 1975. Again, if the servient owner can show that at any time since 1189 the dominant and servient tenements were owned and occupied by the same person, any easement would have been extinguished and the claim at common law would fail. For this reason, claims to prescription at common law rarely succeed, and claimants prefer to rely on the other two methods. In any event, it seems that in Commonwealth Caribbean jurisdictions there could never be a presumption of user since 1189.[140]

137 Although a tenant cannot acquire an easement by prescription over his own landlord (ie where the landlord is owner of the servient tenement as well as the dominant tenement let to the tenant), he/she may, *where the servient tenement is owned by a third party*, acquire a prescriptive right in fee simple over that land for the benefit of his landlord: see *Baboolal v Ali* (2004) High Court, Trinidad and Tobago, No S1303 of 2003.

138 *Kilgour v Gaddes* [1904] 1 KB 457; *Simmons v Dobson* [1991] 4 All ER 25; *Hobbs v Laurie* (1992) High Court, Barbados, No 217 of 1988.

139 *Darling v Clue* (1864) 176 ER 586.

140 But see S Owusu, *Commonwealth Caribbean Land Law*, 2007, London: Routledge-Cavendish, pp 433, 434.

Prescription under the doctrine of the lost modern grant

In order to avoid the difficulty that a claim to prescription at common law could be defeated by proof that the easement could not have been enjoyed since 1189, the courts developed what has been variously described as the 'very questionable theory'[141] and even the 'revolting fiction'[142] of the lost modern grant. Under this doctrine, if the claimant can show actual enjoyment of an easement for at least 20 years,[143] the court will presume that an actual grant was made at the time when enjoyment began, but that the deed had been lost.

In *Tehidy Minerals Ltd v Norman*,[144] it was held that the presumption of the lost modern grant cannot be rebutted by evidence that no such grant was, in fact, made. The doctrine is a pure legal fiction. In this case, the defendants proved that they had been accustomed to graze their sheep on the servient tenement for more than 21 years. It was held that they had acquired a profit of pasture under the doctrine of the lost modern grant. The court presumed that, sometime between 20 January 1920, when the user began, and 5 October 1921, a grant by deed had been made, but the deed had been lost in circumstances unknown to anyone. Even though it was extremely unlikely that this had happened, the court was prepared, albeit reluctantly, to uphold the fiction.

Prescription under the Prescription Acts

Easements other than light

Section 2 of the Prescription Act 1832 Act (UK) lays down two prescription periods: one of 20 years; the other of 40 years.

> (1)
> Where an easement has been actually enjoyed without interruption for 20 years, it shall not be defeated by proof that it commenced later than 1189, but it may be defeated in any other way possible at common law.

The effect of the subsection is that the claim will not be defeated by showing that the right cannot have been enjoyed since time immemorial, but it can be defeated by proof, for example, that it was enjoyed by force, or secretly, or by permission,[145] or that there was no capable grantor:

> (2)
> An easement which has been enjoyed without interruption for 40 years is to be absolute and indefeasible unless it appears that it was enjoyed by some consent or agreement expressly given by deed or writing.

141 *Op cit*, Cheshire and Burn, fn 73, p 518.
142 *Angus and Co v Dalton* (1877) 3 QBD 85, at 94, *per* Lush J.
143 *Lazzari v Lazzari* [1997] CILR 350, Grand Court, Cayman Islands; *Young v Flemming* (2009) High Court, Trinidad and Tobago, No 292 of 2004, where there was evidence that the claimant, his family and visitors had habitually driven up to his house in their vehicles across a roadway on the defendant's land without interruption, since at least 1981. Boodoosingh J held that an easement of way had been acquired both under the Prescription Act, Ch 5, No 8, and under the lost modern grant doctrine.
144 [1971] 2 All ER 475.
145 Cf *Carson v Silva* (2005) OECS Court of Appeal, Civ App No 19 of 2004 on the interpretation of s 138(1) of the Registered Land Act of the BVI and its relationship with s 3 of the Prescription Act, 1882 (BVI).

Apart from the difference in the period of user, it seems that the only distinction between the 20-year and the 40-year prescription periods is that an oral permission may defeat a claim under the 20-year period, but not one under the 40-year period.[146] In particular, despite the wording 'absolute and indefeasible' in subs (2), it appears that user must be as of right and there must be a capable grantor.

Section 35 of the Limitation and Prescription Act, Cap 232 (Barbados),[147] contains provisions identical to those of s 2 of the 1832 Act, whereas under s 2 of the Prescription Act of Grenada (Cap 252), there is a single prescription period of 20 years, and under s 2 of the Prescription Ordinance, Ch 5, No 8 (Trinidad and Tobago), there is a single period of 16 years.[148] The latter section provides:

> When any claim shall be made to any right of common or pasture, or other pasture, or other profit or benefit, except rent and services, or to any way or other easement, or to any watercourse, or the use of any water, to be taken or enjoyed or derived upon, over or from any land or water of the State, or of any body corporate or person, and such right of common or matter as hereinbefore mentioned shall have been actually enjoyed by any person claiming right thereto without interruption for the full period of sixteen years, the right thereto shall be deemed absolute and indefeasible, unless it shall appear that the same was enjoyed by some consent or agreement expressly given or made for that purpose by deed or writing.

A Caribbean illustration of acquisition of an easement by prescription is *Hart v Pierce*,[149] a case that came before the Barbados High Court. Here, the plaintiffs owned a property called 'Cleveland', situated on the seaward side of the main road at Worthing, Christ Church. The defendant owned a neighbouring house, 'Penrith'. He was also the owner of a narrow strip of land, which he had purchased in 1962, located behind Cleveland and stretching from the main road to the sea. This strip was 20 ft wide and about 280 ft long, and provided the occupiers of Penrith with access to the beach. The plaintiffs claimed that, from 1943 (when they purchased Cleveland) until 1964, they, their children and their servants had habitually walked over the strip to the beach without objection from the owners of the strip and without any permission to do so. The defendant argued that there was uncertainty as to the way over which the easement was claimed, in that it was not clear whether the plaintiffs had habitually walked down the centre of the strip to the beach or whether they had used a 4 ft way running along the eastern portion of the strip.

---

146 See *op cit*, Cheshire and Burn, fn 73, pp 522, 523. In *Jones v Price* (1992) 64 P & CR 404, it was held that oral permission given *within* the 40-year period will negative user as of right; so, also, will a user that continues on a common understanding that the user is and continues to be permissive (*per* Parker LJ, at 407).

147 See also s 3 of Cap 338 (Antigua and Barbuda); s 3 of Ch 158 (The Bahamas); s 3 of Cap 192 (Belize); s 3 of Cap 58 (BVI); s 2 of Cap 131 (Cayman Islands); s 3 of Cap 7:02 (Dominica); s 2 of the Prescription Act, 1973 Rev (Jamaica); s 3 of Cap 60 (St Kitts/Nevis); s 2 of Cap 246 (St Vincent and The Grenadines).

148 See *Robley v Samuel* (1987) High Court, Trinidad and Tobago, No 8 of 1986; *John v Samuel* (1987) High Court, Trinidad and Tobago, No 4147 of 1978; *Abraham v Vincent* (1991) High Court, Trinidad and Tobago, No 1935 of 1987; *Bhopa v Bhopa* (1998) High Court, Trinidad and Tobago, No 1101 of 1997; *Singh v The Incorporated Trustees of the Tackveeyatul Islamic Association of Trinidad* (2000) High Court, Trinidad and Tobago, No 878 of 1998; *Young v Flemming* (2009) High Court, Trinidad and Tobago, No 292 of 2004; *Marcelle v Bain* (2011) High Court, Trinidad and Tobago, No 921 of 2008; *Andrews v King* (2019) High Court, Trinidad and Tobago, No CV 2013–03152.

149 (1967) 11 WIR 179, High Court, Barbados. See also *Murrell v Taylor* (2001) High Court, Barbados, No 1387 of 1989, in which a right of way was held to have been acquired by virtue of 40 years' uninterrupted user during the period immediately before the action.

It was held that the plaintiffs were entitled to a right of way under s 35 of the Limitation and Prescription Act by virtue of their continued use of the strip for 21 years. The uncertainty as to the precise path used by the plaintiffs was not fatal to their claim, and the path that they were entitled to use would be that which constituted the nearest way they could take to the beach. As Douglas CJ explained:

> Mr Forde's point is that there must be certainty as to the way over which the right is claimed. The evidence given by the second plaintiff is that she walked down the centre of the strip of land to the beach and, that notwithstanding, her claim is in respect of a 4 ft way running along the eastern portion of the defendant's land. The first plaintiff's evidence on this point is not precise – she merely says that her family and her servant 'went through the wicket gate and straight down to the beach on the adjoining piece of land'. Later, she speaks about using 'this wicket gate and path' but does not specify where the path was.
>
> I do not think this is fatal to the case of the first and second plaintiffs. In *Wimbledon and Putney Commons Conservators v Dixon*, James LJ said:[150]
>
>> If, from one terminus to another, say from the gate here to the end of a road 200 yds off, persons have found their way from time immemorial across a common, although sometimes going by one track and sometimes by another, I am not prepared to say that a right of road across the common from one terminus to the other may not be validly claimed, and may not be as good as a right over any formed road . . .
>
> This statement is, of course, *obiter*, but seems to accord with principle and with common sense. In the instant case, it must be borne in mind that the entire strip of land was only 20 ft wide, that it was not cultivated, and that the only things on it were some shrubs and grape trees. I would be very surprised to find the claimants using one path for the entire period concerning which evidence is given. It is more likely that they found their way to the beach avoiding the shrubs and bushes and the trees which grew there as best they could.
>
> In respect of the Harts, I am satisfied that they are entitled under the terms of s 35 of the Limitation and Prescription Act, by reason of their continued user since 1943 when they bought, to a right of way over the defendant's land as they have claimed. That way has never been defined and there will be an order of the court declaring that the first and second plaintiffs are so entitled and . . . the path which the successful plaintiffs are entitled to take is that which constitutes the nearest way they can take.

A more recent Caribbean example of statutory prescription is the Grenadian case of *Dean v Doyle*.[151] Here, RD, who operated a mattress factory on premises that also comprised his matrimonial home, approached the defendant, the owner of adjacent land, in 1979 with a view to obtaining an alternative means of access to his property over the defendant's land. RD was given permission to construct a road over the defendant's land and the road was completed in 1980, from which time the road was used by RD, his wife, other members of his family and visitors to their premises up to 20 April 2002, when the defendant blocked the road by erecting a fence. Meanwhile, in 2001, RD had conveyed the matrimonial home into the name of his wife, pursuant to an order of the court ancillary to divorce proceedings.

150 (1875) 1 Ch D 362, at 368, 369.
151 (2007) High Court, Grenada, No 0476 of 2002.

The wife sought a declaration that she was entitled to use of the access road to and from her residence 'over the defendant's adjoining property at all times and for all purposes'.

One of the issues in the case was whether the oral permission to construct and use the road operated to defeat the claim to an easement under the Prescription Act of Grenada, s 2 of which provides that

> when . . . any way or easement . . . a claim to which may be lawfully made at common law by custom, prescription, or grant, has been actually taken and enjoyed . . . over . . . any land of any person . . . without interruption for the full period of twenty years, the right thereto shall, subject to the provisions hereinafter contained, be deemed absolute and indefeasible unless it appears that it was enjoyed by some consent or agreement made or given for that purpose in writing.

Benjamin J held that the oral permission did not defeat the claim: 'Section 2 operates, in the absence of consent or agreement in writing, to confer upon the claimant an absolute and indefeasible right of way, there having been user for in excess of the requisite full period of 20 years'. The claimant was accordingly entitled to the declaration sought.

OTHER PROVISIONS IN THE ACTS

The Prescription Act 1832 and its equivalents contain further requirements, which may be summarised thus:

(a) enjoyment must be for the period 'next before the action' – that is, for 20 or 40 years immediately preceding the action;
(b) enjoyment must be without interruption by the servient owner, but no act of the servient owner will be declared to be a statutory interruption unless acquiesced in by the dominant owner for one year after he had notice of the interruption;[152] and
(c) any period during which the servient owner was under a disability (that is, was an infant, lunatic or tenant for life, or during which an action was pending and diligently prosecuted) must be deducted from the 20-year period. Except for the tenancy for life, these disabilities do not apply to the 40-year period, although any period during which the servient tenement was held for a term of years exceeding three years must be deducted from the 40-year (but not from the 20-year) period.[153]

Enjoyment 'next before action'

The period of user must be the period immediately before and leading up to the action in which the claim to an easement is sought to be established. Thus, for example, if, on 1 July 2014, the dominant owner brings an action in the High Court for a declaration that he is entitled to an easement of way on the basis that he has enjoyed

152 See *Mohammed v Ali* (1998) High Court, Trinidad and Tobago, No 1737 of 1980.
153 Sections 7 and 8 of the Prescription Act 1832 (UK).

the way for 20 years, he must show an uninterrupted user from 2 July 1994 right up to 1 July 2014. It would not be sufficient for him/her to show that he enjoyed the user, for example, from 2 July 1985 to 1 January 2014, for, although the period is 29-and-a-half years, it does not immediately precede the court action, there being a 6-month gap between cessation of the user and commencement of the action.

Unity of ownership or possession

One particular circumstance in which a 20-year period of enjoyment would not satisfy the statutes is where, for part of that period, both dominant and servient tenements came into the ownership or possession of the same person – that is, where there was 'unity of ownership or possession'. The reason for this is that, where there is such unity, any rights exercised over the quasi-servient tenement by the common owner of both tenements are deemed to be exercised not as easements, but by virtue of ownership or possession of the quasi-servient tenement itself. It is an implication of the principle that a person cannot have an easement over his own land. Thus if, for example, the fee simple owner of the dominant tenement proves that he and his predecessors-in-title have enjoyed a right of way over the servient tenement for 35 years, apart from a period of 12 months, five years ago, when his immediate predecessor-in-title took a one-year lease of the servient tenement and occupied a house on the land for that period, a claim under the Acts will fail, because during part of the 20 years immediately before the action there was unity of possession of both tenements. It has been held, however, that a claim to an easement in such circumstances may succeed under the doctrine of the lost modern grant.[154]

Statutory interruption

The Prescription Acts give a special meaning to 'interruption', viz, some overt act, such as the obstruction of a right of way by the erection of a barrier or fence, which shows that the easement is disputed.[155] Interruption will, thus, normally be by the servient owner. However, the Acts go on to provide that no act will be deemed to be a statutory interruption unless it has been submitted to or acquiesced in by the dominant owner for at least one year after he had notice of the interruption and of the person responsible for it. For example, the dominant owner has used a footpath over the servient tenement since 1 January 1994, and, on 1 July 2013, the owner of the servient tenement erects a wall across the footpath, blocking use by the dominant owner. If, on 1 January 2014, the dominant owner brings an action in court for a declaration that he is entitled to an easement of way over the servient tenement and for an injunction restraining the servient owner from interfering with the easement, the dominant owner will be entitled to succeed. The servient owner's act in barring the way is not a statutory interruption, because it has not been submitted to or acquiesced in by the dominant owner for one year, but only for six months. The commencement of the action by the dominant owner is sufficient proof that he does not acquiesce in the interruption. Other ways of establishing non-acquiescence by

154 *Hulbert v Dale* [1909] 2 Ch 570.
155 *Carr v Foster* (1842) 114 ER 629, *per* Parke B.

the dominant owner include removing the obstruction, and protesting clearly and forcefully, with or without the threat of legal proceedings.[156]

Easement of light

Section 3 of the Prescription Act 1832 provides that,

> when the use of light to any dwelling house, workshop or other building shall have been actually enjoyed for the full period of 20 years without interruption, the right thereto shall be deemed absolute and indefeasible, unless the same was enjoyed by some consent given for that purpose by deed or writing.

The main differences between acquisition of an easement of light and acquisition of other easements under the Acts are that, in easements of light:

(a) user need not be as of right;[157] all that the claimant under the Acts needs to show is 20 years'[158] uninterrupted user and absence of a written consent;
(b) user need not be by or on behalf of one fee simple owner against another fee simple owner; thus, the mere fact that the servient tenement has been let to a tenant for the whole period of user does not prevent acquisition of an easement of light[159]– and, further, one tenant (X) can acquire an easement of light by prescription over another tenant (Y) of the same landlord, so that X and his successors will acquire an easement not only against Y, but also against the common landlord and all successors-in-title to the servient tenement; and
(c) none of the disabilities applies to the easement of light.

On the other hand, the same principles regarding interruption apply to the easement of light as to other easements,[160] and the period of user must immediately precede the action.

Right to use a beach

Section 4(1) of the Prescription Act of Jamaica[161] provides:

> When any beach has been used by the public or any class of the public for fishing or for purposes incident to fishing, or for bathing or recreation, and any road, track or pathway passing over any land adjoining or adjacent to such beach has been used by the public or any class of the public as a means of access to such beach without interruption for the full period of 20 years, the public shall, subject to the provisos hereinafter contained, have the absolute and indefeasible right to use such beach, land, road, track or pathway as aforesaid, unless it shall appear that the same was enjoyed by some consent or agreement expressly made or given for that purpose by deed or writing.

---

156 *Glover v Coleman* (1874) LR 10 CP 108.
157 *RHJ Ltd v FT Patten (Holdings) Ltd* [2008] EWCA Civ 151, para 2, *per* Lloyd LJ; *George v Thomas* (2009) High Court, Trinidad and Tobago, No 502 of 1994, para 26, *per* Tiwary-Reddy J.
158 Under s 3 of the Prescription Ordinance, Ch 5, No 8 (Trinidad and Tobago), the period is 8 years.
159 See *Garib v Seepaulsingh* (1997) High Court, Trinidad and Tobago, No 140 of 1992.
160 See *Wilson v Abed and Co Ltd* (1964) High Court, Barbados, No 184 of 1964.
161 This section was originally inserted as s 3A by s 2 of the Prescription (Amendment) Law 1955.

It will be noticed that this section follows, *mutatis mutandis*, the wording of s 3 of the Prescription Act 1832 (UK) and its Jamaican equivalent, s 3 of the Prescription Act (Jamaica), which govern the acquisition of easements of light. Section 4 affords the public a right by prescription to use a beach and any means of access to a beach where uninterrupted user of such beach or access for 20 years is proved.

The effect of the section was considered in *Beach Control Authority v Price.*[162] In this case, the Beach Control Authority, a statutory body,[163] sought a declaration on behalf of the inhabitants of Drapers, a small coastal village, that a right of way existed across the defendant's land as a means of access to a beach, together with a right to use the beach itself. It was established on the evidence before the magistrate that: (a) many villagers of Drapers from 1926 to 1948 had used the beach for the purpose of bathing, and that they had used a pathway across the defendant's land in order to reach a spring where they washed their clothes, and to reach a stream that ran across the beach to the sea, for the purpose of bathing; and (b) between 1949 and 1954, the user of the stream, pathway and beach ceased, except that a few individuals, not exceeding 20, were given personal permission by the overseer in charge to use the beach for bathing.

The Jamaican Court of Appeal held that: (a) under s 4, as in the case of easements of light, it was not necessary for the user of the beach to have been 'as of right'; therefore, the fact that user of the beach may have been by permission did not prevent a prescriptive right from being acquired; but (b) user of the beach by the public or a class of the public as such was necessary, and in this case the evidence showed that the user between 1948 and 1954 was not by the people of Drapers as a group, but rather, by certain individual persons who may or may not have been inhabitants of Drapers. Accordingly, since it could not be shown that there had been 20 years' use by the inhabitants of Drapers immediately before and leading up to the initiation of proceedings, no right to use the beach or the access thereto had been established under s 4.

EXTENT OF EASEMENTS

Having established that an easement has been acquired, it may be necessary to decide how extensive that easement is. For instance, where an easement of way is established, it may be necessary to determine whether it is restricted to use by pedestrians or whether it includes use by vehicles. Another question that commonly arises relates to a change in the circumstances of the user. For example, at the time when the easement commenced, the dominant tenement may have been agricultural land. It may have subsequently been developed as a housing estate, a hotel, or a factory. The question may arise as to whether the dominant owner is entitled to use the way

162 (1961) 3 WIR 115, Court of Appeal, Jamaica. See also *Rosenberg v Sherwood*, Civ App No 70/72, *per* Fox and Edun JJA.

163 Under s 3(1) of the Beach Control Act 1955, all rights in and over the foreshore of Jamaica were declared to be vested in the Crown, save those rights expressly preserved by s 3(2). Section 5(1) prohibits user of the foreshore without a licence granted by the Beach Control Authority (the current licensing authority in the National Environment and Planning Agency (NEPA)), but s 4 entitles the owner or occupier of land adjoining the foreshore, or any member of his family or any private guest of his, to 'use' that part of the foreshore adjoining his land for bathing, fishing or other recreation, and as a means of access to the sea for such purposes.

for the purposes of the present development (for example, as a means of access to a hotel), or whether the easement is confined to its original use – that is, only for the benefit of agricultural land. The answer to these questions depends primarily on the method by which the easement was acquired – whether it was by express grant or reservation, implied grant or reservation, or prescription.

A person who, in purported exercise of a right of way, makes an 'excessive user' of the servient tenement (for example, where he drives his vehicle on a way that is restricted to pedestrian access) commits a trespass and may be restrained from so doing at the instance of the servient owner.[164]

Easements acquired by express grant or reservation

The extent of an easement acquired by this method depends upon the proper construction of the document that created it. For instance, if an *unrestricted* right of way is granted expressly, it will not be confined to the purpose for which the dominant land was used at the time of the grant.

In *White v Grand Hotel (Eastbourne) Ltd*,[165] an unrestricted right of way over the servient tenement, granted expressly to the owner of a private house on the dominant tenement, was held not to be limited to the purposes existing at the time of the grant (that is, use for the benefit of a private house). Thus, when the private house was later converted into a hotel, the owners of the hotel were entitled to use of the way for the general purposes of the hotel. In *Kain v Norfolk*,[166] an easement was granted in 1919 'to pass and repass at all times hereafter with or without horses, carts and agricultural machines and implements'. Subsequently, a sand and gravel pit was opened on the dominant tenement and a large number of trucks were driven across the servient tenement to and from the pit. It was held, following *White v Grand Hotel (Eastbourne) Ltd*, that the easement was not restricted to use by horses and carts, but included use by trucks. In *Bulstrode v Lambert*,[167] it was held that a right 'to pass and repass with or without vehicles' over the servient tenement included a right to park vehicles for the purpose of loading and unloading, as this was an incident of the right of way. In *National Trust v White*,[168] the plaintiff was the grantee of a right of way over a track across the defendant's farm, under a 1921 conveyance, for the purpose of access to a historic site. In 1973, the plaintiff built a large car park at the end of the track. The defendant

---

164 See *Wellington v Grant* (1997) High Court, Trinidad and Tobago, No T 201 of 1991.

165 [1913] 1 Ch 113. Similarly, in *Wilson v Bodden* [1988–89] CILR N 18, Grand Court, Cayman Islands, Collett CJ held that 'the extent of the permitted user of an unrestricted right of way need not be limited to the particular purpose for which it was originally granted'. If that purpose was originally to facilitate personal and domestic access to and from his home, the grantee was entitled to extend the use to accommodate residential and commercial tenants, his employees and their families. He was also entitled to make up the road surface of the right of way so as to make it suitable for private and commercial vehicles of a size and width commensurate with the road's width and surface structure. Any limitation that might be imposed should depend on evidence that the proposed use would be more than the actual road could bear, or that the use interfered unreasonably with the lawful use of the right of way by the other persons having similar entitlements. Cf *Todrick v Western National Omnibus Co Ltd* [1934] Ch 190; *Jelbert v Davis* [1968] 1 All ER 1182; *White v Richards* (1993) 68 P & CR 105; *Jalnarne Ltd v Ridewood* (1989) 61 P & CR 143.

166 [1949] 1 All ER 176.

167 [1953] 2 All ER 728, but see *London and Suburban Land and Building Co (Holdings) Ltd v Carey* (1991) 62 P & CR 480.

168 [1987] 1 WLR 907.

complained of the increase in the volume of traffic using the track, alleging that it adversely affected the enjoyment of the defendant's land. It was held that the user of the easement of way was not excessive, since access to the car park was required not for the enjoyment of the car park itself, but in order to visit the site; the user was ancillary to this purpose and came within the terms of the grant.

The principle in *White v Grand Hotel (Eastbourne) Ltd* was applied in a Barbadian case, *Naime v Rockley Country Club*.[169] Here, M in 1937 conveyed a residential property, 'Worthing View House', to a purchaser, expressly reserving in favour of adjacent land retained by him (which at that time was a disused golf course) an easement over the property 'to go, return, pass and repass by day and night over and along the said portion of land . . . with or without . . . carts, trucks, carriages or motor cars or other motor vehicles of all kinds laden or unladen'. The defendants, who subsequently purchased the dominant land from M, redeveloped the land into a large resort, comprising over 300 apartments, with, *inter alia*, a golf course, tennis courts, swimming pools, restaurants, bars and a disco. The plaintiff, the present owner of Worthing View House, claimed in 1980 that the defendants had caused an unjustified enlargement of the right of way by altering the character, nature and extent of the user. He complained of a constant flow of traffic to and from the resort, including minimokes, private cars, coaches, and even Transport Board buses.

Douglas CJ held, applying the test in *White v Grand Hotel (Eastbourne) Ltd*, that there was nothing in the context of the conveyance of 1937 that limited the words by which the reservation of the right of way was made. As Cozens-Hardy MR had said in that case:[170]

> It is a right of way claimed under a grant and, that being so, the only thing that the court has to do is to construe the grant; and unless there is some limitation to be found in the grant, in the nature of the width of the road or something of that kind, full effect must be given to the grant, and we cannot consider the subsequent user as in any way sufficient to cut down the generality of the grant.

Accordingly, the plaintiff's claim failed.

In any case of difficulty in construing the grant or reservation, for example, where there is a simple grant of a 'right of way' without any words defining the extent of the easement, the physical circumstances of the *locus in quo* must be considered, and the court will, if necessary, examine the land itself in order to decide what the parties must have intended. An example of the application of this principle is *St Edmundsbury Diocesan Board v Clark*.[171] In this case, land adjoining a church was conveyed by the church authorities to the defendant, subject to a reservation of 'a right of way over the land coloured red on the plan to and from St Botolph's Church'. The question was whether the right of way reserved by the church authorities was a right exercisable on foot only, or whether it included user with vehicles. In construing the reservation, the court looked at the circumstances of the land itself. The land over which the right was exercisable was a narrow strip, two-thirds of it being a derelict gravel and sandy path covered with leaves. It was only 4.5 ft wide, and there were two gateposts at the end of it, only 4 ft apart. There was no evidence that the path had been used by vehicles before the time of the grant in 1945. It was held that,

169 (1981) 16 Barb LR 244.
170 [1913] 1 Ch 113, at 116.
171 [1975] 1 All ER 772.

in the light of the surrounding circumstances, the right of way would be construed as being limited to use as a footpath only.[172]

Easements acquired by implied grant or reservation

In *Corporation of London v Riggs*,[173] it was held that a way of necessity is strictly limited to the circumstances of the necessity that existed at the time of the conveyance. In that case, the land conveyed by the vendor to the corporation completely surrounded land retained by the vendor. At the time of the conveyance, the landlocked plot was used for agricultural purposes. It was held that the easement of necessity was limited to those purposes and could not subsequently be used for carrying building materials to and from the dominant tenement on which the owner proposed to build a restaurant. It will be noted that this was a case of implied reservation that, in accordance with the rule that a grantor must not derogate from his grant, was construed strictly against the vendor.[174] Whether a similar decision would have been reached if the case had been one of implied grant is not clear, although it has been suggested that, even in cases of implied grant, the extent of the right will be limited by reference to the established or contemplated use at the time of the conveyance or transfer that gave rise to the easement.[175] Thus, in *Milner's Safe Co Ltd v Great Northern and City Rly Co*,[176] it was held that, where a testator devised adjacent plots to different persons, one of which was later bought by the defendants for conversion into a railway station, a right of way that had been used in the testator's lifetime for domestic purposes could not be converted into a means of access to the station for the general public.

Milner's Safe was followed in a Belizean case, *Card v Card*.[177] Here, T in his will devised one portion of his property (Lot A) to P, and the other portion (Lot B) to D. There was evidence that, up to the date of execution of the will, access to Lot B had been enjoyed on foot and occasionally by bicycle over a three-foot wide pathway across Lot A, but the will did not expressly grant any such right of way. D subsequently acquired a motor vehicle which he began habitually to drive over Lot A without P's consent and in defiance of P's protestations. P brought a claim in trespass against D, and D counterclaimed for a declaration that he had a right of way over Lot A. Moe CJ held that D had acquired an easement of way across Lot A by implied grant, since Lot B was 'so situated that it necessarily depends on Lot A in order to be enjoyed in the state which it was in when it was devised', and 'the devise of Lot B carried with it or implied a devise of the way then used to it'; however, the driving of a vehicle across the way was an excessive user and constituted a trespass, in accordance with 'the principle that a right of way cannot be properly exercised by the dominant owner so as to increase the burden originally cast on the servient tenement and to the detriment of the latter'.

172 Similarly, in *Rhinoceros Co Ltd v Moonhole Co Ltd* (2020) High Court, St Vincent and the Grenadines, No 2017/0184, Byer J held that the surrounding circumstances showed that a 12 foot wide access way was to be utilized as a footpath only, and not for vehicles See also*Bulle v Gallagher* (1987) High Court, St Vincent and the Grenadines, No 38 of 1984.
173 (1880) 13 Ch D 798.
174 See p 162, above.
175 Gravells, *Land Law: Text and Materials*, 1995, London: Sweet & Maxwell, p 595.
176 [1907] 1 Ch 208.
177 (1982) Supreme Court, Belize, No 293 of 1980.

Easements acquired by prescription

Where an easement is acquired by long user, its extent is limited to the purposes for which the land has, in fact, been used during the prescription period. The principle is that the easement cannot be extended to purposes radically different from those enjoyed during the period. Thus, for example, if a right of way over the servient tenement was acquired by 20 years' user, during which time it was used for carrying agricultural produce to and from the dominant tenement, it cannot subsequently be used for transporting heavy machinery to and from a factory that is later built on the dominant tenement.[178]

However, there is no objection to the right of way being used more intensively – that is, as regards the number of people or vehicles using it – provided that the user is not different in character. Thus, for example, where an easement to use a path leading to a shop is acquired by prescription, and there is an expansion of the business and consequent increase in the number of customers coming to the shop, the easement will extend to the increased use, since it is a matter of increase in intensity rather than a change in character of the user.[179] The result was similar where two existing houses on the dominant tenement were replaced by seven modern dwelling units;[180] and a right of way appurtenant to a golf club would not be exceeded merely because the membership of the club, and therefore the user of the way, increased.[181]

In *Cargill v Gotts*,[182] C, the owner of a farm, and his employees had, since 1928, continuously drawn water from a pond on G's land. After 1950, the quantity of water taken from the pond increased greatly, since from that time onwards it was used not only for watering cattle, but also for spraying crops. C sought a declaration that he had acquired an easement by prescription to abstract water from the pond for the general purposes of his farm, and that this extended to use for crop spraying. G, on the other hand, argued that the user required to support prescription must be certain and uniform in its character and extent throughout the prescription period, and that the burden on the servient tenement must remain substantially the same. In the present case, that burden had increased greatly for the past 15 years of the user. It was held, however, that C was entitled to the declaration he sought. The increase in intensity of the user since 1950 did not prevent acquisition of the easement to draw water, since it was not a user of a different character.

An interesting Caribbean case in which the excessive user of an easement was in issue is *Bernard v Jennings*.[183] In this case, TB, the plaintiffs'/appellants' predecessor-in-title, had regularly used a strip of land on the defendants'/respondents' adjacent property for gaining access to his property both on foot and with a mule-drawn cart, which he used for conveying cocoa and copra. After TB died in 1947, the plaintiffs tended TB's land and continued to use the strip of land, but only on foot. In 1962, the plaintiffs conveyed a portion of their land to CA, who built a house thereon. Shortly afterwards, the defendants erected a barbed-wire fence and placed logs across the strip in order to

178 *Williams v James* (1867) LR 2 CP 577, at 582.
179 *Woodhouse and Co Ltd v Kirkland* [1970] 2 All ER 587.
180 *Giles v County Building Constructors Ltd* (1971) 22 P & CR 978.
181 *British Railways Board v Glass* [1964] 3 All ER 418, at 432.
182 [1981] 1 All ER 682.
183 (1968) 13 WIR 501, Court of Appeal, Trinidad and Tobago, followed in *Singh v The Incorporated Trustees of the Tackveeyatul Islamic Association of Trinidad* (2000) High Court, Trinidad and Tobago, No 878 of 1998 and in *James v Thomas* (2009) High Court, Trinidad and Tobago, No T-72 of 2005.

prevent cars from passing along it. The plaintiffs sought a declaration that they were entitled to an easement of way over the strip on foot and with vehicles, under ss 2 and 4 of the Prescription Ordinance (Trinidad and Tobago). The trial judge held that a right of way on foot had been established under the Ordinance, but the enjoyment of the way for animal-drawn vehicles not having been exercised for more than 16 years up to the time of action, the claim to such a right under the Ordinance should fail. He awarded the plaintiffs damages for interference by the defendants with the easement of way, on the ground that the obstruction of the strip made it inconvenient for pedestrians to use it. The Trinidad and Tobago Court of Appeal held that:

(a) the trial judge was correct in his finding that a right of way on foot had been acquired by the plaintiffs under the Prescription Ordinance;
(b) the award of damages was not justified, since the obstruction of the way was not wrongful, being designed to prevent the passage of vehicles and not that of pedestrians; and
(c) if the excessive user of an easement cannot be abated without obstructing the whole user of the easement by the person who is unlawfully exceeding his right, the owner of the servient tenement is entitled to obstruct the whole of that user.

Fraser JA said:

> It is unnecessary to go behind the trial judge's findings of fact. The evidence justified his conclusion that a right of way on foot had been acquired by virtue of the Prescription Ordinance; but it is helpful to understand its implications. The appellants' father had acquired a right to pass on foot and with animal-drawn carts. He used the way largely for agricultural purposes which ceased on his death. The only user which continued thereafter was such as was necessary to provide ingress and egress to the appellants' dwelling. True enough, it was a right of way enjoyed by the dominant tenement over the servient tenement, but in its use after Bernard's death it had become restricted to a way on foot. That this was understood by all the parties concerned is supported by the appellants' requests for the passage of motor vehicles to facilitate the construction of the Chin Aleongs' house. It is nowhere suggested that the respondents at any time attempted to interfere with the appellants' continuing right to pass on foot and it is significant that the interference occurred only after construction of the Chin Aleongs' house. It stemmed directly from the threatened use of the way by the Chin Aleongs for the passage of motor cars.
>
> Clearly, the appellants and their agents, the Chin Aleongs, were seeking to enlarge their right. At the same time, they were attempting to increase the burden on the servient tenement. This they could not legally do. Bovill CJ, in *Williams v James*, said:[184]
>
> When a right of way to a piece of land is proved, then that is, unless something appears to be the contrary, a right of way for all purposes according to the ordinary and reasonable use to which that land might be applied at the time of the supposed grant. Such a right cannot be increased so as to affect the servient tenement by imposing upon it any additional burden.
>
> The same principle was more recently applied by Harman J in *RPC Holdings Ltd v Rogers*, in which, after discussing a number of the relevant authorities, he said:[185]
>
> > It seems to me . . . that the question of the extent of the right is one of fact which I as a juryman have got to determine, but that I am not to conclude from the mere fact that, while property was in one state the way was for all purposes for which it was wanted,

184 (1867) LR 2 CP 577, at 580.
185 [1953] 1 All ER 1029, at 1035.

> therefore, that is a general right exercisable for totally different purposes which only came into existence at a later date. Sitting as a juryman, I can feel no doubt that the way here was a way limited to agricultural purposes, and that to extend it to the use proposed would be an unjustifiable increase of the burden of the easement.

The proper approach to determining the extent of easements of light acquired by prescription was considered in *Allen v Greenwood*, where Buckley LJ said:[186]

> The amount of light to which a dominant owner is entitled under a prescriptive claim is sufficient light . . . for the comfortable or beneficial use of the building in question . . . for such purposes as would constitute normal uses of a building of its particular character. If the building be a dwelling house, the measure must be related to reasonable standards of comfort as a dwelling house. If it be a warehouse, a shop or a factory, the measure must be related to reasonable standards of comfort or beneficial use (for comfort may not be the most appropriate test in the case of such a building) as a warehouse, a shop or a factory, as the case may be.

In a Trinidadian case, *Garib v Seepaulsingh*,[187] the plaintiffs were owners of leasehold premises at No 149, Western Main Road, St James, which they had purchased in 1973. They lived in the upper storey of the building and had let the ground floor for commercial purposes. The defendants resided next door at No 151. The plaintiffs claimed that in 1992 the defendants extended their building by adding two storeys, with the result that the plaintiffs' access to light for three apertures on the wall of the upper storey had been substantially diminished, thus requiring the plaintiffs to use artificial lighting during the day. The plaintiffs claimed an entitlement to the enjoyment of light pursuant to section 3 of the Prescription Ordinance, Ch 5, No 8. In an action by the plaintiffs in the tort of nuisance for interference with their right to light, Warner J said that the easement of light does not consist of a right to continue to enjoy all of the light which had previously come to the windows of the dominant tenement; rather, the test was 'whether the diminution was such as to make the building to a sensible degree less fit than it was before for the purposes of business or occupation, according to the ordinary requirements of mankind', and the nature and extent of the right in the present case was 'to have the amount of light necessary for the comfortable use of the building as a dwelling house'. Another factor in the present case was that the plaintiffs had themselves carried out alterations to No 149 which had reduced the amount of light coming through the windows, and it was an established principle that although a right to light is not lost by the rebuilding or structural alteration of the dominant building, such alterations to the dominant tenement cannot be permitted to increase the burden on the servient tenement. Warner J continued:

> Although the owner of a dominant tenement does not lose or restrict his right to light by non-user, or by not using the full measure of light which the law permits, in my view, the fact that the plaintiffs have tinted the windows, blocked up the decorative bricks with sheets of ply-board, and installed an air conditioning unit, thereby increasing the burden on the servient tenement, must be relevant in determining whether she has proved an obstruction amounting to an actionable nuisance . . . It therefore seems clear to me that if the plaintiffs are complaining that the quality of light which

186 [1980] Ch 119, at 134, 135, following *Colls v Home and Colonial Stores Ltd* [1904] AC 179.
187 (1997) High Court, Trinidad and Tobago, No 140 of 1992. See also *George v Thomas* (2009) High Court, Trinidad and Tobago, No 502 of 1994, a similar case in which Tiwary-Reddy J determined that substantial renovations to the dominant building, including the construction of two additional bedrooms, had increased the burden on the servient tenement and that the servient owner was therefore not liable for interference with the easement of light.

> comes to the windows of their dwelling house has been diminished, some indication as to whether living has been made less comfortable must be determined by examining what they have voluntarily done to the property.

It was accordingly held that the plaintiffs' action failed.

Extinguishment of easements

An easement may come to an end in any of the following ways.

By unity of ownership and possession of the dominant and servient tenements

If the fees simple of both tenements become vested in the same person, and that person is in actual possession of both (for example, where the dominant owner sells the dominant tenement to X, and the servient owner leaves the servient tenement to X in his will and X occupies both plots), then any easement of way across the servient tenement is extinguished.[188] If X later sells the two plots to different persons, the easement is not revived. If there is unity only of ownership, the easement continues until there is also unity of possession; if there is unity only of possession, the easement is merely suspended until the unity of possession ceases. Thus, where the fee simple owner of the dominant tenement acquires a lease of the servient tenement, any easement will be merely suspended and will revive when the lease terminates or is assigned.[189]

By express release by deed

At common law, a deed is required for an express release of an easement.[190] However, in equity, an informal release is effective if, in the circumstances, it would be inequitable for the dominant owner to claim that the easement still exists: for example, where he/she has given verbal consent to his light being obstructed, and the servient owner has expended money in building the obstruction.[191]

By implied release ('abandonment')

If the dominant owner, by his conduct, shows an intention to abandon the easement, then it will be extinguished by implied release. Whether there was an intention to abandon is a question of fact in each case. Conduct showing such intention may take the form of any of the following:

(a) a particular act, such as where the dominant owner has an easement of light to a building, and he/she demolishes the building without any intention to replace it with a new one;[192] or

188 *Buckby v Coles* (1814) 128 ER 709. It was held in *Frett v Frett* (1986) High Court, BVI, No 77 of 1984, that extinguishment occurs also where both dominant and servient tenements become vested in persons as proprietors in common.
189 *Simper v Folly* (1862) 70 ER 1179.
190 *Lovell v Smith* (1857) 140 ER 685.
191 *Waterlow v Bacon* (1866) LR 2 Eq 514.
192 *Ecclesiastical Commissioners for England v Kino* (1880) 14 Ch D 213.

(b) non-user for a period sufficiently long to raise a presumption of abandonment. Twenty years' non-user will normally be sufficient to raise the presumption,[193] but non-user will not suffice if there are other circumstances that show that the dominant owner did not intend to abandon. For example, if the user of a right of way has been discontinued for many years because the dominant owner had a more convenient route over his own land,[194] this may be a satisfactory explanation of the non-user, and there will be no abandonment. In *Swan v Sinclair*,[195] a number of lots were sold and conveyed in 1871 on the terms that each purchaser should have a right of way along a road that was to be constructed on a strip of land at the back of the lots. By 1923, the date of the action, no road had been constructed, fences had been erected across its proposed site, and the owner of lot 1, which was next to the proposed road, had, in 1883, levelled up his plot, thus causing a 6 ft drop between lots 1 and 2. The plaintiff wished to build a garage on lot 2, and he claimed to be entitled to a right of way over the strip of land at the back of lot 1. It was held that the claim failed: the continued existence of the fences and the raising of the level of lot 1 were evidence of an intention on the part of the owners of the various lots to abandon the proposed right of way.

A somewhat similar example of abandonment is the Barbadian case of *Dear v Wilkinson*.[196] Here, the plaintiff and defendant were the fee simple owners of two adjoining properties, known as 'Deal' and 'Bungalow' respectively, which were originally part of a large area in common ownership. The conveyance of Deal to the plaintiff's predecessor-in-title in 1913 included a grant of a right of way to the sea over a pathway that was to be laid out across the Bungalow property. No pathway was ever laid out, and the condition of Bungalow underwent changes, including levelling up, the erection of a sea wall, the planting of trees, and enclosure with a wire fence. The successive owners of Deal were allowed access to the sea across Bungalow by, in one case, written, and in the other, oral permission, on payment of an annual fee. The plaintiff in the present action claimed he had an easement of way across Bungalow under the terms of the 1913 conveyance. The defendant pleaded abandonment.

Field J held that:

(a) there had been a valid grant of an easement of way in the 1913 conveyance; but

(b) the fact of non-user, coupled with the acquiescence of the successive owners of Deal in the conduct of the owner of Bungalow, amounted to abandonment, and the easement had accordingly become extinguished.

193 *Moore v Rawson* (1824) 107 ER 756.
194 *Benn v Hardinge* (1992) 66 P & CR 246.
195 [1924] 1 Ch 254; affirmed [1925] AC 227; followed, on similar facts, in *Patcon Ltd v Dare* (1991) ECS Court of Appeal (St Vincent and the Grenadines), Civ App No 3 of 1990.
196 (1960) 2 WIR 309, Supreme Court, Barbados.

CHAPTER 10

MORTGAGES

A mortgage has been defined as 'a conveyance or other disposition of an interest in property designed to secure the payment of money or the discharge of some other obligation'.[1] A mortgage of land may be legal or equitable, and it may relate to freehold or leasehold land.

A mortgage is essentially a real security for the repayment of money lent. The creditor (the 'mortgagee') obtains rights over the property of the debtor (the 'mortgagor'), which are exercisable in priority to the claims of the debtor's general – that is, unsecured – creditors. Since a real security gives priority over general creditors, it is more attractive to a creditor than a debtor's personal credit or a personal security, such as suretyship, the usefulness or efficacy of which will depend on the solvency of the debtor or guarantor. Another feature of a mortgage is that, so long as the mortgaged property remains worth as much as the amount of the debt, the mortgagee will be sure to receive payment of the debt in full; if, on the other hand, the property depreciates in value so that it becomes worth less than the loan, the mortgagee will recover the value of the property, but, with respect to the balance, he/she will be in no better position than the mortgagor's general creditors.

A charge may be used as an alternative to a mortgage. A charge is the appropriation of real or personal property for the discharge of a debt or other obligation, and differs from a mortgage in that the chargee is not vested with either the general or the special property in the subject matter of the charge, nor does he/she have possession of the subject matter. However, the chargee is entitled to realise his/her security in much the same way as a mortgagee.

In modern times, mortgages and charges are used as security for the purchase of land and dwelling houses by private individuals, or for the purchase of business premises; in the Caribbean, mortgagees are most often banks, building societies (especially in Jamaica), or insurance companies.

FORM

A legal mortgage of unregistered land may be created by a conveyance of the mortgagor's fee simple estate to the mortgagee subject to a proviso that, upon redemption (that is, repayment of the debt), the property should be reconveyed to the mortgagor.[2] Where the mortgagor has only a leasehold estate, a mortgage is created by subdemise, subject to a proviso for cesser on redemption. This method of creating

---

1 Cheshire and Burn, *Modern Law of Real Property*, 15th edn, 1994, London: Butterworths, p 657.

2 In The Bahamas, once the loan is repaid by the mortgagor to the mortgagee, and an acknowledgment or receipt for all the monies due under the mortgage is issued to the mortgagor, endorsed on or annexed to the indenture of mortgage and recorded at the Registry of Records together with the certificate of the Registrar General issued pursuant to s 32 of the Conveyancing and Law of Property Act, Ch 138, the mortgage is vacated and the estate in the property comprised in the mortgage is revested in the mortgagor by operation of law, without the need for an actual reconveyance. See *Wilson Distributors Ltd v Strachan* (2001) Supreme Court, The Bahamas, CL No 1252 of 1998, *per* Osadebay Sr J.

DOI: 10.4324/9781003186946-10

mortgages applies in most Commonwealth Caribbean jurisdictions.[3] In Barbados, a mortgage of a legal estate can be effected only by a charge by deed.[4]

A mortgage of registered land is created by execution of a memorandum of mortgage or charge in the prescribed form, which must be lodged for registration in the Land Registry.[5]

Equitable mortgages are created:

(a) by deposit of title deeds (or deposit of a duplicate certificate of title to registered land),[6] usually with a bank to secure an overdraft or loan;[7]
(b) under the *Walsh v Lonsdale* principle, where there is an agreement to grant a legal mortgage;[8] or
(c) where the mortgagor has only an equitable interest in property, by assignment of the interest to the mortgagee.

RIGHTS OF THE MORTGAGOR

Legal right to redeem

A mortgage deed refers to the loan and conveys the mortgaged property to the mortgagee subject to the right of the mortgagor to redeem (that is, to repay the loan plus interest and recover his/her property) on a fixed date, which is, by tradition, normally six months from the date of execution of the mortgage. There is, therefore, a contractual right to redeem on the stipulated date. At common law, if the mortgagor failed to redeem his/her property on the exact day fixed by the agreement, then the estate of the mortgagee became absolute and the mortgagor's interest in the land

3 See, eg, ss 27, 32–35, 48 of the Conveyancing and Law of Property Act, Ch 56:01 (Trinidad and Tobago); s 17 of the Conveyancing and Law of Property Act, Ch 138 (The Bahamas); s 18 of the Conveyancing Act (Jamaica); cf ss 64 and 65 of the Law of Property Act, Cap 190 (Belize). See also *Canadian Imperial Bank of Commerce v Wells* (1996) Supreme Court, The Bahamas, No 287 of 1995.

4 Section 96 of the Property Act, Cap 236. Unlike in the case of the conventional mortgage, the chargor by deed can create successive legal mortgages (charges) on his/her land.

5 See, eg, s 103 of the Registration of Titles Act (Jamaica); s 75 of the Real Property Ordinance, Ch 56:02 (Trinidad and Tobago); Land Registration Act, Cap 229, Pt VIII (Barbados).

6 See, eg, s 59 of the Title by Registration Act, Cap 279 (St Kitts/Nevis); s 62 of the Title by Registration Act, Ch 56:50 (Dominica). See *Caines v Barclays Bank plc* (2000) High Court, St Kitts/Nevis, No 69 of 1997.

7 In *Mapp v Barclays Bank International Ltd* (1992) 43 WIR 30, Court of Appeal, Barbados, a husband was sole owner at law and trustee of the matrimonial home, but his wife had an equitable interest in the property by virtue of her financial contribution to its purchase. Unknown to the wife, the husband created an equitable mortgage by depositing the title deeds with the respondent bank. Williams CJ held that, in the absence of any fraud or negligence on the part of the wife, her equitable interest, being earlier in time, had priority over the bank's equitable mortgage.

> An equitable mortgagee by deposit is entitled to call for a legal mortgage, even in the absence of an express agreement to execute a legal mortgage, unless the right is excluded by agreement, and a deposit of title deeds by a person other than the debtor is enforceable in the same manner: *Barclays Bank plc v Clarke* (1998) Supreme Court, The Bahamas, No 517 of 1996, *per* Dunkley J (Ag).

8 An example is *Monsegue v First Citizens Bank Ltd* (2013) Court of Appeal, Trinidad and Tobago, Civ App No 224 of 2011, where it was held that a court can decree specific performance of the agreement, ordering the mortgagor to execute a legal mortgage, which can then be entered on the registered title to the land.

was extinguished. In modern mortgages, on the other hand, principal and interest are normally repayable by monthly instalments over a long period: for example, 25 years.[9]

Equitable right to redeem

Equity considered the common law rule – that failure to repay the loan on the day fixed by the mortgage resulted in loss of the mortgagor's estate – to be unduly harsh, bearing in mind that the purpose of a mortgage was merely to afford security for a loan. In the eyes of equity, it was unconscionable that a mortgagor should lose his/her property merely because of his/her failure to make prompt repayment of a loan, since, so long as the property remained intact, the mortgagee would still have his/her security, despite the delay in repayment. In Lord Nottingham's words:[10]

> In natural justice and equity, the principal right of the mortgagee is to the money, and his right to the land is only as a security for the money.

More recently, in *Cukurova Finance International Ltd v Alfa Telecom Turkey Ltd*, Lord Neuberger explained the genesis of the doctrine, thus:[11]

> This right arose because the Court of Chancery, exercising its equity jurisdiction, recoiled from the notion that a borrower who had provided the lender with security, which traditionally was always in the form of land, should lose his land simply because it was late in repaying the loan secured on that land . . . Thus, the equitable right to redeem does not arise until the contractual redemption date has passed . . . So, under a normal form of mortgage, a mortgagor had two rights to redeem: a legal right only exercisable on the contractually stipulated date, and an equitable right exercisable at any time after the contractually stipulated date.

Accordingly, equity permitted a mortgagor to redeem his/her property at any time after the contractual redemption date had passed, and this remains the effect of the equitable right to redeem today.

The equity of redemption

The equity of redemption is the sum total of the mortgagor's interests in the mortgaged property after the mortgage has been created. This arises from his/her right to redeem and, in fact, the concept of equity of redemption is often used interchangeably with the right to redeem, but, technically, they differ in meaning. The equitable right to redeem arises after the contractual redemption date has passed,

9 An instalment mortgage will normally take one of two forms, either:

(a) the mortgagor covenants to repay the whole debt on a nominal redemption date (usually six months from the date of the mortgage) – further clauses provide for repayment by instalments if (as anticipated) there is no repayment on the redemption date; or

(b) there is no nominal redemption date – the mortgagor covenants to repay by instalments, with a proviso that, if he/she becomes in arrears (eg, by two months), the whole capital debt is to become repayable.

10 *Thornborough v Baker* (1675) 36 ER 1000.

11 [2013] UKPC 20 (appeal from the Court of Appeal of the British Virgin Islands), para 72.

whereas the equity of redemption comes into existence as soon as the mortgage is created. The equitable right to redeem is a particular right, while the equity of redemption represents the aggregate of the mortgagor's rights. It is an equitable interest that represents the value of the mortgagor's interest in the property after it has been conveyed to the mortgagee as a security, and is freely transferable.

Clogging the equity of redemption

Equity has always sought to promote fair dealing and to prevent anything that suggests oppression. In particular, equity will not allow a mortgagee to take advantage of the financial circumstances of the mortgagor by:

(a) excluding the mortgagor's right to redeem, for example by reserving an option to purchase the mortgaged property; or
(b) postponing the right to redeem for an unreasonably long time; or
(c) reserving certain benefits ('collateral advantages') to be enjoyed after redemption.

Since the purpose of a mortgage is simply to provide the mortgagee with security for a loan, equity views with disfavour any provision in the agreement that tends to hinder the mortgagor in recovering his/her property upon performance of his/her obligations. In short, the equitable maxim is 'once a mortgage, always a mortgage', and any term in the mortgage agreement that constitutes a 'clog' on the equity of redemption will be void.[12]

It is important to note, however, that the traditional hostility of equity towards clogs on the equity of redemption has diminished somewhat in modern times, especially where mortgagor and mortgagee are business concerns of equal bargaining power, and the principle of sanctity of contract now often overrides the notion of protection of the mortgagor. The modern approach of the courts, therefore, is that a bargain freely entered into by mortgagor and mortgagee must be adhered to, unless there is evidence of harsh and unconscionable dealing or inequality of bargaining power.

Excluding the right to redeem

Any provision that excludes or unduly restricts the mortgagor's right to redeem may be held void: for example, an agreement that only the mortgagor and the heirs of his body should be entitled to redeem;[13] an agreement that rendered part of the mortgaged property absolutely irredeemable; and an agreement that if the mortgagor predeceased his father, the mortgaged property should become the absolute property of the mortgagee.[14]

The position where the mortgage deed grants to the mortgagee an option to purchase the mortgaged property was considered in *Samuel v Jarrah Timber and Wood*

12 *Biggs v Hoddinott* [1898] 2 Ch 307.
13 *Salt v Marquess of Northampton* [1892] 2 Ch 307, at 315.
14 *Davis v Symons* [1934] Ch 442.

Paving Corp Ltd.[15] In this case, there was a mortgage of £30,000 of debenture stock to secure a loan of £5,000 at 6 per cent interest. The mortgagee, Samuel, reserved to himself 'the option to purchase the whole or any part of such stock at 40 per cent at any time within 12 months'. Samuel sought to exercise the option. The company succeeded in its claim to redeem and to have the option declared illegal and void.

In *Reeve v Lisle*,[16] on the other hand, it was held that where an option to purchase the mortgaged property is granted by a subsequent and independent transaction, the option may be held valid. In this case, a ship and other properties were mortgaged to secure a loan. Sometime after the mortgage had been executed, the mortgagees were granted an option to enter into a partnership with the mortgagors, and it was further agreed that if the option should be exercised within five years, the mortgagors should be relieved of liability to repay the mortgage debt and the ship should be transferred free from the mortgage and form part of the partnership assets. The House of Lords considered these two transactions to be separate and independent of each other, and the option was therefore valid and enforceable.

The reasoning in such cases is that equity seeks to protect a borrower who finds him/herself in financial straits and consequently loses his/her bargaining power. If, on the other hand, the loan has been granted and the mortgage executed without any restrictive or oppressive condition, the borrower does not need the protection any longer. Where, therefore, following the execution of the mortgage, the mortgagor enters into a separate and independent transaction whereby he/she gives the mortgagee an additional right over the mortgaged property, he/she cannot claim the protection of equity in his/her efforts to escape from the effect of the second transaction, even if the second transaction destroys his/her equity of redemption completely.

Postponement of the right to redeem

Where a provision in a mortgage precludes the mortgagor from redeeming within a certain period (for example, where it is expressly stipulated that the loan is not to be repaid within a period of seven years from the execution of the mortgage), according to Sir Wilfred Greene MR, 'equity is concerned to see two things – one, that the essential requirements of a mortgage transaction are observed, and the other, that oppressive and unconscionable terms are not enforced'.[17]

The objection to a clause postponing the mortgagor's right to redeem is the familiar one – that a mortgage is merely a security for a loan, and a provision prolonging the security beyond the time when the mortgagor is ready and willing to repay the loan constitutes a clog on the equity of redemption. However, in the leading case of *Knightsbridge Estates Trust Ltd v Byrne*,[18] the English Court of Appeal made it clear that such a clause will be valid, provided that: (a) the mortgage as a whole is not so oppressive and unconscionable that equity would not enforce it; and (b) it does not render the equitable right to redeem illusory. In this case, Knightsbridge had mortgaged a large number of properties, including houses, shops and an apartment

15 [1904] AC 323.
16 [1902] AC 461.
17 *Knightsbridge Estates Trust Ltd v Byrne* [1939] Ch 441, at 457.
18 *Ibid.*

block, to an insurance company to secure a loan of £30,000 at 6.5 per cent interest, on the terms that repayment should be made by half-yearly instalments over a period of 40 years. The mortgagee agreed not to call in the money before the end of this period, provided that the instalments were punctually paid. Six years later, Knightsbridge sought a declaration that it was entitled to redeem the mortgage, arguing, *inter alia*, that it was unreasonable and oppressive that it should be unable to redeem its properties for 40 years. It was held, however, that, in the circumstances, the agreement was fair and not unreasonable, particularly since the agreement was a commercial one 'between two important corporations experienced in such matters, and had none of the features of an oppressive bargain where the borrower is at the mercy of an unscrupulous lender',[19] and 'a contract freely entered into after due deliberation by parties dealing with each other at arm's length is not lightly to be interfered with'.[20]

A provision that renders the right to redeem illusory will be void. In *Fairclough v Swan Brewery Co Ltd*,[21] there was a mortgage of a lease having 17-and-a-half years to run. The mortgagor was precluded by the agreement from redeeming the mortgage until a date six weeks before the lease expired. Although there was no evidence of oppression, it was held that the provision postponing redemption rendered the right to redeem illusory and was void. Accordingly, the mortgagor was entitled to redeem at an earlier date.

Collateral advantages

A collateral advantage in the mortgagee's favour denotes some benefit conferred on him by the mortgagor in addition to repayment of the loan plus interest: for instance, where the mortgagor of a public house agrees to sell on the premises only beer brewed by the mortgagee. Two general rules apply:

(a) the collateral advantage must not be unfair or unconscionable; and
(b) the collateral advantage must not unfairly restrict redemption.

Unfairness and unconscionability

It is a question of fact as to whether a collateral advantage is unfair or unconscionable. It is well established that the courts will set aside 'any oppressive bargain or any advantage exacted from a man under grievous necessity and want of money'.[22] In *Cityland and Property (Holdings) Ltd v Dabrah*,[23] the mortgagor was the mortgagee's tenant and a man 'obviously of limited means'. He undertook in the mortgage agreement to pay a premium that represented either not less than 57 per cent of the amount of the loan, or interest at 19 per cent. It was held that this provision was unconscionable and void. This was not a 'bargain between two large trading concerns', and the mortgagor was entitled to redeem by repaying the loan

19 *Ibid*, at 455, *per* Sir Wilfred Greene MR.
20 *Op cit*, Cheshire and Burn, fn 1, p 675.
21 [1912] AC 565.
22 *Barrett v Hartley* (1866) LR 2 Eq 787, at 795, *per* Stuart VC.
23 [1967] 2 All ER 639.

with reasonable interest fixed by the court. In *Multiservice Bookbinding Ltd v Marden*,[24] on the other hand, Browne-Wilkinson J stressed that, for a collateral advantage to be declared void, it must be unfair and unconscionable and not merely unreasonable, and unfair and unconscionable meant 'imposed in a morally reprehensible manner, that is to say, in a way which affects [the mortgagee's] conscience'.[25] In this case, the mortgagor was a small company, which needed a loan in order to expand its business. The terms of the mortgage were that: (a) interest was payable at 2 per cent above bank rate; (b) the loan was to be irredeemable for ten years; and (c) the value of the capital and interest was to be index-linked to the Swiss franc. After ten years, when the mortgage became redeemable, the total capital repayment had risen from the £36,000 lent to £87,588, because of devaluation of the pound against the Swiss franc, and the average rate of interest amounted to 16 per cent. It was held that the agreement was valid. Although the bargain was a hard one from the mortgagor's point of view, it was not unfair or unconscionable in the sense defined by Browne-Wilkinson J.

Restriction of redemption

A collateral advantage will be void if it unfairly restricts redemption, in the sense that it prevents the mortgagor from redeeming his/her property free from all of the conditions of the mortgage and from being restored to his/her original position. Accordingly, the rule has emerged that a collateral advantage that is not unconscionable is valid until redemption, but not afterwards.

In *Biggs v Hoddinott*,[26] the collateral advantage was to last only during the continuance of the mortgage. Here, the owner of a hotel mortgaged it to a brewer as security for a loan of £7,654. The mortgage was not to be redeemable for five years, and the mortgagor agreed that, during the five-year period, he would sell on the premises no beer other than that produced by the mortgagee. It was held that the agreement was valid, so that the mortgagor was not entitled to redeem the property after only two years and be released from the solus agreement.

In *Noakes v Rice*,[27] on the other hand, the lessee of a public house under a lease that had 26 years to run mortgaged the premises and covenanted that, for the duration of the lease, whether he had redeemed the mortgage or not, he would not sell any malt liquors other than those supplied by the mortgagee. After three years, the mortgagor sought to be released from the covenant on repayment of the loan plus interest. It was held that the mortgagor was entitled to be released from the covenant, on the ground that its effect was that he would still be fettered by the terms of the mortgage after redemption, as he would be redeeming a 'tied house' in place of a 'free house'.

A different approach was taken by the House of Lords in the leading case of *Kreglinger v New Patagonia Meat and Cold Storage Co Ltd*,[28] which shows that the courts, in order not to disturb commercial contracts entered into by business organisations

---

24 [1978] 2 All ER 489. See also *Perot v First Citizens Bank Ltd* (2004) High Court, Trinidad and Tobago, No 5071 of 1996.
25 *Ibid*, at 502.
26 [1898] 2 Ch 307.
27 [1902] AC 24.
28 [1914] AC 25.

enjoying equality of bargaining power, may permit collateral advantages to remain binding even after redemption. In this case, a firm of wool brokers lent £10,000 to a meat company. The security took the form of a floating charge on the borrower's assets. It was agreed that, for five years from the date of the loan, the company would not sell sheepskins to any person without first offering them to the lenders at the full market price, the borrowers further agreeing to pay the lenders a commission of 1 per cent of the sale price of all sheepskins sold to anyone other than the lenders. It was also agreed that the lenders would not call in the loan before the end of the five-year period. After two years, the borrowers paid off the loan and disputed the right of the lenders to enforce their option to purchase the sheepskins. The House of Lords held that the lenders were entitled to an injunction restraining the borrowers from selling sheepskins to third parties during the remainder of the five-year period, notwithstanding that the borrowers would be less free in the conduct of their business after repayment of the loan than they were at the date of the loan. The reasoning of the court was expressed by Viscount Haldane thus:[29]

> The question in the present case is whether the right to redeem has been interfered with. And this must . . . depend on the answer to a question which is primarily one of fact. What was the true character of the transaction? Did the appellants make a bargain such that the right to redeem was cut down, or did they simply stipulate for a collateral undertaking, outside and clear of the mortgage, which would give them an exclusive option to purchase the sheepskins of the respondents? The question is, in my opinion, not whether the two contracts were made at the same moment and evidenced by the same instrument, but whether they were in substance a single and undivided contract or two distinct contracts . . . if your Lordships arrive at the conclusion that the agreement for an option to purchase the respondent's sheepskins was not in substance a fetter on the exercise of their right to redeem, but was a preliminary and separable condition of the loan, the decided cases cease to present any great difficulty.

Restraint of trade

In addition to any objection based on clogging the equity of redemption, mortgages are subject to the doctrine of restraint of trade. Under this doctrine, any stipulation in a contract that imposes an unreasonable restriction on the freedom of a person to engage in trade or to pursue a profession will be *prima facie* void. The onus is on the party imposing the restraint (in this context, the mortgagee) to show that the restraint is reasonable: (a) as between the parties; and (b) in the public interest. Thus, as *Esso Petroleum Co Ltd v Harper's Garage Ltd*[30] shows, a postponement of redemption that is not unconscionable or oppressive may nevertheless be declared void if it constitutes an unreasonable restraint upon the mortgagor's business activities. In this case, a garage was mortgaged to Esso. The mortgagors covenanted that they would not redeem the mortgage for 21 years and, during that period, would sell only fuel supplied by Esso. It was held that the solus agreement was void as being in restraint of trade, and the mortgage was redeemable before the expiration of the 21 years.

29 *Ibid*, at 38. This principle was applied in *Wellesley Ltd v Suto Ltd* (1992) Supreme Court, The Bahamas, No 180 of 1988.
30 [1967] 1 All ER 699.

RIGHTS OF MORTGAGOR IN POSSESSION

A mortgagor who remains in possession of the property has the following rights:

(a) a right to the rents and profits – a mortgagor in possession is not liable to the mortgagee for any such rents and profits, even though he/she may be in default in the payment of interest; the mortgagor is entitled to sue in his/her own name for the recovery of rents and profits;
(b) a right to sue for trespass or any wrong done to the land; and
(c) a right to grant valid leases. At common law, a mortgagor in possession is entitled to grant leases of the property that are binding as between himself and the lessee, but, if made without the consent of the mortgagee, the lease can be set aside by the latter.[31] Section 18 of the Conveyancing Act 1881 granted the mortgagor a statutory right to grant agricultural or occupational leases for any term not exceeding 21 years, and building leases for any term not exceeding 99 years. Such a lease must be made to take effect in possession not later than 12 months after its date, at the best rent reasonably obtainable. The statutory leasing powers may be expressly excluded by the mortgage deed, as, for instance, by a provision requiring the mortgagee's consent before the leasing power can be exercised. Similar provisions have been enacted in some Caribbean jurisdictions.[32]

RIGHTS OF MORTGAGEE

There are five of these, viz:

(a) right to sue on the personal covenant;
(b) right to enter into possession of the mortgaged property;
(c) right to appoint a receiver;
(d) right to sell the mortgaged property; and
(e) right to foreclose the mortgage.

These remedies are both concurrent and cumulative: 'contrary to the general rule that a person liable to be sued is not to be harassed by a multiplicity of actions',[33] the mortgagee can pursue all or any remedies simultaneously as soon as the mortgagor is in default, and, if one remedy proves insufficient to satisfy what is owing to him, he/she may pursue another remedy in order to recover the balance. The only exception is foreclosure, which, once made absolute, extinguishes the other remedies.

---

31 *Iron Trades Employers' Insurance Association v Union Land and House Investors Ltd* [1937] 1 All ER 481; *Quennell v Maltby* [1979] 1 All ER 568. See also *Jamaica Youth Development Foundation v Portfolio International Jamaica Ltd* (2004) Supreme Court, Jamaica, No 2305 of 2004.

32 See, eg, s 21 of the Conveyancing Act (Jamaica); s 37 of Ch 56:01 (Trinidad and Tobago); s 20 of Ch 138 (The Bahamas) (applicable to both mortgagors and mortgagees); cf s 108 of Cap 236 (Barbados).

33 Fisher and Lightwood, *Law of Mortgages*, 2nd edn, pp 386–387; cited with approval by Anderson J in *Foote v Capital and Credit Merchant Bank Ltd* (2010) Supreme Court, Jamaica, No 3328 of 2008.

Action on the personal covenant

The mortgagor will normally covenant[34] expressly to repay the loan on a certain date (usually six months from the date of the mortgage) and to pay interest on the loan at a certain date; alternatively, the loan may be stated to be repayable by instalments falling due on a particular day of the month. As soon as the date stipulated for repayment (including the date for payment of an instalment)[35] has passed, the mortgagee may sue on the covenant to recover the principal sum and any arrears of interest. The mortgagor remains liable on the covenant, even if he/she has transferred his/her equity of redemption; he/she should, therefore, take an indemnity from the transferee.

Right to enter into possession

As Harman J emphasised in *Four Maids Ltd v Dudley Marshall (Properties) Ltd*, a legal mortgagee has a right to take possession of the mortgaged property 'before the ink is dry on the mortgage', unless there is something in the contract whereby he has contracted himself out of that right; and 'the right of the mortgagee to possession ... has nothing to do with default on the part of the mortgagor'.[36]

In practice, a mortgagee will not take possession of the mortgaged property except as a preliminary to exercising its statutory power of sale after a default by the mortgagor. Where there has been such default, it will, in most cases, be essential for the mortgagee to exercise its right so that it may sell with vacant possession. Where the mortgagor is in possession of the property, it will be necessary for the mortgagee to bring an action for recovery of possession.

After an amendment to the Rules of the Supreme Court (UK) in 1936, which assigned proceedings for possession from the King's Bench Division to the Chancery Division,[37] it became possible for mortgagors to obtain equitable relief in possession actions, and the master thus had a discretion to refuse a possession order if it was just and equitable to do so. This discretion was apparently terminated, in *Birmingham Citizens' Permanent Building Society v Caunt*,[38] by Russell J, who declared that the equitable discretion was without legal foundation. He said:[39]

> Where (as here) the legal mortgagee under an instalment mortgage ... is entitled to possession, the court has no jurisdiction to decline the order or to adjourn the hearing, whether on terms of keeping up payments or paying arrears, if the mortgagee cannot be persuaded to agree to this course. To this the sole exception is that the application

34 The mortgagor also normally enters into the following covenants: for title; to insure; to repair; to pay rates and taxes. By s 97(1) of Cap 236 (Barbados), similar covenants are implied, in the absence of express covenants in the memorandum of mortgage.

35 It is common, in an instalment mortgage, for the mortgage deed to stipulate that, on failure to pay an instalment by the due date, the whole amount of the debt shall become due: see, eg, *Halifax Building Society v Clark* [1973] 2 All ER 33.

36 [1957] 2 All ER 35, at 36. This common law right has been abolished in Barbados by s 98(2)(b) of the Property Act, Cap 236. The subsection provides that a mortgagee may apply to the court for a possession order. See, eg, *Holders Ltd v St Hill* (1980) 15 Barb LR 206.

37 See Cousins, *Law of Mortgages*, 1989, London: Sweet & Maxwell, p 244.

38 [1962] 1 All ER 163. In England and Wales, the courts have a wide discretionary jurisdiction under s 36 of the Administration of Justice Act 1970 and s 8(1) of the Administration of Justice Act 1973 to postpone possession orders with respect to dwelling houses.

39 *Ibid*, at 182.

> may be adjourned for a short time to afford to the mortgagor a chance of paying off the mortgagee in full or otherwise satisfying him; but this should not be done if there is no reasonable prospect of this occurring.

In the Bahamian case of *Bank of Nova Scotia v Morrison*,[40] the mortgagor was in default of her monthly mortgage payments to the tune of $17,079 principal and $1,752 interest, in respect of which a demand notice had been served. When the mortgagor continued to be in default, the mortgagee sought possession of the mortgaged property with a view to putting it up for sale. Osadebay J, following the judgment of Russell J in *Caunt*, held that he had no power to deprive the mortgagee of its right to possession. He said:

> The nature of the defence in this matter has been such that this court could not adjourn the hearing, whether on terms of keeping up payments or paying arrears, without the request of the [mortgagor] and the concurrence of the [mortgagee].

On the other hand, it was the view of Lord Denning MR in *Quennell v Maltby*[41] that a court of equity may restrain a mortgagee from recovering possession where the action is not brought in good faith for the purpose of enforcing his security. In this case, Q mortgaged his house to a bank. Under the mortgage agreement, Q was prohibited from granting tenancies of the property without the consent of the bank. In breach of this covenant, Q granted a tenancy to M, a student, who subsequently became a statutory tenant under the Rent Restriction Acts. The tenancy was binding on Q, but it was void as against the bank. Q wished to recover possession of the premises in order to sell with vacant possession, and he asked the bank to bring a possession action against M. When the bank declined to do so, Q's wife paid off the loan and procured a transfer of the mortgage from the bank. She then sought possession as mortgagee, but her action failed. Bridge and Templeman LJJ held that she could not recover, because she was acting as agent of Q who, as mortgagor, was not entitled to possession as against M. Lord Denning MR, on the other hand, expressed a wider principle, holding that Q's wife could not recover possession, because her purpose in bringing the action was not to enforce her security as mortgagee, but simply to evict M. He said:[42]

---

40 (1995) Supreme Court, The Bahamas, No 1579 of 1991. In another Bahamian case, *Citibank NA v Major* (2001) Court of Appeal, The Bahamas, No 28 of 1996, Ganpatsingh JA emphasised that:

> the position . . . is that where, under a legal mortgage, being an instalment mortgage, the whole mortgage money becomes payable by reason of the default of the mortgagor, and the legal mortgagee is entitled to possession of the mortgaged property, the court has no jurisdiction to refuse to make an order for possession or to adjourn the summons, either on terms or not on terms as to keeping up payments or paying arrears, if the mortgagee does not agree to that course; but this does not exclude power to direct an adjournment for a short time to enable the mortgagor to pay off the mortgage in full or otherwise satisfy the mortgagee if there is a reasonable prospect of the mortgagor being able to do so . . . It is pellucidly clear that there could be no power in the court to vary contractual rights or to deny one party the benefit of the remedies which flow from the default of the mortgagor.

See also *British American Bank (1993) Ltd v Ellis* (2004) Supreme Court, The Bahamas, No 1375 of 2002; *Finance Corporation of Bahamas Ltd v Miller* (2007) Supreme Court, The Bahamas, No 92 of 2006; *Colina Imperial Insurance Co Ltd v Bethel* (2011) High Court, Trinidad and Tobago, No 166 of 2010.

41 [1979] 1 All ER 568.

42 *Ibid*, at 571.

> The objective is plain. It was not to enforce the security or to obtain repayment or anything of the kind. It was in order to get possession of the house and to overcome the protection of the Rent Acts . . . Equity can step in so as to prevent a mortgagee, or a transferee from him, from getting possession of a house contrary to the justice of the case. A mortgagee will be restrained from getting possession except when it is sought *bona fide* and reasonably for the purpose of enforcing the security, and then only subject to such conditions as the court thinks fit to impose.

It is extremely difficult to reconcile the wide proposition enunciated by Lord Denning with the principle that the mortgagee has a right to take possession of the mortgaged property 'before the ink is dry on the mortgage'. Lord Denning's approach suggests that taking possession exists only as a remedy to enforce the security, rather than as a right, and this is also at variance with the principle expressed by Russell J in *Birmingham Citizens' Permanent Building Society v Caunt*.[43]

Lord Denning's outlook, if not his approach, can be discerned in the judgment of Narine J in a Trinidadian case, *Baksh General Wholesalers Ltd v Republic Bank Ltd*,[44] in which the mortgagee bank took possession of commercial premises without any proven default on the part of the mortgagor. The learned judge held that, in view of the well-established legal right of the mortgagee to take possession, no action in trespass was maintainable by the mortgagor; however, 'it does not follow from this that the bank will not be liable for damages that the mortgagor has incurred by reason of the bank's possession of the premises, which prevented the [mortgagor] from operating his business'. He continued:

> The court must be mindful of the purpose and the commercial reality of the mortgage transaction. Clearly, the mortgage is intended to give security to the mortgagee pending repayment of a debt owed by the mortgagor. Unless there is default on the part of the mortgagor, or the bank requires possession in order to protect its security, one would hardly expect the mortgagee to exercise its right to possession which, of course, is an incident of the legal title it holds. If it were the case that the mortgagee would be expected to exercise its right to possession at any time during the subsistence of the mortgage, this would be a commercial hazard and a disincentive to would-be mortgagors. The commercial reality is that the mortgagee is not expected to exercise his right to possession in the absence of default of the mortgagor.

Accordingly, the bank was held liable for damages for loss of profit during the period of its 'wrongful' possession of the mortgaged premises.[45]

It is certainly arguable that Narine J's judgment has little authority in the case law to support it; however, it is respectfully submitted that it shows commendable pragmatism, in the manner of Lord Denning himself, and is a good example of the willingness of some members of the judiciary in Caribbean jurisdictions to develop legal principles suited to the societies in which they operate. The approach can, in any event, be rationalised by saying that, in mortgages of commercial property, a term should be implied that the mortgagee will not take possession unless there is a default by the mortgagor that puts the mortgagee's security in jeopardy.

43 [1962] 1 All ER 163.
44 (1999) High Court, Trinidad and Tobago, No 1555 of 1998.
45 The decision was subsequently overturned by the Court of Appeal of Trinidad and Tobago on other grounds. The Privy Council agreed with the Court of Appeal: (2004) Privy Council Appeal No 19 of 2003 (judgment delivered on 6 October 2004).

Another reason why a mortgagee will not usually take possession, except as a prelude to selling, is that equity requires a mortgagee in possession to account strictly not only for what it has actually received from the property while in possession, but also for what it ought to have received by better management. Thus, for example, if the mortgagee, having entered into possession, grants a tenancy at a rent which is lower than the market rent,[46] it will be liable not only for the rent actually obtained but also for the difference between that amount and the value of the market rent; and if the mortgagee leaves the property vacant when it might have let it, it will be liable for the amount of an occupational rent.[47] In *White v City of London Brewery Co*,[48] the mortgagee took possession of the mortgaged premises and let them to a tenant subject to a restriction that he should purchase his entire beer supply from the mortgagee. It was held that the mortgagee was accountable for the additional rent it would have obtained if it had let the premises without such a restriction (that is, as a 'free house' instead of as a 'tied house').

On the other hand, it was held by Osadebay J in *Davis v Finco Corp (Bahamas) Ltd*[49] that *Jones v Foley*[50] reflected 'the common law position in The Bahamas that a mortgagee who takes possession in exercise of his rights under the mortgage is not obliged to look after chattels left on the premises pending their removal', subject to the duty of the mortgagee to allow the mortgagor to remove them, assuming the mortgagee has no claim over them.

Right to appoint a receiver

Mortgagees have a statutory right to appoint a receiver of the mortgaged property, where the mortgage is made by deed.[51] The appointment must be made in writing. The right to appoint a receiver arises and is exercisable in the same circumstances as the statutory power of sale.[52] On appointment, the receiver is deemed to be the agent of the mortgagor, so that the sole responsibility for his/her acts and defaults rests on the mortgagor.

The advantage of appointing a receiver is that, where interest payments are in arrears, he may intercept any rents and profits from the land and apply them towards paying off the arrears. In order to achieve this purpose, it is better for the mortgagee to appoint a receiver than to go into possession himself, because of the liability of the mortgagee in possession to account strictly, as explained above.[53]

A receiver is required by the statutes to apply any money received by him in the following order:

(a) in discharge of rents, taxes, rates and outgoings;
(b) in keeping down annual sums and the interest on principal sums having priority to the mortgage;

46 *Blaize v National Insurance Board* (2014) High Court, Trinidad and Tobago, No CV 2010–03239.
47 *Marriott v Anchor Reversionary Co* (1861) 45 ER 846.
48 (1889) 42 Ch D 237.
49 (1998) Supreme Court, The Bahamas, No 1160 of 1995.
50 [1891] 1 QB 730.
51 Sections 39–45 of Ch 56:01 (Trinidad and Tobago); ss 110–16 of Cap 236 (Barbados); ss 21–23 of Ch 138 (The Bahamas); ss 38–44 of Cap 220 (BVI); ss 39–45 of Cap 54:01 (Dominica); ss 9–12 of Cap 64 (Grenada); ss 22–25 of the Conveyancing Act, 1973 Rev (Jamaica); ss 30–33 of the Conveyancing Act 1983 (Bermuda); ss 39–45 of Cap 271 (St Kitts/Nevis).
52 See p 201 *et seq*, below.
53 See fn 48, above.

(c) in payment of his/her own commission and insurance premiums and, if so directed in writing by the mortgagee, the cost of repairs;
(d) in payment of the interest under the mortgage; and
(e) if so directed by the mortgagee, in discharging the principal sum lent; otherwise, it must be paid to the person who would have received it if the receiver had not been appointed – that is, to the mortgagor.

Any residue that remains after discharging the above liabilities must be paid to the mortgagor.

Power of sale

Statutory provisions[54] give a mortgagee power to sell the mortgaged property out of court, provided that the mortgage is made by deed. The statutory power enables the mortgagee to vest the fee simple in a purchaser, notwithstanding that the mortgagee may have only a term of years or a legal charge. The power *arises* as soon as the date fixed for repayment has passed or, in the case of a mortgage repayable by instalments, as soon as an instalment is due and unpaid, but the power becomes *exercisable* only when:

(a) notice requiring repayment of the mortgage money has been served on the mortgagor and default has been made in payment of part or all of it for three months thereafter; or
(b) some interest under the mortgage is two months or more in arrears; or
(c) there has been a breach of some provision contained in the Acts or in the mortgage deed (other than the covenant for payment of the mortgage money or interest), which should have been observed or performed by the mortgagor or by someone who concurred in making the mortgage. (Thus, for example, the power will become exercisable if the mortgagor is in breach of an undertaking to keep the premises in repair.)

It was held in *Derrick v Trinidad Asphalt Holdings Ltd*[55] that the statutory restrictions governing exercise of the power of sale may be negated or varied by the mortgage deed, and this is indeed the accepted practice in most jurisdictions. On the other hand, where land is registered, support for the view that the statutory provisions designed to protect mortgagors cannot be expressly excluded by mortgage agreements can be found in the decision of the Jamaican Court of Appeal in *Jobson v Capital and Credit Merchant Bank*.[56] In Jamaica, ss 105 and 106 of the Registration of Titles Act 1973 govern the arising and exercise of the power of sale in relation to registered land. Section 105 provides that, where there is a default by the mortgagor in payment of principal or interest, or in the performance or observance of any express or implied covenant, and such default continues for one month (or for such other period as may be fixed by the mortgage), the mortgagee 'may give to the

54 Sections 39–45 of Ch 56:01 (Trinidad and Tobago); ss 110–16 of Cap 236 (Barbados); ss 21–23 of Ch 138 (The Bahamas); ss 38–44 of Cap 220 (BVI); ss 39–45 of Cap 54:01 (Dominica); ss 9–12 of Cap 64 (Grenada); ss 22–25 of Conveyancing Act, 1973 Rev (Jamaica); ss 30–33 of Conveyancing Act 1983 (Bermuda); ss 39–45 of Cap 271 (St Kitts/Nevis).
55 (1979) 33 WIR 273.
56 (2005) Court of Appeal, Jamaica, Civ App No 113 of 2002.

mortgagor . . . notice in writing to pay the money owing . . . or to perform or observe the aforesaid covenants' and, by s 106, if such default continues for one month after service of the notice (or such other period as may be fixed), the mortgagee may sell the land, or part thereof, altogether or in lots, by public auction or private contract. There has been much debate as to whether the provision as to the giving of notice is mandatory or merely directory, bearing in mind that s 105 states that the mortgagee 'may' give notice. If the giving of notice is not a mandatory requirement, the reference in s 106 to default in payment or performance for one month will apply only where notice has in fact been given.

The Jamaican Court of Appeal in the *Jobson* case disagreed with the view of the trial judge that the words 'may give' were merely permissive, for 'if this were correct, then that part of section 106 which deals with when the power of sale by a mortgagee becomes exercisable would have been quite unnecessary'. Cooke JA expressed the view that, in construing both sections, the words 'may give' should be interpreted to mean that the mortgagor 'is entitled' to notice if the power of sale is contemplated. Accordingly, the giving of a notice in writing, if the circumstances so warranted, was a mandatory obligation placed on a mortgagee before the power of sale became exercisable, and the practice of expressly excluding the requirement of notice in mortgage agreements was not lawful. The statutory requirement for notice was 'for the benefit of the mortgagor: a last chance to protect his equity of redemption', and it was impermissible to 'contract out' of the mandatory statutory provisions.

On further appeal, the Privy Council rejected the reasoning of the Court of Appeal. Lord Hoffmann pointed out[57] that section 128 of the Act, which had apparently been overlooked by the courts below, provided that 'every covenant and power to be implied in any instrument by virtue of this Act may be negated or modified by express declaration in the instrument'. This was interpreted by the Privy Council to mean that the statutory notice provision could indeed be expressly excluded by the mortgage agreement. The justification for this interpretation of the section, according to Lord Hoffmann, was that the Registration of Titles Act was 'concerned with an efficient system of conveyancing rather than social legislation to give mortgagors a degree of protection against mortgagees which they did not have at common law or equity'. It was further noted that, in the unregistered system, section 21(2) of the Conveyancing Act 1889 (Jamaica) provided that the power of sale conferred on mortgagees of unregistered land could be 'varied or extended by the mortgage deed' without any restriction, and there was no logical justification for giving mortgagors of registered land greater protection than that given to mortgagors of unregistered land. It seems, therefore, that further legislation would be required[58] in order to

57 [2007] UKPC 8, paras 8–22.

58 In The Bahamas, where there is no system of registration of title, the Homeowners' Protection Act, section 4(3) provides that 'where a mortgagor is in breach of the mortgage agreement, the mortgagee shall not institute proceedings before the Court in respect of the breach, unless there has been served upon the mortgagor either personally or by registered post at least 30 days prior to instituting such proceedings a notice in writing' stating, *inter alia*, (i) the nature of the breach of any covenant in the mortgage, (ii) the amount of arrears owed by the mortgagor, (iii) the actions to be taken by the mortgagor to cure the breach in order to avoid foreclosure and sale, (iv) the rights of the mortgagor under the Act, including the right to apply to the Court for relief under section 5, (v) the willingness of the mortgagee to negotiate an agreement with the mortgagor for redress, including modification of the terms of the mortgage agreement. See *RBC Royal Bank (Bahamas) Ltd v Hall* (2020) Supreme Court, The Bahamas, No CLE/gen/236.

vindicate the approach taken by the Court of Appeal, and to ensure that a mortgagor under the Registration of Titles Act retains a degree of protection when the mortgagee is exercising its power of sale.

It remains to be seen whether, in relation to registered and unregistered land, the courts in other Caribbean jurisdictions will follow the lead of the Jamaican Court of Appeal in regarding the statutory provisions designed to protect the mortgagor as mandatory and not susceptible to exclusion by the express terms of mortgage agreements.

Mode of sale

The mortgagee may sell the property, or part thereof, either subject to prior charges or not, and either together or in lots, by public auction[59] or by private contract, and subject to such conditions respecting title or other matters as it thinks fit.[60]

Effect of sale

As soon as a contract for sale has been concluded, the mortgagor's equity of redemption is extinguished[61] and the subsequent conveyance operates to pass the mortgagor's legal fee simple or lease, as the case may be, to the purchaser. The rights of subsequent mortgagees are also extinguished, but the rights of any prior mortgagees remain intact and the purchaser takes subject to them.[62]

Protection of purchaser

The difference between the power of sale arising and becoming exercisable is that where the power has not arisen, the mortgagee has no right to sell, but so long as the power has arisen, he/she can pass a good title to a purchaser notwithstanding that the power has not become exercisable. A purchaser is, therefore, only concerned to see that the power has arisen, and he need not inquire into whether it has become exercisable or it has been properly exercised,[63] although it has been held that if the purchaser 'becomes aware . . . of any facts showing that the power of sale is not exercisable, or that there is some impropriety in the sale, then . . . he gets no good

59 In advertising an auction of land, the general practice in Jamaica is to have two inserts in suitable publications such as national newspapers. Also, sufficient time should be allowed for responses and for any persons interested to view the land: *Jobson v Capital and Credit Merchant Bank Ltd* (2005) Court of Appeal, Jamaica, Civ App No 113 of 2002, *per* Cooke JA.

60 Section 21 of Ch 138 (The Bahamas); s 22 of the Conveyancing Act and s 106 of the Registration of Titles Act (Jamaica); s 110 of Cap 236 (Barbados); s 39 of Ch 56:01 (Trinidad and Tobago).

61 Accordingly, once a valid contract of sale has been concluded, it is too late for the mortgagor to tender the mortgage money and become entitled to have the property reconveyed to him: *Lord Waring v London and Manchester Assurance Co Ltd* [1935] Ch 310, 318, *per* Crossman J; *Edelweiss Chalets Condominium Association v Davis* (1998) Supreme Court, The Bahamas, No FP 160 of 1997, *per* Osadebay J; *Bloomfield v National Development Foundation of Jamaica* (2004) Supreme Court, *Jamaica*, No 00945 of 2004, *per* Sykes J.

62 Section 23(1) of Ch 138 (The Bahamas); s 24(1) of the Conveyancing Act (Jamaica); s 112 of Cap 236 (Barbados).

63 See s 114(1) of Cap 236 (Barbados); s 42 of Ch 56:01 (Trinidad and Tobago); s 23 of Ch 138 (The Bahamas); s 24(2) of the Conveyancing Act (Jamaica).

title on taking the conveyance'.[64] The latter proposition has been explained on the ground that to hold otherwise would be to allow a statute to be used as an instrument of fraud.

The Jamaican courts have considered the issue of protection of purchasers in the context of section 106 of the Registration of Titles Act which, unlike the Property and Conveyancing legislation applicable to unregistered land, makes no distinction between a power of sale arising and becoming exercisable, but simply provides that where there has been an alleged default by the mortgagor and the mortgagee has exercised its power of sale,

> no purchaser shall be bound to see or inquire whether such default as aforesaid shall have been made or have happened, or have continued, or whether such notice as aforesaid shall have been served, or otherwise into the propriety or regularity of any such sale; and the Registrar upon production of a transfer made in professed exercise of the power of sale conferred by this Act or by the mortgage or charge shall not be concerned or required to make any of the inquiries aforesaid; and any persons damnified by an unauthorized or improper or irregular exercise of the power shall have his remedy only in damages against the person exercising the power.

In *Broomfield v National Development Foundation of Jamaica*,[65] Sykes J very helpfully summarised the position under the Jamaican Registration of Titles Act, in the light of the previous decision of the Court of Appeal in *Sheckleford v Mount Atlas Estate Ltd*,[66] thus:

(i) The signing of the sale agreement extinguishes the mortgagor's equity of redemption, so that a subsequent tender of the amount owed to the mortgagee will not assist the mortgagor.

(ii) Provided the purchaser from the mortgagee is a *bona fide* purchaser for value who has no *actual notice* of any impropriety on the part of the mortgagee, no injunctive relief will be given to the mortgagor, since section 106 of the Act relieves the purchaser from enquiring whether (a) the mortgagor defaulted, (b) notice was given to the mortgagor under section 105, and (c) the sale was proper and regular.

(iii) Assuming some impropriety on the part of the mortgagee exists, the mortgagor's only remedy is an action for damages against the mortgagee.[67]

(iv) Once the agreement for sale is signed, the effect of section 106 is that although the mortgagor is still the registered proprietor, the mortgagee is treated *as if he were the registered proprietor*, and the mortgagor is eliminated from the equation.

In the later case of *Jobson v Capital and Credit Merchant Bank Ltd*,[68] the Court of Appeal applied similar reasoning, in holding that the sale to the purchaser in that case could not be set aside, since there was 'no evidence that the purchasers had notice that the power of sale was improperly or irregularly exercised', so that there was no question

64 *Bailey v Barnes* [1894] 1 Ch 25, at 35; *Waring (Lord) v London and Manchester Assurance Co Ltd* [1935] Ch 310, at 318.
65 (2004) Supreme Court, Jamaica, No 00945 of 2004.
66 (2001) Court of Appeal, Jamaica, Civ App No 148 of 2000.
67 See *Farquharson v Everglades Farms Ltd* (2011) Supreme Court, Jamaica, No 820 of 2010, *per* Brooks J.
68 (2005) Court of Appeal, Jamaica, Civ App No 113 of 2002.

of conversion of the provisions of the statute into an instrument of fraud; and in *Foote v Capital and Credit Merchant Bank Ltd*,[69] Anderson J (whose ruling was subsequently upheld by the Court of Appeal[70])stated that in the *Sheckleford* case the Court of Appeal was saying that, in order to deny the purchaser his section 106 protection, it was necessary for the purchaser to have had actual knowledge of the irregularity or impropriety in the exercise of the power of sale by the mortgagee.[71]

Application of proceeds of sale

A mortgagee who sells the mortgaged property under his/her statutory power is a trustee of the proceeds of sale and must apply them in the following order:[72]

(a) in paying all expenses incidental to the sale;
(b) in paying to himself the principal, interest and costs due under the mortgage; and
(c) in paying the balance to the next subsequent mortgagee[73] or, if none, to the mortgagor.

Bad faith

In *Lord Waring v London and Manchester Assurance Co Ltd*, Crossman J said:[74]

> After a contract has been entered into, however, it is in my judgment perfectly clear . . . that the mortgagee (in the present case, the company) can be restrained from completing only on the ground that he has not acted in good faith and that the sale is therefore liable to be set aside.

'Bad faith' has never been exhaustively defined, but it has been said that 'good faith' connotes a 'duty to act honestly and without a reckless disregard of the interests of the mortgagor'.[75]

A number of cases have come before the Trinidadian courts in which mortgagors have sought to restrain mortgagees from selling under their powers of sale, on the ground that the mortgagees had acted in bad faith. One such case is *Seepersad v Colonial Life Insurance Co (Trinidad) Ltd.*[76] Here, the mortgagor had fallen behind in his mortgage payments, and the mortgagees were proposing to sell the land under their statutory power. There was evidence that one Mrs B, who was employed

---

69 (2010) Supreme Court, Jamaica, No 3328 of 2008.
70 [2012] JMCA App 14, *per* Morrison JA.
71 See also *Div Deep Ltd v Tewani Ltd* (2011) Court of Appeal, Jamaica, Civ App No 126 of 2010, where Panton P stated that the combined effect of sections 71, 106 and 108 of the Registration of Titles Act is that the position of the purchaser is 'untouchable – barring fraud'.
72 *Lord Waring v London and Manchester Assurance Co Ltd* [1935] Ch 310, at 318, *per* Crossman J.
73 See *Samuel Keller (Holdings) Ltd v Martins Bank Ltd* [1970] 3 All ER 950.
74 [1935] Ch 310, at 318.
75 *Cuckmere Brick Co Ltd v Mutual Finance Ltd* [1971] 2 All ER 633, at 653, *per* Cairns LJ; *San Fernando Medical Centre Ltd v Republic Finance and Merchant Bank Ltd* (1995) 3 TTLR 807, at 824, High Court, Trinidad and Tobago, *per* Blackman J; *Scotia Bank (Belize) Ltd v Fairweather* (2016) Supreme Court, Belize, No 479 of 2010; *Trethewey v Scotia Bank (Belize) Ltd* (2018) Supreme Court, Belize, No 284 of 2017, para 12, *per* Young J.
76 (1990) High Court, Trinidad and Tobago, No 404 of 1990. See also *San Fernando Medical Centre Ltd v Republic Finance and Merchant Bank Ltd*, above.

by the mortgagees as a debt collector, had suggested to the mortgagor that if he paid his arrears, the mortgagees would not proceed with the sale. The mortgagor accordingly paid part of the arrears, but the mortgagees nevertheless entered into an agreement to sell the land by private treaty. The mortgagor contended that the agreement should be set aside, on the ground that Mrs B had misled him into believing that the mortgagees would not go ahead with the sale, and that, by entering into the contract of sale in these circumstances, the mortgagees had acted in bad faith. Lucky J held the mortgagor's argument to be unsupportable: Mrs B was not an agent of the mortgagees 'for purposes of binding the company by her actions or her words . . . she was simply an agent for the purpose of collecting debts'. He continued:

> In the *Waring* case, it has been held that a mortgagee's exercise of his power under s 101 of the Law of Property Act 1925, which is equivalent to s 39 of our Act, to sell the mortgaged property by public auction or private contract is binding on the mortgagor before completion, unless it is proved that he exercised it in bad faith; and there is no evidence, in my view, that there is any bad faith in this case . . .
>
> In the *Waring* case, it is to be noted that while the plaintiff is still entitled to redeem, that is to have the property re-conveyed to him, he can only have the property re-conveyed to him on payment of principal, interest and costs. A mortgagee, strictly speaking, is not a trustee with respect to the power of sale: it is a power given to him for his own benefit to enable him to realise his debt. If he exercises it for that purpose, without corruption or collusion with the purchaser, the court ought not to interfere even though the sale may be very disadvantageous, unless indeed the price is so low as in itself to be evidence of fraud.

On the other hand, in *Alpras Investments Ltd v National Commercial Bank of Trinidad and Tobago Ltd*,[77] bad faith was found to be present. In this case, the mortgagor company, which was in arrears with its payments, had applied to the court for an order permitting it to redeem the mortgaged property upon payment to the mortgagees of a sum of money to be obtained from a sale of the property by the mortgagor; alternatively, for an extension of time to repay the mortgage debt. Whilst the summons was pending before the court, with the mortgagees' attorney attending, the mortgagees proceeded to exercise their power of sale and sold the property, without providing the mortgagor with any account or statement as to the amount owing to the mortgagees. Wills J held that the mortgagees had acted in bad faith. He said:

> In my judgment, a mortgagee who intends to exercise his powers of entry and sale must do so in good faith. And while he is, in general, entitled to exercise such powers in a way conducive to his best interest, subject to any express conditions contained in the mortgage instrument, he must act in good faith and not capriciously. Furthermore, while to him it may be commercially necessary to sell the mortgaged property primarily for his own benefit to recover the money lent, he is not entitled to ignore the interests of the mortgagor with impunity. At law, the mortgagee is not a trustee of the power of sale for the mortgagor. And while he has a right to look after his own interest, he is not at liberty to act either recklessly or with wilful disregard or indifference, sacrificing the interest of the mortgagor.

77 (1992) High Court, Trinidad and Tobago, No 2389 of 1991, see also *Hearn v Republic Bank Ltd* (1991) High Court, Trinidad and Tobago, No 3738 of 1990.

> The circumstances of this case seem to follow a trend which is prevalent at times like these when there appears to be economic recession, during which the principles of equity seem to be ignored by financial institutions. I find that the property in this case has been sold in questionable circumstances, but I am constrained by the remedy sought in the summons from granting the kind of remedy which in my view might have been available to the plaintiff.
>
> In the circumstances of this case, I find the defendant's conduct in proceeding to exercise its power of sale was, to say the least, draconian, and its effect was such as to make the memorandum of mortgage a deed of defeasance. The defendant bank, in acting as it did, clearly demonstrated a reckless and/or conscious indifference as to whether or not its act of selling the mortgaged property could or could not interfere with the proper dispensation of justice.
>
> Not only has the defendant proceeded to sell the property in the face of the pending proceedings, but failed to provide the plaintiff with an account when it should be obvious to the lender bank and/or its advisers that in law, on a sale being completed, it becomes trustee of any surplus in its hands. It ought also to be aware that, on the completion of the sale, interest ceases to run against the mortgagor.

Restraining exercise of the power of sale

It was emphasised by Gonsalves-Sabola CJ in the Bahamian Supreme Court in *American British Canadian Motors Ltd v Imperial Life Assurance Co of Canada*[78] that the court will not grant an interlocutory injunction to restrain exercise of a mortgagee's power of sale, except on the terms of the mortgagor paying into court the amount sworn by the mortgagee to be due for principal, interest and costs. He continued:

> I agree with the submission of counsel for the defendant that to allow any other course would create havoc in the marketplace. A mortgagor, fat with the mortgagee's funds, who seeks to avoid the mortgage instrument when the power of sale it confers is sought to be exercised, has no right to come empty-handed to court to restrain the mortgagee. Had the rule been otherwise, it requires but little imagination to foresee how a succession of defaulting mortgagors, temporising with technical objections, could employ the interlocutory injunction to constipate the cash flow in the mortgagee's business and frustrate its normal course, with all the serious implications that that entails.

The same principle is applied in Jamaica, where it is known as 'the *Marbella* principle', having been enunciated in *SSI (Cayman) Ltd v International Marbella Club SA*.[79] In *Alexander House Ltd v Reliance Group of Companies*,[80] the trial judge, Batts J, had acceded to the mortgagor's application for an injunction to restrain the mortgagee from exercising its power of sale but, in keeping with the *Marbella* principle, only on the condition that the mortgagor should pay into court the sum of US $747, 908. The mortgagor appealed to the Court of Appeal, contending that the mortgage was void for illegality and that an injunction to restrain sale should have been granted

---

78 (1990–91) 4 Carib Comm LR 258, at 261, following *Macleod v Jones* (1883) 24 Ch D 289. See also *Inglis v Commonwealth Trading Bank of Australia* (1972) 126 CLR 161. Thus, the mortgagee will not be restrained from exercising its power of sale on the ground, for example, that the amount due is in dispute, or because the mortgagor objects to the manner in which the sale is being arranged: 32 *Halsbury's Laws* 332, [725]. Cf *Arts Centre Ltd v Brown* (2006) Supreme Court, Jamaica, No 00132 of 2006.

79 (1987) Court of Appeal, Jamaica, Civ App No 57 of 1886, *per* Rowe P.

80 [2018] JMCA Civ 18. See also *Scott v VGI Finance Investments Ltd* (2011) Supreme Court Jamaica No 5348 of 2009, *per* Sykes J.

without imposing the *Marbella* condition. McDonald-Bishop JA, delivering the judgment of the Court of Appeal, considered whether the present case came within any of the exceptional types of circumstance, suggested by Morrison JA in *Mosquito Cove Ltd v Mutual Security Bank Ltd*,[81] in which the *Marbella* principle may be departed from, such as:

(i) where the terms of the mortgage deed are peculiar or unusual;
(ii) in a case of forgery of the mortgagor's signature;
(iii) where questions arise as to the validity of the mortgage document;
(iv) where, on the face of the mortgage, the mortgagee's claim is excessive.

Morrison JA had further opined that:

> While other or further exceptions to the rule are no doubt to be found in the books and will also emerge in the future, it seems to me that . . . the court will only sanction departures from the general rule in highly exceptional cases, based on very special facts, such as the existence of a fiduciary relationship between mortgagor and mortgagee or, perhaps, in cases of forgery. I naturally intend these as examples only, which are by no means exhaustive.

In the *Alexander House* case, the Court of Appeal declined to disturb Batts J's order, considering that the issue of the illegality or otherwise of the mortgage was essentially a question of fact that ought to be investigated at trial and could not properly be resolved at the interlocutory stage. Accordingly, the learned judge could not be faulted for applying the *Marbella* principle.

Mortgagee's duty of care

A mortgagee, as we have seen, is a trustee of the proceeds of sale,[82] but he is not a trustee of the power of sale itself,[83] which he is entitled to exercise in his/her own interest. Thus, for instance, if at the time he wishes to sell the property the market is depressed, he is not obliged to wait for a rise in market prices,[84] even though it is clear that by selling immediately there will be a smaller surplus to hand over to the mortgagor; nor is he obliged to put the property in a better state of repair in order to obtain a higher price;[85] nor to attempt to sell by auction before selling by private

81 (2010) Court of Appeal, Jamaica, Civ App No 57 of 2003, paras 57–63.
82 See p 205, above.
83 *Kennedy v De Trafford* [1897] AC 180. See *Jamaica Citizens Bank Ltd v Reid* (1995) 32 JLR 1, Supreme Court, Jamaica; *First Citizens Bank Mortgage and Trust Co Ltd v Anthony* (1997) High Court, Trinidad and Tobago, No 708 of 1996; *Christian v Republic Finance and Merchant Bank Ltd* (1997) High Court, Trinidad and Tobago, No 2494 of 1990; *Blake v First Jamaica National Bank* (1994) 31 JLR 450, Supreme Court, Jamaica; *Bank of Butterfield (Cayman) Ltd v Crang* [1992–93] CILR 409, Grand Court, Cayman Islands. In The Bahamas, the mortgagee's duties were summarised by Frazer J in *Evans v Commonwealth Bank Ltd* [2016] 2 BHS J No 95, para 29. See also *Finance Corporation of The Bahamas Ltd v Johnson* (2019) Supreme Court, The Bahamas, No 2015/CLE/gen/01149, *per* Thompson J.
84 *Davey v Durant* (1857) 26 LJ Ch 830; *Bank of Butterfield (Cayman) Ltd v Crang*, above; *Island Life Insurance Co Ltd v Mangertz* (2006) Supreme Court, Jamaica, No CL 2000/1–072. On the other hand, it was held in *Palk v Mortgage Services Funding plc* [1993] 2 All ER 481, that the court has a discretion to order a sale at a depressed market price, even against the wishes of the mortgagee, since where the value of the property is less than the amount of the loan, a sale will terminate the mortgage and relieve the mortgagor of mounting interest payments.
85 *Waltham Forest London Borough v Webb* (1974) 232 EG 461.

contract. As Salmon LJ explained, in the leading case of *Cuckmere Brick Co Ltd v Mutual Finance Ltd*:[86]

> It is well settled that a mortgagee is not a trustee of the power of sale for the mortgagor. Once the power has accrued, the mortgagee is entitled to exercise it for his own purposes whenever he chooses to do so. It matters not that the moment may be unpropitious and that, by waiting, a higher price could be obtained. He has the right to realise his security by turning it into money when he likes. Nor, in my view, is there anything to prevent a mortgagee from accepting the best bid he can get at an auction, even though the auction is badly attended and the bidding exceptionally low. Provided none of those adverse factors is due to any fault of the mortgagee, he can do as he likes. If the mortgagee's interests, as he sees them, conflict with those of the mortgagor, the mortgagee can give preference to his own interests, which of course he could not do were he a trustee of the power of sale for the mortgagor.

Later in his judgment, Salmon LJ said:[87]

> It is impossible to pretend that the state of the authorities on this branch of the law is entirely satisfactory. There are some *dicta* which suggest that, unless a mortgagee acts in bad faith, he is safe. His only obligation to the mortgagor is not to cheat him. There are other *dicta* which suggest that, in addition to the duty of acting in good faith, the mortgagee is under a duty to take reasonable care to obtain whatever is the true market value of the mortgaged property at the moment he chooses to sell it: compare, for example, *Kennedy v De Trafford*[88] with *Tomlin v Luce*.[89]
>
> The proposition that the mortgagee owes both duties, in my judgment, represents the true view of the law . . .
>
> I accordingly conclude, both on principle and authority, that a mortgagee in exercising his power of sale does owe a duty to take reasonable precautions to obtain the true market value of the mortgaged property at the date on which he decides to sell it. No doubt in deciding whether he has fallen short of that duty, the facts must be looked at broadly, and he will not be adjudged to be in default unless he is plainly on the wrong side of the line.

In *Cuckmere Brick*, the mortgagee was held liable in damages for negligence because, in advertising the property for sale, it carelessly omitted to mention that planning permission had been granted for the erection of apartments on the mortgaged land, and it thus obtained a lower price than it ought to have obtained.[90] The mortgagee was thus liable for the difference between the price obtained and the proper market value of the property. *Cuckmere Brick* is, accordingly, authority for the proposition that the mortgagee must take reasonable care to obtain the true market value of the property. More recent authorities,[91] however, have suggested that the mortgagee's

86 [1971] 2 All ER 633, at 643.
87 *Ibid.*
88 [1897] AC 180.
89 (1889) 43 Ch D 191.
90 But in *Island Life Insurance Co Ltd v Mangertz* (2006) Supreme Court, Jamaica, No CL 2000/1–072, Sinclair-Haynes J (Ag) held that, in this case, the failure to state in advertisements that building permission had been obtained did not affect the interest generated in the property, as the market was generally 'lukewarm' towards properties in the district.
91 See *Downsview Nominees Ltd v First City* [1993] AC 295, at 315, *per* Lord Templeman; *Daley v RBTT Bank (Jamaica) Ltd* (2007) Supreme Court, Jamaica, No D162 of 1995, *per* Sykes J; *Khiatani Jamaica Ltd v Sagicor Bank Jamaica Ltd* [2018] JMSC Comm 10, *per* Sykes J; *Rampersad v Agricultural Development Bank* (2009) High Court, Trinidad and Tobago, No CV 2007–01083, *per* Bereaux J. On the other hand, in *Williams v First Global Bank Ltd* [2017] JMCC Comm 39, Batts J opined (at paras 27, 28) that in the great majority of situations the result will be the

duty of care has its doctrinal basis not so much in the law of negligence as in principles of equity, which require the mortgagee to act in a prudent and business-like manner, with a view to obtaining as high a price as may fairly and reasonably be obtainable in the circumstances of the case.

A sale by a mortgagee must be genuine. A 'sale' by the mortgagee to himself, either alone or with others, is not a true sale and may be set aside, even though the price offered is the full value of the property.[92] A sale to a company in which the mortgagee is a shareholder will not necessarily be set aside,[93] but where the company is managed and controlled by the mortgagee, the 'sale' may be set aside as a sham, especially where it is at a gross undervalue.[94] The onus is on the mortgagee to show that the sale was *bona fide*[95] and that he took precautions to obtain the best price reasonably obtainable.

The principle in *Cuckmere Brick Co Ltd v Mutual Finance Ltd* was applied by the Jamaican Court of Appeal in *Dreckett v Rapid Vulcanizing Co Ltd*.[96] In this case, the appellant mortgaged his land, with house thereon, of which he was registered proprietor, to the respondent company to secure a loan of $6,400. The appellant fell into arrears with the mortgage payments, resulting in the respondent exercising its power of sale. The property was sold by public auction to DP, a real estate broker, for $6,400. Some nine months later, DP resold the property for $14,400 to CM, and the property was duly registered in the purchaser's name. The appellant claimed that the respondent had been negligent in failing to ascertain the current market value of the property at the time of the sale to DP, and in failing to fix a reserve price at the auction. Wolfe J, in the lower court, held that the appellant had failed to show negligence on the part of the respondent within the *Cuckmere Brick* principle, and this decision was upheld by the Court of Appeal. Carberry JA said:[97]

> the crucial question in the case is, what was the market value of this land when sold by the mortgagees at the auction? Was it sold at an undervalue? And if so, by how much? If the mortgagor was to gain any redress in this action in respect of his complaint that the premises had been sold recklessly or negligently at an undervalue, he had the onus

---

same whichever rationalisation is followed. He accordingly refused to strike out the mortgagor's claim insofar as it referenced negligence, pointing out that the administration of law and equity has been fused for over 100 years and 'it matters not whether one sues at law or in equity'.

92 *National Bank of Australasia v United Hand-in-Hand and Band of Hope* (1879) 4 App Cas 391.

93 *Tse Kwong Lam v Wong Chit Sen* [1983] 1 WLR 1394; *Paradise Manor Ltd v Bank of Nova Scotia* [1985] CILR 437, Court of Appeal, Cayman Islands, at 473.

94 *Dickson v Playa del Sol Ltd* (1982) 1 BLZR 370, Supreme Court, Belize, at 375.

95 *Mungroo v Westmaas* (2018) Court of Appeal, Trinidad and Tobago, Civ App No 1/2014, paras 47–51, *per* Mendonca JA.

96 (1988) 25 JLR 130. In *Cornwall Agencies Ltd v Bank of Nova Scotia (Jamaica) Ltd* (2008) Supreme Court, Jamaica, No 1652 of 2003, Beswick J found that the defendant bank had failed to take reasonable precautions to obtain the true market value of the mortgaged property at the date on which it decided to sell: the Court of Appeal [2016] JMCA Civ 49, *per* Panton J (at paras 55–57), overruled the trial judge, finding that, after a 'disastrous' auction at which the auctioneer had 'no respectable or acceptable bid', and no interest shown by any entity or individual in purchasing the property for a higher price, the bank waited for about a year before selling to the eventual purchaser. In these circumstances, 'the bank could not have been expected to wait into eternity to recoup its losses'. See also *Davis v Franklyn* (1994) Supreme Court, Jamaica, No E 148 of 1982, in which Malcolm J emphasised that 'a mortgagee's duty on sale is to take reasonable precautions to obtain a proper price, not the best price'; *Davis v Finco Corp (Bahamas) Ltd* (1998) Supreme Court, The Bahamas, No 1160 of 1995; *Scotia Bank (Belize) Ltd v Fairweather* (2016) Supreme Court, Belize, No 479 of 2010; *Foote v JMMB Merchant Bank Ltd* [2018] JMSC Civ 13.

97 (1988) 25 JLR 130, at 133, 134, 140.

> of producing evidence to establish what was the market value of 6 Tangerine Road on or about 2 December 1970.

Carberry JA found that there was no evidence as to the value of the property at the material time, and, after reviewing the case law on the subject of exercise of the mortgagee's power of sale, he continued:

> It is fair to say that [the law] is not in a very satisfactory state. The authorities that have been cited, and there were many, show that the courts have alternated between showing concern for the mortgagor and a wish to protect him against a mortgagee who recklessly sells off the mortgaged premises, concerned only to recover his money on the borrower's default, and that the object of the mortgage was to enable this to be done speedily and at the mortgagee's convenience.
>
> The instant case was conducted on the basis that the *Cuckmere*[98] case should be adopted and followed by the courts in Jamaica, and if there was any doubt on the matter I think it should be received and followed by the courts of Jamaica.[99] In fact, the industry of counsel discovered a first instance case in which Rowe J (as he then was) followed and applied the *Cuckmere* case. See *Rose Hall Ltd v Chase Merchant Bankers (Jamaica) Ltd.*[100]
>
> I have reluctantly come to the conclusion that the mortgagor has failed to discharge the burden of establishing that the property was sold at under the market value of the property at the time of the sale, or to show that for some identifiable reason the auction here failed to realise a proper price or the market value at the date of the auction.

Campbell JA said:

> The view of Salmon LJ in the *Cuckmere Brick* case is most apposite. He said:[101]
>
>> Nor, in my view, is there anything to prevent a mortgagee from accepting the best bid he can get at an auction, even though the auction is badly attended and the bidding is exceptionally low. Providing none of those adverse factors is due to any fault of the mortgagee, he can do as he likes.
>
> Thus Salmon LJ was saying that, consistent with the principle which he later enunciated,[102] an auction which has not been manipulated by the mortgagee is evidence of reasonable precaution taken by the mortgagee to obtain the true market value of the mortgaged property on the date on which he decides to sell. The view expressed by Salmon LJ negatives any obligation of the mortgagee to fix, or have fixed, a reserve price (in circumstances where he does not bid at the auction), because he has the right to accept the highest bid, even if it was below what was the ascertained true market value. Equally, the mortgagee is not obliged to obtain an independent prior valuation to determine the market value on the basis of which to fix a reserve price when the sale is by auction. He can properly rely on the independent competitive biddings at the auction to obtain the true market value, and even if this is not obtained through poor attendance at the auction and/or exceptionally low bids, he is not on that account *per se* liable to his mortgagor for breach of any duty to take reasonable

98 [1971] 2 All ER 633.

99 Carberry JA also pointed out (at 140) that the instant case concerned land under the Registration of Titles Act, which provided in s 105 that the registration of a mortgage does not, unlike at common law, operate as a transfer of the title to the land, and, if the mortgagee wishes to realise the mortgage by sale, he must comply with ss 105 and 106.

100 (1976) Supreme Court, Jamaica, No E 211 of 1976. See also *Bank of Nova Scotia Co of Trinidad and Tobago Ltd v Manswell* (1992) High Court, Trinidad and Tobago, No 1324 of 1989.

101 [1971] 2 All ER 633, at 643.

102 *Ibid*, at 646.

> precautions to obtain the true market value. To the contrary, the mortgagee could say that he had taken the reasonable precautionary steps to protect the mortgagor by having an auction which has been conducted without any impropriety.
>
> In the present appeal, no impropriety as to the conduct of the auction is alleged or proved. The bases on which the mortgagee is being held to have failed in its duty are that it failed to ascertain the then current market value by valuation prior to the auction, and failed to fix a reserve price. These failures, I have already said, do not individually or collectively constitute breaches of duty, particularly in an auction sale in which the mortgagee has not participated and where no impropriety in relation to the auction itself has been alleged or appears on the evidence. The situation fits neatly into the case postulated by Salmon LJ of poor attendance and exceptionally low bids.

In *Adams v Workers Trust and Merchant Bank Ltd*,[103] the circumstances were that the mortgagee, having made an abortive attempt to sell by public auction, sold the property to X by private treaty. The mortgagee had obtained a valuation of the property, but took no steps to advertise before selling. In addition, the mortgagee had rejected a higher offer, in the erroneous belief that it was contractually bound to sell to X.[104]

James J (Ag), in the Jamaican Supreme Court, took the view that, 'by advertising, the property could have been exposed to prospective purchasers in the open market', and the mortgagee's failure to advertise, coupled with its mistake of law, led to the conclusion that it had 'fallen short of the standard of the duty of care owed' to the mortgagor, and it was therefore liable for the loss incurred.

More recently, in *International Trust and Merchant Bank Ltd v Gardiner*,[105] Bingham JA in the Jamaican Court of Appeal stated that, in the case of a sale by private treaty, the following pre-conditions had to be satisfied: (i) a current market valuation[106] of the

103 (1992) 29 JLR 447, Supreme Court, Jamaica. See also *Gardiner v International Trust and Merchant Bank Ltd* (2000) Supreme Court, Jamaica, No CLG 056 of 1996. In *Paradise Manor Ltd v Bank of Nova Scotia* [1985] CILR 437, Grand Court, Cayman Islands, it was held that the mortgagee bank had made every reasonable effort and had taken all of the necessary steps to obtain a sale of the property (a partially completed hotel complex requiring major capital investment to complete it, and described as 'not an attractive proposition' and a 'white elephant'), and 'took reasonable precautions to obtain the best price reasonably obtainable at the time of the sale'. The bank had advertised extensively in the national and international press and sought (without success) to interest major hotel chains in acquiring the site. The site was ultimately sold by private treaty after a long period.

104 In *Khiatani Jamaica Ltd v Sagicor Bank Jamaica Ltd* [2018] JMSC Comm 10, the bank, in the exercise of its power of sale, entered into a contract of sale with H for a price that was insufficient to pay off the debt in full and which would leave no surplus for the mortgagor. Meanwhile, a higher price, which would have covered the debt and left a surplus, had been firmly offered by C. The agreement with H contained a clause making time of the essence and entitling the bank to rescind the contract for failure to make timely payments. Although H was in breach of the time clause, the bank declined to rescind and went ahead with the sale. Sykes J held that, by not taking the opportunity to rescind the agreement with H, so that it would be free to contract to sell to C for the higher price, the bank was in breach of its equitable duty to consider the interests of the mortgagor by obtaining the best price reasonably obtainable.

105 (2004) Court of Appeal, Jamaica, Civ App No 111 of 2000.

106 In *Daley v RBTT Bank Jamaica Ltd* (2007) Supreme Court, Jamaica, No D 162 of 1995, Sykes J stated that the absence of a current valuation in the context of a sale by private treaty was powerful evidence that the bank had failed to take reasonable precautions to obtain the true market value of the mortgaged property at the date at which it had decided to sell. However, it has also been emphasised that property valuation is not an exact science: see *National Commercial Banking Corp of Australia v Solariowski* (1984) NSW Conv R 55–194. See also *Bank of Nova Scotia (Jamaica) Ltd v Rosegreen* (2008) Supreme Court, Jamaica, No B 240 of 1998, in which Jones J held that a valuation obtained two years prior to the sale could not be considered to have been 'current', but that by itself was not evidence that the sale was at an undervalue, as the bank had shown that it had acted in good faith and the sale price was only slightly below the 'forced sale' price. According to Jones J, 'one has to examine the facts "in the round" '.

mortgaged property; (ii) a proper advertisement of the mortgaged property with a view to attracting potential purchasers; and (iii) a sale of the property so carried out as to obtain the market value of the property or, failing this, the best price reasonably obtainable. The plaintiff in this case claimed that, as a result of the negligence of the defendant and its agents, he had lost the sum of $2.6m on the sale of his duplex house, and that this had occurred because the defendant had failed to obtain a valuation and failed to advertise the property adequately. The Court of Appeal upheld the decision of the trial judge, awarding the plaintiff damages amounting to the difference between the valuation price of $4.5m and the sale price of $1.9m.

Right to foreclose

As we have seen,[107] after the contractual redemption date has passed, the mortgagor has an equitable right to redeem. In order to balance the rights of the parties, equity gives the mortgagee a simultaneous right to foreclose the mortgage – that is, to bring an action in court in order to extinguish the equitable right to redeem and to acquire for himself the legal and equitable title to the property, freed from the equity of redemption. The right to foreclose does not arise until repayment has become due at law,[108] which includes not only the case in which the contractual redemption date has passed, but also cases in which the mortgage deed expressly provides that repayment is to fall due on the breach of any term of the mortgage (for example, failure to pay an instalment of interest or principal) and such breach has occurred.[109]

A foreclosure action can be brought by any mortgagee, whether he is a first or subsequent mortgagee or an assignee of an original mortgagee. The effect of a foreclosure order absolute is to foreclose all subsequent mortgagees, but to leave intact the rights of prior mortgagees. Thus, for example, if land is mortgaged to A, B, C and D, and B forecloses, the interests of C and D as well as that of the mortgagor will be extinguished, whilst A's interest will be unaffected. Where there are several mortgagees, the court, in the order *nisi*, may direct that any subsequent mortgagees be given an opportunity to redeem by paying the amount due to the foreclosing mortgagee on the date appointed. Accordingly, subsequent mortgagees must be made parties to the foreclosure action.

Foreclosure is in two stages. First, the court makes a foreclosure order *nisi*, which directs that accounts be taken and provides that, if the mortgagor pays the money due by a fixed day (which is normally six months from the settling of the accounts), the mortgage will be discharged, but that if the mortgagor fails to pay, a motion may be brought to make the foreclosure absolute.

Reopening of a foreclosure

An order of foreclosure absolute may be 'reopened' in certain circumstances: for instance, where the mortgagee, after obtaining an order absolute, proceeds to bring an action on the personal covenant;[110] where a mishap at the last moment prevents

107 See p 190, above.
108 *Williams v Morgan* [1906] 1 Ch 804.
109 *Kidderminster Mutual Benefit Building Society v Haddock* [1936] WN 158.
110 *Perry v Barker* (1806) 33 ER 269.

the mortgagor from repaying the debt; where there is a marked difference between the value of the property and the amount of the debt; and where the property is of special value to the mortgagor (for example, where it is an old family estate).[111]

Sale in lieu of foreclosure

The court has a statutory power to order a sale instead of a foreclosure at the request of any person interested[112] (for example, a later mortgagee or the mortgagor). The power is most likely to be used where the value of the property far exceeds the amount of the mortgage debt. In such a case, the court may order a judicial sale, the effect of which is that each mortgagee is paid what is due to him in order of priority, and the balance is given to the mortgagor.[113]

Foreclosure under the Registration of Titles Act (Jamaica)

Sections 119 and 120 of the Act provide that a mortgagee may make an application for a foreclosure order[114] to the Registrar of Titles where the mortgagor has defaulted in payment of principal or interest for six months after becoming due. The application must be in writing and attest to the following:

(i) the mortgagee's default in payment for the requisite period;
(ii) that the mortgaged property was offered for sale at a public auction, conducted by a licensed auctioneer;
(iii) that the highest bid at the auction was not sufficient to satisfy the amount due under the mortgage and the expenses incurred;
(iv) that written notice of the mortgagee's or transferee's intention to apply for foreclosure had been served on the mortgagor and any other person entered on the Register as having an interest in the property.

The application must also be accompanied by the auctioneer's certificate.

Upon receipt of the application, the Registrar may cause a notice offering the property for private sale to be advertised on three successive weeks in at least one newspaper published in Kingston, and the Registrar will fix a time for issuing a foreclosure order, which must be not less than one month after the date of the first

---

111 See *Campbell v Holyland* (1877) 7 Ch D 166, at 173, *per* Jessel MR.
112 Section 49 of Ch 56:01 (Trinidad and Tobago); s 27 of Ch 138 (The Bahamas); s 28(2) of the Conveyancing Act (Jamaica); s 101 of Cap 236 (Barbados).
113 That is, the proceeds are applied in the same way and in the same order as in the case of a sale under a mortgagee's power of sale. See p 205, above.
114 In *Harley v Harley* [2019] JMSC Civ 8, para 35, Laing J pointed out that, since a foreclosure order extinguishes the mortgagee's right to sue on the personal covenant, it is not commercially sensible to obtain an order for foreclosure 'where the outstanding debt is significantly greater than the value of the property. The foreclosure order can be a double edged sword. The mortgagee may end up with property which has greater value than the outstanding debt, or with property the value of which is substantially less. That is a risk which the mortgagee bears, but that is the nature of the remedy. What is clear is that there is no obligation on him to account to the mortgagor for any amount in excess of the debt, should he be so fortunate as to make a profit on a later sale'. See *Dunbar v St Catherine Co-operative Credit Union Ltd* [2018] JMCC Comm 27, where the outstanding debt was $4,735 million, while the land was valued at $15 million. Batts J pointed out that the mortgagee was entitled to retain the entire net proceeds of sale (para 17). See also *Atkinson v Development Bank of Jamaica* [2015] JMSC Civ 161, paras 20–23, *per* Evan Brown J.

advertisement. In the event that the property is not sold during the period for a sufficient amount to satisfy principal, interest and all expenses, The Registrar will proceed to issue the foreclosure order to the applicant. When entered in the Register Book, the foreclosure order will vest the property in the mortgagee or his/her transferee, free from the equity of redemption of the mortgagor or any person claiming through him/her. The mortgagee or his/her transferee will thus become the new proprietor of the property. The Registrar will then cancel the previous certificate of title, and register a new one in the name of the mortgagee or transferee.

RIGHTS OF EQUITABLE MORTGAGEE

The equitable mortgagee's right to sue for the money due is the same as for a legal mortgagee. He may also foreclose in the same way as a legal mortgagee. Since the equitable mortgagee has no legal estate, the court's order absolute will direct the mortgagor to convey the land to the mortgagee free from the right to redeem.[115] An equitable mortgagee is entitled to exercise the statutory powers of sale and appointment of a receiver only where his/her mortgage is made by deed,[116] as where there is a deposit of title deeds accompanied by a memorandum of deposit made by deed. Where there is no statutory power of sale out of court, the court may order a sale and vest a legal term of years in the mortgagee so that he can convey a legal estate to a purchaser. It seems that an equitable mortgagee has no right to possession of the mortgaged property,[117] but the court has power to make an order of possession in his favour,[118] and the mortgage agreement may expressly grant such right.[119]

Since an equitable mortgagee has no legal estate to convey to the purchaser in exercising his/her statutory power of sale, it may be necessary to employ one or the other of the following conveyancing devices:

(a) insertion of an irrevocable power of attorney in the memorandum, empowering the mortgagee or his/her assigns to convey the legal estate; or
(b) insertion of a declaration of trust in the memorandum, whereby the mortgagor declares that he holds the legal estate upon trust for the mortgagee, and empowering the mortgagee to appoint someone, including himself, as trustee in place of the mortgagor. This will enable the mortgagee to vest the legal estate in himself or the purchaser.

TACKING AND CONSOLIDATION

Right to tack further advances

It is a common practice for banks not only to undertake to lend money for a present purpose, but also to agree to make further advances in the future on the same

115 *James v James* (1873) LR 16 Eq 153.
116 As in *Imperial Life Assurance Co of Canada v M & P Investments Ltd* (1999) Supreme Court, The Bahamas, No 141 of 1998.
117 Since he has no legal estate.
118 *Barclays Bank Ltd v Bird* [1954] 1 All ER 449.
119 *Ocean Accident and Guarantee Corp Ltd v Ilford Gas Co* [1905] 2 KB 493.

security. In certain circumstances, where the mortgagor creates a later mortgage in favour of a third party, the bank as first or prior mortgagee may be entitled to 'tack' further advances so as to obtain priority for them over the intervening mortgage or mortgages. For example, in January, B mortgages his land to X Bank to secure an overdraft of $20,000. It is a term of the mortgage deed that 'this mortgage secures a loan of $20,000 and any further advance that the mortgagee chooses to make'. In March, B grants a mortgage of the same land to Y to secure a loan of $10,000, and in April, another mortgage to Z to secure a loan of $15,000. In May, X Bank consents to an increase of the overdraft to $50,000. X Bank may be entitled to obtain priority over Y and Z, so that it will recover its $50,000 before Y and Z receive anything.

Tacking is permitted under the general law:[120]

(a) where the intervening mortgagee agrees to tacking; or
(b) where the prior mortgagee holds the legal title, and has no notice of the intervening mortgage at the time of making the further advance.[121]

Where the prior mortgagee is under an obligation to make further advances and has no notice of the intervening mortgage, registration of the intervening mortgage in a land or deeds registry does not, in itself, constitute notice.

Statutory provisions enacted in Barbados,[122] and modelled on s 94 of the Law of Property Act 1925 (UK), have modified the general law in two respects:

(a) registration of the intervening mortgage in the Land Registry constitutes actual notice of the mortgage, except where the prior mortgage expressly secures not only the original loan, but also further advances or a current account (in which case, the position is the same as under the general law); and
(b) where the prior mortgage imposes an obligation on the mortgagee to make further advances, tacking will apply to such advances notwithstanding that, at the time of making them, the prior mortgagee had notice of the intervening mortgage.

Right to consolidate

Where two or more mortgages have become vested in the same mortgagee, he has the right to refuse to allow one mortgage to be redeemed unless the other or others are also redeemed.[123]

This is often cited as an illustration of the maxim that 'he who seeks equity must do equity'. For example, X has mortgaged both Redacre and Greenacre to Y to secure loans of $100,000 on each property. At the time the mortgages were created, both properties were worth $130,000. Later, the value of Greenacre appreciates

120 *Brace v Duchess of Marlborough* (1728) 2 P Wms 491; *Taylor v Russell* [1892] AC 244. But it was held by Langrin J, in *Geon Contractors and Associates Ltd v National Commercial Bank (Jamaica) Ltd* (1991) 28 JLR 409, that the doctrine of tacking does not apply to mortgages under the Registration of Titles Act, as 'tacking and consolidation have no place under the Torrens system' (at 412).
121 *Freeman v Laing* [1899] 2 Ch 355.
122 Section 104 of Cap 236.
123 *Jennings v Jordan* (1881) 6 App Cas 698, at 700.

to $200,000, but that of Redacre sinks to $80,000. It would be unfair to the mortgagee, Y, if X were allowed to redeem Greenacre and to leave Redacre unredeemed. Accordingly, equity will allow Y to consolidate – that is, to insist that the two properties be treated as one and redeemed together, or not at all.

Statutory provisions in most jurisdictions provide that there shall be no right to consolidate unless a contrary intention is expressed in one or more of the mortgage deeds.[124] Accordingly, it is usual for mortgage deeds expressly to grant the right to consolidate.

124 See, eg, s 20 of the Conveyancing Act (Jamaica); s 103 of Cap 236 (Barbados); s 19 of Ch 138 (The Bahamas); s 35 of Ch 56:01 (Trinidad and Tobago).

CHAPTER 11

ADVERSE POSSESSION

The concept of adverse possession is rooted in the theory that the basis of title to land in English law is possession. The fact of possession gives a title to the land, which is good against all persons except one who has a better right to possession. All titles to land are relative in the sense that a person's title, including a documentary (or 'paper') title, is only good in so far as there is no other person who can show a better title. The effect of adverse possession is that a person who is in possession as a mere trespasser or 'squatter' can obtain a good title if the true owner fails to assert his superior title within the requisite limitation period[1] in the particular jurisdiction.[2]

Limitation of actions in this context expresses the idea that, whilst it may seem unjust that a wrongdoer should, after expiry of the limitation period, be allowed to retain the land as against the true owner, it would be detrimental to the public interest if persons were to be allowed to bring 'stale' claims. In the words of Lord St Leonards:[3]

> All statutes of limitation have for their object the prevention of the rearing up of claims at great distances of time when evidences are lost; and, in all well-regulated countries, the quieting of possession is held an important point of policy.

Accordingly, after the limitation period has expired, the true owner who has 'slept on' his rights will be barred from asserting them against the person in adverse possession, and his rights will be extinguished. The squatter in possession will then have the best claim to the land, and will be able to acquire a good title by registration,[4] or he/she may simply remain in possession, which could no longer be disturbed. In either case, he/she will have acquired a fee simple interest in the land.[5]

---

1 This passage in the text was cited by Charles J in *Gosine v Gosine* (2012) High Court, Trinidad and Tobago, No CV2009–04135.

2 *Treloar v Nute* [1977] 1 All ER 230, 234, *per* Pennycuick J. See, eg, s 6(3) of the Limitation Act, Cap 43 (BVI) (12 years); *Dessuit v Farrington* (1993) High Court, BVI, No 51 of 1990; s 19 of the Limitation Law 1991 (Cayman Islands) (12 years); s 16(3) of the Limitation Act 1995 (The Bahamas) (12 years); *High Point Estates Ltd v Higgs* (2000) Supreme Court, The Bahamas, No 246 of 2000; *Impco Properties (Bahamas) Ltd v EAH Investments Ltd* (2004) Supreme Court, The Bahamas, No 2002/01788; *Hitzhusen v Riley* (1999) Supreme Court, The Bahamas, No 664 of 1994; *Re Knowles* (2010) Supreme Court, The Bahamas, No 1353 of 2008. See also s 25 of the Limitation of Actions Act 1997 (Barbados) (10 years); s 3 of the Limitation of Actions Act 1973 Rev (Jamaica) (12 years); s 17 of the Limitation Act, Cap 90 (St Vincent and the Grenadines) (12 years); *Belvedere Holdings Ltd v Matthews* (2008) High Court, St Vincent and the Grenadines, No 27 of 2005; s 2 of the Real Property Limitation Act, Cap 54:07 (Dominica) (12 years); s 16 of the Limitation Act, Title 8, Item 42 (Bermuda) (20 years); s 5 of the Title to Land (Prescription and Limitation) Act, Cap 60:02 (Guyana) (12 years); s 4 of the Limitation of Actions Act, Cap 173 (Grenada) (12 years); s 3 of the Real Property Limitation Ordinance, Ch 56:03 (Trinidad and Tobago) (16 years); *Richardson v Lawrence* (1968) 10 WIR 234, 237; *Poplow v Mahabir* (1994) High Court, Trinidad and Tobago, No 3254 of 1988; *Highgate Development Co Ltd v Lawrence* (1994) High Court, Trinidad and Tobago, No 4878 of 1985; *Benoit v Taylor* (2004) High Court, Trinidad and Tobago, No 94 of 1998; *Salamat v Rajack* (2009) High Court, Trinidad and Tobago, No S-1103 of 1994. See generally LM Jackson, (2002) 7(2) Carib LB 1–18.

3 *Dundee Harbour Trustees v Dougall* (1852) 1 Macq 317.

4 See, eg, Registration of Titles Act (Jamaica), ss 85, 87; *Pottinger v Raffone*, Privy Council Appeal No 64 of 2005.

5 In The Bahamas, s 3 of the Quieting of Titles Act 1959, provides that 'any person who claims to have any estate or interest in land may apply to the court to have his title to such land

DOI: 10.4324/9781003186946-11

The possession of a series of adverse possessors may be aggregated in order to make up the appropriate limitation period. Thus, if O, the original 'paper' owner, is dispossessed by X who, in his turn, is dispossessed by Y, Y may aggregate the period of X's possession with that of his own to defeat O's action for recovery of the land,[6] although X may recover the land from Y before the latter's independent period of adverse possession has lasted for the length of the limitation period.

In order that the periods of adverse possession may be aggregated, they must be continuous. Thus, if X abandons his adverse possession within the limitation period and, after an interval of, say, two months, Y begins to possess adversely, Y cannot add his period of possession to that of X, as the periods were not continuous. The break in the adverse possession will have the effect of restoring the full rights of the paper owner, and the limitation period will start afresh with the commencement of Y's adverse possession.[7]

DISPOSSESSION OF TENANT

Where a tenant is dispossessed by a squatter during the term of the lease, the adverse possession of the squatter begins to run immediately as against the tenant and, after expiry of the relevant limitation period, the tenant's lease will be extinguished; but time does not begin to run against the landlord until the date of expiry of the lease.[8] Accordingly, the landlord is entitled to evict the squatter on the expiration of the lease·[9] Further, in *Ralph v Bernard*,[10] Mendonca JA, in the Trinidad and Tobago Court of Appeal, stated that, just as the landlord is entitled to evict the squatter on the expiration of the lease, so also are those claiming through the landlord, since their right to possession is derived from the landlord's title. Therefore, where the old lease is extinguished by a squatter's adverse possession, and the landlord subsequently grants a new lease, the tenant under the new lease (whether or not he was tenant under the old lease) can evict the squatter, provided the new

---

investigated and his nature and extent thereof determined and declared in a *certificate of title* to be granted by the court'. Application is by way of petition, which must state the facts and circumstances grounding the claim to the estate or interest alleged.

The court then makes an order for publication of notices requiring any 'adverse claims' to be filed by a certain date. Claims to entitlement to certificates of title under the Act are often based on adverse possession: see *Re Rolle* (2011) Supreme Court, The Bahamas, No 1978 of 2003; *Re Malcolm Allotments* (1981) Supreme Court, The Bahamas, No 593 of 1965; *Re O'Brien Loans Ltd* (1987) Supreme Court, The Bahamas, No 21 of 1986; *Re Simms* (2001) Supreme Court, The Bahamas, No 14 of 1992; *Re Edwards (No 2)* (1971–76) 1 LRB 521; *Re Smith* (1998) Supreme Court, The Bahamas, No 2 of 1996; *Re Knowles* (2010) Supreme Court, The Bahamas, No 1353 of 2008; *Armbrister v Lightbourn* [2012] UKPC 40. For a full account of the Quieting of Titles jurisdiction, see *Bannerman Town, Millars and John Millars Eleuthera Association v Eleuthera Properties Ltd* [2018] UKPC 27, paras 33–42, *per* Lord Briggs.

6 *Trustees, Executors and Agency Co Ltd v Short* (1883) 13 App Cas 793, 798, *per* Lord Macnaghten; *Ocean Estates Ltd v Pinder* [1969] 2 AC 19, PC appeal from the Court of Appeal of The Bahamas, 24, *per* Lord Diplock; *Re Malcolm Allotments* (1981) Supreme Court, The Bahamas, No 593 of 1965; *Lashley v Marchong* (2017) Court of Appeal, Trinidad and Tobago, Civ App No 266 of 212).

7 *Perry v Woodfarm Homes Ltd* [1975] IR 104; *Re Malcolm Allotments*, above; *International Hotels (Jamaica) Ltd v Proprietors Strata Plan No 461* [2013] JMCA Civ 45, para 85, *per* Morrison JA.

8 *Tichborne v Weir* (1892) 67 LT 735, at 737; *Jordan v Lucas* (2012) Court of Appeal, Trinidad and Tobago, Civ App No 189 of 2009, *per* Jamadar JA.

9 *Ralph v Bernard* (2016) Court of Appeal, Trinidad and Tobago, Civ App No 131 of 2011, *per* Mendonca JA.

10 *Ibid.*

lease was *not* granted pursuant to an option to renew contained in the old lease, since, according to *Chung Ping Kwan v Lam Island Development Co*,[11] where the new lease is granted pursuant to an option to renew in the old lease, the tenant's right to possession under the new lease will also be statute-barred.

The effect of a tenant surrendering his lease to the landlord following the tenant's dispossession by a squatter was considered in *Fairweather v St Marylebone Property Co Ltd*,[12] where the facts were essentially as follows: L granted a 99-year lease of a house and garden, containing a shed, to T. The shed was occupied by a neighbour, S, for more than 12 years adversely to T. While the lease had about 33 years still to run, T surrendered the lease to L. The question was whether L, as fee simple owner, was entitled to resume possession immediately (since L was unaffected by S's adverse possession), or whether he had no such right until the lease came to an end by effluxion of time, ie in 33 years' time. The House of Lords held that the effect of T's surrendering the lease was that L was entitled to resume possession immediately, and was not bound to wait until expiry of the lease. The decision in *Fairweather* has been justly criticised on the ground that if T's lease had been extinguished by S's adverse possession, T had nothing to surrender to L, so that the purported surrender should have been declared void, thus leaving L with no right to resume possession before the date of expiry of the lease. Nonetheless, to date, *Fairweather* has not been overruled and, despite its doctrinal anomalies, it may perhaps be justified on the ground that it would be repugnant to common sense and fairness if, in the case of a very long lease (for example, one of 99 years) a landlord were compelled to accept a squatter as his tenant until the date of its expiry.

An adverse possessor who dispossesses a tenant cannot be sued directly by the landlord for rent or for damages for breach of covenant, as the squatter is not an assignee of the lease and there is no privity of estate between him/her and the landlord.[13] However, in the event of a breach of covenant, the landlord may decide to bring forfeiture proceedings, and since an adverse possessor has no right to seek relief against forfeiture, such proceedings are likely to result in his eviction.[14]

INCHOATE RIGHTS OF ADVERSE POSSESSOR

Another manifestation of the principle of relativity of title is that an adverse possessor acquires inchoate rights, even before expiry of the limitation period, which are good against all persons except the paper owner or any person who can show a superior title.[15] The adverse possessor is deemed to have a fee simple estate from the moment he/she enters into possession of the land, notwithstanding that his entry may have been wrongful, and notwithstanding that his possession is liable to be terminated by legal action before expiry of the limitation period.[16] Such estate may be assigned by the adverse possessor *inter vivos*, or may be disposed of by his will.[17]

---

11 [1997] AC 38.
12 [1963] AC 510.
13 *Tickner v Buzzacott* [1965] Ch 426, at 434.
14 See p 80 *et seq*, above.
15 *Asher v Whitlock* (1865) LR 1 QB 1, at 5.
16 *Wheeler v Baldwin* (1934) 52 CLR 609, at 632.
17 *Asher v Whitlock* (1865) LR 1 QB 1. See *Welch v Broomes* (1981) 16 Barb LR 177, High Court, Barbados.

An assignee may add the period of his possession to that of the assignor in order to establish completion of the limitation period.[18]

REQUIREMENTS FOR ACQUISITION OF TITLE BY ADVERSE POSSESSION

There is a strong presumption that possession is retained by the paper owner or by some person claiming through him/her,[19] and a person claiming title to land by adverse possession must show either:

(a) discontinuance of possession by the paper owner followed by possession by the claimant or his predecessor; or
(b) dispossession – that is, ouster of the paper owner.

The difference between 'dispossession' and 'discontinuance' of possession

> might be expressed in this way: the one is where a person comes in and drives out the others from possession; the other case is where the person in possession goes out and is followed into possession by other persons.[20]

Sufficiency of possession by adverse possessor

Before the ruling of the House of Lords in *JA Pye (Oxford) Ltd v Graham*,[21] it had been held in a number of cases that, in order to succeed in a claim of adverse possession, the claimant had to show 'positively that the true owner has gone out of possession of the land, that he has left it vacant with the intention of abandoning it',[22] and the mere fact that the paper owner was shown to have made no use of the land during the period did not necessarily amount to discontinuance of possession,[23] nor would there be discontinuance of possession in cases in which another person was in occupation of the land, if there was evidence that the paper owner intended to retain the land for some specific use at a later date.[24] In *Pye*, however, Lord Browne-Wilkinson stressed[25] that it is not the intention of the paper owner regarding his future use of the disputed land that determines the sufficiency of the squatter's possession for the purpose of obtaining a possessory title, but rather the intention of the squatter to exercise acts of possession and control over the land. Accordingly, under the modern law, a squatter can obtain a title by adverse possession notwithstanding that his

18 Even without an assignment of the fee simple, the next successive squatter may add his period of possession to that of the previous squatter in order to complete the limitation period. See fn 6, above.
19 *Powell v McFarlane* (1977) 38 P&CR 452, at 470.
20 *Rains v Buxton* (1880) 14 Ch D 537, 539, *per* Fry J. Cf *Lewis v Swan* (1999) Court of Appeal, Bermuda, Civ App No 23 of 1998, *per* Cons JA.
21 [2003] 1 AC 419.
22 *Archer v Georgiana Holdings Ltd* (1974) 12 JLR 1421, at 1426, *per* Swaby JA.
23 *Leigh v Jack* (1879) 5 Ex D 264, 271; *Archer v Georgiana Holdings Ltd* (1974) 12 JLR 1421, at 1426, Court of Appeal, Jamaica, *per* Swaby JA. Thus, 12 years' non-activity by the paper owner on ruinate land might not mean that he had given up ownership: *Green Valley Estates Ltd v Lazarus* (1991) 28 JLR 399, Supreme Court, Jamaica.
24 *Leigh v Jack* (1879) 5 Ex D 264; *Johnson v Myers* (1988) 25 JLR 74, at 77 (Court of Appeal, Jamaica).
25 [2003] 1 AC 419, at 438.

user of the land is not inconsistent with the paper owner's future intentions. In his Lordship's view:

> The highest that it can be put is that, if the squatter is aware of a special purpose for which the paper owner uses or intends to use the land, and the use by the squatter does not conflict with that use, that may provide *some support*[26] for a finding as a question of fact that the squatter had no intention to possess the land in the ordinary sense but only an intention to occupy it until needed by the paper owner. For myself, I think there will be few occasions in which such inference could properly be drawn in cases where the true owner has been physically excluded from the land. But it remains a possible, if improbable, inference in some cases.

In *Pye*,[27] the House of Lords stated that legal possession by the adverse possessor requires (i) a sufficient degree of physical custody and control (factual possession), and (ii) an intention to exercise such custody and control on one's own behalf and for one's own benefit (intention to possess, or *animus possidendi*).

Factual possession

The factual possession required must be (i) *nec clam* (ie, open and unconcealed), and (ii) *nec precario* (ie, not by permission or consent).[28] These characteristics are similar to those required for a claim to an easement by prescription,[29] except that it has been recently held by the Privy Council in a Bahamian case, *Higgs v Leshel Maryas Investment Co Ltd*,[30] that the third requirement for acquisition of an easement by prescription, *nec vi* (not by force), is 'not applicable to the possession of land for possessory title purposes'. Lord Scott, delivering the judgment of the Board, went on to say that the remedy of a paper owner whose attempts to re-enter into possession were forcibly resisted by a squatter[31] would be either to commence legal proceedings for possession (the commencement of which would stop time running), or, if it were possible to do so without breach of the criminal law, 'to re-enter, take possession and throw the squatter out'; but 'simply to accept the barring by the squatter of the desired re-entry and do nothing to disturb the squatter's possession cannot . . . stop time running'. In short, Lord Scott's analysis seems to mean that the fact that a squatter has forcibly resisted re-entry by the paper owner will not prevent the squatter from acquiring a title by adverse possession, if the paper owner fails to take court proceedings to assert his title.

The requirement of openness means that the possession of the claimant must be 'notorious and unconcealed',[32] for otherwise the paper owner would not be made

26 Italics supplied.

27 [2003] 1 AC 419; *Lares v Lares* [2020] UKPC 19, para 3, *per* Lord Leggatt. See also *Smith v Benjamin* (2009) 78 WIR 421 (Court of Appeal, Trinidad and Tobago), *per* Mendonca JA.

28 These requirements were recently confirmed by Best J in *Pooran v Roop* (2010) High Court, Trinidad and Tobago, No 4114 of 2006.

29 See Chapter 9, above.

30 [2009] UKPC 47.

31 It has been suggested that although an adverse possessor must not resort to unreasonable violence in order to maintain himself in possession, it may be that aggressive defence of the boundaries of the land will reinforce, rather than weaken, the adverse possessor's claim: Gray, *Elements of Land Law*, 3rd edn, p 268.

32 *Lord Advocate v Lord Lovat* (1880) 5 App Cas 273, at 291, 296; *Nottingham v Deposit Insurance Corporation* (2010) High Court, Trinidad and Tobago, No 58 of 2006, *per* Moosai J; *Morris v Bethell* (2013) Court of Appeal, The Bahamas, Civ App No 96 of 2012, *per* Allen P.

aware of the need to challenge the adverse possessor before expiry of the limitation period. In the words of Cooper J in *McDonell v Giblin*:[33]

> The possession which is claimed to be adverse to [the paper owner's] rights must be sufficiently obvious to give to such owner the means of knowledge that some person has entered into possession adversely to his title and with the intention of making a title against him; it must be sufficiently open and manifest that a man reasonably careful of his own interests would, if living in the same locality and passing the allotment from time to time, by his observations have reasonably discovered that some person had taken possession of the land.

The requirement that possession must not be by permission or consent is inextricably linked with the concept of 'adverse' possession. Possession cannot be adverse if it is enjoyed by the permission or consent of the paper owner, so that any possession that is concurrent with that of the paper owner will not qualify,[34] nor must possession be founded on a licence[35] or lease[36] granted by the paper owner, nor be by way of family arrangement,[37] as, in all such cases, the possession will not be adverse, but by consent.[38] Claims to acquisition of title in the Commonwealth Caribbean have often failed on the *nec precario* ground: as, for example, where the claimant was the half-brother of the paper owner who was allowed to occupy and enjoy the fruits of the land in return for his paying the rates and taxes,[39] and where the claimant was the daughter of the owner and lived in the house as the 'guest' of her mother until the latter's death.[40]

The common law principles have been modified by statute in some jurisdictions, as has been emphasised in two Privy Council decisions in cases originating from Trinidad and Tobago and Jamaica respectively. In the first of these, *Ramnarace v*

---

33 [1904] NZLR 660, at 662, cited with approval by Moosai J in *Nottingham v Deposit Insurance Corporation*, fn 32 above, holding that 'clandestine' acts of occupation by the claimant of a small portion of the disputed land did not evince an intention to occupy the whole of the land.

34 *Treloar v Nute* [1977] 1 All ER 230.

35 *Wallis's Cayton Bay Holiday Camp Ltd v Shell-Mex and BP Ltd* [1974] 3 All ER 575; *Sookraj v Sookraj* (2010) High Court, Trinidad and Tobago, No 550 of 2000; *Hepburn v Hanley* (1981) Court of Appeal, The Bahamas, No 17 of 1980; *Burke v Whitters Worldwide Properties Ltd* (1993) 30 JLR 6, 10, Supreme Court, Jamaica, *per* Langrin J ('where a person takes possession under a licence or permission, time cannot begin to run until the licence or permission has been terminated'); *Clarke v Swaby* (2007) Privy Council Appeal No 13 of 2005, *per* Lord Walker ('It is perfectly clear that under the law of Jamaica, as under the law of England, a person who is in occupation of land as a licensee cannot begin to obtain a title by adverse possession so long as his licence has not been revoked. Unless and until it is revoked, his occupation of the land is to be ascribed to his licence, and not to an adverse claim').

36 *Johnson v Myers* (1988) 25 JLR 74, at 76, Court of Appeal, Jamaica; *Poochoon v White Ridge Farm Ltd* (2010) High Court, Trinidad and Tobago, No S 1069 of 2003. Equally, possession under the Land Tenants (Security of Tenure) Act, 1981 prevents time from running for the purposes of adverse possession: *Ramdial v Kerry*, (2004) Court of Appeal, Trinidad and Tobago, Civ App No 10 of 2002; *Revero v Ramdath* (2017) High Court, Trinidad and Tobago, No 2015–02052. However, it has been held that, in Trinidad and Tobago, a 16-year possession, even though it is by virtue of a tenancy, operates to dispossess the paper owner if no rent is paid, title is not acknowledged, and the paper owner takes no action to evict the possessor: *Rampersad v Dwarka* (2020) Court of Appeal, Trinidad and Tobago, Civ App No S077 of 2015.

37 *Murphy v Murphy* [1980] IR 183; *Riley v Brathwaite* (1979) WIR 66, Court of Appeal, Barbados.

38 See *McMillan v Grant* (2011) High Court, Trinidad and Tobago, No 69 of 2003.

39 *Scantlebury v Young* (1948–57) 1 Barb LR 23, Court of Error, Barbados.

40 *Greaves v Barnett* (1978) 13 Barb LR 129, High Court, Barbados. Permission to occupy land ceases on the death of the landowner, after which time begins to run for purposes of adverse possession: *Baldie v Cargill* [2020] JMSC Civ 218, para 54, *per* Thomas J.

Lutchman,[41] R had in 1974 been allowed into possession of a piece of land owned by her uncle on the understanding that she would buy the property when she had sufficient funds. After the uncle's death in 1977, L, who was a beneficiary of his estate, purported to give R notice to quit on two occasions, in 1978 and 1985, but did not take steps to enforce either notice. Meanwhile, R had built a concrete house on the land and, in 1990, she erected a chain-link fence, with an iron gate, around the disputed land. L thereupon used a wrecker to pull down the fence, and he cut down R's gate with a cutting torch. R claimed she had acquired a title by adverse possession, and L counterclaimed for possession. The Court of Appeal of Trinidad and Tobago held that R had entered into occupation of the land as a mere licensee and that her licence had been terminated by the service of the notice to quit in 1985. Accordingly, R had not been in adverse possession of the land for the 16-year period required to extinguish L's title under section 3 of the Real Property Limitation Ordinance (now Real Property Limitation Act, Ch 56:03). The Privy Council, however, agreed with the trial judge's finding that R was not a licensee, but a tenant at will[42] because she had entered into possession not merely by virtue of an act of generosity[43] on the part of her uncle, but as an intended purchaser of the land. The case fell to be decided in accordance with section 8 of the Ordinance, which provided, as an exception to the principle that possession is not adverse if it is enjoyed with the consent of the true owner, that where a person is in possession as a *tenant at will*, the right of the true owner to bring an action to recover the land 'shall be deemed to have first accrued' at the expiration of one year from the commencement of the tenancy, at which time the tenancy 'shall be deemed to have determined'. The effect, as Lord Millett explained, was that:

> If a tenancy at will is determined during the first year, the owner's right of action accrues immediately; otherwise it accrues automatically by virtue of section 8 at the end of the first year, and any later determination of the tenancy is ineffective for limitation purposes unless a new tenancy is created . . . The effect of sections 3 and 8 of the Ordinance taken together is that if no action is taken by the true owner, his title is extinguished after the expiration of 17 years from the commencement of the tenancy, even though the possession of the occupier is permissive throughout. It was the deliberate policy of the legislature that the title of owners who allowed others to remain in possession of their land for many years with their consent but without paying rent or acknowledging their title should eventually be extinguished.

The Privy Council accordingly restored the trial judge's decision to the effect that, by virtue of section 8 of the Ordinance,[44] R's tenancy must be deemed to have determined in July 1975, one year after its commencement, and that since R had

41 [2001] 1 WLR 1651.

42 In *Simonette v Ahoy* (2009) Court of Appeal, Trinidad and Tobago, Civ App No 156 of 2005, Warner JA noted that 'difficulties sometimes arise in distinguishing a licence from a tenancy at will, since both may share the characteristic of a grant of exclusive possession. A person cannot, however, be a tenant at will where it appears from the surrounding circumstances that there was no intention to create legal relations'. See also Chapter 4, above.

43 For an example of possession attributable to an act of family generosity, see *Moorjani v Kirpalani* (2009) High Court, Trinidad and Tobago, No 485 of 2007.

44 Section 9 of the Real Property Limitation Act, Ch 56:03, provides a special rule for the running of time for periodic tenancies where there is no written lease, viz: if rent is not paid, and remains unpaid, time starts to run for limitation purposes at the end of the first rent period in which rent was not paid. See *Ramroop v Ishmael* [2010] UKPC 14, where it was also held that it is possible to establish title by adverse possession to part only of a building.

remained in exclusive possession of the land without interruption, by July 1991 L's title was extinguished by the operation of section 3.

Another significant modification of the common law principles is to be found in those sections of the limitation statutes of Commonwealth Caribbean jurisdictions which provide, contrary to the common law rule, that the possession of one co-owner is not to be treated as the possession of the other co-owner(s). In *Re Hollingsworth*,[45] Boyce J, in the Supreme Court of The Bahamas, stated that the effect of s 12 of the Bahamian Real Property Limitation Act 1833 (now replaced by s 19 of the Limitation Act 1995, Ch 83) was that 'one co-tenant [whether joint tenant or tenant in common] can bar the title of another co-tenant by separate possession, that is by occupying the land for his own benefit for the prescribed limitation period', as the Privy Council had confirmed in an earlier Bahamian case, *Re Paradise Beach and Transportation Co.*[46] The equivalent Jamaican provision, section 14 of the Limitation of Actions Act 1973 Rev, was applied by the Privy Council in *Wills v Wills.*[47] This case concerned a married couple, G and E, who had acquired two properties in Jamaica, which were conveyed to them as joint tenants. The parties separated in the early 1970s, and E went to live permanently in the USA, leaving nothing behind except her wedding ring. The joint tenancies were never severed. After E had left, G formed a relationship with M, whom he eventually married, having divorced E. After E's departure, G kept all of the rental income from the properties and never accounted to E for any of it. The last occasion that E visited the properties was in 1976. G died in 1992 and M obtained letters of administration to G's estate. E claimed to be entitled to the two properties as surviving joint tenant. M claimed that E's titles had been extinguished under the Limitation of Actions Act. Chester Orr J and the Jamaican Court of Appeal found in favour of E, being of the view that she had not discontinued her possession nor been dispossessed, but the Privy Council reversed those findings, basing its decision on section 14 of the Act, which had altered the common law rule that the possession of one co-tenant was deemed to be the possession of the other or others, by providing that

> when any one or more of several . . . joint tenants or tenants in common shall have been in possession or receipt of the entirety . . . of such land or of the profits thereof . . . for his own benefit or for the benefit of any person(s) other than the person(s) entitled to the other share of the same land or rent, *such possession or receipt shall not be deemed to have been the possession or receipt of or by such last mentioned person(s).*
>
> (emphasis added)[48]

In other words, as applied to the circumstances of the present case, the possession of the two properties by G since 1976, at the latest, was to be treated as his own individual possession and not the joint possession of G and E. Accordingly, since E had been out of possession for more than the 12 years' limitation period laid down by section 3 of the Act, her title had been extinguished.

45 [1971–76] 1 LRB 482, at 503. See also *Re Royal Island Bahamas Ltd* (2011) Supreme Court, The Bahamas, No 605 of 2008; *Higgs v Leshel Maryas Investment Co Ltd* [2009] UKPC 47. The position is the same in Trinidad and Tobago under section 14 of the Real Property Limitation Act, Ch 56:03: see *Lares v Lares* [2020] UKPC 19, para 4.
46 [1968] 1 All ER 530. See LM Jackson (2002) 7(2) Carib LB 9–11.
47 (2003) Privy Council Appeal No 50 of 2002.
48 Section 14 of the Real Property Limitation Ordinance, Ch 5, No 7 (Trinidad and Tobago) is similarly worded: see *Ramsawan v Ramsawan* (2003) High Court, Trinidad and Tobago, No 915 of 1995, *per* Mohammed J.

In the course of his judgment, Lord Walker referred to the House of Lords decision in *JA Pye (Oxford) Ltd v Graham*,[49] in which Lord Browne-Wilkinson had emphasised that

> the suggestion that the sufficiency of the [squatter's] possession can depend on the intention not of the squatter but of the true owner is heretical and wrong. It reflects an attempt to revive the pre-1833 concept of adverse possession requiring inconsistent user.[50]

Lord Walker then went on to say that the conclusion that E had not discontinued her possession or been dispossessed had been reached by the courts below only because they had proceeded on the 'heretical and wrong' supposition that it was E's state of mind, and not G's, which (together with G's actions) was decisive. He continued:

> E no doubt wished to maintain her claim to co-ownership, not least because she expected to outlive G and hoped to take by survivorship. But such an intention, however amply documented, cannot prevail over the plain fact of her total exclusion from the properties. After 1976, at the latest, G occupied and used the former matrimonial home and enjoyed the rents . . . as if he were the sole owner, except in so far as he chose to share his occupation and enjoyment with M.

As for the suggestion that a decision against E would be likely to cause trouble for the large numbers of Jamaican citizens who work overseas and contribute to their families' welfare and the island's economy, Lord Walker suggested that:

> most of them will come home on a fairly regular basis, will retain the bulk of their possessions at home, and will not (on coming home) be treated as guests in their own houses. But if (as must sometimes happen) a Jamaican working overseas forms new attachments and starts a new life, and entirely abandons the former matrimonial home, he or she will (within the ample period of 12 years) have to consider the legal consequences of that choice.[51]

In order to qualify as sufficient adverse possession, the acts of the claimant must not be 'trivial'[52] or 'equivocal',[53] and, in determining whether the claimant has shown sufficient factual possession to found a claim to title by adverse possession, regard must be had to the circumstances of the individual case. Acts that might be held to be sufficient in one case will not necessarily be sufficient in another. In *JA Pye (Oxford)*

---

49 [2003] 1 AC 419, at 438.

50 Followed in *Ali v Tobago House of Assembly* (2010) Court of Appeal, Trinidad and Tobago, Civ App No 43 of 2008, *per* Kangaloo JA.

51 This rationalisation was applied to similar facts by Batts J in *Farrington v Walters* [2013] JMSC Civ 157 Supreme Court, Jamaica.

52 For example, merely parking vehicles on the land: *Johnson v Myers* (1988) 25 JLR 74, Court of Appeal, Jamaica; *Tecbild Ltd v Chamberlain* (1969) 20 P&CR 633; or setting of traps for doves, and playing of 'doll house' by little girls: *Thompson v Incorporated Trustees of the Ethiopian Orthodox Church of Trinidad* (2013) High Court, Trinidad and Tobago, No CV 2007–02417.

53 An 'equivocal act' was defined by Graham-Perkins JA in *Farrington v Bush* (1974) 12 JLR 1492, at 1493, as 'an act of such a nature as to provide an equal balance between an intention to exclude a true owner from possession and the intention to merely derive some enjoyment or benefit from the land wholly consistent with such use as the true owner might wish to make of it'; see also *Harriram v Gopaul* (2011) High Court, Trinidad and Tobago, No S 1785 of 2002, *per* Harris J. In *Powell v Mc Farlane* (1977) 38 P&CR 452, at 476–477, Slade J characterised as 'equivocal' any use of the disputed land that 'did not necessarily, by itself, betoken an intention on his part to claim the land as his own and exclude the true owner'. The question of equivocality is thus an aspect of the *animus possidendi* requirement (see p 227 *et seq*, below).

Ltd v Graham,[54] Lord Browne-Wilkinson approved the following passage from the judgment of Slade J in *Powell v McFarlane*:[55]

> The question what acts constitute a sufficient degree of exclusive physical control must depend on the circumstances, in particular the nature of the land and the manner in which land of that nature is commonly used or enjoyed . . . Everything must depend on the particular circumstances, but broadly, I think what must be shown as constituting factual possession is that the alleged possessor has been dealing with the land in question as an occupying owner might have been expected to deal with it and that no-one else has done so.

Factual possession signifies an appropriate degree of control: 'the squatter must take control of the land and make use of it without interference from anyone'. Acts showing sufficient factual possession would include, *inter alia*, 'living on the land, building on the land, and fencing the land – the more things done on the land, the more convincing the case for adverse possession'.[56] In particular, it is accepted that enclosure of the land by a wall[57] or fencing[58] will usually be sufficient evidence of factual possession by the adverse possessor, so long as there is also a sufficient *animus possidendi*; and, in a Bahamian case, *Dean v Rolle*,[59] it was held that acts of clearing a neighbouring lot and storing a fishing boat, motor vehicles and building materials on the lot, and using fill and soil from the land, were sufficient acts of factual possession, in the light of the fact that the paper owner 'had not bothered to visit her lot for more than 26 years'.

On the other hand, it has been held that the payment of rates and taxes pertaining to the disputed land does not, by itself, advance a claim founded on adverse possession for, as Moosai J pointed out in a Trinidadian case, *Nottingham v Deposit Insurance Corporation*,[60] such payments are

> not payable necessarily by an owner or occupier. Anyone who chooses to pay, officiously or otherwise, may do so. The issuance of receipts, whether by government or a local authority, in such circumstances accordingly confer no rights on the person making the payment.

Animus possidendi

In addition to factual possession, there must exist the necessary *animus possidendi* on the part of the claimant. This was defined by Slade J, in *Powell v McFarlane*,[61] as

> the intention, in one's own name and on one's own behalf, to exclude the world at large, including the owner with the paper title in so far as is reasonably practicable and so far as the processes of the law will allow.

---

54 [2003] 1 AC 419, at 436.
55 (1977) 38 P&CR 452, at 470–471.
56 *Boodhai v Rambarran* (2009) High Court, Trinidad and Tobago, No 804 of 2007.
57 See *Flowers v Forbes* [1971–76] 1 LRB 340, Supreme Court, The Bahamas.
58 *Buckinghamshire County Council v Moran* [1989] 2 All ER 225, at 236. See *Kadir v Katwaroo* (2009) High Court, Trinidad and Tobago, No 1279 of 2007; *Joseph v Rattan* (2009) High Court, Trinidad and Tobago, No 779 of 2004. In *Blake v Hunt* ((2011) Supreme Court, Jamaica, No 1773 of 2008, Brooks J opined that 'few things more emphatically demonstrate an intention to possess land and to dispossess others of that land, than the erection of a fence around that land'.
59 (2010) Supreme Court, The Bahamas, No 168 of 2009.
60 (2010) High Court, Trinidad and Tobago, No 58 of 2006, following *Richardson v Lawrence* (1966) 10 WIR 234 (Court of Appeal, Trinidad and Tobago).
61 (1977) 38 P & CR 452, at 471, 472.

More recently, in *Buckinghamshire CC v Moran*,[62] it was held that it is sufficient that the squatter should have shown an intention to exclude the paper owner *for the time being*, so that the requirement of *animus possidendi* was satisfied where there was an intention to continue in possession of the land only until such time as the paper owner decided to build a proposed highway across it. Accordingly, the adverse possessor was able to acquire a title on expiry of the limitation period, notwithstanding the 'temporary' nature of the possession. Further, in a recent Trinidadian case,[63] Rajkumar J stated that *Ocean Estates Ltd v Pinder*[64] is authority for the proposition that:

> a squatter may enter into occupation prepared to pay rent or to move out if challenged, and after sufficient time has elapsed may, notwithstanding their initial intent to recognize a superior title, occupy adversely to the rights of the documentary title holder, sufficient to acquire title by adverse possession.

On the other hand, in *Pollard v Dick*,[65] in which it was clear that the paper owner had no intention to part with possession, Davis CJ, in the OECS Court of Appeal, St Vincent and the Grenadines, held that the adverse claimant had failed to show the necessary *animus possidendi*, as he had entered the land, not with an intent to dispossess the owner, but in the expectation of purchasing it from someone who purported to be the true owner and, according to the learned judge, such evidence was fatal to the claim based on adverse possession. Similarly, the claim in *Farrington v Bush*[66] failed on the ground that the claimant had taken possession in the erroneous belief that the land had been conveyed to him, rather than with the intention to exclude the owner. Graham-Perkins JA, in the Jamaican Court of Appeal in *Farrington* said:[67]

> It is a mistake to think that mere entry upon and user of the land of another can, without more, be equated with an assumption of possession. It must be possession of such a nature as to amount to an ouster of the original owner of the land . . . To support a finding of adverse possession, there must be positive and affirmative evidence of acts of possession, unequivocal by their very nature and which are demonstrably consistent with an attempt, and an intention, to exclude the possession of the true owner . . . In this context, an equivocal act means an act of such a nature as to provide an equal balance between an intention to exclude a true owner from possession and an intention merely to derive some enjoyment or benefit from the land wholly consistent with such use as the true owner might wish to make of it.

The approach taken by the Jamaican Court of Appeal in *Farrington* has been followed in a number of Caribbean cases. In *Dolly v Sookoo*,[68] for instance, Jamadar J took the view that 'possessory title under the Real Property Limitation Act [of Trinidad and Tobago] is only established when both the fact of possession and the intention to possess by dispossessing the *legal owner*[69] are proven'. Citing the *dicta* of Graham-Perkins JA in *Farrington*, Jamadar J held that the requisite *animus*

62 [1989] 2 All ER 225.
63 *Moses v Charles* (2011) High Court, Trinidad and Tobago, No 4869 of 2008.
64 [1969] 2 AC 19. The principle was also confirmed by Mendonca JA in *Smith v Benjamin* (2009) Court of Appeal, Trinidad and Tobago, Civ App No 67 of 2007.
65 (1977) 2 OECSLR 239. See also *Gordon v Andrews* (2000) High Court, St Vincent and the Grenadines, No 137 of 1994, *per* Mitchell J; *James v Fortune* (2008) High Court, Antigua and Barbuda, No 0590 of 2002, *per* Blenman J.
66 (1974) 12 JLR 1492.
67 *Ibid*, at 1493.
68 (2006) High Court, Trinidad and Tobago, No 1587 of 1997.
69 Italics supplied.

possidendi had not been established, since 'all of the alleged acts of occupation relied on by the defendant would have been done in the belief that his father and he were the owners of the lands, and not with the intention of excluding or dispossessing the [claimant] or anyone else. The defendant's acts of occupation were therefore not adverse to the [claimant]'. A similar approach was taken by Boodoosingh J (Ag) in *Maraval Heights Development Co Ltd v Global Shelters Ltd*,[70] where the defendant had occupied and developed the disputed land under the mistaken belief that he was the owner, and indeed stated in oral evidence that he had 'no intention to squat on or steal' the claimant's land. This, according to the learned judge, was the clearest obstacle to the defendant acquiring a title by adverse possession.

There is, however, another line of cases[71] in which, following *dicta* of Lord Browne-Wilkinson in *Pye*,[72] it has been held that it is not necessary for the adverse possessor to have had an intention to dispossess or exclude the paper owner: on this view, the only intention which has to be demonstrated is an intention to occupy and use the land as one's own: there is no need for an '*animus dispossessendi*' or a conscious intention to dispossess the true owner. The House of Lords in *Pye* rejected 'the old notions of adverse possession' involving 'acts of disseisin, ouster and inconsistent use by the squatter'.[73] On this approach, cases such as *Farrington, Dolly*, and *Maraval Heights* would be decided differently,[74] as it would be immaterial whether the squatter occupied the land in the mistaken belief that he had a good title to it, or whether he knew that he was a trespasser. The correctness of this approach has since been confirmed by the Privy Council in a Bahamian case, *Armbrister v Lightbourn*,[75] where it was held that the fact that the appellants had acted openly as owners, in the erroneous belief that they had a good title to the land was sufficient factual possession on which to found their claim to a possessory title.[76] Further, it has been said that a cogent argument against the *Farrington* approach is that it would be unjust for a *mala fide* user of land (that is, one who knew he was a trespasser) to be in a better position regarding an adverse possession claim than a *bona fide* user (that is, one who believed he had a good title);[77] indeed, it has also been pointed out that, in a suitable case, the fact that an occupier of land believed he was the true owner might very well be suitable evidence of his intention to possess the land. It thus appears that the balance

70 (2009) High Court, Trinidad and Tobago, No 1750 of 1998.
71 See, eg, *Re Rattan* (2010) High Court, Trinidad and Tobago, No 960 of 2004, *per* Ventour J; *Warner v Thomas* (2009) High Court, Trinidad and Tobago, No 1437 of 2007, *per* Delzin J; *Harriram v Gopaul* (2011) High Court, Trinidad and Tobago, No S 1785 of 2002, *per* Harris J; *Maharaj v Persad* (2009) High Court, Trinidad and Tobago, No S 944 of 2000, *per* Rajnauth-Lee J; *Anoop v Dhani* (2011) High Court, Trinidad and Tobago, No 964 of 2007, *per* Tiwary-Reddy J.
72 [2003] 1 AC 419, at 434–438.
73 See *Re Rattan*, above, at para 5.
74 In *Recreational Holdings Ltd v Lazarus* [2014] JMCA Civ 34, para 37, Morrison JA doubted that the reasoning in *Farrington v Bush* represented the modern law of adverse possession. See also *Anderson v Thompson* [2015] JMCA Civ 51, paras 49, 50, *per* Phillips JA.
75 [2012] UKPC 40. See also *Bannerman Town, Millars and John Millars Eleuthera Association v Eleuthera Properties Ltd* [2018] UKPC 27, para 51, *per* Lord Briggs; followed in *Goberdhan-Watts v Boodoo* (2020) Court of Appeal, Trinidad and Tobago, Civ App No PO 14 of 2016, *per* Mendonca JA.
76 Similarly, it has been held that the fact that a person erroneously believes he/she has the owner's consent to be in possession, does not defeat his *animus possidendi*: *Wretham v Ross* [2005] EWHC 1259; *Dipnarine v Dipnarine* (2017) Court of Appeal, Trinidad and Tobago, Civ App No 43 of 2010.
77 See *Warner v Thomas*, above, fn 71, at para 27.

of current authority is in favour of the 'more relaxed' rule[78] relating to the *animus possidendi* requirement as explained in *Pye* and other cases, and that 'the question is simply whether the . . . squatter has dispossessed the paper owner by going into ordinary possession of the land for the requisite period without the consent of the owner'.[79]

User of part of the land

The question of whether acts of usage exercised over part only of the disputed land can constitute adverse possession of the whole has been in issue in the Commonwealth Caribbean. In the Guyanese case of *West Bank Estates Ltd v Arthur*,[80] the respondents sought to establish a prescriptive title to land under s 3 of the Title to Land (Prescription and Limitation) Act, Cap 184 (Laws of British Guiana),[81] which provided that:

> Title to land . . . may be acquired by sole and undisturbed possession, user or enjoyment for 30 years, if such possession, user or enjoyment is established to the satisfaction of the court and was not taken or enjoyed by fraud or by some consent or agreement expressly made or given for that purpose.

In this case, the respondents, who were peasant farmers, claimed a prescriptive title to an area of land by virtue of various acts, such as cutting timber, fishing and growing rice on the land, throughout the prescription period. The trial judge, Bollers J, held that these acts were insufficient to prove the sole possession that was required, and they were not inconsistent with the enjoyment of the land by the person entitled. The Federal Supreme Court, on the other hand, took the view that the respondents had proved that they had made what was, for persons of their means and class, normal use of the land, and their actions were sufficient to establish adverse possession. The Privy Council preferred the view of Bollers J. In the words of Lord Wilberforce:[82]

> Admitting the utility of the respondents' operations, and that they did what was normal for small peasant farmers, this still does not establish a sufficient degree of sole possession and user to satisfy the Ordinance, to carry the matter beyond a user which remains consistent with the possession of the true owner. What is a sufficient degree of sole possession and user must be measured according to an objective standard, related no doubt to the nature and situation of the land involved but not subject to variation according to the resources or status of the claimants.

The second issue that arose in this case was whether proof of the respondents' user of part of the land was evidence of their possession of the whole. Lord Wilberforce stated that the true question was as to the extent of the land the respondents did in fact use and occupy, and, in determining whether acts of use of part could be evidence of possession of the whole, a distinction had to be drawn between, on the one hand, an area of land surrounded by hedges, and, on the other, one that lacked defined boundaries. In the former, acts done in one part would be evidence of the

78 See *Harriram v Gopaul*, above, fn 71, at para 23.
79 *JA Pye (Oxford) Ltd v Graham* [2003] 1 AC 419, at 434, *per* Lord Browne-Wilkinson.
80 [1967] AC 665.
81 Now, Laws of Guyana, Cap 60:02, s 3.
82 *West Bank Estates Ltd v Arthur* [1967] AC 665, at 678.

possession of the whole,[83] but in the latter, no such inference could be drawn. In the present case, the boundaries of the land were undefined, and Bollers J was correct in finding that there was insufficient evidence of possession of the whole by the respondents.

In the Bahamian case of *Higgs v Nassauvian Ltd*,[84] there was evidence that, at various dates during the 20-year period laid down by the Real Property Limitation Acts 1833 and 1874,[85] the claimants' predecessors and their tenants had farmed parts of the disputed land, producing vegetables and other small crops, the practice of the farmers being to cultivate a small area, to reap the harvest, and then to move on to another area, leaving the first to become overgrown. The land was, for the most part, arable, although some of it consisted of pine barren. It was not fenced or otherwise enclosed, but the boundaries were known and were not disputed.

The Privy Council upheld the findings of fact by the trial judge, supported by the Court of Appeal of The Bahamas, that there was insufficient evidence of possession by the adverse claimants; however, Sir Harry Gibbs, delivering the judgment of the Board, emphasised that, unlike in *West Bank Estates Ltd v Arthur*, in which the boundaries of the land were disputed and undefined, in the present case, although the land was unfenced, its boundaries were known and undisputed and, accordingly, possession of the whole by the claimants might have been established by acts done on part of it. He continued:[86]

> The members of the Court of Appeal were wrong in viewing [*West Bank Estates*] as laying down a general principle that to establish possession of an area of land, a claimant must show that he has made physical use of the whole of it, or as deciding that a farmer can never establish possession of an area of land over parts of which he works in rotation. It is clearly settled that acts of possession done on parts of a tract of land to which a possessory title is sought may be evidence of possession of the whole.
>
> This rule is not applicable to a question of undefined and disputed boundary, but this does not mean that acts done on part of the land are only relevant to prove possession of the whole if the land is enclosed by a wall or other physical barrier. The property claimed by possession may be sufficiently defined in other ways, for example, where the claim is to trees in a belt of woodland,[87] to the bed or foreshores of a river,[88] or to the right to fish in a river.[89]

RESUMPTION OF POSSESSION BY PAPER OWNER

In order to prevent an adverse possessor from acquiring an indefeasible title under the Limitation Acts, the paper owner must show that, before expiry of the limitation

83 *Clark v Elphinstone* (1880) 6 App Cas 164.
84 [1975] 1 All ER 95.
85 See now s 16(3) of the Limitation Act 1995, which has reduced the limitation period to 12 years.
86 [1975] 1 All ER 95, at 101, followed in *Re Hollingsworth* (1971–76) 1 LRB 498, Supreme Court, The Bahamas. See also *Dipnarine v Dipnarine* (2009) High Court, Trinidad and Tobago, No 1599 of 2003 (grazing cattle, constructing an outhouse and depositing earth-fill on the disputed land, held insufficient acts of possession).
87 *Stanley v White* (1811) 104 ER 630.
88 *Jones v Williams* [1835–42] All ER Rep 423.
89 *Lord Advocate v Lord Lovat* (1880) 5 App Cas 273, at 289.

period, he performed acts amounting to dispossession of the squatter and resumption of possession by him. Mere entry upon the land is not sufficient.[90]

In *Markfield Investments Ltd v Evans*[91] Simon Brown LJ listed the circumstances in which adverse possession may cease:

(i) where the squatter vacates the premises;
(ii) where the squatter gives a written acknowledgment of the true owner's title;[92]
(iii) where the true owner brings proceedings for possession that result in final judgment in his favour;
(iv) where the true owner grants a tenancy or licence to the squatter; or
(v) where the true owner physically re-takes possession of the land.

90 See *Bent v Williams* (1976) 14 JLR 122, Court of Appeal, Jamaica (entries by the paper owner to pick mangoes and in unsuccessful attempts to collect rent were held to be insufficient to prevent title from being acquired by adverse possession); *Barnes v Campbell* [2019] JMSC Civ 178 (entries into the property to ask for rent). On the other hand, it has been emphasised by the Privy Council that 'the slightest acts by the person having title to the land or by his predecessors-in-title, indicating his intention to take possession, are sufficient to enable him to bring an action for trespass against a defendant entering upon the land without any title, unless there can be shown a subsequent intention on the part of the person having the title to abandon the constructive possession so acquired': *Ocean Estates Ltd v Pinder* [1969] 2 AC 19, at 25, *per* Lord Diplock, PC appeal from the Court of Appeal of The Bahamas.

91 [2001] 1 WLR 1321, at 1324; *Roach v Jack* (2013) Court of Appeal, Trinidad and Tobago, Civ App No 132 of 2009, *per* Bereaux JA; *Singh v Sinaswee-Manwaring* (2019) High Court, Trinidad and Tobago, No CV2017–01944, *per* Margaret Mohammed J.

92 *Browne v Perry* (1991) 40 WIR 165. Where there is such an acknowledgment, the limitation period begins to run from the date of the signed document: see Limitation of Actions Act, s 16 (Jamaica); *Pottinger v Raffone* (2007) Privy Council Appeal No 64 of 2005 ('the relevant twelve year period of possession for acquiring title runs from the date of any document signed by the person in possession acknowledging the title of the person entitled to the land' – *per* Lord Rodger).

CHAPTER 12

SALE OF LAND

In Caribbean jurisdictions, as in England, the transfer of land by sale is essentially a two-stage process: (i) a binding *contract of sale* is drawn up and signed by both vendor and purchaser; (ii) 'completion' takes place by means of a *conveyance* of the legal title by the vendor to the purchaser (in the case of unregistered land), or a *transfer* of the title by the appropriate form (in the case of registered land). In unregistered land, the conveyance of the legal estate has the effect of immediately vesting the legal title in the purchaser; in registered land, the transfer of title is not final and complete until it is recorded in the Land Register.[1]

DEALINGS BEFORE THE CONTRACT IS SIGNED

During the period before the contract of sale is signed, the parties will negotiate (usually through their attorneys)[2] the terms of the agreement, such as the purchase price, and the precise extent of the property to be sold. The boundaries of the property should be established by a qualified surveyor and, if the property comprises a substantial building, the prospective purchaser may be well advised to employ a civil engineer to carry out an inspection. If the purchaser requires mortgage financing to make the purchase, he/she will need to secure a mortgage offer from a bank or other institutional lender. Also, the purchaser's attorney will need to peruse the title deeds and inspect the land itself in order to be satisfied that there are no patent problems or defects associated with the property, such as lack of access or drainage rights. However, more intensive and detailed investigation of the title normally occurs *after* the signing of the contract, since the parties will normally desire to reach a concluded contract as early as possible, subject to the purchaser's right to rescind in the event that the vendor cannot show a 'good unencumbered title'.

Any correspondence between the parties' attorneys in the course of negotiating the terms of the contract will normally be headed with the words 'Subject to Contract'. These words may be described as a 'magic formula' to postpone contractual liability until a formal document has been drafted by the parties' attorneys and signed by both parties.[3] Similarly, in a Trinidadian case, *Seechan v First Citizens*

1 See, eg, s 63 of the Registration of Titles Act (Jamaica); s 44 of the Real Property Ordinance, Ch 56:02 (Trinidad and Tobago); *Jaikaran v Binda* (1991) 2 TTLR 105, at 120, *per* Gopeesingh J; *Molyneau v Alphan* (1955) 15 Trin LR 71.

2 It is customary for vendor and purchaser to have their own attorneys. It is possible for one attorney to be instructed by both parties (which may save some expense), but this is highly inadvisable because of the obvious conflict of interest, and indeed the Jamaican Court of Appeal has emphasised that it is 'practically impossible for [an attorney] to do his duty to each client properly when he tries to act for both vendor and purchaser', and 'it may be that [an attorney] who tries to act for both parties puts himself in such a position that he must be liable to one or the other, whatever he does': *Palmer v Golding* (2000) Court of Appeal, Jamaica, Civ App No 46 of 1998 (unreported), *per* Downer JA, quoting Dankwerts J in *Goody v Baring* [1956] 2 All ER 11, at 12, and Scrutton LJ in *Moody v Cox* [1917] 2 Ch 71, at 91. A similar view was expressed by Douglas CJ in the Barbados High Court in *Straker v Maraj* (1984) 39 WIR 22, at 25, and by Richards J in *Moore v Callender* (2013) High Court, Barbados, No 1774 of 2005.

3 *Sherbrooke v Dipple* (1980) 41 P & CR 173, CA.

DOI: 10.4324/9781003186946-12

Bank,[4] in which a bank, in the exercise of its power of sale as mortgagee, offered to sell the mortgaged property to the plaintiff, such offer being 'conditional until a purchase agreement is signed', Jamadar J held that, in the absence of such written, signed agreement, the bank was not bound to sell.

STATUTORY FORMALITIES – WRITTEN NOTE OR MEMORANDUM

The effect of sections 2 and 4 of the Statute of Frauds 1677 (in force in most Caribbean jurisdictions)[5] and their modern equivalents (such as section 47 of the Property Act, Cap 236 (Barbados), section 4(1) of the Conveyancing and Law of Property Act, Ch 56:01 (Trinidad and Tobago),[6] and section 55(1) of the Property Act, Cap 190 (Belize)), is that a contract for the sale of land must be either *in writing or evidenced by a sufficient written note or memorandum* of the oral agreement, and signed by the party to be charged or his agent. It is the normal practice for the contract of sale itself to be in writing but, under the statutes, as an alternative, an oral contract will be valid and binding provided that it is evidenced by a written memorandum comprising all of the terms of the agreement.

CONTENTS OF THE MEMORANDUM

The written memorandum must contain the following:[7]

Description of the parties

The memorandum must state the names of the vendor and the purchaser, or at least describe them sufficiently to allow them to be identified. It is not sufficient, however, to describe the purchaser or vendor as 'our clients',[8] and parol evidence is not admissible to establish the identity of a party not named or sufficiently identified in the memorandum.[9]

Description of the property

The property to be purchased must be sufficiently identified. In the case of a dwelling house, the postal address would normally be sufficient. It has been held that, where the vendor owns only one house, it would be sufficient to describe it as 'my

---

4 (2001) High Court, Trinidad and Tobago, No CV 696 of 1998; cf *Singer Sewing Machine Co v Montego Bay Cooperative Credit Union Ltd* (1997) 34 JLR 251, Court of Appeal, Jamaica, in which it was held that there was a concluded agreement to lease, notwithstanding that correspondence between the parties had stated that 'details are to be worked out by lawyers in binding contract'.

5–6 In Jamaica, for example, 'it is settled law that, by virtue of s 41 of the Interpretation Act, the English Statute of Frauds, 1677 applies to this jurisdiction': *per* Smith JA in *Brady & Chen Ltd v Devon House Development Ltd*
(2010) Court of Appeal, Jamaica, Civ App No 62 of 2009. In Trinidad and Tobago, section 4 of the Conveyancing and Law of Property Act, Ch 56:01 applies: see *Bahadursingh v Dansteel Ltd* (2020) High Court, Trinidad and Tobago, No CV 2017–01216.

7 See, eg, *Potgieter v Mayacan Development Co Ltd* (2013) Supreme Court, Belize, No 68 of 2013.

8 *Strada Investments Ltd v Temora Investments Ltd* [1996] CILR 246, Grand Court, Cayman Islands.

9 *Lovesy v Palmer* [1916] 2 Ch 223.

house',[10] but where he/she owns more than one, those words would not satisfy the requirements of the memorandum.

In a Jamaican case, *Brown v Simpson*,[11] in which there was a dispute as to the precise boundaries of the land being sold, Ellis J emphasised that

> every valid agreement for the sale of land must contain a description of the subject matter, but it is not necessary that it should be so described as to admit of no doubt what it is, for the identity of the actual land and the land described may be shown by extrinsic evidence.

Accordingly, in this case, in which the purchaser contended that the northern boundary of the land agreed to be sold was in a straight line, but the vendor maintained that it was not, extrinsic evidence in the form of a subdivision plan was admitted in order to show the true facts, viz, that the boundary was indeed straight.

Price

The memorandum must either state the agreed price or identify the means by which it can be fixed.

Other terms

The memorandum must also include any other terms agreed between the parties, such as the completion date (if it has been fixed), a term relating to stages of payment of the purchase money,[12] and any term regarding payment of a deposit by the purchaser.[13] All relevant terms should be included for the memorandum to be effective; however, terms that will be implied into the contract (such as the implied term that an unencumbered freehold interest is being sold) need not be included in the memorandum.[14]

Signature by the party to be charged

The memorandum must be signed by 'the party to be charged' – that is, the party against whom the agreement is being enforced, or by his agent. An auctioneer has implied authority from both vendor and purchaser to sign a memorandum, but signature on behalf of the purchaser must be contemporaneous with the sale.[15]

It has been held by the Privy Council that where the vendor's attorney or solicitor receives a deposit from the purchaser as stakeholder, he/she is not precluded from subsequently signing a memorandum of the agreement on behalf of the vendor.[16]

10 *Cowley v Watts* (1853) 22 LJ Ch 591.
11 (1982) 19 JLR 389, at 392.
12 *Tweddle v Henderson* [1975] 2 All ER 1096; *Sawyer v Sawyer* (2004) Supreme Court, The Bahamas, No 1203 of 2001.
13 In *McLean v Espeut* (1991) 28 JLR 92, Supreme Court, Jamaica, the memorandum was silent on the question of payment of a deposit and was therefore held to be ineffective.
14 *Timmins v Moreland Street Property Co Ltd* [1957] 3 All ER 265, CA, at 277, *per* Romer LJ.
15 *Bell v Balls* [1897] 1 Ch 663.
16 *Elias v George Sahely and Co (Barbados) Ltd* [1982] 3 WLR 956, followed in *Taylor v Cox and Co Ltd* (2004) Supreme Court, The Bahamas, No 1396 of 2002, *per* Davis J.

JOINDER OF DOCUMENTS

The memorandum need not be in any special form. Any written evidence, such as a letter (or series of letters)[17] or a purchase receipt, will suffice, provided that it is signed by the defendant or his agent. The requisite evidence need not be contained in one document, but can be collected from several, and the various documents can be joined together to make one complete memorandum, provided that the document that is signed by the defendant expressly or impliedly refers to the other document(s) or to some other transaction.[18] If there is such reference, parol evidence is admissible to identify the other document(s) referred to or to explain the other transaction and identify any document relating to it. Further, it was pointed out by Murphy J, in a Cayman case, *Strada Investments Ltd v Temora Investments Ltd*,[19] that the requirement that the document signed by the defendant must contain some reference to some other document or transaction 'effectively means that the incorporated document must pre-date or be contemporaneous with' the signed document.

The principles relating to joinder of documents were applied by the Privy Council in the leading case of *Elias v George Sahely and Co (Barbados) Ltd*.[20] Here, the plaintiff had for several years been a tenant of the defendant, occupying commercial premises in Bridgetown in which he operated a retail store. The defendant agreed orally to sell the freehold to the plaintiff, and on the same day the plaintiff's attorney wrote a letter to the defendant's attorney confirming the oral agreement and setting out its terms. He also enclosed a cheque for the deposit, 'payable to you as stakeholder pending completion of the contract of sale'.

As requested, the defendant's attorney signed and sent back a receipt, which stated that the money had been received as deposit on the property 'agreed to be sold' by the defendant to the plaintiff. Lord Scarman, delivering the judgment of the Privy Council, held that the trial judge had rightly admitted in evidence: (a) the letter from the plaintiff's attorney; (b) the receipt; and (c) parol evidence from the plaintiff's attorney that the receipt had been given in response to the letter. The letter contained all of the terms of the concluded oral contract; it could be read together with the receipt; and since the two documents together constituted a sufficient signed memorandum, the contract was enforceable.

ABSENCE OF SUFFICIENT MEMORANDUM

If there is no sufficient memorandum, the contract is *unenforceable*, but not void. This means that:

(a) no action can be brought for damages at common law for breach of the agreement;

(b) no action can be brought for specific performance of the agreement in equity, unless there is a sufficient act of part performance; and

17 *Bahadursingh v Dansteel Ltd* (2020) High Court, Trinidad and Tobago, No CV 2017–01216.
18 *Timmins v Moreland Street Property Co Ltd* [1957] 3 All ER 265, CA.
19 [1996] CILR 246, at 261.
20 [1982] 3 WLR 956.

(c) rights that do not require action in court to enforce them remain valid – thus, where the purchaser unjustifiably refuses to complete, the vendor may retain any deposit paid.

PART PERFORMANCE

In equity, an oral contract for the sale of land may be specifically enforced despite the absence of a written memorandum, where the plaintiff (that is, the party seeking to enforce the agreement) has done *a sufficient act of part performance of the contract.* The principle underlying the doctrine of part performance is that

> if one party to an agreement stands by and lets the other party incur expense or prejudice his position on the faith of the agreement being valid, he will not then be allowed to turn round and assert that the agreement is unenforceable. Using fraud in its older and less precise sense, that would be fraudulent on his part, and it has become proverbial that courts of equity will not permit the statute to be made an instrument of fraud.[21]

In order to amount to a sufficient part performance, the acts of the plaintiff:

> must be such that they point unmistakably and can only point to the existence of some contract such as the oral contract alleged. But of course the acts of part performance need not show the precise terms of the oral contract . . . The terms of the oral contract must be proved by acceptable evidence, but effect to them can only be given if and when acts of part performance establish that there must have been some such contract. Until then, the door is, so to speak, closed against them.[22]

Put in another way, to amount to part performance, the acts must be capable of explanation only by the existence of a contract, and must be consistent with the particular contract which is alleged to exist.

The most common acts of part performance in the context of sale of land are: (a) the vendor giving up possession; or (b) the purchaser taking possession.[23] Carrying out repairs to the property may also be a sufficient act of part performance.[24] On the other hand, the payment of money, for example payment of the deposit by the purchaser,[25] will not usually amount to part performance,[26] although in *Steadman*

21 *Steadman v Steadman* [1976] AC 536, at 540, *per* Lord Reid.
22 *Ibid*, at 546, *per* Lord Morris. See also *Daulia Ltd v Four Millbank Nominees Ltd* [1978] 2 All ER 557; *McCook v Hammond* (1988) 25 JLR 296, Court of Appeal, Jamaica; *Sagar v Mungroo* (2011) High Court, Trinidad and Tobago, No 2831 of 2007.
23 *Phillips v Bisnott* (1965) 8 WIR 299, Court of Appeal, Jamaica. Similarly, where there is entry into possession coupled with a receipt for payment: *Francis v Mines* (2001) Court of Appeal, Jamaica, Civ App No 94 of 1998, *per* Langrin JA. In *Fitz-Gordon v Spence* (1996) 33 JLR 112, Supreme Court, Jamaica, however, Harris J came to the conclusion that the plaintiff's possession of the property was in the capacity of a tenant and not in pursuance of an option to purchase the property.
24 *Eldemire v Honiball* (1991) 28 JLR 577, PC; *Mattar v Salmon* [2020] JMSC Civ 8, paras 67, 68, *per* D Fraser J. *Northover (WG) and Associates Ltd v Astoria Development (Jamaica) Ltd* [2020] JMSC Civ 184, para 44, *per* Lindo J.
25 But see *Medford v Cumberbatch* (1987) 22 Barb LR 253, High Court, Barbados, in which Husbands J held that payment of a deposit was sufficient part performance of an oral contract of sale.
26 Because the party who merely pays money has not 'altered his position to a point where the court cannot undo what has been done', since the court can order repayment of the money: *Maddison v Alderson* (1883) 8 App Cas 476, *per* Lord Selborne LC. See also *Sawyer v Sawyer* (2004) Supreme Court, The Bahamas, No 1203 of 2001, *per* Lyons J.

v Steadman[27] it was held that the payment of arrears of maintenance did constitute part performance of an agreement between husband and wife with respect to maintenance and the transfer of the matrimonial home. In this case, the part of the agreement relating to transfer of the matrimonial home was rendered enforceable.

A Barbadian case in which there were sufficient acts of part performance is *Jackman v Jones*.[28] Here, by an oral agreement, V agreed to sell his house to P for $18,200 and on the same day P paid that amount to V. V put P into possession of the property. The question to be decided was whether the agreement was unenforceable on the ground of absence of written evidence thereof, as required by s 47 of the Property Act, Cap 236, or whether it could be enforced against V by virtue of part performance by P. It was held that the payment of the purchase price coupled with entry into possession of the property amounted to sufficient part performance of the oral agreement and it would accordingly be specifically enforced. On the other hand, in a Jamaican case, *McLean v Espeut*,[29] it was held that the payment of electricity bills and the cutting of grass by P on the property allegedly agreed to be sold to P (which was adjacent to property already owned by P) were equivocal acts not referable to an agreement to sell, as P's motive for doing so was 'probably for security (considering the proximity to his [existing] residence), or . . . to bolster his claim'.

FORMAL CONTRACT OF SALE

The normal, modern practice in sales of land is for the vendor's attorney to draft a formal contract, which will be perused by the purchaser's attorney before he/she advises his client to sign. (See Appendix 1 for a specimen formal contract.)

'OPEN' CONTRACTS FOR THE SALE OF LAND

There are few rules concerning the form and content of a binding contract for the sale of land, so long as there is agreement as to the essential terms concerning parties, property and price. Many contracts of sale are 'closed' contracts, which incorporate certain standardised conditions relevant to land transactions; however, a contract of sale may be 'open', which means that it 'may provide expressly for nothing beyond the identity of the parties, the definition of the subject matter and the price to be paid. The rights and duties of vendor and purchaser under an open contract are then determined with reference to the general law of property'.[30] In a Trinidadian case, *Chaital v Ramlal*,[31] Sir Martin Nourse, delivering the judgment of the Privy Council, explained that the position in English law, with regard to an open contract of unregistered land that did not specify a date for completion or for the performance of any other obligation, was that the contract must be construed as containing implied terms that: (a) the vendor had a good and marketable title to the land; (b) the vendor would deliver an abstract of title to the purchaser within a

27 [1976] AC 536.
28 (1987) 22 Barb LR 54.
29 (1991) 28 JLR 92.
30 Gray, *Elements of Land Law*, 2nd edn, 1993, London: Butterworths, p 253.
31 (2003) 62 WIR 449.

reasonable time from the date of the contract; and (c) both vendor and purchaser would proceed to completion within a reasonable time from the contract date. However, it would not be until the vendor had delivered an abstract of title that the purchaser would come under an obligation to complete. As to whether these principles were applicable to the conveyancing process in Trinidad and Tobago, Ibrahim JA, in the Court of Appeal, had explained that since there was a system of registration of deeds in Trinidad, a vendor seldom, if ever, had in his possession an abstract of title as a vendor in England would.[32] At most, he might be expected to have copies of his title documents. What, therefore, happened in practice was that the vendor supplied the purchaser with information that evidenced the vendor's acquisition of the land, and the purchaser's attorney would use that information as a starting point to search the title. Thus, while the onus remained on the vendor to produce a proper title, in reality it was the purchaser's attorney who confirmed whether the vendor's title was good or not. In the light of these observations, Sir Martin Nourse concluded that the practice in Trinidad and Tobago, as described by Ibrahim JA, did impose an obligation on the vendor to supply the purchaser with the appropriate information as to title (such as with a copy of the conveyance vesting the title in the vendor) and, in the absence of such information, the purchaser was under no obligation to complete.

Requisitions on title

If there is any information regarding the title which the purchaser's attorney needs to know, he/she may serve 'requisitions on title' on the vendor's attorney in the form of questions regarding aspects of the title. Under an open contract, requisitions must be raised within a reasonable time of delivery of the abstract. It was held by the Court of Appeal in *Williams v Blaize*[33] that in Trinidad and Tobago there will be implied in the agreement for sale a term that the vendor is bound to properly answer all reasonable requisitions and inquiries within a reasonable time, so as to enable the purchaser to satisfy himself on the matters raised and to arrange his finances so as to be ready to complete on the date fixed.

PAYMENT OF DEPOSIT

In contracts for the sale of land there is invariably a term that, on the signing of the contract, a deposit (such as 10 per cent of the purchase price) shall be payable by the purchaser: 'The traditional deposit paid by a buyer when he enters into a contract is an earnest for the performance of the contract, and can be retained by the seller if the buyer defaults'.[34] A provision for payment of a deposit is not treated by equity as a penalty against which relief can be granted, so long as the amount is reasonable as earnest money.[35] Therefore,

32 *Ibid*, at 456, 457.
33 (2016) Court of Appeal, Trinidad and Tobago, Civ App No 226 of 2011, para 34, *per* Narine JA.
34 *Howe v Smith* (1884) 27 Ch D 89; *Faria v Osborne* (1968) 19 Trin Lt R (Pt IV) 38, at 42, Court of Appeal, Trinidad and Tobago; *Bidaisee v Sampath* (1995) 3 TTLR 668, at 675, PC Appeal from the Court of Appeal of Trinidad and Tobago, *per* Lord Nicholls.
35 *Workers Trust and Merchant Bank Ltd v Dojap* (1992) 42 WIR 253, PC Appeal from the Court of Appeal of Jamaica.

> if a contract provides for a deposit over and above the customary and accepted 10% and contains a forfeiture clause in the event that the purchaser is in breach of his contractual obligations, the vendor must show special circumstances which justify such a deposit.[36]

A defaulting purchaser will thus be liable to forfeit his deposit. On the other hand, where it is the vendor who is in default, the purchaser is entitled to the return of his deposit, and statutory provisions, such as s 7(2) of the Conveyancing and Law of Property Act (Trinidad and Tobago), Ch 56:01, reinforce the position by giving the court a wide discretion 'where the court refuses to grant specific performance of a contract, or in any action for the return of a deposit' to order repayment to the purchaser.

THE POSITION PENDING COMPLETION

- As soon as a specifically enforceable contract is signed by the parties, the *equitable interest* in the property passes from vendor to purchaser and, until completion, the vendor holds the legal estate on trust for the purchaser.[37]
- The vendor, subject to any contractual stipulation to the contrary, is entitled to retain possession of the property until all of the purchase money is paid.[38] He/she is also entitled to the rents and profits until the date of completion.[39] On the other hand, as trustee, he/she is under a duty to maintain the property until completion. Whether or not he/she has parted with possession, he/she is entitled to a lien on the property for the unpaid purchase money.[40]
- Notwithstanding the vendor's duty to maintain the property as trustee, the risk of *damage* to the property passes to the purchaser from the date of the contract.[41] The purchaser should therefore take out his/her own insurance on the property from that date.

VENDOR'S DUTIES REGARDING TITLE

In a sale of unregistered land, the vendor is under a two-fold duty as regards the *title* of the property he/she is selling. First, he/she must disclose to the purchaser, before entering into the contract, all latent defects in title,[42] except those of which the purchaser is aware.[43] 'Patent' defects need not be disclosed.[44]

36 *Pompey v Mahadeo* (2002) 61 WIR 293, Court of Appeal, Guyana, at 299, *per* Bernard C.
37 *Lysaght v Edwards* (1876) 2 Ch D 499, at 506, *per* Jessel MR; *Riverton City Ltd v Haddad* (1986) 40 WIR 236, at 258–60, Court of Appeal, Jamaica, *per* Campbell JA.
38 *Ibid.*
39 *Ibid.*
40 *Ibid.* See also *Ken's Sales and Marketing Ltd v Cash Plus Development Ltd* [2015] JMCA Civ 14, paras 15–26, where Brooks JA explained the scope and effect of a vendor's lien in the context of registered land, including the right of a vendor to lodge a caveat to protect his lien.
41 *Rayner v Preston* (1881) 18 Ch D 1.
42 *Reeve v Berridge* (1880) 20 QBD 523.
43 *McGrory v Alderdale Estate Co Ltd* [1918] AC 503, at 508.
44 *Bowles v Round* (1800) 5 Ves 508.

A defect is not patent merely because the purchaser has constructive notice of it.[45] It must be a defect that 'arises either to the eye, or by necessary implication from something which is visible to the eye',[46] such as a right of way evidenced by a worn track. On the other hand, restrictive covenants[47] and tenancies[48] would be considered to be latent. The rationale of the duty to disclose latent defects in title is that the state of the vendor's title is a matter exclusively within his knowledge and it is reasonable to expect that the purchaser will rely on the vendor to disclose such defects.[49] Where a vendor is in breach of this duty, the purchaser may treat the contract as repudiated and sue the vendor for damages.[50] Moreover, although non-disclosure *per se* does not amount to misrepresentation, a 'suppression of the truth may contain a suggestion of falsity'[51] rendering the vendor liable in damages for misrepresentation: as where a vendor, in answering pre-contract inquiries as to the existence of boundary disputes, failed to disclose a long-standing boundary dispute that he erroneously believed to have been settled.[52]

Second, the vendor in a contract for the sale of land in fee simple is obliged 'to make a good title to the whole legal and equitable interest in the freehold free from incumbrances',[53] and to prove that fact. The vendor's attorney should prepare an 'abstract of title', which may be described as

> a statement of the material parts of all deeds and other instruments by which the property has been disposed of during the period in question, and also of all facts, such as births, deaths and marriages, which affect the ownership of the land.[54]

In addition to the abstract, the vendor's attorney must produce either the actual documents in question or the best possible evidence of them.

However, as explained by Ibrahim JA in the Trinidad and Tobago Court of Appeal in *Chaitlal v Ramlal*,[55] this procedure is modified in those jurisdictions in which there is a system of registration of deeds, since under this system all documents of title are kept in the Registry and the vendor will normally have in his possession, at most, only copies of the deeds and so may not be in a position to prepare an abstract. This puts the onus on the purchaser's attorney to search the title in the Registry, and 'while the onus remains on the vendor to produce a proper title, in reality the purchaser's attorney is the one who confirms whether the title is good or not'.[56]

45 *Cabellero v Henty* (1874) 9 Ch App 447.
46 *Yandle and Sons v Sutton* [1922] 2 Ch 199, at 210.
47 *Re Stone and Savilla's Contract* [1963] 1 WLR 163.
48 *Pagebar Properties Ltd v Derby Investment Holdings Ltd* [1972] 1 WLR 1500.
49 *Yandle and Sons v Sutton* [1922] 2 Ch 199.
50 *Pips (Leisure Productions) Ltd v Walton* (1980) P & CR 415.
51 *McKeown v Boudard Peveril Gear Co Ltd* (1896) 74 LT 712, at 713, *per* Rigby LJ.
52 *Walker v Boyle* [1982] 1 WLR 495.
53 *Leominster Properties Ltd v Broadway Finance Ltd* (1981) 42 P & CR 372, at 380, *per* Slade J; *Blaize v Chankadyal* (2011) High Court, Trinidad and Tobago, No 2852 of 2006, *per* Tiwary-Reddy J.
54 Cheshire and Burn, *Modern Law of Real Property*, 15th edn, 1994, London: Butterworths, p 62.
55 (2003) 62 WIR 449, PC, at 456 (discussed in the judgment of Sir Martin Nourse); *Blaize v Chankadyal*, fn 53, above.
56 *Ibid.*

GOOD 'ROOT OF TITLE'

The vendor must be able to trace the title starting with a good 'root of title', for example at least 20 years old.[57] Documents that would serve as a good root of title for the purpose of a sale of a fee simple include a conveyance on sale, a legal mortgage, a voluntary conveyance, and an assent made by a personal representative. A squatter's title – that is, one obtained by adverse possession for the requisite statutory period (12 years in most jurisdictions) – must also be proved from a good root of title, by revealing the full title of the paper owner and then proving the adverse possession.[58]

Having shown a good root of title of the requisite age, the vendor must then trace the title through all of the later transactions leading up to the time when he/she him/herself acquired the property, unless of course the property has been in the vendor's ownership for more than the statutory period.

The effect of establishing a good root of title is that a purchaser may not make any inquiry or objection about matters previous to the date of the root of title, and if he/she discovers by chance that there is some previous defect, he/she is nevertheless bound to take the property as it stands.[59] On the other hand, if the purchaser shows that the title is wholly bad, and that the vendor has no title at all, or that 'the property is subject to some undisclosed but irremovable latent incumbrance of a substantial character',[60] then the court will refuse specific performance, as it will not compel the purchaser to 'buy an immediate lawsuit'. The vendor will thus be confined to an action for damages.

PURCHASER'S DUTY TO INVESTIGATE

Having received the abstract of title from the vendor's attorney, the purchaser's attorney will peruse it, as it is his duty to advise his client as to whether the vendor has shown a good title to the exact interest the vendor has agreed to sell. The purchaser's attorney

> must satisfy himself that the abstract exhibits an ordered sequence of all the documents and events which have disposed of or affected the interest during the last [20] years, and if he observes any omissions, he must requisition the vendor on the matter. He must compare the abstract with the original deeds which are produced by the vendor's [attorney], and put in requisitions on points of discrepancy.[61]

The purchaser's attorney must also search the Land Registry in order to discover incumbrances and other adverse interests affecting the title.

57 See, eg, Property Act, Cap 236, s 50(1) (Barbados); Conveyancing and Law of Property Act, Ch 56: 01 (Trinidad and Tobago) (amended in 2009). In many Caribbean jurisdictions, the period is 40 years. See, eg, Conveyancing and Law of Property Act, Cap 271, s 5 (St Kitts/Nevis); Vendor and Purchaser (Land) Act, Cap 462, s 2 (Antigua and Barbuda); Vendors and Purchase Act, s 2 (Jamaica).

58 *Re Atkinson and Horsell's Contract* [1912] 2 Ch 1. See, generally, Chapter 11, above.

59 *Re Scott and Alvarez's Contract* (No 1) [1895] 1 Ch 596.

60 Megarry and Wade, *Law of Real Property*, 6th edn, 2000, London: Sweet & Maxwell, para 12–078.

61 *Op cit*, Cheshire and Burn, fn 151, p 755.

As well as investigating the title, the purchaser must also *inspect the land itself*, making such inquiries as a reasonable purchaser would make, as he/she will be deemed to have constructive notice of any rights that are reasonably discoverable.[62] In particular, he/she should inquire as to the status of any person in *actual occupation* of the land,[63] as he/she will have constructive notice of all of the rights of such person. Thus, in the well-known case of *Hunt v Luck*,[64] it was held that 'a tenant's occupation is notice of all that tenant's rights',[65] and

> if a purchaser or a mortgagee has notice that the vendor or mortgagor is not in possession of the property, he must make inquiries of the person in possession – of the tenant who is in possession – and find out from him/her what his rights are, and, if he does not choose to do that, then whatever title he acquires as purchaser or mortgagee will be subject to the title or right of the tenant in possession.[66]

In *Cowie v Moses*,[67] the plaintiff, who was living overseas, purchased a two-acre parcel of land in Trinidad from his uncle's wife, without inspecting it. He claimed that when he did inspect the land, after the purchase, he found the defendant living in a house that she had built on a portion of the property. It transpired that the defendant had an equitable interest in the house and land. Hamel-Smith J held that the plaintiff must be deemed to have had constructive notice of the defendant's interest and was bound by it. He said:

> [The plaintiff] never inspected the land before he purchased it, nor did he attempt to make any enquiries . . . He acted in a reckless and imprudent manner when he set sail for Trinidad to complete the purchase of land, the boundaries of which he was unaware. The reasonable thing to have done was to determine precisely the extent and boundaries before completing the purchase. Had he done so, he would have discovered that [the defendant's] house fell on the two-acre parcel of land. Enquiries would then have revealed the basis of the occupation. Needless to say, in such latter circumstances he must be taken to have had constructive notice of [the defendant's] occupation of the land at the relevant time.

On the other hand, if, in response to the purchaser's inquiry, the person in possession gives a misleading or evasive answer, he will be estopped from asserting that the purchaser had constructive notice of his rights.[68]

REGISTERED LAND

Where the title to the land being sold is registered, the requirements up to and including the contract stage are the same as for unregistered land, but the investigation of

62 *Hervey v Smith* (1856) 52 ER 1123.
63 In some registered land systems, the rights of a person 'in actual occupation' of registered land are protected as 'overriding interests'. See, eg, Registered Land Act, Cap 194 (Belize), section 31 (1) (g) and *Tiabo v Flowers* (2018) Supreme Court, Belize, No 722 of 2017.
64 [1901] 1 Ch 45; affd [1902] 1 Ch 428, CA.
65 [1901] 1 Ch 45, at 51, *per* Farwell J.
66 *Hunt v Luck* [1902] 1 Ch 428, CA, 433, followed in *Lutchmansingh v Soogrim* (1994) High Court, Trinidad and Tobago, No 607 of 1973; *Chaitlal v Ramlal* (2003) 62 WIR 449, Privy Council Appeal from Trinidad and Tobago, 460; *Anoop v Dhani* (2011) High Court, Trinidad and Tobago, No 964 of 2007.
67 (1990) 1 TTLR 371.
68 *Midland Bank Ltd v Farmpride Hatcheries Ltd* (1980) 260 EG 493.

the title is radically different. In registered conveyancing, the vendor does not need to, and indeed is not entitled to, trace the history of the transactions dealing with the property, since the Register is conclusive evidence of the estate owner's title.[69] The Register, which is a public document, contains all of the information that would be found in title deeds under the unregistered system, such as the owner's name, a description of the property, and the estate held by the owner. Incumbrances, such as mortgages, easements and restrictive covenants, are usually noted on the Register.

69 See Chapter 13, below.

CHAPTER 13

REGISTRATION OF TITLE

The nature of the system of registration of titles in Jamaica was succinctly explained by Lord Millett, delivering the judgment of the Privy Council in *Half Moon Bay Ltd v Crown Eagle Hotels Ltd*:[1]

> The Registration of Titles Act, 1889 introduced a Torrens system of land registration to Jamaica. The general features of such a system are very familiar. Title to land and incumbrances affecting land are entered or notified in the Register Book, and everyone who acquires title *bona fide* and in good faith from a registered proprietor obtains an indefeasible title to the land, subject to the incumbrances entered or notified in the Register Book but free from incumbrances not so entered or notified, whether he has notice of them or not. The Register Book consists of the original certificates of title, each of which forms a separate folium of the book. The registered proprietor is given a duplicate of the certificate bearing the number of the volume and folium of the Register Book in which the original is entered (RTA, s 55).[2] An instrument purporting to affect land is taken to be registered when it is produced for registration, provided that it is subsequently entered both on the relevant folium and on the duplicate (RTA, s 58). There are further provisions to ensure that every entry on the original certificate is matched at all times by a like entry on the duplicate.

Although most other Caribbean jurisdictions also have Torrens-style registration systems, the vast majority of judicial decisions (including numerous Privy Council judgments) on Torrens registration are concerned with the interpretation and application of the Registration of Titles Act of Jamaica. The discussion in this chapter will accordingly focus on the Jamaican Registration of Titles Act, with reference to the equivalent provisions in the other jurisdictions, wherever relevant.[3]

THE REGISTRATION PROCESS

Bringing land under the Act

Sections 24 and 25 provide that land may be brought under the operation of the Registration of Titles Act by the Registrar registering the title of some person as the proprietor in the manner prescribed by the Act. Such title may be either absolute or qualified.

---

1 (2002) 60 WIR 330, at 336.

2 By s 65, two or more persons may be registered as joint tenants or tenants in common. In the case of the former, one certificate is issued; in the case of the latter, separate certificates representing the undivided shares may be issued. Cf *Re Dunbar* (1984) 21 JLR 41, at 43, *per* Bingham J.

3 It was emphasised by Sir Terence Etherton in the Privy Council in *Arthur v Attorney General, Turks & Caicos Islands* [2012] UKPC 30, paras 13–15, that 'the Torrens system has been implemented in different countries with varying degrees of flexibility', and 'it is necessary, when considering the effect of legislation implementing the Torrens system in any particular jurisdiction, to focus on the provisions of the particular jurisdiction in question, and to take special care when considering the relevance and usefulness of judgments in cases in other jurisdictions where the legislation, policy considerations and general principles of law may be different'.

DOI: 10.4324/9781003186946-13

Effect of registration of proprietor with absolute title

Section 26 contains the important provision, fundamental to the Torrens system of title registration, that a person registered with absolute title 'shall be entitled to hold such land in fee simple, together with all rights, privileges and appurtenances, belonging or appurtenant thereto, subject . . .

(a) to the incumbrances (if any) entered on the certificate of title; and

(b) to such liabilities, rights and interests as may under the provisions of this Act subsist over land brought under the operation of this Act without being entered on the certificate of title as incumbrances, but *free from all other estates and interests whatsoever . . .*'.[4]

Requirements for an application to have land brought under the Act

Section 28 lists the categories of person who may, by application to the Registrar in the form specified in the First Schedule, have land brought under the operation of the Act. Among such persons are: (a) persons individually or collectively claiming to be owners of the fee simple, either at law or in equity;[5] (b) persons having the power of appointing or disposing of the fee simple; (c) trustees for the sale of the fee simple; and (d) guardians of minors and committees of the estates of persons of unsound mind. The section also contains the proviso that (i) a mortgagor is not entitled to make an application unless the mortgagee consents, and (ii) a mortgagee may not do so except for the purpose of the exercise of its power of sale, and only if the certificate of title is directed to be issued in the purchaser's name.

By s 29, every application to have land brought under the Act must be accompanied by the deeds, documents or other evidence relied upon to support the application, as well as the fees payable and certificates or receipts relating to payment of all quit rents, property taxes and succession duties.

Section 30 provides that the land sought to be brought under the Act must be identified either (a) by plat or diagram, or (b) by metes and bounds.

Some interesting procedural issues were raised in *Registrar of Titles v Adela International Financing Co.*[6] Here, a mortgagee, in the exercise of his/her power of sale, agreed to transfer the mortgaged property to the purchaser and applied to the Registrar to have the certificate of title issued in the name of the purchaser. An unusual feature of the case was that the application for registration was in fact one to re-register the land by plat or diagram, the original registration being by metes and bounds, so that the application fell within s 54(1) of the Act. Section 54(2) provides that such an application shall be treated as if it were an initial application to register.

4 The words 'free from all other estates and interests whatsoever' are echoed in s 70, which is worded, 'absolutely free from all other incumbrances whatsoever'. It was pointed out by Carberry JA in *Wood v Wood* (1982) 19 JLR 404, at 409, that s 26 was 'seldom relied on as compared with section 70'. In *Pottinger v Raffone*, Privy Council Appeal No 64 of 2005, Lord Rodger pointed out that, by virtue of s 26, a person whose title is registered 'is entitled to hold the land in fee simple'.

5 See, eg, *Grant v Tapper* (2002) Court of Appeal, Jamaica, No 83 of 1999 (unreported); *Re Dunbar* (1984) 21 JLR 41.

6 (1992) 29 JLR 352.

The Referee, upon a reference to him by the Registrar, ruled that the correct method of transfer of land[7] already registered under the Act was that which was clearly prescribed by s 88, requiring the use of one of the forms set out in the Fourth Schedule. He further ruled that the clause in the application directing the Registrar to issue a certificate of title in the purchaser's name was misconceived, and that it should be deleted to enable title to be issued in the name of the applicant (mortgagee), after which a transfer to the purchaser could be effected. The mortgagee objected and refused to comply with the Referee's ruling, asserting that a direction to the Registrar nominating a purchaser as the new proprietor was valid and sanctioned by long practice. The Referee remained unmoved and the matter eventually came to court.

Harrison J held that although s 54 does not in its wording explicitly permit the applicant to give directions to the Registrar, the proviso to s 28 (which concerns original applications) does speak of the entitlement of a mortgagee exercising its power of sale to direct the issue of a certificate of title in the purchaser's name, and s 174 (dealing with payment of stamp duty) also expressly contemplates such a direction. Harrison J concluded that the Act 'has to be interpreted as a whole', and he accordingly upheld the applicant's contentions.

The Jamaican Court of Appeal agreed with that conclusion, but held that, in order to give effect to ss 33 and 54(3), only provisional approval for the issue of the certificate of title in the purchaser's name would be given in the first instance, so that the Registrar could cause notification thereof by advertisement in the *Gazette* or in an appropriate newspaper.

Carey P (Ag) had this to say:[8]

> The proviso [to s 28] expressly mentions the position with respect to a mortgagee exercising a power of sale under the mortgage and desirous of having title issued by the Registrar of Titles in the purchaser's name. In my opinion, the combined effect of the proviso and section 28(iii) is that an application to re-register by a mortgagee exercising his power of sale where the certificate is to be issued in the purchaser's name is in all respects akin to an original application to register. This is, I suggest, the true meaning of the section and, if that be so, then the respondents would be correct that a special document 'transfer' forms no part of the procedure required where a mortgagee who has exercised his power of sale seeks to have the purchaser's name placed on the certificate of title . . . Plainly, if the exercise being performed by any of the categories of persons named in [s 88] is a transfer of the interest of which he is proprietor, then resort to Forms A, B, C in the Fourth Schedule, which are forms of transfer, would be appropriate. The respondents, however, were not the proprietors of land which they were transferring, nor were they the proprietors of any mortgage which they were transferring: they were mortgagees who had exercised their power of sale and were acting thereafter pursuant to those powers as provided for by law. Strictly speaking, *nemo dat quod non habet.* In my judgment, section 88 is not applicable to a mortgagee who has exercised his power of sale and is transferring the land to a purchaser . . . If the Act is read as a whole, then it is clear that a direction for the certificate of title to be issued in the purchaser's name can operate as a transfer. If that be right, then a transfer cannot be insisted upon by the Registrar or Referee as being a mandatory

7 An unregistered transfer does not confer any estate or interest in land. The transferee becomes proprietor only when the transfer is registered: *National Import-Export Bank of Jamaica v Montego Bay Investment Co Ltd* [2017] JMSC Civ 67, paras 44, 45, *per* Wint-Blair J.

8 *Ibid*, at 356.

requirement of the Act. The conclusion is inevitable not only that the direction allowed by the proviso to section 28 of the Act amounts to a transfer, but also that the legal rights created by sections 106, 108 and 114 are likewise applicable where such a direction is given. In my judgment, Harrison J came to the correct decision and for the right reasons. The requisition raised by the Referee of Titles is, for the reasons I have given, misconceived. A transfer is not necessary: a direction in the terms stated in the present application to the Registrar is the correct procedure.

Gordon JA said:[9]

Section 54(2) [Re-registration of registered land by plan] declares that the application must be treated in all respects as if it were an original application and requires the cancellation of the former registration before the new certificate registering the land by plan is issued. Therefore, there is a period of time, however brief, when there is no registered title in existence for that land. With what then are we left? There is no title that the mortgagee can transfer, but there is an application for a new title with a direction that it be issued in the name of the purchaser from the mortgagee of the former title. Section 54(3) declares the procedure to be followed by the Referee. The proviso to section 28 requires that the mortgagee, in applying for a title in the exercise of his power of sale, must direct that the title be issued in the name of the purchaser. Section 54 provides that an application thereunder shall be dealt with as if it were an original application to register land, and section 174 recognises the validity of both section 28 and section 54. Section 174 accepts that a direction to issue title in the name of another can operate as a transfer on sale for valuable consideration. I find that in this case the direction of the respondent was intended to and does operate as a transfer. I agree with the learned trial judge and hold that the Act must be construed as a whole. The provisions of section 54 make the execution of a transfer under section 106 in the form provided by section 88 unnecessary.

Role of the Referee of Titles

Section 31 provides that the Registrar must submit the application, together with the deeds, documents or other evidence, to a Referee for his/her consideration as to whether the applicant is a person entitled to make an application under the Act, and is 'in possession by himself or a tenant of the land described or identified in the application, and that he would be entitled to maintain and defend such possession against any other person claiming the same or any part thereof'. If the Referee concludes that these requirements have been satisfied, he/she must provisionally approve the registration of the title of the applicant or his/her nominee, with absolute title. Thus, for example, in *Lynch v Ennevor*,[10] the Referee directed that the land in question be registered provisionally and that a certificate of title be issued in the name of the applicant's nominee. He further directed that notice of the provisional approval be given by advertisement to be published once in the *Jamaica Gazette* and once a week for three weeks in the *Gleaner* newspaper, and by service upon the owners and persons in possession, occupation or charge of all adjoining lands. The certificate of title was to be issuable at or after the expiration of seven weeks from the appearance of the first of the advertisements unless, in the meantime, a caveat were duly lodged.

9 *Ibid*, at 366.
10 (1982) 19 JLR 161.

In *Re Dunbar*,[11] the Referee ruled that it was not permissible to transfer various portions of land to various transferees pursuant to a single application under the Act; rather, each transaction required a separate and distinct application. The Referee's ruling was affirmed by the Supreme Court, *per* Bingham J, who characterised the application in this case as an ingenious device to circumvent the provisions of s 174, whereby each application for registration is subject to a one-third *ad valorem* duty on the consideration price before the applicant or his nominee can be registered as proprietor.

Title to be registered

Section 37 provides that if, at the expiration of the time limited in the notice of provisional approval, no caveat has been received by the Registrar forbidding the bringing of the land under the operation of the Act, the Registrar shall bring such land under the Act in accordance with the directions of the Referee, by registering the title of the applicant or of the person in whose name he/she may have been directed to issue the certificate of title. Registration must be as an absolute or a qualified title, as may have been determined by the Referee, with such description or identification of the land as may have been approved by the Referee.

Possession of and dealing with documents evidencing title

Section 42 provides that, upon registering a certificate of title, the Registrar shall retain in his/her custody all deeds, instruments and documents evidencing the title of the person registered, and no person shall be entitled to inspect those documents except upon the written order of the persons who originally deposited them, or of some person claiming through the latter, or upon the order of a judge. In *Wheatle v Donalds*,[12] the Jamaican Court of Appeal, *per* Patterson JA, held that the court's power under s 42 to order inspection of documents lodged with the Registrar of Titles 'should not be exercised unless good cause is shown to lift the veil of confidentiality reposed in the Registrar', and the court would not order inspection where, as in the present case, the 'application for inspection may properly be described as a trip on a fishing expedition with the hope of catching a defence'.

Bringing land under the operation of the Act

Under s 55, land is brought under the Act by the Registrar preparing a certificate of title in duplicate. One copy is entered in the Register Book by binding up or filing it in the Book. The duplicate copy, marked with the volume and folium number where the certificate is entered, is given to the proprietor. Registration is deemed to be effective when the Registrar marks the volume and folium number on the duplicate certificate.

11 (1984) 21 JLR 41.
12 (1996) 33 JLR 272.

Section 59 contains the important provision that instruments purporting to affect the same estate or interest shall be entitled to priority as between themselves according to the time of registration and not according to the date of the instrument.[13]

CAVEAT AGAINST FIRST REGISTRATION

Sections 43–45 of the Act are concerned with caveats against bringing land under the Act – that is, *caveats against first registration* – whereas ss 139–143 are concerned with caveats against dealings with land already registered.

Under s 43, any person claiming any estate or interest in the land described in the advertisement may in person or by agent, within the time appointed by the Referee under s 33, lodge a caveat with the Registrar, in the form in the Second Schedule, forbidding the bringing of such land under the Act. The caveat must be signed by the caveator or his/her agent and must particularise the estate or interest claimed. The Registrar may also require the caveator to make a statutory declaration stating the nature of the title under which the claim is made and to deliver an abstract of his/her title to such estate or interest.

Section 44 provides that the Registrar, on receipt of the caveat, must notify the applicant for registration and must suspend proceedings in the matter until such caveat has been withdrawn or has lapsed, or until an order in the matter has been obtained from the Supreme Court or a judge.[14] Thereafter, the applicant may summon the caveator to attend before the Supreme Court or a judge in chambers to show cause why the caveat should not be removed, and the Court or judge may make such order as it or he/she thinks fit.

The main issue in *Rodney v Rodney-Seale*[15] was whether a caveat ought to be removed on the ground that the caveator did not have a sufficient interest in the disputed land to support the caveat. The background to the case was that one HK died in 1958, leaving a will in which she appointed her eldest son, PR, as sole executor and gave her land, comprising 107 acres, to her ten children in equal shares, directing that the distribution be 'amicably handled, and any proceeds from the said land be equally divided among the ten children'. PR subsequently allotted portions of the land to himself, two sisters and a brother, but the remaining portions were never allotted. PR died, having appointed his wife, MR, executrix of his will. Since the administration of HK's estate had not been completed before PR's death, the effect in law was that MR became trustee of HK's land until such completion. MR applied to the Registrar of Titles to have the portion of land that PR had allotted to himself registered under the Act. JR, one of the daughters of HK and a beneficiary under the will, who had never been allotted any land, lodged a caveat against registration. JR contended that MR was seeking to register in her name more land than to which she was entitled, while MR argued that JR had not established an interest in the land sufficient to support the caveat. The Jamaican Court of Appeal, upholding the trial judge's decision, held that JR did have a sufficient caveatable interest, and the caveat

13 See *Registrar of Titles v Ramharrack* (2005) Court of Appeal, Jamaica, Civ App No 80 of 2002.
14 In *Thomas v Johnson* (1992) 29 JLR 95, affirmed (1995) 32 JLR 196, it was held that an order of specific performance by the court in favour of a purchaser had the effect of discharging the caveat, so that the Registrar was entitled to register a transfer of the land despite the caveat lodged.
15 (1994) 31 JLR 674.

should not be removed until there had been a resolution of all of the issues of fact, law and equity, so that the administration of the estate could proceed.

Forte JA explained:[16]

> In my view, the evidence disclosed in the affidavits leaves it abundantly clear that the administration of Henrietta's estate has not been completed and, more importantly, the beneficiaries, some of whom have never benefited from the estate, have never been in agreement with the purported allotment attempted by Percival and in particular an allotment to himself of so many acres abutting the main road. Consequently, I would conclude that to allow the registration to proceed in the face of such allegations would, as the respondents contend, deprive the beneficiaries of their chance to place before a court all the evidence in order to determine the manner in which the administration of the estate should now proceed, given the death of Percival and the inactivity in its administration since then. In this regard, a passage cited by [counsel] for the respondents, from the text *Registration of Title to Land Throughout the Empire*, by JE Hogg, dealing with the Torrens system throughout the Commonwealth including Jamaica, is of significant relevance. It reads:
>
>> The necessity for protecting unregistered interests by means of injunctions, and the close resemblance that the caveat bears to an injunction, justify the general principle of giving an extended meaning to the 'interest' which will support a caveat. It must of course be borne in mind that 'interest' includes a claim to an interest; the whole system of caveats is founded on the principle that they exist for the protection of alleged as well as proved interests, and of interests that have not yet become actual interests in the land.
>
> In my view, there is in the affidavits overwhelming evidence that demonstrates ample reasons why the caveat should not be removed until there is a resolution of all the issues of fact, law and equity in the appropriate jurisdiction. If there is any *bona fide* question of law or equity to be decided as to the right of the caveator to the estate or interest claimed under the caveat, such question should be disposed of in an action to be brought in which to decide such question.

Section 45 provides that a caveat will be deemed to have lapsed one month from the date of its receipt by the Registrar, unless in the meantime the caveator has taken proceedings in a court of competent jurisdiction to establish his title to the estate or interest specified in the caveat; nor may a caveat be renewed by or on behalf of the same person in respect of the same estate or interest.

CAVEAT AGAINST DEALINGS

Under s 139, any beneficiary or other person claiming an estate or interest in registered land may lodge a caveat[17] with the Registrar in the form in the Thirteenth Schedule, forbidding the registration of any person as transferee or proprietor, or the registration of any instrument affecting such estate or interest. By s 40, on receipt of such caveat, the Registrar must notify the transferee or proprietor, who may summon the caveator to attend before the Supreme Court or judge in chambers to show cause why the caveat should not be removed. By the same section, a caveat will be

16 *Ibid*, at 683.
17 In some jurisdictions, the term used is 'caution'. See, eg, Registered Land Act, Cap 229, ss 127–131 (BVI).

deemed to have lapsed after a period of 14 days from the date of such notice being given to the caveator.

Section 142 provides that so long as a caveat against dealings remains in force, the Registrar must not enter in the Register any change in the proprietorship or any transfer or instrument presented for registration subsequent to the date on which the caveat was lodged, unless the caveator consents.[18]

It was emphasised by Lord Wilberforce in *Rose Hall Ltd v Reeves*,[19] a Jamaican case that went before the Privy Council, that a caveat against dealings has the effect of preventing any dealings with the land while it remains effective, and it cannot be argued that a caveat is 'void' on the ground that the person who lodged it had no interest to protect: 'A caveat is simply a fact – it may be justified in law or not – and whether it is either, must be decided through the procedure laid down in the Registration of Titles Act'.[20] In *Wakefield v Dostey*,[21] on the other hand, Anderson J accepted as correct the view that, to be caveatable, the interest claimed by the caveator must be either a legal estate (or interest) or an interest in respect of which equity will give specific relief against the land itself. Such relief may be by way of an order that the interest claimed be satisfied out of the land itself, for example by an order

18 In *Thomas v Johnson* (1997) 52 WIR 409, a caveat against dealings was lodged in the names of the plaintiffs, claiming an interest in the land as donees from the registered proprietor. Gault J, delivering the judgment of the Privy Council, pointed out (at 412) that this 'should have had the effect of preventing registration of any dealings against the title'.

Sample caveat against dealings:
Caveat against the registration of any change in proprietorship or of dealing
To: The Registrar of Titles
TAKE NOTICE THAT I, CINDY SMITH, of 45 Reservation Mount, Port Antonio, in the parish of Portland, claim to have an estate or interest, to whit an agreement to purchase ALL THAT parcel of land being the Lot numbered 85 on the plan to Northanger Trust deposited in the Office of Titles on the 1st day of August 1967 and being the lands registered at Volume 1074 Folio 387 and we forbid the registration of any person as transferee or proprietor and of any instrument affecting such estate or interest until after notice of the intended registration or dealing be given to me or unless such instrument be expressed to be subject to my said claim.
I APPOINT the office of Elton, Keyes and Carey of Nos 131–134 Church Street, Kingston, Attorneys-at-Law, as the place at which notices and proceedings relating hereto may be served.
[Section 139 provides that 'no caveat shall be received unless some address or place within the City of Kingston shall be appointed therein as the place at which notice and proceedings relating to such caveat may be served . . .'.]
For an example of lapse of such a caveat, see a Trinidadian case: *Crease v Voisin* (1980) High Court, Trinidad and Tobago, No 1997 of 1971.
An example of lapse of a caveat against dealings under s 140 is *Vehicles and Supplies Ltd v Financial Institutions Services Ltd* (2005) PC Appeal No 7 of 2004.

19 (1972) Court of Appeal, Jamaica, Civ App No 37 of 1968.

20 Cf *Patrick v Emmanuel* (1994) Court of Appeal, OECS (Dominica), Civ App No 9 of 1994, *per* Liverpool JA.

21 (2002) Supreme Court, Jamaica, No E-510 of 2000. In *National Insurance Board of Trinidad and Tobago v Moses* (2010) High Court, Trinidad and Tobago, No 1625 of 2000, the right of an individual to lodge a caveat under section 125 of the Real Property Ordinance, Ch 56:02, was challenged. The section provides that 'any beneficiary or other person claiming any estate or interest in land under the provisions of this Ordinance . . . or by devolution of law or otherwise . . . may lodge a caveat with the Registrar . . . forbidding the registration of any person as transferee or proprietor of and of any instrument affecting such estate or interest . . .' The caveator lodged her caveat on the basis that she was the sole beneficiary under the will of the deceased proprietor of certain registered land. It was held that the caveator was entitled to lodge the caveat, despite the fact that the deceased's estate had not yet been administered, so that her interest had not crystallised but was 'at best, a floating equity'. Considering the matter to be strictly one of statutory interpretation, Myers J (Ag) opined that the purpose of section 125 was to protect a person's interest (or claim of an interest) in land until such claim was substantiated.

for the sale of the land and the payment out of the proceeds of an amount in respect of which the caveator has a mortgage or charge.

It has also been emphasised[22] that, under a Torrens system, a person who seeks to preserve an unregistered interest (such as, for example, an agreement for the sale of land) against a subsequent inconsistent dealing must, at the very least, lodge a caveat to preserve and maintain it, otherwise that interest will be extinguished and cannot be reasserted later against a subsequent registered proprietor, or against the holder of a later and inconsistent registered interest. This is a consequence of the principle of indefeasibility of registered titles under Torrens systems.

INDEFEASIBILITY OF REGISTERED TITLE

Sections 68–71 of the Act are of central importance in so far as they provide for the indefeasibility of the registered title. In the words of Carey P (Ag):[23]

> That registration of title confers on the proprietor[24] indefeasibility of title, save for fraud, is the very basis of the Torrens system of registration of land and is a matter of settled law.

Section 68[25] speaks of a certificate of title being *conclusive evidence of title* and provides that it cannot be impeached on account of any informality or irregularity in the application process or in the proceedings previous to the registration of the certificate. The section provides:

> No certificate of title registered and granted under this Act shall be impeached or defeasible by reason or on account of any informality or irregularity in the application for the same, or in the proceedings previous to the registration of the certificate; and every certificate of title issued under any of the provisions herein contained shall be received in all courts as evidence of the particulars therein set forth, and of the entry thereof in the Register book, and shall, subject to the subsequent operation of any statute of limitations,[26] be conclusive evidence that the person named in such certificate as the proprietor of or having any estate or interest in, or power to appoint or

22 See *Doig-Warner v Lewis* (2005) Supreme Court, Jamaica, No W070 of 2002, *per* Anderson J; *Anderson v Wan* [2020] JMCA Civ 41, paras 30–40, *per* Morrison P.

23 *Willcocks v Wilson* (1993) 30 JLR 297, at 299.

24 'Proprietor' is defined by s 4 as 'the owner, . . . whether in possession, remainder, reversion expectancy or in tail or otherwise, of land, or of a lease, mortgage or charge'. Accordingly, in *Jamaican Redevelopment Foundation Inc v Capital Solutions Ltd* (2009) Supreme Court, Jamaica, No 02664 of 2008, Mangatal J pointed out that the indefeasibility provisions in the Act applied not only to the holder of the fee simple of land, but also to the owner of a mortgage.

25 Cf Real Property Act, Ch 56:02 (Trinidad and Tobago), s 37: *Bisram v Samaroo* (1983) High Court, Trinidad and Tobago, No 3417 of 1979, *per* Hosein J.

26 This wording provides an exception to the indefeasibility of a registered title, in that its effect is that a squatter in adverse possession of land for 12 years or more, as required by s 3 of the Limitation of Actions Act, may defeat the paper owner's title and obtain the registered title himself under s 85 of the Registration of Titles Act. As Evan Brown J pellucidly explained in *Barnes v Campbell* [2019] JMSC Civ 178, para 62, 'Even a certificate of title issued under the Registration of Titles Act, which is otherwise conclusive evidence that the person named therein is the proprietor of the relevant land, has been made subject to the operation of any statute of limitations (s 68) . . . The cumulative effect of [ss 68 and 85] is that an "indolent" paper owner may be ousted by a trespasser who remains in possession for the requisite limitation period'. See also *Fullwood v Curchar* [2015] JMCA Civ 37, para 30, *per* McDonald-Bishop JA.; *Hayles v McFarlane* [2017] JMSC Civ 5, paras 30,31, *per* Evan Brown J;*McCrea v Lindo* [2020] JMSC Civ 19, paras 56–59, *per* T Hutchinson J (Ag).

dispose of the land therein described, is seised or possessed of such estate or interest or has such power.

Section 70[27] speaks of *preferential and prior rights being defeated in favour of the registered proprietor*, except in cases of *fraud*, and provides that the registered proprietor is bound by those incumbrances that are notified on the Register, but takes

> absolutely free from all other incumbrances whatsoever, except the estate or interest of a proprietor claiming the same land under a *prior registered certificate of title*, and except as regards any portion of land that may by *wrong description of parcels or boundaries* be included in the certificate of title . . .'.

Under the proviso to section 70, 'land which shall be included in any certificate of title . . . shall be deemed to be subject to . . . any rights acquired over such land since the same was brought under the operation of this Act under any statute of limitations. . .'.[28]

Section 71[29] exempts a person, except in the case of fraud, from tracing the root of title of any registered land with which he/she proposes to deal. The section provides that:

> except in the case of fraud, no person contracting . . . or proposing to take a transfer from the proprietor of any registered land, lease, mortgage or charge shall be required . . . to enquire or ascertain the circumstances under . . . which such proprietor or any previous proprietor was registered . . . or shall be affected by notice, actual or constructive, of any trust or unregistered interest, any rule of law or equity to the contrary notwithstanding; and the knowledge that any such trust or unregistered interest is in existence shall not of itself be imputed as fraud.

The effect of the sections has been considered in a number of cases before the Jamaican courts.

A straightforward example of the application of the indefeasibility principle is *Wilcocks v Wilson.*[30] In this case, a mortgagee, in the exercise of its power of sale over the mortgaged property, a dwelling house, sold the house to the respondents and the transfer was registered. The appellant, the widow of the deceased guarantor of the mortgage, continued to reside in the house with her six children. She resisted the respondents' action for possession of the house on the ground, *inter alia*, that fraud on the respondents' part should be inferred from the fact that the respondents knew that the appellant, through court action against the mortgagee, was claiming

27 Cf Real Property Act, Ch 56:02, s 45 (Trinidad and Tobago): see *Republic Bank Ltd v Seepersad* (2015) Civ App No S268 of 2014; *Collins v Dhanasar* (2016) High Court, Trinidad and Tobago, No CV2001–0982; Registered Land Act, Cap 194, s 26 (Belize).

28 In *Recreational Holdings Ltd v Lazarus* [2016] UKPC 22, it was held that this proviso explicitly subordinates the title of the registered proprietor to such unregistered rights under the Limitation Acts (ie, rights acquired by adverse possession) as have begun to accrue since first registration under the Act, and no exception is made (as is made elsewhere in the Act) for the registered proprietor who can claim to have been a *bona fide* purchaser for value (para 34), *per* Lord Wilson. The same principle has been applied in Trinidad and Tobago under section 45 of the Real Property Act. See *Collins v Dhanasar*, fn 27, above, *per* Charles J, following *Republic Bank Ltd v Seepersad* (2015) Court of Appeal, Trinidad and Tobago, Civ App No S268 of 2014, *per* Mendonca JA.

29 Cf Real Property Act, Ch 56:02, s 141 (Trinidad and Tobago)Registered Land Act, s 41 (Belize); Registered Land Act s 38 (BVI). See also *Racoon Ltd v Turnbull* (1996) Privy Council Appeal No 33 of 1995.

30 (1993) 30 JLR 297, at 299, cited by Morrison JA in *Bancroft v Cookhorne* (2009) Court of Appeal, Jamaica, Civ App No 15 of 2008. See also *Francis v Graham* [2017] JMCA Civ 39.

a beneficial interest in the house. The Court of Appeal of Jamaica held that the appellant's contention was misconceived since the effect of s 71 of the Act was that, in the absence of proof of fraud, the respondents' registered title was indefeasible. As Carey P explained:[31]

> I understood the appellant to be saying that the [respondent] purchasers by reason of their knowledge of the dispute [with the mortgagee] should have been put on enquiry. But, assuming without accepting that conclusion, it is pertinent to ask what such an enquiry would reveal. It would disclose an action by the appellant in which no allegation of fraud was being made against the mortgagee. It seems to me that, unless the enquiry disclosed fraud, the respondents would be *bona fide* purchasers for value without notice. That registration of title confers on the proprietor indefeasibility of title, save for fraud, is the very basis of the Torrens system of registration of land . . . It is plain from the [wording of s 71] that even knowledge of the existence of a trust or other unregistered interest is not fraud . . . If knowledge of a claim to a trust or unregistered interest is not fraud, then an allegation that such a claim is being asserted by a court action can have no more significance . . . It is right to point out that fraud in this Act means actual fraud, ie dishonesty.[32] The claim to an interest in the house, which the appellant put forward, was based on the fact that she had contributed substantial amounts to the purchase price of the house. This claim was never established during the lifetime of her common-law husband and thus remains to be proved, if that is at all possible, at this stage. Howsoever that might be, it cannot affect the interest of the title of the respondents.

Another clear illustration of the indefeasibility of a registered title is *Wedderburn v Capital Assurance Building Society Ltd.*[33] Here, the building society granted a loan on mortgage to the sole registered proprietor of matrimonial property, without having investigated whether the proprietor's spouse had any interest in the property. The spouse had in fact filed a suit under the Married Women's Property Act, claiming an equitable interest in the property (under a resulting trust) by virtue of her contribution to the purchase. The essential question before the Jamaican Court of Appeal was, in the words of Langrin JA:

> If the intended mortgagee, upon receiving an application, fails to investigate whether the spouse of the intended mortgagor has an interest in the matrimonial property or fails to obtain the consent of the spouse to the pledging of the intended security (the matrimonial home), is the said mortgage voidable, and is the court entitled to declare the said mortgage void? . . . The matter does not concern the validity of the registered title but touches and concerns the validity of the mortgage held by the mortgagee which was obtained in circumstances where the mortgagee knew or ought to have known (if there was due diligence) of the interest of the proprietor of the unregistered interest in the property.

31 *Ibid*, at 299.

32 *Boothe v Cooke* (1982) 19 JLR 278 is another example of indefeasibilty of a registered title. Here, H, the registered proprietor of a parcel of land, entered into an agreement to sell to B. B failed to keep to the agreed payment schedule and H, after warning B of his intention to find another buyer, eventually sold the property to C, who was registered as proprietor. C later sought an injunction to restrain trespass by B, relying on his status as registered proprietor. B's only defence to the injunction was an unsubstantiated allegation that H was in fact dead and that the transferor to C was a fictitious person. Accordingly, in the absence of proof of any actual fraud, C's title was indefeasible, and he was entitled to the injunction sought. See also *De Mercado* v *McKenzie* (1997) 34 JLR 433.

33 (1999) Court of Appeal, Jamaica, Civ App No 77 of 1998.

Langrin JA held that the Registration of Titles Act conferred on the registered proprietor indefeasibility of title. This was the fundamental basis of the Torrens system of registration of land and was a matter of settled law. Section 71 of the Act provided that no person contracting with a registered proprietor was affected by notice,[34] actual or constructive, of any trust or other unregistered interest, and knowledge of the existence of any such interest was not to be imputed as fraud. He continued:

> [Section 71] provides adequate protection to parties dealing with the registered proprietor. The law in relation to notice as it may affect purchasers or mortgagees of unregistered land has no application to registered land. The system of registration of title is designed to free the purchaser or mortgagee from the hazards of notice, real or constructive, which in the case of unregistered land involved him in enquiries failing which he might be bound by equities. Even knowledge that a claim is being asserted by court action, as shown by the appellant filing suit under the Married Women's Property Act against her husband, can have no legal consequence against the validity of the mortgage, since her right would have to be postponed to the rights of the mortgagee . . . [As Lord Buckmaster LC said] in *Waimiha Sawmilling Co Ltd v Waione Timber Co Ltd*:[35] 'Litigation is the means by which a disputed interest in land can be established. If knowledge of the interest itself does not affect a registered proprietor, knowledge that steps are being taken to assert that interest can have no more serious effect'.

Meaning of 'fraud'

It was established by the Privy Council in the leading case of *Assets Co Ltd v Roihi*,[36] decided under the Land Transfer Act of New Zealand, on provisions that are similar to those of the Jamaican Act, that:

> by fraud in these Acts is meant actual fraud, ie, dishonesty of some sort,[37] not what is called constructive or equitable fraud . . . Further, it appears . . . that the fraud

34 See also *Creque v Penn* [2007] UKPC 44.
35 [1926] AC 101, at 108.
36 [1905] AC 176.
37 See *Harley Corporation Guarantee Investment Co Ltd v Daley* [2010] JMCA Civ 6, paras 51, 52, *per* Harris JA; *Brilliant Investments Ltd v Messado* [2019] JMCC Comm 26, paras 60–63, *per* Laing J. This definition of fraud has also been applied in Trinidad and Tobago in interpreting ss 45 and 143(b) of the Real Property Ordinance, Ch 56:01. See, eg, *Roberts v Toussaint* (1963) 6 WIR 432, at 433, *per* Wooding CJ; *Gobin v Ishahack* (1985) High Court, Trinidad and Tobago, No 1323 of 1977, *per* Blackman J; *Crease v Voisin* (1980) High Court, Trinidad and Tobago, No 1997 of 1971; *Jaikaran v Binda* (1991) High Court, Trinidad and Tobago, No S2928 of 1986; *Annisette v Chunisingh* (2001) High Court, Trinidad and Tobago, No 2349 of 1994; *Bobscombe v Hills* (1999) High Court, Trinidad and Tobago, No 2431 of 1994; *Gayapersad v Gayapersad* (2015) High Court, Trinidad and Tobago, No CV 2012–00164; *Graham-Joseph v Williams* (2019) High Court, Trinidad and Tobago, No CV2018–01785. Among Jamaican cases in which actual fraud was established are: *Reid v Wilson* (1994) 31 JLR 123, in which the plaintiff procured the registration of his title to certain land, knowing that the defendants were already registered as proprietors of the same land (Malcolm J said: 'Where fraud is alleged, as in this case, it must be strictly proved . . . It must be established that Mr Reid obtained material advantage by unfair and wrongful means'); *Lynch v Ennevor* (1982) 19 JLR 161, in which J entered into an agreement to sell to E an area of land of approximately half an acre, knowing that this area included a portion of land belonging to L that had been encroached upon. J falsely represented to the Registrar of Titles that he was the owner of the entire area, falsely declaring that he was not aware that any other person had an estate or interest in the land. Similarly, in a Trinidadian case, *Charles v Seeratan* (2012) High Court, Trinidad and Tobago, No 2008–02579, Rajkumar J held that fraud was established where registration of title had been procured after (i) non-disclosure of the inventory of a testator's estate, (ii) non-disclosure or concealment of claims to the land by other parties, and (iii) false sworn assertions

> which must be proved in order to invalidate the title of a registered purchaser for value . . . must be brought home to the person whose registered title is impeached or his agent . . . The mere fact that he might have found out fraud if he had been more vigilant and had made further inquiries which he omitted to make, does not of itself prove fraud. But if it be shown that his suspicions were aroused, and that he abstained from making enquiries for fear of learning the truth,[38] the case is very different, and fraud may be properly ascribed to him . . . A person who presents for registration a document which is forged or has been fraudulently or improperly obtained is not guilty of fraud if he honestly believes it to be a genuine document which can be properly acted upon.

The principle in *Assets Co* was confirmed by the same court in *Frazer v Walker*,[39] in which mortgagees lent money to a wife on the security of a registered property jointly owned by her and her husband, and registered the mortgage. Unknown to the mortgagees, the husband's signature on the mortgage document had been forged by the wife. When the wife defaulted in repayment, the mortgagees in the exercise of their power of sale sold the property by auction to an innocent purchaser who had no knowledge of the forgery. The new registered proprietor sued the husband for possession of the property. The husband counterclaimed on the basis of the forgery of his signature to the mortgage document, arguing that his interest in the property was not affected, that the mortgage was a nullity, and that the Registrar should cancel the consequential entries in the register. The counterclaim was dismissed on the ground that it was in effect an action for recovery of possession. The New Zealand courts and the Privy Council held that the husband's counterclaim was in effect an action for recovery of possession under s 63 of the New Zealand Land Transfer Act 1952 (similar to s 161 of the Jamaican Act), and since it did not fall within any of the exceptional cases mentioned by the section, the action failed. The purchaser at the auction sale had accordingly obtained an indefeasible title as registered proprietor.

IN PERSONAM LIABILITIES

Frazer v Walker also established the important principle that the indefeasibility sections of the statutes 'in no way deny the right of a plaintiff to bring against a registered

concerning the land taxes allegedly paid with respect to the land. On the other hand, in *Faulknor v Pearjohn Investments Ltd* (2000) Supreme Court, Jamaica, No CL 1994/F 007, no fraud was established. Here, the plaintiff, in possession of land under an alleged contract for sale, failed to lodge a caveat on the title. The defendant was subsequently registered as transferee, knowing of the plaintiff's possession, but believing he was in possession merely as tenant of the previous owner. Smith J emphasised that 'section 71 provides that mere knowledge of any trust or unregistered interest shall not be imputed as fraud', and 'fraud within the meaning of sections 68, 70 and 71 of the Act implies some act of dishonesty which must not be assumed merely by reason of knowledge of an unregistered interest or trust. It must be strictly pleaded and proved . . . It was the plaintiff's duty to protect any equitable interest which he may have had by lodging a caveat on the title to the said land'. The absence of such caveat might have led the defendant to 'form a *bona fide* view that the plaintiff had no agreement for sale or that, if there was an agreement, it was not valid'. See also *Timoll-Uylett v Timoll* (1980) 17 JLR 257; *Grier v Bancroft* (2001) Court of Appeal, Jamaica, Civ App No 16 of 1997; *Bent v Evans* (2009) Supreme Court, Jamaica, No 1993/B 115; *Mastay v Ross* (2012) High Court, Trinidad and Tobago, No 2008–02106.

38 Sometimes referred to as 'wilful blindness' or 'contrived ignorance'. See the comprehensive analysis by Sykes J in *Daley v RBTT (Jamaica) Ltd* (2007) Supreme Court, Jamaica, No D 162 of 1995.

39 [1967] 1 AC 569.

proprietor a claim *in personam*, founded in law or in equity, for such relief as a court acting *in personam* may grant'.[40]

Put in another way:

> a registered proprietor who has incurred personal obligations cannot plead the indefeasibility provisions of the land registration statute in order to escape the enforcement of those obligations.
>
> . . . The doctrine of indefeasibility is designed to protect a proprietor from defects in the title of the transferor and earlier predecessors-in-title, not to free the proprietor from personal obligations with which he has burdened himself.[41]

Thus, in *Gardener v Lewis*,[42] Lord Browne-Wilkinson pointed out that although under s 68 the land certificate was conclusive as to the *legal interests in the land*, that did not mean that personal claims (for example, for breach of contract to sell, or to enforce trusts affecting the registered land against the trustee, or where the registered proprietor acts in breach of an undertaking given to the court) could not be enforced against the registered proprietor.[43]

Again, in *Oh Hiam v Tham Kong*,[44] Lord Russell explained that 'The Torrens system is designed to provide simplicity and certitude in transfers of land, which is amply achieved without depriving equity of the ability to exercise its jurisdiction *in personam* on grounds of conscience'. In *Oh Hiam*, because of a mistake common to vendor and purchaser, certain land was erroneously included in a transfer to the purchaser. The Privy Council held that the land should be re-transferred to the vendor, as it would have been unconscionable for the purchaser to retain lands that he knew were mistakenly transferred to him.

ACTIONS AGAINST REGISTERED PROPRIETOR

Another section that supports the indefeasibility of the registered proprietor's title is s 161,[45] which provides that 'no action of ejectment or other action, suit or proceeding for the recovery of any land shall lie . . . against the person registered as proprietor', except in the following cases:

---

40 *Ibid*, at 585.

41 Cooper, SAA, *Conveyancing Law and Practice in the Cayman Islands*, 2nd edn (2006), p 16.

42 (1998) 53 WIR 236.

43 Thus, in *Haughton v Haughton* (2004) Supreme Court, Jamaica, No E476 of 2001, Sykes J held that a registered proprietor who had procured a transfer of land to her from her father by undue influence was 'not outside of the jurisdiction of the courts of equity. She is not immunised from any equitable claim that can be made against her personally. The nature of the claim against her is that she has committed an inequitable act for which she is being called to account. The fact that the remedy may have the effect of causing the register to be altered to reflect the remedy granted by the court cannot change the picture'. Again, in *Stephens v The Administrator General of Jamaica* [2020] JMSC Civ 20, paras 94–96, Lindo J held that, as a result of errors in the conveyancing process, there had been a misdescription of the parcel of land purchased by the claimant, as reflected in the certificate of title, which was 'within the *in personam* exception referred to by Lord Wilberforce'.

44 Privy Council Appeal No 22 of 1978. Mendonca JA in *Lewis v Sookdeo* (2016) Court of Appeal, Trinidad and Tobago, Civ App No 236 of 2012, paras 27–32, considered the decision in *Oh Hiam* to be an example of the *in personam* jurisdiction being invoked in response to unconscionable conduct.

45 Cf the equivalent s 143 of the Real Property Ordinance, Ch 56:02 (Trinidad and Tobago). See also *Bobscombe v Hills* (1999) High Court, Trinidad and Tobago, No 2431 of 1994, *per* Moosai J.

(a) action by a mortgagee against a mortgagor in default;
(b) action by an annuitant against a grantor in default;
(c) action by a lessor against a lessee in default;
(d) action by a person deprived of any land by fraud as against the person registered as proprietor through fraud, or as against a person deriving otherwise than as a transferee *bona fide* for value from or through a person registered through fraud;[46]
(e) action by a person deprived of or claiming land included in a certificate of title of other land by misdescription of such other land, or of its boundaries, as against the registered proprietor of such other land, not being a transferee *bona fide* and for value;
(f) action by a registered proprietor with an absolute title, claiming under a prior certificate of title, where two or more certificates of title have been registered in respect of the same land.

CANCELLATION OR CORRECTION OF CERTIFICATE OF TITLE

The Act contains two important sections dealing with cancellation of certificates of title.

Section 153[47] provides that if it appears to the Registrar 'that any certificate of title or instrument has been issued in error, or contains any misdescription of land or of boundaries, or that any entry or endorsement has been made in error on any certificate of title or instrument, or that any certificate, instrument, entry or endorsement has been fraudulently or wrongfully obtained', he/she may require the person to whom the document has been issued or by whom it has been retained to deliver it up for cancellation or correction.

Section 158(2)[48] provides that:

> in any proceeding . . . in relation to land under the operation of this Act, the court or a Judge may . . . make an order directing the Registrar–
>
> (a) to cancel the certificate of title to the land and to issue a new certificate of title and the duplicate thereof in the name of the person specified for the purpose in the order; or
>
> (b) to amend or cancel any instrument, memorandum or entry relating to the land in such manner as appears proper to the court or a Judge.

46 To succeed under s 161(d), the claimant must show actual fraud on the part of the defendant; constructive fraud does not suffice. Fraud in this context means 'conduct of a dishonest nature on the part of the defendant, and the standard of proof is that required in a criminal case, viz, proof beyond a reasonable doubt': *Grier v Bancroft* (2001) Court of Appeal, Jamaica, Civ App No 16 of 1997, *per* Bingham JA; see also *Bancroft v Cookhorne* (2009) Court of Appeal, Jamaica, Civ App No 15 of 2008, *per* Morrison JA. In *Robinson v Nunes* (1994) 31 JLR 142, Langrin J regarded undue influence as a species of actual fraud sufficient to invalidate a certificate of title within s 161(d). In *Honiball v Alele* (1993) 43 WIR 314, the Privy Council held that fraud was established where, for the purpose of instituting proceedings for the recovery of land against the registered proprietor under s 161(d), and with the intention of persuading the court to authorise the execution of a judgment by the issue of a writ of sale, a lawyer swore an affidavit of value in relation to the land without having any honest belief in its accuracy. The equivalent subsection in the Real Property Ordinance, Ch 56:02 (Trinidad and Tobago) is s 143(b). See *Charles v Seeratan* (2012) High Court, Trinidad and Tobago, No 2008–02579.

47 Cf Title by Registration Act, Cap 231 (BVI), s 140.

48 Cf Registered Land Act, Cap 374 (Antigua and Barbuda), s 140(1).

The nature and extent of the Registrar's power under s 153 and its relationship with the indefeasibility provisions of ss 68–71 and with s 80 (Registrar's power to amend the register) were considered by the Privy Council in *Thomas v Johnson*.[49] In this complex but interesting case, D (vendor) had entered into a written agreement to sell land to the respondents. D purported to determine the contract before the completion date, but the respondents elected to enforce the agreement and obtained an order for specific performance from Langrin J, who designated the Registrar of the Supreme Court as authorised to sign the transfer on behalf of the vendor. A transfer was duly executed by the Registrar of the Supreme Court, but before the transfer was registered, a caveat was lodged in the name of the appellants claiming an interest in the land as donees from D. As Gault J, delivering the judgment of the Privy Council, pointed out, the lodging of the caveat should have had the effect of preventing registration of any dealings against the title; however, it appeared that the caveat was not in fact noted on the Register, as the transfer in favour of the respondents was subsequently registered. The appellants sought to have the certificate of title in the name of the respondents cancelled and a new certificate issued in their own names as donees. In separate proceedings before the Court of Appeal, it was held that the proceedings before Langrin J were a nullity because they had been wrongly commenced by way of originating summons instead of the mandatory writ, with the result that 'any subsequent proceeding based upon the order for specific performance would be itself a nullity'. The orders of Langrin J were accordingly set aside. But that was not the end of the matter, for the respondents obtained a judgment in their favour from Pitter J – subsequently upheld by the Court of Appeal – in which the learned judge held that even if the appellants' caveat had been on the title, the Registrar of Titles had correctly registered the transfer to the respondents, as it had been executed pursuant to a court order then extant (the order of Langrin J). The caveat must be taken to have been, in effect, discharged pursuant to the court order. Further, on the authority of *Frazer v Walker*,[50] the respondents' title, once registered, was indefeasible, even if it had been secured by a void instrument. The saga continued.

The present proceedings before the Privy Council had been brought by the appellants, who argued that s 70 must be read with s 153, under which, as we have seen, the Registrar is empowered to cancel or correct a certificate of title where it has been issued in error, wrongfully obtained, or wrongfully retained. The appellants contended that the respondents' certificate of title was both issued in error (because it should have been prevented by the appellants' caveat) and wrongfully obtained (because the entire proceedings leading to the orders made by Langrin J were, as held by the Court of Appeal, 'bad and a nullity'). Gault J pointed out that the Jamaican Act differed from the New Zealand Land Transfer Act in that, under the Jamaican Act, the Registrar's power under s 80 to amend the Register was limited in scope. Under that section, the power is confined to amendments as to: (a) the description of the land; (b) entries that no longer affect the land or the title; (c) the names of roads and the number on a road by which the land is designated; and (d) the name, address or occupation of any person that has been incorrectly entered. In the view of Gault J, the amendment power 'does not seem to extend to

49 (1997) 52 WIR 409.
50 [1967] 1 AC 569.

the cancellation of an entry as to proprietorship'. This view was reinforced by the positioning of s 153 in a separate part of the Act under the heading 'Practice and Procedure'. It was

> unlikely that the legislature would have intended by such a section – directed to the procedure for requisitioning outstanding instruments and certificates – to confer power on the Registrar to determine proprietorship of land and interests therein, when the Registrar's powers to amend the primary record, the register, are so confined.

As to whether the registration of their proprietorship could be said to have been 'wrongfully obtained' by the respondents, the meaning of 'wrongfully' in the corresponding section of the New Zealand Act had been left open by the Privy Council in *Frazer*, but it had been suggested in more recent cases that 'wrongful conduct' involved 'acting other than honestly and in good faith' and, in the present case, 'merely employing the wrong procedure without any intentional objective of defeating the rights of others' would not amount to wrongful conduct.

The view expressed by the Privy Council concerning the scope of s 153 was strongly supported by Panton JA (dissenting) in *American Jewellery Co Ltd v Commercial Corp Jamaica Ltd.*[51] He said:

> In my view . . . section 153 is concerned with proceedings by the Registrar. As I see it, the section provides for action, first and foremost, by the Registrar. There is no record of any application having been made by the appellant to the Registrar. It would be a very dangerous precedent for this Court to allow an appellant, who has not pleaded fraud, to use section 153, while alleging some vague misconduct, to shake the principle of the indefeasibility of the registered title . . . The principle of the indefeasibility of the registered title is sacrosanct. There should be no tinkering with it.

The question of the scope and effect of s 153 was again considered by the Privy Council in *Pottinger v Raffone.*[52] Here, an investment company had been registered proprietor of 34 parcels of land, but the appellant claimed to have been in undisturbed possession of the land for more than 12 years within s 3 of the Limitation of Actions Act. On the basis of this adverse possession, he applied to the Registrar under s 85 of the Registration of Titles Act to be registered as proprietor of the land in fee simple, the application being accompanied by various documents including a declaration by himself setting out the circumstances on which he relied to show that he had been in possession for the requisite 12-year period. The necessary advertisements were duly published in the newspaper. The application was successful and the Registrar, under the powers given to him by s 87 of the Registration of Titles Act, cancelled the certificates showing the company as proprietor and issued new certificates in the name of the appellant. The respondent thereupon claimed that the company had previously entered into an agreement to sell the land to her and that the appellant had fraudulently deprived her of the title. She argued that the case

51 (2004) Court of Appeal, Jamaica, Civ Apps Nos 155 and 156.
In a similar vein, Harrison JA explained that 'the statutory duty placed on the Registrar is restricted to discernible cases of errors or omissions in registration or proven fraud or wrongdoing in the case of a registered proprietor. There is no responsibility on the Registrar to decide the competing claims of parties nor the ownership of the land': *Registrar of Titles v Ramharrack* (2005) Court of Appeal, Jamaica, Civ App No 80 of 2002.

52 (2007) Privy Council Appeal No 64 of 2005.

fell within s 161(d) of the Act and sought cancellation of the appellant's certificate of title. The Jamaican Court of Appeal held that the respondent had not proved fraud within s 161(d), but that the court nevertheless had the power to cancel the appellant's certificate of title under s 153 on the ground that it had been 'wrongfully' obtained.

Lord Rodger, delivering the judgment of the Privy Council, disagreed that s 153 could be employed in this way to cancel an existing certificate of title. In his view, s 153 was not concerned with the fundamental matter of the validity of the title of the proprietor[53] whose name appeared on the register, but rather with providing the Registrar with essentially administrative powers to deal with 'significant, but less fundamental, problems relating to the certificates which evidence that title', such as cases of loss or destruction of a certificate, clerical errors, misdescription of boundaries, or wrongful retention of a certificate by a third party. In principle, when s 153 refers to a certificate of title being 'fraudulently or wrongfully obtained', 'it is referring quite specifically to the certificate rather than the title'. As Lord Oliver had emphasised in *Honiball v Alele*,[54] 'registration confers an "unassailable title" on the proprietor shown in the certificate of title, save in the specific cases enumerated in section 161. Paragraph (d) speaks of a person being deprived of land by fraud and of a person being registered as proprietor through fraud and nothing else', and 'the same policy of confining the attack on title to cases of fraud is reflected in sections 70 and 71'. Thus, in the absence of any proof of fraud on the part of the appellant, the respondent's claim failed.

ACTIONS AGAINST THE REGISTRAR

Under the scheme of the Registration of Titles Act, the Registrar enjoys a limited immunity from suit, and legal action can be brought against him/her only where certain preconditions are satisfied. Section 160 provides that

> the Registrar shall not, nor shall the Referee or any person acting under the authority of either of them, be liable to any action, suit or proceeding, for . . . any act or matter *bona fide* done or omitted to be done in the exercise or supposed exercise of the powers of this Act'

'The section thus exempts the Registrar and the Referee of Titles from suit in respect of any act done pursuant to the provisions of the Act 'without fraud, collusion or complicity in wrongdoing'. Section 162 provides that any person deprived of land or any interest in land by fraud may recover damages in the first instance from the person on whose application the land was brought under the operation of the Act or who acquired the title to the land through such fraud, but that where such person is dead, or bankrupt, or cannot be found, such damages may be recovered together

---

53 Likewise, in *Smith v Small* [2018] JMSC Civ 150, it was held that, on the facts, there was nothing fraudulent or wrongful about the way in which the certificate of title had been obtained by the defendant; rather, the error alleged by the claimants was that by inadvertence the wrong parcel of land had been transferred as sold to the defendant. 'The certificate of title was duly and regularly obtained in the course of those dealings. The concern is therefore not the way the certificate was obtained but in relation to the underlying error alleged, which affects the validity of the title itself that the certificate represents—a situation section 153 was not designed to address'. See para 64, *per* D Fraser J.

54 (1993) 43 WIR 314, at 320.

with costs out of the Assurance Fund, the Registrar acting as nominal defendant. Further, by s 164, a person wrongfully deprived of land or any interest therein through the mistake, omission or misfeasance of the Registrar or any other officer, or by the registration of any other person as proprietor, can bring an action against the Registrar as nominal defendant for the recovery of damages where the person deprived of the land is barred by the Act from bringing an action for the recovery of the land, or where the remedy for recovery of damages is inapplicable.

The effect of these provisions was in issue in *Registrar of Titles v Melfitz*,[55] in which the main issue was whether a person wrongfully deprived of land through the operation of the Act could bring an action against the Registrar, in circumstances in which it was possible to recover the land from the person who had fraudulently brought about the deprivation. In this case, the plaintiff company brought an action against the Registrar in which it claimed damages, a declaration and cancellation of the certificate of title issued to R, alleging that R had fraudulently caused the company's land to be transferred to himself and that the Registrar had been negligent and in breach of her statutory duty. The Jamaican Court of Appeal held that the action against the Registrar was misconceived since:

(i) by s 158, in an action for the recovery of land from a person registered as proprietor, the court may direct the Registrar to cancel or correct any certificate of title or any entry in the register;[56] the section clearly empowered the court to grant the remedies of declaration and cancellation of certificate of title sought in the instant case, and there was no need for the Registrar to be a party to the suit;

(ii) by s 164, the company was not entitled to bring an action against the Registrar as nominal defendant because it was possible to sue R, the registered proprietor, who was the person who had allegedly deprived the company of the land, and R had in fact been sued; and

(iii) by s 162, where fraud is alleged and the recovery of the land is not possible, the person deprived of such land may bring an action for damages against the Registrar only where the person against whom the fraud is alleged is dead or bankrupt or cannot be found, which was not so in the present case. Further, by s 165, an application in writing to the Registrar for compensation is a condition precedent to the commencement of proceedings for the recovery of damages against the Registrar pursuant to ss 162 and 164 and, by s 166, a notice in writing of such action must be served on the Registrar as nominal defendant at least one month before the commencement of the action.

55 (2005) Court of Appeal, Jamaica, Civ App No 9 of 2003. See also *Attorney General v International Trust Ltd* (2009) Court of Appeal, Jamaica, Civ App No 16 of 2008.

56 Cf Land Registration Act 1984, s 98(1) (St Lucia). See *Heirs of Hamilton La Force v Attorney General* [1996] ECLR 246.

APPENDIX 1

GLOSSARY OF LEGAL TERMS IN PROPERTY LAW

Absolute: not conditional or determinable (in relation to estates)
Advancement: (i) gift by parent or husband to provide for child or wife; (ii) power of trustee to advance capital to a beneficiary
Alienation: the act of disposing of or transferring property by sale or gift
Appurtenant: attached to land by act of the parties
Assignment: a transfer, eg of a lease
Beneficial owner/beneficiary: a person entitled for his/her own benefit and not, eg, as a trustee
Bona vacantia: goods without an owner
***Cestui que trust*:** a beneficiary under a trust
Charge: an incumbrance securing the payment of money (similar to a mortgage)
Chattel(s): tangible personal property, goods
Chattel real: leasehold interest
Chose in action: an intangible right in personal property (eg company shares, copyright, trade mark) enforceable by court action
Codicil: a supplementary will
Collaterals: blood relations who are neither ancestors nor descendants
Condition precedent: a condition which must be fulfilled before a grant or disposition can take effect
Condition subsequent: a condition which may defeat a grant after it has taken effect (a grant 'cut short in mid-flight')
Constructive: inferred or implied
Contingent: operative only on the occurrence of a future, uncertain event
Conveyance: a deed transferring land
Corporeal: capable of physical possession
Covenant: a promise contained in a deed
Deed: a document signed, sealed and delivered
Demise: a transfer, usually by the grant of a lease (not to be confused with 'death' of a person)
Determine: terminate, come to an end
Devise: a gift of land by will
Disseisin: dispossession of land
Distrain, Distress: the lawful seizure of a tenant's chattels for arrears of rent
Dominant tenement: land to which the benefit of an easement is attached
Easement: a right over land for the benefit of neighbouring land (eg a right of way)
Effluxion of time: expiration of a lease for a fixed term through the passage of time
Ejectment: legal action for the recovery of land
Emblements: growing crops which an outgoing tenant may take
Entail: an estate or interest descending only to the issue (ie children and grand-children) of the grantee
Equity of redemption: the sum total of a mortgagor's rights over mortgaged property

Escheat: the Crown's (State's) right to ownerless real property
Estate: (i) the extent of an interest in land measured by its duration; (ii) an area of land; (iii) the whole of the property owned by a deceased person
Estate contract: a contract for the sale or lease of land
Estoppel: prohibition of a party from denying facts which he/she has led another to assume to be true
Estovers: wood which a tenant may take for domestic and other purposes
Executors: persons appointed by a testator to administer his estate
Fee simple: the largest freehold estate, equivalent to absolute ownership
Fee tail: [same as 'entail']
Freehold: an estate of uncertain maximum duration; ie fee simple, fee tail, life estate (nowadays treated as synonymous with a fee simple)
Hereditaments: inheritable rights in property
Incorporeal: not capable of physical possession
Incumbrance: a liability burdening land (eg, mortgage, restrictive covenant)
Intestacy: the failure to dispose of property by will
Jus utendi, jus fruendi, jus abutendi: the rights to use, to enjoy the fruits, and to alienate land
Lapse: failure of a gift, especially by the beneficiary predeceasing the testator
Letters of administration: authorisation to administer the estate of a deceased person who has not appointed an executor
Licence: a permission to enter on land
Lien: a form of security for unpaid money
Limitation of actions: the statutory barring of rights of action after a period of years
Limited owner: an owner with an estate less than a fee simple
Mesne: middle, intermediate
Mortgage: transfer of property as security for a loan
Notice: actual or presumed knowledge
Parol: by word of mouth, oral
Periodic tenancy: a tenancy from year to year, month to month, week to week
Personal representatives: executors or administrators of a deceased's estate
Possibility of reverter: the grantor's right to the land when a determinable fee determines
Prescription: the acquisition of easements or profits by long user
Pur autre vie: an estate for the life of another person
Remainder: the interest of a grantee subject to a prior life interest
Restrictive covenant: a covenant restricting or limiting the use of land
Reversion: the interest remaining in a grantor after granting a lesser estate (eg, the fee simple owner's reversion where he has granted a lease or life estate)
Right of re-entry: the right to regain possession of land following occurrence of a condition subsequent or a breach of covenant
Root of title: a document from which ownership of land is traced
Seisin: the possession of land by a freeholder
Servient tenement: land burdened by an easement or restrictive covenant
Settlement: a trust for persons in succession (eg, 'upon trust for for X for life, remainder to Y and Z absolutely)
Severance: the conversion of a joint tenancy into a tenancy in common
Socage: freehold tenure involving agricultural services

Squatter: a person wrongfully occupying land and claiming title to it
Subinfeudation: alienation of land by creating a new tenure
Substitution: alienation of land by outright transfer
***Sui juris*:** of full age and capacity
Survivorship: a surviving joint tenant's right to the entire property
Tenure: the holding of land in return for certain services
Term of years: lease for a fixed period
Terra nullius: uninhabited land
Time immemorial: dating from the year 1189
Title: the evidence of a person's right to property
Undivided share: the interest of a tenant in common
User: the use or enjoyment of land
Vested: unconditionally owned (ie, not contingent on a future uncertain event)
Volunteer: a person who has not given value for property
Waiver: the abandonment of a legal right
Waste (voluntary, equitable, permissive): a tenant's obligations not to damage or destroy property or allow it to fall into disrepair

APPENDIX 2

SAMPLE PROPERTY SALE AGREEMENT

AGREEMENT FOR SALE OF PROPERTY OF
[PROPERTY ADDRESS]

DATE: the_________ day of _________, **[2005]**.
PARTIES:

1 **[name of seller]** of **[address of seller]** in the Island of Trinidad ('the Vendors'); and

2 **[name of buyer]** of **[address of buyer]** in the Island of Trinidad ('the Purchaser').

THE PROPERTY:

The Vendors are possessed of the Freehold Hereditaments ('the Property') described in the Schedule hereto.

OPERATIVE PROVISIONS:

SALE OF PROPERTY:

(1) The Vendors shall sell and the Purchaser shall buy the Property on the following terms and conditions.

PURCHASE PRICE AND MANNER OF PAYMENT:

(2) The Purchase consideration for the Property shall be **$[purchase price]** payable as follows:

A deposit of **$[amount of deposit]** ('the Deposit') shall be paid on or before the signing of this agreement, the receipt of which the Vendors hereby acknowledge.

The balance of **$[balance of purchase price]** shall be paid on the date set for Completion in clause 3.

In this Agreement time shall be of the essence of the contract but no party shall be entitled to pursue its remedies upon a default unless and until it has given the other party not less than ten (10) days' notice to remedy the default.

This Agreement shall not become effective unless and until it is signed by both parties and the Deposit had been paid to the Vendors.

This Agreement is not a deed and has not been executed by the parties to it as a deed.

COMPLETION:

(3) Completion shall take place not later than____________________day of _______________________**[2005]**, ('the Completion Date') at the offices of _______________________Attorneys for the Purchaser.

(4) At Completion:

(a) the Purchaser shall pay to the Vendors the balance of the purchase price in the sum of **$[balance of purchase price]**;

(b) vacant possession of the Property shall be given to the Purchaser; and

(c) the Vendors will execute a Deed or Memorandum (as appropriate) in favour of the Purchaser or the Purchaser's nominee transferring ownership in the Property to the Purchaser or as the Purchaser shall direct. That document will be prepared and perfected by the Purchaser's Attorney-at-Law.

FEES COSTS AND CHARGES:

(5) The Vendors shall bear costs for the preparation stamping and registration of the Releases/Discharges in respect of all existing mortgages or other encumbrances over the Property.

(6) The Purchaser shall bear the costs for:

(a) the preparation of this Agreement;

(b) the investigating and reporting on the title to the Property;

(c) the preparation and registration of the Deed or Memorandum referred to in 4(c); and

(d) all stamp duty, registration and other incidental charges.

CONDITIONS OF SALE:

(7) This contract shall be subject to and conditional upon:

(a) the Vendors showing a good and marketable title to the Property free from all encumbrances, to the satisfaction of the Purchaser's Attorney-at-Law;

(b) the Vendors:

(i) obtaining all consents required to transfer the Property (if any);

(ii) settling all rates, taxes, assessments, rents, charges and other outgoings for the Property up to the Completion Date;

(iii) obtaining a clearance certificate to be issued by the Water and Sewerage Authority; and

(iv) producing receipts or adducing satisfactory evidence to assure the Purchaser that the said charges have been paid and everything in this regard is properly in order; and

(c) the Vendors providing the Purchaser's Attorney-at-Law with:

(i) the Releases/Discharges of all existing mortgages on the Property;

(ii) the redemption statement from each mortgagee indicating the amount due to effect the Releases/Discharges; and

(iii) a copy of the invoice for the legal charges payable on each Release/Discharge or a receipt for payment of same; and

(iv) a copy of the consent/s in writing to the sale of the Property to the Purchaser.

REPRESENTATIONS AND WARRANTIES OF THE VENDORS:

(8) The Vendors hereby represent and warrant to the Purchaser that:

(a) they are the owners of and have title and power to sell the Property and that all information supplied by them is accurate in all respects;

(b) as at the Completion Date, there are no liens, judgments, mortgages, charges or other encumbrances on the Property or material to its title; and

(c) as at the Completion Date, the Property is in the same condition it was in at the date of this Agreement (fair wear and tear excepted).

(9) At least one week prior to the Completion Date, the Vendors will provide reasonable access to the Purchaser for the purpose of allowing the Purchaser to inspect the Property.

(10) The Vendors undertake to do all such acts and things and to execute all such deeds and documents as may be necessary fully and effectively to vest the Property in the Purchaser free from all charges, liens and other adverse interests.

(11) The Vendors acknowledge that the Purchaser has entered into this Agreement in reliance on the above representations and warranties. The Vendors undertake to disclose forthwith in writing to the Purchaser or his Attorney-at-Law any matter that may arise or become known to them that is inconsistent with any of the representations or warranties herein or which is material to be known by a purchaser for value in respect of the Property.

FORFEITURE OF DEPOSIT AND RESALE ON PURCHASER'S DEFAULT:

(12) If for any reason, not being the fault or responsibility of the Vendors, the Purchaser fails to complete the purchase by the Completion Date or is otherwise unable to fulfil the terms and conditions of this Agreement, the Vendors' sole and exclusive remedy shall be to rescind this Agreement and the Purchaser's Deposit shall be forfeited.

PURCHASER'S REMEDIES:

(13) If the Vendors fail to complete the sale by the Completion date the Purchaser shall have a right of action for specific performance and/or damages for breach of contract.

(14) The Purchaser shall be entitled at his option to rescind this Agreement in any of the following cases:
   (a) if the title of the Property is found to be defective and as a consequence the Vendors are unable to complete the sale by the Completion Date; and
   (b) if the Vendors for any reason fail, refuse or are unable to complete the sale by the Completion date.

(15) In the event that the Purchaser exercises his option under clause (14) to rescind the agreement, he shall be entitled to an immediate refund of the Deposit (together with interest on the Deposit at 10% per annum from the date of this Agreement to the date the refund is received by the Purchaser). The Vendors shall also reimburse the Purchaser the costs incurred by the Purchaser in investigating the title to the Property and conducting a valuation thereon (if a valuation was done at the Purchaser's expense), and any other costs and expenses reasonably incurred by the Purchaser in the course of his proposed purchase of the Property.

(16) The above provisions are without prejudice to any other right or remedy lawfully available to the Purchaser.

ADMINISTRATIVE AND MISCELLANEOUS PROVISIONS:

ASSIGNS AND SUCCESSORS:

(17) This Agreement shall be binding upon and enure to the benefit of the parties and their respective heirs, administrators, successors and assigns.

ENTIRE AGREEMENT AND VARIATIONS:

(18) This agreement constitutes the entire agreement between the parties. Each party confirms that he has not relied upon any representation not recorded in this document inducing him to enter into this Agreement.

(19) No variation of these terms and conditions will be valid unless confirmed in writing by authorised signatories of both parties on or after the date of this Agreement.

(20) The Parties hereto have read, agreed and understood the terms and conditions of this Agreement before appending their respective signatures.

SEVERABILITY:

(21) If any of the provisions of this Agreement is judicially or otherwise held illegal, invalid or unenforceable, or if the parties mutually agree in writing to any variation or revision of this Agreement, the remainder of the Agreement and its application shall not be affected or prejudiced and it shall remain in full force and effect.

WAIVER:

(22) The waiver or forbearance or failure of a party in insisting on any one or more instances upon the performance provisions of this Agreement shall not be construed as a waiver or relinquishment of that party's rights to future performance of such provision, and the other party's obligations in respect of such future performance shall continue in full force and effect.

CHANGE OF ADDRESS:

(23) Each of the parties shall give notice to the other of change of any address or contact number as soon as practicable and in any event within 48 hours of such change or acquisition.

NOTICES:

(24) Without prejudice to the right to serve notices by other means, any notice under this Agreement shall be in writing.

(25) Unless otherwise expressly directed, all notices and other correspondence shall be sent to the addresses noted in this Agreement.

AGREEMENT TO CO-OPERATE:

(26) Each of the parties hereby undertakes to the other that he shall execute such further documents and perform such further acts and generally use their best endeavours in good faith to give full effect to the provisions of the Agreement.

INTERPRETATION:

(27) In this Agreement the singular shall include the plural and vice versa and words in the masculine shall include the feminine and neuter genders.

SCHEDULE

Address of Property:	**[address]**
Tenure:	Freehold
Description:	**[description]**

ALL AND SINGULAR

Made in Duplicate
Signed by the parties
the day and year first above written.

[name of seller]
Signature of Witness:..
Name of Witness:...
Occupation of Witness:..
Address of Witness:..
....
....
....

[name of buyer]
Signature of Witness:..
Name of Witness:...
Occupation of Witness:...
Address of Witness:..
....

APPENDIX 3

SAMPLE LEASE AGREEMENT

LEASE AGREEMENT

THIS AGREEMENT is made this__________day of__________, [2005], BETWEEN the Party described in Item 1 of the Schedule hereto (hereinafter called 'the Landlord') of the ONE PART and the Party described in Item 2 of the said Schedule (hereinafter called 'the Tenant') of the OTHER PART.

WHEREBY it is agreed as follows:

1 PREMISES AND LETTING: The Landlord lets and the Tenant takes the more particularly described in Item 3 of the said Schedule hereto (hereinafter called 'the rented premises').

2 TENANCY: The Landlord shall grant and the Tenant shall accept a lease of the rented premises for the term set out in Item 4 from the______ day of______[year] at the monthly rental set out at Item 5 of the Schedule and payable in a manner provided therein.

3 TENANT'S COVENANTS: The Tenant agrees:

(1) to pay the rent at the times hereinbefore mentioned;

(2) to pay a security deposit of **$[amount]** at the commencement of the term hereby created, to be held by the Landlord throughout the duration of the term of the tenancy for the purpose of defraying therefrom any expenses incurred or the costs of remedying any damage caused by the Tenant, for example damage to the rented premises, which the Tenant has been requested but has failed to make good. If the Tenant defrays all expenses incurred by her and has performed all and singular her obligations hereunder at the end of the term of the tenancy, then the said security deposit will be returned to the Tenant at the end of the said term, free of interest;

(3) to keep and maintain the interior of the rented premises including all windows, walls, electrical and sanitary

equipment, water apparatus, drains, fittings, carpets, furniture and fixtures, gardens and fences in a good and tenantable state of repair and condition and shall apply at least one coat of paint to the interior walls on the termination of this tenancy;

(4) to rectify any damage done by her, her agents, employees or servants to the rented premises;

(5) to pay all costs of electrical power, gas, water and telephone bills that may accrue during the tenure and not to cause any of these services to be discontinued for non-payment of bills;

(6) not, without the written consent of the Landlord, to make or cause to be made any structural alterations or additions to the rented premises;

(7) not to assign, sublet or part with the possession of the rented premises or any part thereof without the written consent of the Landlord;

(8) to use the rented premises as a private residence only;

(9) to have insects exterminated from the rented premises during the term of the lease or any renewal thereof;

(10) to permit the Landlord, his agents, servants, and/or workmen to enter the rented premises at any reasonable hour during the day for the purpose of periodical inspection and to effect necessary repairs upon giving three (3) days' written notice of such intention; and

(11) to yield up the premises with all fixtures, carpets (other than Tenant's fixtures) and additions at the expiration or sooner determination of the tenancy, in good and tenantable repair.

4 THE LANDLORD'S COVENANTS: The Landlord hereby covenants with the Tenant as follows:

(1) to insure and keep insured the rented premises during the existence of this Agreement;

(2) to pay all property tax imposed in respect of the rented premises; and

(3) to keep and maintain the foundations, roof, ceilings, walls, beams and other structural parts of the building(s) in the rented premises and all fixtures and integral parts thereof in good condition and in proper state of repair.

5 MUTUAL AGREEMENTS: It is mutually agreed that in the event that fire, riot, civil commotion, Act of God or the Queen's enemies shall render the rented premises unfit for use as a private residence, then the tenancy hereby created shall forthwith cease. Should the rented premises be rendered only partially unfit for use, then the rent shall abate in proportion to the damage done until the premises are restored as originally let.

6 OPTION TO RENEW: If the Tenant shall be desirous of continuing the tenancy hereby created for a further term of three (3) years as from the expiration of the term hereby granted and shall give two (2) months' notice prior to the expiration of this Lease to the Landlord of such desire and there shall not at the time of such request be any existing breach or non-observance of any of the covenants herein contained on the part of the Tenant, then the Landlord may grant the Tenant a further term of three (3) years subject in all respect to the same conditions and stipulations as are herein contained, save and except this clause for renewal, at an increased rent in keeping with the market rental prevailing at that date.

7 POSSESSION: The Tenant observing the terms of this Agreement shall have quiet and peaceable enjoyment of the rented premises free from any interruption from the Landlord or any person or persons rightfully claiming under or in trust for him.

8 FORFEITURE: If any rent shall be thirty (30) days or more in arrears (whether lawfully demanded or not) or if the Tenant shall omit to perform or observe any stipulation contained in this Agreement after receiving not less than thirty (30) days' previous written notice specifying such omission

or non-observance, the Landlord, or any person duly authorised by him, may re-enter upon and take possession of the Leased Premises: upon such re-entry the tenancy shall absolutely determine but without prejudice to the other rights and remedies of the Landlord.

9 COSTS: The legal cost of preparation of this Agreement and stamp duty payable thereon shall be borne by the Landlord and Tenant in equal shares.

SCHEDULE

ITEM 1: **[name of Landlord]**

ITEM 2: **[name of Tenant]**

ITEM 3: **[description of premises]**

ITEM 4: A term of three (3) years commencing on the______day of___ ____, [2010], renewable by giving two (2) months' notice.

ITEM 5: FOUR THOUSAND DOLLARS ($4,000.00) payable in advance on or before the first day of each month.

AS WITNESS the hands of the parties hereinbefore mentioned.

[signatures of the parties]

APPENDIX 4

SAMPLE MEMORANDUM OF MORTGAGE

(under Real Property Ordinance, Ch 27, No 11)

WHEREAS **[name of proprietor]** of **[address of proprietor]** in the Island of Trinidad is registered as Proprietor of an estate in fee simple (hereinafter called 'the Landowner') subject however to such mortgages and encumbrances as are notified by memorial underwritten or endorsed herein in the parcel of land described in the Schedule hereto.

AND WHEREAS **[name of borrower]** of **[address of borrower]** in the Island of Trinidad (hereinafter referred to as 'the Borrower') has requested the **[name of mortgagee bank]**, a Company duly incorporated in Trinidad and Tobago with its registered office situate at **[address of mortgagee bank]** in the Island of Trinidad (hereinafter called 'the Bank', to make and/or continue to make advances and/or give and/or continue to give accommodation to me and/or other persons as the Bank may hereafter in its discretion and, if and so long as it shall think fit to do so, and/or continue to make advances and/or give accommodation to me and/or other persons in compliance with such request upon having the same and such other monies and liabilities as are hereinafter mentioned secured to it in manner hereafter appearing.

NOW THEREFORE I, the Borrower aforesaid, in pursuance and in consideration of the premises do hereby jointly and severally covenant with the Bank that I shall pay to the Bank on demand in writing the balance which on my account with the Bank shall for the time being (and whether on or at any time after such demand) be due and owing to the Bank by either solely or jointly with any other persons firms or companies, and whether as principal or surety for or in respect of bills or notes discounted or paid or other lands payments credit or advances on banking account or otherwise made to or on account of or for the accommodation of or at my request or for interest discount commission or other lawful charges in respect of any of the matters aforesaid or for keeping my account, and will thereupon also retire all bills or notes that may for the time being be under discount with the Bank and which I am party to either as drawer acceptor, maker or indorser without any deduction whatsoever.

AND I the Borrower do hereby further covenant with the Bank that I will at all times hereafter during the continuance of this security pay and discharge all rates, charges and assessments that shall become due, payable or imposed on or in respect of the said lands and all of the buildings thereon, and will also keep and maintain all of the said buildings in good, complete and substantial repair and condition and will at all reasonable times allow and permit the Bank and its agents and servants to enter into and upon the said lands and buildings thereon and to view and inspect the state and condition thereof, and if when required will repair and remedy any defects that may be found therein, and also will insure and keep all of the said buildings insured against loss or damage by fire (and during war if possible against loss or damage by aircraft or arising out of aerial warfare or if the Bank shall think necessary by bombardment by hostile guns not landed on the Island of Trinidad) in its proper values in some insurance office approved of by and in the name of the Bank, and will pay the premiums in respect of such insurance as and when the same shall become due and payable, and will on demand produce to the Bank the policy or policies of such insurance and the receipt for every such premium, AND in case I shall at any time refuse neglect or omit to pay such rates, taxes, charges or assessments as aforesaid and/or keep and/or maintain all such buildings in good and substantial repair and condition and/or to remedy when required by the Bank any defect that may be found therein and/or pay any premium upon any such policy of insurance as aforesaid, it shall be lawful but not obligatory upon the Bank to pay the said rates, taxes, charges and assessments and/or put all such buildings in good and substantial repair and condition and/or to remedy any defect that may be found therein, and/or to pay any premium that may be due upon any such policy of insurance as aforesaid, and all monies that the Bank shall disburse for any of the purposes aforesaid shall be chargeable to me with interest at the rate for the time being charged on the account with the Bank for which I am liable.

PROVIDED ALWAYS AND IT IS HEREBY AGREED AND DECLARED THAT:

(i) A demand for payment or any other notice under this security may be made by any Manager or Officer of the Bank by letter sent by post addressed to or in care of me at the address above given at my last known place of abode or business in the Island of Trinidad, and every demand or notice so made shall be deemed to have been made or given on the date after the letter is posted.

(ii) This Security shall be a continuing security of the Bank notwithstanding any settlement of account or other matter or thing whatsoever and shall prejudice or affect any security that may have been created by any deposit of title deeds and other documents that may have been made with the Bank prior to the execution hereof relating to all or any other premises or any other security that the Bank may now or at any time hereafter hold in respect of the monies hereby secured or any of them or part thereof respectively.

(iii) The Bank shall be at liberty from time to time to give time for payment of any bills of exchange promissory notes or other securities that may have been discounted for or received on account from me on which I shall or may be liable thereon or thereto as the Bank in its absolute discretion shall think fit without releasing me or affecting any liability under these presents.

(iv) All costs, charges and expenses properly incurred herein or by exercise of any of the powers hereunder by the Bank and all other monies properly paid by the Bank in respect of the said costs, charges and expenses or otherwise together with interest thereon aforesaid shall be charges on all of the premiums hereby mortgaged or charged, provided that the charge hereby conferred shall be in addition and without prejudice to any and every other remedy, lien or security that the Bank may or, but for the said charge, would have for the monies hereby secured or any part thereof.

(v) No lease or tenancy made by me during the continuance of this security of the lands, buildings or premises hereby mortgaged or charged or any part thereof shall have effect by force or virtue of any statute unless the Bank shall consent thereto in writing.

(vi) The statutory power of sale conferred upon mortgagees by the Conveyancing and Law of Property Ordinance, Chapter 27, Number 12, shall apply to this security but without the restrictions therein contained as to giving notice or otherwise and so that for the purpose of exercising the said power of sale the mortgage monies hereby secured shall be deemed to have become due and payable immediately upon the execution of these presents, but as between the Bank and me the Bank shall not exercise the said power of sale until the payment of the monies hereby secured has been demanded and default has been made in paying the same, but this provision is for the protection only of myself and shall not affect a purchaser or put him upon enquiry whether such default has been made. The statutory power to appoint a receiver may be exercised at any time after the payment of monies hereby secured has been demanded and default has been made in paying the same. The Bank shall be entitled to retain possession of the Certificates of Title and/or Crown Grants for the parcels of land hereby charged so mortgaged until payment of the mortgage only and all interest hereby secured. The provisions of section 35 of the Conveyancing and Law of Property Ordinance, Chapter 27, Number 12 restricting the right of consolidation of the Bank shall not apply to this security.

(vii) The Landowner hereby attorns and becomes tenant at will of the Bank of the said parcel of land described in the Schedule hereto at a peppercorn rent during the continuance of this security, but nothing in this clause contained shall prevent the Bank from any time entering on and taking possession of the said parcel of land and so determining the tenancy, but neither the tenancy created nor the receipt of the said rent shall render the Bank liable as mortgagee in possession.

(viii) And for the better securing to the Bank the repayment in the manner aforesaid of the said principal sum and interest, I the registered proprietor hereby mortgage to the Bank all my estate and interest in the said parcel of land described in the Schedule hereto.

(ix) The Borrower shall carry on its/his business properly and efficiently and in compliance with all applicable laws.

IN WITNESS WHEREOF We have hereunto subscribed our names this______ day of______in the Year of Our Lord 20__.

THE SCHEDULE HEREIN REFERRED TO:

[Description of the land]

[Signatures of the parties]

APPENDIX 5

SAMPLE MORTGAGE BY CHARGE

THIS DEED OF CHARGE by way of Legal Mortgage is made the______day of______2005.

BETWEEN______AB______of______in the parish of______in Barbados (hereinafter called "the Mortgagor") of the **ONE PART** and XYZ Ltd, having its registered office at______which has been licensed in accordance with the provisions of the Financial Institutions Act 1996-16 of the Laws of Barbados (hereinafter called "the Mortgagee") of the **OTHER PART**.

WHEREAS the Mortgagor is the estate owner of the fee simple absolute in possession in the property described in the First Schedule hereto subject only as is stipulated in the Second Schedule hereto but otherwise free from incumbrances.

AND WHEREAS the Mortgagor is entitled to the Policy of Assurance the particulars of which are set out in the Third Schedule hereto.

AND WHEREAS the Mortgagor intends to construct a dwelling house on the property described in the First Schedule hereto (hereinafter called "the building works") in accordance with the drawings and specifications which have been lodged with and approved by the Mortgagee.

AND WHEREAS the mortgagor has obtained all necessary planning approval and the other consents in respect of the building works.

AND WHEREAS the Mortgagor has applied to the Mortgagee for a loan of______for the purpose of refinancing an existing land loan and providing funds to assist with the construction of a house at______as described in the First Schedule hereto which the Mortgagee has consented to make upon having the repayment thereof secured in manner hereinafter appearing and upon the terms and conditions herein contained and hereunder implied.

NOW THIS DEED WITNESSETH as follows:

1. In this mortgage:

"Appropriate rate" means the sum of______per centum per annum calculated on the basis of annual rests or such increased or reduced rate of interest as may from time to time be in force under a variation notice given by the Mortgagee to the Mortgagor as hereinafter provided;

"Building" shall include boundary walls gates and fences;

"Principal sum" means the moneys lent and advanced by the Mortgagee to the Mortgagor and secured by this mortgage;

"Policies of Assurance" where the context so admits and/or requires means and/or includes the Policy or Policies of Life Assurance the particulars of which are set out in the Second Schedule hereto and/or any policy or policies substituted for the same as hereinafter provided;

"Variation notice" means a notice given as herein provided to vary the rate of interest payable;

The masculine gender includes the feminine and the singular includes the plural and vice versa;

Whenever an obligation under this mortgage is enforceable against two or more persons the liability of such persons shall be joint and several;

All references to dollars and cents shall be to the currency of Barbados.

The provisions and definitions contained in or implied by the Property Act Chapter 236 of the Laws of Barbados shall apply and extend to this mortgage subject to any expressed provisions to the contrary herein contained.

2. In pursuance of the said recited agreement and in consideration of the principal sum of______lent and advanced to the Mortgagor by the Mortgagee (the receipt whereof is hereby acknowledged by the Mortgagor) the Mortgagor hereby covenants with the Mortgagee;

(1) to pay to the Mortgagee interest at the appropriate rate on the principal sum such interest to accrue from day to day;

(2) to pay to the Mortgagee such interest on the principal sum from the______ day of______;

(3) to pay to the Mortgagee the principal sum and interest thereon by **Two hundred and forty (240)** monthly instalments of______each (or such other monthly instalments as may from time to time be payable in accordance with the provisions herein contained) on the last day of the month following the month referred to in sub-clause (2) hereof and continuing on the last day of each succeeding month thereafter until the principal sum with all interest thereon at the appropriate rate and all other moneys hereby secured have been paid in full; And it is hereby agreed that such instalments shall be applied first in payment of interest on the amount of the principal sum remaining owing immediately before the payment of each such instalment and then in reduction of the principal sum;

(4) that notwithstanding the provisions of sub-clauses (1), (2) and (3) of this clause the principal sum and all the interest thereon and all other moneys owing hereunder shall become immediately due and payable by the Mortgagors to the Mortgagee in any of the following events:

(a) if default is made for a period of fourteen days (as to which time shall be of the essence) in the payment of any instalment or interest or other sum of money payable to the Mortgagee under these presents (whether or not notice requiring payment thereof shall have been served upon the Mortgagors);

(b) if the Mortgagor fails to perform or observe any expressed or implied covenant agreement or obligation on the part of the Mortgagor contained or implied in these presents;

(c) if the Mortgagor commits any act of bankruptcy or makes any assignment for the benefit of or enters into any arrangement or composition with the Mortgagor's creditors;

(d) if the Mortgagor shall sell or otherwise dispose of (otherwise than by testamentary disposition) the property or any part thereof without the prior written consent of the Mortgagee or if the property or any part thereof shall be compulsorily purchased acquired or requisitioned;

(e) if any other creditor shall proceed against the property.

(1) The Mortgagee may from time to time in writing at the absolute discretion of the Mortgagee permit the Mortgagor to repay principal and interest by

instalments other than those herein provided for the payment of any money hereby secured or with the approval of the Mortgagor generally make such other arrangements as to the mode and time of payment of any money (whether principal interest or otherwise) as the Mortgagee may think fit Provided that no such arrangement shall affect the power of sale and other powers hereby or by any statute conferred on the Mortgagee or render the Mortgagee liable in damages or otherwise for the exercise of any such power in any case where if the arrangement had not been made no such liability would have arisen.

(2) Notwithstanding anything to the contrary hereinbefore contained for payment of the principal sum and interest if there shall then be no subsisting breach of any covenant agreement stipulation or condition herein contained or hereunder implied on the part of the Mortgagor to be observed or performed and subject to the Mortgagor making the payment mentioned in one of the next succeeding sub-clauses hereof the Mortgagor shall be at liberty to repay to the Mortgagee on the last day of any month the whole or a portion of the principal sum hereby secured not being less than Five thousand dollars ($5,000.00) or any multiple thereof at anyone time subject to the following conditions:

(a) In the case of a repayment of the whole or a portion of the principal sum at any time during the first five years from the date of this mortgage the Mortgagor shall pay to the Mortgagee a sum equal to six months' interest on the principal money so repaid together with a further sum by way of penalty computed at the rate of One (1) per cent per annum on the principal money so repaid; or

(b) In the case of a repayment of the whole or a portion of the principal sum at any time during the next five succeeding years thereafter the Mortgagor shall pay to the Mortgagee a sum equal to six months' interest on the principal money so repaid; or

(c) In the case of a repayment of the whole or a portion of the principal sum at any time thereafter the Mortgagor shall pay to the Mortgagee a sum equal to three months' interest on the principal money so repaid.

3. In further pursuance of the said agreement and for the consideration aforesaid the Mortgagor as Mortgagor and as beneficial owner hereby **MORTGAGES** the estate in fee simple absolute in possession of the Mortgagor in **ALL THAT** the property described in the First Schedule hereto to the Mortgagee with the payment in accordance with the covenants herein contained or implied of the principal sum interest and other moneys hereby expressly or impliedly covenanted to be paid by the Mortgagor.

4. In further pursuance of the said recited agreement and for the consideration aforesaid the Mortgagor as Mortgagor and as beneficial owner hereby **ASSIGNS TRANSFERS and SETS OVER** unto the Mortgagee **ALL THOSE** the Policies of Assurance the particulars of which are contained in the Second Schedule hereto and all moneys including bonuses accrued and to accrue hereafter which shall be payable under the said Policies **TO HOLD** the said Policies and moneys unto the Mortgagee by way of legal mortgage and charged with the payment of the principal sum and interest thereon and all other moneys hereby covenanted to be paid by the Mortgagor.

5. The Mortgagor hereby covenants with the Mortgagee in manner following that is to say:
   (1) That during the continuance of this security the Mortgagor will keep the buildings subject hereto insured in his names against loss or damage under a full comprehensive policy from such risks as may be required by the Mortgagee under a policy of insurance to the full insurable value thereof and will cause the interest of the Mortgagee to be noted on the said policy and will duly pay all premiums payable for those purposes and immediately deliver to the Mortgagee the said policy or policies of such insurance respectively and on the day each premium becomes due produce the receipt for each payment. And that if the Mortgagor shall make default in any of the above matters the Mortgagee may in its absolute discretion insure and keep insured all or any of the said buildings in manner aforesaid and it is hereby agreed and declared that all moneys received under or by virtue of any such insurance as aforesaid shall at the option of the Mortgagee either be forthwith applied in or towards substantially rebuilding reinstating or repairing the buildings destroyed or damaged or in or towards payment of the moneys for the time being secured by this mortgage including any premiums paid under the aforesaid power and that the Mortgagor will hold any moneys received by the Mortgagor under any such insurance as aforesaid in trust for the Mortgagee and for any of the purposes mentioned in this sub-clause.
   (2) That the Mortgagor will give to the Mortgagee such particulars relating to the buildings subject hereto or any part thereof and such assistance as the Mortgagee shall require for the purpose of effectuating any such insurance as aforesaid.
   (3) That if the Mortgagee shall give to the Mortgagor particulars of any insurance effected by the Mortgagee in respect of any buildings subject hereto then and in such event the Mortgagor will not while such insurance remains in force except with the written consent of the Mortgagee effect or keep in force any other policy insuring the same building or any part thereof against the same risks.
   (4) That the Mortgagor will immediately inform the Mortgagee of any circumstances which may affect the validity of and/or the premium payable under any policy of insurance.
   (5) That during the continuance of this security the Mortgagor shall and will keep all buildings subject hereto in good and substantial repair and condition and permit the Mortgagee and the agents of the Mortgagee at all reasonable times during the day time and without any further consent to enter into and upon the property subject hereto and inspect the same and view the state thereof and upon receipt of notice in writing from the Mortgagee immediately to remedy restore repair amend and make good all such defects decays wants of reparation amendment and upkeep of the property subject hereto as the Mortgagee may require and if the Mortgagor shall neglect to do so the Mortgagee may at the discretion of the Mortgagee enter upon the property from time to time in order to repair and keep in repair the same and without thereby becoming liable as a Mortgagee in possession.

(6) Not without the written consent of the Mortgagee first had and obtained to mortgage, charge or otherwise encumber, let lease or part with possession of the property.

(7) Not without the written consent of the Mortgagee first had and obtained to make or permit or suffer to be made any material change or addition whatsoever to the property subject hereto or the use thereof.

(8) Not without the written consent of the Mortgagee first had and obtained to use or occupy or permit to be used or occupied the property or any part thereof otherwise than for the purpose of a dwelling house.

(9) Not to do or permit or suffer to be done or permitted anything in consequence whereof the property may in any way deteriorate or lessen in value or any policy of insurance effected in pursuance of the provisions of this mortgage be avoided or the amount of any premium payable for any such policy of insurance be increased.

(10) Punctually to pay all rates assessments charges taxes and other outgoings in respect of the property.

(11) To comply with all enactments and regulations under the Town and Country Planning Act Chapter 240 of the Laws of Barbados for the time being in force and with all by-laws whether under that Act or any other legislation which may affect the property from time to time.

(12) To comply with the provisions of the Landlord and Tenant (Registration of Tenancies) Act Chapter 230A of the Laws of Barbados or any amendment thereto, or any Act in substitution thereof in the event of the property being let.

(13) Immediately on receipt of any notice order or similar matter affecting or likely to affect the property whether sent to the Mortgagors by a competent authority or any other person to notify the Mortgagee in writing of such receipt and send the same or a copy thereof to the Mortgagee and to supply to the Mortgagee all information within the possession of the Mortgagor relating to the matters mentioned or dealt with in such notice order or other similar matter and on the grant or issue of any permission consent licence or other document affecting the property to deliver the same to the Mortgagee to be kept with the deeds and documents of title relating to the property.

(14) That the said Policies of assurance are valid and that nothing shall be done or suffered whereby the Mortgagee may be prevented from receiving the moneys payable thereunder or any part thereof.

(15) That if the said Policies of Assurance shall become voidable or void the Mortgagor will forthwith at his own cost do all such things as may be necessary for keeping the same on foot (if only voidable) or for effecting or for enabling the Mortgagee to effect (as it is hereby authorised to do) a new policy on the Mortgagor's life (if it shall become void) for such sum as would have been payable under the Void policy if the life of the insured had ceased immediately before the same became void such policy or policies to be effected in the name of the Mortgagee or in such other name or names and in such insurance company or with such underwriters as the Mortgagee may direct.

(16) That every such new policy or policies and the moneys to be assured thereby shall be subject to this security and to the powers and provisions herein contained or implied by statute and applicable thereto as fully and to all intents as the said policy hereby assigned.

(17) That the Mortgagor will during the continuance of this security punctually pay all premiums for keeping on foot the said Policy of Assurance hereby assigned and/or any new or substituted policy or policies as aforesaid within fourteen days after the same shall from time to time fall due and will deliver the receipts for every such payment to the Mortgagee forthwith.

(18) If the Mortgagor shall at any time make default in payment of any of the premiums it shall be lawful for the Mortgagee to pay the same and any sums so paid or expended by the Mortgagee in effecting any new policy or policies in place of any policy or policies which may become void shall be repaid to the Mortgagee on demand and if not so repaid shall in the meantime be added to the principal sum for the time being owing on this security and bear interest accordingly at the appropriate rate from the time or respective times of payment and be charged upon the property and the Policies hereby assigned and upon every new policy or policies effected hereunder in the same manner as if they had originally formed part of the principal sum.

(19) To repay to the Mortgagee immediately on demand all money expended by the Mortgagee:

(a) in carrying out repairs to or work upon the property as authorised by this mortgage;

(b) in paying all charges in connection with any inspection of the property for the purposes of this mortgage or in connection with any further advance which the Mortgagor may have requested;

(c) in paying any assessments charges or outgoings which may be assessed charged or imposed upon or payable in respect of the property;

(d) in effecting any insurance policy on the buildings;

(e) in taking recovering and keeping possession of the property and generally in any other proceedings taken to realise the moneys hereby secured or in perfecting or protecting the security for the said moneys together with a proper allowance for the time and services of any person appointed by the Mortgagee and all Attorneys-at-Law and agent's charges and commissions for or in respect of the collection of any overdue interest principal sum insurance premiums taxes and/or any other moneys whatsoever payable by the Mortgagor hereunder and in relation to any other matter hereunder whether any action or other judicial proceeding to enforce such payment has been taken or not.

(20) That all money expended by the Mortgagee as aforesaid shall unless it is repaid within fourteen days after demand therefor (as to which time shall be of the essence) carry interest at the appropriate rate and shall be a charge on the property.

(21) That all money expended by the Mortgagee as aforesaid shall unless it is repaid within fourteen days after demand therefor (as to which time shall be of the essence) carry interest at the appropriate rate and shall be a charge on the property and the Policies of Assurance.

(22) That all water heaters television antennae electrical light fittings window blinds screen doors and windows storm doors and windows and air conditioning ventilating electrical plumbing cooling lighting and heating equipment now or hereafter in any way affixed annexed or attached whether permanently or otherwise to the property shall for all purposes of this mortgage form part of the said property.

6. It is hereby agreed and declared as follows:

(1) The Mortgagee may from time to time by notice in writing to the Mortgagor (hereinafter called "variation notice") increase or reduce the rate of interest payable hereunder and in this connection the following provisions shall apply and have effect:

(a) the rate of interest shall not be increased above the rate permitted by the Rate of Interest Act Chapter **316** of the Laws of Barbados and the regulations made thereunder or any Act or regulations amending or substituted for the same respectively;

(b) the rate of interest shall not be increased above the rate at which when the variation notice is given interest is currently charged on new advances made by the Mortgagee and which are of the same type as the advances secured by this mortgage;

(c) any variation in the rate of interest shall take effect from the date specified in the variation notice (which date in the case of an increase in the rate of interest shall not be earlier than one month after the date on which such notice is served on the Mortgagor) and from and after such date the increased or reduced rate of interest shall be payable;

(d) any variation notice shall specify an increased or reduced monthly instalment calculated in accordance with sub-clause 1 (b) hereof to be payable on each monthly instalment date after the date when the variation in the rate of interest is to take effect and in such event the increased or reduced monthly instalment shall be payable accordingly;

(e) if any variation notice shall stipulate a new rate of interest which is not acceptable to the Mortgagor the Mortgagor shall be at liberty to repay the outstanding balance due under this mortgage at the expiration of the variation notice upon giving to the Mortgagee written notice of such intention within thirty days of receipt of the Mortgagee's variation notice.

(2) The Mortgagee may at any time transfer this mortgage to any person and in such case the transferee shall have the benefit of all the covenants and provisions herein contained and may at any time thereafter exercise all the rights and remedies of the Mortgagee.

(3) All moneys payable hereunder by the Mortgagor to the Mortgagee shall be paid to the Mortgagee without any deductions whatsoever at the Mortgagee's principal place of business in Barbados or at such other

place in Barbados as the Mortgagee may from time to time designate for the purpose.

(4) Any notice hereunder shall be deemed to be duly served in the case of notice to the Mortgagor if it is addressed to the Mortgagor at and left at or posted by registered post to the property or the Mortgagor's last address known to the Mortgagee and in the case of notice to the Mortgagee if it is addressed to the Mortgagee at and left at or posted by registered post to the Mortgagee's principal place of business in Barbados or the place if any for the time being designated by the Mortgagee for the payment of moneys hereunder. Any such notice which is posted as aforesaid shall be deemed to have been served forty-eight hours after the posting thereof.

(5) No delay in exercising or omission to exercise any right power or remedy available to the Mortgagee upon any default under this mortgage shall impair such right power or remedy or be construed as a waiver thereof or as acquiescence in such default nor shall any act or omission of the Mortgagee in respect of any default or any acquiescence by the Mortgagee in any default affect or impair any right power or remedy of the Mortgagee in respect of any other default.

(6) All legal fees and expenses incurred in the preparation of this mortgage (including the Mortgagee's Attorneys-at-Law fees) shall be borne by the Mortgagor and may be deducted from the amount of the principal sum.

(7) The Mortgagor shall not be entitled to exercise any powers of leasing or accepting surrenders of leases given by statute in that behalf except with the consent in writing of the Mortgagee.

(8) If the Mortgagor shall pay to the Mortgagee the principal sum and interest hereby secured in accordance with the covenants hereinbefore contained and shall likewise pay to the Mortgagee on the day on which the same ought to be paid under the foregoing covenant in that behalf every further sum which may be advanced by the Mortgagee on behalf of the Mortgagor with interest at the appropriate rate the charge on the Policies of Assurance hereby created shall be discharged and the Mortgagee will thereafter at the request and cost of the Mortgagor reassign the Policies of Assurance to the Mortgagor or as the Mortgagor shall direct.

7. The provisions of any statute restricting the Mortgagee's right of consolidation shall not apply to this mortgage.

8. At any time after any moneys hereby secured shall have become payable the Mortgagee may by writing under the hand of an Attorney or Manager for the time being of the Mortgagee in the said Island of Barbados or any person authorised by anyone of them in writing appoint any person or persons (whether an officer of the Mortgagee or not) to be a receiver or receivers of the property hereby charged or any part thereof upon such terms as to remuneration or otherwise as the Mortgagee shall think fit and remove any receiver or receivers so appointed and appoint another or others in his or their place. Any receiver or receivers so appointed shall be deemed to be the agent of the Mortgagor (who shall alone be responsible for his or their acts or defaults and for his or their remuneration) and the Mortgagee and

any receiver so appointed shall have power at any time after the moneys hereby secured shall have become due and payable as aforesaid (and without obtaining any further consent of or giving any notice to the Mortgagor):

(a) to take possession of collect and get in any property (including any Policies of Assurance) hereby charged and for that purpose to take any proceedings in the name of the Mortgagor or otherwise as may seem expedient;
(b) to carry on manage or concur in carrying on and managing the property of the Mortgagor or any part thereof and for any of those purposes to raise or borrow any moneys that may be required upon the security of the whole or any part of the property or the Policies of Assurance hereby charged in priority to this mortgage or otherwise;
(c) to sell or concur in selling (but where necessary with the leave of the Court) and to let or concur in letting and to accept surrenders of leases or tenancies of all or any of the property or the Policies of Assurance hereby charged or mortgaged and to carry any such sale letting or surrender into effect by conveying leasing letting or accepting surrenders in the name and on behalf of the Mortgagors or other the estate owner. Any such sale may be for cash debentures or other obligations shares stock or other valuable consideration and may be payable in a lump sum or by instalments spread over such period as the receiver or receivers shall think fit;
(d) to make any arrangement or compromise which he or they shall think expedient;
(e) to make and effect all repairs renewals and any improvements of the Mortgagors' property and effects and to maintain or renew all insurances;
(f) to appoint managers agents officers servants and workmen for any of the aforesaid purposes at such salaries and for such periods as the receiver or receivers may determine; and
(g) to do all such other acts and things as may be considered to be incidental or conducive to any of the matters or powers aforesaid and which he or they lawfully may or can do as agent for the Mortgagors.

All moneys received by such receiver or receivers shall after providing for his or their remuneration and for all costs and expenses in carrying on the business of the Mortgagor or the sale or disposal of the whole or any part of the property or Policies of Assurance hereby charged or mortgaged be applied in providing for:

(a) all rents taxes rates assessments and outgoings whatever affecting the property or Policies of Assurance hereby charged;
(b) all annual sums or other payments and the interest on all principal sums (if any) having priority to this security;
(c) all premiums on the Policies of Assurance and on fire or other insurances and the cost of executing repairs renewals and improvements of the Mortgagor's property; and
(d) in or towards satisfaction of the money hereby secured and the receiver shall pay the residue (if any) of the moneys received by him to the Mortgagor.

9. The Mortgagor hereby irrevocably appoints the Mortgagee and any receiver or receivers appointed by the Mortgagee and the persons deriving title under them and their substitutes to be jointly and also severally the attorney and attorneys of the Mortgagor for them and in their name and on their behalf and as their act and deed or otherwise to sign seal and deliver and otherwise perfect any such legal or formal mortgage as aforesaid or (without executing any such mortgage) any deed assurance or act which may be required or may be required or may be deemed proper on any sale lease or disposition by the Mortgagee or by any such receiver or receivers as aforesaid of the said property the Policies of Assurance or any part thereof or any other property or assets of the Mortgagor under any power of sale leasing or other disposition applicable thereto.
10. The Mortgagor shall not during the continuance hereof have power to enter into agreements for leases or to accept or surrender the same without the written consent of the Mortgagee but it shall not be necessary to express such consent in any lease agreement or surrender.
11. The security hereby created is in addition to any other security or securities which the Mortgagee may now or from time to time hold or take from the Mortgagor.
12. The taking of a judgement or judgements on any covenant or covenants herein contained shall not operate as a merger of the said covenant or covenants or affect the Mortgagee's right to interest at the rate and time herein set forth.
13. And the Mortgagor hereby certifies as follows:
    (a) that the consideration stipulated in this mortgage represents the fair market value of the mortgage interest in the property which is hereby transferred;
    (b) that the Mortgagor is resident in Barbados for the purposes of the Exchange Control Act Chapter 71 of the Laws of Barbados; and
    (c) that this mortgage is security for moneys lent and advanced by the Mortgagee to the Mortgagor and applied by the Mortgagor to purchase the property described in the First Schedule.

IN WITNESS whereof this Deed of Charge by way of legal mortgage is executed under seal the day and year first before written.

THE FIRST SCHEDULE TO THE FOREGOING DEED OF CHARGE BY WAY OF LEGAL MORTGAGE

ALL THAT land situate in the district known as______in the parish of______in Barbados (and being the lot numbered 19 on the third key Plan) containing by admeasurement 709.6 square metres or thereabouts (inclusive of 85.8 square metres in the area a of the private road hereinafter mentioned) Abutting and bounding on the lots numbered 20B on the Third Key Plan on the lot numbered 21 on the Second Key Plan on that portion of the lot numbered 15 on the Second Key Plan which is now shown on the Third Key Plan as the lot numbered 15B and on the private road 8.0 metres wide which leads to______and to the Highway or however else the same may abut and bound together with the messuage or dwelling house thereon and all other erections and building thereon.

THE SECOND SCHEDULE TO THE FOREGOING DEED OF CHARGE BY WAY OF LEGAL MORTGAGE

The covenants, conditions, stipulations and reservations mentioned and/or contained in a Deed of Conveyance dated 14 April 2000 (recorded on the 17th day of April as Deed no. 1623) and made between______(as Vendor) of the One Part and the mortgagor (as Purchaser) of the Other Part.

THE THIRD SCHEDULE TO THE FOREGOING DEED OF CHARGE BY WAY OF LEGAL MORTGAGE

Policy Number:
Date of Issue:
Plan:
Sum Assured:
Beneficiary:
Insured:
Insurer:

SIGNED SEALED AND DELIVERED by
the said

in the presence of

Witness:

APPENDIX 6

SAMPLE CERTIFICATE OF TITLE

JAMAICA

Certificate of Title under the Registration of Titles Act

DANIEL DOE of 23 West Street, Ocho Rios in the parish of Saint Ann, Accountant, RICHARD ROWE of Lot 44 Rio Bravo, Tower Isle in the parish of Saint Mary, Haulage Contractor, and STEPHEN SCULLY of Broadlands, Chalky Ridge Estate, Ocho Rios in the parish of Saint Ann, Engineer, are now the proprietors of an estate as joint tenants in fee simple subject to the incumbrances notified hereunder in ALL THAT parcel of land part of ANTILLEAN PARK formerly part of TOWER HILL in the parish of SAINT MARY being the lot numbered FIFTEEN on the plan of part of Antillean Park aforesaid deposited in the Office of Titles on the 4th day of August, 1961 of the shape and dimensions and butting as appears by the plan thereof hereunto annexed and being the land comprised in Certificate of Title formerly registered at Volume 555.

DATED this day of Two Thousand and Four
[signed]
Deputy Registrar of Titles

Incumbrances above referred to:

The land above described (hereinafter called "the said Land"] is subject to the undermentioned restrictive covenants which shall run with the said land and shall bind as well the registered proprietor their heirs personal representatives and transferees as the registered proprietor for the time being of the said land their heirs, personal representatives and transferees and shall enure to the benefit of and be enforceable by the registered proprietor or proprietors for the time being of the lands or any portion thereof now or formerly comprised in Certificate of Title registered at Volume 333 Folio 22.

1. There shall be no sub-division of the said land.

2. Antlllean Park Limited shall not at any time be liable for an part of the cost of any fence dividing the said land from other lands belonging to the said Caribbean Park Limited.

3. No **bath water, sullage water or water used for domestic purposes in respect of the said** lands or any part thereof or any water except storm water shall be permitted or allowed to flow from the said lands or any part thereof on the remaining portion of the said lands or any road or street adjacent thereto but that all such water as aforesaid shall be got rid of by being run into an absorption pit or pits or any evaporation or absorption or percolation on the said lands.

4. There shall be erected on the said land water closets discharging into a cess or absorption pits constructed in accordance with the regulation of the Public Sanitary Authority.

5. No building or erection shall be nearer than thirty feet to any road, the main wall of no building nearer than ten feet from the boundary of any adjoining lot, and doors, gates or windows in any fence on any road shall open inwards.

6. No fence, hedge or other construction of any kind nor any tree or plant of a height of more than four feet six inches above road level shall be erected grown or permitted to be within fifteen feet of any road intersection and the Road Authority shall have the right to enter upon the said land and clean, repair, improve and maintain all or any of the drains, gullies or water courses which may be thereon and remove, cut, trim any fence, hedge or other construction and any tree, plant which may be erected, placed or grown upon the said land in contravention of this restrictive covenant without liability for any loss or damage thence arising and the registered proprietor shall pay to the Road Authority the cost incurred by reason of the matters aforesaid.

7. Development of the said land must be submitted to the Local Planning Authority (Clarendon Parish Council) in the form of an application with detailed drawings for approval before any such development is completed.

8. No sign or hoarding or other advertisement shall be erected on the said land except as are specifically permitted by the Local Planning Authority.

9. The registered proprietors shall be responsible for the supply of their own domestic water.

[signed]

Deputy Registrar of Title

APPENDIX 7

QUESTIONS AND ANSWERS

QUESTION 1

Victor has recently sold and conveyed the fee simple of a large mansion, Moonbury House, to Pamela. On taking possession, Pamela was horrified to discover that Victor had removed:

-an expensive fitted carpet from the living room

-an air-conditioning unit from the study

-a heavy statue which had stood in the middle of the front lawn

-a chattel house located at the rear of the property and used as accommodation for the housekeeper.

Advise Pamela as to whether she may be legally entitled to recover the aforementioned items, assuming that the contract of sale of Moonbury House makes no mention of any of them.

Suggested answer

In advising whether Pamela may recover the items removed by Victor, it is necessary to determine whether the items were chattels or fixtures, as only items classed as fixtures will have passed to Pamela under the conveyance to her. Put in another way, because of the maxim *quicquid plantatur solo, solo cedit* ('whatever is attached to the land becomes part of the land'), the conveyance of Moonbury House to Pamela will be deemed to have included all fixtures in the property. Items classed as chattels, on the other hand, belong to Victor and were removable by him.

In deciding whether items are fixtures or chattels, the courts use two tests, (i) the 'degree of annexation' test, and (ii) the 'purpose of annexation' test. According to the degree of annexation test, an item is a fixture if it is attached to the land or building in some substantial manner, and the greater the degree of attachment, the more likely it is to be considered as a fixture. Thus, for example, in *Holland v Hodgson* (1872) LR 7 CP 328, looms bolted to the floor of a mill were held to be fixtures, as was an automatic car-wash machine bolted to the ground in *Lombard and Ulster Banking Ltd v Kennedy* [1974] NI 20, and panel doors and three-phase tubing in *National Business Printing Ltd v Carib Spray Ltd* (1994) 31 JLR 653. On the other hand, items resting on the ground by their own weight will usually be held to be chattels under the degree of annexation test, because of the lack of affixation to the land.

However, the degree of annexation test is not conclusive as to the status of an item, for the court may also apply the 'purpose of annexation' test, whereby an item substantially attached to the land will be regarded as a chattel if the purpose of the attachment was to enable it to be enjoyed as a chattel rather than to benefit the land. On this test, for instance, 'white goods' such as an oven or a dishwasher will be regarded as chattels even if they are part of the overall design of a 'fitted' kitchen, because they do not permanently improve it.

The status of the items in the present problem will be considered *seriatim:*

(i) The fitted carpet in the living room

Under the degree of annexation test, the carpet would be considered a chattel, as it rests on the floor by its own weight, perhaps with the assistance of light tacks or staples at its corners to prevent it from lifting. Also, the purpose of fitting it is arguably to enjoy it as a carpet and not to enhance the value of the property. Thus, in *Botham v TSB Bank plc* (1996) 73 P&CR D1, fitted carpets in a residential flat were held to be chattels, and indeed it is customary in the sale of residential property for the price of carpets and curtains to be separately negotiated by the parties. By contrast, in *La Salle Recreations Ltd v Canadian Camdex Investments Ltd* (1969) 4 DLR (3d) 549, it was held that, notwithstanding the minimal degree of attachment, wall-to-wall carpeting in a hotel was a fixture, since the purpose of its installation was the better use of the building as a hotel rather than the better use of the carpeting. In the present case, Moonbury House is clearly a residential property and so, following the *Botham* case, Pamela is advised that the carpet is a chattel removable by Victor.

(ii) The air-conditioning unit in the study

Pamela is advised that it is likely that the air-conditioning unit will be held to be a fixture, that Victor was not entitled to remove it, and that she is entitled to recover it as purchaser of the property. The reasons for this conclusion are (i) that (at least if the air-conditioning unit is of the conventional kind), there will have been a substantial degree of annexation to the land, and (ii) that the purpose of fitting it was to make the study a more comfortable place to work, rather than to enjoy the item for its own sake. This view is supported by *Aircool Installations v British Telecommunications plc* [1995] CLY 821.

(iii) The statue on the lawn

Applying the degree of annexation test, the fact that the statue rested on the ground by its own weight suggests that it should *prima facie* be considered a chattel. On the other hand, on the purpose of annexation test, if the statue had been placed on the lawn as part of the landscaping and architectural features of the property, then it would be regarded as a fixture. In *Hamp v Bygrave* (1982) 266 EG 720, for instance, stone and lead garden ornaments resting by their own weight were held to be fixtures because the vendors regarded them as 'features of, and part and parcel of, the garden', and a similar conclusion was reached in *Berkley v Poulett* [1977] EGLR 86 in relation to a heavy marble statue of a Greek athlete standing on a plinth. However, in the absence of any information as to the purpose for placing the statue on the lawn, the prima facie presumption that it is a chattel will stand and it will therefore belong to Victor and be removable by him.

(iv) The chattel house

Chattel houses are unique to Caribbean jurisdictions and there are a number of cases which have examined the question whether they are to be regarded as chattels or as fixtures. It appears from the judgment of Wooding CJ in *Mitchell v Cowie* (1964) 7 WIR 118 that, applying the 'degree of annexation' test, if a chattel house is of the type that rests by its own weight and is easily removable either wholly or in sections for installation elsewhere, it will be regarded as a chattel; but if it is of a kind that is attached more substantially to the land and cannot be removed without its total destruction, then it will be considered a fixture; and, on the 'purpose of annexation' test, if the chattel house has been placed on the land for a temporary purpose it will be treated as a chattel, but if it was intended to be a permanent residence for its occupants, it will be a fixture (*Massiah v Hutson* (1961–63) 3 Barb LR 11. On the other hand, it was also pointed out by Georges JA in *O'Brien Loans Ltd v Missick* (1977) BLR 49 that where a yearly tenant of a 'house spot' places a chattel house on the land, it will be regarded as a chattel and removable (notwithstanding that there is a substantial degree of attachment to the land), because a yearly tenant would not have any intention of benefiting the owner of the land. The situation in the present case is somewhat unusual in that the chattel house was installed by Victor or his predecessor for the specific purpose of providing accommodation for the housekeeper (whoever happened to be employed as such) at Moonbury House, unlike in the aforementioned decided cases where it was the owner of the chattel house (not the owner of the land) who installed the house for his own benefit as a residence. In the present case, it is clear that the chattel house was intended to be a permanent and not a merely temporary addition to the land, and so on the 'purpose of annexation' test and irrespective of the degree of annexation, it will be regarded as a fixture to which Pamela is entitled.

In conclusion, Pamela is advised that, as purchaser, she is entitled to recover possession of the air-conditioning unit and the chattel house, but not the carpet or the statue.

QUESTION 2

Vinnie is selling his suburban house, No. 13 Elm Street, to Peter. Vinnie is a keen carpenter in his spare time and has installed a work bench in the garage, bolted to the floor. He has also erected a free-standing bicycle shed in the back yard. In the dining room, there is an ornate chandelier hanging from the ceiling and a painting of 'Dido and Aeneas' attached to hooks on the wall. There is a fitted kitchen with integral stove, dishwasher and washing machine. Also, on an inspection visit to No 13 last week, Peter picked up a gold bracelet that he found lying under a bush in the garden.

Consider, on the sale of No 13 (in the absence of relevant terms in the sale agreement), who will be entitled to:

(i) The work bench
(ii) The bicycle shed
(iii) The chandelier
(iv) The painting
(v) The stove, dishwasher and washing machine
(vi) The gold bracelet

Suggested answer

Since there are no terms in the agreement of sale specifying which items are to pass on the sale to Peter, the entitlement to such items will be decided according to whether a particular item is to be classified as a fixture or as a chattel. Fixtures will be deemed to be part of the land and building and will pass to Peter; chattels will remain the property of Vinnie. The two tests employed for deciding whether an item is a chattel or a fixture are (i) the degree of annexation test and (ii) the purpose of annexation test. According to the *degree of annexation test*, an item is a fixture if it is attached to the land or building in some substantial manner, and the greater the degree of attachment the more likely it is to be held to be a fixture. According to the *purpose of annexation test*, an item which is substantially attached to the land will be regarded as a chattel if the purpose of the attachment was to enable it to be enjoyed as a chattel rather than to benefit or enhance the value of the land.

The status of the items in the problem will be considered *seriatim*:

(i) *The work bench.* Since the work bench has been bolted to the floor, there has been a substantial degree of attachment and, according to the degree of annexation test, it would be *prima facie* classed as a fixture, like the looms bolted to the floor of the mill in *Holland v Hodgson* (1872) LR 7 CP 328. However, in this case the work bench was not installed in a factory or mill but in the garage of a private house and we are told that Vinnie was a 'keen carpenter', which suggests that carpentry was his pastime or hobby, and that he installed the workbench in the garage, not to benefit or increase the value of the house but rather for its more convenient use as a chattel. On this analysis, Vinnie would be entitled to remove and keep the work bench for himself.

(ii) *The bicycle shed.* On the degree of annexation test, this would be a chattel, as we are told it is 'free standing' and therefore not attached to the ground. It has been held that a greenhouse (*Dibble v Moore* [1970] 2 QB 181), printing machinery (*Hulme v Brigham* [1943] KB 152), and a mobile home (*Royal Bank of Canada v Beyak* (1981) 119 DLR (3d) 505), all of which rested on the ground by their own weight, were to be classed as chattels. On the other hand, in applying the purpose of annexation test, it must be asked whether Vinnie's purpose in erecting the bicycle shed in the back yard was to enhance the value of the property or rather to enjoy it as a chattel. It could be argued that the purpose of a bicycle shed is not to enjoy it as an item in itself but rather to store and protect bicycles used by persons living in the premises. To that extent, it could be said to be for the permanent benefit of the property. Should that argument be accepted, the shed would pass to Peter as purchaser.

(iii) *The chandelier.* A chandelier, being an ornate, heavy fitting suspended from the ceiling, will require a high degree of attachment in order to guard against its falling and causing serious injury or damage to persons or property. So, on the degree of annexation test, it would be classed as a fixture. It could also be classed as a fixture under the purpose of annexation test if it served as part of the overall design of the room and was intended to enhance a particular decor and ambience. On that premise, it would pass to Peter as purchaser.

(iv) *The painting.* A painting attached to hooks will *prima facie* be held to be a chattel and therefore removable by Vinnie, on both degree and purpose of annexation tests. The degree of annexation is minimal, as the picture is merely suspended from hooks attached to the wall, and the purpose of the attachment is to enjoy the painting as a work of art and not to enhance the value of the property. In *Leigh v Taylor* [1902] AC 157, it was held that tapestries fixed to a framework of wood and canvas nailed to a wall never

lost their character as chattels. There was no other way that they could be enjoyed except by fixing them to the wall. On the other hand, as in the case of the chandelier, if the painting were intended to be a feature of the overall design of the dining room, it could be considered as a fixture.

(v) *The stove, dishwasher and washing machine.* The status of such common household objects was considered in *Botham v TSB Bank plc* (1996) 73 P&CR D1, applying the test whether or not they were, objectively, intended to be a permanent and lasting improvement to the house. It was held that, whereas fitted kitchen units, including cupboards and storage spaces, were usually fixtures, 'white goods' such as stoves, refrigerators and washing machines were to be treated as chattels because they could readily be removed without significant damage to the house. Accordingly, Vinnie is entitled to remove these items and keep them for himself.

(vi) *The gold bracelet.* The first point to note here is that Peter was a lawful visitor to No. 13 and, in inspecting the garden, he was not trespassing in any unauthorised area. Any chattel found on land by a wrongdoer cannot, on policy grounds, be claimed by the finder (*Hibbert v McKiernan* [1948] 2 KB 142, where golf balls lost by players were found by a trespasser on the golf course: held, he was not entitled to keep them as finder). Accordingly, assuming that the owner of the bracelet cannot be traced, the question is whether Peter is entitled to keep it as the finder, or whether Vinnie is entitled to it because it was found on his land. It is established that, on the basis of the *quicquid plantatur solo, solo cedit* maxim, any chattel that is found *under or attached to land* belongs to the person in possession of the land, whether as fee simple owner or leaseholder (assuming the owner cannot be traced), and not to the finder (*South Staffordshire Water Co v Sharman* [1896] 2 QB 44); but where a chattel is found lying on and unattached to land, the position is less clear. In *Parker v British Airways Board* [1982] QB 1004, a passenger who found a gold bracelet lying in the defendant's executive lounge at London Heathrow Airport was held entitled to keep it, as finder, as against the defendant. The court held that the finder of a chattel who was not a trespasser acquired the right to keep it against all but the true owner if the chattel had been abandoned or lost, unless the occupier of the building, in which the chattel was found, had shown an intention to exercise exclusive control over the building and the things which were in it and, in the circumstances, the defendant had not shown such intention. In the present case, it can be argued that, unlike in *Parker*, where the airport lounge was open to the public, it should be inferred that Vinnie intended to exercise control over his own private residence, including the garden, and anything found there, so that he would be entitled to the gold bracelet as against Peter.

QUESTION 3

Consider the effect of the following devises made by will:

(i) *Blackacre to Anna in fee, 'until Anna should marry'*

(ii) *Whiteacre to Brian in fee, 'but if Brian should cease to be a Jehovah's Witness, then to Lorna'*

(iii) *Blueacre to Casper, 'for so long as Mary shall live'*
(iv) *Brownacre to Desmond in fee, 'provided that Desmond does not mortgage the land'*
(v) *Yellowacre to Ernest in fee, so long as he continues to reside in Jamaica*
(vi) *Orangeacre to Gregory in fee, 'until Gregory becomes bankrupt or attempts to alienate the land'*
(vii) *Redacre to Henry in fee, 'provided that he never sells the land out of the family, and, if he does so, then to Quincy absolutely*
(vii) *Pinkacre to Irene 'so long as she remains a spinster'*

Suggested answer

(i) A devise 'to Anna in fee, until Anna should marry' is a determinable interest and is valid. Therefore, if Anna did marry, the fee simple in Blackacre would revert to the testator's estate.

(ii) A devise 'to Brian in fee, but if Brian should cease to be a Jehovah's Witness, then to Lorna' is a conditional interest followed by a gift over on the fulfillment of the condition. The main issue here is whether the condition, ie, that Brian should remain a Jehovah's Witness, is valid. The courts have been unwilling to strike down 'religious discrimination' conditions, because it has been held that it is not against public policy for an adherent of a particular religion to discriminate in disposing of his own property, in view of the broad principle of freedom of testamentary disposition (*Blathwayt v Lord Cawley* [1975] 3 All ER 625, 636). On the other hand, such a condition will be void for *uncertainty* if it is not possible to determine whether the condition has been fulfilled (*Re Tegg* [1936] 2 All ER 878). In this case, if it would be possible to determine conclusively that Brian had ceased to be a Jehovah's Witness (for example, by removal of his name from a register of members), then the condition would be valid and, were Brian to cease to be a member, the gift over to Lorna would take effect. If, on the other hand, it were not possible to decide conclusively whether or not Brian had ceased to be a Jehovah's Witness, then the condition would be void and would be struck out, causing Brian's fee simple interest in Whiteacre to become absolute.

(iii) The devise of Blueacre to Casper 'so long as Mary shall live' should be interpreted not as a conditional or a determinable interest but as an estate 'pur autre vie', ie for the life of another (Mary), which will come to an end on Mary's death. It is accordingly a species of life estate. If Casper predeceases Mary, his personal representatives will hold his interest in Blueacre on trust for the persons entitled under his will or intestacy.

(iv) The devise of Brownacre to Desmond 'provided that he does not mortgage the land' is a conditional interest because of the words, 'provided that'. The condition is void on the ground that it is a restraint on alienation (*Ware v Cann* (1830) 10 B&C 433: condition prohibiting alienation by mortgage held void). Accordingly, the condition will be struck out and Desmond will have an absolute interest in Brownacre.

(v) The devise of Yellowacre to Ernest is a determinable interest because of the words 'so long as'. Determinable interests, like conditional ones, are subject to the requirement of certainty, so that if there is uncertainty as to what will terminate the estate, the whole interest will be void. In this case, there is uncertainty regarding the word 'reside'. In *Sifton v Sifton* [1938] AC 656, it was held that the words 'so long as [the beneficiary] shall reside in Canada' were too vague to be enforced, for there were many forms and degrees of residence and it was impossible to say precisely which form of residence was being referred to. It has been held, however, that if the words 'permanent residence' are used, they may be sufficiently certain, as 'permanent' implies an intention to live in a place for life, as opposed to a temporary or fixed period of residence (*Re Gape* [1952] Ch 743). Further, 'permanent residence' is defined in many immigration statutes. In the present case, the determinable interest will be void for uncertainty and Yellowacre will revert to the testator's estate.

(vi) The devise of Orangeacre to Gregory creates a determinable interest. The two alternative determining events are (a) bankruptcy and (b) attempted alienation. It was established in *Re Leach* [1912] 2 Ch 422, that a fee simple which is made determinable on the bankruptcy of the grantee, or on his attempt to alienate his interest, is valid, so that, if either of those events occurs, the estate will automatically come to an end and, in the case of bankruptcy, there will be nothing to vest in the grantee's trustee in bankruptcy. On occurrence of the determining event, the fee simple in Orangeacre will revert to the grantor's estate. On the other hand, if Gregory dies without either event having occurred, his fee simple will become absolute and will pass to his estate.

(vii) The devise of Redacre to Henry is a conditional interest because of the words 'provided that'. The condition that Henry 'shall not sell the land out of the family' is only a *partial* restraint on alienation which was held in *Re Macleay* (1875) LR 20 Eq 186 to be valid. Therefore, if Henry does purport to sell to a non-family member, the condition will take effect and Quincy will be able to exercise his right of entry and claim the property.

(viii) The devise of Pinkacre to Irene 'so long as she remains a spinster' can be interpreted as a total restraint on marriage but, because the interest is determinable (through the words 'so long as') and not conditional, the restraint is valid. Therefore, if Irene does get married, her interest will automatically come to an end and Pinkacre will revert to the testator's estate.

QUESTION 4

(A) 'Equitable rights are neither quite rights in rem nor rights in personam, but a hybrid, being neither entirely the one nor entirely the other'.

Discuss

(A) Earlier this year, Moses purchased from Jacob a large suburban house, 'Casa Blanca', paid the purchase price of $400, 000 (US), and went into possession. The following matters have since come to light:

(a) In 2018, Jacob had agreed in writing to let the upper floor of 'Casa Blanca' to his cousin, Ruth, for five years at an annual rent of $12,000. No formal lease was ever

drawn up, but Ruth entered possession under the agreement. Moses knew that Ruth was Jacob's cousin and therefore assumed that Ruth was living in the house as a family guest;

(b) 'Casa Blanca' was originally the property of Ezra, who sold it to Jacob in 2015 for the sum of $300,000. At that time, Jacob paid only $30,000 of the purchase price but the receipt clause in the conveyance executed by Ezra acknowledged that the purchase price of $300,000 was fully paid at the time of the conveyance to Jacob. Jacob never paid the balance of the purchase price, and Ezra is now threatening to have 'Casa Blanca' sold in order to recover the amount owed to him.

Moses is alarmed at these matters and seeks your advice. Advise him.

Suggested answer

(A) In discussing this statement, it is necessary to refer to the origins of equity and its relationship with the common law, particularly in the context of the development of the trust as a creation of equity. Trusts (or 'uses') were developed from mediaeval times in England. A use or trust arose whenever land was conveyed to T (the trustee) on T's undertaking to hold it 'to the use and benefit' of B (the beneficiary) in circumstances such as where B, the beneficial owner of an estate in land, was about to go abroad on a crusade and it was necessary for the land to be held by another person on his behalf, who could perform and receive feudal services. In such a case, the common law would not recognise any rights in B at all, but would regard T, to whom the legal title had been conveyed, as alone beneficially entitled. The Court of Chancery, on the other hand, regarded it as unconscionable that B should be excluded and, although it would not deny T's legal title, it would act *in personam* against T by issuing a 'common injunction' restraining T from enforcing or exercising his legal right. Disobedience to such an injunction was punishable by imprisonment for contempt of court. By this method, equity ensured that the rights of a beneficiary under a trust were protected. Accordingly, in a trust of land, T is the 'legal owner' and B the 'equitable owner.' The land is vested in T, but since the beneficial title is in B, T is said to have only the 'bare legal estate' in the land and the beneficial interest belongs to B.

Because the rights of B, the beneficial owner, were enforced by courts of equity originally only against T (the trustee), those rights were said to be *in personam* (ie, 'against a person'), in much the same way as contractual rights are exercisable only *in personam*, ie, against the other contracting party. Legal ownership, on the other hand, has always conferred a right *in rem*, ie, a proprietary right in the land itself which can be enforced against the whole world. Equitable ownership at first conferred only a right *in personam* against the trustee, but later the Court of Chancery extended the categories of persons against whom the trust would be enforced, and ultimately it came to be the rule that an equitable interest under a trust was enforceable against *anyone who took a conveyance of the land with notice of the trust.* Put in another way, equitable ownership ultimately became almost, but not quite, a right *in rem*, since it became enforceable not only against the trustee but also against all other persons to whom the land was conveyed, *except* a bona fide purchaser for value of a legal estate in the land who had no notice of the existence of the trust. Accordingly, equitable rights under trusts never achieved the impregnable or indefeasible status of legal rights, because they were vulnerable to being defeated by the bona fide purchaser of the legal title without notice of the trust, though, by developing the concept of 'constructive notice', equity was able to severely limit the circumstances in which a purchaser could claim to be without notice. It is also significant that the same principles apply to equitable rights other than those arising under trusts, such as restrictive covenants, estate contracts and equitable mortgages.

In conveyancing practice, in order not to be affected by constructive notice, a purchaser of land is under a duty to investigate both the title deeds and the land itself, in order to be assured that there are no equitable interests over the land, and he will be deemed to have constructive notice of any interests that such investigation would have revealed. However, the doctrine of notice is of importance only in relation to unregistered conveyancing and does not apply to registered land, where equitable interests must be entered on the register in order to be protected; if they are not so entered, they will be void against a purchaser of the registered land, whether the purchaser had notice of them or not. Accordingly, it can be said that the doctrine of notice is inapplicable to registered land.

In conclusion, the hybrid nature of equitable rights is clear. In the light of equity's extension of those who were bound, from the trustee alone (right *in personam*) to all other persons except the bona fide purchaser of the legal estate without notice, equitable interests almost, but not quite, achieved the status of a right *in rem*. It is thus correct to say that equitable rights are not entirely rights *in personam* nor entirely rights *in rem* but a hybrid, having characteristics of both.

(B) First, it is clear that when Moses went into possession of 'Casa Blanca' last year, he had acquired the legal title to the property from Jacob. A person acquiring the legal fee simple bona fide and for value will take free from (ie, will not be bound by) any prior equitable interests of which he had no actual, constructive or imputed notice. He will, however, be bound by any prior legal interests in the property, whether he had notice of them or not.

In (a), we are told that, two years ago, Jacob agreed in writing to let the upper floor to his cousin, Ruth, for five years, at an annual rent of $12,000 (US). In most jurisdictions, in order to be valid at law, a lease for more than three years must be made by deed. In this case, no formal deed of lease was drawn up, but there was a written agreement and Ruth went into possession, paying a yearly rent. In *Walsh v Lonsdale* (1882) 21 Ch D 9 and the Trinidadian case of *Metcalf and Eddy Ltd v Edghill* (1963) 5 WIR 417, it was held that a lease for more than three years which was not valid at law for lack of a deed would nevertheless take effect in equity as an agreement for a lease (or 'equitable lease'), and the lessee would acquire an equitable interest in the property. Accordingly, Ruth acquired an equitable interest in 'Casa Blanca'. The next question is whether, when he purchased 'Casa Blanca' last year, Moses had actual, constructive or imputed notice of Ruth's interest. If he did, then he will be bound by it; if not, he will take free from it.

It is well established that a purchaser of property must inspect the land itself, making such inquiries as a reasonable purchaser would make, as he will be deemed to have constructive notice of any rights that are reasonably discoverable (*Hervey v Smith* (1856) 52 ER 1123). In particular, he should inquire as to the status of any person *in actual occupation* of the property, as he will have constructive notice of all the rights of such person. In the leading case of *Hunt v Luck* [1901] 1 Ch 428, it was held that 'a tenant's occupation is notice of all that tenant's rights', and

> if a purchaser has notice that the vendor is not in possession of the property, he must make inquiries of the tenant who is in possession and find out from him what his rights

> are, and, if he does not choose to do that, then whatever title he acquires as purchaser will be subject to the title or right of the tenant in possession.

Thus, in the present case, Moses was at fault in assuming that Ruth was only a family guest, and he ought to have made serious inquiries as to her true status. Of course, if the tenant, when asked pertinent questions, makes false, misleading or evasive answers, he/she will be estopped from asserting that the purchaser has constructive notice of his/her rights (*Midland Bank Ltd v Farmpride Hatcheries Ltd* (1980) 260 EG 493). Therefore, Ruth has a right in equity to remain in possession of the upper floor of 'Casa Blanca' as tenant until expiry of the equitable lease in three years' time.

In (b), it is established that if a vendor of land parts with possession before he receives full payment of the purchase price from the purchaser, he has an equitable lien on the land which entitles him, if he cannot obtain payment, to seek an order of sale from the court (*Mackreth v Symmons* (1808)15 Ves 329). In this case, Ezra has an equitable lien over 'Casa Blanca', because he has received only $30,000 out of the total of $300,000. The lien, as an equitable interest, will be binding on Moses, if, and only if, he had actual, constructive or imputed notice of it at the time when he purchased 'Casa Blanca' last year. In some jurisdictions, registration of a lien as a land charge will constitute notice to the world. We are not told anything about registration in Ezra's case, and so the position will be governed by the doctrine of notice. The critical fact in this case is that the receipt clause in the conveyance executed by Ezra in 2015 acknowledged (albeit wrongly) that the purchase price of $300,000 had been fully paid, and consequently Moses, as a bona fide purchaser without notice of the lien, took the property free from it. A court would therefore deny Ezra's application for a sale.

QUESTION 5

Under the will of Daniel, who died in 2015, Blackacre was devised to his children, Ruth, Simon, Timothy, Ursula and Victor as joint tenants beneficially. In 2016, Ruth died, having made a will leaving her 'share' in Blackacre to Mary. In 2017, Simon sold his 'share' to Nigel and, the following year, Timothy died intestate, his wife Olive being entitled to his estate. Last year, Ursula wrote to Mary, Nigel, Olive and Victor stating that she wished Blackacre to be sold and to be paid her 'share' of the proceeds. Victor, who actually lives in Blackacre, has objected on the ground that he is disabled and has spent his own money in making alterations to Blackacre to fit his particular needs. The others all agree to a sale taking place.

Advise Ursula generally as to the legal position.

Suggested answer

Daniel devised Blackacre to Ruth, Simon, Timothy, Ursula and Victor as beneficial joint tenants. Accordingly, the *ius accrescendi* (right of survivorship) applies, and if any joint tenant dies without having severed his interest, it will pass to the survivors. On the other hand, if a joint tenant severs his interest during his lifetime, he (or his assignee) will become a tenant in common of his share. Three methods of severance were laid down by Page Wood V-C in *Williams v Hensman* (1861) 70 ER 862, 867, viz, (i) 'act of the joint tenant operating on his own share', ie, alienation; (ii) mutual agreement; and (iii) course of dealing (mutual conduct). Two additional methods are, (iv) acquisition of an additional estate in the land, and (v) written notice, provided by section 36(2) of the Law of Property Act (UK) and copied in two Caribbean jurisdictions, namely Barbados (in section 43(1) of the Property Act, Cap 236) and Belize (in section 38(2) of the Property Act, Cap 190).

In the present problem, Ruth purported to leave her 'share' in Blackacre to Mary by her will; however, since she did not sever her interest in the joint tenancy during her lifetime, when she died in 2016 her 'share' passed to the other joint tenants (Simon, Timothy, Ursula and Victor) by survivorship, and so she had no interest to leave to Mary by her will. Mary therefore has no interest in the land and she drops out of the picture.

The next event occurred in 2017 when Simon sold his 'share' to Nigel. A sale by a joint tenant of his interest to a purchaser causes a severance of the joint tenancy under the first of the *Williams v Hensman* categories ('act of a joint tenant operating on his share'), so the effect of Simon selling his interest to Nigel was that Nigel became a tenant in common with Timothy, Ursula and Victor, while they remained joint tenants *inter se*.

When Timothy died intestate one year later, his share passed by survivorship to the remaining joint tenants (Ursula and Victor), with the result that his estate, which was inherited by Olive, did not include any interest in Blackacre.

The next issue is whether Ursula's communication to Mary, Nigel, Olive and Victor had the effect of severing the joint tenancy held by her and Victor. First, it is clear that if these events took place in Barbados or Belize, the written communication would be effective to sever the joint tenancy, within section 43 (1) of Cap 236 (Barbados) and section 38 (2) of Cap 190 (Belize), but in other jurisdictions which have not enacted this statutory method of severance, the position is less clear. There are some judicial statements which suggest that a unilateral declaration by one joint tenant communicated to the others is sufficient to cause a severance within the third of the *Williams v Hensman* categories (course of dealing), whether or not the others are in agreement. In *Hawkesley v May* [1956] 1 QB 304, for instance, Havers J held that a letter from a joint tenant to a co-tenant requesting that his dividends be paid into a particular account caused a severance, and in *Re Drapers Conveyance* [1967] 3 All ER 853, Plowman J stated that 'a declaration by one of a number of joint tenants of his intention to sever operates as a severance'. This view is supported by some text writers (eg, Snell, *Equity*, 30th edn, p 38), but it is submitted that the weight of authority is against the view that a unilateral declaration can constitute a severance, since such a declaration can hardly be described as a 'course of dealing' or 'mutual conduct', and if severance could have been effected at common law by a unilateral declaration there would have been no need for the provision in the UK's 1925 legislation of the 'new' method of severance by written notice; further, it would render redundant the 'mutual agreement' method of severance. In *Nielson-Jones v Fedden* [1974] 3 All ER 38, where a husband and wife were joint tenants of their matrimonial home, the wife signed a memorandum authorising her husband to sell the house so that the proceeds could be used to provide a new home for himself. It was held that the document did not sever the joint tenancy since, according to Walton J, 'a mere unilateral declaration does not in any way shatter any one of the essential unities [of possession, interest, title and time]'. This view is supported by text writers such as Gray, *Elements of Land Law*, 3rd edn, p. 862, and has been followed in Australia and Canada. It seems, therefore, that the better view is that Ursula remains a joint tenant.

The next issue concerns the proposed sale of the property. Co-owners, whether joint tenants or tenants in common, may agree to the partition of their co-owned property, the effect of which would be that the property would be divided up into several parcels, each former co-owner becoming a single owner of his parcel. At common law, partition was not possible without the consent of all the co-owners, but the Partition Acts 1539 and 1540 (UK) conferred a statutory right to seek an order of partition from the court. Such an order could be granted on the application of any co-owner, even against the will of the other co-owners. Much later, by the Partition Act 1868, the court was given jurisdiction to order sale of the property in lieu of partition, which would be a more desirable solution in cases where, for instance, the property was too small to be conveniently partitioned amongst the co-owners.

These statutory provisions regarding partition and sale have been reproduced in most Commonwealth Caribbean jurisdictions. In the present case, we are told that all the co-owners agree to a sale, but that Victor opposes sale, on the ground of his special needs and his expenditure incurred on Blackacre in making alterations to accommodate those needs. In order to advise Victor, it is necessary to consider the effect of the Partition Acts. For instance, section 4 of the Partition Act, Ch 27, No 14 of Trinidad and Tobago provides that where application for sale is made to the court by a party holding a half share or more in the property, the court *must* order a sale unless there is good reason for not doing so, whereas by section 3, where the applicant has less than a half share in the property, the court *may* order sale after taking into consideration various factors, viz, the nature of the property, the number of parties interested in the property, the absence or disability of some of the parties, or whether sale would be more beneficial to the parties than partition. It should be noted that the 'shares' mentioned in the Partition Acts are not restricted to the 'true' shares held by tenants in common, but must also be taken to include the proportionate 'shares' held by joint tenants in property owned under joint tenancy.

In the present case, those who wish to sell, namely Nigel and Ursula, hold more than half of the 'shares' in Blackacre. Nigel is a tenant in common holding one share (purchased from Simon); Ursula and Victor are joint tenants holding the remaining four shares of the property. Ursula and Nigel together are thus entitled to three-fifths of the property, while Victor is entitled only to two-fifths. Accordingly, since Ursula and Nigel own more than half of the 'shares' in the property, the court must order sale, unless there is 'good reason to the contrary'. Victor may argue that his disability and the fact that he has spent his own money in making alterations to the property to fit his particular needs is 'good reason' for the court to decline to order sale. On the other hand, the court may take the view that to refuse an order of sale would be unfair to Ursula and Nigel who wish to turn their portions into cash, and that since section 4 primarily enjoins the court to order sale, the interests of the majority should prevail (*Pena v Pena* (2000) HC T&T, unreported).

A better solution, however, is provided by section 5, which enables the party or parties wishing to retain the property to 'buy out' the party or parties who apply to the court for an order of sale. The section provides that where those wishing to retain 'undertake to purchase the share of the party requesting a sale . . . the court may order a valuation of the share of the party requesting a sale'. In this case, it is open to Victor to offer to purchase the 'shares' of Ursula and Nigel at a valuation. The only remaining question would be whether, after valuations of their respective 'shares', they would then be bound to sell to Victor at those prices. This question was considered in *Pitt v Jones* (1879–80) 5 App Cas 651, where a majority in the House of Lords held that the party or parties applying for sale would not be bound to accept the valuation and sell to the other co-owners at those prices. According to Lord Watson, 'the provisions of section 5 cannot be enforced, except at the instance of the party requesting a sale and *voluntarily* offering, as an alternative, to sell his own share to the other parties interested, at a price to be fixed by the court'. This principle was later applied by Mendonca J in a Trinidadian case, *Superville v Superville* (1999) HC, T&T (unreported).

In conclusion, Victor is advised that he may offer to 'buy out' the shares of Ursula and Nigel within section 5 of the Partition Act, so that he may retain possession of and continue to occupy Blackacre. If the 'buy out' negotiations prove to be unsuccessful, Victor will have to convince the court not to exercise its power to order a sale under section 4, on the ground that there is 'good reason' for not so ordering.

QUESTION 6

Dominic, a wealthy businessman and bachelor who was in a poor state of health, owned a large house,' El Gringo', in an exclusive suburb. While attending the outpatients' clinic at the local hospital, he met Beatrice, a young nurse, and they formed a relationship. Shortly afterwards, Dominic suggested to Beatrice that she should give up her hospital job, leave the small flat which she was renting, and come to live with him, telling her that she would have a more comfortable place to live, with no financial worries, and that on his death she would inherit 'El Gringo' and the rest of his estate. Beatrice resigned from her job, gave up her flat and moved into 'El Gringo'. Several months later, Dominic's health took a turn for the worse, and Beatrice nursed him for two years until he eventually died earlier this year. Beatrice has discovered that Dominic neglected to make a will and that, under the intestacy laws, his entire estate will be inherited by his next-of-kin.

Advise Beatrice.

Suggested answer

Clearly, as title to 'El Gringo' was in the sole name of Dominic, it will pass at law under his intestacy, and Beatrice, not being among Dominic's next-of-kin, will have no claim. However, it is likely that Beatrice will have a good cause of action under the equitable doctrine of proprietary estoppel, whereby a person who has suffered a detriment in reliance upon an assurance given by another will acquire an 'equity' which the court will satisfy by making an appropriate order against that other or his estate. In the modern law, the three requirements for the application of proprietary estoppel are: (1) an assurance, (2) a detriment, and (3) reliance on such detriment.

First, as to the requirement of an assurance, it is clear that Dominic gave Beatrice an assurance that she could come and live in 'El Gringo', implicitly for an indefinite period and rent-free; that she would have no financial worries; and that she would inherit 'El Gringo', together with the rest of Dominic's estate, implicitly under Dominic's will. There is thus no doubt that the requirement of assurance has been satisfied.

The second requirement for proprietary estoppel is that Beatrice must have suffered a detriment, which may consist of expenditure of money or some other detriment, such as performing services without pay, as in *Greasley v Cooke* [1980] 3

All ER 710, where the claimant worked as a maidservant in a household without pay for over 30 years. In the present problem, it can be argued that the detriment suffered by Beatrice was in giving up her job and moving from her own accommodation, thereby depriving herself of her source of income and her independence. She did, admittedly, obtain the benefit of rent-free accommodation at 'El Gringo' and an arguably more comfortable lifestyle, but that was more than outweighed by the further detriment in that she nursed Benedict for two years without pay until his death.

Similar contentions concerning detriment arose in a St Lucian case, *Henry v Henry* [2010] UKPC 3. Here, one of the issues discussed in the Privy Council was whether the claimant, who had lived with and cared for G, an elderly relative, for many years, on the faith of a firm assurance that she would leave her share in a plot of land to him in her will, had in fact suffered a detriment. The trial judge had held that the claimant had not acted to his detriment since he had lived on the plot rent-free for decades; the plot had been his source of livelihood; and he had reaped the produce and sold and kept the proceeds. The ECS Court of Appeal had taken a different view, holding that the claimant had acted to his detriment, and awarded him G's promised share of the land—his 'expectation interest'. The Privy Council, revisiting the issue of detriment, stated that, in order to determine the matter, it was necessary to weigh the advantages against the disadvantages suffered by the claimant in relying on G's assurance. The Privy Council ultimately determined that the claimant had shown a detriment because, by working on the land (which other family members had declined to do), caring for G, and providing food for her, he had 'effectively deprived himself of the opportunity of a better life elsewhere, and that detriment was not outweighed by the advantages mentioned by the trial judge, such as the claimant's rent-free accommodation and enjoyment of the land.

The third requirement is that the detriment must have been incurred in reliance upon the assurance given by Dominic. Here, the case of *Greasley v Cooke* (above) will be of assistance to Beatrice, because it was established in that case that, where a detriment has been proved, the court will presume that it was incurred in reliance on the assurance. In other words, proof of an assurance and a detriment gives rise to a rebuttable presumption of reliance on that assurance which shifts the burden on to the other party to prove that the detriment was incurred for reasons other than reliance on the assurance. In the present case, the court will presume that Beatrice gave up her job and accommodation and later nursed Dominic during his illness in reliance on the assurances given by Dominic. Could that presumption be rebutted on the facts? In order to rebut the presumption, Dominic's next-of-kin might argue that Beatrice's motive for her actions was 'natural love and affection' for Dominic, and that she would have acted in the same way even if there had been no assurances. This argument is unlikely to succeed, however, particularly with respect to the very substantial detriment incurred in providing free nursing services for Dominic for two years.

Having established the elements of assurance, detriment and reliance, the next task for the court is to 'decide in what way the equity can be satisfied' (Lord Denning in *Ives v High* [1967] 1 All ER 504, 507). Beatrice will no doubt contend that she is entitled to receive Dominic's entire estate, because that was what he promised her, and there are indeed cases in which the court has used the expectation created in the claimant's mind as the basis for determining what is needed to satisfy the equity (for example, in *Khan v Khan* (1994) HC, T&T (unreported)), where the claimants had spent money on the defendant's house on the faith of an assurance that the defendant would leave his share of the house to the claimants by his will, the court held that the claimants' equity would be satisfied by granting them the fee simple of the property in remainder; and in *Re Basham* [1987] 1 All ER 405, where the claimant worked for the defendant without payment in the belief, induced by the defendant, that she would inherit his estate when he died, the court held that the equity would be satisfied by awarding the claimant the entire estate). In other cases, however, the courts have taken the approach that the criterion for satisfying the claimant's equity is the amount of the detriment suffered, which is to be quantified in monetary terms (as in *Seymour v Ebanks* [1980–83] CILR 252). Further, in at least two more recent cases, it has been held that the criterion for satisfying the equity was not necessarily the expectation of the claimant but rather the court's assessment of the *minimum required in order to do justice* in the case. Thus, in *Gillett v Holt* [2000] 3 WLR 815, where the claimant farm worker had worked on H's farm for over 40 years without pay on the faith of an assurance that 'all this (meaning the farm) will be yours' after H's death, the court, after H's decease, declined to grant the claimant the entire farm and awarded him only a part of it, plus the sum of 100,000 pounds sterling, to satisfy his equity, which was the minimum required to do justice. This approach was confirmed in *Jennings v Rice* [2003] 1 P&CR 8, where the claimant, who had acted as a gardener, handyman and part-time carer for an elderly woman for over 20 years without pay, in the expectation of receiving her entire estate (worth 1.3 million pounds) on her death, was awarded only 200,000 pounds by the court in satisfaction of his equity. Walker LJ emphasised that the essence of proprietary estoppel was the avoidance of an unconscionable result, and a disproportionate remedy should be avoided. The monetary award in *Jennings* was accordingly assessed on the basis of the cost of full-time nursing care for the relevant period.

On this basis, it is probable that the court in the present problem would order that Dominic's estate be liable to pay to Beatrice the amount equivalent to the cost of providing nursing services for the period of over two years during which Beatrice looked after Dominic.

QUESTION 7

Discuss the extent to which it is correct to state that 'an agreement for a lease is as good as a lease'.

Suggested answer

A lease that does not comply with the necessary statutory formalities, such as execution of a deed of lease, is void at common law, but it has long been the rule that if the intended tenant goes into possession with the landlord's consent, a tenancy at will arises, and if the tenant then pays rent, which is accepted, he becomes a yearly or other periodic tenant depending on the period with reference to which rent is paid (*Martin v Smith* (1874) LR 9 Ex 50). Thus, for example, if T goes into possession under a lease that is void for lack of formality and pays rent monthly, he becomes a monthly tenant at law.

In equity, on the other hand, a lease that fails to satisfy the statutory formalities will nevertheless take effect as *an agreement for a lease*, which, if specifically enforceable, will be effective as between the parties. Such an informal lease is known as an 'equitable lease'. The relationship between an agreement for a lease in equity and a yearly tenancy at law is illustrated by the leading case of *Walsh v Lonsdale*. In this case, L agreed in writing to grant to T the lease of a mill for seven years. It was agreed that a deed should be executed containing, *inter alia*, a term that, on demand, T would pay one year's rent in advance. No deed was executed, but T was let into possession and paid rent, in arrears, for a year and a half, thereby becoming a yearly tenant at law. L then demanded a year's rent in advance and, upon refusal by T, distrained for the amount. T brought an action for, *inter alia*, damages for illegal distress and an injunction to restrain the distress.

T argued that he was under no obligation to pay rent in advance since he was, at law, only a yearly tenant and the payment of rent in advance was inconsistent with a yearly tenancy, which could be determined by half a year's notice; L's distress was, therefore, illegal. It was held, however, that a tenant who holds under an agreement for a lease of which specific performance will be decreed is in the same position vis-à-vis the landlord (as regards rights and liabilities) as if a formal lease had been executed ('equity regards that as done which ought to be done') and, since L would have been entitled to distrain for rent had the lease agreed upon been granted by deed, the distress was lawful in equity. In so far as there was a conflict between the position at law (in which there was a yearly tenancy) and the position in equity (where there was an equitable lease for seven years), the equitable rule prevailed.

The principle in *Walsh v Lonsdale* was applied by the Trinidad and Tobago Court of Appeal in *Metcalfe and Eddy Ltd v Edghill* (1963) 5 WIR 417. In this case, there was an oral agreement for a lease for a period of 3 years and 15 days. The tenant went into possession of the landlord's premises, paying $350 a month as rent in accordance with the agreement. The oral agreement was subsequently reduced into writing and signed by both parties, but no deed, as required by section 3 of the Landlord and Tenant Ordinance, Ch 27, No 16, was executed. Shortly afterwards, the tenant gave one month's notice to quit and, on expiry of the period of notice, vacated the premises. The landlord disputed the validity of the notice and claimed specific performance of the agreement. The tenant argued that he had entered into possession under a monthly tenancy that had been validly determined, and this argument was accepted by the trial judge.

It was held that, under the rule in *Walsh v Lonsdale*, there was a binding contract to execute a lease for the fixed term stated therein (ie, 3 years and 15 days), and it was specifically enforceable as such.

As between the landlord and the tenant, 'an agreement for a lease may be as good as a lease', particularly having regard to the rule that the stipulations in the agreement are as binding on the parties as if they had been contained in a formal lease valid in law. However, in the following two respects, an agreement for a lease is not as effective as a lease:

(1) An agreement for a lease depends for its effectiveness on the willingness of the court to grant specific performance of the agreement (*Warmington v Miller* [1973] 2 All ER 372, 377). Specific performance, like other equitable

remedies, is discretionary, and if, for any reason, the court will not grant the remedy, an agreement for a lease will be ineffective. Examples where the court may refuse the remedy are where the tenant is unable to perform the covenants to be contained in the lease because he is insolvent, or where he has already been in breach of a covenant that formed part of the lease (*Coatsworth v Johnson* (1886) 55 LJQB 220).

(2) An agreement for a lease is not as effective as a formally drafted lease where third parties are involved. This is so in two respects:
   (a) Since an agreement for a lease creates a mere equitable interest, it may be defeated by a *bona fide* purchaser for value of a legal estate in the land (*Broadway Import and Export Ltd v Levy* (1996) 33 JLR 26). Thus, for example, if L agrees to grant a five-year lease of Blackacre to T, and one week later L sells and conveys the fee simple to P, who has no notice of the agreement, P will take free of the agreement, which will be extinguished. If, on the other hand, it is possible in the particular jurisdiction to protect equitable interests by an entry on the land register, and the agreement is entered on the register before conveyance of the fee simple, the purchaser will take subject to it.
   (b) In a lease, there is privity of estate between landlord and tenant, and those covenants which 'touch and concern' the land are enforceable by and against assignees of the lease, but in an agreement to lease the normal principle of contract law applies, which is that only benefits, and not burdens, are assignable. Thus, for example, where T1 assigns his equitable lease to T2, T2 may enforce the landlord's covenants since they are benefits to him, but he is not liable on the tenant's covenants – for example, the covenant to pay rent (*Purchase v Lichfield Brewery Co* [1915] 1 KB 184).

In conclusion, it is correct to state that, as between a landlord and a tenant, an agreement for a lease, of which a court would grant specific performance, is as effective as a formally drafted lease, and the parties will have the same enforceable rights and obligations as if the lease had been formalised; though specific performance is a discretionary remedy and the court may, in certain circumstances, refuse to grant it. On the other hand, the statement is not correct when third parties are brought into the picture, whether that third party is a purchaser of the fee simple without notice of the equitable lease, or an assignee of the lease.

QUESTION 8

Discuss the legal effect of the following transactions:

(a) *Brian engages Sleepy as his chauffeur and handyman, paying him a weekly wage that includes the use of a small apartment behind Brian's garage*

(b) *After entering into an agreement for the sale of his house to Peter, Vince allows Peter to occupy the house pending completion, requiring Peter to pay $500 (US) per month for his occupation*

(c) *Sabre Tooth Dental Services Inc ('Sabre Tooth') employs Keisha as a receptionist. When Keisha was evicted from her previous lodgings, Sabre Tooth allowed her to occupy the apartment above Sabre Tooth's premises which was unoccupied at the time. Sabre Tooth deducted a monthly 'rent' from Keisha's wages. Keisha has now found another job in the area but wishes to continue to occupy the apartment*

(d) *Terence occupies a studio apartment attached to Lorna's dwelling house on terms of payment of $150(US) per week. Lorna is responsible for cleaning and changing linen.*

Suggested answer

(a) An important fact here is that Sleepy's occupation of the apartment behind Brian's garage was treated as part of his weekly wages for working as a chauffeur and handyman for Brian. Sleepy's occupation was therefore a 'service occupancy', which takes effect as a licence and not as a tenancy, Brian being the licensor and Sleepy the licensee. The legal analysis of such licence is that it is not an interest in land and it may be revoked by Brian at any time. The arrangement is a licence and not a tenancy because Brian has granted possession of the apartment to Sleepy in consequence of his employment, and for the purpose of enabling Sleepy to carry out his duties as chauffeur and handyman more effectively; possession was not given merely for the convenience of Sleepy (*Smith v Sedghill Overseers* (1875) LR 10 QB 422; *Hekmati v Scherer* (1998) SC Bah (unreported)).

(b) In this case, Vince granted a licence, not a tenancy, to Peter, because the right to occupy the house was granted pursuant to a binding contract for the sale of the house between licensor (the vendor) and licensee (the purchaser). The occupation of a purchaser who enters into possession pursuant to a contract of sale is said to be 'ancillary and referable to' his equitable interest in the property arising from the contract and takes effect as a licence(*Essex Plan Ltd v Broadminster* (1988) 56 P&CR 353, 356). On the other hand, there is some earlier authority for regarding such occupation as a tenancy at will rather than a licence (*Wheeler v Mercer* [1957] AC 416, 425).

(c) This is a 'service tenancy' because it was granted by the employer, Sabre Tooth, to its employee, Keisha, not in order that Keisha could carry out her duties as a receptionist more effectively but rather for the convenience of Keisha, who had been evicted from her home. The arrangement takes effect as a monthly tenancy because rent was deducted from Keisha's salary each month, and the tenancy may be terminated by one month's notice to quit by either Sabre Tooth as landlord or Keisha as tenant. Keisha will be entitled to continue in occupation unless and until Sabre Tooth serve her with a valid notice to quit.

(d) This is a contractual licence to occupy the studio apartment and not a tenancy, because of the term concerning the provision of cleaning and linen changing by the owner. The effect of such provision is that Terence will be regarded as a 'lodger' (ie, a licensee) and not a tenant because, in order to provide the cleaning and linen changing services, Lorna will have unrestricted access to the apartment, which derogates from what would otherwise have been exclusive possession by Terence (*Street v Mountford* [1985] AC 809, 818). In *Huwyler v Rudder* (1996) 72 P&CR D3, the provision of cleaning and linen changing once a week, involving only 20 minutes' labour, was held to amount to 'unrestricted access'.

QUESTION 9

In January, 2016, Luke granted to Titus a 5-year lease of 'Bethany', a suburban dwelling house of which he was registered proprietor. During Hurricane Herod in September, 2019, part of the roof blew off and the area of the front porch subsided by six inches, causing severe cracks in the floor and walls. There was no evidence as to the state of the house at the time of the commencement of the lease, but expert evidence has disclosed that the damage to the property would not have occurred had there not been serious faults in the roof and the structure at the time of the storm.

Advise Titus as to his liability to repair 'Bethany' in the event that

(a) the lease contains a covenant binding the lessee to keep the premises in 'good tenantable repair'

(b) the lease makes no provision for repair.

Suggested answer

Luke granted a valid 5-year lease of 'Bethany' to Titus.

(a) If the lease contains a covenant binding the lessee 'to keep the premises in a state of repair', Titus will be bound, after the hurricane damage, to restore the property to its previous state, and the standard of repair required at common law is that 'which a prudent owner might reasonably be expected to keep his property, due allowance being made for the age, character and location of the premises at the commencement of the lease' (*Lurcott v Wakely* [1911] 1 KB 905).

The evidence as to the likelihood of serious faults in the roof and structure at the time of the storm raises the difficult issue as to the extent of the repairs required to be carried out by Titus. The general principle is that the lessee may be bound to *renew or replace* parts of a building that fall into disrepair, but he is not bound to reconstruct the entire building, and it is always a question of degree whether what the lessee is being asked to do can properly be described as 'repair', or whether it amounts to reconstruction. In a Jamaican case, *International Hotels Ltd v Cornwall Holdings Ltd* (1996) 33 JLR 314, Harris J held that the lessee is obliged to keep the premises in a good state of repair 'even if they were not in a state of tenantable repair at the inception of the tenancy, so long as it will not involve giving back to the landlord a wholly different thing from that which he demised'. There is also the principle in *Ravenseft Properties Ltd v Davstone (Holdings) Ltd* [1979] 1 All ER 929, in which it was held that where an inherent defect in a building has caused damage, the lessee may be under an obligation to rectify not only the damage but also the *cause* of the damage, even though it is an inherent defect, if it is necessary to do so in order to do 'the job properly, once and for all'. Thus, in *Ravenseft*, in which the stone cladding on a building became cracked, owing to the absence of expansion joints, which had not been included in the original design, the lessee was obliged not only to replace the stone cladding but also to insert expansion joints in order to prevent recurrence of the problem. Application of the *Ravenseft* principle in the present case would mean that

Titus would be liable not only to repair the immediate damage to the roof, the porch area and the cracks in the floor and walls, but also to remedy the inherent faults in the roof and structure of the building, so that there would not be a recurrence of the damage.

(b) If the lease makes no express provision for repair, Titus, as lessee, will at common law be liable to repair the property under the *doctrine of waste*. Under this doctrine, a tenant for a fixed term of years, as in Titus' case, is liable for both voluntary and permissive waste, so that Titus will *prima facie* be bound to restore the property to the condition in which he took it at the commencement of the lease. However, there is some uncertainty as to the extent of a tenant's obligation under the doctrine of waste, perhaps because modern leases normally contain express repairing obligations. Indeed, in *Warren v Keen* [1954] 1 QB 15, 20, Lord Denning denied any general duty to repair under the doctrine. Further, in Barbados, section 157 (c) of the Property Act, Cap. 236, implies a covenant by the landlord 'to keep in repair the roof, main walls and main drains', and section 158 (c) imposes an obligation on the tenant 'to keep the interior of the leased premises in good repair, reasonable wear and tear excepted'.

QUESTION 10

In January, 2018, Lance granted a 21-year lease of commercial premises to Troy at a monthly rent of $3,000 (US). The lease contains a clause entitling the lessor to forfeit the lease in the event of a breach of any covenant by the lessee. In the lease, the lessee covenanted

(i) to keep the premises 'in good and substantial repair, fair wear and tear excepted';

(ii) not to assign, sublet or part with the possession of the premises without the prior written consent of the lessor; and

(iii) not to use the premises for any purpose other than a hardware store.

In March, 2019 Troy sublet the basement area of the premises to Seunath without seeking Lance's consent, and since that time Seunath has been using the area as a bar and pool room. Also, the roof of the premises is in a bad state of repair and, in consequence, the outer walls have been affected by rainwater and have become damp and mildewed.

Since August, 2019 Lance has refused to accept any rent from Troy but in January, 2020, Lance's secretary mistakenly opened an envelope containing Troy's rent cheque and she immediately paid it into Lance's bank account.

Advise Lance.

Suggested answer

Lance has granted a valid legal lease of commercial premises to Troy. In advising Lance, it must first be determined whether Troy is in breach of any of the three covenants contained in the lease, by which he is bound as lessee of the premises. If Troy is in breach of any of the covenants, then Lance must be advised as to what remedies he may have against Troy.

The repairing covenant

With respect to the first covenant, by which Troy is bound to keep the premises 'in good and substantial repair, fair wear and tear excepted', we are told that the roof is now in a bad state of repair and that, in consequence of the failure to repair, the outer walls have become damp and mildewed. Has there been a breach of the covenant by Troy? The answer lies in the interpretation of the phrase 'fair wear and tear excepted'. It has been established that the effect of this phrase is to absolve the tenant (who has undertaken to repair) from liability for (a) damage due to the ordinary operation of natural causes, such as wind and rain, and (b) disrepair resulting from the reasonable use of the premises. On the other hand, it is also settled that although the lessee is not liable for the *original* damage or deterioration constituting fair wear and tear, he is liable for any *consequential* damage resulting from his failure to rectify the original damage, where it should be obvious to a reasonable person that, if not rectified, further and lasting damage would ensue. Talbot J in *Haskell v Marlow* [1928] 2 KB 45, 58 gave the example of a tile falling off the roof (which would amount to fair wear and tear for which the lessee would not be liable), followed by further damage to the building caused by the lessee's failure to replace the tile (for which he would be liable). In the present problem, Troy has covenanted to keep the premises in 'good and substantial repair' and, through his neglect to repair the roof, consequential damage to the outer walls of the building has occurred. He is therefore bound to remedy that damage under the repairing covenant.

The covenant against assignment and subletting

Troy covenanted not to assign the lease or sublet the premises without the lessor's prior written consent. The facts show that, without seeking Lance's consent, he sublet the basement area of the property to Seunath in March, 2019. Was this a breach of the covenant? There is a principle that covenants in leases are construed strictly against the lessor, so that a covenant must by its express wording cover the breach complained of, and any ambiguity will be interpreted in favour of the lessee. In *Cook v Shoesmith* [1951] 1 KB 752, followed in *Montrichard Enterprises Ltd v Attorney General of Trinidad and Tobago* (1998) HC, T&T (unreported), it was held that a covenant 'not to sublet the premises' is not broken by a subletting of *part only* of the premises, which is the case here (Troy sublet only the basement area). It seems, therefore, that the subletting to Seunath was not a breach of covenant.

The user covenant

Although the subletting to Seunath was, on the authorities cited above, not a breach of covenant, it is submitted that, by permitting Seunath to open a bar and pool room on the premises, which was a purpose other than that permitted by the lease, Troy was in breach of the covenant not to use the premises for any purpose other than a hardware store.

Remedies available to the lessor

Since the lease includes a forfeiture clause, Lance may be able to forfeit the lease on account of Troy's breaches of covenant. Before issuing a claim against Troy, however, Lance must first serve a statutory notice on Troy (within, eg, section 17(1) of the Conveyancing Act 1973 (Jamaica)), (a) specifying the breach complained of, (b) requiring the lessee to remedy the breach, if it is capable of remedy, and (c) requiring the lessee to pay compensation for the breach. The question as to whether or not a breach is capable of remedy is important since, if it is so capable, the lessee must, under the statute, be given a reasonable time to remedy it. Three months is normally regarded as a reasonable time for remedying breach of a positive covenant such as a covenant to keep the premises in good repair. On the other hand, if the breach is a 'once and for all' one which the courts regard as incapable of remedy, such as breach of a covenant against assignment or subletting, or breach of a covenant against immoral user which has caused a 'stigma' to be attached to the premises, then the question of giving the lessee time to remedy it becomes superfluous and it has been held that in such a case the lessor may proceed with the forfeiture after only 14 days (*Scala House and District Property Co Ltd v Forbes* [1973] 3 All ER 308). In the present problem, the breach of the repairing covenant is clearly capable of remedy, and in the statutory notice Troy should be given three months to carry out the necessary repairs to the property. As for the breach of the user covenant, it is significant that it was Seunath, the sublessee, who breached the covenant by using the basement area for a bar and pool room. Although the headlease is equally liable to forfeiture whether it was Troy or Seunath who actually committed the acts constituting the breach, and such a breach would normally be regarded as being incapable of remedy, the fact that Seunath was the guilty party may be relevant in that there is authority for the view that if the lessee, on discovering the breach by the sublesssee, takes immediate steps to forfeit the sublease, the breach may be regarded as capable of remedy (*Glass v Kencakes Ltd* [1964] 3 All ER 807), and the lease will not be forfeited. This approach may be contrasted with that taken in the *Scala House* case (above), where it was held that the breach of the covenant against subletting without consent could not be remedied, even by obtaining a surrender of the sublease from the sublessee. On balance, it is submitted that Lance would have a good case for forfeiture of the lease both on the ground of failure to repair and on the ground of breach of the user covenant. In addition, Lance is entitled to claim damages for any loss he has incurred as a result of Troy's breaches of covenant.

Possible defences

In any case in which a lessor has served his statutory notice, the lessee may apply to the court for relief against forfeiture. The court's jurisdiction to grant relief was originally an equitable one, but it is now enshrined in statutory provisions which provide that the court may grant or refuse relief as, having regard to the conduct of the parties and all other circumstances, it thinks fit. In other words, the court has a wide discretion in the matter of granting or refusing relief (eg, in Conveyancing Act 1973, section 17(2) (Jamaica)), and the courts have deliberately avoided laying down firm rules, so that it is impossible to predict what the court might order in a particular case. Further, the court, in granting relief, may impose whatever conditions it deems appropriate. In the present problem, it is unlikely that the court would give relief against forfeiture of the lease should Troy fail to carry out repairs to the property within the time-frame stated in the statutory notice. On the other hand, the court may be willing to grant relief to Troy with respect to breach of the user covenant, on condition that Troy takes steps to cause Seunath to stop using the basement for unauthorised purposes. It may also be mentioned that the statutes in addition give a sublessee or mortgagee the right to seek relief against forfeiture of the headlease, which might be a suitable course for Seunath to take, should Troy fail to carry out the necessary repairs to the property.

Another defence which Troy may seek to rely on is that of 'waiver of forfeiture', whereby a lessor who has demanded, sued for, or accepted rent falling due after a breach of covenant is precluded from proceeding with the forfeiture, on the reasoning that, by his actions, he is deemed to have shown an intention that the lease should continue (*Bates v Sylvester* (1960)3 WIR 136). Although Lance refused to accept rent from Troy after August, 2019, we are told that his secretary mistakenly accepted one of Troy's rent cheques in January, 2020, by paying the amount into Lance's bank account. That action by the secretary would have had the effect of waiving Lance's right to forfeit the lease on account of any previous breaches of covenant, notwithstanding (as was held in *Central Estates (Belgravia) Ltd v Woolgar (No 2)* [1972] 3 All ER 610) that the acceptance of the rent was in error. However, it is settled law that a waiver of a breach of covenant extends only to the particular breach in question, and does not extend to future breaches, ie, those occurring after the act of waiver and, by the same token, where the breach is a 'continuing' one, such as a continuing failure to carry out repairs, an acceptance of rent will waive the right to forfeiture only up to the date of the acceptance, and will not preclude the lessor from forfeiting the lease if the breach continues. In the present problem, both the failure to repair and the unauthorised user are continuing breaches, so the acceptance of the rent by Lance's employee will not affect Lance's right to forfeit the lease.

Accordingly, Lance is advised that the outcome in this case will depend upon whether the court will be willing to grant Troy relief against forfeiture. It should also be mentioned that, although forfeiture is the most effective remedy open to a lessor who has been adversely affected by a lessee's breach of covenant, he also has the common law remedy of damages which can be awarded in all cases of breach of covenant, on contractual principles. Lance is therefore advised to demand compensation in his statutory notice and, if compensation is not paid to his satisfaction, he may bring an action in court for damages in respect of the breaches of the repairing and the user covenants.

QUESTION 11

In 2018, Lenny granted to Terry a 7-year lease of a house, 'Casa Blanca', which is divided into two self-contained apartments. Terry lives in the lower apartment, and he has sublet the upper one to Steve on a quarterly tenancy.

The lease contains, inter alia, a covenant by the lessee 'not to do, or cause to be done, anything which might be a nuisance or annoyance to occupiers of neighbouring property', and a proviso for re-entry by the lessor on breach of any covenant. Rent of $2,000 (US) is payable monthly.

On March 1, 2020, Lenny sold his reversionary interest in 'Casa Blanca' to Michelle. Steve has been using his apartment as a nocturnal rendez-vous for local 'ladies of the night', but, as Terry is himself a night-shift worker, he knew nothing of this. Several of the neighbours have now complained to Michelle about the 'activities' at Steve's apartment, and Michelle has also discovered that Terry paid no rent between 1 October 2019 and 28 February 2020, though he has paid into Michelle's bank account all rent falling due since she purchased the reversion on March 1.

Advise Michelle as to what legal remedies, if any, are available to her.

Suggested answer

There are two covenants in Terry's lease that fall to be considered: (i) the covenant to pay a monthly rent of $2,000 (US), and (ii) the covenant 'not to do, or cause to be done, anything which might be a nuisance or annoyance to occupiers of neighbouring property', which is a species of user covenant. Both covenants are clearly binding on Terry, and, since the lease also contains a forfeiture clause, Michelle will be able to exercise her right of re-entry in the event of breach of either covenant.

Before considering the issue of breach of covenant and the remedies available, it is necessary to state that the effect of Lenny's sale of his reversionary interest to Michelle in March, 2020, was that, at that date, Michelle replaced Lenny as landlord and, in effect, 'stepped into his shoes' by virtue of statutory provisions (eg, Conveyancing Act (Jam), sections 12 and 13) which provide that, on assignment of a landlord's reversion, the benefits of the tenant's covenants and the burdens of the landlord's covenants *'go with'* the reversion. In the present case, both the user covenant and the covenant to pay rent are 'tenant's covenants', and so the benefit of those covenants passed to Michelle on the date of the assignment. Accordingly, if there has been a breach of any of the tenant's covenants by Terry, Michelle (and only Michelle) will have the right to sue for damages and/or forfeiture, whether such breach occurred before or after the assignment to Michelle: *London & County Ltd v Wilfred Sportsman Ltd* [1970] 2 All ER 600 (covenant to pay rent); *Re King* [1963] 1 All ER 781 (covenant to repair).

It appears that the use of the upper apartment as a meeting place for prostitutes constitutes a 'nuisance or annoyance to occupiers of neighbouring property' and is a breach of covenant, since we are told that several neighbours have complained about these activities. The fact that the activities were facilitated by Steve and that Terry knew nothing about them is no defence, though the circumstances of Terry's lack of knowledge (a) may be relevant in determining whether the breach was remediable, and (b) be taken into account by the court in deciding whether to grant him relief against forfeiture.

In consequence of this breach, Michelle may bring an action for damages and forfeiture of the lease (the lease contains a forfeiture clause), but she must first serve a statutory notice on Terry, (i) specifying the breach, (ii) requiring the breach to be remedied, if capable of remedy, and (iii) seeking damages. If, within a reasonable time, Terry fails to remedy the breach (if capable of remedy) and pay reasonable compensation to Michelle, Michelle may proceed with an action of ejectment. The main difficulty here is whether the breach is capable of remedy. Some judges have taken the view that all breaches of *negative* covenants, such as the user covenant in this case, are incapable of remedy (*Hoffmann v Fineberg* [1949] Ch 245, 254, *per* Harman J; *Scala House and District Property Co Ltd v Forbes* [1974] QB 575, 588, *per* Russell, LJ), because one cannot undo forbidden conduct that has already occurred, unlike with a positive covenant (such as a covenant to repair) which can normally be remedied (such as by carrying out the repairs). This view, however, has been disapproved in more recent cases (*Expert Clothing Service and Sales Ltd v Hillgate House Ltd*

[1996] 2 EGLR 65, 67), and in *Akici v L R Butlin Ltd* [2005] EWCA Civ 1296, Neuberger LJ opined that *Scala House* might be binding authority on whether the breach of a covenant against assignment or subletting can be remedied, but it should not be given any wider authority.

In the present case, there is the further factor of 'immoral user'. On the one hand, it may be argued that the prostitution has caused a 'stigma' to be attached to the premises which cannot be erased by cessation of the activity, so that the breach is incapable of remedy (*Rugby School Governors v Tannahill* [1935] 1 KB 87); on the other hand, it has been held that where an action for forfeiture is brought against the tenant in respect of immoral user permitted not by him but by his subtenant, the tenant may take immediate steps to put a stop to the wrongful user and enforce forfeiture against the wrongdoer and, if he does so within a reasonable time of learning the facts, the breach will be regarded as capable of remedy (*Glass v Kencakes Ltd* [1964] 3 All ER 807).

The practical significance of the question whether the breach of the user covenant is capable of remedy is that, if it is so capable, the tenant must be given a reasonable time to remedy the breach, which is generally considered to be three months from the service of the statutory notice. If, after expiry of the three month period, the breach has not been remedied, the landlord may proceed with an ejectment action. On the other hand, if the breach is incapable of remedy, the landlord may proceed with the ejectment action after 14 days (*Scala House*, above).

As soon as the landlord has served his statutory notice, the tenant may apply to the court for relief against forfeiture, which is a discretionary remedy, being derived from equity, though now statutory in some jurisdictions (eg, Belize, Landlord and Tenant Act, Cap. 189, section 15 (2)). The court may grant or refuse relief, taking into account the conduct of the parties and all other circumstances, as it thinks fit. The discretion is wide, and there are no firm rules upon which relief may be granted or refused, although it has been held that, where the breach involves immoral user, relief will be granted only in rare cases (*Central Estates (Belgravia) Ltd v Woolgar* [1971] 3 All ER 647,647). Where a headlease is forfeited, any subtenancy will automatically be destroyed, since the sublease depends for its existence on the headlease, being, so to speak, 'carved' out of the headlease. Accordingly, a subtenant may also apply to the court for relief against the forfeiture of the headlease (*Doe d Wyatt v Byron* (1845) 135 ER 685). In the present case, in view of the fact that it was Steve who was guilty of promoting the immoral conduct, it seems inconceivable that a court would grant him relief; however, the court would probably take a more favourable view towards Terry, since he has a plausible reason for not being aware of the immorality, and may grant him relief, possibly on the terms that he either causes the immorality to cease forthwith or forfeits Steve's sublease, or both.

The other breach of covenant is the non-payment of rent by Terry during the period 1 October 2019 to 28 February 2020. This breach occurred before Michelle became Terry's landlord, and we are told that Terry is not in arrears with any rent due to Michelle. Nonetheless, the effect of the property statutes (eg, Conveyancing Act, sections 12 and 13 (Jam)) is that the right to recover rent has 'gone with the reversion' to Michelle, and Lenny has lost whatever right he might have had to recover the amount (*London & County Ltd v Wilfred Sportsman Ltd* [1970] 2 All ER 600). Michelle may bring forfeiture proceedings against Terry for breach of the covenant to pay rent, but the court will readily grant a tenant relief, if he is able to pay all the arrears and costs forthwith. Accordingly, it would be incumbent on Terry to settle the outstanding rent in order to avoid forfeiture.

QUESTION 12

In 2015, Leonard, the freehold owner of residential premises, granted a 21-year lease of the premises to Terence. In the lease (which contained the usual forfeiture clause), the lessee covenanted not to assign the lease or sublet or part with the possession of the premises without the lessor's written consent, such consent not to be unreasonably withheld. The lease also contained a clause granting the lessee an option to purchase the freehold at any time during the term of the lease 'at a price to be agreed, taking into account the state of the property market at the date of the exercise of the option'.

In 2018, Leonard sold his reversionary interest to Donald. In 2020, Terence assigned the lease to William, although Donald had refused his consent to the assignment. Donald gave no reasons for his refusal, but it is common knowledge that Donald's partner had left him and is living with William. Immediately after the assignment, William gave notice to Donald that he wished to exercise the option to purchase the freehold. Donald refuses to sell and claims possession of the premises.

Advise William.

Suggested answer

The three relevant clauses in this lease are: (a) the clause prohibiting assignment, subletting or parting with possession of the premises without the lessor's consent, such consent not to be unreasonably withheld; (b) the usual forfeiture clause; and (c) the clause granting to the lessee an option to purchase the reversion. In order to advise William, it is necessary to consider, first, whether there has been a breach of the covenant against assignment and, if so, the consequences of breach; second, whether the option to purchase is enforceable against Donald.

With respect to the covenant against assignment without consent, it is significant that, by the express terms of the lease, the lessor's consent was 'not to be unreasonably withheld'. The effect of such a stipulation is that if the lessor does refuse consent but the lessee nevertheless proceeds with the assignment, the court can examine the reasonableness of the refusal and, if the court considers the refusal to be unreasonable, it can hold the assignment to be valid; if, on the other hand, the refusal is found to be reasonable, then the lessor will be entitled to forfeit the lease on account of the breach of covenant. In this case, since Terence sought Donald's consent and Donald refused consent, then, provided the court finds that the refusal of consent was in fact unreasonable, Terence will incur no liability whatsoever for breach of covenant. So the question is, was the consent unreasonably withheld? It is for Terence to prove unreasonableness. There are no fixed rules as to what is unreasonable, and it is a question of fact in each case. Tomlin J in *Houlder Bros v Gibbs* [1925] 1 Ch 575 suggested that refusal of consent will be reasonable if it is connected either with the personality of the assignee or with the manner in which he proposes to use the premises. The lessor must have some fair, solid and substantial cause for disallowing the assignment. The test is probably objective, not subjective, and therefore depends on what a reasonable lessor would think. In this case, Donald gave no reasons for his refusal. It seems that, at common law, the lessor is not bound to state any reasons for withholding his consent.

[It may be noted that under the Landlord and Tenant Act, 1988 (UK), the lessor is required to give reasons for refusal of consent, but this provision has not been enacted in Caribbean jurisdictions]. On balance, it seems likely in this case that Donald's refusal will be held to have been unreasonable, especially in the light of the evidence of a possible malicious motive for the refusal, namely that Donald resented the fact that his partner had left him and was living with the assignee (William). If the court finds Donald's refusal of consent to have been unreasonable, Terence will incur no liability for breach of covenant. On the other hand, if the refusal were held to be reasonable in the circumstances, then there would have been a breach of covenant on Terence's part, and the question as to what remedies were available against Terence and his assignee, William, would arise.

It may be noted, first of all, that in 2018 the original lessor (Leonard) sold his reversionary interest to Donald, and that the assignment of the lease took place while Donald was the lessor. At common law, since there is privity of contract between Leonard and Terence (as original lessor and lessee respectively), Terence remains liable to Leonard for any breach of covenant for the duration of the lease. However, it appears that the common law position has been overturned by the property statutes (eg, Conveyancing Act (Jam), sections 12 and 13), which provide that the benefits of covenants entered into by a lessee, and having 'reference to the subject-matter of the lease, *go with* the reversion', which has been interpreted as meaning that where a reversion is assigned, the assignee is the only person entitled to sue the lessee (or his assignee) for any breaches of covenant, whether the breach occurred before or after the assignment of the reversion: *Re King* [1963] 1 All ER 781; *London and County Ltd v Wilfred Sportsman Ltd* [1970] 2 All ER 600; *Arlesford Trading Co Ltd v Servansingh* [1971] 3 All ER 1130. Accordingly, only Donald, as assignee of the reversion, and not Leonard can sue Terence for breach of the covenant against assignment and subletting without consent. Donald could sue Terence for damages for breach of covenant and, since the lease contains a forfeiture clause, he could also bring proceedings for forfeiture of the lease. In order to obtain these remedies, he would first need to serve a statutory notice (a) specifying the breach, (b) requiring the breach to be remedied, if capable of remedy, and (c) claiming damages. Since it has been held that breach of a covenant against assignment or subletting is a 'once-and-for-all' breach which is incapable of remedy, Donald would not need to give the lessee time to remedy the breach (normally a period of at least three months), but could issue a claim for possession within 14 days (*Scala House and District Property Co Ltd v Forbes* [1973] 3 All ER 308). It would then be for the court to decide whether to grant William relief against forfeiture, a matter which is entirely within the discretion of the court and with respect to which there are no firm rules. As to service of the statutory notice, it has been held that, where the lease has been assigned, the statutory notice must be served on the assignee (William in this case), not on the assignor (Terence): *Old Grovebury Farm Ltd v W Seymour Plant Sales & Hire Ltd (No 2)* [1979] 3 All ER 504.

With respect to the option to purchase the freehold at any time during the term of the lease, the nature of such an option was described by Langrin J in a Jamaican case, *Broadway Import and Export Ltd v Levy* (1996) 33 JLR 26, 28 as

> the right to purchase a particular estate in land for a particular sum within a particular period. The option agreement constitutes an irrevocable offer to sell, and once the [lessee] has accepted that offer by exercising the option, a contract has come into being.

It is established that such an option (unlike an option to renew a lease) is not a covenant which 'touches and concerns' the land, since it affects the parties *qua* vendor and purchaser, not *qua* lessor and lessee; it is collateral to the lease and, as such, cannot run as a matter of course with the lease (*Woodall v Clifton* [1905] 2 Ch 257). Accordingly, the benefit of the option in this case does not run automatically to the assignee of the lease (William). However, it has also been held that, provided an option to purchase does not infringe the rule against perpetuities (the option in the present case clearly does not infringe the rule, since it cannot be exercised outside the perpetuity period of 21 years), its effect is to confer upon the assignee of the lease an equitable interest which, like any other property interest, is freely assignable unless the terms of the grant show that it was intended to be personal to the original lessee (*London & South Western Rly Co v Gomm* (1882) 20 Ch D 562). Thus it may be inferred that the benefit of the option passed to William on the assignment of the lease in 2010, even if the assignment made no mention of the option (*Griffith v Pelton* [1957] 3 All ER 75) and would, *prima facie*, be enforceable by William against the assignee of the reversion (Donald), provided that, at the time of assignment of the reversion in 2018, Donald had notice of it; and indeed Donald would have had such notice as the option was an express term of the lease.

It remains to consider what effect, if any, a breach of covenant by Terence would have had on the exercise of the option. It is submitted that even if Terence was in breach of covenant by assigning the lease to William, such breach would not invalidate the option unless, by the express terms of the lease, exercise of the option was made conditional on the due performance of covenants by the lessee (*Bassett v Whiteley* (1982) 45 P & CR 87).

In conclusion, (a) Donald may seek to forfeit the lease and claim damages against Terence for breach of the qualified covenant against assigning the lease without consent, but William has a good chance of defeating Donald's action by showing that Donald's consent was unreasonably withheld; alternatively, if the court does find Terence in breach, William can seek relief against forfeiture of the lease which, if granted, would put a stop to the forfeiture; (b) William is entitled to exercise the option to purchase the reversion from Donald, unless (i) the exercise of the option was made conditional on the due observance of the lessee's covenants, and (ii) the court finds that there was a breach of covenant.

QUESTION 13

Lucy, the freehold owner of 'Caribee House', a residential property comprising two separate apartments, enters into the following transactions:

(i) By a written agreement, dated 15 March, 2019, she lets Apartment No.1 to Trinny on a monthly tenancy commencing on 'April Fools' Day', and Trinny goes into possession; and

(ii) By a letter, signed and dated 20 April 2019, she lets Apartment No.2 to Vincent for a 7-year term, commencing on 1 May 2019, and Vincent goes into possession on the latter date.

Early in August, 2019, Lucy receives a most attractive offer from Guy to purchase the freehold of 'Caribee House' with vacant possession.

Accordingly, on 15 August, 2019, Lucy serves on Trinny's common law wife, Dominique, a document headed 'Notice to Quit' which states that Trinny is required to vacate Apartment No.1 'on or before 15 September, 2019'.

On the same day (15 August, 2019), Lucy approaches Vincent in order to persuade him to surrender his lease in return for a monetary sum. Vincent refuses the offer, whereupon Lucy causes the power company to disconnect the power supply to Apartment No. 2.

Discuss (a) whether the notice to quit served on Trinny is valid; and (b) whether Vincent may have any cause of action against Lucy.

Suggested answer

(a) Whether the notice to quit served on Trinny is valid

In (i), Lucy has granted Trinny a monthly tenancy commencing on 'April Fools' Day, 2019'. A court would take judicial notice of 'April Fools' Day' as meaning 1 April. Although the agreement is dated 15 March, 2019, the tenancy commences and Trinny goes into possession on 1 April 2019. In the absence of a contrary stipulation in the agreement, a monthly tenancy can be terminated by a one calendar month's notice to quit served either by the landlord or by the tenant. Such notice must be unconditional, in the sense that there must be 'plain, unambiguous words' claiming to determine the existing tenancy at a certain time. In this context, it has been held that a notice to quit 'on or before' a certain date is void if given by a tenant, but valid if given by a landlord (*Dagger v Shepherd* [1946] KB 215; *Chang v Empire Flats Ltd* (2006) HC, T&T (unreported).

A notice to quit must expire on the corresponding day in any month following the date of commencement, or on the preceding day. For instance, a tenancy commencing on 5 June, 2019 may be validly terminated by a notice to quit expiring on the 5th or the 4th December, 2019. In a Trinidadian case, *Pollonais v Gittens* (1975) CA, T&T (unreported), a monthly tenancy commenced on 3 April 1969. On 10 February 1973, the landlord served a notice on the tenant to quit 'at the end of one full month which will expire on 9th March, 1973'. The notice was held invalid, because the date of expiry was not at the end of a current period of the tenancy, which ran from the third of each month to the third of the following month. Similarly, in the present case, the notice to quit served on 15 August to expire on 15 September is invalid, as the expiry date does not correspond with the end of a current period of the tenancy, which would be the 1 day of a month, or the previous day.

Regarding service of a notice to quit, the best practice is to serve it on the tenant personally; however, it was held in *HV Holdings Ltd v Jumadeen* (1988) CA, T&T (unreported) that service on a member of the tenant's household, such as his 'common law' wife or some other person left in control of the premises, was sufficient, though in *Williams v CLICO (Trinidad) Ltd* (2008) HC, T&T (unreported), it was held that such service gave rise only to a rebuttable presumption of service on the tenant.

In the present case, in the light of the foregoing, the notice to quit served by Lucy is ineffective, since it is stated to expire on an incorrect date.

(b) Whether Vincent has any cause of action against Lucy

Lucy's letter, signed and dated 20 April 2019, would not be sufficient to grant a legal 7-year lease of Apartment No.2 to Vincent in most jurisdictions, because a fixed-term lease for 3 years or more must generally be made by deed. However, the lease will take effect as an equitable one, under the *Walsh v Lonsdale* (1882) 21 Ch 9 principle, which means that Lucy and Trinny will have, under the agreement, the same rights and obligations as if the lease had been formally made by deed. One of the implied obligations of a landlord is the covenant for quiet enjoyment, which is that the tenant shall be put into possession and have 'quiet enjoyment' of the premises during the continuance of the lease. A tenant is entitled to recover damages and/or an injunction from a landlord who substantially disturbs or physically interferes with the tenant's enjoyment of the land, such as by disconnecting the power supply, as the landlord did in a Jamaican case, *Tapper v Myrie* (1968) 11 JLR 102. Accordingly, Lucy will be liable to Vincent for her vindictive act of cutting off Vincent's power supply.

QUESTION 14

Lawrence is the fee simple owner of three properties, Blueacre, Greenacre and Yellowacre. On 15 February, 2019, Lawrence let Blueacre to Brian on a monthly tenancy, and Greenacre to Crystal Cove Ltd on a 7-year lease for the purpose of operating a casino. On 1 September 2019, Lawrence executed a declaration of condominium in relation to Yellowacre. Subsequently, the following events occurred:

- *(i) On 31 January 2020, Lawrence served on Brian's common law wife a notice to quit addressed to Brian in the following terms: 'Take notice that you are required to quit and deliver up possession of Blueacre which you hold of me as a monthly tenant on or before the 14 March, 2020'*
- *(ii) On 1 April 2020, legislation was enacted which prohibited casino gambling for a period of four years*
- *(iii) Debbie, a postgraduate law student who purchased a condominium unit in Yellowacre two months ago, has discovered (a) that the declaration of condominium relating to Yellowacre does not state the conditions to be fulfilled for amendment of the declaration, and (b) that the management of the body corporate is composed entirely of personal friends of Lawrence.*

Advise Brian, Crystal Cove Ltd and Debbie as to the legal effects of the above.

Suggested answer

In (i), Brian had been in possession of Blueacre on a monthly tenancy since 15 February 2019. Such a tenancy can be terminated by either the landlord or the tenant by service of a valid 'notice to quit'. Unless and until such a notice has been served, the tenancy will continue indefinitely. The issues in this case, therefore, are, first, whether the notice addressed to Brian was valid and, secondly, whether it was sufficient to serve Brian's common law wife rather than Brian himself. As to the validity of the notice, the first requirement is that a notice to quit must be unconditional, and there must be 'plain, unambiguous words claiming to determine the existing tenancy at a certain time' (*Gardner v Ingram* (1889) 61 LT 729,730). Lawrence's notice stated that Brian was to deliver up possession 'on or before the 14th March, 2020'. Did the use of the words 'on or before' render the notice void for uncertainty? According to Megarry & Wade, *Law of Real Property*, 6th edn, para 14–073, a notice to quit 'on or before' a certain date is valid when given by a landlord, since the tenant can be in no doubt as to when he is required to leave. Accordingly, Lawrence's notice is sufficiently certain. The second requirement is that, in a monthly tenancy, unless there is an express agreement to the contrary, one calendar month's notice must be given, which has been interpreted to mean that (i) the notice must expire on the corresponding day of the month following the month of the notice or, it seems, on the previous day (for example, a notice to quit served on the 10 March must expire on the 10 April or on the 9 April: *Crate v Miller* [1947] KB 946), and (ii) the notice must expire on the day of a month (or the previous day) which corresponds to the day of the commencement of the tenancy. This latter requirement is illustrated by *Pollonais v Gittens* (1975) CA, T&T (unreported). In this case, a monthly tenancy commenced on 3 April, 1969. On 10 February 1973, the landlord served a notice on the tenant to quit 'at the end of one full month which will expire on 9th March'. It was held that the notice was void, as the date of expiry did not correspond with the end of a 'current period of the tenancy', which ended on the 3rd of the month (the day of the month on which the tenancy commenced). For the notice to have been valid, it should have expired on the 3rd of a month or the previous day. In *Mohammed v Radoo* (2007) HC, T&T (unreported), however, it was held that provided the date of expiry corresponds with the end of a current period of the tenancy, a notice served more than a month before the end of the period will be valid. In that case the tenancy commenced on the 11th of a month. The landlord served a notice to quit on 22 July 2003, to expire on 11 September 2003. The tenant argued, citing *Pollonais*, that the notice was bad, as it should have been served exactly one month prior to the date on which it expired. The court held, however, that the notice was valid; it expired on the correct day of the month; there was no requirement that it should be served exactly one month before its expiry; what the law required was that the tenant must be given *at least* one month's notice, not exactly one month.

Applying these principles to the present problem, Brian's monthly tenancy commenced on 15 February 2019; therefore, to be valid, a notice to quit would have to be served at least one month before its expiry, and the date of expiry would need to be the 15th or the 14th of a month. This requirement was satisfied, as Lawrence's notice was expressed to expire on 14 March, 2020 and, on the authority of *Mohammed v Radoo* (above), the fact that it was served more than a month before its date of expiry does not invalidate it.

The second issue regarding the notice to quit is whether its validity was affected by the fact that it was served not on Brian personally but on his common law wife. It was held in *Ramlal v Chong* (1990) CA,T&T (unreported) that 'a notice to quit need not be served on the tenant personally; it may be served on a person constituted the agent of the tenant for the purpose of receiving the notice', and in *HV Holdings Ltd v Jumadeen* (1988) HC, T&T (unreported), it was held that service of a notice to quit on the tenant's common law wife, as a member of his household, was valid. More recently, in *Williams v CLICO (Trinidad) Ltd* (2008) HC,T&T (unreported), a distinction was made between service on an agent of the tenant (such as a solicitor or attorney appointed for that purpose), which is deemed to be service on the tenant, and service on a member of the tenant's household, which gives rise only to a presumption of service on the tenant which is rebuttable by proof that the notice did not come to his attention. In the present problem, in the absence of evidence that the notice did not actually reach Brian, it will be held to have been validly served.

Brian is accordingly advised that the notice to quit is valid in law and that it was validly served on him.

In (ii), the issue is whether the passage of legislation in April, 2020, prohibiting casino gambling, has caused frustration of the 7-year lease of Greenacre to Crystal Cove Ltd, so that the lease should be regarded as having come to an end. Traditionally, case law has denied that the doctrine of frustration can apply to a lease, as a lease is not merely a contractual obligation but is also an interest in land. It has thus been held, for example, that a building lease for 99 years commencing in May, 1936 was not frustrated (and rent remained payable) when war-time legislation prohibited building (*Cricklewood Property and Investment Trust Ltd v Leighton's Investment Trust Ltd* [1945] AC 221), and tenants have been held to remain liable to pay rent where, for instance, buildings on the demised properties were destroyed by fire (*Matthey v Curling* [1922] 2 AC 180), or enemy bombs (*Redmond v Dainton* [1920] 2 KB 256), or requisitioned by the government (*Eyre v Johnson* [1946] 1 All ER 719). Lord Simon in the *Cricklewood* case went to so far as to suggest that a lease of land could be frustrated perhaps only 'where some vast convulsion of nature swallowed up the property altogether, or buried in the depths of the sea'. More recently, however, the House of Lords in *National Carriers Ltd v Panalpina Northern* Ltd [1981] 1 All ER 161, took a more liberal view, suggesting that a lease could be frustrated by a supervening event which was so far beyond the contemplation of the parties that it would be unjust to enforce the lease. In the *National Carriers* case, where there was a 10-year lease of a warehouse, it was held that there was no frustration and rent remained payable by the tenant when the local authority closed the only access road to the warehouse, rendering it unusable for a 20-month period; but the court suggested that a longer interruption might have frustrated the lease, the matter being treated as one of degree.

In the present problem, Lawrence granted a 7-year lease of Greenacre to Crystal Cove Ltd for the specific purpose of operating a casino. The statutory prohibition of casino gambling is to last for four years. According to *National Carriers*, it is a matter of degree as to whether the interruption was so far beyond the contemplation of the parties that it would be unjust to enforce the lease. On balance, although the period of interruption is substantial and much greater than that in the *National Carriers* case, it is submitted that the prohibition of casino gambling would not have been beyond the contemplation of the parties, as casino gambling is a controversial issue and a frequent subject of debate, and is indeed illegal in several Caribbean jurisdictions. Crystal Cove Ltd is therefore advised that the lease is not frustrated and rent remains payable for the entire period of the lease.

Regarding (iii) (a), it was emphasised by Henry J in *Goodyear v Maynard* (1983) SC, Bah (unreported) that 'the declaration is the foundation stone on which the entire legal edifice in the [Law of Property and Conveyancing (Condominium) Act, Ch 139, Laws of The Bahamas] was built, and if the declaration is defective, the edifice must fall'. In the present problem, Debbie has discovered that the declaration does not state the conditions to be fulfilled for its amendment. This is contrary to section 4(1) of the Act, which states that a declaration must provide for 'the methods . . . to be observed and the conditions to be fulfilled for the amendment of the declaration by the unit owners'. The effect of the section was discussed in the *Goodyear* case, where Henry J, approving the view taken earlier by Costa J in *GLT Corp Ltd v Bank of Nova Scotia*, No E 56 of 1980 (unreported), held that the provisions of section 4(1) of the Act were mandatory and, in the absence of suitable provisions relating to amendment, the declaration was void, rendering all the titles in the particular condominium scheme defective. Debbie is accordingly advised to inform Lawrence of the need to draw up a new declaration incorporating the provisions required by section 4(1).

Regarding (iii) (b), the composition of the body corporate depends on section 13 (1) of the Act and on the bylaws of the particular condominium scheme. Section 13 (1) provides that, as from the date of the recording of the declaration, all the owners from time to time of the units in a condominium scheme constitute the body corporate, with responsibility for operating the condominium scheme, and the bylaws (as set out in the Schedule to the Act) give the unit owners the sole power to elect the members of the board of directors. In the present problem, Debbie has discovered that the board of management is composed entirely of personal friends of Lawrence, but that in itself does not indicate that the proper procedure for the appointment of the directors was not followed, which, it is submitted, is the crucial factor. This issue arose in *Cannes Resort (Freeport) Ltd v Gaudet* (2004) SC, Bah (unreported), where a clause in the declaration purported to reserve to 'the company' the right 'to appoint the majority of the directors of the body corporate until such time as all the units in the condominium have been sold', whereas the bylaws gave the unit owners the sole power to elect the members of the board. The unit owners held a meeting at which the defendants were duly elected to the board. Representatives of the company then sought the determination of the court as to whether the defendants were entitled to exercise the powers of the board to the exclusion of the company. It was held that the terms of the declaration purporting to give the company the power to appoint the directors of the body corporate could not be reconciled with the provisions of the Act and the bylaws without every unit owner being a member of the company, and none of the unit owners were in fact members. The court characterised the situation as a thinly veiled attempt by the plaintiffs, who drafted the declaration, to exercise control over the scheme, which they were not entitled to do under the Act, and it was accordingly held that the defendants had been validly appointed.

In the present problem, Debbie, as a unit owner, has power under section 23 (3) of the Act to bring an action to enforce compliance with the bylaws. If the bylaws applicable to Yellowacre are those contained in the Schedule to the Act, and if Debbie can prove that the members of the board of management were not properly appointed, she may obtain an injunction to restrain them from acting in that capacity.

QUESTION 15

Serena is the fee simple owner of a unit on the 5th floor of 'Wimbledon Condos' in Grand Bahama. She complains:

(i) That the lifts and the garbage disposal chutes in the building have been out of order for the past six months, with the result that she has been obliged to walk up and down five flights of stairs each day in order to dispose of her trash;

(ii) That Venus, the owner of the apartment immediately above Serena's has, in breach of the condominium bylaws, been in the habit of hanging her washing on her balcony rail, with the result that water constantly drips into Serena's apartment below;

(iii) That, late one evening, when returning home, Serena was 'mugged' and injured by a masked bandit in the condominium car park. There was no security guard on duty at the time, and the lighting was out of order.

Serena seeks your advice as to whether she may withhold her condominium assessments and fees until the matters of which she complains have been remedied; alternatively, what other remedies may be available to her, and against whom.

Suggested answer

(i) Under section 14 (1) of the Law of Property and Conveyancing (Condominium) Act of The Bahamas, it is the duty of the condominium's body corporate:
   (a) to operate the property for the benefit of all unit owners and to be responsible for the enforcement of the bylaws;
   (b) to keep the common property in good repair; and
   (c) to insure the building to its replacement value against fire, hurricane and sea wave.

The body corporate is thus at fault within section 14(1)(b) in failing to keep the lifts and garbage schutes, which are part of the 'common property' in the condominium, in a sufficient state of repair, so that unit owners, such as Serena, would not be inconvenienced by having to walk up and down the stairs in order to dispose of their trash. It should be remembered, however, that such repair costs are likely to be significant, and the body corporate would be financially able to meet them only if the unit owners in the condominium were up-to-date in payment of their maintenance contributions, or 'common assessments', which is the fund available to the body corporate for carrying out their management duties.

(ii) As we have seen, under section 14(1)(a) the body corporate is 'responsible for the enforcement of the bylaws'. Accordingly, the management committee should take steps to ensure that Venus ceases her practice of hanging her washing on her balcony rail in breach of the bylaws. If Venus persists in her breach, the body corporate has power under section 23(3) to bring an action 'on behalf of the unit owners' to enforce compliance with the bylaws, and the section gives the same power to any 'aggrieved unit owner'. Accordingly, if the body corporate fails to commence proceedings against a recalcitrant Venus, then Serena herself may sue. It was held in *Strachan v The Owners, Strata Corporation VR574* (1992) 28 RPR (3d) 279, that, under section 40 of the Condominium Act of British Columbia, a unit owner could apply to the court for a mandatory injunction to compel the body corporate ('strata corporation') to enforce the bylaws against other unit owners who were in breach of the bylaws. Section 23 (3) of the Bahamian statute, unlike the British Columbia statute, does not specifically mention a mandatory injunction as a remedy, but there seems no reason why it should not be interpreted as contemplating such an application on the part of an aggrieved unit owner, as the only available judicial remedy.

(iii) As in the case of repairs to the lift and garbage chutes, it is the duty of the body corporate under section 14(1)(b) to provide sufficient security and lighting for the condominium car park, as part of the 'common property'. Again, its ability to do so will depend upon the financial resources available through the assessment fees and contributions due from unit owners. This point was emphasised by the court in *Maillis v Town Court Ltd* [1989–90] 1 LRB 184, a

Bahamian case where a unit owner had been robbed and shot by a masked bandit in the condominium car park when she returned home one evening. It was held that, in the circumstances, the body corporate had not been at fault in failing to provide a higher degree of security and illumination, since there was insufficient evidence that it had the resources to do so. On the authority of *Maillis*, Serena will have no remedy against the body corporate unless there is evidence of sufficient financial resources being available to it.

(iv) As to whether Serena may withhold her condominium assessments and fees until the matters of which she complains are remedied, the answer is clear: no, she cannot. In *Towers Condominium Association v Lawrence* [1995] VIR 185, it was held that the alleged breaches of duty by the association in failing to maintain the buildings, facilities and common areas of the condominium did not justify the unit owners' withholding of the common charges payable by them. It was emphasised by Meyers J that 'nowhere in the declaration, the bylaws or the Condominium Act is a unit owner authorised or permitted to withhold the payment of common assessments for any reason. This payment is mandatory, without any exceptions'. A unit owner's duty to pay contributions was conditional solely on his acquisition of title, and, if he was involved in a dispute with the association concerning its services and operations, he was not entitled to 'exert leverage in the controversy by withholding payment, but must seek other remedy'. The obligation to pay assessments or contributions is thus independent of the body corporate's obligation to carry out repairs, and Serena is not entitled to withhold her payments.

QUESTION 16

In 2017, Vincent, the owner in fee simple of the Mont Cenis Plantation, sold and conveyed a large plot ('Greenacre') to Peter for use as a nature reserve. A road passed along one side of Greenacre, and round the other three sides Vincent erected a fence separating Greenacre from the remainder of the plantation. Vincent covenanted with Peter and his successors-in-title to keep the fence in a good state of repair and not to use any part of his retained land as a nature reserve.

For his part, Peter covenanted with Vincent and his successors-in-title not to build on Greenacre and to pay half the cost of keeping the fence in repair.

In 2019, Peter sold Greenacre to Quincy, who now proposes to build on the land. Further, Quincy refuses to contribute towards the cost of maintaining the fence. Quincy has also learned that Terence, who purchased a one-acre lot ('Redacre') from Vincent in 2020, is using his lot as a nature reserve.

Advise Quincy.

Suggested answer

The first fact to note in this problem is that on the sale of Greenacre by Vincent to Peter, both Peter and Vincent entered into covenants with one another. Vincent covenanted with Peter (i) to keep the fence on three sides of the 2-acre lot in a good state of repair (a positive covenant) and (ii) not to use any part of his retained land as a nature reserve (a negative covenant). These are freehold covenants, enforceable at common law by Peter (the covenantee) against Vincent (the covenantor). For his part, Peter covenanted with Vincent (i) not to build on his lot (a negative covenant) and (ii) to pay half the cost of keeping the fence in repair (a positive covenant). Similarly, these freehold covenants are enforceable at common law by Vincent (as covenantee) against Peter (as covenantor).

In 2019, Peter sold his lot to Quincy, who now proposes to build on it. Further, Quincy refuses to contribute towards the cost of maintaining the fence. The question to be determined, therefore, is whether Quincy, as successor-in-title to Peter, is bound by these covenants. He will be bound only if the burden of the covenants has passed to him. At common law, the burden of freehold (as opposed to leasehold) covenants never passes to successors-in-title of the original covenantor (*Austerberry v Oldham Corp* (1885) 29 Ch D 750), but the burden will pass in equity under the rule in *Tulk v Moxhay* (1848) 41 ER 1143, provided the following requirements are satisfied:

(1) The covenant must be 'restrictive', ie, negative in substance. This means that performance of the covenant must not involve expenditure of money by the covenantor and his successors. The covenant in *Tulk v Moxhay* itself (to keep the covenantor's lot 'in an open state, uncovered by any buildings') was a negative covenant, even though expressed in partly positive form, because it meant that the covenantor was *not to build* on the land. Equity favoured negative covenants because, if a breach were threatened, all the court needed to do would be to issue an injunction restraining the breach and there would be no question of the court having to supervise the performance of positive acts, which courts of equity were always reluctant to do.

(2) The covenant must have been made for the protection of other land retained by the covenantee. Since the law of restrictive covenants is based on 'dominancy and serviency' (a concept borrowed from the law of easements), there must be a 'dominant' land which is capable of deriving a benefit from the restriction on the use of the 'servient' land. If, at the time the covenant was entered into, the covenantee retained no adjacent land capable of being protected by the covenant, the burden would not run to assignees of the covenantor, but would be enforceable only against the original party to the covenant (the covenantor) on contractual principles, and it would not be an incumbrance on the land binding the covenantor's successors-in-title (*Formby v Barker* [1903] 2 Ch 539; *London County Council v Allen* [1914] 3 KB 642).

(3) It must have been the common intention of the parties that the burden of the covenant should run with the covenantor's land. In some jurisdictions, eg, in Barbados (Property Act, Cap 236, section 84(1)), Belize (Law of Property Act, Cap 190, section 22 (1)), Bermuda (Conveyancing Act 1983, section 22(1)), it is provided that, unless a contrary intention appears, covenants relating to the covenantor's land are deemed to have been made by the covenantor on behalf of himself, his successors-in-title and other persons deriving title under him or them. In other words, it will be inferred that the burden of a restrictive covenant was intended to run with the covenantor's land and to be binding on his successors, unless the conveyance expressly provides to the contrary. In other jurisdictions, which have no equivalent statutory provisions, it would be necessary to prove affirmatively that the parties intended the burden on the servient land to be binding on successors.

(4) The covenant must 'touch and concern' the dominant land, in the sense that it must 'either affect the land as regards mode of occupation or affect the value of the land'(Farwell J in *Rogers v Hosegood* ([1900] 2 Ch 388).
(5) Since a restrictive covenant is an equitable interest, it will not be automatically binding on purchasers of the servient land; more precisely, in common with other equitable interests, it will not be binding on a bona fide purchaser of the servient land without notice of the covenant. Where title to the servient land is registered, the dominant owner should ensure that the covenant is protected by entry of a memorandum on the certificate of title or by a caution or caveat imposed on the registered title, depending on the proper procedure in the particular jurisdiction.

A. The covenants entered into by Vincent

It is necessary to decide whether the two covenants entered into by Vincent satisfy the above requirements. The first covenant – to keep the fence in a good state of repair – is a positive covenant involving expenditure of money and clearly does not satisfy the first requirement. The burden of this covenant will not run to Terence (the purchaser of Redacre), though Vincent remains liable (as original covenantor) to Peter (as original covenantee) under their contractual relationship. The second covenant (not to use any part of the land retained by Vincent as a nature reserve), is clearly negative in substance and the burden will have run to Terence if the other four requirements are satisfied. The second requirement is satisfied, on the assumption that the covenant was taken for the benefit of the lot sold to Peter. The third requirement will be satisfied if it was intended by the parties (Vincent and Peter) that the burden should pass. In those jurisdictions where there is legislation equivalent to section 79 of the English Law of Property Act (Property Act, Cap 236, section 84(1) (Barbados); Law of Property Act, Cap 190, section 62(1) (Belize); Conveyancing Act, 1983, section 22(1) (Bermuda)), an intention that the burden should run is presumed, provided there is no contrary intention expressed, but in other jurisdictions there must be evidence of such intention. In the present problem, there is clearly an intention that the *benefit* should run (Vincent covenanted 'with Peter and his successors-in-title'), but no positive evidence of an intention that the *burden* should run. This would mean that, in those jurisdictions which do not have the equivalents to the section 79 provisions, the burden of the covenant forbidding use of any part of the Mont Cenis Plantation as a health farm would not be binding on Terence, though Vincent would remain contractually bound to Peter.

As to whether the restrictive covenant entered into by Vincent is enforceable by Quincy, the present freehold owner of Greenacre, the answer depends on whether the equitable rules for the running of the benefit of freehold covenants are satisfied (the common law rules for the running of the benefit are inapplicable in this case, because the alleged servient land (Redacre) is no longer owned by the original covenantor (Vincent)). Under the equitable rules, it must be shown that the benefit of the covenant has passed to Quincy either (a) by annexation, or (b) by express assignment, or (c) under a scheme of development. Methods (c) and (b) can be discounted in this case because there is no scheme of mutually enforceable obligations, nor any indication of an express assignment of the covenant. Quincy must therefore be able to show that the benefit of the covenant has been annexed to the dominant land (Greenacre). Were there express words of annexation? It seems that there were not, as the covenant was made 'with Peter and his successors-in-title', with no express mention of the land (Greenacre) to be benefited. Such a lack of reference to a dominant tenement was held to preclude annexation in *Renals v Cowlishaw* (1878) 9 Ch D 125, in *Pass v Ramsahoye* (1986) HC, Barb (unreported) and (at first instance) *in Halfmoon Bay Ltd v Crown Eagle Hotels Ltd* (1996) 33 JLR 103. On the other hand, in those jurisdictions which have legislation equivalent to section 78 of the Law of Property Act, 1925 (UK), namely Barbados (section 83(1) of the Property Act, Cap 236), Belize (section 61 of the Law of Property Act, Cap 190) and Bermuda (section 21 of the Conveyancing Act, 1983), it can be argued that, on the authority of *Federated Homes Ltd v Mill Lodge Properties Ltd* [1980] 1 All ER 371, no express words of annexation were necessary, since the statutory provisions have the effect of automatically annexing the benefit of restrictive covenants to the dominant land. This argument is not guaranteed to succeed, however, as Brightman LJ in *Federated Homes* appeared to leave open the question whether it is necessary for the covenant to identify the dominant tenement.

B. The covenants entered into by Peter

Regarding the covenants entered into by Peter, the first one (to pay half the cost of keeping the fence in repair) is positive and the burden therefore does not run to Quincy under *Tulk v Moxhay*, but it may be binding on Quincy under the principle in *Halsall v Brizzell* [1957] 1 All ER 371, which is that a person who wishes to take advantage of a shared service (such as access roads, drains and, as in this case, a shared fence) must comply with any corresponding obligation to contribute to the cost of maintaining it; in Lord Denning's words, 'He who takes the benefit must accept the burden' (*Ives v High* [1967] 1 All ER 504). If the evidence shows that Quincy does in fact benefit from the existence of the fence, he will be bound in equity to observe the covenant to contribute to the cost of its maintenance: *Rhone v Stephens* [1994] 2 All ER 65. The second covenant entered into by Peter, not to build on his lot, is very similar to the actual covenant in *Tulk v Moxhay*, where Elms covenanted to keep the lot purchased by him forever in an open state, uncovered by any buildings. This is a classic negative covenant, which satisfies the first requirement for the running of the burden. The second requirement is also satisfied, as the covenant was taken for the benefit of the land retained by Vincent. The third requirement, that the parties should have intended the burden to run with the servient land will, as in the case of the covenant entered into by Vincent, be satisfied by statute (as discussed above) in those jurisdictions which have copied section 79 of the Law of Property Act; in other jurisdictions, in the absence of positive evidence of such intention, the burden will not run to Quincy. Accordingly, it is unlikely that Quincy can be restrained from building on his lot.

The final point is that, since Vincent (as original covenantee) is still the owner of the Mont Cenis Plantation, there is no issue as to the running of the benefit of the covenant entered into by Peter.

QUESTION 17

Arawak Investments Ltd ('Arawak') were the fee simple owners of a disused dockland area. In 2016, Arawak converted a number of derelict warehouses on the site into townhouses with a view to future sale.

In 2017, the rest of the dockland area, including a private wharf, was sold by Arawak to Carib Inc ('Carib') for conversion into a water sports and leisure centre. Carib covenanted in the conveyance on behalf of itself and its successors-in-title

(1) *To use the property exclusively for the purpose of a water sports and leisure centre, including the mooring of small boats*
(2) *To maintain the wharf and its installations in proper working order*
(3) *Not to berth or permit to be berthed any vessel having a gross tonnage in excess of 75 tons.*

All three covenants were duly protected by entry on the registered title of the land sold.

In March and April 2019, Arawak sold the town houses to various purchasers in fee simple.

Three months ago, Carib went into liquidation and its assets were sold to the Maya Oil Company ('Maya'). The wharf is now in a dangerous condition and Maya proposes to demolish it. Maya is also seeking planning permission to convert the leisure centre into an oil storage depot to be served by large tankers.

Advise the owners of the townhouses as to whether they can prevent Maya from going ahead with its proposals.

Suggested answer

In 2017, having previously converted some derelict warehouses into town houses with a view to future sale, Arawak Ltd sold the rest of the dockland area, including a private wharf, to Carib Inc. As purchaser, Carib Inc entered into three covenants in the conveyance on behalf of itself and its successors-in-title. All three covenants, being equitable interests, were duly protected by entry on the registered title of the land sold. These are 'freehold' covenants, since they were entered into between two fee simple owners, namely Arawak and Carib.

In order to advise the owners of the town houses as to whether they can prevent the Maya Oil Company from going ahead with its proposal to demolish the wharf and convert the leisure centre into an oil storage depot, it is necessary to determine whether (a) the burden of the covenants has passed to Maya, as successor-in-title of the covenantor (Carib), and (b) whether the benefit of the covenants has passed to the townhouse owners, as successors-in-title to the covenantee (Arawak).

Regarding the running of the *burden*, it is well established that the burden of a freehold covenant never runs at common law, but it may run *in equity* if the following requirements are satisfied:

(i) The covenant is restrictive (ie negative) in substance (*Tulk v Moxhay* (1848) 41 ER 1143)
(ii) The covenant was made for the protection of other land retained by the covenantee (*London County Council v Allen* [1914] 3 KB 642)
(iii) It was the common intention of the parties that the burden should run with the covenantor's land.

As to whether these requirements are satisfied in this case, firstly it is clear that covenants (i) and (iii) are negative in substance (even though covenant (i) is expressed in a positive form of words) because they *prohibit* the covenantor from certain conduct. Covenant (ii), on the other hand, is clearly positive because it requires the covenantor to take positive action which will require effort and expenditure of money. Secondly, the covenants were made for the protection of other land retained by the covenantee (the area on which the townhouses were erected). Thirdly, it seems to have been the common intention of the parties that the burden of the covenants should run, since the covenantor, Carib, expressly covenanted 'on behalf of itself and its successors-in-title'. Indeed, in some jurisdictions, statutory provisions provide that, unless a contrary intention appears, covenants relating to the covenantor's land are deemed to have been made by the covenantor on behalf of himself, his successors-in-title, and persons deriving title under him or them (eg, Barbados, Cap. 236, section 84(1), Belize, Cap. 190, section 62(1)), which means that, in those jurisdictions, the intention that the burden of covenants should run will be automatically implied, unless a contrary intention is shown.

Accordingly, the burden of covenants (1) and (3) will have run to Maya, as successor-in-title to the original covenantor, Carib, and the covenants will be binding on Maya. On the other hand, since covenant (2) is positive, in that it requires effort and expenditure on the part of the covenantor, the burden will not run to Maya, either at common law or in equity, and so it will not be binding on Maya, though it will remain binding on the original covenantor, Carib.

The next question is whether the *benefit* of the covenants has passed to the owners of the townhouses, as successors-in-title to the original covenantee, Arawak. There are three possible methods whereby the benefit of a restrictive covenant can run in equity: (i) By 'annexation' to the dominant land, using express wording in the conveyance of the dominant land to a purchaser; (ii) By express assignment of the benefit to a purchaser of the dominant land; (iii) Under a 'scheme of development' (or 'building scheme'). We are not told anything about the wording of the conveyances of the townhouses to the various purchasers in March and April, 2019, so there is no evidence of annexation; nor are we told that there were any express assignments of the benefit of the covenants; nor are we told that Arawak had an intention to create or did create a scheme of development in relation to the town houses. Therefore, none of the traditional requirements for the running of the benefit of the covenants has been satisfied.

However, in at least three Caribbean jurisdictions, the principle in *Federated Homes Ltd v Mill Lodge Properties Ltd* [1980] 1 All ER 371 will enable the dominant owners to establish that they are entitled to the benefit of the covenants. It was held in that case that the wording of section 78 of the Law of Property Act 1925 (UK) had the effect of automatically annexing the benefit of a restrictive covenant to the dominant land, without the need for express words of annexation. The wording of section 78 has been substantially reproduced in Barbados (Cap 236, section 83(1)), Belize (Cap 190, section 61) and Bermuda (Conveyancing Act 1983, section 21). However, it seems that in other Caribbean jurisdictions, where the property legislation is based not on LPA 1925 but on the earlier Conveyancing Act 1881, the *Federated Homes* principle will not apply, since it was held in *J Sainsbury plc v London Borough of Enfield* [1989] 1 WLR 590 that the wording of the earlier statute was significantly different and insufficiently precise to annex the benefit of a covenant to the dominant land.

In conclusion, although the burden of the two negative covenants, nos. (1) and (3), has run to Maya, the owners of the townhouses will be unable to enforce the covenants against Maya because the benefit of the covenants has not run to them, unless the events occurred in Barbados, Belize or Bermuda. Accordingly, except in the latter jurisdictions, the townhouse owners will be unable to prevent Maya from carrying out its proposal to convert the leisure centre into an oil storage depot to be served by large tankers. Regarding covenant (2), Maya is not bound to maintain the wharf and its installations because the covenant is a positive one and the burden cannot run, and unless Arawak, as original covenantee, is willing to enforce the covenant against Carib, it seems that Maya will be free to demolish the wharf.

QUESTION 18

In 2005, Job, a Jamaican property developer, purchased a large area of land, 'Babylon Heights', which he divided into 12 lots [Lots A-L] and sold to various purchasers, subject to covenants:

(i) not to erect more than one dwelling house on each lot

(ii) not to carry on any trade or business on any lot

(iii) in the case of lots K and L only, not to create a nuisance on the land.

Noah, the present owner of Lot A, which he purchased last year from Cain, and of Lot B, which he purchased two years ago from Abel, has obtained planning permission to construct on the two lots a resort complex comprising four buildings with a swimming pool and tennis courts. Moses, the present owner of Lot C, objects to the proposed resort construction by Noah, claiming that it would constitute a breach of the covenants.

Discuss:

(i) Whether Moses is entitled to enforce the covenants against Noah;

(ii) Whether Noah may obtain a discharge or modification of the covenants.

Suggested answer

(i) In order to determine whether Noah is liable on the covenants, the first point to note is that Noah is not an original covenantor (having purchased his lots from Cain and Abel), and therefore will be liable only if the burden of the covenants has passed to him. The covenants in this case are freehold ones, as they came into being when Job sold and conveyed the 12 lots to purchasers in 2005. It is well established that the burden of a freehold covenant never runs at common law (*Austerberry v Oldham Corporation* (1885) 29 Ch D 750), but it may run in equity under the rule in *Tulk v Moxhay* (1848) 41 ER 1143 provided (i) it is negative in substance, (ii) it was made for the protection of other land retained by the covenantee (*London County Council v Allen* [1914] 3 KB 642; *Formby v Barker* [1903] 2 Ch 539), (iii) the covenant touches and concerns the land, and (iv) the burden was intended to run. It appears that all four requirements were satisfied with respect to the covenants (not to build more than one dwelling house on each lot, and not to carry on any trade or business on a lot), so that the burden will have passed to Noah. As to whether Moses can enforce the two covenants against Noah, Moses would no doubt seek to show that Babylon Heights was subject to a scheme of development (building scheme). If there is a scheme of development, the effect will be that each purchaser and his assignees will be able to sue or be sued on the covenants by every other purchaser and his assignees. The existence of a scheme of development thus makes it unnecessary to show that the benefits of the covenants were annexed to the dominant land or that they had been expressly assigned to the person seeking to enforce them. Is there a scheme of development in this case? The question may be answered with reference to the requirements for the existence of a building scheme laid down by Parker J in *Elliston v Reacher* [1908] 2 Ch 374: viz, (a) both plaintiff and defendant in the action must have derived their titles from a common vendor; (b) the common vendor must have laid out his estate for sale in lots subject to restrictions that were intended to be imposed on all the lots, and which were consistent only with some general scheme of development; (c) the restrictions must have been intended to be for the benefit of all the lots sold, and if the restrictions were obviously calculated to enhance the value of each lot, the intention will be readily inferred; (d) the original purchasers must have bought their lots on the understanding that the restrictions were to be for the benefit of the other lots; (e) the geographical area of the scheme must be ascertained with reasonable certainty. The principles in *Elliston* are still good law, but the courts have not always applied them strictly (eg, in *Re Dolphin's Conveyance* [1970] 2 All ER 664, a scheme of development was held to exist despite the absence of both a common vendor and prior lotting), and the modern approach seems to require only two necessary characteristics, (i) that the land to which the scheme relates must be identified, and (ii) that there was a common intention on the part of the purchasers that there should be 'reciprocity of obligation'. In a Trinidadian case, *Emile Elias and Co Ltd v Pine Groves Ltd* [1993] 1 WLR 305, the Privy Council denied the existence of a scheme of development on the grounds, first, that the area of the scheme was not sufficiently defined and, second, that the covenants imposed on some of the lots differed substantially from those imposed on others. In Lord Browne-Wilkinson's words, 'it is not sufficient that the common vendor has himself defined the area. In order to create a valid building scheme, the purchasers of all the land within the area of the scheme must also know what the area is'. Further,

> if, as in the present case, the lots are all of a similar nature and all intended for high-class development consisting of one dwelling on a substantial plot, a disparity in the covenants imposed is a powerful indication that there was no intention to create reciprocally enforceable rights.

In the present problem, it is not clear from the facts whether, at the time of the sales of the lots to the various purchasers in 2005, the latter were aware that Job intended to create a building scheme but, assuming that the purchasers did have knowledge of such intention and of the precise area of the scheme, there is the further objection that there was a disparity in the covenants, in that the covenant not to create a nuisance on the land applied only to lots K and L. In the *Emile Elias* case, two of the lot owners had similarly covenanted not to create a nuisance on the land while the others were free of such a covenant, which is similar to the situation in the present problem. However, the disparity was greater in *Emile Elias* in that, in that case, some lots were subject to a restriction that any building erected thereon was to be used only as a private dwelling, while others were free of such restriction – a significant difference, opening up the possibility that the area could become substantially commercialised. In the present problem, the only discrepancy concerns the non-nuisance covenant imposed on lots K and L, and it is arguable that the discrepancy between the covenants is not so great as to lead the court to deny the existence of a scheme of development, especially since the first three of the *Elliston v Reacher* requirements have clearly been satisfied. If the court were to hold that a building scheme was indeed established in 2005, Moses, as a lot owner within the scheme, will be entitled to enforce the restrictions against Noah.

(ii) In order to obtain a discharge or modification of the restrictive covenants, so as to enable him to construct a resort complex, Noah would have to establish one or more of the grounds laid down by section 3(1) of the Restrictive Covenants (Discharge and Modification) Act of Jamaica, namely

(a) that, by reason of changes in the character of the property or the neighbourhood, the restriction ought to be deemed obsolete; or
(b) that the continued existence of such restriction, or its continued existence without modification, would impede the reasonable user of the land for public or private purposes, without securing to any person any practical benefits sufficient to justify the continued existence of the restrictions, or their continued existence without modification; or
(c) that the persons entitled to the benefits of the restrictions have agreed, either expressly or impliedly, by their acts or omissions, to discharge or modification; or
(d) that the proposed discharge or modification will not injure the persons entitled to the benefit of the restrictions.

Unfortunately for Noah, the courts have interpreted these provisions restrictively and it is very difficult to obtain a discharge or modification on any of the statutory grounds. It has been held, for instance, that ground (a), obsolescence, can be established only where there is proof that the original purpose for which a covenant was imposed can no longer be achieved (*Re Truman, Hanbury, Buxton and Co's Application* [1955] 3 WLR 704), and the Jamaican courts have taken the view that, in order to obtain a discharge or modification on this ground, it must be shown that there has been a fundamental change in the character of the neighbourhood such as to render the covenants obsolete. It is not sufficient, for example, to show evidence of a tendency to subdivision of lots in the neighbourhood resulting in differences in the style, appearance and arrangement of the buildings (*Re 48 Norbrook Avenue* (1994) SC, Jam, unreported); nor, it has been held, does the fact that many lot owners have followed a practice of letting residential property to vacationing tourists as a commercial enterprise amount to a fundamental change in the character of the neighbourhood from residential to commercial (*Stephenson v Liverant* (1972) 18 WIR 323). It is true that, more recently, the courts in Jamaica and Barbados, where the statutory provisions governing discharge and modification are similarly worded, have been more willing to grant discharge or modification on the ground of obsolescence, especially where, in response to growing urbanisation, there has been an increase in the number of multi-unit dwellings, such as apartment complexes, and a decrease in the number of large single dwelling houses: *Re Boyce* (2005) HC, Barb (unreported); *Re 30 Dillsbury Avenue, St Andrew* (2011) SC, Jam (unreported), In the present problem, however, there is no indication of any such change in the character of the neighbourhood, and so it is likely that discharge or modification would be refused.

An application for discharge or modification based on ground (b) (impeding the reasonable user of the land) is also likely to fail. In *Stannard v Issa* [1987] AC 175, the Privy Council, endorsing the 'powerful' dissenting judgment of Carey JA in the Jamaican Court of Appeal, confirmed that, in order to succeed on this ground, it must be shown that the restrictions have 'sterilised' the reasonable use of the land; the court must be satisfied not only that the permitted use of the land is a reasonable one, but also that the applicant's proposed use is the *only* reasonable one; it was not sufficient merely to show that the neighbourhood was in a tourist area and that the proposed development would be in harmony with it. In the present problem, an application on this ground also would be likely to fail.

There is no evidence of express or implied agreement to modify within ground (c). As for ground (d) (no injury to objectors), the courts have again taken a restrictive view, holding that, in order to discharge or modify, the court must be of the view that the objections raised to the proposed development are 'insubstantial' or 'vexatious': *Ridley v Taylor* [1965] 2 All ER 51; *Re System Sales Ltd's Application* (1992) 43 WIR 19. Where the neighbourhood is a 'quiet and peaceful enclave', a proposed development which envisages a resort complex with amenities such as tennis courts and swimming pools is likely to substantially interfere with the 'peace and quiet' of the area, and an objection to such a development is unlikely to be considered insubstantial or vexatious.

In conclusion, it is submitted that Job established a scheme of development in 2005, that the covenants are binding on Noah, and that Moses may bring an action for an injunction to restrain Noah from proceeding with his proposed development. Further, it is unlikely that Noah would obtain a discharge or modification of the covenants.

QUESTION 19

Usain was the fee simple owner of two adjacent plots of agricultural land, Yellowacre and Greenacre. Usain built a farmhouse on Yellowacre where he lived and, although a highway passed directly in front of the farmhouse, Usain frequently preferred to take a short cut on foot across Greenacre, which was an open field, to a nearby mini-mart. Last year, Usain sold Yellowacre to Don and this year he sold Greenacre to Shelly-Ann. Upon taking possession of Greenacre, Shelly-Ann noticed that Don was in the habit of driving his tractor across Greenacre. Moreover, she discovered that a shed on Greenacre, which Usain had used to store lumber, was being used by Don as a shelter for his goats.

Shelly-Ann seeks your advice as to whether she can lawfully prevent Don from driving his tractor across Greenacre and from using the shed in the aforementioned manner.

How would your advice differ if the sale of Greenacre to Shelly-Ann had preceded the sale of Yellowacre to Don?

Suggested answer

The essential question in this case is whether Don has acquired easements to (i) drive his tractor across Greenacre and (ii) use the shed on Greenacre as a shelter for his goats. If the answer is in the affirmative, then Shelly-Ann should be advised that she cannot lawfully prevent Don from exercising those rights.

The first issue is whether those rights are capable of existing as easements in law. Are the necessary characteristics of an easement as laid down in *Re Ellenborough Park* [1955] 3 All ER 667 satisfied? Requirement (1) is that there must be dominant and servient tenements. This requirement is clearly satisfied: Yellowacre is the dominant tenement to be benefited and Greenacre the servient tenement over which the rights are to be exercised. Requirement (2) is that the rights must 'accommodate' the dominant tenement, in the sense that the rights claimed must be sufficiently connected with the enjoyment of the dominant tenement and must be for its benefit. This requirement is potentially satisfied in this case, in so far as rights of way and rights of storage are well recognised as accommodating a dominant tenement. Requirement (3) is that the right must be 'capable of forming the subject matter of a grant', which has various elements, such as (a) the right must not be too vague, (b) it must not substantially deprive the servient owner of possession of the servient tenement, and (c) there must be a capable grantor and a capable grantee. In the present case, it could not reasonably be contended that if Don drives his tractor across Greenacre or uses the shed to shelter his goats, he is substantially depriving Shell-Ann of possession of Greenacre or of the shed itself, nor are either of these rights too vague to be recognised as easements. Further, Usain is a capable grantor and Don a capable grantee. Accordingly, it seems that the *Ellenborough Park* requirements are satisfied in this case.

The next issue is whether Don has legally acquired the rights of way and storage. An easement can be acquired (i) by express grant (or reservation), (ii) implied grant (or reservation), or (iii) prescription. There was no express grant of the easements by deed in this case, nor a 20 years' user of the rights as required for prescription. Don, however, can claim that he has acquired the rights as implied easements under the rule in *Wheeldon v Burrows* (1879) 12 Ch D 31. The rationale for the rule is that where X owns two adjoining tenements, Redacre and Blueacre, and he is in the habit of walking or driving across Blueacre as an alternative means of access from Redacre to the outside world, one cannot speak of X enjoying an easement over Blueacre, as X is merely exercising his right as owner of Blueacre itself; but if X sells Redacre to Y, the doctrine of non-derogation from grant requires that Y should not be in a less favourable position than X was, and Y may become entitled to an easement of way over Blueacre. In this context, X's enjoyment of the access across Blueacre may conveniently be called a quasi-easement, which, on the sale of Redacre, ripens into a full legal easement. Thus, under *Wheeldon v Burrows*, upon the grant of part of the grantor's land, there will pass to the grantee as easements all quasi-easements over the land retained that:

(a) were continuous and apparent; and
(b) were necessary to the reasonable enjoyment of the land granted; and
(c) had been, and were at the time of the grant, used by the grantor for the benefit of the part granted.

'Continuous' under the rule means that the enjoyment on the part of the previous owner must have been at least regular, though not necessarily constant, and 'apparent' means that there must be some obvious and permanent mark on the land itself which can be seen on a careful inspection of the property, such as a made road or a worn track (*Hansford v Jago* [1921] 1 Ch 322). 'Necessary to the reasonable enjoyment of the land' is not to be equated with an easement of necessity, and the requirement will be satisfied despite the presence of some alternative means of access (like the highway passing in front of Yellowacre in the present case) (*Horn v Hiscock* (1972) 223 EG 1437, 1441). We are not told in the present case whether there was a worn track across Greenacre where Usain was in the habit of walking, but the other *Wheeldon v Burrows* requirements appear to have been satisfied since the 'short cut' to the mini-mart clearly enhanced the enjoyment of Yellowacre, and it was used by Usain right up to the time he sold Yellowacre to Don.

With respect to the shed, it would appear that all the *Wheeldon* requirements were satisfied. Usain continuously stored his lumber there, right up to the time of the sale of Yellowacre to Don; the shed was apparent on a visual inspection of Greenacre; and the use of the shed for storage was necessary to the reasonable enjoyment of Yellowacre.

On the assumption that Don, when he purchased Yellowacre from Usain, acquired an easement of way across Greenacre and an easement of storage in the shed on Greenacre, the next question is (i) whether Don is entitled not only to cross Greenacre on foot but also to drive across it with his tractor, and (ii) whether he is entitled to use the shed as a shelter for his goats rather than for storage of lumber. This issue essentially concerns the *extent* of the easements acquired by Don. It has been held that where an easement is acquired by implied grant, as in this case, the extent of the easement is limited by reference to its established use at the time of the conveyance of the dominant tenement (*Milner's Safe Co Ltd v Great Northern Railway Co* [1907] 1 Ch 208). Thus, in a Belizean case, *Card v Card* (1982) SC, Bel (unreported), it was held that where an easement of way had previously been enjoyed on foot or with a bicycle, the driving of a vehicle across the land was an excessive user and constituted a trespass, in accordance with the principle that 'a right of way cannot be properly exercised by the dominant owner so as to increase the burden originally cast on the servient tenement and to the detriment of the servient owner'. Accordingly, in the present case, Don is not entitled to drive his tractor across Greenacre, since the user by Usain was on foot only. Accordingly, Shelly-Ann may obtain an injunction to restrain Don from driving his tractor across Greenacre. As for the use of the shed, it is submitted that the user by Don (sheltering his goats) is not markedly different from the user enjoyed by Usain (storing lumber) and does not increase the burden on the servient tenement. Accordingly, Shelly-Ann will have no cause of action in relation to the shed.

Finally, if the sale of Greenacre to Shelly-Ann had preceded the sale of Yellowacre to Don, the rule in *Wheeldon v Burrows* would not have applied, so that no implied easements of way or storage would have been acquired by Don. This is because the rule is based on *'non-derogation from grant'*, and where the quasi-servient tenement is sold first, no easements will be implied in favour of the quasi-dominant owner because that would not be a case of implied grant but of implied reservation. Accordingly, when the quasi-dominant tenement is then sold, the purchaser will not be in any better position than the vendor.

QUESTION 20

In 2011, Laura granted a 7-year lease of a self-contained apartment on the upper floor of her house to Terry, and Laura retained possession of the ground floor area, garden and yard. Since they were on good terms, Laura gave Terry permission to hang his washing on a clothes line in the garden; to use her greenhouse to grow whatever he wished; and to park his car in her garage whenever she was away on any of her frequent business trips. In 2018, Laura renewed Terry's lease in writing for a further 7-year term, the renewal making no mention of the use of the clothes line, greenhouse or garage.

In 2019, Terry's uncle, Nigel, who owns the adjacent property, Brownacre, on which there is a paved road over which Laura has a right of way to the public highway, opened a factory on the land, constructing ramps on the road to reduce the speed of vehicles. Laura complains that on account of the numbers of heavy vehicles passing along the road and the existence of the ramps, it is no longer convenient for her to exercise her right of way. In retaliation, she has forbidden Terry the use of her clothes line, greenhouse and garage.

Advise the parties as to the legal position.

Suggested answer

During the first 7-year lease (2011–2018), Laura gave her tenant, Terry, licences to use her clothes line, greenhouse and garage. By virtue of statutory provisions modelled on section 6(1) of the Conveyancing Act, 1881 and section 62 of the Law of Property Act, 1925 (UK) (such as section 66 of the Property Act, Cap 236 (Barbados), section 6 of the Conveyancing and Law of Property Act, Ch 138 (The Bahamas), and section 9 of the Conveyancing Act, 1973 Rev. (Jamaica)), such licences, if capable of existing as easements, will have been converted into fully fledged easements on the renewal of the lease in 2018. The statutory provisions state that 'a conveyance of land shall be deemed to include, and shall . . . operate to convey with the land all buildings, erections, fixtures . . . ways, watercourses, liberties, privileges, easements, rights and advantages whatsoever . . . appertaining to the land'. The word 'conveyance' has been held to include the renewal of a lease, provided the renewal is in writing (as was the case in the present problem). Thus, eg, in *Wright v Macadam* [1949] 2 All ER 565, an oral permission granted by the landlord to his tenant to store her coal in a shed on land in the possession of the landlord, was converted into an easement of storage when he granted her a new lease by an unsealed document that made no reference to the shed. This was the unintended result of the operation of the statutory provision. It is therefore advisable for a landlord who is about to renew a lease to take care to first revoke any licences which he has given to the tenant, so as to prevent any further enjoyment of them, or alternatively to insert a provision in the new lease to exclude the application of the statutory provision. Apart from the requirement that there must be a 'conveyance' of land, other requirements for the application of the sections are (i) that the right must be capable of being an easement and (ii) there must have been some diversity of ownership or occupation of the dominant and servient tenements prior to the conveyance (*Sovmots Investments Ltd v Secretary of State for the Environment* [1977] 2 All ER 385, 391, 397), though the second of these two requirements was doubted and not applied by the court in *P&S Platt Ltd v Crouch* [2003] EWCA Civ 1110.

In the present problem, as suggested above, the renewal of the lease constituted a 'conveyance' within the sections, and the requirement of diversity of occupation of the dominant and servient tenements is satisfied. It is also significant that the dominant owner (Terry) is a tenant of the servient owner (Lorna), and it is perfectly possible for a tenant to acquire an easement as against his own landlord by implied grant (as in this case, where easements are implied under the statutes), though he cannot do so by prescription.

The next requirement to be satisfied is that the licences should be capable of existing as easements; in other words, they must possess the necessary characteristics stated in *Re Ellenborough Park* [1955] 3All ER 667, which are (i) there must be a dominant and a servient tenement, (ii) the rights must accommodate the dominant tenement, ie, they must be for the benefit of the dominant tenement and sufficiently connected to its enjoyment, (iii) the rights must be capable of forming the subject-matter of a grant (which means that they must not be too vague, or too extensive, or substantially deprive the servient owner of possession of his own land). There clearly are dominant and servient tenements in this case (the upper apartment is the dominant tenement and the relevant areas on the ground floor in the possession of Laura are the servient tenement), and the rights claimed clearly accommodate the dominant tenement. The only doubtful question in this case is whether the rights claimed are too vague or extensive, or whether their exercise could have the effect of depriving Laura of possession of parts of her own land. With respect to the clothes line, there is authority for the view that the right to hang washing on a line is capable of being an easement (*Drewell v Towler* (1832) 110 ER 268; *Pallister v Clark* (1975) 30 P&CR 84); with respect to the use of the greenhouse, it would seem that the right is not too extensive, nor does it deprive Laura of possession of the greenhouse, provided that Laura would be able to continue using it for growing her own plants and vegetables (*Wright v Macadam* [1949] 2 All ER 565, where the right to store coal in a shed was held to be capable of being an easement, the court seemingly accepting that exercise of the right would not prevent the servient owner from using the shed himself). The right to park a car in Laura's garage, on the other hand, cannot exist as an easement, for two reasons: first, it seems to be established that the right to park a car in a defined space (such as a garage, unless it can hold more than one car) amounts to ouster of the owner from possession of the servient tenement and therefore cannot be an easement (*London and Blenheim Estates Ltd v Ladbroke Retail Parks Ltd* [1993] 1 All ER 307); it is otherwise if the right is to park anywhere in a larger parking area, rather than in a defined or reserved space (*Newman v Jones* (1982) Ch Div, unreported). Secondly, there can be no easement of parking in favour of Terry because his licence to park was restricted to times when Lorna was away on her business trips. It is of the essence of an easement that it can be enjoyed at any time the dominant owner wishes; if restrictions are placed on the time for enjoyment, it cannot be an easement (*Green v Ashco Horticulturalist Ltd* [1966] 2 All ER 232). Therefore, whereas the licences to hang washing on the line and to use the greenhouse for growing plants ripened into easements in 2018, and Lorna can be restrained from interfering from their enjoyment, the licence to park cannot qualify as an easement and Lorna is entitled to withdraw it.

Regarding the actions of Nigel, Lorna's claim is essentially one for disturbance of the easement. It is not every interference with the full enjoyment of an easement that amounts in law to a disturbance. There must be some substantial interference with the dominant owner's enjoyment. Where a private right of way is obstructed, as here, the dominant owner cannot complain unless he can prove injury. The test is whether practically and substantially the right of way could be exercised as conveniently as before. In *Keefe v Amor* [1964] 2 All ER 517, Russell LJ required proof of 'substantial interference'. The grant of a private right of way confers only a right to the reasonable use of the way by the grantee in common with others, and whether there has been a substantial interference depends on the circumstances and is a matter of degree. Acts which have been held to actionable disturbance include building on the way and ploughing it up, so as to make the enjoyment more difficult than previously (*Finlayson v Campbell* (1997) 8 BPR 15703, 1709–1711). In the present problem, the interference complained of is the placing of the ramps and the amount of heavy vehicular traffic. On balance, it is arguable that there has been a sufficient interference with Lorna's enjoyment of her right of way to justify the grant of an injunction against Nigel ordering removal of the ramps, and requiring a reduction in the volume of traffic to and from the factory on Brownacre; alternatively, if the court considers the interference not to be sufficiently substantial for the grant of an injunction, it may grant damages in lieu of an injunction under its Lord Cairns' Act power.

QUESTION 21

Since the beginning of this year, Broward Ltd has been the owner in fee simple of a large complex comprising a shopping mall, office accommodation, and a multi-storey car park.

(a) On March 25, 2000, Broward Ltd's predecessor-in-title, Aristide Ltd, granted a 5-year lease of a retail store in the mall to Tudor, simultaneously giving Tudor written permission to park his delivery van in the car park, free of charge. On the expiry of the lease in March, 2005, Aristide renewed the lease for a further 21-year term. Broward Ltd, which is now in financial difficulties, has informed Tudor that henceforth Tudor must pay the normal daily charges for parking his van in the car park.

(b) On 27 March 2000, Aristide let two separate office premises to Verona and Wilma respectively on 99-year leases. Since that date, Verona's employees have used a washroom on Wilma's premises without any objection from Wilma, but last week Wilma put a lock on the door and informed Verona that access to the washroom was in future restricted to Wilma's own employees, to whom she has given keys.

Advise Tudor and Verona, [on the assumption that today's date is 1 August 2020].

Suggested Answer

(a) The issue for determination in (a) above is whether Tudor currently has the right to continue parking his van in the mall car park free of charge, or whether Broward Ltd is entitled to demand payment from Tudor for the privilege. The answer to this question will depend on whether or not Tudor has acquired an easement to park in the car park.

The first issue to be considered is whether the right to park a vehicle in a car park is *capable* of being an easement. The requirements for a valid easement were laid down in *Re Ellenborough Park* [1953] 3 All ER 667. Those that are most relevant to the present problem are: (i) there must be a dominant and a servient tenement; (ii) the right claimed as an easement must 'accommodate' the dominant tenement; (iii) the dominant and servient tenements must not be both owned and occupied by the same person; and (iv) the right claimed as an easement must not substantially deprive the servient owner of possession of the servient tenement.

In the present problem, the retail store let to Tudor is the dominant tenement and the car park is the servient tenement. The right to park a vehicle in the car park clearly 'accommodates' the dominant tenement because it is not merely a personal benefit for Tudor but rather constitutes a benefit to the dominant tenement itself, in that it makes the retail store 'a better and more convenient property' (Megarry and

Wade, *Law of Real Property*, 8th edition, para 27–008). Thus requirements (i) and (ii) in *Ellenborough Park* are satisfied. Requirement (iii) is also satisfied because, although both retail store and car park are within the confines of the shopping mall owned in fee simple by Broward Ltd, they are in fact occupied by different persons (retail store in the possession of Tudor as tenant; car park in the possession of Broward Ltd as landlord). It appears also that requirement (iv) is satisfied, since it has been held that a right to park a vehicle *anywhere* in a car park (as opposed to a right to park in a one-car garage or a particular reserved space) is capable of being an easement (*Newman v Jones* (1982) (unreported)), in that it does not deprive the servient owner of possession of the servient tenement as a whole. In *London & Blenheim Estates Ltd v Ladbroke Retail Parks Ltd* [1993] 4 All ER 157, it was said that

> the essential question is one of degree. If the right granted in relation to the area over which it is to be exercisable is such that it would leave the servient owner without any reasonable use of his land, whether for parking or anything else, it could not be an easement.

More recently, in *Moncrieff v Jamieson* [2007] UKHL 442, Lord Scott disapproved of the test that asked whether or not the servient owner was left with any reasonable use of its land, and preferred a test that asked whether the servient owner retained possession and, subject to the reasonable exercise of the right to park, retained control of the servient land. In the present case, it is submitted that Tudor's parking of his van in the car park would satisfy either test.

The next issue to be considered is whether Tudor has *acquired* an easement to park in the car park. We are told that on 25 March 2000, Aristide Ltd, simultaneously with the grant of a 5-year lease of the retail store, gave Tudor written permission to park his van in the car park free of charge. Since a legal easement can be granted only by deed under seal, Tudor will not have acquired an easement of parking by virtue of the written permission; at most, he will have acquired a licence to park which could be revoked at any time. However, when Aristide Ltd renewed the lease in March 2005 for a further 21-year term, Tudor would at that moment have acquired a legal easement to park, by virtue of statutory provisions modelled on UK legislation and enacted in Caribbean jurisdictions [see, eg, Conveyancing Act 1881, section 6(1) and Law of Property Act 1925, section 62 (1) (UK), Property Act, Cap 236, section 66 (Barbados); Conveyancing and Law of Property Act, Ch 138, section 6 (The Bahamas); Conveyancing Act 1973 Rev, section 9 (Jamaica)]. The sections provide that 'a conveyance of land shall be deemed to include, and shall . . . operate to convey with the land, all . . . liberties privileges, easements, rights and advantages whatsoever appertaining . . . to the land'. The effect of these provisions is that a 'purchaser' of land will automatically acquire the benefit of any licences or privileges previously enjoyed only by way of permission of the 'vendor'. Further, the word 'conveyance' has been interpreted in subsequent case law as including the renewal of a lease by deed or writing, as in *Wright v Macadam* [1949] 2 All ER 565, so that 'purchaser' will include a tenant in whose favour a lease is renewed, and 'vendor' will include the landlord renewing the lease.

Accordingly, Tudor may continue to park his van in the car park free of charge, at least until expiry of his lease in March 2026.

(b) The issues for determination here are (i) whether the right to use a washroom is capable of being an easement, and (ii) if so, whether Verona has

> acquired the easement. As to (i), it was held in *Miller v Emcer Products Ltd* [1956] 1 All ER 237 that the right to use a washroom in an upper apartment was capable of being an easement. It constituted a servient tenement which accommodated a lower apartment (the dominant tenement) because it enhanced the use and enjoyment of the latter. With regard to the question of exclusion of the servient owner from possession, Romer LJ stated that it was 'true that during the times when the dominant owner exercised the right, the owner of the servient tenement would be excluded, but this in greater or less degree is a common feature of many easements (for example, rights of way) and does not amount to such an ouster of the servient owner's rights as was incompatible with a legal easement'.

In the present case, the *Ellenborough Park* requirements are satisfied, in that (i) there are dominant and servient tenements, (ii) the right to use the washroom in the office premises let to Wilma (the servient tenement) accommodates the dominant tenement (the premises let to Verona), (iii) the dominant and servient tenements are in separate occupation, and (iv) as explained above, the use of the washroom will not exclude the servient owner from possession of the servient tenement.

The next issue is whether Verona has *acquired* an easement to use the washroom on Wilma's premises. There was no express grant of an easement to Verona by deed, nor will an easement be implied under the Conveyancing and Property Acts, because there has been no 'conveyance', such as by renewal of Verona's lease. The fact that Verona enjoyed the use of the washroom for more than 20 years without interference from Wilma would at first suggest the possibility of acquisition under the Prescription Acts. However, such a claim would fail because of the rule that, since prescription is a method of acquisition available only in favour of fee simple owners, one tenant (Verona) of a fee simple owner (Broward Ltd) cannot acquire an easement as against another tenant (Wilma) of the same fee simple owner: *Kilgour v Gaddes* [1904] 1 KB 457; *Hobbs v Laurie* (1992) HC, Barb. Therefore, Verona has not acquired an easement to use the washroom; she has enjoyed only a gratuitous licence which Wilma has now revoked.

QUESTION 22

St Monique Investments Inc had for 25 years owned a hotel, the 'Coral Cove', and an adjacent lot, 'Sandyacre', near the sea. The front of the 'Coral Cove' abuts onto a public road, but the hotel guests and staff have habitually walked along a 4-feet wide track across Sandyacre as a short-cut to the beach. Two years ago, St Monique Investments sold and conveyed Sandyacre to Donald in fee simple, expressly reserving in the conveyance 'a right of way across Sandyacre' in favour of 'St Monique Investments Inc, its assignees, successors, servants, agents and licensees'. Last year, St Monique Investments sold the Coral Cove to Sunshine Enterprises Ltd which has carried out various extensions and renovations resulting in a threefold increase in the number of guests and staff crossing Sandyacre, some of whom are parking their cars on one side of the track.

Donald complains that the right of way across Sandyacre is now being abused, and he seeks your advice as to whether he can prevent the alleged abuse.

How, if at all, would your advice differ if there had been no express reservation of a right of way in the conveyance of Sandyacre to Donald?

Suggested answer

The two main issues in this problem are (i) whether Donald can prevent what he alleges is an excessive user of the right of way across Sandyacre, and (ii) whether he can prevent the parking of cars on the side of the track.

In order to advise Donald as to whether he can obtain an injunction to prevent the increased number of persons walking across Sandyacre, it is necessary to determine the extent of the easement expressly reserved in favour of St Monique Investments Inc in the conveyance of Sandyacre to Donald two years ago. It is well established that the extent of an easement acquired by express grant or reservation depends on the proper construction of the document which created it and that, in cases of ambiguity, the court may examine the *locus in quo* in order to decide the matter. In this case, a 'right of way across Sandyacre' was expressly reserved in favour of 'St Monique Investments Inc., its servants, agents and licensees'. No restriction was placed on the manner of user or on the number of persons using the way. In *White v Grand Hotel (Eastbourne) Ltd* [1913] 1 Ch 113, an unrestricted right of way over the servient tenement was granted expressly to the owner of a private house on the dominant tenement. The house was later converted into a hotel. It was held that the right of way was not limited to the purposes existing at the time of the grant (ie, use as a private house), and that the owners of the hotel were entitled to the use of the way for the general purposes of the hotel. Similarly, in *Wilson v Bodden* [1988–89] CILR N18, Collett CJ emphasised that 'the extent of the permitted user of an unrestricted right of way need not be limited to the particular purpose for which it was originally granted', and if that purpose was originally to facilitate personal and domestic access to and from his home, the grantee was entitled to extend the use to accommodate residential and commercial tenants, his employees and their families. These principles were applied in a Barbadian case, *Nairne v Rockley Country Club* (1981) 16 Barb LR 244. There, M in 1937 conveyed a residential property, 'Worthing View House', to a purchaser, expressly reserving in favour of adjacent land retained by him (which at that time was a disused golf course) an easement over the property 'to go, return, pass and repass by day and night over and along the said portion of land . . . with or without . . . carts, trucks, carriages or motor cars or other motor vehicles of all kinds laden or unladen'. The defendants, who subsequently purchased the dominant land from M, redeveloped the land into a large resort, comprising over 300 apartments, with, *inter alia*, a golf course, tennis courts, swimming pools, restaurants, bars and a disco. The plaintiff, the present owner of 'Worthing View House', claimed in 1980 that the defendants had caused an unjustified enlargement of the right of way by altering the character, nature and extent of the user. He complained of a constant flow of traffic to and from the resort, including mini-mokes, private cars, coaches, and even Transport Board buses.

Douglas CJ held, applying the test in *White v Grand Hotel (Eastbourne) Ltd*, that there was nothing in the context of the conveyance of 1937 that limited the words by which the reservation of the right of way was made. As Cozens-Hardy MR had said in that case:

> It is a right of way claimed under a grant and, that being so, the only thing that the court has to do is to construe the grant; and unless there is some limitation to be found in the grant, in the nature of the width of the road or something of that kind, full

> effect must be given to the grant, and we cannot consider the subsequent user as in any way sufficient to cut down the generality of the grant.

Applying the above principles to the present problem, when the dominant tenement (Coral Cove) was sold last year, the purchaser, Sunshine Enterprises Ltd, acquired an easement of way across the servient tenement, Sandyacre, which was not limited to the amount of user enjoyed by the vendor, St Monique Investments Inc, and there can be no valid objection to the threefold increase in the number of persons using the way. On the other hand, the right of way expressly reserved in the conveyance of Sandyacre to Donald is a right of access or passage and does not include the right to park vehicles on the land. Further, the fact that the track is only 4 feet wide suggests that it was never intended to accommodate even the passage of vehicles, and therefore is to be restricted to use by pedestrians: *St Edmundsbury Diocesan Board v Clark* [1975] 1 All ER 772. Donald should thus be able to obtain an injunction to restrain both the passage and the parking of cars on the track.

If there had been no express reservation of a right of way in favour of St Monique Investments in the conveyance of Sandyacre to Donald, the question would arise as to whether St Monique Investments and its successor-in-title, Sunshine Enterprises, could have acquired an easement of way either by implied reservation or by prescription. It is clear that no easement was acquired by implied reservation since (a) no easement of necessity will be implied, as Coral Cove abuts onto a public road and therefore has access to the outside world; (b) no easement will be implied under the rule in *Wheeldon v Burrows* (1879) 12 Ch D 31, as the rule is based on the principle of non-derogation from grant and thus applies only to cases of implied grant (ie, where the common owner of the two tenements sells and conveys the quasi-dominant tenement and retains the quasi-servient tenement); it does not apply to implied reservation (ie, where the common owner sells the quasi-servient tenement and retains the quasi-dominant tenement, as in the present problem). Equally, there can be no argument that St Monique Investments and its successors have acquired an easement by prescription (based on 25 years' user of the way), as, unlike in *Hart v Pierce* (1967) 11 WIR 179, where the dominant and servient tenements were in separate ownership during the prescription period, St Monique Investments was the owner of both tenements throughout the period, and a person cannot acquire a title by prescription over his own land. Accordingly, in the absence of any express reservation, Sunshine Enterprises would have no easement of way over Sandyacre.

QUESTION 23

Stag is the fee simple owner of Greenacre, a large area of agricultural land with unregistered title which, since 2009, has been let under a 21-year lease to Banks, who in fact lives in Florida. When Piton purchased an adjacent lot, Orangeacre, in 2010, Greenacre was overgrown with bush and appeared to be abandoned. Piton accordingly began to cultivate a 1500 square foot portion of Greenacre ('Red Strip') next to the boundary with Orangeacre, and later enclosed Red Strip in order to prevent his goats from straying. Since Piton died in 2016, Carib, who lives in a neighbouring house, has continued to cultivate Red Strip, and also uses it to store his building materials and a motor boat, as well as for grazing his cows.

In 2007, the Heineken brothers began to cut timber and grow rice on an outlying portion of Greenacre and have been doing so ever since.

Recently, Carib received a letter from Stag's attorney informing him that Banks has surrendered his lease of Greenacre to Stag and demanding that Carib vacate Red Strip immediately. Also, the Heineken brothers have been informed that Stag intends to seek an injunction restraining them from continuing to 'trespass' on Greenacre.

Advise Carib and the Heinekens.

Suggested answer

Stag, the fee simple owner of Greenacre, has let the land to a tenant, Banks, who is not occupying the property but lives overseas. The lease is for a 21-year term and expires in 2030. Piton, the owner of adjoining Orangeacre, started to cultivate a portion of Greenacre ('Red Strip') in 2009, believing it to have been abandoned. He later erected a fence around Red Strip to prevent his goats from straying. After Piton's death in 2016, Carib has continued the cultivation of Red Strip, which he has also been using to store building materials and a motor boat and to graze his own goats.

Now that Carib has received a letter from Stag's attorney demanding that Carib vacates Red Strip, the question arises as to whether Carib has acquired any title to Red Strip by adverse possession. First, Carib must show uninterrupted possession of Red Strip for the statutory period of 12 years (see, eg, Limitation of Actions Act, 1973 Rev, s 3 (Jamaica)) and, in calculating the period, he is entitled to add Piton's 7-year period of possession to his own period of 5 years, provided the user was continuous, with no gap between the two periods (*Ocean Estates Ltd v Pinder* [1969] 2 AC 19, PC). Assuming the 12-year period has elapsed, the next question to determine is whether the two requirements of (i) factual possession and (ii) *animus possidendi* can be demonstrated.

With respect to factual possession, the possession of the adverse claimant must be (i) open and unconcealed and (ii) without the permission of the paper owner (*Clarke v Swaby* [2007] UKPC 1). Both requirements are satisfied here. Next, the possession must not be 'trivial' or 'equivocal' and, in determining whether the claimant has shown sufficient, unequivocal factual possession, regard must be had to the circumstances of the individual case. Acts which might be regarded as sufficient in one set of circumstances might not be held sufficient in another. Above all, according to Slade J in *Powell v Macfarlane* (1977) 38 P&CR 452), it must be shown 'that the alleged possessor has been dealing with the land as an occupying owner might have been expected to deal with it'. Piton's cultivation of Red Strip for an extended period may qualify as a sufficiently unequivocal course of conduct (*Seddon v Smith* (1877) 36 LT 168). With respect to the enclosure, it is well accepted in case law that enclosure by a wall or fencing will usually be sufficient evidence of factual possession and, in a Jamaican case, *Blake v Hunt* (2011) SC Jam, unreported, Brooks J said that 'few things more emphatically demonstrate an intention to possess land and to dispossess others of that land, than the erection of a fence around that land'. This suggests that enclosure of disputed land could satisfy both the requirement of unequivocal factual possession and that of *animus possidendi*, ie, the intention to exclude all others from the land, including the paper owner. There is a problem in the present case, however, in that Piton's purpose in enclosing Red Strip was not to assert his possession and control over Red Strip but rather to prevent his goats from straying, which would mean that Piton's act of enclosure was equivocal and did not *per se* satisfy the factual possession requirement (*Inglewood Investment Co v Baker* [2002] EWCA Civ 1733). As far as Carib's acts are concerned, it was held in a Bahamian case, *Dean v Rolle* (2010) SC, Bah (unreported), that acts of clearing a neighbouring lot, storing a fishing boat, motor vehicles and building materials on the lot, and using fill and soil from the land, were sufficient acts of factual possession, particularly in the light of the fact that the paper owner had not visited his lot for more than 26 years. In the present case, Carib's acts of factual possession were cultivating Red Strip, storing building materials and a motor boat thereon, and grazing his cows. These acts were similar to those in *Dean v Rolle* (above) and, granted that each case must be decided on its own individual circumstances, it seems likely that Carib's actions would collectively be deemed sufficiently unequivocal. It seems also that the requirement of *animus possidendi* has been satisfied, in relation to both Piton and Carib, since both believed Greenacre (including Red Strip) to have been abandoned. In such circumstances, it is easy to infer an intention on the part of both Piton and Carib, each 'on his own behalf, to exclude the world at large . . . in so far as was reasonably practicable' (in the words of Slade J in *Powell v Mc Farlane* (1977) 38 P&CR 452, 471).

Regarding the Heineken brothers, who, since 2007, have been cutting timber and growing rice on an outlying portion of Greenacre, the question whether these acts are sufficiently unequivocal to satisfy the requirement of factual possession may be decided in line with the approach taken by the Privy Council in *West Bank Estates Ltd v Arthur* [1967] AC 665. In that case, the respondents, who were peasant farmers, claimed a prescriptive title to an area of land in Guyana by virtue of various acts such as cutting timber, fishing, and growing rice on the land throughout the statutory limitation period. The trial judge considered these acts to be insufficient to establish the 'sole and undisturbed possession' required by the limitation statute; the Court of Appeal, on the other hand, took the view that the respondents had proved that they had made what was, for persons of their means and class, normal use of the land, and their actions were sufficient to establish adverse possession. The Privy Council preferred the view of the trial judge, holding that, even if the actions of the respondents could be considered normal for peasant farmers, that did not establish a sufficient degree of sole possession and user to satisfy the statute nor 'to carry the matter beyond a user which remains consistent with the possession of the true owner'. In the present case, it is likely that a court would take a similar view and hold the acts of the Heinekens to be equivocal and insufficient to support a claim to the outlying portion of Greenland by adverse possession.

The final issue concerns the significance and effect of Banks surrendering his lease to Stag. The person entitled to possession during the 12-year prescriptive period was Banks, the lessee, and not Stag, since during the continuance of a lease it is the lessee (tenant) and not the lessor (landlord) who is entitled to exclusive possession of the property let. Accordingly, Piton's and Carib's possession of Red Strip will have been adverse to Banks, but not to Stag, whose reversionary interest will be unaffected by such possession. Therefore, although Banks will have lost his legal lease to Carib, Stag's fee simple still subsists and, in effect, Carib will step into Banks's shoes and become Stag's lessee. The effect of a lessee surrendering his lease to the lessor in such circumstances was considered in *Fairweather v St Marylebone Property Co Ltd* [1963] AC 510, where the facts were essentially as follows: L granted a 99-year lease of a house and garden, containing a shed, to T. The shed was occupied by a neighbour, R, for more than 12 years adversely to T. While the lease had about 33 years still to run, T surrendered the lease to L. The question was whether L, as fee simple owner, was entitled to resume possession immediately (since L was unaffected by R's adverse possession), or whether he had no such right until the lease came to an end by effluxion of time, ie in 33 years' time. The House of Lords held that the effect of T's surrendering the lease was that L was entitled to resume possession immediately, and was not bound to wait until expiry of the lease. The decision in *Fairweather* has been justly criticised on the ground that if L's lease had been extinguished by R's adverse possession, he had nothing to surrender to L, so that the purported surrender should have been declared void, thus leaving L with no right to resume possession before the date of expiry of the lease. Nonetheless, since *Fairweather* has not been overruled, it would be applied in the present case, giving Stag the right to resume possession of Red Strip immediately.

Accordingly, (i) Carib will be ordered give up possession of Red Strip to Stag, and (ii) the Heinekens will be ordered to vacate the outlying portion of Greenacre.

QUESTION 24

In 2018, Maurice Morrison, a man of limited means, purchased shop premises with registered title. He paid a deposit of 10 per cent of the purchase price and the balance, $50,000,000 (Ja), was provided by means of an instalment mortgage from the Clarendon Commercial Bank ('the Bank'). The mortgage agreement provides for, inter alia:

- *(i) Payment of interest on the loan at 11 per cent above bank rate*
- *(ii) Index-linking of the value of capital and interest to the US dollar*
- *(iii) The mortgage to be irredeemable for 15 years*
- *(iv) The whole sum of $50,000,000 (Ja)to become payable in the event of non-payment of any instalment within one month of its becoming due.*

Maurice's business has not been successful and he has made default in regard to two months' instalments.

Discuss

- *(a) whether, if Maurice can find a buyer for the premises, he may be permitted to redeem the mortgage immediately*
- *(b) whether the court may vary the terms of the mortgage agreement*
- *(c) what remedies are available to the Bank in order to enforce its security.*

Suggested answer

This question is concerned with the equitable policy of promoting fair dealing between mortgagor and mortgagee. Equity will not allow a mortgagee to take advantage of the financial circumstances of the mortgagor. In the present case, we are told that Maurice Milligan was 'a man of limited means', so that there would be inequality of bargaining power between Maurice and the bank. In such a situation, a court of equity would be concerned to ensure that the terms of the mortgage agreement were not 'unfair and unconscionable' from the mortgagor's perspective.

(a) Is the term that the mortgage should be irredeemable for 15 years 'unfair and unconscionable', in the sense that it unfairly restricts redemption? In much earlier times, the courts tended to regard a mortgagor as 'an impoverished debtor on the brink of ruin, unable to resist the demands of a rapacious lender' (Cheshire and Burn, *Modern Law of Real Property*, 18th edn, p 821), but the more modern approach is to uphold the sanctity of contracts freely entered into by businessmen who may be quite capable of protecting their own interests (*ibid*). It is submitted that a term postponing redemption for 15 years is not unfair or unconscionable, despite the limited means of the mortgagor and the inequality of bargaining power, as modern installment mortgage agreements commonly specify 10-, 20- or 25-year redemption periods. In the present case, it is likely that Maurice will be bound by the 15-year redemption period, though it is common for a term to be included in the agreement permitting earlier redemption on payment of a penalty to the mortgagee. On the other hand, if the Bank decides to take possession of the mortgaged property in order to exercise its power of sale following Maurice's default (see below), it will not be able to prevent Maurice (assuming he can find a buyer) from repaying the loan plus interest and redeeming the property immediately (*Bovill v Endle* [1896] 1 Ch 648).

(b) The term providing for interest on the loan at 12% above bank rate may be said to be unfair and unconscionable, since it is well above the 'normal' rate of about 2% above bank rate. In *Cityland and Property (Holdings) Ltd v Dabrah* [1967] 2 All ER 639, the mortgagor was the mortgagee's tenant and a man 'obviously of limited means'. He undertook in the mortgage agreement to pay a premium that represented either not less than 57 per cent of the amount of the loan, or interest at 19 per cent. It was held that this provision was unconscionable and void. This was not a 'bargain between two large trading concerns', and the mortgagor was entitled to redeem by repaying the loan with reasonable interest fixed by the court. In the present case, it is likely that a court would be prepared to vary the agreement by substituting a lower interest rate for the existing one.

(c) In *Multiservice Bookbinding Ltd v Marden* [1978] 2 All ER 489, Browne-Wilkinson J stressed that, for a term in a mortgage agreement to be declared void, it must be unfair and unconscionable and not merely 'unreasonable'. Unfair and unconscionable meant 'imposed in a morally reprehensible manner, that is to say, in a way which affects [the mortgagee's] conscience'. In *Multiservice*, the mortgagor was a small company which needed a loan in order to expand its business. The terms of the mortgage were that: (a) interest was payable at 2 per cent above bank rate; (b) the loan was to be irredeemable for ten years; and (c) the value of the capital and interest was to be index linked to the Swiss franc. After ten years, when the mortgage became redeemable, the total capital repayment had risen from the £36,000 lent to £87,588, because of devaluation of the pound sterling against the Swiss franc, and the average rate of interest amounted to 16 per cent. It was held that the agreement was valid. Although the bargain was a hard one from the mortgagor's point of view, it was not unfair or unconscionable in the sense defined by Browne-Wilkinson J. On the authority of *Multiservice*, a court in Maurice's case would probably decline to interfere with the index-linking term in the mortgage agreement, so that if the Jamaican dollar has been devalued during the five years since the mortgage agreement was entered into, it is likely that, as in *Multiservice,* Maurice will be bound to repay more than the original debt of $50,000,000 (Ja).

(d) In order to enforce its security in the light of Maurice's default in regard to two months' instalments, the bank should first of all exercise its right to take possession of the property (*Four Maids Ltd v Dudley Marshall (Properties) Ltd* [1957] 2 All ER 35), so that it will be able to sell with vacant possession. The bank may then decide to exercise its statutory power to sell the property under the Registration of Titles Act, sections 105 and 106, which govern the exercise of the power of sale in relation to registered land. Section 105 provides that, where there is a default by the mortgagor in payment of principal or interest, or in the performance or observance of any express or implied covenant, and such default continues for one month (or for such other period as may be fixed by the mortgage), the mortgagee 'may give to the mortgagor . . . notice in writing to pay the money owing . . . or to perform or observe the aforesaid covenants' and, by s 106, if such default continues for one month after service of the notice (or such other period as may be fixed), the mortgagee may sell the land, or part thereof, altogether or in lots, by public auction or private contract. In carrying out a sale, the bank as mortgagee will be under a duty to take reasonable care to obtain the true market value of the property (*Cuckmere Brick Co Ltd v Mutual Finance Ltd* [1971] 2 All ER 633) and, if it decides to sell by private treaty, it must first obtain a current valuation of the property and advertise the property with a view to attracting potential purchasers (*International Trust and Merchant Bank Ltd v Gardiner* (2004) CA, Jam, unreported).

QUESTION 25

Four years ago, Usher executed a mortgage in favour of the BET Bank to secure a loan of $200,000 (US) for the purchase of a two-storey dwelling house, with registered title, in which Usher currently lives. The loan is repayable by monthly instalments of $1,500 over a period of 20 years, the whole capital sum plus interest being immediately repayable in the event of a failure to pay any instalment within 14 days of its becoming due. Last year, contrary to a clause in the mortgage agreement whereby 'the mortgagor shall not grant any lease or tenancy of the property without the prior consent in writing of the mortgagee', Usher granted a 5-year lease of the ground floor of the house to Beyonce. Also, Usher is now two months in arrears with his mortgage payments.

Advise BET Bank:

(a) Whether and, if so, by what method it may recover possession of the house; and
(b) Whether it may sell the house to Alicia, an accountant employed by the Bank, without advertising it for sale to the general public.

Suggested answer

According to the terms of the mortgage agreement between Usher (mortgagor) and BET Bank (mortgagee), if any instalment remains unpaid two months after its becoming due for payment, the whole capital sum of $200,000 plus interest becomes immediately repayable; further, Usher is prohibited from granting any lease or tenancy of the house without the prior written consent of the Bank. The first issue, therefore, is whether Usher is in breach of any one or both of these terms.

It is clear, first of all, that Usher is in breach as to his monthly payments, since we are told that he is now two months in arrears. Secondly, Usher appears to be in breach of the agreement by granting a five-year lease to Beyonce without the written consent of the Bank; however, one line of defence which may be open to Usher is that whereas the agreement states that the mortgagor shall not grant any lease 'of the property', Usher has in fact granted a lease of only part of the property, ie, the ground floor area. He may argue that the term is ambiguous and, by analogy with the principle which applies as between landlord and tenant, the restrictive term should be construed strictly against the party relying on it (the mortgagee), so that it should be interpreted as prohibiting only leases of the whole property and not leases of part. The analogous rule in landlord and tenant law was established in *Cook v Shoesmith* [1951]1 KB 752 and followed in a Trinidadian case, *Montrichard Enterprises Ltd v Attorney General of Trinidad and Tobago* (1998) HC, T&T (unreported). Whether this argument would succeed is doubtful, however, so one may advise BET Bank on the basis that there has been a breach of the term by Usher:

(a) As Harman J stated in *Four Maids Ltd v Dudley Marshall (Properties) Ltd* [1957] 2 All ER 35, 36, a legal mortgagee has a right to take possession of the mortgaged property 'before the ink is dry on the mortgage', and its right to possession 'has nothing to do with default on the part of the mortgagor'. There is thus no doubt that BET Bank has a right to possession of the dwelling house, irrespective of Usher's default, and the only issue concerns the method of obtaining such possession. Since the property is a dwelling house and Usher is currently in actual possession, it would not be feasible or appropriate for the Bank to physically take possession of the premises, as this could amount to 'forcible entry', which is a breach of the criminal law (*Patrick v Beverley Gardens Development Co Ltd* (1974) CA, Jam (unreported); *Duplessis v Moore* (1993) HC, Barb (unreported). Accordingly, BET Bank is advised that it will be necessary to bring an action in court to recover possession of the house.

In England and Wales, the Administration of Justice Acts 1970 and 1973 give the courts a wide discretion to postpone possession orders with respect to dwelling houses, but in Caribbean jurisdictions the common law position applies, which is that a court has no power to deprive the mortgagee of its right to possession by postponing a possession order or adjourning the hearing in order to give the mortgagor more time to pay the arrears. In *Bank of Nova Scotia v Morrison* (1995) Supreme Court, The Bahamas (unrep), where the mortgagor was in default of her monthly mortgage payments to the tune of $17,079 principal and $1,752 interest, and the mortgagee sought possession with a view to putting up the property for sale. Osadebay J held that the court could not adjourn the hearing, whether on terms of keeping up payments or paying arrears, without the concurrence of the mortgagee; and in *Citibank NA v Major* (2001) CA, The Bahamas (unrep), Ganpatsingh JA stated that 'where, under a legal mortgage, being an instalment mortgage, the whole mortgage money becomes payable by reason of the default of the mortgagor, and the legal mortgagee is entitled to possession of the mortgaged property, the court has no jurisdiction to refuse to make an order for possession or to adjourn the summons, either on terms or not on terms as to keeping up payments or paying arrears, if the mortgagee does not agree to that course', although he did go on to say that, following *Birmingham Citizens' Permanent Building Society v Caunt* [1962] 1 All ER 163, the court had power to direct an adjournment 'for a short time' to enable the mortgagor to pay off the mortgage in full or otherwise satisfy the mortgagee, if there is a reasonable prospect of the mortgagor being able to do so.

(b) Unlike the right to take possession (a common law right which the mortgagee can exercise whether or not there has been a default on the part of the mortgagor), the mortgagee's statutory power to sell the mortgaged property is governed by the legislation which creates the power. For instance, section 105 of the Registration of Titles Act (Jamaica) (applicable where the title of the property is registered, as in the present problem), provides that where there is a default by the mortgagor in payment of principal or interest, or in the performance or observance of any express or implied covenant, and such default continues for at least one month, the mortgagee must give to the mortgagor notice in writing to pay the money owing or to perform the covenants (as the case may be) (*Jobson v Capital and Credit Merchant Bank* (2005) CA, Jam (unreported)), and if the default continues for one month after service of the notice, the mortgagee may sell the property by public auction or private contract.

Thus, in the present problem, Usher, who is two months in arrears of the mortgage payments, will be given one month after service of the statutory notice to pay the arrears, failing which the Bank would be able to exercise its power of sale. A further difficulty for Usher is that he is also arguably in breach of the term in the mortgage agreement requiring the Bank's consent to the granting of leases of the property, and it seems that this breach cannot be remedied by Usher, unless he can obtain a surrender of the lease by Beyonce. Thus, it seems that the most likely consequence is that the Bank will be entitled to sell the property.

As to whether the Bank can sell to Alicia without advertising the property for sale to the general public, this will depend on whether the sale to Alicia is at a 'fair market value' within the principle in *Cuckmere Brick Co Ltd v Mutual Finance* Ltd [1971] 2 All ER 633, 643, where a mortgagee was held liable in damages for negligence because, in advertising the mortgaged property for sale, it had carelessly omitted to mention that planning permission had been granted for the erection of apartments on the land, and thus obtained a lower price than it ought to have obtained. The mortgagee was held liable for the difference between the price obtained and the proper market value of the property. More recently, the duty to obtain a fair market price has been held to be grounded not so much in the law of negligence as in the mortgagee's equitable duty to act in a prudent and business-like manner (*Daley v RBTT Bank (Jamaica) Ltd* (2007) SC, Jam (unreported)), though, according to Scott V-C in *Medforth v Blake* [2000] Ch 86, 102, it does not 'matter . . . one jot whether the duty is expressed as a common law duty or as a duty in equity: the result is the same'.

In order to assess whether the proposed sale to Alicia is at a fair market price, the Bank will need to obtain a valuation from a qualified valuer since, as Sykes J pointed out in the *Daley* case (above), the absence of a current valuation in the context of a sale by private treaty was 'powerful evidence' that the mortgagee bank in that case had failed to take reasonable precautions to obtain the true market value of the mortgaged property at the date at which it had decided to sell. The need for a valuation in cases of sale by private treaty was also emphasised by Bingham JA in the Jamaican

Court of Appeal in *International Trust and Merchant Bank Ltd v Gardiner* (2004) CA, Jam (unreported), where it was also stated that property being sold by private treaty should also be properly advertised, with a view to attracting potential purchasers. In the present problem, however, it is submitted that advertisement will not be necessary provided that there is a valuation and that the price being offered by Alicia is comparable to the current valuation, bearing in mind that the duty is to obtain a 'fair' price, not necessarily the 'best' price (*per* Malcolm J in *Davis v Franklyn* (1994) SC, Jam (unreported), and that property valuation is not an exact science, and one has to examine the facts 'in the round' in deciding whether the mortgagee has satisfied the *Cuckmere Brick* principle (*Bank of Nova Scotia (Jamaica) Ltd v Rosegreen* (2008) SC, Jam (unreported), *per* Jones J).

A final point is whether a sale to Alicia would be vitiated by the fact that she is an employee of the mortgagee. In the first place, it is established that a mortgagee cannot sell to himself/itself alone, or to his attorney or solicitor (*Martinson v Clowes* (1882) 21 Ch D 857,860), or to his agent (*Downs v Grazebrook* (1817) 36 ER 77, 80), even if the sale price is the full market value, because a sale by a person to himself is 'no sale at all'. On the other hand, a sale by a mortgagee to a less closely associated person such as a business acquaintance will not be set aside, though the court will scrutinise it carefully and may set it aside if it finds the sale was not *bona fide* (*Tse Kwong Lam v Wong Chit Sen* [1983] 1 WLR 1349). In the present problem, it is submitted that the proposed sale to Alicia would be upheld by the court unless it found that, for some reason, the sale was not 'genuine'.

In conclusion, BET Bank is advised that (a) it may obtain a court order for possession, and (b) it may sell to Alicia without advertising the property for sale, provided it first obtains a valuation and provided that the selling price represents the true market value of the property.

INDEX